To Tom

WEBSTER'S
WINE
GUIDE
1991
SEVENTH EDITION

[signatures]

Contributors to *Webster's Wine Guide 1991*

Burton Anderson, the world's leading authority on Italian wine and the author of *Vino*, lives and works in Tuscany; **Tim Atkin**, twice winner of the Glenfiddich Wine Writer of the Year award, is the wine correspondent for *The Guardian*; **William Bolter** is the author of several books on Bordeaux, where he lives and owns his own vineyard. **Stephen Brook** is wine author, novelist and travel writer whose diverse credits include *Honkytonk Gelato* and *Liquid Gold*, a guide to the world's dessert wines. **Gordon Brown** writes regularly on wine and whisky and is currently writing a book on brandy; **Nicholas Faith** is the author of books on Champagne and Cognac as well as the classic study of the Bordeaux wine trade, *The Wine Masters*. He is also a regular contributor to *The Independent on Sunday*. **James Halliday** is Australia's top wine writer, author of *The Australian Wine Compendium* and the annual *Australian Wine Guide*, who now runs his own winery at Coldstream Hills in Victoria; **Giles MacDonogh**, historian and wine writer, writes regularly for *The Financial Times*, WINE and *Decanter* magazines; his latest book is about the life and times of the great French gastronome Brillat-Savarin. **Kathryn McWhirter**, former editor of *Wine & Spirit* magazine and *Which? Wine Guide*, now appears in *The Independent on Sunday*. **Charles Metcalfe** is the associate editor of WINE magazine. He and Kathryn McWhirter are the joint authors of several books on wine and food and are leading authorities on Iberian wines. Their book *The Wines of Spain and Portugal* won a recent Glenfiddich award. **Anthony Rose** is the wine correspondent for *The Independent* and California-based **Larry Walker** is the managing editor of *Wines and Vines* magazine and a leading commentator on the California wine scene.

Reviews of previous editions

'... the guide gets better with every vintage. Clarke writes with enthusiasm virtually steaming off the page. Here is someone who loves wine' *The Guardian*

'*Webster's Wine Guide 1990* is the book I would choose to have at my elbow throughout the year ... for sheer spot on, razor-sharp, inside-track, up-to-the minuteness' *Punch*

'Oz Clarke's annual *Webster's Wine Guide 1990* is an enthusiastic, opinionated and entertaining survey of the world's wines and a price guide to wines on the shelves of Britain' *The Sunday Times*

'... typically up-to-date, irreverent but informative' *The Independent*

'Scholarly, funny and thought-provoking' Robert Parker

'his sixth edition of *Webster's Wine Guide 1990* is both passionate and quite unpretentious, in true Oz Clarke fashion' *The Newcastle Journal*

— WEBSTER'S —

WINE GUIDE 1991

SEVENTH EDITION

**THE
COMPLETE
WINE-BUYER'S
HANDBOOK**

**WRITTEN AND EDITED
BY**

OZ CLARKE

**Associate Editor
ROSEMARY GEORGE MW**

**WEBSTERS/MITCHELL BEAZLEY
LONDON**

Managing Editor Sandy Carr
General Editor Fiona Wild
Price Guides Editor Mary Pickles
Deputy Editor Nicholas Bevan
Art Editor Alison Donovan
Editorial Assistant Siobhan Bremner
Database and Word-Processing Assistants
Suzi Pattinson, Monica Maxted Jones
Database and DTP Consultant
Alexandra Boyle
Indexer Naomi Good
Cover illustration Mathew Cook, Artworks
Back cover photograph Steve Shipman

Created and designed by
Webster's Wine Price Guide Limited,
Axe and Bottle Court, 70 Newcomen Street,
London SE1 1YT;
in association with Mitchell Beazley
International Limited, Artists House,
14/15 Manette Street, London W1V 5LB

Webster's Wine Guide 1991 Edition
© Webster's International Publishers
and Mitchell Beazley Publishers 1990

ISBN 0 85533 850 4

Cover reproduction by Scantrans,
Singapore
Printed and bound in the UK by
William Clowes Ltd, Beccles

CONTENTS

INTRODUCTION

This is a year when you're going to need all the help and advice *Webster's* can give you. The summer of 1989 produced phenomenal grape ripeness right across northern Europe, and equally phenomenal amounts of hot air and hype to go with them. French journalists were already tapping out the tired old Vintage of the Century routine when the grapes were still on the vine, and the vintners gleefully seized on the opportunity to puff the reputation of their wines.

It sounds a bit silly, but 1989 was *too* hot in many places to make great wines. Only two areas of France achieved white wine greatness despite the heat – two areas where overripeness is positively prized – in the Loire for Chenin wines and in Alsace. Elsewhere – well the Mâconnais in Burgundy had the chance to make great '89s but the Burgundians have a supreme talent for slaughtering geese which lay golden eggs. Champagne produced splendid wine – at a price.

1989 *did* produce some splendid red wine in France, especially in the Loire. Beaujolais and Burgundy were upstaged in pricing strategy by Bordeaux. Some great wine, some good and some downright dull has been flooding on to the market at unprecedented prices, the merchants in this country claiming that we, the consumers, are forcing them to buy 1989s they might not otherwise sniff at!

And that's just France. Doesn't it all add up to a year when you need *Webster's* more than ever before? Many prices are getting out of control. Should you buy? If so, what, where, when, how? We'll tell you, because our first concern is for the wine drinker and wine drinking pleasure.

This year for the first time we asked a line-up of top wine experts to give us their news and views on what's happening in the world's wine regions. From Tuscany to the Napa Valley, from the Médoc to the Yarra, *Webster's* brings you more in-depth assessment than ever before. And we bring you the *real* stories. The massive hyping of the 1989 Bordeaux reds threatened to swamp the news of the genuine revolution that is happening there – that of white wines, sweet and dry. Some of the world's greatest whites are now being made in Bordeaux. A few Sauternes apart, you wouldn't have found many takers for that view ten years ago. *Webster's 1991* has the story as of now.

Italy is finally getting around to overhauling the wine laws which put declassified Chianti and £25-a-bottle Sassicaia into the same bracket of *vino da tavola*. Room is going to be made for identifying the best vineyard sites and a real pyramid system reflecting sheer wine quality should soon begin to take shape. *Webster's 1991* brings you up to date.

In Portugal there are finally signs that the stranglehold of the co-ops may be being challenged to some effect. But are the new demarcated areas going to work? *Webster's 1991* tells you why the Soares Franco family is sceptical.

The wine world has never been more exciting than it is today. The New World wine revolutions which were spawned so far away in California and Australia are now coming home to roost in the heartlands of tradition in France, Italy and Spain, with every sign that as the decade progresses they will open up the almost limitless potential of Eastern Europe and Russia. In the 1980s we enjoyed the heady salad days of modern wine's adolescence. In the 1990s the modern world of wine – *our* world of wine – is reaching maturity. The '80s were fun. The '90s will be even better.

ENGLISH WINES

I have been fascinated by English wine for the best part of a decade now. And, early in 1990, support for my enthusiasm came from an English household slightly older than mine. On an archaeological site in Dorset the boffins were sifting through the prehistoric garbage left by a family of local Neanderthals when they discovered an ancient grape pip. Somehow they have decided it was a 'cultivated' grape pip. So there we have it. Neolithic man in Dorset was cultivating the grape vine.

What he did with his grapes isn't clear, but there's no doubt at all that when the Romans arrived, they planted vineyards in the warmer spots of southern England, just as they did in the more favoured areas of Spain, France and Germany. And they planted them for wine. All the prime Roman plantations in these countries have been accorded praise and respect for centuries. But what about ours? Where are the proud, jingoistic defenders of the local faith, who aggressively assert the superiority of Bordeaux over Burgundy, of Côte de Nuits over Côte de Beaune, of Volnay over Pommard, of his vines over hers? Where are our world-famous labels? Where is the rush to purchase, the gloating pride in possession of Albion's greatest growths? Nowhere. It doesn't exist.

Or it *didn't* exist. However loudly I shouted encouragement, I felt it was so much hot air belched into a winter squall. No one wanted to know that English vineyards were on the march again. No one wanted to listen when English wines in fair and square blind tasting competition beat their fabled rivals from France and Germany, Italy and Spain. The release of the 1989 wines on to the market in the last couple of months signals that this is the time English wine *must* stand up and shout its own praise, bark its own wares to people all too willing to recall the pleasures of the long hot summer of '89.

THE FIRST AND THE LAST

It's a last chance for some. One of the West Country's leading winemakers was lamenting to me this summer, half in resignation, half in anger. Talking about our signal lack of enthusiasm for home-grown talent and home-grown produce he railed against hoteliers and restaurateurs for their total lack of support for what he called 'our fragile industry'. He then went on to say – 'Sadly, enthusiasm is not an English trait, and I fear many of us are about to founder for lack of sales at the sort of price that will pay for the cost of production.'

But it's a first chance for others. We've had good summers before – a few of us still bear the sunburn scars from 1976, and in 1984 our summer was about the only reasonable one throughout Europe. But in 1976, the wine boom which has swept this country was still in its infancy: a growing number of people were becoming excited about wine in general, but they had to get some experience of more exotic creations from Germany and France, Spain and Portugal, Australia even, and New Zealand, before they had gained enough confidence and curiosity to try their own backyard brew. In 1990, there's a potential market for English wines of millions of drinkers – if we can shout loud enough for them to try just *one* bottle. If only 10 per cent of Britain's wine drinkers tried just *one* bottle before Christmas, we'd have virtually sold out of the entire stock.

1976's heat was the spur which persuaded many people to take up vine-growing. The dismal summers of 1977, 1978 and 1980 must have made them think they were mad; but the vines were in the ground already, so most persevered. Those vines are now mature. In 1976 there were few mature vineyards around, and despite the baking summer, the wines I've tasted were of the 'hmm, interesting, er encouraging, um shows potential ...' variety. In 1990 those kind of remarks won't wash any more.

Internationally experienced winemakers are going to be necessary to run the wineries if some of our grander schemes get off the ground. Wellow Vineyards cover 80 acres in Hampshire. They intend to make 400,000 bottles of wine a year. Barkham Manor is a new 40-acre venture at Piltdown in East Sussex, while Chiltern Valley intend to build up a 100-acre operation in the Thames Valley. However these are all dwarfed by the ambitious designs of Denbies, just south of Box Hill near Dorking. There 250 acres of vines are creeping towards maturity on a ridge of limestone chalk very similar to that found in Champagne. And rather than be content with the usual melange of Reichensteiner and Müller-Thurgau, substantial blocks are given over to classic Champagne grapes Pinot Noir and Chardonnay.

FUTURES MARKET

Whether Denbies will work remains to be seen, but the encouraging thing is that it does look as though some thought has gone into identifying the potential market, not just planting the odd vine – hoping someone will roll up to buy the wine a few years down the track.

If there is truth in the 'Greenhouse Effect' predictions for Britain, we're going to need those vineyards of Pinot Noir and Chardonnay because the grapes we have right now are mostly planted for their ability to attain some vague sort of semi-ripeness in the coolest and dampest of years. 1989 showed that grapes like Siegerrebe, Madeleine Angevine and, frequently, Müller-Thurgau couldn't hold on to their acid and fruit flavours as the hot weather sent alcohol levels careering to unheard-of heights. If 1989 is a foretaste of vintages to come, the grapes of Alsace and Champagne are going to be the ones we need to plant to pull English wine to new heights. Mainland Europe may begin to suffer from sweltering vintages every year. For the lighter, more refreshing and aromatic styles – England may become the prime source.

Until the Continentals begin to beat an impassioned path to our doors, however, we have still got to find a way of selling the stuff. By far the most profitable way is to sell it at the winery gate. You can charge a straightforward retail price and keep all the profit for yourself. Some years ago, if a national chain had placed a large order for your wine, you'd have been turning cartwheels. Now you may just as easily tell them – sorry, no deal. Majestic wanted 400 cases of Bruisyard's Suffolk Whites. The owners said no; they could sell every bottle to the 30,000 visitors they attract each year.

CHARACTERS IN SEARCH OF A WINEMAKER

This is all very well – so long as the wine is good. Well, the 1989 vintage seemed to us at *Webster's* to provide an excellent chance to sift through the wide range. We also decided that maybe the time had come to try to pinpoint some regional characteristics. There are dramatic differences between, say, the dry but windswept conditions of Cambridge and East Anglia, and the far warmer but much wetter vineyards of the South West. Funnily enough, this was much more difficult than we'd expected, for several reasons. Firstly the overripe condition of many of the grapes had the same effect in England as it does in France or Germany – local characteristics are swamped by the fat richness of alcohol and extract. Secondly, many growers are still using a 'sweet reserve' of grape juice to sweeten their wine. Often this is of German origin, and it effectively masks any regional characteristics with sugar. Thirdly, and positively, the winemakers' styles are frequently more evident than any local peculiarities, or, indeed, than the particular flavour of a single grape type. Kit Lindlar's 'English Vineyard' is a classic example. Though based in Kent, Lindlar works with grapes from as far afield as Devon. His English Vineyard wine is made from Huxelrebe, Faber, Seyval Blanc and Müller-Thurgau grapes, but tasting it in the summer at the International Wine 2000 symposium in Cambridge, the general feeling was that it resembled a damned good Sauvignon from the Loire. That's the winemaker, not the grapes or the local conditions doing the talking.

RED WINES

Things are still pretty rudimentary here, and though we didn't see any wines we positively liked *yet*, there were a couple of extremely hopeful signs. *Mumford* near Bath have produced a big juicy red from Triomphe d'Alsace with a flavour like cranberries and bruised damsons. And *Beenleigh Manor* at Totnes in Devon has been growing Cabernet Sauvignon and Merlot in plastic polytunnels. When it has done its malolactic fermentation and rested a few months in barrel – but not too long, please – the Beenleigh red will be very pleasant.

We expected to see more good rosés, as 1989 should have been an ideal year for them. Even so, we found a few with just the right balance of fruit and acidity to be good high summer tipples. *Bardingley* is still fairly acid, but has a pleasant smoky apple fruit and a bit of balancing softness. *Headcorn* is off-dry, appley and mild, but perfectly nice. And just down the road, the tiny *Conghurst* has made a delightful light smoky apple pink with a gentle creamy finish.

WHITE WINES

We'll divide these up geographically to see if any pattern emerges.

EAST ANGLIA This is one area which has definitely begun to develop a regional style. Maybe it's all those chill winds from the Urals, but almost all the best East Anglian wines are bitingly dry, and as such many of these '89s, though ready to drink now, will age extremely well for anything up to ten years!

Elmham Park Müller-Thurgau is high acid, but attractively rounded out with a herby grassiness and a touch of honey. Their Kerner is remarkably full and soft, a taste of greengage and Cox's apples, with good acidity too; and their Madeleine Angevine is fascinating with a bouquet of lilies and soft bananas, and an almost glycerine softness. *Lexham Hall's* best offering is their Müller-Thurgau, which has a good lean apple and flowering currant style quite reminiscent of French Sauvignon. *Gifford's* Dry White, made by Kit Lindlar, has the flowering currant sharpness again, made fresh and attractive by a perfume of elderflower. *Bruisyard* is its usual excellent bitingly dry lemon and lime pith self, while *Shawsgate* is the same idea, lemon sherbet and peardrops, but just a little softer.

KENT A lot of our most mature vineyards are in Kent, as well as some of our most talented winemakers. The combination should have been perfect, but in fact the Kent wines we saw were mostly a little disappointing. This may simply be due to the stage in their development, since the modern Kent style is dry, but with a little more fruit than East Anglia. Or it may be that drought was a severe problem in '89 and the grapes didn't come in with quite the perfect ripeness levels everyone hoped for. The best wine by far was *Chiddingstone* Pinot Gutedel, a remarkable full white, full of fresh English orchard fruit, but with a lovely spicy oak influence. It really does taste like a good quality Chardonnay from somewhere like the Loire. *Staple's* Huxelrebe is also good, albeit still too young with a spicy honey softness and a grapiness too which makes it resemble Alsace wine. *Mount Ephraim* is another good dry wine, with a flavour of grapefruit and passion fruit and a slight muskiness which again, despite the high acidity, puts the style in the Alsace camp. *Lamberhurst's* wines were all good, but none were special, since they all tasted just a little bland, even the dry, lemony Seyval Dry – the mildly muscatty Müller-Thurgau.

SUSSEX Most of Sussex's vineyards are in the east, and are some of the country's most mature. Again, the influence of the individual winemakers is strong here, Stephen Skelton of Lamberhurst, David Carr Taylor, and Kit Lindlar all having different views of what they're after. In general Sussex wines have a little more rounded fruit and perfume than Kent wines, and the trend towards super-dry is not so dominant, with the exception of *Breaky Bottom* where Peter Hall swears he tries to make his wines 'mean and military'. He doesn't succeed. Much to his disgust, his '89s are already delicious. The Müller-Thurgau has a beautiful mix of floral perfume and fizzy lemon sherbet dosed with honey, while the Seyval Blanc tries to be 'beetle-browed' but fails totally, with a big, mouthfilling flavour of apples and lemon, elderflower and white peaches topped off with Sauvignon grassiness. Sorry, Peter, it's delicious.

Nutbourne is another good Sussex producer, further west. They make a lovely Schönburger with the mouthwatering crisp grapiness of just plucked Muscat grapes. Their Bacchus is fiercer, impressively filled with grapefruit. *Carr Taylor* is Sussex's biggest operation, and milder in manner. They get some flavour out of Gutenborner, which not many do; theirs is a nice green elderflowery sort of wine. Their Schönburger, by comparison, is round and full with a rich flavour of toffee and peach skins. Peaches crop up again in *Hidden Spring's* Ortega which is full and golden and honeyed, very similar to the soft, glyceriney *Barkham Manor* Medium Dry.

HAMPSHIRE is where the revival of English commercial grape-growing started after the war, and Hampshire is where *Wellow's* giant operation hopes to swing English marketing and wine-making into the 21st century. They're not doing too badly so far. The Ortega is soft and fresh with a taste of pears, the Bacchus is gently scented with nectarines and their commercial 'Medium Dry' is a good straight grassy white. Even their Chardonnay tastes like the real thing. If they keep this up, they'll be a welcome addition to the English scene. But for more intense flavours, you'll have to go to smaller outfits. *Barton Manor* Dry has a whiff of Gewürztraminer rose petal about it, but good citrous lemon peel to keep it snappy. *Lymington* don't believe in half measures. Their Medium Dry is a brilliant blend of everything that shouldn't work – guavas and underripe mangoes being the most obvious. Their Schönburger is more mainstream, with an excellent full aromatic style, all ripe pink grapefruits and lemon peel.

DEVON has some of the warmest vineyards, and some of the most ambitious winemakers – that *Beenleigh Manor* Cabernet/Merlot, and a red from *Yearlstone* that has an almost Syrah blackberry fruit, for a start. But the best wines are still the whites. *Loddiswell's* Reichensteiner has a strangely confected smell but is very pleasant despite that. Their Medium is attractive pears and peaches stuff, while their Müller-Thurgau is far better than average with a big, dry, fragrant taste something like greengage skins. Yearlstone's Madeleine Angevine is round and fat, tasting of leather and guavas in a quite un-English way.

But the big guns are mostly in SOMERSET, another county which manages to blend mature vineyards with good local expertise, in particular Colin Gillespie of *Wootton*. If anything, Somerset wines are marked out by their strong varietal characteristics, and both Wootton and *Pilton Manor* frequently produce the cleanest examples of their grape types in the country. In all my tastings this year, Somerset has regularly achieved the highest overall standard.

Wootton's Schönburger is dead straight dry wine, tasting of green apple peel and musky crunchy table grapes. The Auxerrois shows how this Alsace relation of Pinot Blanc might be very effective in England, being quite weighty in the mouth, but beautifully dry and likely to go creamy with a bit more age. Seyval Blanc is probably our best widely planted non-aromatic variety: again, the bone dry but soft and pear-fruited Wootton shows it can be a top quality producer. Pilton Manor's Huxelrebe catches exactly the mixture of pure grapefruit softened with honey that this variety should show more often. The Special Reserve blend has an exhilarating, startlingly fresh taste of green apples much like wines from the Mauzac grape.

Other Somerset producers are also getting it right. *Moorlynch* manages to get some unnervingly original flavours into its wines. Their Medium Dry has an aroma of lavender and really green fruit in a very dry wine. Their Faber has a smell just like the rather attractive sensation of warm steam when you're ironing in the depths of winter. Against all the odds it's extremely enjoyable! *Staplecombe* are slightly less off the wall, and their Kerner, ripe and round, with good lime acidity, and very pleasant flavour of grape and honeycomb shows how this Riesling imitation may yet be an important grape here. *Coxley's* Schönburger is gently floral with an attractive flavour of guava and peach. Their Seyval seems to be earthy and flat – but I remember the Breaky Bottom of a few years ago: this will simply need time in order to turn into a lovely dry wine, scented by apple blossom and smoke.

Heading back north, WALES does have a few fledgling vineyards, and I've always got a soft spot for *Monnow Valley's* gentle Loire-like white.

There aren't many vineyards in HEREFORD AND WORCESTER, but what there is consistently score well. *Astley's* Madeleine Angevine has a lovely perfumed mose like floral talcum powder, and a soft ripe fruit of greengages and apples. *Three Choirs* Bacchus is softly dry, but with a green grass acidity more like Sauvignon or Colombard, and a most attractive greengage fruit.

Which brings us back to BERKSHIRE and the Thames Valley. *Thames Valley's* Schönburger Medium is extremely good, with elderflower perfume and a soft ripe flavour of peaches. But they don't just follow the pack here. They make sweet wine. And I mean sweet – genuinely, noble-rottedly sweet. The Scheurebe Late Harvest is mouthfilling, mixing elderflower perfume with honey and grapefruit. Just down the road, *Chiltern Valley* have bottled a Noble Bacchus in beautiful clear glass half-bottle flutes. To be honest, the nose is a bit volatile at the moment, but the wine is so luscious and syrupy and intensely rich, I decided I couldn't care less. It's a sensational dessert wine, and yet further evidence that we finally have a real full-blown wine-growing fraternity in this country, prepared to take risks, eager to excel.

A YEAR OF CHARDONNAY

I hadn't really expected the kangaroo tails to be up to much, so when James Halliday, Australian wine guru and my host for the evening, leaned dangerously over his barbecue and asked how I would like my kanga done – rare, but not extinct, I replied, quick as a flash – I had no high expectations of a gastronomic revelation. Barbied roo quickly proved itself to be the most astonishingly succulent yet gamey meat I had ever encountered. But what do you drink with kangaroo? Something utterly exotic, virtually unobtainable and preferably only just this side of illegal is what I hoped for – and, wow, did I get that! The most astonishing mouthfilling, mouth-coating, almost mouth-consuming Chardonnay I'd had all year. Nicholson River Chardonnay 1988, a couple of hundred cases made at the end of civilization as even the Australians know it in the wilds of Victoria's East Gippsland. Nicholson River? East Gippsland? Where, what, why? I know. But it's been that sort of year. I've been researching a new book and have been lucky enough to spend most of the year travelling the world's wine regions. In the process I've stumbled across all kinds of weird and wonderful concoctions in the most unlikely of places. They may not be classics yet, but they will be, just give them time. These are going to be the *new* classic wines.

CHALLENGING BURGUNDY

Chardonnay is a grape which sprang to fame in its own right a dozen or more years ago as the variety responsible for the heady, intoxicating brilliance of luscious yet dry flavours that marked out the great wines of Burgundy as the world's finest dry whites. Growers didn't aim for subtlety, they aimed for magnificence. The wines were so rich, so honeyed, so hazelnutty, and even so they were genius-flawed with whiffs of sour cream and hayricks untended in the suffocation of a summer noon. Yet there is now hardly a Burgundy made which makes the heart leap with such a scary intensity.

For a brief while the great names of the New World did produce their Meursault look-alikes, but as marketing strategies and insatiable demand have taken over from the misty-eyed dreams of wine men, Chardonnay is in danger of becoming just a generic term for dry white wines. Yet the flame which Chardonnay first lit does still burn, in all kinds of places. People describe it as the greatest white wine grape. There are still winemakers determined their wines will live up to that ideal.

California is in the grips of a marketing-led wine-making style, a toned-down, held-back style – but where there's a passionate winemaker, he'll still produce passionate wine in the full confidence that great wine markets itself. The sprawling giant Franciscan winery in California's Napa Valley produced fewer than 6000 bottles of a Cuvée Sauvage 1988 Chardonnay which really *is* wild stuff. Kent Rasmussen has so tiny a winery you can't do a proper barrel tasting – there all the casks are piled higgledy-piggledy on top of each other in a lean-to and even the winemaker doesn't know which is which until he throws open the doors in spring and hauls them all out, blinking and bleary into the pale Carneros sun. But what a Chardonnay he makes! So fat, so luscious, syrupy deep yet perfectly dry.

Another California shed – bigger, but just as ugly – and I taste the Au Bon Climat Reserve '88 Chardonnay and again my heart lifts at the intense, viscous syrup richness, the courage and the vanity of such impressive wine. And a barn this time – Chalone – way up a winding track in the Gavilan mountains – and the '89 Reserve is taking shape in barrel – ah, toast dripping butter, a spice box shaken on to the surface of the wine and a richness of peach and syrup and lime. Now I remember why Chardonnay can be supreme.

But sadly, these wines are all difficult to obtain and expensive to buy. Some of Australia's best are too. Lake's Folly '88 is rare but outstanding, mixing the perfumes of late Sunday morning toast with the chewy creaminess of a brazilnut, the piercing acidity of a lime. Dalwhinnie is rare too, brooding magnificently as it slowly unfurls the smoky, nutty intensity that Burgundy once thought was all its own. Brown Brothers Whitlands vineyard is the highest in Australia. It's only just coming into production. The Puligny-like dry intensity of their '87 Chardonnay shows one more passionate wine is about to take wing.

Yet Australia does manage to produce succulent, mouth-coating Chardonnays in quantity too – and often for not much more than £5 a bottle. Lindeman produce unbelievably good Hunter Valley Chardonnay which, inexplicably, is not available here in the UK. The Cowra region near the Hunter Valley is packed with Chardonnay grapes just dripping with lush, golden honeyed flavours. Rothbury's Cowra is startlingly good, drops of glistening honey swirled with pineapple and barley sugar. Brilliance at £5 a bottle from a flat stretch of desert in the middle of nowhere, only brought to life in the early morning sun by the glistening mile-long streaks of the irrigation lines.

THE STUFF OF DREAMS

And passion is flaring closer to home. Miguel Torres has taken to the hills above Barcelona and produced his Milmanda Chardonnay after years of trying. As good as Puligny? Yes. Better maybe, because you can taste the passion. Maurizio Castelli, Italian winemaker extraordinary, has swept up to the German-speaking Tyrol, bristling with Latin pride, and produced a Portico dei Leoni Chardonnay full of citrous lime attack, scented like leather gloves still warm from a dainty pair of hands, mint mingled with a salad and the caressing lusciousness of butterscotch and cream. Latin passion.

And the surging will to excel is breaking fresh ground as winemakers new to Chardonnay revel in the chance to fire our imaginations as the Burgundians used to do. Vipava make wine in Yugoslavia, right by the Italian border. Their Chardonnay is proud, smacking of lemongrass, the tang of a beach bar lime, resin from bark. In the empty hills of Limoux in south-west France, where in a single moment of glory centuries back, winemakers just managed to beat Dom Pérignon to the discovery of sparkling wine, producers have planted Chardonnay, crushed the grapes into expensive oak barrels and produced fabulously spicy, unctuous wine, excitingly fresh as well as invitingly decadent. The best barrels were auctioned off for the local church spire fund. Parish Passion.

And even in England the tinder box is struck. Wellow Vineyards in Hampshire last year produced a pale, wispy, unsteady foal of a Chardonnay so light it seemed like water, and yet as I swallowed I saw just the tiniest flicker of beauty, a moment, no more, to show that even the English yeoman can feel his heart race a little at the challenge of Chardonnay, the greatest white wine grape in the world.

IDEAL CELLARS

When people ask you, 'Do you have a cellar?', you can't help but feel that they don't mean the jumble of cardboard boxes in the understairs cupboard that constitutes the sum total of your own precious wine stocks. A cellar, surely, is a dark, cool cavern, lined with stamped wooden cases and floor-to-ceiling racks.

The Russian Imperial Cellar that was auctioned at Sotheby's in 1990 fitted into this vision. Tsar Nicholas II possessed a cellar of awesome proportions: 11 galleries over three floors, the lowest level over 200 feet underground, the whole carved out by Siberian coal miners. Now that's what you could call a Real Cellar.

The reality today, from house to house, is a little different. We had a phone call in the *Webster's* offices earlier this year from a journalist who wanted to write about wine experts without cellars. He seemed pretty disappointed to hear that Oz Clarke had moved house and was no longer the proud possessor of a jumbled, blanket-lined cupboard, but the owner of a real, underground cellar.

But Oz is living proof that it is perfectly possible to survive with or without the perfect storage conditions. It has never stopped him hoarding wine. Below, *Webster's* wine merchants and contributors dream about their own Ideal Cellars.

ALLAN CHEESMAN

SAINSBURY'S

—————— £100 ——————

With frightening price increases due to costs, currency and duty, this £100 limit is becoming more difficult, but it's still possible to put together a good 'start-up' cellar.

Sainsbury's Alsace Pinot Blanc *A continuing favourite; as versatile as ever and tremendous value.* **6 for £18.90**

Sainsbury's Vin de Pays des Côtes du Tarn *Crisp dry white in the new style from the south-west. Price unbelievable.* **6 for £14.10**

1989 Sainsbury's Côtes du Lubéron Rosé, Domaine de la Panisse *Dry, fresh rosé with delicate flavour.* **6 for £19.14**

Sainsbury's Montepulciano d'Abruzzo *Rich, meaty Italian red, ideal for rich, full-flavoured stews. Will keep too.* **6 for £15.54**

1988 Sainsbury's Côtes du Frontonnais, Château Bellevue-la-Forêt *A new find from north of Toulouse. Soft style.* **6 for £19.14**

Sainsbury's Arruda *The old favourite from north of Lisbon – still amazing value and quality.* **6 for £13.14**

Total cost: £99.96

—————— £500 ——————

A mix of drinking for the year plus some to put away for a year or two.

Sainsbury's Alsace Pinot Blanc *See above.* **12 for £37.80**

Sainsbury's Chardonnay Alto-Adige *This stylish Tiefenbrunner Chardonnay has been a favourite for years and continues to please. It develops well too.* **12 for £46.68**

1988 Sainsbury's Chablis *In spite of the price, this fuller-flavoured, classic wine is a sure winner in any cellar. It will repay keeping.* **12 for £77.80**

1989 Sainsbury's Côtes du Lubéron Rosé, Domaine de la Panisse *See above.* **12 for £38.28**

Sainsbury's Arruda *See above.*
12 for £26.28

1986 Sainsbury's Chianti Classico *Still from Ricasoli, this 1986 shows all the style and power of Chianti.* **12 for £41.88**

1988 Sainsbury's Minervois, Château de Gourgazaud *Estate bottled, this rich, almost spicy red is ideal all year round, from summer barbecues to cold winter evenings!* **6 magnums for £36.54**

1985/86 Château Tourteau-Chollet *Classic red Graves; mellow and mature with good fruit and tannin balance.* **12 for £65.40**

1987 Herdade de Santa Marta Alentejo *A Sainsbury 'find' in 1990. This Peter Bright red from the centre of Portugal is a blend of local varieties, fermented in oak, with that Australian 'know-how'.* **12 for £41.40**

Sainsbury's Crémant de Bourgogne *White or rosé at the same price! An excellent alternative to the real thing and almost half the price.* **12 for £70.20**

Total cost £482.26

One bottle of 1985 Sainsbury's Vintage Champagne will make up the £500.

――――――― **£1000** ―――――――

Fifteen cases in total ranging widely across the quality and price spectrum.

1989 Domaine Grandchamp, Bergerac Sauvignon *From the Ryman stable, this crisp, fruity, almost juicy white Sauvignon is a great food wine.* **12 for £59.40**

1989 Gavi, Bersano *The vogue Italian white from Cortese grapes. Stylish and characterful.* **12 for £53.40**

Sainsbury's White Burgundy – Chardonnay *From the house of Rodet. A 'hardy annual'; drinking well now, and worth keeping too.* **12 for £53.88**

1988 Craigmoor Chardonnay, Mudgee *Rich, buttery Chardonnay from northern New South Wales.* **12 for £72.40**

1988 Serriger Vogelsang Riesling QbA, Staatsweingut Trier *Classic Riesling with a touch of sweetness. Ideal aperitif wine, worth keeping too.* **12 for £42.60**

1987/88 Clos St-Georges Graves Supérieures *Still good value in today's Sauternes market and comparable with many Classed Growths.* **12 for £63.00**

Sainsbury's Côtes du Lubéron Rosé, Domaine de la Panisse *See above.*
12 for £38.28

1988 Sainsbury's Côtes du Frontonnais, Château Bellevue-la-Forêt *See above.*
12 for £38.28

1987 Herdade de Santa Marta Alentejo *See above.* **12 for £41.40**

1985 Sainsbury's Rioja *Soft, buttery style, yet with good fruit.* **12 for £39.00**

1982 Castello di San Polo in Rosso, Chianti Classico Riserva *A real stunner and excellent example of modern Chianti wine-making. Outstanding.* **12 for £65.40**

1987 La Crema Pinot Noir *One of California's newest wineries, making real, Burgundy-like Pinot Noir. With a touch of style too!* **12 for £95.40**

1986/87 Domaine André Brunel, Châteauneuf-du-Pape *Spicy, rich and robust, a single-estate wine that we've followed for a number of years.*
12 for £81.00

1984/86 Château Maucaillou, Moulis *One of the best bourgeois clarets around today, with that classic cedar, oak and blackcurrant balance. Excellent.*
12 for £113.40

1985 Sainsbury's Vintage Champagne *Still affordable (just) and showing all the rich biscuity style you could wish for.*
12 for £138.60

Total cost: £995.44

A case of Sainsbury's Monastère Belgian Spring Water will just round off the £1000.

Sainsbury's Vintage Selection.
good restaurant. Until

If you're a wine buff who's been buffeted by rising prices you'll welcome our Vintage Selection.

You'll find the quality familiar and the prices, quite often, nostalgic. All our wines have been tasted and tested by our wine buyers who have been working on this selection for 7 years. All of the wines are ready to drink now though some are suitable for laying down.

Many come with established reputations like Paul Jaboulet Aîné.

Some are more unusual like the Portuguese Quinta da Bacalhôa or Vernaccia di San Gimignano from the small family-owned estate of San Quirico.

Many are virtually exclusive to Sainsbury's and they all bear our Vintage Seal on the label.

You'll find the complete list in our larger stores and most carry a good selection.

We hope that you'll enjoy reading about the wines below and that you'll be tempted to turn a wine list into something more satisfying.

A shopping list.

1. **Le Sec de Rayne Vigneau 1989, Bordeaux.** A crisp, dry white wine produced from Sauvignon and Semillon grapes grown on the alluvial soils of Château Rayne Vigneau, a property more widely known for its rich Sauternes.

2. **Château Mayne des Carmes 1987, Sauternes.** This delicious wine is the 'second wine' of Château Rieussec, the premier cru Sauternes property which now forms part of the Domaines Baron de Rothschild. It is made from a blend of 80% Semillon and 20% Sauvignon grapes. It is piercingly rich and honeyed. Serve lightly chilled either as a dessert wine or with pâté de foie gras.

3. **Château de Davenay 1987, Montagny Premier Cru.** Château de Davenay is a single estate situated near the village of Montagny in the Côte Challonaise area of Burgundy. Made from Chardonnay grapes, the wine is matured in oak barrels for 6 months in order to develop its supple and slightly nutty style.

4. **Quincy 1989, Duc de Berri.** Quincy, a small village in the Upper Loire, is among the smallest of appellations in France but deserves greater recognition for its lively and attractive wine. Crisp and dry, the Sauvignon grape gives a distinctive aroma of blackcurrant leaves. It traditionally partners chevre (goat's cheese) but is more often served with white meats or fish.

5. **Kaseler Herrenberg Riesling Kabinett 1988, Reichsgraf von Kesselstatt.** The estate of Reichsgraf von Kesselstatt has vineyards in many of the finest areas of the Mosel region. The Herrenberg vineyard is situated on the hills above Kasel, a small village on the River Ruwer. Kaseler wines have a delicate floral style and elegant flavour which makes them most appealing. Serve lightly chilled as a perfect aperitif.

It reads like the wine list in a you come to the prices.

6. **Vernaccia di San Gimignano 1989, San Quirico.** This distinguished white wine is produced on an estate of 22 hectares near the beautiful mediaeval town of San Gimignano in Tuscany. The estate is run by Andrea Vecchione whose family have owned the property for 120 years. The wine is dry and full bodied with a crisp and elegant style which makes it ideal for serving with antipasti, hors d'oeuvres or fish.

7. **Firestone Chardonnay 1987, Santa Ynez.** The Firestone Estate was established nearly 20 years ago by Brooks Firestone of the famous tyres family. The Chardonnay wines from Firestone have a justified reputation for quality. Having been matured in French oak barrels, the wine has an elegant flavour with a mellow, oaky touch.

8. **Château Maucaillou 1984, Moulis.** Château Maucaillou was founded in 1875. It is situated in the Médoc region of Bordeaux between Margaux and St Julien. The wine is a classic medium-bodied claret which has been made from grapes grown on the gravelly soil of the district. The flavour is enhanced by ageing the wine in oak casks for 18 months before bottling. Serve with red meats, particularly lamb, or well-flavoured cheeses.

9. **St Joseph le Grand Pompée 1988, Paul Jaboulet Aîné.** Made from Syrah grapes grown on the steep granite hillsides, St Joseph is one of the most robust and flavoursome wines of the Rhône Valley. The 1988 vintage has produced an excellent example of St. Joseph at its best: rich, dark, spicy and peppery it has a full-bodied flavour which will develop with keeping.

10. **Vino Nobile di Montepulciano 1986, Fattoria di Casale.** Montepulciano is a small and picturesque hilltop town in southern Tuscany where this robust and complex wine is made from a blend of up to 6 grape varieties. The 1986 vintage produced a wine which is still very youthful and which will continue to improve over the next 5 years.

11. **La Crema Pinot Noir 1987.** The La Crema winery, founded in 1979, produces premium quality wines of great elegance. The La Crema wine is a delicious example of the standard of excellence that can be achieved with this notoriously difficult grape. It has a wonderfully rich bouquet and a stylish flavour which is full and mellow.

12. **Quinta da Bacalhôa 1986.** The beautiful wine estate of the Quinta da Bacalhôa at Azeitão in central Portugal dates from 1480 and is a national monument. The vineyard is planted with Cabernet Sauvignon and Merlot and the resulting wine is matured in oak barrels. Its classic style and distinguished flavour can be enjoyed now as a partner for red meat dishes or will benefit from further ageing.

Good wine costs less at Sainsbury's.

NICHOLAS BEVAN

DEPUTY EDITOR

£100

Thirst and mood come to mind. Something for everyday drinking, one selection with a little more substance and one with a light fizz.

Sainsbury's Vinho Verde *Easy going, light fridge wine. Refreshing, cooling, fruity and easy on the mind.*   **6 for £15.54**

1989 Château La Place, Côtes de Duras, Sauvignon Blanc *Sharp, snappy, tingling taste that rounds out into a fruity clean sensation which slides down peacefully without an awful burning aftertaste, characteristic of the nasty versions.*   **6 for £20.10**

Vin de Pays Haute Vallée de l'Aude, Merlot *Soft and round, not quite Rubensesque, without being overbearing. Plummy with a hint of fruit from the summer hedgerow.*   **6 for £15.54**

1986 Seaview Cabernet Sauvignon *Wonderful, confident Australian at a price that belies its quality. Brilliant scent, full blackcurrant fruit with an undercurrent of firm tannin and acidity. It has never let me down.*   **6 for £23.94**

Yalumba Angas Brut Rosé *Australian pink fizz. Soft, delicate flavour in contrast to some of the blowsy sparklers of the past.*   **6 for £29.94**

Total cost £105.06

£500

Wines for winter Sunday lunch and for those times when cheques arrive in the post.

1985 Château de Marbuzet, Ste Estèphe *Some merchants tell me that I should be keeping this but I think it's hokum. It will of course last but it's tremendous drinking now.*   **12 for £113.40**

1985 Riesling Grand Cru AC, Brand *Slaty, fruity but dry, full-bodied but light in the mouth and great to drink with Thai food – it's often a problem finding a wine that is!*   **12 for £95.88**

1989 Orlando RF Chardonnay *THE Australian Chardonnay for me. It may not be perfect but it has such an accomplished array of mega tastes, powerful with a zing of fruit only found in the succulence of an oriental mango, rich, seductive and a catalyst to thirst.*   **12 for £52.68**

NV Jacquesson, Blanc de Blancs, Brut, Magnums *Buttery, balanced, explosive Champagne from the fifth oldest Champagne House of all. Clean with a fresh, sensational delivery.*   **12 for £174.00**

1985 Torres Gran Sangredetoro, Penedes *Not a tart plonk but an intense, aromatic, ripe wine. Miguel Torres is synonymous with consistency in the Spanish market.*   **12 for £59.88**

Total cost £495.84

£1000

Serious wine for serious money.

1989 Sancerre, Les Perriers *A magnificent, dry and friendly Sauvignon, intense in perfume. A wonderful vintage when the grapes were in top condition, producing a wine that is drinkable within a couple of months of bottling.*   **12 for £83.40**

1986 Seaview Pinot Noir/Chardonnay *Another Australian sparkler that reminds me of my childhood but this is no island wine. Deep in flavour; an elegant mix of grapes.*   **12 for £83.88**

1985 Chateau d'Angludet, Margaux AC *Classic half price Médoc if I'm looking at ordinary Classed Growths. Large, beautiful fruity wine from a fantastic year.*   **12 for £111.60**

1988 Semillon/Sauvignon, Cape Mentelle *The Semillon fills out and massages the brisk Sauvignon into a smoothness which makes for urgent drinking.* **12 for £80.40**

1985 Gewürztraminer 'Altenbourg', P. Blanck *A fine vintage which is now tasting terrific, peppery and full-flavoured.* **12 for £84.60**

1984 Firestone Pinot Noir *My Burgundian taste-alike at half the price. Very alert and fruity varietal from the USA.* **12 for £77.40**

1988 Selvapiana Chianti Rufina *A wonderful year in Tuscany, and a wonderful wine – from Rufina, north of Florence. Elegant drinking.* **12 for £59.88**

1987 Semillon Selaks, Kumeu Estate *Lavish, light, overripe apricotty taste, with an aftertaste of baked fresh apple and blackcurrant – a palate buster.*
12 for £87.00

Mumm Crémant de Cramant *Rich, creamy, delicious with a hint of sweet nuts giving a mouth warming, filling sensation.*
12 for £220.80

1983 Dow's Port *For laying down*
1983 Château des Tours, Ste Croix du Mont *The alternative Sauternes – for drinking – full, rich and dripping with sweetness.*
6 bottles of each for £132.90

Total cost: £1021.86

PHILIP CONTINI

VALVONA & CROLLA

———— £100 ————

The efforts to improve quality over the last ten to fifteen years are starting to pay dividends in Italy. A wealth of indigenous grape varieties, previously used for blending, are being singled out and developed as wines in their own right. The intention is to give the wine lover the opportunity to taste new flavours as well as improve the quality of the better-known varieties. If Italy can only hang on to a sensible quality/price ratio, success is guaranteed. I have chosen well-made, everyday wines for the £100 cellar.

1988 Pinot Grigio, Ca' Donini *Zesty, fragrant white from the Veneto. This producer is part of a large group. Their pooled skills are exemplified in this well-made wine with good fruit / acid balance.*
6 for £19.74

1988 Montepulciano d'Abruzzo, Bianchi *Off-dry, quaffing red from the Abruzzi, packed full of ripe fruit with a deep ruby colour and a long aftertaste. One of the largest producers of Montepulciano, Bianchi are noted for the quality of their large production.* **6 for £19.14**

1987 Cirò, Librandi *From Calabria (the big toe of Italy). Made from an obscure grape variety, Gaglioppo. Rich, earthy and spicy red, bursting with fruit.* **6 for £20.34**

1989 Bianco di Sciacca, Enocarboj *A stunner from this well equipped co-operative in south-west Sicily. Full-flavoured, fragrant white made from local Inzolia grapes.* **6 for £19.74**

1989 Dolcetto d'Acqui, Viticoltori dell'Acquese *The rich fruit aromas just burst out of the glass. The light colour of this red wine belies the intensity of flavour. Simply delicious when drunk at around 10 degrees.* **6 for £21.54**

Total cost: £100.50

———— £500 ————

Italy has so many excellent wines to offer in the £3–6 bracket.

1988 Bianco d'Arquata, Adanti *This family-run azienda produces some of the most exciting wines from Umbria. This full, dry white wine, made primarily from Garganega and Grechetto, has generous fruit with a hint of lemon.* **12 for £55.08**

1986 Montefalco Rosso d'Arquata, Adanti *Signor Adanti and his winemaker Alvaro have worked hard to produce this deep, rich spicy red. Made primarily with the Sagrantino grape.*   **12 for £55.08**

1987 Barbera Oltrepò Pavese, Fugazza *The two Fugazza sisters have taken over the reins of their late father's estate, Castello di Luzzano. This red is robust, full-bodied and made as organically as wine can be. Should be drunk young.*   **12 for £50.28**

1989 Orvieto, Marchesi Antinori *Generous, appealing with plenty of fresh, tangy fruit.*   **12 for £46.68**

1987 Campo ai Sassi, Marchesi de' Frescobaldi *This Rosso di Montalcino is of medium weight with forward fruit and a tannic backbone.*   **12 for £62.28**

1985 Montepulciano d'Abruzzo, Barone Cornacchia *One of the really serious small producers in the Abruzzi. This wine is excellent value for money. Really concentrated flavours.*   **12 for £62.28**

1986 Rosso Conero, Mario Marchetti *Dottore Marchetti's wine is almost 'hand-made'. Earthy and spicy with tannic grip – it will blossom over the next couple of years.*   **12 for £55.08**

1988 Chianti Rufina, 'Banda Blu' Gianfranco Grati *The lively fruit of this wine is as delicious an example of young Chianti as I have come across.*
12 for £43.08

1986 Barolo, Giacomo Ascheri *A forward style of Barolo with a good balance between fruit and tannin.*   **12 for £77.88**

Total cost: £507.72

── **£1000** ──

So much mature Italian wine never reaches our shores mainly because the Italians drink it all and, more often than not, when it is still too young. Well, the buck stops here. Let you and I put away some liquid jewels to enjoy and appreciate in the years to come.

1988 Teroldego Rotaliano, Roberto Zeni (Trentino Alto-Adige) *Probably the most exciting red in the region. The Teroldego grape is unique to the Rotaliano plain and must be tasted to be believed. Drink over the next two to three years.*   **12 for £62.28**

1985 Sagrantino, Domenico Adanti (Umbria) *Made from 100 per cent Sagrantino grapes with a short time in new oak. This red is a knockout! Give it a couple of years to soften.*   **12 for £74.28**

1985 Chianti Classico Riserva, Vigneto Bellavista, Castello di Ama (Tuscany) *I think this Chianti will just go on and on. Robust, yet gentle. Concentrated, ripe, sweet fruit yet dry with plenty of tannin to see it through to the turn of the century.*
12 for £166.68

1985 Tignanello, Marchesi Antinori (Tuscany) *Tignanello was the original 'Super-Tuscan' and it's still my favourite. Start drinking in six or seven years.*
12 for £167.88

1987 Recioto di Soave dei Capitelli, Roberto Anselmi (Veneto) *Please leave a few bottles of this deep golden, sweet nectar for your grandchildren. Not wishing to compare this with better-known dessert wines, I will only say that this would certainly be one of my desert-island wines.*   **12 for £178.68**

1985 Brunello di Montalcino, Fattoria dei Barbi (Tuscany) *The rich fruit is still shrouded in tannin but over the next ten years or so the tannin will recede and you will be drinking one of the great wines of the 1980s.*   **12 for £148.08**

1988 Barbaresco Santo Stefano, Castello di Neive (Piemonte) *The cask samples I tasted showed great promise. A medium-weight Barbaresco with the tannins easing off over the mid 1990s. Drinking brilliantly in spring 2000?*   **12 for £120.00**

1985 Aglianico, Fratelli d'Angelo (Basilicata) *From the Aglianico grapes, one of the great wines of southern Italy. For drinking in the mid 1990s.*   **12 for £79.08**

Total cost: £996.96

ROSEMARY GEORGE MW

ASSOCIATE EDITOR

————— **£100** —————

This is for topping up on wines for everyday drinking, friendly uncomplicated bottles that provide immediate quaffable enjoyment.

Vin de Pays des Côtes de Gascogne, Domaine de San Guilhem *This* vin de pays *is the rising star of south-west France, with a dramatic improvement in the wine-making following the fall in sales of Armagnac. (The grapes that are no longer used for the spirit now go into the wine.)*
12 for £36.00

Asda Côtes du Frontonnais *This is a simply delicious own-label wine, from one of the main producers in this little-known region near Toulouse. Négrette is the principal grape variety, lending some spicy cherry flavours.*   **12 for £36.00**

Yalumba Angas Brut Rosé *One of the best pink sparklers around, just for fun, and very much better value than anything from France.*   **6 for £29.94**

Total cost: £101.94

————— **£500** —————

This is going to be devoted to my Tuscan cellar. Tuscany is today a region of exciting wine-making. The following are mainly from the excellent 1985 vintage.

1985 Vino Nobile di Montepulciano, Avignonesi *This splendidly fruity red comes from one of Montepulciano's best producers.*
12 for £108.00

1985 Carmignano Riserva, Capezzana
12 for £120.00

1985 Chianti Classico Riserva, Fontodi
12 for £112.00

1985 Fontalloro *A pure Sangiovese vino da tavola from a leading Chianti estate, Felsina Berardenga, and a brilliant example of the quality of this grape variety.*
12 for £132.00

1986 Morellino di Scansano, le Pupille *Morellino is another name for Sangiovese and Scansano is an isolated hilltop town in the heart of the Maremma of southern Tuscany. The taste is not dissimilar to Chianti.*
6 for £29.00

Total cost: £501.00

────────── **£1000** ──────────

This is the chance for real long-term indulgence, with a few choice bottles for laying down.

1986 Meursault Charmes 1er cru, Henri Germain *Actually I would have to be very strong-minded not to drink all this soon, as it is already delicious, with lovely toasted fruit. I'll try and be resolute though – it can only get even better.*
12 for £232.20

1988 Nuits-St-Georges 1er cru, les Pruliers, Domaine Boillot *Wonderfully rich, concentrated, chocolate Pinot Noir fruit, from a superb vintage.*
12 for £230.00

1988 Chablis 1er cru, Chapelot, Raveneau *An excellent vintage and my favourite producer.*
12 for £115.00

1989 Château Trotanoy, Pomerol *Ex-cellars means that there's duty and VAT to pay when it is eventually shipped. We heard lots about the 1989 vintage in Bordeaux. This really is great wine.*
12 for £350.00EC

1988 Crozes-Hermitage, Domaine Pochon *A stunning mouthful of concentrated, blackcurrant gum fruit, which needs time to develop. The same small grower's Château Curson is even better – but it's £1 a bottle more expensive.*
12 for £79.00

Total cost: £1006.20

BRUCE KENDRICK

HAUGHTON FINE WINES

────────── **£100** ──────────

Let's get off to those relatively unknown *vins de pays* from southern France, stopping off in Bergerac and ending up on the flat sea-shore in Fitou.

1988 Vin de Pays du Val de Montferrand, Domaine Belles Croix Robin *Redolent of dark red fruits, full and stylish and organic to boot.*
6 for £22.14

1988 Vin de Pays des Côtes de Gascogne, Domaine de Mathalin *Plenty of colour, a sound aromatic style from classic red grape varieties as well as the local Négrette. Good blackcurrant fruit.*
6 for £20.52

1988 Bergerac Blanc Sec, Domaine de Libarde *Excellent fruit acidity with fresh, gooseberry aromas.*
6 for £20.52

I've got £36.82 left. The rules say at least six bottles per style so I've chosen nine ...

1987 Fitou Domaine Aimé Fontanel *A whopper with firm red fruit.* **9 for £36.45**

Total cost: £99.63

────────── **£500** ──────────

What about a varietal cellar with up-front, ripe fruit flavours at reasonable prices? Antipodean of course ...

1989 David Wynn, Chardonnay, Australia *New to the UK. No oak character whatsoever, just bags of light, mellow citrus fruits.*
12 for £78.36

1988 Schinus Molle, Shiraz, Australia *New-style Shiraz with soft, peppery, spicy fruit and lingering finish.*
12 for £83.88

1986 David Wynn, Cabernet Sauvignon, Australia *Deep red-purple colour, distinctive, unoaked Cabernet fruit and texture.* **12 for £67.44**

1989 Sauvignon Blanc, Rongopai, New Zealand *Not the 'standard' grassy character, but more complex with creamy tone and texture. Rich, full of gooseberry flavour.* **12 for £101.04**

1987 Riesling, Hollick's, Coonawarra, Australia *This wine is just emerging from one of those frustrating dormant periods but the wait has been worthwhile. Bags of butterscotch with a pleasingly crisp finish.* **12 for £80.16**

1988 Semillon, Neudorf Vineyards, Nelson, New Zealand *Herbaceous nose, unusual in a Semillon but not in New Zealand. The true character comes through on the palate with those full, green fruit flavours.* **12 for £90.84**

Total cost: £501.72

─────── **£1000** ───────

These wines are for keeping and I'm going to include some top-whack Australasian goodies along with the more conventional, if a little obscure, French delights. All have at least three years' cellaring potential.

1986 Coteaux d'Aix en Provence Les Baux, Mas de Gourgonnier, Réserve du Mas *This is great wine with another three years of life at least if the '83 is anything to go by. Classic red varieties Cabernet and Syrah as well as Mourvèdre. A full and round wine with elegant, clean fruit.* **12 for £64.68**

1989 Pouilly Fumé, Domaine Didier Pabiot, Cuvée Tradition *Grassy and fragrant with a rich creaminess which anticipates the extra complexity on the palate. Great cellaring potential.* **12 for £92.52**

1986 Savennières, Domaine du Closel *Some traces of late-picked Chenin Blanc show through well. Apples, honey and rich complexity.* **12 for £70.08**

1986 Château Patache d'Aux, Cru Grand Bourgeois, Médoc *The depth of flavours are so impressive from this, my favourite petit château. The wines seem to improve with each vintage.* **12 for £78.60**

1986 Saumur-Champigny, Clos Rougeard *Wood-ageing for two years was a match for this massive Cabernet Franc. Now softer, but still with keen fruit. The best vintage for a while. Organic too!* **12 for £95.88**

1986 Hautes-Côtes de Nuits, Domaine Alain Verdet *New oak, spicy, heavy raspberry fruit character, plenty of vanilla and tannins which are integrating well...* **12 for £130.20**

1988 Martinborough Pinot Noir, New Zealand *Strictly rationed in the UK. Complex, rich raspberry fruit. The nearest thing I've come across to perfect Pinot at the price.* **12 for £128.40**

1989 Mountadam Chardonnay, High Eden Ridge, Australia *Stunning, elegant, rich, complex, balanced. I like the way it always surprises the taste buds.* **12 for £131.88**

1988 Dromana Estate Cabernet Merlot, Mornington Peninsula, Australia *Lifted cherry and berry aromas. Concentrated, complex blackcurrant flavours with a soft tannin centre. Excellent.* **12 for £127.68**

1984 Banyuls Grand Cru, L'Etoile *This is great value, fortified wine with bags of medium-sweet, fleshy fruit and a nuttiness on the nose.* **12 for £84.96**

Total cost: £1004.88

WILLIE LEBUS

BIBENDUM

£100

If anybody is mad enough to give you £100 or £500, let alone £1000, you owe it to the giver to go mad. Therefore, cast aside inhibitions and use the money to buy wines which you would otherwise never dream of getting.

The first sign of madness is extravagance, so £100 buys but 12 bottles. The second sign is Alsace because it used to be reserved for wine merchants. Now even human beings like the stuff.

1987 Tokay-Pinot Gris Réserve, Rolly Gassmann *If Gewürz is too strong, try this. The Rolly Gassmanns make an elegant yet powerful wine. This is wonderful with food.*
6 for £53.22

1987 Gewürztraminer Réserve, Rolly Gassmann *If this is an off-vintage, save me from the good ones! To achieve intensity of fruit whilst keeping balance is hard enough. With Gewürz, it's nigh impossible. This has so much length it could sing 'God Save the Queen' twice over.*   **6 for £44.88**

Total cost: £98.10

£500

Five cases of weird wines coming up...

1983 Vouvray Clos de Bourg Demi-Sec, Gaston Huet *Huet's organic Demi-Sec is most other producers' Sec. Appley fruit, strident grip, real length. Great with fish (not chips).*   **12 for £97.29**

1985 Gigondas, Domaine les Pallières *Sadly for us, other countries have sussed this wine so hurry, hurry, hurry!! The 1985 vintage has produced intense, richly fruity wine with characteristic, earthy spiciness.*
12 for £105.02

1983 Brauneberger Juffer-Sonnenuhr, Riesling Auslese, Max Ferd Richter *A*

million miles from Liebfraumilch. Light years away. This wine manages to combine heady concentration with stalky, lemony Riesling fruit. And yes, what length!
12 for £132.76

1985 Sangioveto del Borgo, Citterio (Tuscany) *Too cheap, but a real aristocrat. 100 per cent with no Cabernet anywhere to be seen. Rich, sweet fruit, some raisiny character. Yum, yum.*   **12 for £58.10**

1985 Grande Escolha, Champalimaud *This is wine for grown-ups, watching Friday 13th Part 65. Authentic, full-bodied Portuguese red with excellent tannin. This one will keep for ages.*   **12 for £98.26**

Total cost: £491.43

£1000

Now, for some serious **madness, one case each of...**

NV Henri Billiot Champagne *Proper Champagne this. Almost entirely made of Pinot Noir, it has bags of flavour and rich fruit and you can sit on it for years and watch it change for the better.*
12 for £188.65

1988 Sancerre Rouge, Domaine de Montigny, H Natter *Huge and intense; almost Burgundian wine which is far better than most. Big vanilla flavour from the oak and nice background acidity.*
12 for £115.23

1988 Condrieu, Pierre Dumazet *Take a bottle from the cellar, not the fridge, open it, pour a good amount into the glass and sip it for four hours, noting the amazing change in flavour. Dumazet makes ten barrels of this nectar, cheap at the price.*
12 for £194.03

1987 Nuits-St-Georges 1er Cru, Les Pruliers, Boillot *The ambitious Boillot brothers have wonderful vineyards in Nuits*

and Gevrey. They practise minimum handling of the wines, relying on the tiny yield from their uniformly mature vineyards. For vintage star gazers, try this 1987 and destroy all plastic charts.
12 for £188.23

1985 Barolo, Domenico Clerico *Not renowned for subtlety, Barolo has a new champion in Clerico. He has managed to produce massive concentration without big, tannic structure. This has the power of Barbaresco with the majesty of Barolo. Stunning wine.*
12 for £207.00

Just one Chardonnay creeps in – and who would have believed it a decade ago; wines from the other side of the world – it's from ... New Zealand!!

1989 Hawke's Bay Chardonnay, Yales Vineyard, Collards *Possibly the best Chardonnay I have had from outside Montrachet on a Wednesday. Seriously, it has mountains of rich fruit, great length and taut structure provided by fruit acidity. Unbelievably good!!*
12 for £137.45

Total cost: £1030.59

JAMES ROGERS

FULHAM ROAD WINE CENTRE

—————— £100 ——————

All these cellars have been chosen to include some wines to drink now and others to lay down. First, two reds and a white.

1982 Château Musar *The remarkable Lebanese wine that will improve both in quality and value.*
6 for £36.00

1985 Remelluri *One of only two single vineyard Rioja estates. This will drink well for five years.*
6 for £46.00

1988 Tokay-Pinot Gris, Caves de Turckheim *The remarkable wine from Alsace that drinks way above its price.*
6 for £25.00

Total cost: £107.00

—————— £500 ——————

The perfectly balanced cellar – a white, a fizz, three reds and a sweet Barsac. Something for everyone.

1989 Wynns Coonawarra, Chardonnay *Consistently one of the very best from Australia.*
12 for £72.00

1989 Rully, Louis Jadot *One of the stars of this vintage from this highly regarded Burgundian négociant.*
12 for £140.00

NV Le Mesnil *No cellar should be without Champagne. 100 per cent Chardonnay from a 100 per cent rated village.*
12 for £160.00

1986 Domaine Richeaume, Côtes de Provence *One of the rare organic wines with class. Rich and long lasting.*
12 for £72.00

1985 Château Beaumont, Haut-Médoc *A lovely wine from a very attractive vintage that will age well for ten years.* **6 for £60.00**

1988 Château Piada, Barsac *A dessert wine with both richness and elegance that will age well for 20 years.*
6 for £84.00

Total cost: £588.00

—————— £1000 ——————

These wines have been chosen with a serious millennium dinner party in mind. Please ask me!

1985 Le Mesnil *A wonderfully rich yet elegant Champagne that will be at its glorious peak as we move into the year 2000.*
12 for £190.00

1989 Puligny-Montrachet, Les Folatières, Maroslavac-Leger *A perfectly balanced wine from an outstanding vintage, made by one of Burgundy's new stars.* **6 for £140.00**

1985 Château Pichon-Longueville-Baron, 2ème cru classé Pauillac *Pichon 'Baron' has really 'come good' in the recent vintages. The new owners are determined to match the quality of the more celebrated Pichon-Lalande. They certainly managed it in 1985.*   **12 for £190.00**

1981 Château de Beaucastel, Châteauneuf-du-Pape *One of the really great Rhône reds that will be quite exceptional by the year 2000.*   **12 for £230.00**

1986 Château Rayne-Vigneau, Sauternes *Beautifully rich fruit with the acidity to ensure a venerable life. Classic dessert wine made in a year when noble rot swept through the vineyards.*   **6 for £90.00**

1983 Cockburn's Vintage Port *A reasonably light year will mean that this wine will be reaching its peak by the turn of the century.*   **6 for £130.00**

Total cost: £970.00

RICHARD TANNER

TANNERS

—————— £100 ——————

I never cease to wonder how fortunate we are to have France and her best wines so near at hand. At lower price levels it is hard to find such value for money further afield.

Saumon Blanc, Tanners *Fresh and with good fruit, this crisp white comes from the rolling foothills of the Pyrenees, inland from the Mediterranean.*
   6 for £17.10

Bécasse Rouge, Tanners *With character and soft, well-defined fruit, this hails from the same area as the Saumon Blanc.*
   6 for £17.10

1989 Côtes de St-Mont, Producteurs Plaimont *This full-flavoured, stylish white from Gascony is made from a number of local grape varieties.*   **6 for £19.38**

1989 Domaine de Limbardie, Vin de Pays des Coteaux de Murviel *The 1988 vintage of this delicious red was a gold medal winner in the WINE magazine 1990 International Wine Challenge. The 1989 is just as good.*   **6 for £20.40**

> **Webster's** *is an annual publication. We welcome your suggestions for next year's edition.*

1989 Château du Grand Moulas, Côtes du Rhône-Villages *Half Grenache and half Syrah, this is something to enjoy drinking in three to five years' time.*   **6 for £28.50**

Total cost: £102.48

—————— £500 ——————

If I have chosen few New World wines it is because I tend to purchase the cooler climate North European wines: I prefer their elegance and natural acidity to the power, higher strength and ripeness that is often found in New World wines.

1989 Domaine Cauhapé, Jurançon Sec, Henri Ramonteau *Made from local grape varieties at the foot of the Pyrenees, this has masses of fruit and excellent length.*
   12 for £75.12

1988 Macon-Clessé Quintaine, M. & P. Guillemot *An elegant, light and extremely well-made Chardonnay from an area where quality has much improved.*   **12 for £76.32**

1988 Rheingau Riesling Kabinett, Langwerth Von Simmern *A classic Rheingau Riesling from a top German estate that has been in the same family's hands since 1469.*   **12 for £63.24**

1983 Château Ruat-Petit-Poujeaux, Moulis *An extremely well-made* bourgeois *Médoc of a classic vintage. Expert winemaker and* négociant *Pierre Coste advises the proprietor here.* **12 for £95.64**

1986 Châteauneuf-du-Pape, Domaine de Vieux Télégraphe, H. Brunier et Fils *Made from Grenache, Syrah and Mourvèdre grapes at one of Châteauneuf-du-Pape's top domaines, this magnificent, complex wine can be enjoyed in between three and 12 years' time (the 1987 is good current drinking).* **12 for £94.80**

1987 Givry, Gérard Mouton *Delicious Pinot Noir from a producer of excellent quality Burgundy in the Côte Chalonnaise, an area less fashionable – and therefore less expensive – than the Côte d'Or.* **12 for £89.76**

Total cost: £494.88

——————— **£1000** ———————

My enthusiasm for French wines prevented me from venturing any further before my £1000 was spent. Had we been allowed six bottles of each, or £1500, there would have been non-European wines before now.

1988 Riesling Réserve Millésime, Rolly Gassmann *Made entirely from the domaine's own grapes, grown on slopes above Rorschwihr and Bergheim. Elegant, aromatic wine. The quality is superlative, the vintage is perhaps the best year since 1983.* **12 for £83.52**

1988 Meursault, Domaine Henri Germain *From a small, dedicated producer, this Chardonnay wine has fine flavour, elegance and length.* **12 for £201.12**

1983 Château Léoville-Barton, 2ème cru St-Julien *Delicious Classed Growth claret from a family-run estate that consistently produces top quality.* **12 for £185.64**

1988 Beaune Bressandes 1er cru Domaine Henri Germain *Another wine from Henri Germain's three-hectare domaine; he is our favourite grower and does almost everything himself. The wine is cherry red in colour and has delicious Pinot Noir fruit.* **12 for £149.16**

1989 Château du Basty, M. Perroud, Beaujolais Regnié *Until its recent promotion to cru status Tanners sold this wine as Beaujolais-Villages; wonderful concentrated fruit from steep, south-east facing slopes; an excellent vintage.* **12 for £79.68**

Bordeaux Clairet, J.P. Moueix *With good fruit, this is made from pure Merlot and more akin to a light red wine than a rosé.* **12 for £49.56**

1983 Duval Leroy, Fleur de Champagne Brut *This vintage Champagne has ample flavour and is excellent value for money.* **12 for £170.40**

1988 Bonnezeaux, Château de Fesles, Jacques Boivin *Superb Chenin Blanc dessert wine from a wonderfully situated Loire vineyard matured in secondhand, two-year-old d'Yquem casks. If you can resist drinking it now, it will be magnificent in ten and 20 years' time.* **12 for £135.60**

Total cost: £1054.68

Please ask for our fine wine list and details of our many services, local and countrywide.

TANNERS WINES LTD,
FREEPOST, 26 WYLE COP,
SHREWSBURY SY1 1BR.
Telephone: (0743) 232400

Branches at:
Welshpool, Bridgnorth,
and Hereford

WINE MERCHANTS & SHIPPERS
TANNERS
ESTABLISHED 1842

FIONA WILD

GENERAL EDITOR

£100

My current favourites. I've chosen three half-cases, two from France's Rhône valley – both reds – and a great Italian fizz. Not so special you feel obliged to fuss over them, but so good they're bound to improve the day.

1986 Côtes du Rhône, Guigal *I liked the 1985 and was reluctant to see the last bottle go. Fortunately the '86 isn't doing a bad job at filling the gap. Clean, clear Syrah at its most gulpable.*   **6 for £29.34**

1989 Château du Grand Moulas, Côtes du Rhône-Villages *Still in the Rhône, this is a regular provider of sound, fruity drinking. Pay a little extra for the 'Villages' version, there's more Syrah in it. A colleague says this would be her desert-island wine; I'm inclined to agree.*   **6 for £28.50**

Prosecco di Conegliano, Carpené-Malvolti *Off-dry fizz for every occasion: friends arriving, lunch party, evening party, birthdays, the first cuckoo, the day BR runs on time, European harmony ...* **6 for £35.70**

Total cost: £93.54

£500

1987 Castello di Cacchiano, Chianti Classico *Immediately attractive Sangiovese, not from a great year, but one that is drinking well now while we wait for '85s and '88s to mature.*   **12 for £68.28**

1987 Dolcetto Gagliassi, G Mascarello *I loved the vibrant fruit of the 1985, then the '86 was just delicious, the '87 sumptuously concentrated, the '88 ... Don't worry about the vintage; this wine will always be good.*   **12 for £75.48**

Tio Pepe, Gonzalez Byass *Top standard* fino *sherry, a vital item in anyone's fridge. Nothing else is quite as good with very fresh prawns, or with light stir-fried Chinese food, or just by you on the ledge while you're cooking.*   **12 for £67.08**

1986 Pinot Noir, Matua Valley *Deliciously fresh rosé from one of the top New Zealand producers. Drink cool, rather than cold.*   **12 for £69.48**

Lindauer, Montana *New this year in the UK, softly creamy sparkling wine with good depth and without that icing sugar taste you sometimes get with Australian equivalents. There's now so much good fizz around at the £5–7 mark, who needs cheap Champagne?*   **12 for £70.68**

1988 Tilley's Vineyard Semillon/Sauvignon, Henschke *An Australian friend introduced this into the household during the summer and it was the star of the evening. Full but not over rich, beautifully balanced.*
   12 for £87.00

1989 Moscato d'Asti, Ascheri *Grapy, fresh and wonderfully light – a much better idea at the end of the meal than anything fortified. Perfect with puddings.*
   12 for £50.28

   Total cost: £488.28

─────── **£1000** ───────

Even with all this money to spend in my imagination I can't bring myself to shell out more than £20 a bottle. The following bottles are scarcely cheap, but they are all utterly special.

1986 Mompiano Spumante Brut, M Pasolini *Delicately creamy, softly fruity fizz. Fine bubbles, sheer class.*   **12 for £135.48**

1988 Roussanne Vieille Vigne, Château de Beaucastel *Made from old vines of Roussanne, this shows just what the variety can do at its best. 'Vieille Vigne' appears in thin type across the label. You will know which is the plain white Château de B (also very good) when you get the bill. Peachy, apricotty, full-flavoured yet dry – for a stunner of a white wine, there is little to beat it.*   **12 for £211.80**

1989 Pinot Grigio, Collio DOC, Puiatti *Clean, elegant fruit with good depth of flavour. This is from Italy's north-east, still the leader for white wine quality. I first tasted this in Florence. Happy days. You don't have to travel that far to find it now, though.*   **12 for £111.00**

1988 L'Eremo, Isole e Olena *Lurking behind the anonymity of the name is a glorious wine bursting with rich, concentrated Syrah fruit, Tuscan-born and bred. An expensive joy, but a joy all the same.*   **12 for £225.48**

1989 Moscato d'Asti, Rivetti *Essence of fresh-crushed grapes, greenhouse-new, yet not sticky-sweet. A wonderful palate-refresher after a long meal.*   **12 for £72.00**

NV Alfred Gratien Champagne *For richness and finesse in your Champagne, there can be little to beat Gratien. Don't turn down their vintage fizz if anyone offers you any.*   **12 for £222.60**

   Total cost: £978.36

MARCEL WILLIAMS

THE WINE SOCIETY

─────── **£100** ───────

The most important thing in starting a cellar is balance and variety. I hope therefore that I am forgiven for nominating two mixed cases of different French red and white wines

– two bottles of each – rather than stick to the original brief of no fewer than six bottles of any wine.

The two cases are selected by The Society's buying team to offer a wide choice of styles with their overriding theme being value for money.

The Wine Society's French Country Wine, Red Case:
The Society's French Country Red, Corbières
1988 Merlot, Vin de Pays de l'Hérault
1988 Château La Tour du Pech, La Clape
1988 Domaine de Roquecourbe, Côtes de Roussillon-Villages
1989 Syrah, Vin de Pays des Côtes de Thongue
1988 Cuvée L'Arjolle, Vin de Pays des Côtes de Thongue.   **12 for £39.00**

The Wine Society's French Country Wine, White Case:
The Society's French Country White, Corbières
1989 Château La Besage, Bergerac Sec
1988 Grenache Blanc, Vin de Pays de l'Hérault
1988 Sauvignon, Vin de Pays des Côtes de Thongue
1989 Château Calabre, Montravel Sec
1989 Domaine Jean Cros, Blanc Sec, Gaillac Perlé.   **12 for £42.00**

Total cost: £81.00

──────── **£500** ────────

The Society's Sauvignon de Touraine (Oisly et Thésée) *This is a good example of fresh dry Loire Sauvignon, with a herbal scent and crisp, dry flavour.*   **12 for £51.00**

1989 Château Bel Air, Bordeaux Blanc *A delicious discovery this year, round and delicately fruity.*   **12 for £49.80**

1982 The Society's Celebration White Burgundy, Remoissenet *A concentrated, rich-tasting white Burgundy. This is the proper stuff and at a bargain price.*
12 for £115.80

1985 Château Pitray, Bordeaux Supérieur, Côtes de Castillon *A full, ripe-tasting claret with ample fruit.*   **12 for £52.80**

1988 Château des Applanats, Beaumes-de-Venise, Côtes du Rhône-Villages *Apart from the famous dessert Muscat, Beaumes-de-Venise also produces strong reds. This is dark and rich, yet quite round and a good match to a spicy casserole.*   **12 for £58.20**

Domaine de Limbardie, Vin de Pays des Coteaux de Murviel, Boukandoura et Hutin *Dark coloured with a rich Merlot flavour. A good alternative to claret.*
12 for £40.20

1987 Cabernet del Trentino, Ca'vit *This is an excellent full-bodied aromatic Cabernet from north-east Italy.*
6 magnums for £39.00

1988 Taja, Jumilla *Jumilla is inland from Alicante. This deep-flavoured Spanish red is packed with fruit.*   **12 for £50.40**

1985 Concha y Toro, Cabernet Sauvignon *An exceedingly fruity Cabernet from Chile.*
12 for £44.40

Total cost: £501.60

──────── **£1000** ────────

Five cases of top quality French wines selected from three recent good vintages.

The Society's Blanc de Blancs Champagne *An elegant Champagne made exclusively from Chardonnay grapes from the* premier cru *Côtes des Blancs village of Le Mesnil. Flowery and delicately fruity.*
12 for £166.20

1988 Riesling Cuvée Tradition, Hugel *An abundance of fruit makes this a memorable glass of wine. 1988 was an excellent vintage in Alsace.*   **12 for £102.00**

1987 Château Duhart Milon Rothschild, Pauillac *The wines from this fourth growth property, acquired by the Château Lafite Rothschilds in 1964, improve each year. This is beautifully made with concentrated fruit flavours.*   **12 for £264.00**

1985 Vosne Romanée, Bourée *A richly-flavoured old-fashioned red Burgundy from a great vintage.*   **12 for £234.00**

1985 Côte-Rôtie, Guigal *Guigal's '85 Côte-Rôtie is outstanding; deep in colour and flavour, it will last for years.* **12 for £205.40**

Total cost: £971.60

New Mitchell Beazley Wine Books
Autumn 1990

Oz Clarke's
Essential Wine Book
An indispensable guide
to the wines of the world
£12.99 – Co-published
with Websters

Now available in paperback, this is a completely revised and updated edition of OZ CLARKE'S WINE FACT FINDER.

This conversational encyclopaedia of wine gives descriptions and evaluations of the world's wines by one of the world's most gifted winetasters. Oz Clarke's approach is unashamedly consumerist and refreshingly unsnobbish.

Harrods Book of
Fine Wine
Editor: Joanna Simon
£19.95

Here is a wine guide for people who appreciate fine wine and who wish to know more about the people who make it and the fascinating places where it is made.

Edited and introduced by Joanna Simon, wine correspondent of *The Sunday Times*, it includes expert contributions from twenty-four of the world's foremost writers on wine.

Hugh Johnson's
Pocket Wine Book 1991
£6.95

For 1991 Hugh Johnson has once again completely revised and refreshed this outstandingly useful guide.

Vintage data has been reappraised and information on the revival of fine wine in Germany and on the good value wines of the New World is included.

This is the book every wine drinker, beginner or connoisseur, needs.

The Wine Atlas of Italy
Burton Anderson
£25

Following the success of THE WINE ATLAS OF FRANCE and THE ATLAS OF GERMAN WINES, here is the complete guide to Italy.

Designed for use while exploring Italy and as a guide to the wines themselves, this is the first book to contain detailed maps of the wine zones in Italy.

The Mitchell Beazley
Red Wine and White
Wine Guides
Jim Ainsworth
£5.99 each

These two books work on the simple premise: "if you enjoy this wine, here are some others you'll probably like".

Using an innovative and friendly approach, the guides encourage the reader to enjoy a wider selection of wines and offer key facts on why wines taste as they do, where they come from and other alternatives available in three quality and price bands.

FRANCE

I t looks as though France, in most areas, got 1989 just about as right as it could. It wasn't just the long, warm summer – vines like a good growing season, but they like a drop of water too, at the right time. And that's what they got, rain in early spring, sufficient to last the roots through the summer months. Then from May, when calm weather is needed for the flowering, that's what they got too. The fruit set in dry, warm conditions and the sun then shone, day after day, until the grapes were brought to full ripeness a good month earlier than usual in some areas. Some red grapes were being harvested in Bordeaux in August, an event unknown in this century!

The unusual warmth brought its own problems, quite apart from arousing great interest in *en primeur* buying all over again. In Alsace the crop was brought in in such hot weather that it was difficult to control fermentation temperatures, unless you had the right equipment for cooling tanks and vats. But Alsace never normally needs this kind of technology. In Bordeaux the grapes were reluctant to leave the vines even when analytically ripe, because the tannins needed a bit longer to develop fully.

In the Loire, grapes known for crisp acidity, like Muscadet, ripened so well that growers had to wrestle with overripeness and the possibility of flabby wines. Who knows, could this be the year to try Gros Plant without fearing for your gums? Will the Loire's dentists be disappointed?

In Champagne, harvesters were sent out into the vineyards before the official harvesting date. Now that's a thing that's never happened before in *that* region. There's going to be a lot of lovely 1989 Champagne around in years to come, if anyone can still afford to buy it.

Burgundy had more rain than Bordeaux, but good producers have made delicious wines, especially whites, and this was a year when the personalities really shone – the wines' personalities, that is, not the producers. You can really see the differences between sites.

QUALITY CONTROL

The French have the most far-reaching system of wine quality control of any nation. The key factors are the 'origin' of the wine, its historic method of production and the use of the correct grape types. There are three defined levels of quality control – AC, VDQS, and *Vin de Pays*.

Appellation d'Origine Contrôlée (AC, AOC) To qualify for AC a wine must meet seven requirements:
Land Suitable vineyard land is minutely defined. **Grape** Only those grapes traditionally regarded as suitable can be used. **Degree of alcohol** Wines must reach a minimum (or maximum) degree of natural alcohol. **Yield** A basic permitted yield is set for each AC, but the figure may be increased or decreased year by year after consultation between the growers of each AC region and the Institut National des Appellations d'Origine (INAO).
Vineyard practice AC wines must follow rules about pruning methods and density of planting. **Wine-making practice** Each AC wine has its own regulations as to what is allowed. Typically, chaptalization – adding sugar during fermentation to increase alcoholic strength – is accepted in the north, but not in the south. **Tasting and analysis** Since 1979 wines must pass a tasting panel.

Vin Délimité de Qualité Supérieure (VDQS) This second group is, in general, slightly less reliable in quality. It is in the process of being phased out. No more *vins de pays* are being upgraded to VDQS but there is still no news on when existing ones will be upgraded to AC (or downgraded to *vin de pays*).

Vin de Pays The third category gives a regional definition to France's basic blending wines. The rules are similar to AC, but allow a good deal more flexibility and some wonderful cheap wines can be found which may well surprise.

Vin de Table 'Table wine' is the title for the rest. No quality control except as far as basic public health regulations demand. *Vins de pays* are always available for approximately the same price, and offer a far more interesting drink.

RED BORDEAUX

For Bordeaux, 1989 was a year of excesses. The weather was remarkable, the harvest astonishingly early and the reactions to the wines bordered on the hysterical. It was a vintage for superlatives and exclamation marks, headlines and telegraphic pithiness, purple prose and glittering verse. What follows is a sober description, a black and white report on the multi-coloured pattern of the 1989 harvest.

The great difficulty that those of us who live in Bordeaux have is that the year did not feel so enormously hot or sunny at the time. We did not feel the need for pith-helmets or fear that our cars would explode from over-heating. If the weather archivists at the meteorological office had not reminded us of the fact, and if the grapes had not sometimes developed so much sugar that they had to be picked very early, no one would have noticed that records for this century's weather were being broken.

But the records *were* being broken, and we all now know that it was the earliest harvest since 1893, a year which did produce truly remarkable wines. None of the wines were sampled young by tasters now alive, though, making comparisons of the fledgling wines impossible.

This gives a journalistic tag to the vintage as being the year of the early harvest, but it may not say quite as much about the quality or even the style of the wines as appears at first. A hot year is a year of ripe grapes and therefore of wines with a good alcoholic content, but it may not be a year when the alcohol is balanced by the acidity or the wine given depth and lasting qualities by tannins.

These were the considerations which encouraged caution on the part of growers when the harvest was brought in. They looked at the analyses of the vats and marvelled at the alcoholic strength and wondered how it would turn out. We were all still wondering about this when the wine drinker, the lawyer in St Louis, the factory manager in Milton Keynes and the stockbroker in Osaka started to encourage their wine merchants to buy 1989 clarets. Faxes and telexes started hurtling towards château-owners and wine shippers in Bordeaux in December, people were so anxious to buy the vintage at the earliest possible moment.

This was unusual, even in such a curious business as the wine trade. The last time there was such interest in a vintage was in 1983, when the 1982 vintage caught the public's eye.

If the excitement originated anywhere other than in Bordeaux, the late date at which the wines were offered for tasting by journalists contributed to increase the sense of breathless anticipation about the vintage. Until 1989, châteaux-owners had allowed journalists to taste their wines from January on, asking them only to remember that they were tasting very young wines. Since 1989, tasting of many of the most famous properties' wines has been permitted only after the end of March. This may or may not have had the desired result of ensuring that the wines were less difficult to taste, but it has certainly had the effect of creating a build-up for the harvest, a roll of drums to draw attention to the tastings given in major cities of the wine-drinking world to the press.

The excitement nearly reached the point where only single word descriptions of the vintage were asked for or accepted. 'Great' was possible and so, in all fairness, was 'Bad!'. 'Very good' was not an answer, however, any more than

'Interesting'. The answer most headline writers wanted was probably 'Pow!!!'

Such vulgar reactions are not for the readers of *Webster's*. Serious students of the vine should know that the red wines had uniformly deep colour, an attractive perfume and an appealingly warm taste. The best displayed depth of flavour, the very best great concentration. The best, again, had a long and powerful finish.

But there was considerable variation in quality. The very few downright poor wines will probably not appear on British shelves, but they do exist. Some of that part of the vintage which was hollow and therefore dull to taste and without attraction or length on the finish will reach Britain, however, and will disappoint us all in five or six years' time. This part of the crop reminded me of 1983.

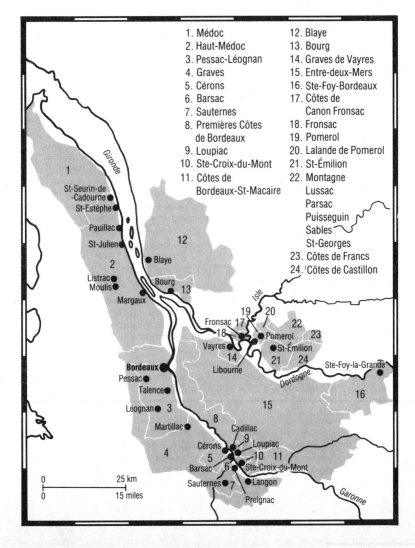

1. Médoc
2. Haut-Médoc
3. Pessac-Léognan
4. Graves
5. Cérons
6. Barsac
7. Sauternes
8. Premières Côtes de Bordeaux
9. Loupiac
10. Ste-Croix-du-Mont
11. Côtes de Bordeaux-St-Macaire
12. Blaye
13. Bourg
14. Graves de Vayres
15. Entre-deux-Mers
16. Ste-Foy-Bordeaux
17. Côtes de Canon Fronsac
18. Fronsac
19. Pomerol
20. Lalande de Pomerol
21. St-Émilion
22. Montagne
    Lussac
    Parsac
    Puisseguin
    Sables
    St-Georges
23. Côtes de Francs
24. Côtes de Castillon

Most of the crop was very good, with the power, depth and length which claret gives at its best. The very best of the vintage, from perhaps one château in ten, was great: with those qualities of depth and length and authority that correspond to the greatest vintages of Bordeaux.

The best wines did not come from any single region. There were outstanding wines from the Médoc, Pomerol, St-Émilion and the Graves. Wines with a high Merlot content (particularly the right bank wines of St-Émilion and Pomerol) were made with grapes which were appreciably riper than those made in the Médoc or Graves, where the Cabernet Sauvignon was not always so enormously rich in sugar.

The best of the Pomerol and St-Émilion wines were huge, their tannins well hidden by deep concentration of fruit and by the warmth which high alcohol brings to a wine. The best of the Médoc wines were typical of that narrow peninsula, more restrained and with more evidence of subtlety.

Margaux and the southern Médoc seemed to fare slightly less well than the areas going north from St-Julien, and the Graves (including the new Léognan and Pessac *appellation*) also seemed to have been rather less successful than the other districts, but there were mighty exceptions, and the Haut-Brion is one of the outstanding wines of the vintage.

There is wild variety among commentators as to which previous vintage most closely resembles 1989. Of the wines made in the last decade, the most similar is clearly the 1982 vintage, where the summer was hot, the harvest early and the wines big, powerful and with very obvious charms. In my notes, the 1982 vintage was more uniformly successful, the Médocs less typically Médoc in the sense that they frequently lacked subtlety, although this did not make them less good wines.

The other parallel year which seems to crop up a good deal in discussion is the 1988 vintage. Although the wines were dissimilar in style, it is fascinating that one property's wine in five was better in 1988 than in 1989, another property's wine better in 1989 than in 1988 and the other three, of the five, displayed little variation from one year to the next.

One element which was not generally taken into account by commentators was the size of the vintage. Unlike other famous 'hot' years, including 1982, the harvest in 1989 was a very large one, and very few properties thinned their crop by cutting off bunches of grapes. It is no chance coincidence that the properties which did cut back their production in this way, produced remarkable wines.

EN PRIMEUR BUYING

Because the world thirst for 1989s was so huge, because the law of supply and demand applies as much to wine as to anything else and because the pound was (and is) weak against the franc, the 1989s went on offer at high prices.

Most wines on offer at £8 a bottle or less were only 10–20 per cent more expensive than 1988 from the same property. This is perhaps an acceptable increase in price, and won't have put off the well-heeled wine buyer.

It was the wines that sell at more than £200 a case which, at 30–40 per cent more than the previous vintage, should have caused some soul searching. For the worrier, there was always the possibility that the pound would start to fly again. There was a lot of wine, even First Growth wine, in 1989, and where would a Japanese businessman find room to store such wine in his tiny flat? The American wine-lover may have space, but he is also suffering from a weak currency, and the American economy seems weak, too.

Moreover, the vintage was NOT the vintage of the century, excellent though its best wines may be. What should the serious wine lover do? Buy or wait?

The answer to this lies more in the psychology of passions, in this case a passion for wine, rather than in a serious analysis of the pros and cons of purchasing wine. It has become part of the lore of wine-buying that good claret is best bought early. The advice which the buyer will heed is that he consult his wine merchant rather than his banker. Whether the story in ten years' time is that this 1989 was bought then at one-tenth what it would cost today or twice what it would cost at the local off-licence, the story is the story of wine-buying and horse-backing. Make sure you buy wines you are fairly certain of.

CLASS STRUCTURE IN BORDEAUX

One of the more exhilarating experiences in Bordeaux over the last ten years has been the rise in quality of all wines. Winemakers are better informed and more willing to make efforts to obtain better quality than they were. Ironically, this has had the effect of making the gap between most of the Classed Growths and most *bourgeois* Growths greater and clearer.

With very few exceptions, the two groups of properties are marching to different drums. Since the Classed Growths can readily command distinctly higher prices than the *bourgeois* Growths if the quality of their wines is perceived as being superior, they are vinifying their wines for subtlety and depth to an extent and at a cost which the owner of a *bourgeois* Growth cannot match.

The *bourgeois* Growth still works in most years with the intention of making a wine which will be drunk five years after the vintage, less for a year like 1987, more for a tannic year like 1986. The producer making a Classed Growth has his sights on a wine to be drunk eight years or more after the harvest.

The *bourgeois* Growths which choose to make wine for the long haul produce good wine, but wine which is generally short of the best a major Growth could produce. The significance of the land on which a wine is produced is currently being played down, but it may be that this basic difference is simply demonstrating the importance of soil on quality.

THE RETURN FROM OAK

The 1980s also saw the rise and fall of new oak. The use of the traditional Bordeaux *barrique* of 225 litres for ageing wine does two things: it adds an oaky, tannic taste to the wine and it encourages faster evaporation than storage in vats.

As the fine wine trade went from good to better during the 1980s and winemakers were no longer haunted by the dreadful days of 1973-1976, when good wine found no buyer, they experimented with the use of an ever higher proportion of new oak. These experiments coincided with those made in the New World, where the strong oak flavour underlying the powerful, fully-ripe taste made for heavyweight wines for heroes. The Bordeaux wines aged to a considerable extent in new oak proved extremely popular in the mid 1980s, but began to pall as the vintage character of a wine became less clear and the taste of wood seemed to overtake the taste of wine.

The position at the moment seems to be that new oak to an extent of not more than 20 per cent is considered desirable in most non-Classed Growths, although ageing in older wood, which gives off less tannin, is also very acceptable. In the world of Classed Growths there is less enthusiasm than five years ago to leave a very oaky taste in the bottled wine. **WILLIAM BOLTER**

GRAPES & FLAVOURS

Fine claret has the most tantalizing and unlikely combination of flavours of any red wine. There's the blast of pure, fragrant blackcurrant essence as the basic fruit, and then the exotic, dry perfumes of lead pencil shavings, fresh-wrapped cigars and the intense smell of cedar resin to weave an endlessly fascinating balance of sweet and dry tastes. Increasingly nowadays this is also blended with the buttersweet overlay of new oak barrels, the whole adding up to one of the most absorbing tastes the world possesses.

Bordeaux's vineyards are so poised on the knife-edge of being able to ripen their grapes or failing to do so that every vintage is fascinatingly, absorbingly different. The relatively temperate air in this coastal region is a crucial factor. In all but the very hottest years, the sunshine is tempered by cool breezes off the Atlantic. If the year nevertheless gets too hot, as in 1959 and 1976, and in some cases 1982, the flavour will be rich, strong and burnt, more like the Californian or Italian attempts at claret. If the summer rains and autumn gales roll in off the Bay of Biscay and the grapes can't ripen, then the taste may be thin and green and rather raw, resembling the Cabernets of the Loire valley. But in the years of balance, like 1966, '70, '78, '83, '85, '86 and '88, those astonishing sweet and dry, ripe and raw flavours all mix together to produce the glory that is claret.

CABERNET SAUVIGNON It comes as a surprise that this world-famous Bordeaux grape variety covers only a fifth of the region's vineyards. In the Médoc and Graves, however, more than half the vines grown are Cabernet Sauvignon, and the grape has a much more pronounced influence on flavour here than elsewhere in Bordeaux. The crucial factors in a wine built to age well are balanced amounts of tannin and acidity, and the fruit and extract to keep up with them. The Cabernet Sauvignon has all these in abundance. It gives dark, tannic wine with a strong initial acid attack, and a stark, pure blackcurrant fruit. When aged in new oak, its blackcurrant fruit combined with cedary, cigar-like perfume is stunning. It's the dominant grape of the famous châteaux of the Haut-Médoc, but other varieties are always blended in to soften it.

CABERNET FRANC A lesser Cabernet, giving lighter-coloured, softer wines than the Cabernet Sauvignon, sometimes slightly earthy but also with good, blackcurranty fruit. It's always blended in Bordeaux. In St-Émilion and Pomerol it can give very fine flavours and is widely planted since Cabernet Sauvignon rarely ripens fully on their clay soils.

MERLOT Bordeaux has more Merlot than Cabernet Sauvignon. It covers almost a third of the land under vine, and is the dominant variety in St-Émilion and Pomerol, whereas in the Médoc and Graves it's used to soften the Cabernet. It ripens early and gives a gorgeous, succulent, minty, honeyed, blackcurrant- or plum-flavoured wine, which explains why Pomerols and St-Émilions take less effort to enjoy than Médocs. Merlot makes a less long-lived wine than Cabernet Sauvignon, so Pomerol and St-Émilion wines with a high proportion of Merlot are likely to reach their peak and fade sooner.

MALBEC A rather bloated, juicy grape, not much seen nowadays in Bordeaux, though it forms a small part of some blends, especially in Bourg and Blaye. In Bordeaux it tastes rather like a weedy version of Merlot, soft and low in acidity, though up-river in Cahors it has real style, which probably explains why there's lots of it in Cahors and little in Bordeaux.

PETIT VERDOT A dark, tough, acid grape with a liquorice and plums taste, used to add firmness and colour. Not much planted, but on the increase in the Médoc, because it adds quality in a ripe year.

WINES & WINE REGIONS

BORDEAUX ROUGE, AC Unless qualified by one of the other *appellations* below, this is the everyday wine of Bordeaux, either from co-ops, from properties in undistinguished localities, or wine disqualified from one of the better *appellations*. It can come from anywhere in Bordeaux. Quite cheap (but by no means a bargain any more), for drinking young, it is a delicious, appetizing meal-time red when good, and a miserable palate-puckering disappointment when bad.

BORDEAUX SUPÉRIEUR, AC Similar to Bordeaux Rouge but, in theory, a bit more interesting. It must have a little more alcohol and be produced from vines with a slightly lower yield. The same comments on quality apply here, but from a well-run single château the wines can be delicious – and age for a number of years. Best results are increasingly coming from properties producing white Entre-Deux-Mers (AC) and from the Premières Côtes on the right bank of the Garonne river. Best châteaux: *Brethous, Cayla, Domaine de Terrefort, Fayau, la Gabory, le Gay, Grand-Moüeys, Gromel Bel-Air, Jalousie-Beaulieu, Jonqueyres, du Juge, Lacombe, Lamothe, Méaume, Peyrat, Pierredon, Reynon, la Roche, Tanesse, Thieuley, de Toutigeac, de la Vieille Tour.*

CÔTES DE BOURG, AC A reasonable-sized area across the river to the east of the Médoc, with its best vineyards looking directly across the Gironde to Margaux. Their rather full, savoury style is backed up by sweet Merlot fruit and just occasionally a touch of new oak. As Médoc and St-Émilion prices spiral, Bourg wines are slowly coming into their own. Best châteaux: *de Barbe, du Bousquet, Brûle-Sécaille, la Croix, Dupeyrat, Grolet, Guionne, Haut-Guiraud, Haut-Rousset, de Millorit* and wines from the co-op at *Tauriac.*

CÔTES DE CASTILLON, AC and **CÔTES DE FRANCS, AC** Two small regions east of St-Émilion on the road towards Bergerac, which are turning out an increasing number of exciting wines. Although the Castillon wines can suffer from being a little too earthy, at their best they combine a slightly grassy Cabernet Franc freshness with a gorgeous, juicy, minty Merlot sweetness, which can even be honeyed in the best châteaux. Many merchants now list examples, and you can expect to see a lot more of these wines. Côtes de Francs produces tiny amounts as yet but the quality is so exciting from the best properties that I'm tipping this mini-AC as Bordeaux's fastest rising star. The presence of several sons of top Pomerol and St-Émilion châteaux owners is providing the driving force behind this surge. Best Castillon châteaux: *Beau-Séjour, Belcier, Brisson, Canon-Monségur, Ferrasses, Fonds Rondes, Grand Taillac, les Hauts-de-Grange, Lessacques, Moulin-Rouge, Parenchère, Pitray, Rocher-Bellevue.* Best Francs châteaux: *la Claverie, de Francs, Lauriol, du Moulin-la-Pitié, la Prade, Puygueraud.*

CÔTES DE FRONSAC, AC (now usually called simply Fronsac) with the theoretically superior **CANON-FRONSAC, AC**, is a small area a couple of miles west of Pomerol. The wines can be excellent, often having the smooth, sweet fruit of St-Émilion, the minerally depth of Pomerol, and a slightly cedary perfume, too. Their general standard is higher than that of several better known areas, and their price is lower. It seems impossible that we won't start seeing more of them, especially in view of the keen interest being shown in the area by the firm of *Jean-Pierre Moueix* of Château Pétrus in Pomerol. What has been holding them back up till now has been proprietors' lack of ambition, which means that there has been infrequent evidence of efforts to improve properties and upgrade wine-making techniques. Best châteaux: *Canon-de-Brem, Canon-Moueix, Cassagne Haut-Canon, Dalem, de la Dauphine, Fonteuil, Mayne-Vieil, Mazeris, Moulin Haut-Laroque, Plain Point, la Rivière, la Truffière* (super since 1985), *Toumalin, la Valade.*

GRAVES, AC The huge area of the
Graves, south of Bordeaux town, built up a
bad reputation as a white wine area, which
it has taken a decade of struggle and
determination to overcome. Now, every
new vintage brings another clutch of
properties who have invested in stainless
steel and new oak barrels and taken the
advice of a decent winemaker, with the
result that the Graves, at single château
level, is now one of France's most exciting
white wine areas. Even four years ago I'd
have promised to drink nothing but
Liebfraumilch for a month rather than
admit that!

However, it's the reds that are still
more important. The Graves run the whole
gamut of claret flavours, and are less easy
to generalize about than any of the other
regions. There are various different soils,
and though the Cabernet Sauvignon is the
dominant grape, as in the Médoc, there's
just a little less emphasis on Cabernet, a
little more on Merlot, which makes for
slightly softer styles of wine. They tend to
have some of the blackcurrant and cedar of
the Médoc, but without the sheer size of,
say, Pauillac: they have some of the full,
plummy richness of St-Émilion yet that
never dominates; and there *is* a slightly
gravelly quality in many of them, too. The
top half a dozen châteaux are superb, and
as expensive as any Médoc. But the less
well-known châteaux are cheapish, and
increasingly good in a variety of styles.
Local merchant Pierre Coste has developed
a style of young-drinking Graves which is
deliciously drinkable, and reasonably
available in the UK (at Adnams, Haynes,
Hanson & Clark, Tanners and others).

A new AC, Pessac-Léognan, was
declared in 1987 for the northern part of
the Graves. Mature bottles will still bear
the words AC Graves, but all newer
vintages will be 'Pessac-Léognan'. Best
châteaux: *Cabannieux, Carmes-Haut-
Brion, Cruzeau, Domaine de Chevalier,
Domaine de Gaillat, Domaine la Grave,
Ferrande, de Fieuzal, Haut-Bailly, Haut-
Brion, Haut-Portets, la Louvière, Malartic-
Lagravière, la Mission-Haut-Brion, Pape-
Clément* (since 1985), *Rahoul, Rochemorin,
Roquetaillade-la-Grange, de St-Pierre,
Smith-Haut-Lafitte* (since 1988), *la Tour
Martillac, Tourteau-Chollet.*

HAUT-MÉDOC, AC Geographically, the
prestigious southern part of the Médoc,
nearest Bordeaux – stretching from
Blanquefort in the south to St-Seurin de
Cadourne in the north. The AC itself covers
the slightly less exciting vineyard sites
between these two points because there are
six separate ACs within the region where
the really juicy business gets done. These
are Margaux, St-Julien, Pauillac, St-
Estèphe, Listrac and Moulis. Even so, the
AC Haut-Médoc has five Classed Growths
including two superb ones – *Cantemerle*
and *la Lagune* – and an increasing number
of fine *bourgeois* properties like *Beaumont,
de Castillon, Cissac, Hanteillan,
Lamarque, Lanessan, Liversan, Pichon,
Sociando-Mallet* and *la Tour-du-Haut-
Moulin* – plus lots of lesser châteaux, such
as *Bernadotte, Cambon-la-Pelouse,
Coufran, le Fournas, Grandis, du Junca,
Larose-Trintaudon, Malescasse,
Maucamps, Moulin de Labarde, Quimper,
Sénéjac* and *Verdignan.*

LALANDE-DE-POMEROL, AC
Pomerol's northern neighbour, a region as
tiny as Pomerol itself, is often accused of
being overpriced, but since it can produce
rich, plummy wines with a distinct
resemblance to Pomerol at a distinctly less
painful price, this criticism is not entirely
fair. Best châteaux: *Annereaux, Bel-Air,
Belles-Graves, Bertineau-St-Vincent, Clos
des Moines, Clos des Templiers, la Croix
Bellevue, la Fleur St-Georges, Grand
Ormeau, Haut-Ballet, les Hauts-Tuileries,
Lavaud-la-Maréchaude, Siaurac, les
Templiers, Tournefeuille.*

LISTRAC, AC One of the less prestigious
communes of the Haut-Médoc, just to the
west of Margaux. Generally tough, rather
charmless, only slightly perfumed wines,
lacking the complexity of the best
communes, but the meteoric rise in quality
amongst the *bourgeois* wines since the '82
and '83 vintages has made its mark here
too, though without quite the same show of
fireworks. But some properties rise above
this. *Clarke* is the best, followed by *la
Bécade, Cap-Léon-Veyrin, Fonréaud* (since
1988), *Fourcas-Dupré, Fourcas-Hosten,
Fourcaud, Lestage* and the *Grand Listrac
co-op.*

MARGAUX, AC Of the famous Haut-Médoc communes, this is the nearest to Bordeaux, covering various villages producing rather sludgy, solid wines at one extreme, and at the other extreme the most fragrant, perfumed red wines France has yet dreamed up. The great Margaux wines come from round the village of Margaux itself. People pay high prices for them and still get a bargain. Best châteaux: *d'Angludet, la Gurgue, d'Issan, Labégorce-Zédé, Margaux, Monbrison, Palmer, Prieuré-Lichine, Rausan-Ségla, du Tertre*. Next best châteaux: *Brane-Cantenac, Durfort-Vivens, Giscours, Kirwan, Malescot-St-Éxupéry, Marquis d'Alesme-Becker, Marquis de Terme, Siran, la Tour-de-Mons*.

MÉDOC, AC This name covers the whole of the long (80km) tongue of land north of Bordeaux town, between the Gironde river and the sea, including the Haut-Médoc and all its famous communes. As an *appellation*, it refers to the less highly regarded but important lower-lying northern part of the area, traditionally known as the Bas-Médoc. AC Médoc reds, with a high proportion of Merlot grapes, are drinkable more quickly than Haut-Médocs and the best have a refreshing, grassy, juicy fruit backed up by just enough tannin and acidity. Easily the best property is *Potensac*, making wine of Classed Growth standard. Other good wines are *le Bernadot, Cardonne, du Castéra, la Gorce, Greysac, Grivière, Haut-Canteloup, Lacombe-Noaillac, Noaillac, Ormes-Sorbet, Patache d'Aux, la Tour-de-By, la Tour-St-Bonnet, Vieux-Château-Landon*. Most of the wine from the co-ops – especially *Bégadan, Ordornac* and *St-Yzans* – is good fruity stuff.

MOULIS, AC Another lesser commune of the Haut-Médoc next door to, and similar to, Listrac, but with more potentially outstanding properties and a softer, more perfumed style in the best examples which can equal a Classed Growth in quality. Best châteaux: *Bel Air Lagrave, Brillette, Chasse-Spleen, Duplessis-Fabre, Dutruch-Grand-Poujeaux, Grand-Poujeaux, Gressier-Grand-Poujeaux, Maucaillou, Moulin-à-Vent, Poujeaux*.

PAUILLAC, AC The most famous of the Haut-Médoc communes, Pauillac has three of the world's greatest red wines sitting inside its boundaries, *Latour, Lafite* and *Mouton-Rothschild*. This is where the blackcurrant really comes into its own. The best wines are almost painfully intense, a mixture of blackcurrant and celestial lead pencil sharpenings or cigar box wood that sends well-heeled cognoscenti leaping for their cheque books. Best châteaux: *Grand-Puy-Lacoste, Haut-Bages-Avérous, Haut-Bages-Libéral, Lafite-Rothschild, Latour, Lynch-Bages, Mouton-Baronne-Philippe, Mouton-Rothschild, Pichon-Lalande*. Next best châteaux: *Batailley, Clerc-Milon-Rothschild, Duhart-Milon, Fonbadet, Grand-Puy-Ducasse, Haut-Bages-Monpelou*.

PESSAC-LÉOGNAN, AC An AC in its own right since September 1987 for the area traditionally thought of as the Graves' best and containing all the *crus classés*. It's a large area in the north of the Graves, running right up into the suburbs of Bordeaux. The AC covers ten communes but only 55 châteaux.

POMEROL, AC Tiny top-class area inland from Bordeaux, clustered round the town of Libourne to the right of the river Dordogne. The Merlot grape is even more dominant in Pomerol than in nearby St-Émilion, and most Pomerols have a deeper, rounder flavour than St-Émilions, the plummy fruit going as dark as prunes in great years, but with the mineral backbone of toughness preserving it for a very long time. Pomerol has no classification, but it harbours the world's greatest red wine, *Château Pétrus*. Any vineyard that has been picked out by *Jean-Pierre Moueix* or influenced by *Michel Rolland*, can be regarded as being of good Classed Growth standard. Best châteaux: *le Bon Pasteur, Bourgneuf Vayron, Certan-de-May, Certan-Giraud, Clinet, Clos René, Clos du Clocher, Clos l'Église, la Conseillante, la Croix de Gay, l'Église Clinet, l'Évangile, le Gay, la Grave-Trigant-de-Boisset, Lafleur, Lafleur-Gazin, Lafleur-Pétrus, Lagrange à Pomerol, Latour-à-Pomerol, Petit-Village, Pétrus, Trotanoy, le Pin, Trotanoy, Vieux-Château-Certan*.

PREMIÈRES CÔTES DE BLAYE, AC
There is now a shift to red in this large, historically white wine area north of Bourg, across the river from the Médoc. The wines are too frequently a little 'cooked' in taste and slightly jammy-sweet. They're cheap, but they still have a lot more improving to do. Good properties: *Bas Vallon, Bourdieu, Charron, Crusquet-Sabourin, l'Escadre, Fontblanche, Grand Barail, Haut-Sociando, Jonqueyres, Peybonhomme.*

PREMIÈRES CÔTES DE BORDEAUX,
AC This long, south-facing slope stands opposite Bordeaux town and slides down the river Garonne to about opposite Barsac. Its rather grand name is not overly justified, since its only claim to fame until recently has been the production of rather half-baked Sauternes look-alikes. The area is also producing some fairly sturdy reds. The 1985 and '88 vintages, in particular, produced numerous wines with a surprising amount of soft fruit and durability. Best châteaux: *de Berbec, Brethous, Cayla, Fayau, Grands-Moüeys, du Juge, de Lucat, Peyrat, la Roche, Reynon, Tanesse.*

ST-ÉMILION, AC
Soft, round, rather generous wines are the norm in St-Émilion, near Pomerol, inland from Bordeaux, because the dominant grape is the Merlot, assisted a little more than in Pomerol by the Cabernet Franc and Malbec, and only to a small extent by the Cabernet Sauvignon. St-Émilions don't always have the minerally backbone of Pomerol, and the sweetness is usually less plummy and rather more reminiscent of butter, toffee or sometimes raisins. The top wines add to this a minty, blackcurranty depth. It's such a well-known name, yet there are very few famous châteaux. It has its own classification, but such a sprawling one that it has never really done the cause of St-Émilion much good, and recent changes to the classification have made little difference. It has two of Bordeaux's best châteaux, *Cheval-Blanc* and *Ausone*, and a dozen others of top quality. There are also numerous areas annexing the name St-Émilion, like St-Georges-St-Émilion or Puisseguin-St-Émilion. They're often OK, if sometimes a little solid, and would be better value if they didn't trade greedily on the St-Émilion handle. Best bets in satellites: *St-Georges, Montaiguillon, Tour du Pas St-Georges (St-Georges-St-Émilion); Haut-Gillet, de Maison Neuve (Montagne-St-Émilion); Bel Air, la Croix-de-Berny (Puisseguin-St-Émilion); Lyonnat* (since 1983) *(Lussac-St-Émilion).*
Best châteaux: *l'Angélus, l'Arrosée, Ausone, Beauséjour-Duffau-Lagarosse, Canon, Cheval-Blanc, Clos des Jacobins, la Dominique, Figeac, Fonroque, Larmande, Magdelaine, Pavie, Pavie Decesse, Soutard, Tertre-Rôteboeuf.* Next best châteaux: *Balestard-la-Tonnelle, Belair, Berliquet, Cadet-Piola, Canon-la-Gaffelière, Cap de Mourlin, Cardinal Villemaurine, Carteau, Côtes Daugay, Corbin-Michotte, Clos Fourtet, Couvent des Jacobins, Destieux, de Ferrand, Fombrauge, Franc-Mayne, la Gaffelière, Gaillard, Grand-Mayne, Gravet, Haut-Quercus, Haut-Mazerat, Magnan-la-Gaffelière, Mauvezin, Monbousquet, Pavie-Macquin, Rolland-Maillet, la Rose Pourret, Tour-des-Combes, la Tour-du-Pin-Figeac, Trappaud, Troplong-Mondot, Villemaurine.*

ST-ESTÈPHE, AC
This northernmost of the great Haut-Médoc communes is regarded as a rather everyday performer. There aren't many famous names, and most of the wines are relatively cheap. Best châteaux: *Calon-Ségur, Chambert-Marbuzet, Cos d'Estournel, Haut-Marbuzet, Lafon-Rochet, Marbuzet, Meyney, Montrose, les Ormes-de-Pez, de Pez.* Next best châteaux: *Andron-Blanquet, Beausite, du Boscq, Cos Labory, le Crock, Lavillotte, Phélan-Ségur.*

ST-JULIEN, AC
There are two main styles. One is almost honeyed, a rather gentle, round, wonderfully easy-to-love claret. The other has glorious cedar-cigar-box fragrance mixed with just enough fruit to make it satisfying as well as exciting. Best châteaux: *Beychevelle, Ducru-Beaucaillou, Gruaud-Larose, Lagrange* (recent vintages), *Lalande-Borie, Langoa-Barton, Léoville-Barton, Léoville-Las-Cases, St-Pierre, Talbot.* Next best châteaux: *Branaire-Ducru, Gloria, Hortevie, Léoville-Poyferré* (recent vintages), *Terrey-Gros-Caillou.*

THE 1855 CLASSIFICATION

This is the most famous and enduring wine classification in the world – but it was never intended as such, merely as a one-off guide to the different Bordeaux wines entered for the Great Paris Exhibition of 1855, made up by various local brokers and based on the prices the wines had obtained over the previous century or so. Those brokers would be dumbfounded if they returned today to find we still revered their rather impromptu classification.

An interesting point to note is that the *wine name* was classified *not* the vineyard it came from. Some of the vineyards that make up a wine are now completely different from those that merited classification in 1855, yet, because the 'brand name', expressed as 'Château' this or that, got into the lists, the level of classification remains. There are endless arguments about the quality ratings – which châteaux deserve promotion, which ones should be demoted and so on, but the only change so far occurred in 1973, when Mouton-Rothschild got promoted from Second to First Growth level after *50* years of lobbying by its late owner! In general, those properties which *are* classified do deserve their status, but the arguments about which ones do and which don't fit their ranking can be one of the more enjoyable aspects of wine!

First Growths (1ers Crus)
Latour, *Pauillac*; Lafite-Rothschild, *Pauillac*; Margaux, *Margaux*; Haut-Brion, *Pessac-Léognan* (formerly Graves); Mouton-Rothschild, *Pauillac* (since 1973).

Second Growths (2èmes Crus)
Rausan-Ségla, *Margaux*; Rauzan-Gassies, *Margaux*; Léoville-Las-Cases, *St-Julien*; Léoville-Poyferré, *St-Julien*; Léoville-Barton, *St-Julien*; Durfort-Vivens, *Margaux*; Lascombes, *Margaux*; Gruaud-Larose, *St-Julien*; Brane-Cantenac, *Cantenac-Margaux*; Pichon-Baron, *Pauillac*; Pichon-Lalande, *Pauillac*; Ducru-Beaucaillou, *St-Julien*; Cos d'Estournel, *St-Estèphe*; Montrose, *St-Estèphe*.

Third Growths (3èmes Crus)
Giscours, *Labarde-Margaux*; Kirwan, *Cantenac-Margaux*; d'Issan, *Cantenac-Margaux*; Lagrange, *St-Julien*; Langoa-Barton, *St-Julien*; Malescot-St-Exupéry, *Margaux*; Cantenac-Brown, *Cantenac-Margaux*; Palmer, *Cantenac-Margaux*; la Lagune, *Ludon-Haut-Médoc*; Desmirail, *Margaux*; Calon-Ségur, *St-Estèphe*; Ferrière, *Margaux*; Marquis d'Alesme-Becker, *Margaux*; Boyd-Cantenac, *Cantenac-Margaux*.

Fourth Growths (4èmes Crus)
St-Pierre, *St-Julien*; Branaire-Ducru, *St-Julien*; Talbot, *St-Julien*; Duhart-Milon-Rothschild, *Pauillac*; Pouget, *Cantenac-Margaux*; la Tour-Carnet, *St-Laurent-Haut-Médoc*; Lafon-Rochet, *St-Estèphe*; Beychevelle, *St-Julien*; Prieuré-Lichine, *Cantenac-Margaux*; Marquis-de-Terme, *Margaux*.

Fifth Growths (5èmes Crus)
Pontet-Canet, *Pauillac*; Batailley, *Pauillac*; Grand-Puy-Lacoste, *Pauillac*; Grand-Puy-Ducasse, *Pauillac*; Haut-Batailley, *Pauillac*; Lynch-Bages, *Pauillac*; Lynch-Moussas, *Pauillac*; Dauzac, *Labarde-Margaux*; Mouton-Baronne-Philippe, *Pauillac* (formerly known as Mouton d'Armailhacq); du Tertre, *Arsac-Margaux*; Haut-Bages-Libéral, *Pauillac*; Pédesclaux, *Pauillac*; Belgrave, *St-Laurent-Haut Médoc*; de Camensac, *St-Laurent-Haut-Médoc*; Cos Labory, *St-Estèphe*; Clerc-Milon-Rothschild, *Pauillac*; Croizet-Bages, *Pauillac*; Cantemerle, *Macau-Haut-Médoc*.

Webster's is an annual publication. We welcome your suggestions for next year's edition.

CHÂTEAUX PROFILES

These properties are valued according to how they are currently performing; a five-star rating means you are getting a top-line taste – not just a well-known label. Some big names have been downgraded, some lesser-known properties are promoted – *solely* on the quality of the wine inside the bottle. A star in brackets shows that the wine can achieve the higher rating but does not always do so.

The £ sign shows which wines are offering particularly good value for money – although given the current inflated prices for Bordeaux in general, that does *not* mean any of these wines will exactly be cheap.

L'ANGÉLUS *grand cru classé St-Émilion*
★★★(★) One of the biggest and best known *grands crus classés*. They have a lot of Cabernet in the vineyard, which makes the wine reasonably gutsy, although the taste is rich and soft. Since 1979 new barrels have contributed to flavour. The 1985 and 1986 are, by a street, the finest yet, with excellent '87, '88 and '89.

D'ANGLUDET *cru bourgeois supérieur exceptionnel Margaux* ★★★ £ *Bourgeois* easily attaining Classed Growth standards. Owned by an Englishman, Peter Allan Sichel, the wine has much of the perfume of good Margaux without ever going through the traditional tough, lean period. Fairly priced. Tremendous value. The 1980s have seen Angludet on a hot streak. The '83 is the property's finest wine *ever*, and the '85, '86, '88 and '89 are big and classy.

AUSONE *1er grand cru classé St-Émilion* ★★★★★ The phoenix rises from the ashes. For many years, people have been referring to Ausone as they would to a slightly mad and distinctly embarrassing maiden aunt, who then marries the most popular boy in town. The boy in question is Pascal Delbeck, who has been at the château since 1976 and has worked at returning Ausone to its proper position as one of St-Émilion's two First Growths. Great wine at its best and very expensive. The 1985 and '86 are especially good, but the '82 and '83, although they started out well, are going through a decidedly *odd* phase just now. Let's hope it passes.

BATAILLEY *5ème cru classé Pauillac* ★★★ £ Batailley's reputation has been of the squat, solid sort rather than elegant

and refined, but recently the wines have performed that extremely difficult Pauillac magician's trick – they've been getting a great deal better, and the price has remained low. They drink well young, but age well too. The 1983, '85, '86, '88 and '89 are excellent, available – and affordable.

BELAIR *1er cru classé St-Émilion* ★★★ The arrival of Pascal Delbeck at Ausone had a dramatic effect on Belair too, since it's under the same ownership. It looked as though it was rapidly returning to a top position as a finely balanced, stylish St-Émilion, but some recent bottles have been strangely unconvincing.

BEYCHEVELLE *4ème cru classé St-Julien* ★★★★ Certainly the most expensive Fourth Growth, but deservedly so, since traditional quality puts it alongside the top Seconds. It takes time to mature to a scented, blackcurranty, beautifully balanced – and expensive – wine. Its consistency during the 1980s has been dramatic, with marvellous '82, '83, '85, '88 and '89 wines, as well as good '87s, '86s and '84s, a better than average '80, and delicious '78 and '79.

BRANAIRE-DUCRU *4ème cru classé St-Julien* ★★(★) Used to be soft, smooth wine with a flavour of plums and chocolate, gradually achieving a classic, cedary St-Julien dry perfume in maturity. The 1981, '82, '85 and '86 are good. But the 1980s have been very erratic, with rather dilute flavours and unclean fruit. '82, '85 and '86 were quite good, but '83, '87 and '88 were strangely insubstantial. 1989 saw a welcome return to form, with wine of sturdy fruit and backbone.

BRANE-CANTENAC *2ème cru classé Margaux* ★★(★) This is a big and famous property which has been underachieving, when most of the other Second Growths are shooting ahead. It has had chances in the last eight years to prove its greatness and despite some improvements which give grounds for optimism, ('89 showed much better intensity of flavour) this Growth has been falling behind the rest of the field. Even its supposedly inferior stable-mate Durfort-Vivens produced better wine in '87 and '88. The mature bottles still on the shelves should be avoided.

CALON-SÉGUR *3ème cru classé St-Estèphe* ★★★ The château with the heart on its label. This is because the former owner, Marquis de Ségur, though he owned such estates as Lafite and Latour, declared 'my heart belongs to Calon'. On present showing, it's certainly good, but doesn't set many hearts a-flutter. '86 and '88 were promising though.

CANON *1er grand cru classé St-Émilion* ★★★★ Mature Canon reeks of the soft, buttery Merlot grape as only a top St-Émilion can. Recently, it has been getting deeper and tougher, and although we'll probably miss that juicy, sweet mouthful of young Merlot, the end result will be even more exciting. The wines seem to get better and better; marvellous 1982s and '83s were followed by a stunning '85 and a thoroughly impressive '86. '87 and '88 were excellent. '89 should keep up the run of good years.

CANTEMERLE *5ème cru classé Haut-Médoc* ★★★(★) Since 1983 the Cordier company has controlled this Fifth Growth and the wine is now often up to Second Growth standards, although sometimes a little light. The 1988 and '89 are the best recent vintages by a long way, and the '83 was really good, but though the '85 and '86 are beautifully perfumed, they are a little loose-knit. Interestingly, the perfumed style quite suits the '87.

CHASSE-SPLEEN *cru grand bourgeois exceptionnel Moulis* ★★★(★) £ A tremendously consistent wine, at the top of the *bourgeois* tree, and a prime candidate

for elevation in any new classification. The wines have been impressive, chunky and beautifully made right through the 1980s, except for a rather 'over-elegant' 1985. Choose 1982 and '86, followed by lovely '87 and tip-top '88. The signs are that the inky-black '89 will be terrific.

CHEVAL-BLANC *1er grand cru classé St-Émilion* ★★★★★ The property stands on a grand outcrop right next to Pomerol, and seems to share some of its sturdy richness, but adds extra spice and fruit flavour that is impressively, recognizably unique. Good years are succulently good. Lesser years, like 1980 and 1987, can be great successes too, and only 1984 hasn't worked here recently. The 1982 is unbelievably good, and the '81, '83, '85 and '86 are not far behind. '88 is one of the top wines of the vintage, and '89 packs tremendous power into the intense but subtle blend of blackcurrant and vanilla.

CISSAC *cru grand bourgeois exceptionnel Haut-Médoc* ★★★ £ Traditionalists' delight! This is one of the best known *bourgeois* growths, dark, dry and slow to mature with lots of oak influence, too – the oak perhaps a little more apparent than the fruit. It is best in richly ripe years like 1982 and '85, and can be a little lean in years like '86. '88 and '89 were very good indeed.

COS D'ESTOURNEL *2ème cru classé St-Estèphe* ★★★★(★) Now the undoubted leader of St-Estèphe in quality terms, this property has rapidly acquired much of the fame of the top Pauillacs just down the road. The wines are dark, tannic and oaky – classically made for long ageing despite a high percentage of Merlot in the vineyard. They are deservedly among the most expensive Second Growths. In fact the quality was so good in '85, '86, '88 and '89 that they are probably undervalued. Second label Château Marbuzet is good.

DOMAINE DE CHEVALIER *cru classé Pessac-Léognan* ★★★★(★) The red and white are equally brilliant. The red possesses a superb balance of fruit and oak, and the white is simply one of France's great white wines. You have to book ahead even to see a bottle of the white but you might find some red. Buy it. It's expensive and worth every penny. The hottest years are not always the best here, and despite an impressive richness in 1982, the '81, '83, '85, '86 and '88 may yet turn out better. 1987 is a resounding success in a light vintage, as is 1984. 1989 was another classy year in an area of Bordeaux where results seem a little uneven.

DUCRU-BEAUCAILLOU *2ème cru classé St-Julien* ★★★★(★) One of the glories of the Médoc. It has now distanced itself from most other Second Growths in price and quality, yet the flavour is so deep and warm, and the balance so good, it's worth the money every time. With its relatively high yields, it has a less startling quality when young than its near rivals Léoville-Las-Cases and Pichon-Lalande, but as Beychevelle also shows just down the road, if the balance is right, the wine can age impressively and beautifully without extra concentration. 1982, '85, '86, '88 and '89 are all top drawer and marvellously complex, while '81, '79 and '78 are also remarkably good and fit for the long haul.

L'EVANGILE *Pomerol* ★★★★(★) First-class Pomerol, lacking the sheer intensity of its neighbour Pétrus, but perfumed and rich in a most irresistible way. Output isn't excessive, demand is. 1982, '85, and '88 are quite exceptional, with first-rate '87 too. '89 is packed with multi-layered, firm, luscious fruit. Wonderful stuff.

DE FIEUZAL *cru classé Pessac-Léognan* ★★★★(★) A rising star. A perfect blend of high-tech knowhow and traditional values. The red starts plum-rich and buttery, but soon develops typical earthiness and cedar perfume allied to lovely fruit. It made one of the finest 1984s, outstanding '85s and '86s as well as lovely '87s and thrilling '88s. '89 was absolutely top-notch. The white, though unclassified, is scented and exciting. One to watch.

FIGEAC *1er grand cru classé St-Émilion* ★★★★(★) Figeac shares many of the qualities of Cheval-Blanc (rare gravelly soil, for a start) and sometimes makes an even better wine, but it's always ranked as the star of the second team. A pity, because

the wine has a beauty and a blackcurranty, minty fragrance not common in St-Émilion. High quality. High price. Figeac is always easy to drink young, but really deserves proper ageing. The excellent 1978 is just opening out, and the lovely '82, '85, '86 and '88 wines will all take at least as long. '89 is already marvellously seductive.

LA FLEUR-PÉTRUS *Pomerol* ★★★★ This wine is in the top flight, having some of the mineral roughness of much Pomerol, but also tremendous perfume and length. Real class. We don't see much of this in the UK since the Americans got their teeth into it, but the 1982 is without doubt the best recent wine, since the '85 and '86 seem to lack that little 'extra' class.

GAZIN *Pomerol* ★★★ This can produce the extra sweetness and perfume Nenin usually lacks. Although fairly common on the British market, it wasn't that great up to about 1985. Now controlled by Moueix, '87 and '88 are back on form, and '89 is really very fine, so we can all start buying it again.

GISCOURS *3ème cru classé Margaux* ★★★ This property excelled right through the 1970s and into the 1980s, and made some of Bordeaux's best wines in years like '75, '78 and '80. But something's gone wrong since 1982. Although 1986 is good, and '87 is very attractive, '83, '85 and '88 are really not up to par if Giscours wants to remain a candidate for the top rank. 1989 showed a welcome return to form.

GLORIA *cru bourgeois St-Julien* ★★(★) Owing to the high-profile lobbying of its owner, Henry Martin, Gloria has become expensive and renowned. The quality of this quick-maturing wine has not always been faithful to the quality of the rhetoric. 1986, '88 and '89 show some signs that Monsieur Martin is now trying to make a wine worthy of the price he asks.

GRAND-PUY-DUCASSE *5ème cru classé Pauillac* ★★★ £ Every recent vintage has been a success, and, with a price that is not excessive, its slightly gentle but tasty Pauillac style is one to buy. The 1979 is lovely now, and the '82 and '83 are very nice without causing the hand to tremble in anticipation. Since 1984 there has been a discernible rise in tempo and '85 and '86 look to be the best wines yet.

GRAND-PUY-LACOSTE *5ème cru classé Pauillac* ★★★★ £ This wine manages to combine perfume with power in a way that shows top Pauillac at its brilliant best. Few châteaux achieve this as consistently as Grand-Puy-Lacoste. The blackcurrant and the cigar-box perfume are rarely in better harmony than here. Not cheap but worth it for a classic. The 1978 is sheer class, the '82, '83, '86 and '88 top wines, and the '84, though very light, is gentle and delicious. 1989 is deliciously perfumed with robust fruit – a real star.

GRUAUD-LAROSE *2ème cru classé St-Julien* ★★★★(★) Another St-Julien that often starts rich, chunky and sweetish but will achieve its full cedary glory if given time, while still retaining a lovely sweet centre. Gets more exciting with every vintage and the remarkable run of 1982, '83, '84 and '85 continued with a great '86, an attractive '87 and exceptionally impressive '88 and '89.

HAUT-BAILLY *cru classé Pessac-Léognan* ★★★★ Haut-Bailly tastes sweet, rich and perfumed from its earliest youth, and the high percentage of new oak adds to this impression even further. But the wines do age well and, though expensive, are of a high class. 1981, '82, '85, '86 and '88 are the best recently.

HAUT-BATAILLEY *5ème cru classé Pauillac* ★★★ Once dark, plummy and slow to sweeten, Haut-Batailley is now a somewhat lighter, more charming wine. In some years this has meant it was somehow less satisfying, but 1989 is the best yet, marvellously concentrated. 1986 and '88 are the best of earlier wines, with '82, '83 and '85 all good, but just a touch too diffuse and soft.

HAUT-BRION *1er cru classé Pessac-Léognan* ★★★★★ The only non-Médoc red to be classified in 1855. The wines are not big, but are almost creamy in their gorgeous ripe taste, uniquely so. If anything, they slightly resemble the great Médocs. Although 1982 is strangely insubstantial, the next four vintages are all very fine and '88 and '89 are outstanding. There is also a delicious white Haut-Brion – the 1985 is spectacular.

D'ISSAN *3ème cru classé Margaux* ★★★★ One of the truest Margaux wines, hard when young (though more use of new oak recently has sweetened things up a bit), but perfumed and deep-flavoured after 10 to 12 years. Fabulous in 1983 and '88, first rate in '85 and '86, with a good '87 too. 1989 has excellent fruit underneath the tannin.

LAFITE-ROTHSCHILD *1er cru classé Pauillac* ★★★★(★) The most difficult of all the great Médocs to get to know and understand. It doesn't stand for power like Latour, or overwhelming perfume like Mouton. No, it stands for balance, for the elegant, restrained balance that is the perfection of great claret. And yet, till its day comes, Lafite can seem curiously unsatisfying. I keep looking for that day. I keep being unsatisfied. 1989 and '88 are undoubtedly the best recent vintages, followed by 1982 and '86 but this fabled estate does seem to be dishing up fairy tales in the place of the real stuff that dreams are made of.

LAFLEUR *Pomerol* ★★★★★ This tiny property is regarded as the only Pomerol with the potential to be as great as Pétrus. So far, they couldn't be further apart in style, and Lafleur is marked out by an astonishing austere concentration of dark fruit and an intense tobacco spice perfume. The 1982 almost knocks you sideways with its naked power, and the '83 and '85 are also remarkable. 1989 is superbly fruity and displays tremendous finesse already. It should be a good buy.

LAFON-ROCHET *4ème cru classé St-Estèphe* ★★★(★) £ Since the 1970s, an increasingly good St-Estèphe, having as much body, but a little more perfume than most of them. It's a good bargain buy, given its quality. 1982, '83 and '85 are all good, though none of them stunning, while '86, '87, '88 and '89 show lots of class and a welcome consistency of style.

LAGRANGE *3ème cru classé St-Julien*
★★★(★) Much berated for its quality, but
this château has been described by Bruno
Prats, one of the Médoc's most dedicated
winemakers, as having the best vineyard of
all of the still sub-par châteaux. Until its
purchase by the Japanese Suntory whisky
group in 1984, Lagrange had always lacked
real class, though '82 and '83 were good.
But investment is making its presence felt;
'85 and '86 are impressive and '87 was good
too. Another bandwagon is set to roll. Make
sure you concentrate on new vintages
though.

LA LAGUNE *3ème cru classé Haut-Médoc*
★★★★ Certainly making Second Growth
standard wine, with a rich, soft intensity. It
is now becoming more expensive, but the
wine gets better and better. The 1982 is a
wonderful rich, juicy wine, with '85 and '88
not far behind, and '83 not far behind that.
1986 is burly but brilliant stuff, as is '89.
1987 is more delicate but good.

LANESSAN *cru bourgeois supérieur Haut-
Médoc* ★★★ 'Grand Cru Hors Classe' is
how Lanessan describes itself. This could
be a timeless reminder of the fact that a
previous owner felt it unnecessary to
submit samples for the 1855 Classification,
and so its traditional ranking as a Fourth
Growth was never ratified. Nowadays, the
wine is always incredibly correct, if
sometimes slightly lacking in personality.
But this may be because the owner
resolutely refuses to use new oak and
therefore his wines *are* more discreet when
tasted young. The '82 and '83 are both
exhibiting classic claret flavours now, '88
looks set for the same path and first
tastings of '89 reveal a wine of balance and
depth.

LANGOA-BARTON *3ème cru classé St-
Julien* ★★★★ This wine is very good. It is
in the dry, cedary style, and although
sometimes regarded as a lesser version of
Léoville-Barton, this is patently unfair
since the wine has exceptional character
and style of its own, and is always
reasonably priced. '82 and '85 are exciting,
'86 and '87 very typical, but the '88 may be
the best Langoa for 30 years, and the '89
almost matched Léoville for elegance.

LASCOMBES *2ème cru classé Margaux*
★★★ Lascombes made its reputation in
America, and that's where it still likes to be
drunk. Very attractive early on, but the
wine can gain flesh and character as it
ages. It's been a little inconsistent recently,
but the 1985 and '83 are good, and the '86
is the most serious effort for a long time.
'87 is also good, but '88 is so light you'd
think they'd included every grape on the
property.

LATOUR *1er cru classé Pauillac* ★★★★★
This is the easiest of all the First Growths
to understand. You may not always like it,
but you understand it because it is a
massive, dark, hard brute when young,
calming down when it ages and eventually
spreading out to a superb, big,
blackcurrant and cedar flavour. It used to
take absolutely ages to come round, but
some recent vintages have seemed a little
softer and lighter, yet usually retaining
their tremendous core of fruit. Let's hope
they age as well as the previous ones,
because the 1984 was more true to type
than the '85! And though the '82 is a

classic, both '83 and '81 are very definitely not. '86 and '88 seem to be back on course, and '89 looks splendidly powerful. But it's worrying. Are they heading into the mire of inconsistency that has been plaguing local rival Lafite recently?

LÉOVILLE-BARTON *2ème cru classé St-Julien* ★★★★(★) £ The traditionalist's dream. Whoever described claret as a dry, demanding wine must have been thinking of Léoville-Barton. Despite all the new fashions and trends in Bordeaux, Anthony Barton simply goes on making superlative, old-fashioned wine for long ageing, and resolutely charging a non-inflated price for it. All the vintages of the 1980s have been attractive, but the 1982, '83, '85 and '86 are outstanding, the '87 delicious, and the '88 is one of the best wines of the Médoc. 1989 keeps up the standard. All are *wonderfully* fairly priced.

LÉOVILLE-LAS-CASES *2ème cru classé St-Julien* ★★★★★ With Ducru-Beaucaillou, this is the most brilliant of the St-Juliens, combining all the sweet, honeyed St-Julien ripeness with strong, dry, cedary perfume. The wine is justly famous, and despite a very large production, the whole crop is snapped up at some of the Médoc's highest prices. The 1982 is more exciting every time a bottle is broached, and all the vintages of the 1980s are top examples of their year. The second wine, Clos du Marquis, is better than the majority of Classed Growths.

LÉOVILLE-POYFERRÉ *2ème cru classé St-Julien* ★★(★) The Léoville that got left behind, not only in its unfashionable reputation, but also in the quality of the wine, which usually has a dull, indistinct flavour and an unbalancing dryness compared with other top St-Juliens. Things are now looking up with new investment and new commitment but progress is still patchy, and it's difficult to feel confident about this property yet. The 1982, '85, '86 and even the '87 are considerable improvements, and '89 is perhaps the best yet, so could it be time to stop feeling wary?

LOUDENNE *cru grand bourgeois Médoc* ★(★) The château is owned by Gilbey's and the wine is seen a lot in such chains as Peter Dominic. The red always seems pleasant, but unmemorable and a little too soft to lay down for long.

LYNCH-BAGES *5ème cru classé Pauillac* ★★★★(★) This château is so well known that familiarity can breed contempt, and its considerable quality be underestimated. It is astonishingly soft and drinkable when very young, and yet it ages brilliantly, and has one of the most beautiful scents of minty blackcurrant in all Bordeaux. The most likely to show that character are the 1986 and '83, and, remarkably, the '87, but for sheer exuberant starry-eyed brilliance, the '88, '85 and particularly the '82 are the ones. '89 is unusually big and powerful, less extrovert and more intense.

MAGDELAINE *1er grand cru classé St-Émilion* ★★★★ A great St-Émilion, combining the soft richness of Merlot with the sturdiness needed to age. They pick very late to maximize ripeness, and the wine is made with the usual care by Jean-Pierre Moueix of Libourne. Expensive, but one of the best. 1982 and 1985 are both classics, '88 and '89 tremendously good.

MALARTIC-LAGRAVIÈRE *cru classé Pessac-Léognan* ★★★ £ While its near neighbour, Domaine de Chevalier, hardly ever produces its allowed crop, this property frequently has to declassify its excess. Even so, the quality is good, sometimes excellent, and while the white is very attractive young, the red is dry and herby, and capable of long ageing. Usually good value. 1987, '86, '85, '83 and '82 are all successful, with '88 and '89 the finest yet.

MALESCOT-ST-EXUPÉRY *3ème cru classé Margaux* ★★(★) A property which seems to have lost its way. Traditionally it started out quite lean and hard and difficult to taste, but after ten years or so it began to display the perfume and delicate fruit only bettered by such wines as Palmer and Margaux. A good Malescot would happily last 25 years. Yet after tasting and re-tasting the wines of the 1980s, sadly the conclusion is that they are now being made too light and lacking in depth for this thrilling perfume ever to develop.

MARGAUX *1er cru classé Margaux*
★★★★★ Since 1978 a succession of great wines have set Margaux back on the pedestal of fragrance, refinement and sheer, ravishing perfume from which it had slipped a dozen or so years before. Many vintages of the 1970s were pretty feeble, but the new Margaux is weightier than before, yet with all its beauty intact. 1978 and 1979 were the exciting harbingers of this new 'Mentzelopoulos era', the '80 was startlingly good in a tricky vintage, and '82, '83 and '86 are just about as brilliant as claret can be, while the '88 may well be the wine of the vintage. The deep, concentrated '89 doesn't seem to match up to the '88.

MEYNEY *cru grand bourgeois exceptionnel St-Estèphe* ★★★(★) £ This epitomizes the 'reliable' style of St-Estèphe, yet is better than that. The wine is big, meaty, and strong, but never harsh. Vintages in the 1970s lacked a little personality, but the recent wines are increasingly impressive and although the wine is difficult to taste young, the '82, '83, '85, '86, '88 and '89 are remarkable and the '84 and '87 also exceptionally good.

LA MISSION-HAUT-BRION *cru classé Pessac-Léognan* ★★★(★) La Mission likes to put itself in a class apart, between Haut-Brion and the rest. Yet one often feels this 'hors classe' position relies more on weight and massive, dark fruit and oak flavours than on any great subtleties. For those, you go up to Haut-Brion, or across to Domaine de Chevalier. '82, '85 or '86 are recommendable of recent vintages.

MONTROSE *2ème cru classé St-Estèphe* ★★★ Traditionally famous for its dark, tannic character, and its slow, ponderous march to maturity. For a wine with such a sturdy reputation, some recent vintages have seemed faintly hollow. 1986 made amends with a really chewy, long-distance number, and '87 was densely structured, if hardly classic, but it's taken until '89 for the wine to really return to form.

MOUTON-BARONNE-PHILIPPE *5ème cru classé Pauillac* ★★★(★) A wine of very good balance for a Fifth Growth, with the perfume particularly marked, this obviously benefits from having the same ownership as Mouton-Rothschild. Seems to be improving each year. 1986 and '83 are very good, with '82 not bad either.

MOUTON-ROTHSCHILD *1er cru classé Pauillac* ★★★★★ After 50 years of well-orchestrated lobbying, Baron Philippe de Rothschild managed to raise Mouton to First Growth status in 1973. Of course it should be a First Growth. But then several Fifths should probably be Seconds. The wine does have an astonishing flavour, piling an intense cigar-box and lead-pencil perfume on to the rich blackcurrant fruit. The 1982 is already a legend, the '86 and '89 are likely to join '82, and the '85, '84 and '83 are well worth the asking price for brilliant wine.

NENIN *Pomerol* ★★ A thoroughly old-fashioned wine. It quite rightly pleases the royal family, who order rather a lot of it. But in fact it is rather chunky and solid and has quite a tough core for a Pomerol, which doesn't always disperse into mellow fruitfulness. The 1985 and '86 aren't bad, but, really, the '82, the '83 and the '88, all good vintages, were pretty feeble.

PALMER *3ème cru classé Margaux* ★★★★(★) 'Most expensive of the Third Growths?' asks one of Palmer's owners. 'No. Cheapest of the Firsts.' The way things are going, there's a lot of truth in that. Palmer used to out-Margaux Margaux for sheer beauty and perfume. And it still can out-perform some of the First Growths in tastings. It was consistently brilliant in the 1960s and 1970s (excepting '64), but the 1980s have seen Palmer lose some of its sure touch, and even the '83 lacks the class of some of its neighbours in what was very much a Margaux year. 1985 and '86 are both extremely good. '87 and '88 are very good too, but are close in style to out-Beychevelling Beychevelle. '89 is cedary and elegant, rich but tannic, in a year when not all Margaux wines had great depth of fruit.

PAPE-CLÉMENT *cru classé Pessac-Léognan* ★★★★ One of the top properties in Pessac-Léognan, capable of mixing a considerable sweetness from ripe fruit and new oak with a good deal of tough structure. 1975 was great, but then we had a very poor decade until 1985. The last five vintages are outstanding.

PAVIE *1er grand cru St-Émilion* ★★★(★) The biggest major property in St-Émilion, with high yields, too. Until recently good without being wonderful, stylish without being grand. Still, Pavie does have the true gentle flavours of good St-Émilion and recent releases are showing a deeper, more passionate style which suits it very well. 1989, '88, '87, '86 and '85 are good examples of the new Pavie, '82 of the old.

PETIT-VILLAGE *Pomerol* ★★★★ A fairly pricy wine, it is not one of the soft, plummy Pomerols, and until recently there was a fair amount of Cabernet giving backbone. The wine is worth laying down, but the price is always high. 1985, '83 and the absurdly juicy '82 are all very good, but the '88 and '89 look likely to be the best yet.

PÉTRUS *Pomerol* ★★★★★ The world's most expensive red wine, and frequently the world's greatest. Astonishingly, its reputation, though surfacing briefly in 1878, has been made since World War Two, and in particular since 1962, when the firm of Jean-Pierre Moueix took a half-share in the property. This firm has given the kiss of life to many Pomerol properties, turning potential into achievement, and with Pétrus it has a supreme creation. Christian Moueix says his intention is to ensure no bottle of Pétrus ever disappoints anyone. 1982 was shamelessly, stupendously great. 1985 isn't far off it, nor is '81 and the only example from the last 20 years which seemed atypical is the rather Médoc-like 1978. Can they keep it up in the face of blistering world demand?

DE PEZ *cru bourgeois supérieur St-Estèphe* ★★★ One of the most famous *bourgeois* châteaux of Bordeaux, the wine is almost always of Classed Growth standard, big, rather plummy and not too harsh. 1982 and '83 were very attractive, though some prefer the slightly more unashamed St-Estèphe wines made during the 1970s, which saw something of a comeback with the excellent '86.

PICHON-LONGUEVILLE *2ème cru classé Pauillac* ★★★★ (since 1987) Often described as more masculine than its 'sister', Pichon-Lalande, this tremendously correct but diffident Pauillac (formerly Pichon-Longueville-Baron) was until 1987 only hinting at its potential. Drier and lighter than Lalande, it was also less immediately impressive, despite ageing well. 1987 saw the property being bought by the Axa insurance company and the supremely talented Jean-Michel Cazes of Lynch-Bages being brought in to run it. The '87 was very good, the '88 superb, the '89 *tremendous*, broodingly intense.

PICHON-LALANDE *2ème cru classé Pauillac* ★★★★★ Pichon-Lalande announced its intentions with a stunning 1970, and since then has been making a rich, oaky, concentrated wine of tremendous quality. Its price has climbed inexorably and it wishes to be seen as the equal partner of St-Julien's leading pair, Léoville-Las-Cases and Ducru-Beaucaillou. Well, the wines are now so consistently remarkable, those two may end up having to join Lalande's club. 1982, '83 and '84 all brim with exciting flavours, '85 is quite superb, and they think '86 is even better. '87 and '88 don't quite reach the same standards, but '89 is velvety, elegant and seductively fruity. With the revival of Pichon-Longueville, over the road, I look forward to the future rivalry between these properties with enormous enthusiasm.

PONTET-CANET *5ème cru classé Pauillac* ★★ Famous but unpredictable property, still trying to find its traditionally reliable form, with only mixed results. 1985 and '86 are hopeful, '87 and '88 less so.

POTENSAC *cru grand bourgeois Médoc* ★★★(★) £ The most exciting of the Bas-Médoc properties, since it is owned by Monsieur Delon of Léoville-Las-Cases, and a broadly similar style of wine-making is pursued. This gives wines with a delicious, blackcurrant fruit, greatly improved by a strong taste of oak from once-used Las-Cases barrels. Not expensive for the quality. 1982 is way up the *crus classés* in quality and each vintage since has also beaten many *crus classés* for sheer flavour.

PRIEURÉ-LICHINE *4ème cru classé Margaux* ★★★ One of the more reliable Margaux wines, and in years like 1970, 1971 and 1975 it excelled. Recently it has been fairly priced and although not that perfumed, a good, sound Margaux. 1983, '86, '88 and '89 are the best recent vintages.

RAUSAN-SÉGLA *2ème cru classé Margaux* ★★★★(★) What an astonishing transformation. Up to and including the 1982 vintage this lovely property, rated second only to Mouton-Rothschild in the 1855 Second Growths, had been woefully underachieving for a couple of generations. It might have merited two stars, certainly not more. But a dynamic change of ownership in 1983 saw a triumphant return to quality – in the very first year! Many proprietors moan that it takes 10 or 20 years to improve a property's performance. Pichon-Longueville and Rausan-Ségla are proof it can be achieved in a single vintage. 1983, '85 and '86 were triumphs. 1987 was declassified as Château Lamouroux but is still delicious and the '88 is a supreme achievement which the '89 matches.

RAUZAN-GASSIES *2ème cru classé Margaux* ★★ Right behind Rausan-Ségla, this should only be an arm's length away from Mouton in quality. But in fact the wine is leagues below Mouton and most Second and Third Growths in quality, and so far hasn't taken the hint from its neighbour Ségla that quality pays in the end. But the soil is as good as ever, so I'm still hoping. Slight signs with the '86.

ST-PIERRE *4ème cru classé Médoc* ★★★★ Small St-Julien property making superb, underrated old-fashioned claret. Used to be under-priced too, but not any more since the image-conscious Henri Martin of Gloria bought it in 1982. Still, the quality is worth the asking price, and while the 1970 and '75 were underrated stars, the wines of the 1980s are possibly even better.

> *The price guides for this section begin on page 246.*

DE SALES *Pomerol* ★★★ An enormous estate, the biggest in Pomerol by a street. This vastness may show a little in a wine, which, though it is good round claret, doesn't often excite. The 1985 is very nice, the '83 and '82 are very nice.

SIRAN *cru bourgeois supérieur Margaux* ★★★ Sometimes mistaken for a Classed Growth in blind tastings, this property is indeed mostly made up from the land of Dauzac and Giscours. The '85 and '83 are the most successful recently, but all recent vintages have been good. The '88 was a bit clumsy though '87 is OK.

TALBOT *4ème cru classé St-Julien* ★★★★ One of the most carefully made and reliable of the fleshier St-Juliens, suffering slightly only in comparison with its sister château, Gruaud-Larose, and always offering value for money and tremendous consistency. Maybe the name Talbot just lacks the right ring? Whatever the reason, you must seek out the exciting 1986, the super-classy '85, '83 and '82 and the ultra-stylish '84, as well as the lovely '87 and the impressive '88 and then there's the big, rich '89 ... just taste the wine.

DU TERTRE *5ème cru classé Margaux* ★★★(★) This wine is unusually good, with a lot of body for a Margaux, but that weight is all ripe, strong fruit and the flavour is direct and pure. Funnily enough, it's not cheap for a relative unknown but neither is it expensive for the quality. The '85 is rich and dense and yet keeps its perfume intact, while the '86, '83 and '82 are rich and blackcurranty – already good and sure to improve for ten years more. '88 not quite so good, for some reason, '89 back to normal.

TROTANOY *Pomerol* ★★★★ If you didn't know Château Pétrus existed, you'd say this had to be the perfect Pomerol – rich, plummy, chocolaty fruit, some mineral hardness, and tremendous fat perfume. It's very, very good, and makes Pétrus' achievement in eclipsing it (in a friendly way) all the more amazing. The '82 is brilliant, and although the '85 is also wonderfully good, the mid and late 1980s haven't been as thrilling as the previous vintages.

SECOND WINES

The second wines from the major Bordeaux châteaux can be defined, approximately, as being wines from the same vineyard as the *grand vin* (the wine with the château name) which, for various reasons, have been 'selected out' of the top wine. Legally they could be included, but to maintain quality certain barrels are put on one side when the final selection is made.

These may be the produce of particularly young vines, which won't have the concentration and staying power demanded from an expensive Classed Growth. They may be from sections of the vineyard that, owing to the vagaries of the weather, didn't produce quite the right style, or that are just traditionally less good. Or they may include first-class wine from mature vines and good parts of the vineyard that just doesn't fit into this particular vintage of the *grand vin* style. For example, if the Merlot grape produces an enormous crop and the tougher Cabernet falls a bit short on quantity, then a winemaker may decide to use less Merlot, so as to preserve the balance he wants. In which case he'll beef up his second wine with wine of first-class quality.

Then there is another form of second wine. Sometimes a major château buys up a lesser property nearby, and begins to use its label for its second wine. Since it is in the same *appellation* this is perfectly legal. Cos d'Estournel uses the seven-hectare vineyard of Château Marbuzet like this, and Lynch-Bages uses Haut-Bages-Avérous in the same way.

If you talk to retailers about the relevance of the Classed Growth Bordeaux maker in England, more and more will tell you that the actual purchase of a remotely ready to drink *grand vin* from a Classed Growth property is gradually becoming an almost irrelevant part of their business. Apart from a few old-established companies and one or two new up-market specialists, very few retailers now sell more than token amounts of mature *grand vin* claret. But the desire to trade up and drink so called 'classy claret' is as strong as ever. It's just the ridiculous price which people balk at.

And that's where the second wines have made phenomenal inroads during the last 12 months. If we leave out wine such as Pavillon Rouge du Château Margaux and Les Forts de Latour, which are usually priced at the £15 plus mark, the other top Bordeaux properties are able to offer their second wines at between £7 and £9 a bottle. Sure, that *is* a lot, but given the seemingly innate desire of the British to drink decent claret as their 'high days' wine whenever possible, and given the fact that at three to four years old, the second wine of a property like Léoville-Barton, Pichon-Longueville, Pichon-Lalande, Palmer or Lynch-Bages can be outstandingly attractive – far less tannic than the main wine, but fleshy and soft and reasonably oaky too – consumers can really *taste* the class they are buying. Marks and Spencers really got the ball rolling last year with their smartly turned out but simply labelled generics – Pauillac, St-Estèphe, St-Julien etc – all top second wines – and they sold like hot cakes right through the year, and especially at Christmas. As top properties declassify more and more of their wine to maintain the densely structured, dark, long distance style which is popular with the Château owners and the trade at the moment, the second wines will play a bigger and bigger part in our market. In years like '83, '85, '86 and '88 top properties might declassify as much as 40 per cent. Twenty years ago many of them wouldn't declassify at all, and more than ten per cent was very rare.

We should take immediate advantage. Not only to drink now, but also to lay down. Now good second wines *do* have a ten year life expectancy from the good vintages of the '80s, although there are lighter styles – like some of the AC Margaux properties, and the delicious but delicate wines of a label like Lacoste-Borie (Grand-Puy-Lacoste) which are so good at five years old it seems a pity to wait. But if you've got the wherewithal – try a bottle of the *grand vin* next to a bottle of the second wine. This is a wine lover's game we'll also see a lot more of in the next decade or so. There no question of not being able to tell them apart. The second wine almost always lacks a little of the drive, a little of the lingering, tantalizing flavour of the *grand vin*. The flavours that shout at you in the *grand vin* are more likely to whisper in the second wine. But they'll be ready to drink much more quickly, and that is often their chief virtue. They give you a suggestion, within four or five years of the vintage, of the glorious flavours the *grand vin* may take 20 years to achieve. Indeed, for some châteaux making lighter wine, five or six years may be more than the second wine wants.

THE NAME GAME

Just one word of caution. The number of second wines appearing on the market has mushroomed. If you see an unfamiliar name on a bottle with a familiar *appellation contrôlée*, look at the small print on the bottom of the label. If it's a real château it'll just say something like 'Propriétaire Mme Thatcher et Fils' or something like 'Société Civile' of the main name on the label. But it may also say 'Société Civile' of one of the well-known properties in the AC. In which case it is almost certain to be a second wine of that property. Some proprietors own more than one property in the AC – M Lurton of Brane Cantenac and Durfort Vivens is an example – in which case it may say something like 'Domaine Lurton' on the second wine label.

And another cautionary note. There are a lot of ambitious properties in lesser ACs – like Listrac, Moulis, Haut-Médoc, St-Émilion, Lalande-de-Pomerol, even Côtes de Francs. Many of these are starting to utilize second labels for their lesser cuvées. That's fine; the wine can be good and not expensive. But make a rule – *don't* buy the second wine of a property you don't think is up to much in the first place. It'll just be a worse example of a not very good wine. And, despite the pronouncements of one or two leading Bordeaux figures about '87 being *the* year for second wines – *don't* buy second wines from indifferent vintages. To take 1987 as an example, the properties who cared to make fine wine in 1987 did so because they declassified as much as half their wine. Almost all of this would be the unripe Cabernet Sauvignon hit by vintage-time rains. There is nothing less likely to give you drinking pleasure in the short term than unripe, dilute Cabernet Sauvignon. So don't touch it. (The exception I would make is Château Lamouroux which is the declassified Rausan-Ségla – but they declassified *all* their wine and the result is delicious. And Palmer and Angludet sold some extremely attractive wine to large groups in the UK for drinking at less than two years old which was also a delight.) Anyway, 1987 is the year we can afford to buy the *grand vin* – so whatever the Bordelais try to tell us in the next 12 months, what we *don't* want is their '87 slops. 1985 was basically a year when Merlot and Cabernet both overproduced and the second wines are absolutely lovely for now and to keep. A 1987 Classed Growth *grand vin* would be better than '86 and not necessarily much more expensive, but there should be some good '89s to look forward to in future years, and '88s to keep us going until then.

RECOMMENDED WINES

Because of the importance of second wines for *Webster's* readers, we have considerably expanded our list of available wines and starred the wines we feel are the best bets. Most of them are from the Haut-Médoc, since properties there are larger and the opportunities for selection much greater. In any case the right bank wines are likely to be ready for drinking much more quickly. An increasing number of large retail groups are now doing 'generic' wines which are in fact classy second wines. These are usually very good buys. And don't feel you're buying a second rate modern invention. You're not. A good second wine provides very classy drinking. And the idea is scarcely new. Château Margaux produced its first Pavillon Rouge du Château Margaux in 1908, and Léoville-Las-Cases created *its* second label, Clos du Marquis – in 1904!

Haut-Médoc

1st Growth: ★les Forts-de-Latour (Latour), le Moulin-des-Carruades (Lafite-Rothschild), ★Pavillon-Rouge-du-Château Margaux (Margaux).

2nd Growth: ★le Baronnet-de-Pichon (Pichon-Longueville), ★Clos du Marquis (Léoville-Las-Cases), ★la Croix (Ducru-Beaucaillou), la Dame de Montrose (Montrose), Domaine de Curebourse (Durfort-Vivens), ★Lamouroux (Rausan-Ségla), ★Marbuzet (Cos d'Estournel), Moulin-Riche (Léoville-Poyferré), Notton (Brane-Cantenac), ★Réserve de la Comtesse (Pichon-Lalande), ★St-Julien (Léoville-Barton), ★Sarget de Gruaud-Larose (Gruaud-Larose), ★les Tourelles-de-Pichon (Pichon-Longueville).

3rd Growths: ★Fiefs de Lagrange (Lagrange), ★St-Julien (Langoa), de Loyac (Malescot St-Exupéry), Ludon-Pomies-Agassac (la Lagune), Marquis-de-Ségur (Calon-Ségur), ★Réserve du Général (Palmer).

4th Growths: de Clairefont (Prieuré-Lichine), ★Connétable-Talbot (Talbot), des Goudat (Marquis de Termes), Moulin-de-Duhart (Duhart-Milon-Rothschild), ★Réserve de l'Amiral (Beychevelle), St-Louis-le-Bosq (St-Pierre).

5th Growths: Artique-Arnaud (Grand-Puy-Ducasse), Enclos de Moncabon (Croizet-Bages), ★Haut-Bages-Avérous (Lynch-Bages), les Hauts-de-Pontet (Pontet-Canet), ★Lacoste-Borie (Grand-Puy-Lacoste), ★Villeneuve-de-Cantemerle (Cantemerle).

Good Bourgeois Châteaux: Abiet (Cissac), ★Admiral (Labégorce-Zédé), Bellegarde (Siran), Bory (Angludet), ★Clos Cordat (Monbrison), Domaine de Martiny (Cissac), Domaine Zédé (Labégorce-Zédé), Ermitage de Chasse-Spleen (Chasse-Spleen), Granges-de-Clarke (Clarke), Labat (Caronne-Ste-Gemme), ★Lartigue-de-Brochon (Sociando-Mallet), ★Lassalle (Potensac), Moulin d'Arrigny (Beaumont), ★Prieuré de Meyney (Meyney), Réserve du Marquis d'Evry (Lamarque), ★la Salle-de-Poujeaux (Poujeaux), ★Tour-de-Marbuzet (Haut-Marbuzet).

Graves, Pessac-Léognan

★Abeille de Fieuzal (Fieuzal), Bahans-Haut-Brion (Haut-Brion), ★Batard-Chevalier (Domaine de Chevalier), ★Coucheroy (la Louvière), ★Hauts de Smith-Haut-Lafitte (Smith-Haut-Lafitte), ★la Parde-de-Haut-Bailly (Haut-Bailly).

St Emilion

Beau-Mayne (Couvent des Jacobins), ★Domaine de Martialis (Clos Fourtet), ★Franc-Grace-Dieu (Canon), ★la Grangeneuve-de-Figeac (Figeac), Jean du Nayne (Angélus), ★des Templiers (Larmande).

Pomerol

Chantalouette (de Sales), Clos Toulifaut (Taillefer), ★Fleur de Clinet (Clinet), la Gravette-de-Certan (Vieux-Château-Certan), Monregard-Lacroix (Clos du Clocher), ★la Petite Église (l'Église Clinet).

Bordeaux Supérieur Côtes de Francs,

les Douves de Francs (de Francs), ★Lauriol (Puygueraud).

PETITS CHÂTEAUX

'Petit château' means 'little castle', and that's a pretty fair description, because these are the properties out of the mainstream, away from the grand Classed Growths of the Médoc, St-Émilion, Pessac-Léognan and the high-fliers of Pomerol, the areas where prices cannot be inflated and quality often goes unrewarded, yet which have a definable personality of their own.

Not that long ago, most small properties would sell off their produce to be blended in bulk by a merchant or co-op who would then simply slap on a label saying 'claret' or 'Bordeaux', sometimes 'Bordeaux Supérieur'. The price would be controlled by the market place, and would be negotiated on a take-it-or-leave-it basis – the grapes really were a commodity.

Production of Bordeaux Rouge rose year by year. Successful harvest followed successful harvest. Vineyard land spread and many farmers uprooted white grapes for which they could get no price at all, and planted reds in the hope of cashing in on a claret boom. And prices fell. As they gazed enviously at the escalating prices of the top châteaux and at their own dwindling resources, the growers realized that one way of making money would be to ape the great châteaux. Basically a château need be no more than a cottage, a shed, at very best a simple farmhouse. Many of Bordeaux's famous châteaux may comprise wonderful vineyards, expensive wine – and a squat little bungalow rejoicing under the name 'château'. (*Château* literally means 'castle', which makes it all the more bizarre.) Indeed, French law says that so long as you have a building of a vaguely residential sort on your vineyard, you can call your wine 'Château X, Y or Z'. And that is exactly what these farmers do.

IMPROVEMENTS IN THE VINEYARDS

As soon as your own name and your own property is identified on the label, it's only human nature for you to try harder to make good wine. As soon as you can charge 10 to 15 francs a bottle for your wine instead of three or four francs, you are in a position to improve your wine-making equipment, install a few oak barrels, and hire a bottler to come to your property and 'château-bottle' your wine. You may even involve yourself in 'whole grape' vinification – a sort of Beaujolais method of wine-making which cuts down the tannin and squeezes some fruit character out of even the most menial grapes.

In other words, suddenly you have options open. The poverty trap which afflicts most growers of ordinary basic Bordeaux no longer has to strangle you. The mass of *petits châteaux* now on the UK market reflects this. Some are nothing more than plonk with a pretty label, but an increasing number are honest, fruity claret, so far without too many frills. And there's no doubt that as techniques improve and vineyards mature, there are going to be some exceptional wines from the ranks of the, as yet, unknowns.

After all, some of Bordeaux's lesser areas were growing grapes when the Médoc was simply an undrained bog. But 300 years ago, things evolved slowly. Now, a decade can transform a property and an area. Just think. Pomerol is now one of the most famous areas of Bordeaux but 50 years ago no one had ever heard of it, let alone bought the wine.

The opportunities for the small vineyard owner to gain in reputation are increasing with both the growth of the *petits châteaux* and a huge improvement in the quality of service offered by the co-ops. The *Union des Producteurs* at St-Émilion, for instance, has got itself organized with good quality vinification equipment that can make and bottle separately the wines from each of its 58 members' estates. A great plus for the producer and drinker.

It is, however, a long, long haul if you want to break away from the realms of *petits châteaux* and reach even the middle rank of *bourgeois*, let alone the top flight of *crus classés*.

First, there's your soil and microclimate. Now, a lot of Californians have been beefing on recently about how soil doesn't matter. And quite a few Bordelais have been doing the same. The funny thing is, the Californians who are most vociferous are those most desperate to prove that they are the 'equals', the 'peers' of those champions of vineyard sites, the great Bordeaux Classed Growths, and who end up saying – look what we do without your soil. Frequently they do brilliantly well, but it's brilliantly *different*. The other most vociferous group are those Bordeaux proprietors who *don't* possess Classed Growth land. Not surprisingly, they are also likely to proclaim the site and soil are irrelevant.

TERROIR

Well, they're wrong. The soil is crucial. It gives extra flavours to the wine and, vitally for Bordeaux, it provides early ripening conditions and good drainage – if it is the right kind. For the Cabernet Sauvignon grape, that means at least a modicum of gravel. Most of Bordeaux is clay – in which case you won't get the extra-exciting Cabernet flavours and your fruit will *never* taste like great Pauillac. Yet some people go on proclaiming their parity with the great. There's one property, la Rivière in Fronsac, which sometimes seems to do well in taste-offs versus the classics: I can't think of anyone else.

Second, investment counts. Unless the owner is dramatically rich by other means, can he afford to put in expensive oak barrels, top-class fermenting equipment, all that sort of thing? Can he afford to hire a top-line oenologist? Or to cut out between 20 per cent and 50 per cent of each year's crop to concentrate and intensify the remaining vats into a true *grand vin* as the *grands crus classés* do? Of course he can't!

And then you need commitment. It took Baron de Rothschild 50 years of obsessive, exhausting self-promotion to raise Mouton-Rothschild from a Second to a First Growth. Clearly Mme de Lencquesaing is embarked on the same self-sacrificial course as she tours the world promoting the patently brilliant qualities of Pichon-Lalande. Would anyone listen if the owner of a property in the Côtes de Bourg did that?

Certainly we are going to see many more 'small' châteaux raise their standards and strive towards more renown. But the world is choc-a-bloc with 'Grand' wine right now, and it's fairly crowded with second tier 'Bourgeois' wine, trying to become 'Grand'. There isn't that much demand for even more properties trying to charge higher prices for wines which will always just lack that touch of class. But there *is* a great demand for good, true claret, without frills and at an affordable price and that is what the *petits châteaux can* do best. But, sadly, that is *precisely* what never made any proprietor rich. It doesn't seem fair does it?

CLARETS OUT OF THEIR CLASS

Make up a classification for something, and in no time you'll be deluged with cries of 'not fair'. People will dredge up a sackful of candidates who should have been included, and they'll whisper and jeer at numerous inclusions of which they don't approve. Nowhere is this more true than in Bordeaux.

It's virtually a regional pastime trying to rearrange the Classification of 1855. It effectively condemned as second best any Médoc château that wasn't on the list, which, even so, includes many examples of wines at Fifth Growth level that people say should be Second or Third, and there are some at Second or Third that people feel should be Fourth or Fifth.

One of the most exciting things for a claret devotee is to catch a château at the beginning of a revival in its fortunes, or to be the first to find a château no-one knew was making great wine. Because while a reputation is being built or re-built, the quality will always keep ahead of the cost, and you can get fine wine at a bargain price. However, in the competitive claret market quality does tell, and the price will rise – and while in the old days it might have taken a painstaking decade or two to improve a property's quality, nowadays the employment of a top winemaker who uses state-of-the-art techniques as well as spanking new oak barrels, and a commitment to reject any portions of your wine which are not truly up to scratch mean you can go from mediocrity to magnificence in a bare two or three years.

Webster's puts forward a list – by no means exhaustive – of wines that we consider to be performing 'out of their class'. Since Bordeaux classifications are mostly rigid, wines that have long been thought of as 'out of their class' may now be obtaining far higher prices than the rating would imply.

Médoc

Minor châteaux performing like top bourgeois *wines:* Andron-Blanquet, Cartillon, le Fournas Bernadotte, de Junca, Lamothe, Malescasse, Maucamps, Moulin-de-Laborde, Patache-d'Aux, Peyrabon, Ramage-la-Bâtisse, la Tour-de-By, la Tour-du-Haut-Moulin, la Tour-Pibran, la Tour-St-Joseph, Victoria.

Top bourgeois *performing like Classed Growths:* d'Angludet, Brillette, Chasse-Spleen, Chambert-Marbuzet, Cissac, Clarke, Fonbadet, la Gurgue, Hanteillan, Haut-Marbuzet, Gressier-Grand-Poujeaux, Hortevie, Labégorce-Zédé, Lanessan, Maucaillou, Meyney, Monbrison, les Ormes-de-Pez, de Pez, Potensac, Poujeaux, Siran, Sociando-Mallet, la Tour-de-Mons.

Classed Growths outperforming their classification: Camensac, Cantemerle, Clerc-Milon-Rothschild, Grand-Puy-Ducasse, Grand-Puy-Lacoste, Haut-Bages-Libéral, d'Issan, Kirwan, Lafon-Rochet, Lagrange, la Lagune, Langoa-Barton, Léoville-Barton, Lynch-Bages, Marquis d'Alesme-Becker, Rausan-Ségla, St-Pierre, du Tertre, la Tour-Carnet. Since 1987 Pichon-Longueville has returned to the top flight.

Graves

Outperformers: Cabannieux (white), Domaine la Grave (white), Montalivet (red and white), Rahoul (red), Roquetaillade-la-Grange (red and white).

Pessac-Léognan

Outperformers: Carbonnieux (white), Couhins-Lurton (white), Cruzeau, de Fieuzal (red and white), la Louvière (red and white), Malartic-Lagravière (red and white), Rochemorin, Smith-Haut-Lafitte (white, and red since 1988), la Tour-Martillac.

Pomerol

Outperformers: Bertineau St-Vincent (Lalande-de-Pomerol), Belles Graves (Lalande-de-Pomerol), le Bon-Pasteur, Bourgneuf-Vayron, Certan de May, Clinet, Clos du Clocher, Clos René, L'Eglise Clinet, Feytit-Clinet, la Fleur-St-Georges (Lalande-de-Pomerol), Franc-Maillet, Grand Ormeau (Lalande-de-Pomerol), la Grave-Trigant-de-Boisset, les Hautes-Tuileries (Lalande-de-Pomerol), Latour-à-Pomerol, Lavaud la Maréchaude (Lalande-de-Pomerol), Siaurac (Lalande-de-Pomerol), les Templiers (Lalande-de-Pomerol).

St-Émilion

Outperformers: l'Arrosée, Balestard-la-Tonnelle, Bellefont-Belcier, Berliquet, Cadet-Piola, Cardinal-Villemaurine, la Dominique, de Ferrand, Fombrauge, Larmande, Monbousquet, Montlabert, Pavie-Decesse, St-Georges, la Serre, Tertre-Rôteboeuf, Troplong-Mondot, Vieux-Château-Mazerat.

Sauternes

Outperformers non-classed: Bastor-Lamontagne, Chartreuse, de Fargues, Gilette, Guiteronde, les Justices, Liot, Menota, Raymond-Lafon, St-Amand.

Outperforming Classed Growths: d'Arche, Doisy-Daëne, Doisy-Védrines, de Malle, Nairac.

CLARET VINTAGES

Claret vintages are accorded more importance than those of any other wine; so much so that good wine from a less popular vintage can get swamped under all the brouhaha. We have had a positive parade of 'vintages of the century', although the noise and fuss more often start in Bordeaux itself or on the volatile American market than in the UK's more cautious wine circles.

Vintage is crucial because wines age at different rates according to the vintage they come from; wines may get more delicious or less delicious as they mature; some wines will be better to drink before they are fully mature, because, although their final balance may not be terribly impressive, at least they've got a good splash of young fruit. Wines also mature differently according to the quality level of the property.

This is often expressed in Bordeaux by a 'classification', with *premier grand cru classé* at the top, followed by *grand cru classé*, followed by various forms of *bourgeois*, and then simply a property's name – the 'petit château'. After this come the generic *appellations* – like Bordeaux Supérieur – which rarely need any ageing. So a 1978, for instance, from a *premier cru*, might take twenty years to be at its best, a good *bourgeois* might take ten, and a *petit château* might take five years.

The grape variety is also important. Wines based on the Cabernet Sauvignon and/or Cabernet Franc (many of the Médocs and the Graves) will mature more slowly than wines based on the Merlot (most Pomerols and St-Émilions).

In the following tables, A = quality; B = value for money; C = drink now; D = lay down.

1989 (AD) In a way it's something of a relief to be able to write that this *wasn't* the vintage of the century. Surely we've all had enough of the hackneyed cliché anyway, and it's time for a return to the calm, considered view. Although, even the calmest commentator has to agree that it was a very *unusual* year altogether. By the time the Vinexpo trade fair was held in June 1989, the heat had already been way above average for a month. The mean temperature for May was 19.2, a good four degrees above normal, according to Peter Sichel of Château Palmer. 'Both July and August were hot too, so that the average summer (June to September) temperature (20.9) ended up the same as that of 1947 and over the last 50 years second only to 1949 (21.3)'. If there was a characteristic that united the growers and winemakers of Bordeaux in the autumn of 1989, it was a certain bafflement. All the measurements for sugar and acidity levels said the grapes were ready to pick, yet the experienced eye still hesitated. The sugar was high, the acidity was low and yet those who picked the analytically ripe grapes found that the grape tannins weren't ripe. Picking dates, rather than blend proportions will make a difference to your bottle of 1989 claret.

For those who like to designate a Bordeaux vintage as either a Merlot year or a Cabernet year, this was a year in which the Cabernet Sauvignon couldn't fail to ripen well, and in fact most of the Cabernet grapes brought in were deliciously, juicily ripe. Merlots were more of a problem. Grown to add ripeness and fatness to a possibly lean Cabernet, in 1989 the Merlot grapes were in most cases fully ripe at the beginning of September. It became a balancing act, attempting to catch the grapes *before* acidity got too low but *after* the tannins were ripe. A tricky business, and one which growers in Australia and California have to deal with each year, but which was a novel, and baffling, phenomenon for Bordeaux.

Those who managed the juggling act have produced wines of exceptional colour (especially if there is much Merlot in the blend) and splendidly rich fruit (especially if Cabernet dominates).

But the irregular levels of ripeness led to difficulties in the cellar for many. At Château de Fieuzal in the Graves the technical director was quoted as saying, 'I cannot remember a year as difficult as this to vinify. Ripeness was so irregular that you had to take it tank by tank, bringing the temperature down to make the aromas work'.

1989 will become known as a year when the decisions of the winemaker were crucial to the finished wine. When it came to assessing vats for the final blend, some of the early-picked wines were found to be far too 'green-tasting'. The better châteaux will have eliminated these batches for the *grand vin*, but there will still be a fair number of rawish-tasting wines around when the vintage finally goes on sale. *Petits châteaux* are already looking disappointing.

Prices, needless to say, went up, even though this was a gigantic crop and a record was reached for AC reds at nearly five million hectolitres produced. But the growers of Bordeaux are claiming that the 1988 First Growths have already increased in value by 50 per cent; they must feel little pressure on them to keep price increases minimal. With the interest in the 1989 vintage at fever pitch long before anyone had tasted the wines, the temptation must have been to push the prices even higher.

So to specifics. The wines are still in cask, and you may feel you prefer to hold back until the wines are actually in bottle before you trust tasters' judgment. The risk, as always, is that 1989 wines are bound to cost more by that time, but because of the known variation in quality this maybe well worthwhile. In the Haut-Médoc, Cantemerle stood out from others, followed by La Tour de By, Coufran, Citran and Lanessan. Rausan-Ségla in Margaux is back on form. Giscours, d'Issan, du Tertre, Lascombes and Cantenac-Brown were very successful, but overall it may not prove to be a Margaux year.

Elsewhere in the Haut-Médoc the wines seem juicier, fruitier, better constructed for the long haul. In St-Julien, Langoa-Barton, Léoville-Barton, Beychevelle, Gruaud-Larose, Talbot, Branaire-Ducru were all excellent with Ducru-Beaucaillou a notch above. In Pauillac, Haut-Batailley looks back on form, sturdy, rich Pichon-Longueville a lovely counterpoint to the elegance of Pichon-Lalande, Latour impressively magnificent, combining power with finesse.

In St-Estèphe Montrose attracted attention with a triumphant return to the top, and also successful were Cos Labory, Meyney and Lafon-Rochet.

Over on the right bank, St Émilion and Pomerol defied attempts to call this a Cabernet year by producing Merlot wines of great richness and charm, from First Growth down. Best so far seem to be Canon-la-Gaffelière, Balestard la Tonnelle, Larmande, Cap-de-Moulin, Troplong-Mondot among the good value ranks, elsewhere there is Canon, La Conseillante, Gazin, Clinet, L'Evangile, Clos Fourtet, Pavie, an especially powerful L'Angélus, and a Cheval-Blanc of tremendous concentration and fragrance.

The Graves and Pessac-Léognan produced more uneven levels of quality on the whole, and although Domaine de Chevalier and Pape Clément are as classy as you would hope, only de Fieuzal and Malartic-Lagravière stood out from the rest. Early days yet.

1988 (AD) A wet 'non-winter' and an equally dismal spring meant the vineyards were full of disease before the ripening had ever begun. The good growers were doing regular rounds spraying against rot and mildew. Then on 4 July the rain stopped – totally – until 1 September – when there was a single storm – and then nothing until the end of the month. The summer consisted of three almost rainless months. In fact by September drought conditions were setting in in the more gravelly vineyards and this, allied with the fact that the dry days were surprisingly cool, meant that Cabernet Sauvignon grapes just weren't ripening. And then came rain – a big storm on 29 September. Many growers decided they couldn't risk another 1987, when it rained for three weeks, and cleared their vines.

But the sun did return and apart from some overcast days in the second week of October, the weather was then superb, right into November. All the top growers did their picking in mid to late October and the results were some of the most classically balanced wines of the 1980s. But it was not a *bourgeois* and *petit château* year, because you had to pick late and you had to reject a lot of unripe fruit. Most of this was Cabernet Sauvignon. The Merlot and Cabernet Franc were in general outstanding. There was a lot of tannin but in general there was a lot of colour too, and a lot of ripe but not overripe fruit. A few growers seemed to have added back too much *vin de presse*, which was a pity, and overproduction still seemed to be a problem, especially in Pomerol, but the vintage *could* make the most classically balanced claret of the '80s.

The Graves/Pessac-Léognan yielded a remarkable range of wines, and it really showed how they are getting their act together down there. Special efforts from La Louvière, Larrivet-Haut-Brion, de France, Smith-Haut-Lafitte (a joyous return to the top rank), Fieuzal, Olivier (another wine coming out of the shadows), La Tour-Martillac, Malartic-Lagravière, Pape-Clément, Haut-Bailly and Domaine de Chevalier. In the Médoc, La Lagune was good and Cantemerle as good as the inspiring '83. Margaux was less exciting, but there were good wines from Angludet, d'Issan, Tertre, Prieuré-Lichine, Palmer, Durfort-Vivens (at last) and superb efforts from Monbrison, Rausan-Ségla and Margaux. Chasse-Spleen and Poujeaux were the best of the Moulis while St-Julien had beautiful wines from Beychevelle, Gloria, St-Pierre, Talbot, Gruaud, Ducru-Beaucaillou, Langoa-Barton and Léoville-Barton. Pauillac did very well, with Lafite, Grand-Puy-Lacoste, Haut-Bages-Libéral and Pichon-Lalande all excellent, and tip-top Lynch-Bages and the triumphantly resurrected Pichon-Longueville. St-Estèphe made its best vintage for several years, with consistently high quality from Cos d'Estournel, Calon-Ségur, Les Ormes-de-Pez, Meyney, Cos Labory and Lafon Rochet. The northern Médoc was a success too, in particular at Cissac, Hanteillan, Sociando-Mallet, La Tour-de-By, Potensac.

Pomerol made some excellent wines, and should have made more, but overproduction diluted the quality in many cases and they taste rather one-dimensional. Best so far seem to be Clinet, Beauregard, Évangile, Moulinet, l'Enclos, Vieux-Château-Certan, with improved efforts from La Croix-de-Gay and La Pointe. St-Émilion made superb wines, as good as 1985 and '82. Cheval-Blanc and Figeac lead the way, followed by Canon, Pavie, L'Angélus, Larmande, Fonplégade, Canon-la-Gaffelière, Balestard-la-Tonnelle, Couvent-des-Jacobins, Clos des Jacobins.

1987 (BCD) There *are* lean, unbalanced edgy wines in 1987 – often made by the same uninspired proprietors who made mediocre '88s. But the overall style of the vintage is wonderfully soft and ridiculously drinkable, the soft Merlot fruit combining with good new oak to produce light but positively lush reds, totally unlike the other two vintages it tends to be bracketed with, 1984 and 1980. These will happily last up to ten years, but you can start really enjoying them *now*. Best bets: Angélus, Balestard-la-Tonnelle, Beauregard, Bertineau-St-Vincent, Beychevelle, Bon-Pasteur, Canon, Cap de Mourlin, Cheval-Blanc, Clinet, Clos Fourtet, la Conseillante, Cos d'Estournel, Cos Labory, le Crock, Domaine de Chevalier, L'Enclos, Fieuzal, Figeac, Fonbadet, Gazin, Giscours, Gruaud-Larose, d'Issan, Kirwan, Lafon-Rochet, Langoa-Barton, Larrivet-Haut-Brion, Lascombes, Léoville-Barton, Léoville-Poyferré, Lynch-Bages, Malartic-Lagravière, Margaux, Meyney, Monbrison, Montrose, Ormes-de-Pez, Palmer, Pape-Clément, Pavie, Pavie-Decesse, Pichon-Lalande, Pichon-Longueville, Picque-Caillou, Rolland-Maillet, Talbot, La Tour-Martillac, Troplong-Mondot, Villemaurine.

1986 (AD) These wines are not in general heavyweight brutes; if anything inclining to the lean and austere in style, but the fruit does seem to be developing a vintage style in a surprising number of wines – and it is a rather thick, jammy fruit, allied to a slight rasp like the flavour of the grape skin itself. That said, the wines are good, sometimes very good,

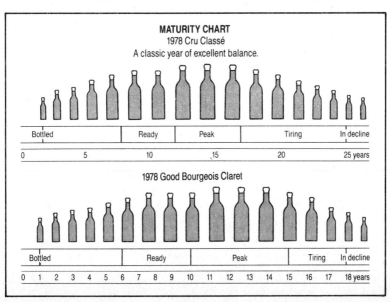

MATURITY CHART
1978 Cru Classé
A classic year of excellent balance.

| Bottled | | Ready | Peak | | Tiring | In decline |

| 0 | 5 | 10 | 15 | 20 | 25 years |

1978 Good Bourgeois Claret

| Bottled | | Ready | | Peak | | Tiring | In decline |

| 0 | 1 | 2 | 3 | 4 | 5 | 6 | 7 | 8 | 9 | 10 | 11 | 12 | 13 | 14 | 15 | 16 | 17 | 18 years |

MATURITY CHART

1982 Cru Classé
A marvellous super-ripe vintage.

Bottled		Ready	Peak		Tiring		In decline

0	5	10	15	20	25	30 years

1982 Good Bourgeois

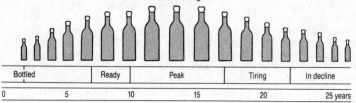

Bottled	Ready	Peak	Tiring	In decline

0	5	10	15	20	25 years

1985 Cru Classé
A delicious, quick-maturing, but well-balanced year.

Bottled	Ready	Peak	Tiring	In decline

0	5	10	15	20	25 years

1985 Good Bourgeois

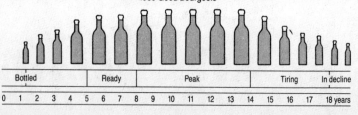

Bottled	Ready	Peak	Tiring	In decline

0	1	2	3	4	5	6	7	8	9	10	11	12	13	14	15	16	17	18 years

and mostly for the 10 to 20 year haul, though some will be attractive in about five years' time. I think you should have some in your cellar, but if I had only one fistful of £5 notes and '86 and '88 to choose between, I'd choose '88.

1985 (ACD) These are so delicious you can drink them now – even the top wines. The top wines will age as long as any sensible person wants to age them – but like, I'm told, 1953, they'll *always* be good to drink. The *petits châteaux* are still gorgeous if you can find them, the *bourgeois* probably the best ever on many properties and most of the Classed Growths and Graves/Pessac-Léognans are soft, and deep and ravishing.

1984 I downgrade this every time I drink an example. What seemed to be quite light, dry – and grossly overpriced – Cabernet clarets are, at present, mostly short, fruitless and tough. They *may* improve with keeping.

1983 (ABD) A true Bordeaux classic, still relatively well-priced. Though tannic now, the wines will flower triumphantly into a lovely dry cedar and blackcurrant maturity – but it'll take another five to ten years. AC Margaux made its best wines for a generation.

1982 (ACD) Fabulous year – unbelievably ripe – loads of wine, fat and juicy and rich. The slow process of maturing means they're going to make great drinking right to their peak in 10 to 20 years' time.

1981 (BCD) Good vintage, but not spectacular. Quite light, classic flavours from top properties which should still age a bit.

1980 (BC) Nice light, grassy claret, which needs drinking up.

1979 (ABCD) Many of these wines demand another five years' ageing at least. So keep your top wines, and hurry up with the lesser ones.

1978 (ACD) Lovely wines. The tip-top wines are a bit tough still, but most Classed Growths are lovely now, and many lesser wines are still good. Graves and St-Émilions are ready too, although Graves will hold.

1976 (C) Rather soft and sweet on the whole. Not inspiring, with a few exceptions in St-Émilion and Pomerol. Drink up.

1975 (A) A difficult vintage. The very harsh tannins frequently didn't have ripe enough fruit to mesh with, but the flavour went stale and brown before the wine had time to soften.

1970 (ACD) Now re-emerging with the fruit intact to make lovely current drinking – but the top wines will age a good decade yet.

1966 (AC) Some say they're tiring, some say they aren't quite ready yet. I say *all* the wines are ready, with many at their peak now. Yet some lesser wines which seemed to be dying out have taken on a new lease of life.

1961 (AC) Still wonderful. I marvel at how great claret can match richness and perfume with a bone-dry structure of tannin and acidity.

Most other vintages of the 1960s will now be risks; '69 and '67 are basically past it, '64 can still be good, rather big, solid wines, and '62, one of the most gorgeous, fragrant vintages since the war, is just beginning to show the ladders in its stockings. If your godfather's treating you, and offers '59, '55 or '53, accept with enthusiasm. If he offers you '49, '47 or '45, get it in writing before he changes his mind.

WHITE BORDEAUX

O nly those who are old enough to have tasted the white Bordeaux of the '60s and '70s can appreciate what a revolution has been wrought in the quality of these wines over the last decade. To those of us who remember the ponderous dry Graves or sickly Sauternes which used to be standard, the wines of the 1980s were a huge delight. It is not unfair to say that the decade has seen both the sweet and dry white wines return to the map of fine wines made in France.

The secret behind the success of the great Sauternes and Barsac wines has been a mixture of luck and intelligent self-interest. Until the 1983 vintage was offered for sale, wine merchants throughout the world had a common reaction to these wines. With little variety of expression and none of inspiration it went, 'I love these wines, but people just won't buy them.' What 'people' *would* buy in the way of sweet white wine was the cheapest; sulphurous as a just-lit match and as artificial as candy floss.

The sheer quality of the 1983 vintage, which may well be the best of the decade, obliged wine merchants everywhere to offer them, if only to demonstrate their respect for quality, and it was found that the consumer reacted to the offer with orders as well as praise. Sauternes was at last back as a great wine.

Since then a series of great vintages (1986, '88 and now '89) has encouraged the growers to make better wine, the merchants in Bordeaux to buy it and the British wine trade to offer it. That there should be such a series of vintages is luck: making fine Sauternes is nearer roulette than poker in that the grower intent on making great wine must wait until October to harvest, and the weather in October may just as easily be awful as good. That a significant number of growers are willing to wait in the hope of making great wine is intelligent self-interest, and it happens to have paid off since 1983 for the grower, the wine lover and the merchant in between.

The technical improvements in making sweet white wines have not been enormous in the last twenty or so years. There is some fascinating research going into the making of artificial 'Eiswein', by concentrating the grape juice before fermentation, but there is a mile of difference between a wine which has been made from grapes infected by noble rot and a wine made from grape must which simply has great concentration of sugar. This is not the case with the making of dry white wines, which has changed very fundamentally over the last ten years. The new vinification takes advantage of technical improvements. The main change however, is that winemakers now wish to produce a different style of wine.

Even 20 years ago, the French market, which is the main market for white Bordeaux, called for off-dry wines of high alcoholic strength. This was true for the British market, and it is true still for a handsome number of consumers in both countries who love and buy wines with enough sweetness to mask the acidity. As taste moved towards drier wines with more fruit and delicacy, the growers reacted by changing, first, the grape variety. Sauvignon Blanc gives more obvious freshness when young than the Sémillon, and in the 1970s a lot of Sauvignon was planted, and a lot picked early while the acidity was still quite high. The result was wines prickly with acidity but only attractive for a year or more in bottle, after which they became disagreeable in the extreme.

The stylistic change which has been so successful lies in producing fresh wines with an elegant perfume, dry without being mouth-puckering, not from different grape varieties but through fermentation at a controlled temperature of less than 20°C. The other main requirement is ripeness. Wine made from unripe grapes is always unsatisfactory. We have all drunk lots of it, but in an ideal world it is wine which should be served with curry or used for cooking or mixed with cassis.

All the lessons of controlled vinification had been learned and assimilated by the men who make the wine before the 1989 harvest was brought in, and there was a general conviction that provided weather conditions permitted, good dry white wine could be produced without difficulty. This remains the confident belief, but in 1989 the growers had to face up to a new and quite original problem. When is a grape ripe for wine-making purposes? In almost all years the measured sugar content of the grape ceases to rise at the same time that the acidity of the grapes levels off. The problem in 1989 was that the sugar was already high beyond belief at the end of August and the acidity was already unusually low. Those growers who had the choice, who had not booked a picking machine or arranged with a band of pickers to come at some specific and, as it turned out, likely to be unsatisfactory date were faced with the problem of whether to pick while the sugar content of the grapes was still increasing daily, and at an earlier date than any other they had any of them known, or to wait.

STERLING VIRTUES

We now know the answer to that question in so far as this class of white wines is concerned; the best wines are those that were picked early, and it is not difficult to distinguish those which were harvested before 7 September, say, and those picked later. The first batches have the lightness of touch, the charm and the wit of good white wine. The wines picked later have the sterling virtues which well-made wine must always have, but little more than alcohol. They are powerful and lacking in personality, wines for Sunday lunch in a cold climate when there is rain outside and nothing much to stir the mind.

The Bordelais adopt a different attitude to wine from the men who make wine in California, and even the most sought-after bottle does not sport a back label with a precise indication of, among other things, the date of picking. You would therefore do well to taste a bottle of any dry white Bordeaux before you buy a case; it may be very good indeed, but you may equally find it somewhat dull. The 1988 dry whites are overall better wines than the 1989s, with much less variation from one property's wine to another's.

The Sauternes and Barsac wines are just as varied in quality as the dry wines, but here it is the wines picked late which are better, given depth by noble rot. The wines picked earlier have the enormous sugar content which makes for lovely and luscious wines, but not that little extra. Here, it is safe to say that £10 is the minimum you will have to pay for first-rate Sauternes: prices have risen quite remarkably, and this may be a good moment to look out for some 1988s, a first-rate vintage for this sort of wine, better overall than 1989.

If you feel the need to accompany your pear or Mars bar with a sweet wine and do not feel that you can afford the new prices for the grand names, you should try one of the sweet *appellations contrôlées* which have not recently been in much evidence in Britain. These wines (Cadillac, Cérons, Loupiac and Ste-Croix-du-Mont) are a very uneven bunch at the moment, but the prospect of a decent price for their product is already working wonders and may be what encourages the next revolution in Bordeaux wine-making.　　　　　　　　　　**WILLIAM BOLTER**

GRAPES & FLAVOURS

SAUVIGNON BLANC There has been a rush to plant more and more of the fashionable Sauvignon Blanc in Bordeaux in recent years, but with a couple of exceptions, such as Malartic-Lagravière, Couhins-Lurton and Smith-Haut-Lafitte, Sauvignon doesn't perform at its best by itself in Bordeaux, often giving rather muddy, tough wine. Even so, many dry white Bordeaux *are* made entirely from Sauvignon, particularly at the cheaper end, and *can* be fresh and flowery if made by careful winemakers like Mau, Dourthe, Ginestet and Coste, but the best are almost always a result of blending with Sémillon. A small proportion of Sauvignon adds acidity and freshness to Sauternes and other sweet whites, too.

SÉMILLON The most important grape of Sauternes. It's very susceptible to noble rot and imparts a rich, lanolin feel to the best sweet wines. Sémillon is a vital ingredient in the best dry wines, too, though it has become very unfashionable. Frankly, given modern wine-making techniques a good Sémillon made bone dry is almost indistinguishable from a Sauvignon, except that it's a little fuller. But ideally, Sémillon and Sauvignon should be blended, with Sémillon the dominant variety. Sémillon gives a big, round dry wine, slightly creamy but with an exciting aroma of fresh apples and leaving a lanolin smoothness in the mouth. From the top properties, fermented cool and aged in oak barrels, the result is a wonderful, soft, nutty dry white, often going honeyed and smoky as it ages to a maturity of perhaps 7 to 15 years, as one of France's great white wines.

MUSCADELLE A very little, up to five per cent, of this headily perfumed grape often goes into the Sauternes blend. In dry white blends a few per cent can add a very welcome honeyed softness. It is now being produced in small quantities as a single varietal, dry, lean, but perfumed.

WINES & WINE REGIONS

BARSAC, AC (sweet) The only one of the Sauternes villages with the right to use its own name as an official *appellation* (it may also call itself Sauternes – or Sauternes-Barsac for that matter). Barsac has chalkier soils than the other Sauternes villages, and tends to make lighter wines. Even so, wines from good properties are marvellously rich despite a certain delicacy of texture.

BORDEAUX BLANC, AC (dry) This AC covers a multitude of sins. It is the catch-all for all white Bordeaux, and as such is the label on some of France's dullest medium-to-dry whites, as well as on many fresh, simple well-made wines. With the sudden surge of interest in Bordeaux's dry whites spurred on by the idiotic pricing shenanigans practised by its rivals in the Loire and Burgundy, the still considerable gallonage of over-sulphured dross is both inexplicable and incredibly short-sighted. Thank goodness every year sees another surge of good guys beating back the bad. Château wines are usually the best and should generally be drunk as young as possible. Recommended producers: *Birot, Grand-Mouëys, du Juge, Lamothe, Reynon*. Good blends are possible from *Coste, Dourthe, Dubroca, Ginestet, Joanne, Lurton, Mau, Sichel* and *Univitis*. Some classy properties in red wine areas make good, dry white wine which is only allowed the AC Bordeaux. Château Margaux's white, for instance, is a simple AC Bordeaux. Many great Sauternes châteaux have started to make a dry wine from the grapes unsuitable for Sauternes. These use the 'Bordeaux Blanc' AC and seem to concentrate on the first letter – as in 'G' of Guiraud, 'R' of Rieussec and 'Y' of Yquem. 'Y' can be spectacular.

BORDEAUX BLANC SUPÉRIEUR, AC (dry) Rarely used, but requires higher basic strength and lower vineyard yield than Bordeaux Blanc AC.

CADILLAC, AC (sweet) In the south of the Premières Côtes de Bordeaux, just across the river from Barsac; can produce lovely sweet whites, but since the price is low, many properties now produce dry white and red – which do *not* qualify for the AC Cadillac. *Château Fayau* is the best property for sweet wines.

CÉRONS, AC (sweet) Enclave in the Graves butting on to Barsac, producing good, fairly sweet whites, but many growers now prefer to produce dry whites, which can sell as Graves. *Château Archambeau* is a typical example, producing tiny amounts of very good Cérons and much larger amounts of good, fresh dry Graves. Other good properties: *Cérons, Grand Enclos du Château Cérons, Haura.*

ENTRE-DEUX-MERS, AC (dry) Large Bordeaux area between the Garonne and Dordogne rivers. The AC is for dry whites, which are of varying quality, but every vintage produces more examples of excellent, fresh, grassy whites. Many properties make red, and these can only be Bordeaux or Bordeaux Supérieur. Best châteaux: *Bonnet, Ducla, de Florin, Fondarzac, Moulin-de-Launay, Tertre du Moulin, Thieuley.*

GRAVES, AC (dry) Famous, or perhaps infamous area south of Bordeaux, on the left bank of the Garonne. The infamy is the result of the endless turgid stream of sulphurous, flabby, off-dry white that *used* to flow out of the region. However, modern Graves is a dramatic improvement. Even at the level of commercial blends it can be sharply fruity and full in style, while at the best properties, with some oak ageing employed, the wines are some of the most delicious dry whites in France. Since the 1987 vintage the wines from the northern Graves bear the *appellation* 'Pessac-Léognan'. Best châteaux: *Archambeau, Cabannieux, Carbonnieux, Domaine de Chevalier, Couhins-Lurton, du Cruzeau, Domaine la Grave, de Fieuzal, la Garance, la Garde, Haut-Brion, Landiras, la Louvière, Magence, Malartic-Lagravière, Montalivet, Rahoul, Respide, Rochemorin, Roquetaillade-la-Grange, Smith-Haut-Lafitte, de St-Pierre, la Tour-Martillac.*

GRAVES SUPÉRIEURES, AC (sweet or dry) White Graves with a minimum natural alcohol of 12 degrees. Frequently made sweet. Best property: *Clos St-Georges.*

LOUPIAC, AC (sweet) These wines from the lovely area of Bordeaux looking across the Garonne to Barsac are not as sweet as Sauternes, and many properties now make dry white and red without the Loupiac AC because of difficulties in selling sweet whites. Best châteaux: *Domaine du Noble, Loupiac-Gaudiet, la Nère, Ricaud.*

PESSAC-LÉOGNAN, AC (dry) The AC for reds and whites declared in 1987 and created out of the best and northernmost part of Graves. Fifty-five estates are involved, including all the *crus classés*, so quality ought to be high. Yields are lower than for Graves and the percentage of Sauvignon is higher (at least a quarter of the grapes used). This might change the style of some estates, but the most important point is that the new AC will provide further motivation for

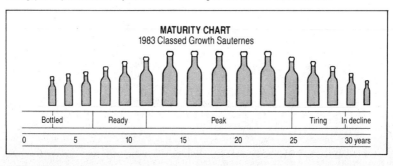

MATURITY CHART
1983 Classed Growth Sauternes

| Bottled | Ready | Peak | Tiring | In decline |

| 0 | 5 | 10 | 15 | 20 | 25 | 30 years |

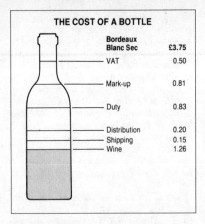

THE COST OF A BOTTLE

Bordeaux Blanc Sec	£3.75
VAT	0.50
Mark-up	0.81
Duty	0.83
Distribution	0.20
Shipping	0.15
Wine	1.26

improvement in what is rapidly becoming one of France's most exciting white wine areas. The best wines start out with a blast of apricot, peach and cream ripeness and slowly mature to a superb nutty richness with a dry savoury finish. Best châteaux: *Bouscaut, Carbonnieux* (from 1988), *Couhins-Lurton, Domaine de Chevalier, de Fieuzal, Haut-Brion, la Louvière, Malartic-Lagravière, Rochemorin, Smith-Haut-Lafitte, la Tour Martillac.*

PREMIÈRES CÔTES DE BORDEAUX,

AC Some very attractive reds and excellent dry whites from the right bank of the Garonne opposite Graves and Sauternes in the bang-up-to-date, fruit-all-the-way style as well as some reasonable sweetish wines. The sweet wines can now take the AC Cadillac, but you still get some under the Premières Côtes mantle, sometimes with their village name added, as in *Château de Berbec* – a Premières-Côtes-Gabarnac.

STE-CROIX-DU-MONT, AC (sweet) The

leading sweet white AC of the Premières Côtes de Bordeaux. Can be very attractive. *Château Loubens* is the best-known wine, but *Lousteau-Vieil* is producing better wine every year, and *Domaine du Tich, Lépine, la Raine, des Tours,* and the sadly minuscule *de Tastes* are also good.

SAUTERNES, AC (sweet) The overall

appellation for a group of five villages in the south of the Graves region, Sauternes, Bommes, Fargues, Preignac and Barsac.

(Barsac wines may use their own village name if they wish.) Concentrated by noble rot, the Sémillon, along with a little Sauvignon and Muscadelle, produces at its glorious best a wine that is brilliantly rich and glyceriny, combining honey and cream, pineapple and nuts when young, with something oily and penetrating as it ages and the sweetness begins to have an intensity of volatile flavours, rather like a peach, bruised and browned in the sun, then steeped in the sweetest of syrups. These are the fine wines. Sadly, owing to economic pressures, much Sauternes outside the top Growths is made sweet simply by the addition of sugar to the juice and the brutal arrest of the fermentation with a massive slug of sulphur. There is a possible way forward for these 'generic' Sauternes. They are now fetching a high price and could invest in the equipment needed to practise 'cryoextraction' – which isn't some form of torture but a method of freezing the grapes before fermentation which can increase the richness of the juice pressed out, particularly from the Sémillon grape. Best châteaux: *Bastor-Lamontagne, Climens, Doisy-Daëne, Doisy-Védrines, de Farques, Gilette, Guiraud, Lafaurie-Peyraquey, Lamothe-Guignard, Raymond-Lafon, Rayne-Vigneau, Rieussec, St-Amand, Suduiraut, d'Yquem.*

1855 CLASSIFICATION OF SAUTERNES

Grand premier cru d'Yquem (Sauternes).

Premiers crus Climens (Barsac); Coutet (Barsac); Guiraud (Sauternes); Haut-Peyraguey (Bommes); Lafaurie-Peyraguey (Bommes); Rabaud-Promis (Bommes); Rayne-Vigneau (Bommes); Rieussec (Fargues); Sigalas-Rabaud (Bommes); Suduiraut (Preignac); la Tour-Blanche (Bommes).

Deuxièmes crus d'Arche (Sauternes); Broustet (Barsac); Caillou (Barsac); Doisy-Daëne (Barsac); Doisy-Dubroca (Barsac); Doisy-Védrines (Barsac); Filhot (Sauternes); Lamothe (Sauternes), Lamothe-Guignard (Sauternes); de Myrat (Barsac) (now extinct); Nairac (Barsac); Romer-du-Hayot (Fargues); Suau (Barsac); de Malle (Preignac).

CHÂTEAUX PROFILES

I have valued these properties according to how they are currently performing; a five-star rating means you are getting a top-line taste – not just a well-known label. Some big names have been downgraded, some lesser-known properties are promoted – *solely* on the quality of the wine inside the bottle. A star in brackets shows that the wine can achieve the higher rating but does not always do so.

The £ sign shows which wines are offering particularly good value for money – although given the current inflated prices for Bordeaux in general, that does *not* mean any of these wines will exactly be cheap.

D'ARCHE *2ème cru Sauternes* ★★★(★) A little-known Sauternes property now beginning to make exciting wine after a long period of mediocrity. 1983, '86, '88 and '89 are particularly good.

BASTOR-LAMONTAGNE *cru bourgeois Sauternes* ★★★ £ Unclassified property making marvellous, widely available, and easily affordable wines, as rich as many Classed Growths. 1981, '82, '83 and '86 epitomize high quality at a fair price.

BROUSTET *2ème cru classé Barsac* ★★(★) A reliable, fairly rich wine, not often seen, but worth trying. The '88 is especially good, the dry white disappointing.

CABANNIEUX *Graves* ★★★ £ One of the new wave of non-classified Graves which is radically improving its white wine by the use of new oak barrels. The red is good, too. 1986, '88 and '89 show the way.

CARBONNIEUX *cru classé Pessac-Léognan* ★★★ This large property used to make decent enough light white for quick consumption, but since 1988 they have been using 50 per cent new oak – and can you taste the difference!

CLIMENS *1er cru Barsac* ★★★★(★) Famous Barsac property making some of the most consistently fine sweet wines in France. 1983, '86, '88 and '89 excel. Also makes delicious second wine called Les Cèdres. M & S used the '84 as their own-label 'Sauternes'.

COUHINS-LURTON *cru classé Pessac-Léognan* ★★★★ 100 per cent Sauvignon dry white fermented in new oak barrels, producing a successful blend of grassy fruit and oaky spice. Recent vintages excellent.

COUTET *1er cru Barsac* ★★★ A great property which in recent years has not been living up to its previous exacting standards.

DOISY-DAËNE *2ème cru Barsac* ★★★(★) A very good, consistent property providing relatively light, but extremely attractive sweet wine. Doisy-Daëne Sec is a particularly good dry white.

DOISY-VÉDRINES *2ème cru Barsac* ★★★★ £ A rich, concentrated wine, which is usually good value. 1980, '83, '86 and '89 are very good.

DOMAINE DE CHEVALIER ★★★★★ (for white). See Red Bordeaux.

DE FARGUES *cru bourgeois Sauternes* ★★★★(★) Small property owned by Yquem, capable of producing stunning rich wines in the best years.

DE FIEUZAL ★★★★(★) The white is unclassified, but, with its burst of apricot fruit and spice, is one of Bordeaux's leading dry whites. See Red Bordeaux.

FILHOT *2ème cru Sauternes* ★★(★) Well-known Sauternes property producing pleasant but hardly memorable wines. 1988 looks a bit more hopeful.

The price guides for this section begin on page 270.

GILETTE *cru bourgeois Sauternes* ★★★★
Remarkable property which ages its wines
in concrete tanks for 20 to 30 years before
releasing them! Usually delicious. The
1955 and 1959 are heavenly, and only just
released. I'm serious!

GUIRAUD *1er cru Sauternes* ★★★★(★)
Fine property owned since 1981 by a
Canadian who has revolutionized the
estate and brought the wines back to peak,
and pricy, form. The wines are difficult to
taste when young but are very special, and
the 1983, '86, '88 and '89 are going to be
outstanding. On the market at the moment.

HAUT-BRION *cru classé Pessac-Léognan*
★★★★ Small quantities of very fine, long-
lived wine, also appealing when young. See
Red Bordeaux.

LAFAURIE-PEYRAGUEY *1er cru
Sauternes* ★★★★(★) Fine property,
returning to top form after a dull period in
the 1960s and '70s. Remarkably good in the
difficult years of '82, '84 and '85, it is
stunning in '83, '86, '88 and '89.

LAMOTHE-GUIGNARD *2ème cru
Sauternes* ★★★ Since 1981, this previously
undistinguished wine has dramatically
improved. 1983, '86 and '88 will show the
improvement and '89 was such a perfect
year it can hardly fail.

LAVILLE-HAUT-BRION *cru classé
Pessac-Léognan* ★★★★ This should be one
of the greatest of all white Pessac-Léognan,
since it is owned by Haut-Brion, but,
despite some great successes, the general
effect is irritatingly patchy – especially at
the crazy prices.

LA LOUVIÈRE *cru bourgeois Pessac-
Léognan* ★★★★ This property has been
making lovely, modern, oak-aged whites for
years but is only now achieving the acclaim
it deserves. Since 1987, the quality has
climbed even higher.

MALARTIC-LAGRAVIÈRE *cru classé
Pessac-Léognan* ★★★(★) £ Tiny quantities
of beautiful, perfumed Sauvignon wine for
drinking young.

DE MALLE *2ème cru Sauternes* ★★(★)
Good, relatively light wine from a very
beautiful property set partly in Graves and
partly in Sauternes. It boasts a
seventeenth-century château.

DRY WHITE BORDEAUX VINTAGES

Using cool fermentation, and a greater percentage of Sauvignon Blanc, many white Bordeaux are
not now being made to age, but all Graves should have at least two to three years, and the best 10
to 20 years.

1989 Unlike 1988, the problem was with overripe rather than underripe grapes. Growers who picked
early have made crisp wines, but those who didn't will provide us with some flabby drinking this
year. In years to come the dry wines will inevitably be overshadowed by the sweet ones.

1988 Some of the 1988 dry whites lack a little oomph. The excessively dry summer retarded ripening
and some producers picked grapes which were not totally ripe. Even so, most 1988s from good
producers are delicious, and some are outstanding.

1987 All the grapes were safely in before the rains arrived which lashed Bordeaux's vineyards and
threatened the red harvest. A slight lack of acidity has meant they have aged quite fast and even
the top wines are already drinking well, although those from Pessac-Léognan can happily take
further ageing.

1986 Basic wines now tiring. Top line properties made outstanding wines which will mature for at
least a decade.

1985 Big, ripe, soft wines now tiring except at the top level.

1984 Good, though not entirely ripe wines which have now reached their peak.

RABAUD-PROMIS *1er cru Sauternes*
★★★(★) At last! The 1986 is excellent and
shows a long-awaited return to First
Growth quality.

RAHOUL *cru bourgeois Graves* ★★★(★) A
leader of the new wave of cool-fermented,
oak-aged whites among the Graves
properties, having an effect, not only on the
Bourgeois properties, but on the Classed
Growths as well. Every year seems to be
better than the one before. Also
increasingly good red. Ownership changes
are worrying me, though, and the '88 was
not as special as previous vintages, though
still good. Domaine Benoit and Château
Constantin also good in same stable.

RAYMOND LAFON *cru bourgeois
Sauternes* ★★★★ Owned by the manager of
neighbouring Yquem, this is fine wine but
not quite as fine as the increasingly
daunting price would imply.

RIEUSSEC *1er cru Sauternes* ★★★★(★)
One of the richest, most exotic of all
Sauternes, making particularly good wines
during the 1980s. The 1982 is good, the '83,
'86 and '88 really special, the '89 wonderful.

ST-AMAND *cru bourgeois Sauternes*
★★★(★) £ Splendid property making truly
rich wines that age well, at an affordable
price. Also seen as Château de la
Chartreuse. Since the 1970s each decent
vintage has produced a delicious example.

SMITH-HAUT-LAFITTE *cru classé
Pessac-Léognan* ★★★★ A late convert to
cool fermentation and oak-barrel ageing,
but since 1985 there have been superb
wines in this new mode. Also good, and
better-known, reds.

SUDUIRAUT *1er cru Sauternes* ★★★★
Rich, exciting wines, frequently deeper and
more intensely perfumed than any other
Sauternes – except for its neighbour,
d'Yquem. A remarkable 1982 was followed
by a fine '83, a very good '85 but slightly
disappointing '86 and ditto in 1988. '89 was
a leap up again though, thank goodness.

D'YQUEM *1er grand cru classé Sauternes*
★★★★★ The pinnacle of achievement in
great sweet wines. Almost every vintage is
a masterpiece and its outlandish price is
almost justified, since d'Yquem at its best is
the greatest sweet wine in the world.

SWEET WHITE BORDEAUX VINTAGES

The 1980s brought Sauternes the good fortune that had been drenching the red wines of Bordeaux with great vintages for a decade. About time too, because 1983 created a much needed surge of interest in these remarkable, super-sweet wines and 1986, '88 and '89 can continue it. The astonishing run of Indian summer vintages that has saved red Bordeaux year after year since 1977 has not always been so kind to Sauternes. In 1978 and 1981, the botrytis just didn't quite develop, and in 1982 the rains came at exactly the wrong time, diluting potentially perfect grapes. But 1988 and '89 are more than making amends. It's worth remembering that Sauternes can be drunk very young or very old, depending entirely on whether you like the startlingly-sweet shock of young wine or the deep, nutty, golden honey of older wines. The best can last a very long time. The *en primeur* prices have the wine merchants listing the best Barsac at around £250 a case and the finest Sauternes at £300. But for mortals a good decent dozen can be purchased for a pound less than £100 – ambitious to say the least even though 'extraordinary' is the overworked quote this year.

1989 A superlative Vintage. Not only did the sun shine so perfectly that the white grapes all ripened beautifully, but the early days of September also brought those early morning mists that noble rot enjoys so much. The growers who waited for the botrytis to spread, praying rain would hold off, made richly succulent wines of great character. Comparing 1989s with '88s is going to be one of life's pleasures in years to come; the signs are that '89 Sauternes are going to be stupendous.

1988 In 1988 every Sauternes and Barsac château and many in Cadillac, Loupiac and Ste-Croix-du-Mont, had the chance to make the greatest wine in a generation. It all depended on each individual's desire to excel, his pride, his passion. It was a dry year and patience was needed while botrytis developed. Sadly, one or two leading properties were seen harvesting long before noble rot had run its full course. Many other producers went through the vines again and again, picking only the well rotted grapes: the wines are already destined to be classics.

1987 The rains came far too early this year, long before noble rot could get going on the grapes. Even so there were some pleasant, light wines made, especially by those properties who used the cryoextraction method of freezing the grapes to concentrate what sugar there was.

1986 Another marvellous year, when noble rot swept through the vineyards, and any proprietor who cared to could make great sweet wines. At the moment the best wines seem to be even better than 1983 and 1988 but it is notoriously difficult to judge young Sauternes, so I could well reverse my opinion in a year or two. By which time the '89s can join the debate.

1985 Quite pleasant lightish wines, but nothing terribly exciting.

1984 Some nice light wine from good properties, but that's about it.

1983 Superbly rich, exciting wines to be ranked alongside 1986 and 1988. Which vintage will finally turn out best is going to entail a large amount of comparative tasting over the next decade. What a jolly thought.

1981/80 Both attractive mid-weight vintages at their peak now.

1976 Fat, hefty, rich. Some haven't quite developed as hoped, but lots of 'lanolin' oiliness and lusciousness in those that have.

1975 Another lovely year. Not quite so utterly indulgent as 1976 but perhaps a little better balanced.

1971/70 Two fine years which need drinking up.

1967 The greatest recent vintage.

Webster's is an annual publication. We welcome your suggestions for next year's edition.

BURGUNDY

S ales are up, prices are up. And Burgundy the golden slope just keeps flowing with milk and honey, or rather Chardonnay and Pinot Noir. Where else can you get such voluptuous reds and irresistible whites? Carneros, Napa Valley, Oregon, Padthaway, Yarra Valley, Tuscany, I hear you say. Yes, but hang on a tick. So quality and prices in the New World are good. But don't tradition and experience count for something? Burgundy may only be a small region, but it's chock-full of illustrious names like Gevrey-Chambertin and Vosne-Romanée, Puligny-Montrachet and Corton-Charlemagne. And where you have a famous name, it is only right and proper, isn't it, that you should be expected to pay a premium for the privilege?

Let's talk figures for a moment. As of the beginning of 1990, prices are up between 20 and 45 per cent for 1989 reds compared with 1988 and between 26 and 32 per cent for whites. And production is up too. By 50 per cent since 1980. Something to do with the soil, I understand. Sales are up too. Exports are up by more than 50 per cent since 1980. And as the old Burgundy saying has it, where two or three Burgundy growers are gathered together at the Crédit Agricole, smiling into their black leather *blousons*, the laws of supply and demand must be working.

Yet all is not well behind the scenes. Last year in these pages Oz complained about the first generic Burgundy tasting in London. As the Bureau Interprofessionel des Vins de Bourgogne press release pointed out before the second London tasting last December, 'Burgundy is often considered to be a region of rare, expensive wines, beyond the means of the average consumer', so the idea behind the tastings was to promote the 'numerous lesser known *appellations*, alongside the better known ones'. Unfortunately, they hadn't read Oz's comments in this section of last year's *Guide*, in which he took the BIVB to task for allowing itself to be hijacked by the fat controllers of Burgundy, the *négociant-éleveurs*. These are the merchants who have for long had the grower in thrall to their power through their skills of buying and selling, not to mention 'improving' on the growers' efforts. A touch of the Midi here, a bag of sugar there. Tradition dies hard in Burgundy.

Despite the laudable efforts of the BIVB to reach a wider audience, the exercise was another missed opportunity. The whites were fair but the reds were by and large the kind of wines about which I feel it would not be constructive to print my tasting notes, as Oz would say. From the chosen *appellations* of the Hautes-Côtes de Nuits, from Savigny-lès-Beaune and Nuits-St-Georges, one bland, boring wine followed another with synthetic, jammy and tinned strawberry fruit flavour. Hang on, flavour is overdoing it. Worse still, there were wines with defects to steam up the spectacles of a Master of Wine examinee. And these were wines supposedly selected by a tasting panel!

Occasionally a grower's wine shone through like a beacon in the dark, a lovely Savigny-lès-Beaune 1er cru Les Guettes 1986 from Machard de Gramont, three Nuits-St-Georges; a 1986 En la Perrière Noblot from Machard de Gramont, Clos des Porets St-Georges 1985 from Henri Gouges and a Les Perrières 1985 from Jean Germain.

But why are so many travesties of Burgundy being made? One major problem

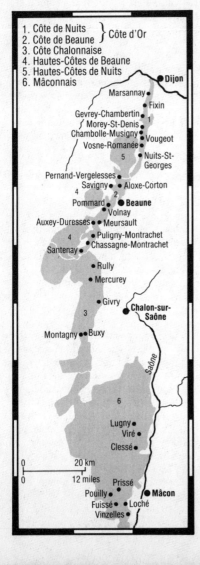

1. Côte de Nuits ⎫ Côte d'Or
2. Côte de Beaune ⎭
3. Côte Chalonnaise
4. Hautes-Côtes de Beaune
5. Hautes-Côtes de Nuits
6. Mâconnais

CLASSIFICATIONS

Burgundy has five different levels of classification:

Non-specific regional appellations with no geographical definition, e.g. Bourgogne, which may come from inferior land or young vines.

Specific regional appellations, e.g. Côte de Beaune-Villages, generally a merchant's blend of wines from one or more villages. Côte de Nuits-Villages is usually better.

Village commune wines Each Burgundian village has its vineyards legally defined. The village names have traditionally been used for vineyards that had not established any special reputation over the years, and are thus usually blended together under the village name. But there is a growing move towards even relatively unknown vineyards appearing on the label. These unclassified vineyards are called *lieux-dits* or 'stated places'. They can only appear on the label in letters half the size of the village name.

Premier cru It's just typical of Burgundy that *premier cru* or 'First Growth' actually means 'Second Growth', because these are the second best vineyard sites. Even so, they contain some of Burgundy's finest wines. They are classified by both village and vineyard names, e.g. Gevrey-Chambertin, Combe-aux-Moines. The vineyard name must follow the village name on the label, and it may be in the same size print. Confusingly, some growers use smaller print for their *premier cru* vineyard names, so unless you're in the know, it's hard to tell from the label whether a vineyard is a *premier cru* or a *lieu-dit*.

Grand cru These are the real top growths, the cream of the vineyards. Not every village has a *grand cru*. The reds are concentrated in the Côte de Nuits, the whites in the Côte de Beaune. A *grand cru* vineyard name can stand alone on the label without the name of the village -- for example, Chambertin from the village of Gevrey-Chambertin. (By long tradition, a Burgundy village is allowed to tack on the name of its *grand cru* vineyard, and use the compound village name for wines that have nothing to do with *grand cru*, for instance Puligny-Montrachet.)

is certainly overproduction. With young, productive clones planted in the vineyards in the 1960s, yields soared and the wines became thinner. The AC laws then did their bit. Until the mid-1970s any wine over the legal production limit for the *appellation* could still be sold as red Burgundy, albeit with an inferior *appellation*. The system was open to abuse. Surplus wine from Nuits-St-Georges vineyards for instance could be sold off abroad and promptly relabelled as Nuits-St-Georges. So the rules were changed. Henceforth anything over the limit had to be sent to the distillery. In return for this sacrifice, growers were allowed a more generous ceiling of more than twice the previous limit. 'Yields are the key to Burgundy', says Robert Denby of Raisin Social in Burgundy. '1988 may be the vintage of the decade for reds, but even so, *ça a pissé le vin*, as they say, and there will still be a lack of concentration in some wines.' This is the legacy of a region in which the balance of power has been held since time immemorial by the *négociant* with business as his priority. If you're paid by the kilo, it's hardly surprising if bunches of grapes take on the appearance of money bags.

Directly allied to the question of yields is the problem of what has been going into Burgundy's hallowed limestone soil these past few decades. There can be little doubt that Burgundy has systematically misjudged the use of fertilizers and weedkiller over a long period. Soils have become potassium-rich, the yields have crept up to levels where the concentration is lacking, the acidity is low and needs boosting, the wine is thin and meagre and has to be bolstered with alcohol. Enter bags of tartaric acid stage left and sugar stage right. Burgundy is defensive about chaptalization, which is perfectly acceptable in the right hands.

SCANDAL IN THE FAMILY

Since the Bouchard Père et Fils case broke, when Claude Bouchard was charged with adding sugar and tartaric acid at the same time to his 1987s (you can do one or the other but not both together), the public reaction from Burgundy has been to close ranks behind the Bouchards while privately breathing a collective sigh of there-but-for-the-grace-of-God-go-I relief. One in the eye for those who thought God divided his time between Bordeaux and Champagne. But what is Burgundy's response to the existing regulations? To keep their heads down? To keep their yields down? No. Burgundy is in the process of applying to the powers that be at the EC for the right to *increase* the capacity to chaptalize up to three degrees of alcohol.

In the eternal struggle between grower and *négociant*, the balance of power is slowly changing. Increasingly, growers like Robert Jayer-Gilles of the Hautes-Côtes de Nuits (where were *his* wines at the BIVB tasting?) are extricating themselves from the tentacles of the *négociant* and going it alone. Life has become more difficult for the *négociant* with growers creaming off the best for themselves. The upshot of the best growers' efforts are wines of character, concentration and individuality.

It would be unfair to depict the *négociant*/grower struggle entirely in black and white terms. In reality, the dividing line is less clear. For one thing, a number of *négociants* wear both devil's cap and halo, owning considerable tracts of vineyard themselves and rightly considering themselves both growers and *négociants* in equal part. An experienced *négociant* like Robert Drouhin may admit ruefully that 'the small-is-beautiful movement has turned the tide of opinion against the *négociant*'. But he is still proud of his unrivalled knowledge of the subtleties of the region. And he believes rightly that the discriminating customer appreciates that the producer's name is a far more significant guarantee of quality, be it grower or *négociant*, than any illustrious village name. Merchants like Joseph Drouhin, Louis Jadot (and new acquisition Champy Père et Fils), Louis Latour (white wines), François Faiveley, Jaffelin, Leroy and Chartron et Trebuchet are all in the first rank of Burgundy *négociants*. Olivier Leflaive is a new arrival on the scene, rapidly making a name for himself as a quality *négociant*. Antonin Rodet, Moillard and Remoissenet are also names to watch for over the next few years.

The new well-travelled, better-schooled generation are more open to the cross-fertilization of ideas from friends within and outside the region, willing to share problems as well as successes. Growers are more aware of the contribution of lower yields and fewer pesticides and herbicides to the modern style of pure, elegant Pinot Noir. Cleaner cellar practice is now considered as important a part of the wine-making process as techniques designed to enhance the quality of the wine: temperature-controlled fermentation, the judicious use of oak barrels in fermentation and maturation, less or even no filtering to avoid evisceration of character and earlier bottling for the preservation of aroma and flavour. In a hundred invisible ways, Burgundy is shuffling off its snail-like shell and progressing towards the millennium with confidence.   **ANTHONY ROSE**

RED WINES

Of all the classic regions' wines, red Burgundy, thanks to the vagaries of climate, the capriciousness of the Pinot Noir grape and the often sullen disposition of the Burgundian grower, is one of the most demanding for the customer.

So, is it worth the candle? If you're after an easy life, the answer is simple: no. But if you've ever tasted a really fine, seductive, sensual red Burgundy oozing gorgeous Pinot Noir character, or if you're prepared to believe in the possibility, then I suggest you venture carefully across the stepping stones watching out for wobbly boulders and snapping piranhas along the way. Yes, there'll be disappointments, but there'll be rewards too.

First things first. To illustrate how chancy this business can be, consider the results of a summer tasting held at *The Independent*. We took 18 bottles of Gevrey-Chambertin 1986, nine from growers and nine from *négociants* and tasted them blind. Admittedly 1986 was the least good vintage out of the last five, but it wasn't too bad in the Côte de Nuits. Anyway, a difficult vintage should sort the men out from the boys and sure enough that's what happened. It resulted in a general thumbs-down for the 'name' of Gevrey and a two-nil victory for the growers. It might have been a five-nil trouncing of the *négociants*, but two of the growers' wines were awful and two of the *négociant* wines weren't bad at all. But the winner, a straight village Gevrey-Chambertin, from the talented young Denis Bachelet, showed what can be done. It was so lovely, so pure, so *Pinot*-like, I just had to snap up a case. Anthony Hanson, the author of *Burgundy* (Faber), tried to see if he could separate the growers from the *négociants*. In all but two instances, he was spot on. How? Because he was looking for Pinot Noir character. That's the simple key.

With Burgundy you need to discriminate to accumulate and seek out the specialists. This is easier than it sounds because of the comparatively few wine merchants who take the trouble to devote much time to Burgundy. The first step is to get hold of the lists of the handful of specialists. It's true they have a product to sell, but the best lists are packed with enough information about the state of play in Burgundy to make them a good and worthwhile read, in particular the lists of Adnams, Berkmann Wine Cellars, Bibendum, Corney & Barrow, Domaine Direct, Haynes Hanson & Clark, Lay & Wheeler, Laytons, Morris & Verdin, Tanners and The Wine Society. Don't expect fantastic value for money. Burgundy is not nine-to-five country. Like Pavarotti, its appeal is to the heart and below, not the head.

For good house Burgundy, on price alone, the wines of the co-op at Buxy or the Cave des Hautes-Côtes, though simple and straightforward, can often be ripe, oaky and juicy. Straight Bourgogne Rouge from the likes of Philippe Rossignol, Michel Lafarge, Aubert de Villaine, Leroy or Olivier Leflaive is worth seeking out. Selected wines from Irancy (Sorin, Bienvenu) west of Chablis, from Marsannay (Charlopin, Bruno Clair, Coillot) at the northern tip of the Côte de Nuits and of Rully (Domaine de la Folie, Château de Rully, Jacqueson), Givry (Gérard Mouton, Pascale Juillot, Baron Thénard) and Mercurey (Château de Chamirey, Michel Juillot, Domaine Hugues de Suremain, Jacqueson) in the Côte Chalonnaise are the closest thing to value-for-money Burgundy has to offer. Once you get into the Côte d'Or itself – the Côte de Beaune and the Côte de Nuits, that is – the mind starts to boggle at the range of choices.

I was disappointed enough by our Gevrey-Chambertin tasting to believe that particular care needs to be taken with a village like Gevrey that has got too big for its boots. Nevertheless there are some excellent producers worth following, notably Denis Bachelet, Joseph Roty (his 1988 Champ-Chenys is a sensual delight), Alain Burguet, Philippe Rossignol, Armand Rousseau (forget the 1986) and the Domaine des Varoilles. And at Nuits-St-Georges, there's star quality from Chevillon, Michelot, Rion and Machard de Gramont.   **ANTHONY ROSE**

GRAPES & FLAVOURS

PINOT NOIR The sulkiest, trickiest, most tempestuous fine wine grape in the world is the exclusive grape in all but a tiny proportion of red Burgundies. It needs a more delicate balance of spring, summer and autumn climate than any other variety to achieve greatness, and one Burgundian maxim is that you must have unripe grapes, ripe grapes and rotten grapes in equal quantities to achieve that astonishing part-rotted, part-perfumed, and part-ethereal flavour.

It used to be true to say that no other part of the world could produce a Pinot Noir to match those of Burgundy. But isolated growers in Oregon, California, New Zealand, Australia and South Africa are now making very fine examples. Even

so, Burgundy is still the only place on earth where fine Pinot Noirs abound. The problem is, awful Pinot Noirs abound too, heavy, chewy and sweet-fruited or thin and pallid. Good Burgundian Pinot Noir should generally be *light*, fragrant, marvellously perfumed with cherry and strawberry fruit, sometimes meatier, sometimes intensely spicy, but, as a rule, *light*.

GAMAY Most Burgundy has by law to be 100 per cent Pinot Noir, but the Gamay (the Beaujolais grape) can be used in wines labelled 'Burgundy' or 'Bourgogne' from the Mâconnais and the Beaujolais regions, or from elsewhere in Burgundy in wines labelled 'Bourgogne Passe-Tout-Grain', 'Bourgogne Grand Ordinaire' or 'Mâcon'.

WINES & WINE REGIONS

ALOXE-CORTON, AC (Côte de Beaune)
Ten years ago, this village at the northern
end of the Côte de Beaune was the best of
all buys for full-flavoured, balanced
Burgundy. Most recent Aloxe-Corton has
been pale stuff indeed. Its production is
overwhelmingly red, and it has the only red
grand cru in the Côte de Beaune, Le
Corton, which is also sold under various
subdivisions like Corton-Bressandes,
Corton Clos du Roi and so forth, and is seen
on the market rather more frequently than
one might expect a *grand cru* to be. Go for
Jadot, Drouhin, Jaffelin, Tollot-Beaut. Also
good: *Chandon de Briailles, Dubreuil
Fontaine, Faiveley, Juillot, Daniel Senard,
Voarick*.

AUXEY-DURESSES, AC (Côte de
Beaune) Backwoods village with a
reputation for full, but fairly gentle, nicely
fruity reds, though there seems to have
been a slump in quality, the wines often
tasting rather lumpish. However, don't let
this hiccup put you off. There are a handful
of good growers which includes *Ampeau,
Diconne, Duc de Magenta, Leroy, Roy,
Prunier* and *Thévenin*. Their '85s are
lovely, but the later '87s and '88s are
good too.

BEAUNE, AC (Côte de Beaune) One of the
few reliable commune wines, usually quite
light, with a soft, 'red fruits' sweetness and
a flicker of something minerally to smarten
it up nicely. The wines are nearly all red.
Beaune has the largest acreage of vines of
any Côte d'Or commune, and they are
mostly owned by merchants. It has no
grands crus but many excellent *premiers
crus*, for example, Grèves, Marconnets,
Teurons, Boucherottes, Vignes Franches
and Cent Vignes. Beaune was more
successful than many communes in 1983,
and there are good wines from *Moillard,
Lafarge, Morot* and *Drouhin*. 1986 and
1987 are pretty good here, but it is still the
1985s which catch the attention; all these
producers excelled themselves: *Besancenot-
Mathouillet, Drouhin, Germain, Jadot,
Jaffelin, Lafarge, Leroy, Moillard, Morot,
Tollot-Beaut*.

BLAGNY, AC (Côte de Beaune) Tiny
hamlet on the boundary between
Meursault and Puligny-Montrachet. The
red wine is usually a bit fierce, but then
this is white wine heartland, so I'm a bit
surprised they grow any red at all. Best
producers: *Leflaive, Matrot*.

BONNES-MARES, AC (Côte de Nuits)
Grand cru of 15.54 hectares mostly in
Chambolle-Musigny, with a little in Morey-
St-Denis. Usually one of the most – or
should I say one of the very few – reliable
grands crus, which ages extremely well
over 10 to 20 years to a lovely smoky,
chocolate and prunes richness. Best
producers: *Bouchard Père et Fils, Clair-
Daü, Domaine des Varoilles, Drouhin,
Dujac, Groffier, Jadot, Roumier, de Vogüé*.

**BOURGOGNE GRAND ORDINAIRE,
AC** Très Ordinaire. Pas Très Grand. Rarely
seen outside Burgundy, this is the bottom
of the Burgundy barrel. It may be made
from Pinot Noir and Gamay, and even a
couple of obscure grapes, the Tressot and
César.

**BOURGOGNE PASSE-TOUT-GRAIN,
AC** Often excellent value, lightish
Burgundy made usually in the Côte d'Or or
the Côte Chalonnaise from Gamay blended
with a minimum of one-third Pinot Noir. In
some years, such as 1985, it may well be
mostly Pinot. The firm of *Leroy* makes an
excellent one, *Rodet* is *very* good in 1988,
Chanson makes it well, but as usual, the
growers make it best, particularly in the
less famous Côte d'Or and Hautes-Côtes
villages; *Rion* in Nuits-St-Georges, *Henri
Jayer* in Vosne-Romanée, *Thomas* in St-
Aubin, *Chaley* or *Cornu* in the Hautes-
Côtes, and many others like them.

BOURGOGNE ROUGE, AC The basic
red AC for the Burgundy region from
Chablis in the north to the Beaujolais *cru*
villages in the south. Unknown Bourgogne
Rouge is best avoided – much of it is very
basic indeed. Most of Burgundy has to
make its Bourgogne Rouge exclusively
from the Pinot Noir, but Gamay can be

used in the Beaujolais (if declassified from one of the ten *crus*) and Mâconnais, and the César and Tressot are permitted in the Yonne around Chablis. Wine from the ten Beaujolais *crus* can be declassified and sold as Bourgogne – and *that* should generally be from the Gamay grape alone. Domaine-bottled Bourgogne Rouge from good growers can be excellent value. Look out for those of *Bourgeon, Coche Dury, Germain, d'Heuilly-Huberdeau, Henri Jayer, Juillot, Mortet, Parent, Pousse d'Or, Rion* and *Rossignol*. Good merchants include *Drouhin, Faiveley, Jadot, Jaffelin, Labouré-Roi, Latour, Leflaive, Leroy, Rodet, Vallet.* The co-op at *Buxy* is also good as is the *Caves des Hautes-Côtes.* These all produced good '85s. Their '87s promise to be delicious, but the '86s often lack fruit.

CHAMBERTIN, AC (Côte de Nuits) Most famous of the eight *grands crus* of Gevrey-Chambertin, this 13-hectare vineyard should make wines that are big, strong and intense in their youth, mellowing to a complex, perfumed, plummy richness.

Good ones need 10 to 15 years' ageing. Best producers: *Camus, Damoy, Drouhin, Faiveley, Ponsot, Rebourseau, Rousseau, Tortochot, Trapet.*

CHAMBERTIN CLOS-DE-BÈZE, AC
(Côte de Nuits) *Grand cru* in the village of Gevrey-Chambertin next door to Chambertin both geographically and in quality. Can keep ten years in a good vintage. The wines may also be sold as Chambertin. Best producers: *Drouhin, Faiveley, Gelin, Rousseau.*

CHAMBOLLE-MUSIGNY, AC (Côte de Nuits) This village towards the southern end of the Côte de Nuits can make light, cherry-sweet, intensely perfumed, 'beautiful' Burgundy, but sadly most commercial Chambolle will be too sweet and gooey to retain much perfume. *Roumier* and *Drouhin* led the '85s. 1987 and 1988 look good too. Other good producers include *Pierre Amiot, Barthod-Noëllat, Dujac, Hudelot-Noëllat, Rion, Serveau, Volpato-Costaille, de Vogüé.*

CHAPELLE-CHAMBERTIN, AC (Côte de Nuits) Small *grand cru* vineyard (5.4 hectares) just south of the Clos-de-Bèze in Gevrey-Chambertin. Typically lighter, more delicate wines than the other *grands crus*. But over-lightness – from over-production – is the curse of the Gevrey-Chambertin *grands crus*. Best producers: *Damoy, Trapet*.

CHARMES-CHAMBERTIN, AC (Côte de Nuits) At 31.6 hectares, this is the biggest of the *grands crus* of Gevrey-Chambertin. It can be fine, strong, sensuous wine, but as with all the Gevrey-Chambertin *grands crus*, it is sometimes disgracefully light. Best producers: *Bachelet, Camus, Rebourseau, Roty, Rousseau, Taupenot, Tortochot*.

CHASSAGNE-MONTRACHET, AC (Côte de Beaune) Down in the south of the Côte de Beaune, well over half the wine Chassagne-Montrachet produces is red, even though its fame lies in its large share of the white *grand cru* Le Montrachet. The reds are a puzzle. I'm frequently disappointed by their rather hot plum-skins and chewy earth flavours, yet because the price is keen, I do keep coming back for more! Best producers: *Bachelet-Ramonet, Carillon, Colin, Delagrange-Bachelet, Duc de Magenta, Gagnard-Delagrange, Albert Morey, Moreau, Fernand Pillot, Ramonet-Prudhon*.

CHOREY-LÈS-BEAUNE, AC (Côte de Beaune) Good lesser village near Beaune, not expensive for soft, fruity reds. Because the village isn't popular, these are some of the few affordable '85s, and '86 and '87 are good here too – and still not expensive. *Germain* and *Tollot-Beaut* are the best producers.

CLOS DE LA ROCHE, AC (Côte de Nuits) Largest and finest *grand cru* of Morey-St-Denis, on the border with Gevrey-Chambertin. When not made too lightweight, this can be a splendid wine, full of redcurrant and strawberry richness when young, but coming to resemble a pretty good Chambertin after ten years or so. Best producers: *Amiot, Dujac, Lignier, Ponsot, Rémy, Rousseau*.

CLOS DES LAMBRAYS, AC (Côte de Nuits) A *grand cru* only since 1981, this nine-hectare vineyard in Morey-St-Denis belongs to a single family (*Saier*), unusual in Burgundy. In the 1970s the estate became very run down and the wines were not only very rare but also not very tasty. Wholesale replanting in 1979 means that no real style has yet emerged, but old-timers say that the Clos des Lambrays could potentially make one of Burgundy's finest, most fragrant reds.

CLOS DE TART, AC (Côte de Nuits) *Grand cru* of Morey-St-Denis wholly owned by Beaujolais merchants *Mommessin*. At its best Clos de Tart is a light but intense wine which lasts a surprisingly long time.

CLOS DE VOUGEOT, AC (Côte de Nuits) This 50-hectare vineyard completely dominates the village of Vougeot. Over 80 growers share the enclosure and, while the land at the top is very fine, the land by the road is not. That rare thing, a good bottle of Clos de Vougeot, is a wonderful fat Burgundy, rich, strong, thick with the sweetness of perfumed plums and honey, unsubtle, but exciting. 1983s are better than the Côte de Nuits average, while 1985s are absolutely first rate. Best producers: *Arnoux, Château de la Tour, Confuron, Drouhin-Laroze, Engel, Grivot, Gros, Jayer, Lamarche, Mugneret, Rebourseau, Rion*.

CLOS ST-DENIS, AC (Côte de Nuits) The village of Morey-St-Denis gets its name from this *grand cru* but the villagers probably should have chosen another *grand cru* – like the much better known Clos de la Roche – because this small 6.5 hectare vineyard has rarely achieved great heights and is probably the least known of all the *grands crus*. I'd give my vote to *Lignier* or *Ponsot*, though *Dujac* is the best known.

LE CORTON, AC (Côte de Beaune) The only red *grand cru* in the Côte de Beaune, on the upper slopes of the famous dome-shaped hill of Corton. Ideally, Corton should have something of the savoury strength of Vosne-Romanée to the north, and something of the mouth-watering, caressing sweetness of Beaune to the south, but the wines labelled Corton have been strangely insubstantial in recent vintages, and wines from subdivisions of Le Corton such as Corton-Pougets, Corton-Bressandes and Corton Clos du Roi more regularly reach this ideal. Best producers: *Bonneau du Martray, Bouchard Père et Fils, Chandon de Briailles, Chevalier, Dubreuil-Fontaine, Faiveley, Gaunoux, Laleur-Piot, Prince de Mérode, Quenot, Rapet, Reine Pédauque, Daniel Senard, Tollot-Beaut, Michel Voarick.*

CÔTE CHALONNAISE The area immediately south of the Côte d'Or. The vineyards come in pockets rather than in one long swathe, but the top four villages of Rully, Mercurey, Givry and Montagny all produce good wines, with a lovely, simple strawberry and cherry fruit.

CÔTE DE BEAUNE The southern part of the Côte d'Or, fairly evenly divided between red and white wines. There is a tiny AC Côte de Beaune which can produce light but tasty reds in warm years. Best producers: *Bouchard Père et Fils, René Manuel.*

CÔTE DE BEAUNE-VILLAGES, AC Catch-all red wine *appellation* for 16 villages on the Côte de Beaune. Only Aloxe-Corton, Beaune, Volnay and Pommard cannot use the *appellation*. Rarely seen nowadays and rarely exciting, it used to be the source of much excellent soft red, as many lesser-known but good villages would blend their wines together. Still, it *is* worth checking out the wines of *Jaffelin, Lequin-Roussot* and *Bachelet.*

CÔTE DE NUITS The northern part of the Côte d'Or, theoretically producing the biggest wines. Frequently it doesn't and many of Burgundy's most disappointing bottles come from the top Côte de Nuits communes. It is almost entirely devoted to Pinot Noir.

CÔTE DE NUITS-VILLAGES, AC An *appellation* covering the three southernmost villages of Prissey, Comblanchien and Corgoloin, plus Fixin in the north. Usually fairly light and dry, they

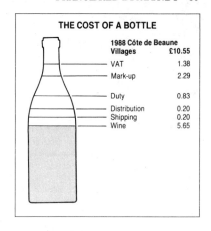

THE COST OF A BOTTLE

1988 Côte de Beaune Villages	£10.55
VAT	1.38
Mark-up	2.29
Duty	0.83
Distribution	0.20
Shipping	0.20
Wine	5.65

can have good cherry fruit and the slightly rotting veg delicious decay of good Côte de Nuits red. Look out for the wines of *Durand, Rion, Rossignol* and *Tollot-Voarick*, and especially *Chopin-Groffiers.*

CÔTE D'OR The source of Burgundy's fame – a thin sliver of land only 30 miles long, and often less than a mile wide, running from Dijon to Chagny. It has two halves, the Côte de Nuits in the north and the Côte de Beaune in the south.

ÉCHÉZEAUX, AC (Côte de Nuits) Large, (relatively) unexciting *grand cru* of Vosne-Romanée. Best producers: *Domaine de la Romanée-Conti, Engel, Faiveley, Louis Gouroux, Grivot, Henri Jayer, Lamarche, Mongeard-Mugneret, René Mugneret.*

EPINEUIL Tiny region near Tonnerre, producing light but fragrant Pinot Noir.

FIXIN, AC (Côte de Nuits) A suburb of Dijon, Fixin can make some of Burgundy's sturdiest reds, deep, strong, tough but plummy when young, but capable of mellowing with age. Such wines are slowly reappearing, but the village's proximity to Gevrey-Chambertin and its mania for over-producing does mean that there's a lot of pretty pallid Fixin too. If you want to feel you're drinking Gevrey-Chambertin without shouldering the cost, Fixin from the following producers could fit the bill: *Bordet, Charlopin-Parizot, Bruno Clair, Fougeray, Gelin, Joliet, Moillard.*

FLAGEY-ÉCHÉZEAUX, AC (Côte de Nuits) Commune that sells its basic wines as Vosne-Romanée but, in Échézeaux and Grands-Échézeaux, has two *grands crus*.

GEVREY-CHAMBERTIN, AC (Côte de Nuits) The start of the big time for reds. Gevrey-Chambertin has eight *grands crus*, and two of them, Chambertin and Chambertin Clos-de-Bèze can be some of the world's greatest wines. They should have rough, plum-skins and damson strength, fierce when young, but assuming a brilliant, wafting perfume and intense, plummy richness when mature. For drinking now there is the decent '82s of *Bachelet, Faiveley, Jaffelin, Maume, Antonin Rodet* and *Rossignol*. For the future, there is loads of brilliant '85 and *Drouhin, Magnien, Maume* and *Rossignol* excelled. 1986 is a little charmless, but '87, '88 and '89 could rival '85 when the producer didn't overcrop. The following also make fine wine: *Burguet, Camus, Domaine des Varoilles, Hospices de Beaune, Humbert, Jacqueson, Leclerc, Rossignol, Roty, Rousseau, Trapet, Voëgeli.*

GIVRY, AC (Côte Chalonnaise) Small but important red wine village. At its best, deliciously warm and cherry-chewy with a slightly smoky fragrance but there are too many mediocre bottles around, especially from *négociants*. *Baron Thénard* is the best estate, but *Chofflet, Clos Salomon, Juillot, Mouton* and *Ragot* are also worth a look.

GRANDS ÉCHÉZEAUX, AC (Côte de Nuits) A slightly second-line *grand cru*, but capable of delicately scented, plum-and-wood-smoke flavours going rich and chocolaty with age. Best producers: *Domaine de la Romanée-Conti, Drouhin, Engel, Lamarche, Mongeard-Mugneret.*

GRIOTTE-CHAMBERTIN, AC (Côte de Nuits) One of the smallest *grands crus* of Gevrey-Chambertin – 5.58 hectares. Best producers: *Drouhin, Pernot, Ponsot, Roty, Thomas-Bassot.*

HAUTES-CÔTES DE BEAUNE and **HAUTES-CÔTES DE NUITS** A happy hunting ground, this hilly backwater behind the line of famous villages and vineyards on the Côte d'Or. The 28 Hautes-Côtes villages make some fairly good, light, strawberry-like Pinot at a decent price. 1985 is fresh, fruity and good, '86 has enormously improved over the last year because vintage rains didn't affect these vineyards, and we may get some pleasant surprises from the last three vintages. Look out in the Hautes-Côtes de Nuits for the wines of *Cornu, Domaine des Mouchottes, Jayer-Gilles, Thévenet* and *Verdet* and in the Hautes-Côtes de Beaune for such growers as *Bouley, Capron Manieux, Chalet, Guillemard, Joliot, Mazilly* and *Plait*. The *Caves des Hautes-Côtes* is beginning to produce some of the best value reds in the whole of Burgundy.

IRANCY, AC Wines made mostly from Pinot Noir from vineyards just to the south-west of Chablis, sometimes with a little of the darker, tougher local grape, the César. Rarely deep in colour, but always perfumed, slightly plummy and attractive, good at two years old and usually capable of ageing several years more. It must legally be labelled 'Bourgogne Irancy'. Good producers: *Léon & Serge Bienvenu, Bernard Cantin, André & Roger Delaloge, Gabriel Delaloge, Jean Renaud, Simmonet-Febvre, Luc Sorin.*

LATRICIÈRES-CHAMBERTIN, AC (Côte de Nuits) Small *grand cru* vineyard in Gevrey-Chambertin and very similar in style to Chambertin though without the power. So long as the producer hasn't pushed the yields too high, it is at its best at 10 to 15 years. Best producers: *Camus, Ponsot, Rémy, Trapet.*

MÂCON ROUGE, AC There's a lot of red wine made in the Mâconnais but it's usually fairly lean, earthy Gamay without the spark of Beaujolais' fruit. If you like that sort of thing, try the wines of *Igé* and *Mancey*, or *Lafarge*'s wine from *Bray*. *Lassarat* is improving things by using new oak, and I'm sure more will follow.

The price guides for this section begin on page 275.

MARSANNAY, AC (Côte de Nuits) A new *appellation* in 1987, replacing the old Bourgogne Rosé de Marsannay. Mostly pleasant rosés from the Pinot Noir, grown on the outskirts of Dijon, but the objective is to concentrate more on red and white. The first results of this new seriousness are most encouraging and some lovely wines are already emerging, usually quite dry and cherry-perfumed, sometimes much more full-blown and exciting. One to watch. Best producers: *Bouvier, Charlopin-Parizot, Bruno Clair, Collotte, Fougeray, Fournier, Geantet-Pansiot, Huguenot, Jadot, Naddeff, Quillardet.*

MAZIS-CHAMBERTIN, AC (Côte de Nuits) 12.5 hectare *grand cru* in Gevrey-Chambertin, far more reliable than most of the neighbouring *grands crus*. Mazis wines can have a superb deep blackberry-pip, damson-skin and blackcurrant fruit which gets deeper and more exciting after 6 to 12 years. Best producers: *Camus, Faiveley, Hospices de Beaune, Rebourseau, Roty, Rousseau, Tortochot.*

MAZOYÈRES-CHAMBERTIN, AC (Côte de Nuits) *Grand cru* of Gevrey-Chambertin, rarely seen since producers generally take up the option of using the *grand cru* Charmes-Chambertin instead.

MERCUREY, AC (Côte Chalonnaise) The biggest Chalonnais village, producing half the region's wines. Indeed many people call the Côte Chalonnaise the 'région de Mercurey'. It's mostly red wines, and these are often fairly full, with a most attractive strawberry fruit and a little smoky fragrance. As with the other Chalonnais reds, Mercurey's problems are infuriating inconsistency of quality, allied to callous exploitation of the name by some *négociants*. *Château de Chamirey, Chandesais, Chanzy, Domaine La Marche, Dufouleur, Faiveley, Jacqueson, Juillot, de Launay, Antonin Rodet, Saier* and *de Suremain* are all good.

MONTHÉLIE, AC (Côte de Beaune) Monthélie shares borders with Volnay and Meursault, but fame with neither. It's a red wine village, and the wines deserve recognition, because they're full, dry,

Webster's is an annual publication. We welcome your suggestions for next year's edition.

rather herby or piney, but with a satisfying rough fruit. Often a good buy but beware the insidious growth of *négociants'* labels from firms who never traditionally noticed the AC. Best producers: *Bouchard Père et Fils, Boussey, Caves des Hautes-Côtes, Deschamps, Doreau, Garaudet, Château de Monthélie, Monthélie-Douhairet, Potinet-Ampeau, de Suremain, Thévenin-Monthélie.*

MOREY-ST-DENIS, AC (Côte de Nuits) Once obscure and good value, the wines of Morey-St-Denis are now expensive and in general suffer badly from overproduction and over-sugaring. They should be wines with less body and more perfume than Gevrey-Chambertin, and a slight savouriness blending with a rich, chocolaty fruit as they age. Most are far too light, but there is a small number of outstanding growers. There were significant rot problems across the board in 1983. *Pierre Amiot, Bryczek, Dujac, Lignier, Marchand, Ponsot, Seysses* and *Tardy* have all made super '85s along with merchants such as *Drouhin* and *Moillard*. 1986s are fair but a bit lean – and again, too many vineyards ended up racked with rot. But the 1987s look back on form and as good as '85, with small yields and intense fruit.

MUSIGNY, AC (Côte de Nuits) Extremely fine *grand cru* which gave its name to Chambolle-Musigny. All but a third of a hectare of the 10.65 hectare vineyard is red, capable of producing Burgundy's most heavenly-scented wine, but few recent offerings have had my hand lunging for the cheque book. Best producers: *Jadot, Leroy, Mugnier, Jacques Prieur, Roumier, de Vogüé.*

NUITS-ST-GEORGES, AC (Côte de Nuits) When it's good, this has an enthralling decayed – rotting even – brown richness of chocolate and prunes rising out of a fairly light, plum-sweet fruit – quite gorgeous, whatever it sounds like. It used to be one of the most abused of all Burgundy's names and virtually disappeared from the export markets, but is now fairly common, expensive but immeasurably better, and increasingly reliable. From companies such as *Jadot, Jaffelin, Labouré-Roi* and *Moillard*, it's even becoming possible to buy good merchants' Nuits once more. *Labouré-Roi* is the most consistent merchant, although *Moillard* and *Jadot* are increasingly good particularly at *premier cru* level. *Henri Jayer* seems to get better every vintage and made a considerable success of 1982 and 1983, as did *Chevillon, Dubois* and *Michelot*. 1985 has produced some beauties, as has 1987, while 1986, though Nuits did get rot problems, has produced a fair amount of lean but honest wine. Other good producers include *Caves des Hautes-Côtes, Jean Chauvenet, Faiveley, Grivot, Jayer-Gilles, Machard de Gramont* and *Rion*.

PERNAND-VERGELESSES, AC (Côte de Beaune) Little-known village round the back of the hill of Corton. Some quite attractive, softly earthy reds. *Besancenot-Mathouillet, Caves des Hautes-Côtes, Chandon des Briailles, Delarche, Dubreuil-Fontaine, Laleure-Piot, Pavelot, Rapet* and *Rollin* are the best producers.

POMMARD, AC (Côte de Beaune) From good producers, Pommard can have a strong, meaty sturdiness, backed by slightly jammy but attractively plummy fruit. Not subtle, but many people's idea of what red Burgundy should be. The *de Montille* and *Gaunoux* wines are the most consistently fine here at the moment, although *Mussy* is also first-class, and *Comte Armand* and *Parent* can be excellent. Also look out for the wines of *Billard-Gonnet, Boillot, Château de Pommard, Comte Armand, Lahaye, Lejeune, Jean Monnier, Pothier* and *Pousse d'Or*.

RICHEBOURG, AC (Côte de Nuits) Exceptional *grand cru* at the northern end of the commune of Vosne-Romanée. It's a wonderful name for a wine – Richebourg – and, at its best, it manages to be fleshy to the point of fatness, yet filled with spice and perfume and the clinging richness of chocolate and figs. Best producers: *Domaine de la Romanée-Conti, Gros, Henri Jayer, Liger-Belair, Charles Noëllat*.

LA ROMANÉE, AC (Côte de Nuits) This *grand cru* is the smallest AC in France, solely owned by the Liger-Belair family and sold by *Bouchard Père et Fils*. It is usually adequate wine, but doesn't begin to get near the quality of the neighbouring vineyards owned by the *Domaine de la Romanée-Conti*.

LA ROMANÉE-CONTI, AC (Côte de Nuits) This tiny *grand cru* of almost two hectares is capable of a more startling brilliance than any other Burgundy. The 7,000 or so bottles it produces per year are seized on by the super-rich before we mere mortals can even get our tasting sheets out and our pencils sharpened. It is wholly owned by the *Domaine de la Romanée-Conti*.

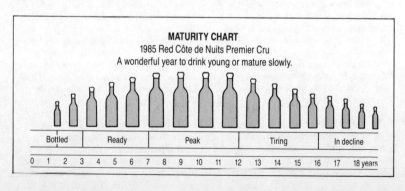

MATURITY CHART
1985 Red Côte de Nuits Premier Cru
A wonderful year to drink young or mature slowly.

Bottled	Ready	Peak	Tiring	In decline

0   1   2   3   4   5   6   7   8   9   10   11   12   13   14   15   16   17   18 years

LA ROMANÉE-ST-VIVANT, AC (Côte de Nuits) 9.54 hectare *grand cru* in the village of Vosne-Romanée. Much less easy to taste when young than its neighbouring *grands crus* and needing a good dozen years to show what can be a dazzlingly delicious, savoury yet sweet personality. Best producers: *Arnoux, Domaine de la Romanée-Conti, Latour, Noëllat.*

RUCHOTTES-CHAMBERTIN, AC (Côte de Nuits) The smallest *grand cru* of Gevrey-Chambertin at 3.1 hectares, making wines of deeper colour and longer-lasting perfumed richness than most of the village's other *grands crus*. Best producers: *Roumier, Rousseau.*

RULLY, AC (Côte Chalonnaise) Village just a couple of miles below Santenay, initially known for its sparkling wine, but gradually gaining a reputation for light but tasty reds and whites. Best producers: *Chanzy, Château de Rully, Delorme, Domaine de la Folie, Duvernay, Faiveley, Jacqueson, Jaffelin, Noël-Bouton.*

ST-AUBIN, AC (Côte de Beaune) Some of Burgundy's best value wines, especially from *Bachelet, Clerget, Lamy, Prudhon* and *Roux*. 1983s are in general good here; the '85s are delicious, and fairly priced, which is a minor miracle in Burgundy for '85s.

ST-ROMAIN, AC (Côte de Beaune) Even more out of the way than St-Aubin. Full, rather broad-flavoured, cherry-stone dry reds. On the whole sold cheaper than they deserve. Look for *Bazenet, Buisson, Thévenin* and *Thévenin-Monthélie*. Go for the '85s rather than the '83s and '86s.

SANTENAY, AC (Côte de Beaune) Rough and ready red. At its best, with a strong, savoury flavour and good strawberry fruit, though frequently nowadays rather lean and mean. Best producers: *Belland, Girardin, Lequin-Roussot, Morey, Pousse d'Or, Prieur-Bonnet, Roux*. Even among these top producers, however, there can be a lot of variation.

SAVIGNY-LÈS-BEAUNE, AC (Côte de Beaune) Not renowned, but pretty reliable reds. Rarely very full, but with an attractive earthiness backing up strawberry fruit. Often good quality at a fair price. Look out for *Bize, Camus-Bruchon, Capron-Manieux, Ecard-Guyot, de Fougeray, Girard-Vollot, Guillemot, Pavelot-Glantenay* and *Tollot-Beaut*. The 1982s are still remarkably good and the '83s are softening, but I'd go for the vastly popular '85s and the exceptionally tasty '87s at the moment.

LA TÂCHE, AC (Côte de Nuits) Another *grand cru* monopoly of the *Domaine de la Romanée-Conti*. As famous as Romanée-Conti, but not so totally unobtainable, since the 6.06 hectare vineyard can produce all of 24,000 bottles a year – that's two bottles each for the world's 12,000 richest people. The wine is heavenly, so rich and heady the perfumes are sometimes closer to age-old brandy than table wine and the flavour loaded with spice and dark autumn-mellow fruits and the swirling acrid richness of dark chocolate.

VOLNAY, AC (Côte de Beaune) Volnay is one of the most perfumed red Burgundies, with a memorable cherry and strawberry spice, but also, in its *premiers crus*, able to turn on a big, meaty style without losing the perfume. The best performers here at the moment are *Lafarge* and *de Montille*, the '83s are better than average, and those '85s are superb. Other good producers include *Ampeau, Blain-Gagnard, Boillot, Clerget, Comtes Lafon, Delagrange, Glantenay, Lafon, Marquis d'Angerville, Pousse d'Or, Vaudoisey-Mutinde, Voillot.*

VOSNE-ROMANÉE, AC (Côte de Nuits) The greatest Côte de Nuits village, right in the south of the Côte. Its *grands crus* sell for more money than any red wine on earth, except for Château Pétrus in Bordeaux, and, remarkably for Burgundy, they are dominated by a single estate, *Domaine de la Romanée Conti*. These vineyards make wines capable of more startling brilliance than any other red wine in France, with flavours as disparate yet as intense as the overpowering, creamy savouriness of fresh *foie gras* and the deep, sweet scent of ripe plums and prunes in brandy. There are also fine *premiers crus*, and the village wines, though not so reliable as they once were, can sometimes reflect their leaders. The 1985s are going to be some of the greatest made in years, but there is also a higher than average amount of good '83 and some decent '84. 1987 is going to cause heart flutters as well. 1988 is bound to outshine '89. Apart from the Domaine, good producers include *Arnoux, Sylvain Cathiard, Engel, Grivot, Jean Gros, Hudelot-Noëllat, Georges Jayer, Henri Jayer, Henri Lamarche, Méo-Camuzet, Moillard, Mongeard-Mugneret, Rouget, Rion* and *Jean Tardy*.

VOUGEOT, AC (Côte de Nuits) A village famous only because of its *grand cru* Clos de Vougeot, at its best plummy and broad, yet more often sweet and sullen, sad to say. However, there are some decent wines made outside the hallowed walls of the Clos – notably from *Bertagna*.

RED CÔTE D'OR VINTAGES

1989 The warm season produced a large crop of healthy, ripe grapes pretty well everywhere. It shouldn't have been necessary to chaptalize and the better growers did not. The anticipation generated by the new vintage in Bordeaux had some knock-on effect in Burgundy, but on the whole the feeling of thrill and excitement just wasn't borne out by the wines themselves. Yes, there were a lot of good wines made, but only a few that might be regarded as exceptional. The wines are softer than the 1988s, and some commentators view them as a kind of cross between 1982 and 1985 in style. Though, having said that, there are some superbly concentrated wines, particularly in the Côte de Beaune, destined to rival the 1988s and, dare I suggest it, surpass them in some cases.

1988 There's no doubt that the potential to make great wine descended on Burgundy in 1988, though it was hardly a textbook year. There was serious drought during the summer, and those who were hoping to increase their yields may well have ended up with grapes rather short on sugar. Those tempted to wait a bit longer were then walloped by the rains! But, having said all this, throughout the Côte d'Or a surprising number of growers did *not* overproduce, *did* pick fully ripe grapes before the rains came, and *have* made delicious wines – more joyously fruity than 1987, and quite a bit deeper and riper than 1986. Truly a great year.

1987 It didn't start out with much of a reputation because no one was enthusiastic about *Bordeaux* '87s and this impression travelled. The good producers made quite small amounts of well coloured, concentrated wine which in some cases is better than the same producers' 1985s. The best '87s are very good indeed, Côte de Beaune having the edge over Côte de Nuits. Further down the quality scale the wines *aren't* as good as '85, but are better than '86.

1986 Over the last year the wines have been shedding toughness, and now exhibit their best feature – perfume – that most elusive yet seductive quality in good Pinot Noir. As with '87 *only* the decent producers made lovely wine, because there was a fair amount of rot around.

1985 Once that riot of juicy fruit and sweet strawberries and redcurrants had lost its first flush of youth, the gorgeous lush juiciness seemed to have shed a little flesh. But this *always* happens, to good and bad vintage alike. When the 1985s were young, they were so good that frankly I wanted to glug them straight from the barrel. Some have gone from strength to strength. Some shot their bolt early.

1984 Nothing special, though not as bad as at first reported.

1983 The best wines display impressive flavour. If you can wait another decade you may have the most impressive old-style Burgundies made in the last 20 years.

1982 Ridiculously over-praised to start with. The best wines are from the Côte de Beaune and are delicate, perfumed, nicely balanced.

1978 Wonderful balance with the fruit and acidity and tannin finally coming together. But as always in Burgundy, the producer's name is absolutely vital because while the best are now utterly delicious, there are distressingly shabby bottles too.

WHITE WINES

I'm taking out an insurance policy with the Crédit Agricole des Vignerons de Bourgogne on my white Burgundy consumption. First I pay a premium – and how. Nothing happens as long as I open a satisfying bottle, but when I don't, I get my money back, plus compensation for irritation and annoyance, from Burgundy. Simple idea. Trouble is, if it worked, Burgundy would be bankrupt and I'd be rich instead of the other way round. Don't get me wrong. If, like now, I always had a fine glass of white Burgundy sitting on my desk, prompting me as I write with fine words like complexity, sensuality, longevity and *terroir*, I daresay I could witter on till the cows come home about how exquisite white Burgundy can be to drink and how there's no other wine on earth made from the Chardonnay grape to beat it.

If on the other hand I felt like I do more often after a taste of white Burgundy, not to mention a glance at the bill, you might find me in a rather different mood, more critical perhaps, more inclined to save my money for a rich Au Bon Climat from Santa Barbara in California, a Leeuwin Estate Chardonnay from Western Australia, a Coldstream Hills Chardonnay from Victoria or a steely Martinborough from Wellington on New Zealand's North Island. It's not that I'm fickle but I have this, er, sort of condition – chardofrenia or chardonfreude, something like that anyway – in which I'm so frequently in two minds.

Who can doubt that at its very best, the finest white Burgundy really is the most exhilarating and sensual wine in the world? Take a Meursault Charmes from Comtes Lafon or a Puligny-Montrachet from Vincent Leflaive, a Bâtard-Montrachet from Louis Latour or a Beaune Clos des Mouches from Joseph Drouhin (you see, I'm not prejudiced against *négociants* when they deliver the goods). Sublime stuff. Expensive yes, but where the production is small and the quality matchless, it's hard to argue against high (as distinct from exorbitant) prices even if most of the best stuff does get poured down the wrong throats.

Meursault is different. For Meursault is the biggest white wine village in the Côte d'Or with almost double the production of Puligny- and Chassagne-Montrachet. Meursault is the just about affordable yardstick by which top white Burgundy can be measured. But despite the efforts of fine producers like Comtes Lafon, Coche-Dury, Bernard Michelot, Guy Roulot and François Jobard, too much Meursault is poor value for money. This year *Decanter* magazine conducted a tasting of Meursault 1986, a good year for white Burgundy. Their conclusion? A huge let-down. 'In the battle between France and the New World, France is not winning on the basis of this tasting', said one experienced taster, a specialist retailer himself of fine white Burgundy.

It's the same old story. The problem begins in the vineyard with overproduction. Both 1986 and 1988 produced good vintages for white Burgundy. But the yields were very high. The production figure for Meursault in 1986 was nearly 50 hectolitres to the hectare, for Pouilly-Fuissé in 1988, 60 hectolitres to the hectare. This is all very well for Mâcon-Villages or generic Chablis at £5–7 a bottle, but unacceptable in wines costing twice as much. When are the Meursaultiens going to twig that in the £8–14 price range California, Australia and New Zealand offer greater consistency and better value? But surely, I hear you say, white Burgundy is a more complex wine than any of those?

Dick Ward of the Saintsbury Winery in Carneros, whose lovely Chardonnay Reserve 1987 retails for around £12.00 doesn't agree. 'New World Chardonnay can be as complex as anything Burgundy can produce,' says Ward. 'The only question mark in my mind is whether they will have the same grace and finesse in ageing.' Can New World Chardonnay compete with white Burgundy as it ages? Tim Atkin, who has been researching Chardonnay, also believes that the New World can achieve equivalent complexity. 'Don't forget,' he says, 'there's a lot of rubbish at high prices in Burgundy. And anyway, who says that white Burgundy always ages so brilliantly? It's a question of balance and the right degree of natural acidity. The New World doesn't chaptalize, Burgundy does, and that can often leave an empty, alcoholic flavour.'

UNSENTIMENTAL HYGIENE

Certainly cellar techniques, though improving, still leave a lot to be desired in Burgundy. While the red winemakers are getting their act together, white wine-making still lags behind. An Australian may go green with envy at Burgundian vineyards, but not at his cellar. Things are changing – slowly. At the basic level, cold fermentation has revolutionized bog-standard Mâcon and Chablis. At the higher level where character is the key, it is gradually dawning on Burgundy that hygiene in the cellar is not an enemy of complexity in the wine, but a friend.

Barrel-fermentation in new oak of different origins, Allier, Tronçais, Limousin, with different treatments once the wine has undergone its alcoholic fermentation, also contributes to the complexity of fine white Burgundy. But if you barrel-ferment water, you still get water, albeit with a vanilla taste. Nothing shall come of nothing, as King Lear said.

Although Burgundy as a whole breaks down into red and white production roughly half and half, red wines outnumber whites by nearly five to one in the heartland of the Côte d'Or. And ordinary white Burgundy, by which I mean Mâcon and Chablis, the kind of stuff we actually drink, outnumbers Côte d'Or white by seven to one. In 1988, the Côte d'Or produced less than seven million bottles against Mâcon's 31 million, Chablis' nearly 20 million, and 2.5 million from Côte Chalonnaise. That's the world of white Burgundy most of us inhabit if we inhabit any part of it: the world in which even spending a fiver on a bottle of wine is an outlay not to be sneezed at. But there ain't much white Burgundy, even at the humblest Mâcon co-op level, for a fiver today.

QUALITY TASTING

At the BIVB tasting in London, it was the real world of white Burgundy that was on show: Mâcon-Villages and St-Véran in the Mâconnais and Rully in the Côte Chalonnaise. Not a Meursault in sight. You still had to pick and choose your way, but there was more consistency and some actual promise here, even without the presence of some of the best producers in the Mâconnais like André Bonhomme, Jean Thévenet and Henri Goyard of Domaine de Roally. In particular the two wines from Domaine Talmard at Mâcon-Uchizy and a Mâcon-Viré from Emilian Gillet were superb. There were some nice wines from St-Véran, which I suppose can no longer be considered exactly poor man's Pouilly-Fuissé now that prices of Pouilly-Fuissé have dipped. Even so, the better wines, from Maison Auvigue-Burrier-Revel, from the co-op at Prissé and from Jean Bernard at Leynes, are worth staking out. Rully was a bit disappointing, lacking its usual body, but I liked Antonin Rodet's Château de Rully and Chartron et Trébuchet's New

Worldy/oaky Rully la Chaume which suited the event.

I wasn't the only one who did. James 'the nose' Rogers of ex-Cullens fame, was inspired by the tasting to start making a little collection of the best value 1988 white Burgundies he could find from the various tastings he went to, to end up as the Barnes Wine Shop's Summer Wine List. What did he end up with? Four Mâconnais whites, a Mâcon Lugny les Genièvres from Louis Latour, Mâcon Charnay from Mançiat-Poncet, St-Véran from Corsin and Pouilly-Fuissé from Mançiat-Poncet. There were three Côte Chalonnaise wines, Faiveley's Mercurey Clos Rochette, Joseph Drouhin's Montagny and that Rully from Chartron et Trébuchet. Finally two Côte d'Or whites, St-Romain and St-Aubin 1er cru Les Charmois from Olivier Leflaive. This is the way forward. Look for the best producers in the most interesting up-and-coming *appellations*, among them St-Aubin 1er cru, Pernand-Vergelesses and Chablis 1er cru. Above all, talk to the specialists, the Morris & Verdins and Haynes Hanson and Clarks and you never know, you just might find that you too end up with an insurance policy of sorts.

ANTHONY ROSE

GRAPES & FLAVOURS

CHARDONNAY In a world panting for Chardonnay, Burgundy makes the most famous Chardonnay of all. Even in the decidedly dicky Burgundian climate, it produces a fair to considerable amount of good to excellent wine almost every year. Its flavour depends on where it is grown, and how the wine is made. Chardonnays made without the use of oak barrels for ageing will taste very different from barrel-aged wines. A Mâcon produced in stainless steel will have rather appley fruit as well as something slightly fat and yeasty or, in a hot year, a slightly exotic peachiness. Côte Chalonnaise Chardonnay is in general rather taut and chalky-dry, but given a little oak, it can become delicate and nutty. Chablis, too, generally produces lean wine, but in riper years and with some oak treatment it can get much rounder and mouth-filling. The Côte d'Or is the peak of achievement for Chardonnay, and a top wine from the Côte de Beaune manages to be luscious, creamy, honeyed yet totally dry, the rich, ripe fruit intertwined with the scents of new oak into a memorable, and surprisingly powerful wine – from the right producer, the world's greatest dry white wine. It is this outstanding accolade that has so enticed the New World wineries into trying to mimic the success of the Burgundian grape with their own examples of fine wine.

ALIGOTÉ Not planted in the best sites – though there are a few vines in Corton-Charlemagne. Aligoté used to be merely sharp, spritzy café wine, but from old vines it can produce a lovely, refreshing wine, scented like buttermilk soap yet as sharp and palate-cleansing as a squeeze of lemon juice.

PINOT BEUROT Known elsewhere as Pinot Gris. Rare in Burgundy, but it produces rich, buttery wine usually blended in to soften the Chardonnay. There is a little unblended Pinot Beurot in the Hautes-Côtes.

PINOT BLANC There is a little of this about in the Côte d'Or – in Aloxe-Corton, for instance, where it makes a soft, rather unctuous, quick-maturing wine. Rully in the Côte Chalonnaise has a good deal and it ripens well in the Hautes-Côtes. There is also an odd white mutation of Pinot Noir – as at Nuits-St-Georges where the *premier cru* La Perrière produces a very savoury white, and in the Monts Luisants vineyard in Morey-St-Denis.

The price guides for this section begin on page 275.

WINES & WINE REGIONS

ALOXE-CORTON, AC (Côte de Beaune)
This most northerly village of the Côte de
Beaune has one of the Côte's most famous
grands crus, Corton-Charlemagne. It can
be a magnificent, blasting wall of flavour,
not big on nuance, but strong, buttery and
ripe, which traditionally is supposed to
require long ageing to show its full
potential. Recent vintages have mostly
been strangely disappointing and one is
left wondering if they're not trying to
produce too much wine.

AUXEY-DURESSES, AC (Côte de
Beaune) Tucked away in the folds of the
hill rather than on the main Côte de
Beaune slope, Auxey-Duresses has never
been well known, but has always had some
reputation for soft, nutty whites. Recently,
though, too many have been
disappointingly soft and flabby, but the
new confidence of the lesser villages is
evident here too and 1989, '88 and '87 have
all produced good wine. 1986, '85, '83 and
'82 can be good. *Ampeau, Diconne, Duc de
Magenta, Jadot, Leroy* and *Prunier* are still
producing pretty decent stuff.

BÂTARD-MONTRACHET, AC (Côte de
Beaune) *Grand cru* of Chassagne and
Puligny lying just below Le Montrachet
and, from a good producer, displaying a
good deal of its dramatic flavour, almost
thick in the mouth, all roasting nuts,
buttered toast and honey. Exciting stuff,
costing rather more than the national
average wage – per bottle, that is – in the
few restaurants that stock it. Good
producers: *Blain-Gagnard, Bachelet-
Ramonet, Leflaive, Pierre Morey, Michel
Niellon, Poirier, Claude Ramonet,
Ramonet-Prudhon, Sauzet.*

**BIENVENUES-BÂTARD-
MONTRACHET, AC** (Côte de Beaune)
Tiny *grand cru* in Puligny below Le
Montrachet, and inside the larger Bâtard-
Montrachet – whose wines are similar
though the Bienvenues wines are often
lighter, more elegant and may lack a tiny
bit of Bâtard's drive. Producers: *Leflaive,
Ramonet-Prudhon.*

BOURGOGNE ALIGOTÉ, AC Usually
rather sharp and green except for
vineyards near Pernand-Vergelesses where
old vines can make exciting wine, but the
Burgundians usually add Crème de Cassis
to it to make Kir – which tells you quite a
lot about its usual character. Look out for
*Coche-Dury, Confuron, Diconne, Jobard,
Monthélie-Douhairet, Rion, Rollin.*

**BOURGOGNE ALIGOTÉ DE
BOUZERON, AC** (Côte Chalonnaise) The
white wine pride of the Côte Chalonnaise is
made not from Chardonnay but from
Aligoté in the village of Bouzeron. The
vines are frequently old – more crucial for
Aligoté than for most other wines – and the
characteristic buttermilk soap nose is
followed by a very dry, slightly lemony,
pepper-sharp wine, too good to mix with
Cassis. It got its own AC in 1979. It owes
its sudden fame to the interest of the *de
Villaine* family, who own a substantial
estate there making very good, oaked
Aligoté. *Chanzy* and *Bouchard Père et Fils*
are also good.

BOURGOGNE BLANC This can mean
almost anything – from a basic Burgundy
grown in the less good vineyards of
anywhere between Chablis and the
Mâconnais to a carefully matured wine
from a serious producer, either from young
vines or from parts of his vineyard that just
miss a superior AC. Best producers:
*Boisson-Vadot, Boyer-Martenot, Boisson-
Morey, Paul Chapelle, Henri Clerc, Coche-
Dury, Dussort, Jadot, Javillier, Jobard,
Labouré-Roi, René Manuel, Millau-
Battault,* and *Buxy co-op (Clos de
Chenoves).*

CHABLIS, AC Simple Chablis, mostly
soft, sometimes acidic, covers the widest
area of the *appellation*. Well it would,
wouldn't it? They've included most of what
used to be Petit Chablis for a start. But at
the rate they're now extending the *premier
cru* status to virtually anything that
moves, maybe *premiers crus* will soon
overtake Chablis in acreage. Chablis covers
a multitude of sins, with a lot of wine going

under *négociants'* labels, and a lot being sold by the co-op – they make most of the *négociants'* stuff too. Some of the co-op's best *cuvées* are outstandingly good, but many of the cheaper *cuvées* are too bland and soft. A good grower is more likely to give you something steely and traditional. Good producers: *Christian Adine, Jean-Marc Brocard, La Chablisienne, Jean Collet, René Dauvissat, Defaix, Jean-Paul Droin, Joseph Drouhin, Jean Durup, William Fèvre, Vincent Gallois, Alain Geoffroy, Jean-Pierre Grossot, Michel Laroche, Bernard Légland, Louis Michel, Guy Mothe, Louis Pinson, François & Jean-Marie Raveneau, Regnard, Simmonet-Fèbvre, Philippe Testut, Robert Vocoret.*

CHABLIS GRAND CRU The seven *grands crus* (Blanchots, Preuses, Bougros, Grenouilles, Valmur, Vaudésir and Les Clos) come from a small patch of land just outside the town of Chablis, on a single slope rising from the banks of the river Serein. The wines *can* be outstanding, though still unlikely to rival the *grands crus* of the Côte de Beaune. To get the best out of them, you need to age them, preferably after oaking, although *Louis Michel's* oak-free wines age superbly. The last three vintages have seen a considerable increase in the use of oak by the better producers, and the results are much deeper, more exciting wine which may well benefit from six to ten years' ageing in bottle.

CHABLIS PREMIER CRU Some 30 names, rationalized into 12 main vineyards. This used to be a very reliable classification for good, characterful dry white, if less intense than *grand cru*, but again, there has been this expansion mania, meaning that many hardly suitable pieces of vineyard are now accorded *premier cru* status. Given that there is a price difference of £3 to £4 a bottle between Chablis and *premier cru* Chablis, the quality difference should be plain as a pikestaff. Sadly it rarely is. However, since 1986 there has been a definite move towards quality by the better growers and La Chablisienne co-op.

CHABLIS VINEYARDS

Grands Crus

Blanchots, Bougros, Les Clos, Grenouilles, Preuses, Valmur, Vaudésir.

Premiers Crus Vineyards

Fourchaume (including Fourchaume, Vaupulent, Côte de Fontenay, Vaulorent, l'Homme Mort); Montée de Tonnerre (including Montée de Tonnerre, Chapelot, Pied d'Aloup); Monts de Milieu; Vaucoupin; Les Fourneaux (including Les Fourneaux, Morein, Côte des Prés-Girots); Beauroy (including Beauroy, Troesmes); Côte de Léchet; Vaillons (including Vaillons, Châtains, Séché, Beugnons, Les Lys); Mélinots (including Mélinots, Roncières, Les Epinottes); Montmains (including Montmains, Forêts, Butteaux); Vosgros (including Vosgros and Vaugiraut); Vaudevey.

CHASSAGNE-MONTRACHET, AC (Côte de Beaune) Well under half the production of this famous vineyard at the south of the Côte de Beaune is white, but that minority share does include a chunk of the great Montrachet vineyard. The *grands crus* are excellent, but the *premiers crus* rarely dazzle quite like those of nearby Puligny-Montrachet. The Chassagne '86s are going to be superb, and are starting to open up, while the '85s here are probably the Côte d'Or's most successful, as were many of the '83s. Best producers: *Bachelet-Ramonet, Blain-Gagnard, Carillon, Chartron et Trebuchet, Colin, Delagrange-Bachelet, Duc de Magenta, Fontaine-Gagnard, Gagnard-Delagrange, Génot-Boulanger, Lamy-Pillot, Laquiche, Moreau, Albert Morey, Ramonet-Prudhon.*

CHEVALIER-MONTRACHET, AC (Côte de Beaune) *Grand cru* vineyard of Puligny, directly above Le Montrachet. The higher elevation gives a leaner wine than Le Montrachet, but one with a fabulous deep flavour as rich and satisfying as a dry white wine can get. Good examples will last 20 years. Best producers: *Bouchard Père et Fils, Jadot, Latour, Leflaive.*

CORTON, AC (Côte de Beaune) Corton-Charlemagne is the white *grand cru* here in Aloxe-Corton, but tiny patches of the Corton *grand cru* grow Chardonnay and Pinot Blanc. The finest wine, the *Hospices de Beaune's* Corton-Vergennes, is all Pinot, and *Chandon de Briailles* makes Corton-Bressandes, half from Pinot Blanc, half from Chardonnay.

CORTON-CHARLEMAGNE, AC (Côte de Beaune) This famous *grand cru* of Aloxe-Corton and Pernand- Vergelesses occupies the upper half of the dome-shaped hill of Corton, where the first of the Côte de Beaune's limestone outcrops becomes apparent. It is planted almost entirely with Chardonnay, but a little Pinot Blanc or Pinot Beurot can add an intriguing fatness to the wine. Good producers: *Bonneau du Martray, Chandon de Briailles, Dubreuil-Fontaine, Hospices de Beaune, Laleure Piot, Latour, Rapet.*

CÔTE CHALONNAISE, AC As the ordered vineyards of the Côte de Beaune swing away and dwindle to the west, the higgledy-piggledy vineyards of the Côte Chalonnaise hiccup and splutter into life as a patchwork of south- and east-facing outcrops. Light, usually clean-tasting Chardonnay predominates among the whites – although at long last the idea of oak-ageing is catching on and some of 1989's most pleasant discoveries have been oak-aged Rullys and Montagnys. But the Côte Chalonnaise has one star that cannot be overshadowed by the famous Côte d'Or: the village of Bouzeron makes the most famous, if not quite the finest Aligoté in all France.

CÔTE D'OR This famous strip of vineyard, running south-west from Dijon for 30 miles, sprouts famous names right along its length, with a fine crop of illustrious whites in the southern portion. But in fact it produces only about 16 per cent of Burgundy's white. (Mâconnais is the chief white producer, with the Côte Chalonnaise chipping in a bit.) Price lunacy for whites has become a fairly common phenomenon in all the Côte d'Or villages, as has complete absence of the wines from many British wine-lovers' cellars. Including mine.

CRÉMANT DE BOURGOGNE, AC What used to be simple, pleasantly tart Burgundian fizz, based on slightly green Chardonnay and Aligoté grapes, excellent for mixing with cassis, is beginning to sharpen up its act. Competition from other wine-producing regions and from neighbouring countries, added to the increase in Champagne prices, has led to co-operatives, such as the *caves* of Viré or St-Gengoux-Clessé in the Mâconnais, and the *Cave de Bailly* in the Yonne and *Delorme* in Rully, producing excellent, affordable fizz, increasingly from 100 per cent Chardonnay. It is becoming a wine that no longer needs disguising.

CRIOTS-BÂTARD-MONTRACHET, AC (Côte de Beaune) Tiny 1.6 hectare *grand cru* in Chassagne-Montrachet nuzzled up against the edge of Bâtard itself. Hardly ever seen but the wines are similar to Bâtard, full, strong, packed with flavour, perhaps a little leaner. Best producers: *Bachelet, Delagrange, Blain-Gagnard, Marcilly.*

MATURITY CHART
1988 White Côte de Beaune Premier Cru
1988 displays a class lacking in the 1986s and 1987s.

Bottled	Ready	Peak	Tiring	In decline

| 0 | 1 | 2 | 3 | 4 | 5 | 6 | 7 | 8 | 9 | 10 | 11 | 12 years |

HAUTES-CÔTES DE BEAUNE, AC and **HAUTES-CÔTES DE NUITS, AC** A lot of reasonably good, light, dry Chardonnay from the hill country behind the Côte de Beaune and Côte de Nuits. Best producers: *Caves des Hautes-Côtes, Chalet, Cornu, Goubard, Jayer-Gilles, Alain Verdet* (organic).

MÂCON BLANC, AC It seemed a few years ago that the spiralling price of Pouilly-Fuissé – the region's only white wine star – was acting as a spur for the producers and, in particular, the co-operatives who dominate production, to improve quality. Sadly, as Pouilly-Fuissé comes spinning back to earth – a wiser but better, and cheaper, wine – upping the price of Mâcon to patently unrealistic levels seems to have been the only effect of the last few years' madhouse.

MÂCON BLANC-VILLAGES, AC One step up from basic Mâcon Blanc, this must come from the 43 Mâcon communes with the best land. The rare good ones show the signs of honey and fresh apples and some of the nutty, yeasty depth associated with fine Chardonnay. You can expect the better wines from those villages, notably **Viré, Clessé, Prissé** and **Lugny**, that add their own village names (Mâcon-Viré, etc). Full, buttery yet fresh, sometimes spicy: look for that and, if you find it, consider paying the price – but only if. Prices went silly for the 1985s, whose taste in no way matches their reputation. Vintages since then have been better, and prices are now merely too high, rather than an insult to our intelligence. Best producers: *Bicheron, Bonhomme, Danauchet, Goyard, Josserand, Lassarat, Manciat-Poncet, Merlin, Signoret, Thévenet-Wicart.*

MERCUREY, AC (Côte Chalonnaise) Village making over half the wine of the Côte Chalonnaise. Most of the production is red – the whites used to be rather flaccid afterthoughts from the less good land, but as the price of white shifts upwards in the Côte de Beaune, several producers have started making a bigger effort with interesting results. Good examples come from *Chartron et Trebuchet, Faiveley* and *Genot Boulanger.*

MEURSAULT, AC (Côte de Beaune) Halfway down the Côte de Beaune, this village is the first, working southwards, of the great white wine villages. It has by far the largest white production of any Côte d'Or village, and this is one of several reasons why its traditionally high overall standard is gradually being eroded. The wines should be big and nutty and have a delicious, gentle lusciousness, and sometimes even peachy, honeyed flavours. Meursault has more producers bottling their own wine than any other village. These are some of the best: *Ampeau, Boisson-Vadot, Boyer-Martenot, Buisson-Battault, Coche-Debord, Coche-Dury, Comte Lafon, Dussort, Jobard, René Manuel, Matrot, Michelet-Buisson, Millot-Battault, Pierre Morey, Prieur, Roulot, Thévenot-Machal.*

MONTAGNY, AC (Côte Chalonnaise) White-only AC in the south of the Côte Chalonnaise. In general the wines are a bit lean and chalky-dry, but now that the use of oak is creeping in, some much more interesting wines will appear. Best producers: *Arnoux*, co-op at *Buxy, Latour, de Montorge, Alain Roy.*

LE MONTRACHET, AC (Côte de Beaune) Finest of fine white *grands crus* in the villages of Puligny and Chassagne, and by that token the finest dry white wine in the world. Funny word – finest. Does it mean most enjoyable, most happy-making? Not really. In fact the flavours in Montrachet can be so intense it's difficult sometimes to know if you're having fun drinking it or merely giving your wine vocabulary an end of term examination. So be brave if someone opens a bottle of Montrachet for you and let the incredible blend of spice and smoke, honey and ripeness flow over your senses. Good producers: *Bouchard Père et Fils, Domaine de la Romanée-Conti, Comtes Lafon, Laguiche, Pierre Morey, Prieur, Thénard.*

MUSIGNY, AC (Côte de Nuits) Just 0.3 hectares of this predominantly red *grand cru* of Chambolle-Musigny are planted with Chardonnay, owned by the *Domaine de Vogüé*, and most of it seems to be consumed on the premises.

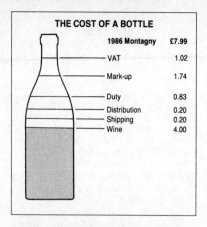

THE COST OF A BOTTLE

	1986 Montagny	£7.99
VAT		1.02
Mark-up		1.74
Duty		0.83
Distribution		0.20
Shipping		0.20
Wine		4.00

PERNAND-VERGELESSES, AC (Côte de Beaune) Little village in the north of the Côte de Beaune. The village wines can be good – it's here you find the best Aligoté in Burgundy, while the Chardonnays are generally fairly lean and need a little time to soften, but can be gently nutty and very enjoyable from a good producer. Best producers: *Dubreuil-Fontaine, Laleure-Piot, Pavelot, Rapet, Rollin.*

PETIT CHABLIS There used to be lots of this grown on the least good slopes. But the growers objected that it made it sound as though their wine was a lesser form of Chablis. Nowadays, of course, pretty well the whole lot is called 'Chablis' – so *we* can't tell what's what, *they're* all richer, they're happy, we're not...I give up.

POUILLY-FUISSÉ, AC (Mâconnais) This once ridiculously overpriced white has, through total lack of orders for its wine, more than halved its price in the last couple of years; and you can find parcels of Pouilly-Fuissé here and there for as little as a fiver. This tumble in price came about partly because the Americans stopped buying, although they were the ones who made it famous in the first place, and partly because the general quality from this co-op-monopolized, *négociant*-abused AC was a disgrace. So the price slid. But snap up any bargains you see; they won't be there for long. Best producers: *Béranger, Corsin, Duboeuf's* top selections, *Ferret, Guffens-Heynen, Leger-Plumet, Loron's les*

Vieux Murs, Manciat-Poncet, Noblet, Vincent at *Château Fuissé.* Adjoining villages **Pouilly-Loché, AC** and **Pouilly-Vinzelles, AC** have borrowed the name of Pouilly. They make similar wines to those of Pouilly at half the price.

PULIGNY-MONTRACHET, AC (Côte de Beaune) At the south of the Côte de Beaune, the peak of great white pleasure is to be found in the various Montrachet *grands crus*. Le Montrachet is a peerless wine, showing in the most perfect way how humble words like honey, nuts, cream, smoke, perfume and all the rest do no honest service to a white wine that seems to combine every memory of ripe fruit and subtly worn scent with a dry, penetrating savouriness quite without equal. There are several other *grands crus*, less intense, but whose wines buzz with the mingling opposites of coffee and honey, and smoke and cream. And, of course, there's a range of *premiers crus* as well. While 'village' Meursault may be good, it's always worth buying a single vineyard wine in Puligny-Montrachet. Much of the wine is sold in bulk to *négociants* whose offerings vary between the delicious and the disgraceful, but look for the wines of *Bachelet-Ramonet, Boyer-Devèze, Carillon, Chapelle, Chartron et Trebuchet, Drouhin, Jadot, Labouré-Roi, Laguiche, Leflaive, Ramonet-Prudhon, Antonin Rodet, Sauzet, Thénard.*

RULLY, AC (Côte Chalonnaise) This village gets my vote for the most improved AC in Burgundy. Originally best known for sparkling wine, then for pale, nutty Chardonnay of no great excitement, the use of oak to ferment and age the wine has transformed many producers' wines into wonderfully soft, spicy Burgundies of good quality – and low price. Best producers: *Bêtes, Chanzy, Cogny, Delorme, Dury, Duvernay, Jacqueson, Jaffelin, Noël-Bouton, Rodet.*

ST-AUBIN, AC (Côte de Beaune) Some of Burgundy's best value white wines, full and racy, come from this tiny, forgotten Côte de Beaune village behind Puligny-Montrachet and Meursault. Two-thirds of the vineyards are *premiers crus* and it really shows. Starting with 1982 it became clear that St-Aubin's *premiers crus* could rival the more famous wines of Meursault and Puligny-Montrachet, and each successive vintage has confirmed this trend. The 1986s from *Prudhon, Roux, Albert Morey* and *Jadot* show superb flavours at affordable prices. Other good producers are *Bachelet, Bouton, Clerget, Colin, Delaunay, Duvernay, Jadot, Jaffelin, Lamy, Albert Morey, Prudhon* and *Roux*.

ST-ROMAIN, AC (Côte de Beaune) Flinty, dry whites from this out of the way Côte de Beaune village up near the Hautes-Côtes are often pretty good value. Best producers: *Bazenet, Buisson, Germain, Gras, Thévenin, Thévenin-Monthélie*.

ST-VÉRAN, AC (Mâconnais) Pouilly-Fuissé's understudy in the Mâconnais, capable of making simple, soft, quick-maturing but very attractive, rather honeyed white Burgundy. The 1986s looked to be exceptional and then they seemed to fall apart – just as the '85s had done after a brief but brilliant reign of about one year. Now the '87s and '88s are looking better than either – but for how long? Best producers: *Corsin, Duboeuf, Grégoire, Lassarat, de Montferrand, Thibert, Vincent*.

SAUVIGNON DE ST-BRIS, VDQS A wine of undoubted AC quality grown around the village of St-Bris-le-Vineux, south-west of Chablis, that languishes as a VDQS because the Sauvignon is not a permitted grape in the area. Often one of the most stingingly nettly, most greeny gooseberryish of all France's Sauvignons, but recent examples have been considerably more expensive and considerably less exciting. Ah well, New Zealand has some nice Sauvignon, and Bordeaux Blanc is really tasty right now, so perhaps I'll drink those. Producers take note. Good producers: *Louis Bersan, Jean-Marc Brocard, Robert & Philippe Defrance, Michel Esclavy, André Sorin, Luc Sorin*.

WHITE BURGUNDY VINTAGES

White Burgundy is far less prone to vintage fluctuation than red, and in most years can produce a fair amount of pretty good wine.

1989 An outstanding year for white Burgundy, in the hands of competent winemakers. It's already being hailed as the best white vintage of the 1980s and the feeling is there hasn't been a year to rival 1989 for quite some time. Almost all the best growers' wines are beautifully balanced, despite the richness of the wine. Most wines have avoided being over-alcoholic, although the occasional batch lacks acidity. As one Burgundy importer put it: 'a richer version of the structured and seriously undervalued 1985s'. Best of all, individual vineyard characteristics seem particularly pronounced in 1989.

1988 The fruit was, if anything, a little cleaner and fresher than in 1987 and the wines may yet turn out like those of 1982. Which would be very nice – but remember 1982 was a year of record yield and the wines never attained real complexity. Numbers of Mâconnais wines have a bright fresh fruit not seen down that way for a few years. Chablis prices went up by 10 to 15 per cent, but you couldn't say that quality went up in parallel.

1987 There's a lot of very pleasant '87 white around, but it hasn't got the extra dimension of the red. As in 1988, the Chardonnay failed to get into overdrive and in a tricky autumn just never quite ripened. Even so, good producers made attractive, quite light wines, sometimes with a slightly lean streak of acidity. Try the exciting new growers in the Côte Chalonnaise and Mâconnais. The Côte d'Or produced wines that were often frankly dull, but with time, Chablis is turning out to be good.

1986 There's an interesting debate beginning to develop over the relative qualities of '86 and '85. Initially 1985 was hailed as a super year, but then '86 was given an even better reception because, whereas 1985 seemed to rely on sheer power for its effect, 1986 seemed to have finer acidity, a more focussed fruit and even a hint of richness from noble rot on the grapes (that's the stuff which makes Sauternes so sweet, and it can add a really luscious honeyed edge even to a dry white). The balance has redressed a bit now because, while the good 1985s have proved to be much better balanced than previously thought, the '86s have closed up somewhat. Whether they finally outshine the '85s will make for some interesting tasting over the years – if we can a) find, and b) afford any of the wines to join in the fun. Chablis is extremely good for '86 and they do exhibit that classic blend of leanness and restrained ripeness which can make good Chablis the logical, if not the emotional choice for so many fish dishes. They're hitting peak from about now, except for *grands crus*, which will need several years yet. This was the first year we saw increasing signs of a return to new oak barrels on more than a very isolated scale in Chablis. The Mâconnais promised so much, but few bottles really delivered much satisfaction. Still, it was a watershed vintage as some growers saw that quality first was the way forward.

1985 This is on the way back. Along with the strength are increasing signs of a proper acid balance and an outstanding concentration of fruit. Pity nobody waited to find out because most '85s were consumed long ago. If you do see one from a good producer, go for it – well, perhaps not, I've just remembered the price it'll be. Chablis started out with a lesser reputation, but wines from good producers are still improving by the minute. Mâconnais 1985s never really fulfilled their potential.

1984 Not too bad, some well-made, rather lean wines but as they age, the unripe acidity can dominate. Chablis are still good, and typical, but not showstoppers.

1983 In 1983 there was a serious rot problem and a lot of grapes were also seriously overripe. The result is frequently heavy, rather unrefreshing, soggy-flavoured wines. Interestingly some good growers still rate their '83s as classics. The Chablis were wonderful, but except for the top *crus* are now beginning to fade.

1982 A lovely vintage, almost entirely consumed by now, of easy outgoing clean-flavoured wines. If they hadn't overproduced so grossly, this would have been a classic; as it was, it still gave a great deal of pleasure. Wines from good producers should still be lovely, if tiring a little.

BEAUJOLAIS

In a complicated world, Beaujolais used to be one of those things you could depend on to be straightforward. Something cheap, reliable and fruity to drink with friends, rarely more. Until recently the region itself was similarly accommodating: charming, open and uncomplicated.

Over the last few years there have been signs of a distressing change in attitude. Beaujolais has begun to develop pretensions, ridiculous ones in some instances. The transformation is rather sad, like watching one of the Carry On team struggling to play King Lear.

In common with most French *appellations*, Beaujolais increased its prices after the 1989 harvest. Some of the increases were plain silly, irrespective of the quality of the vintage. Beaujolais Nouveau, the ultimate quaffing wine, has broken the £5 barrier. Most of the ten *crus* – notably Fleurie and Moulin-à-Vent – are at least 15 per cent more expensive this year. If anything, producers of Beaujolais-Villages have been even more greedy, although some can at least claim that their vineyards were badly damaged by hail in July 1989.

If things go on like this, I fear we could be paying £10 for a bottle of bog-standard Fleurie before long. Last year we were worried about it being £8. You see what I mean about silly? Some feel Beaujolais is already in danger of pricing itself out of the market, and the same could be said of Muscadet. In such a climate, the behaviour of certain growers and *négociants* has been reprehensible. As the English Beaujolais specialist Roger Harris puts it, 'my enduring memories of 1989 will be of acrimony, avarice and double dealing'.

WHAT PRICE THE WINE?

But back to the wines. Are the 1989s worth the extra money? Yes and no. 1989 was a ripe, early vintage. Quite the best year in Beaujolais since, well … since 1988, actually. Remember what we were told then? Marvellous vintage, sublime wines, the works. Well, now we've had two very good vintages on the trot. Both have produced some excellent wines. Neither, in my opinion, is as consistently good as 1985, despite the hyperbole.

The 1988s are still cheaper than the 1989s in many cases. They should also last longer. A wine like René Passot's 1988 Morgon, Domaine Les Rampaux (available from Haughton Fine Wines at £4.57) has profited from more time in bottle. On the other hand, the same importer's 1989 Fleurie, Les Roches du Vivier (£6.49) is fresh, lively and packed with such juicy young fruit that you want to guzzle it straightaway.

One of the pleasing things about the 1989 vintage was the high natural sugar levels. Some producers were picking grapes with 13 per cent potential alcohol. This removed the need for excessive chaptalization, the continuing blight of Beaujolais. At last the authorities are doing something about this. In March the president of one of the region's leading co-operatives was charged with over-chaptalization. In the street outside 500 growers staged a demonstration. Let them protest. Meanwhile we can get on with drinking some excellent Beaujolais – a unique taste, at its best.

More than 85 per cent of the region's wines is sold by merchants, a lot of whom produce rather dull, overchaptalized wines. Some more reliable names to seek out are Duboeuf, Dépagneux, Loron, Champclos, Jadot, Sarrau, Mommessin and Tête. On the whole, though, I'd be tempted to stick to wines from individual domaines. As a rule, avoid Fleurie and Moulin-à-Vent and plump for cheaper, less popular *crus* like Juliénas and Côte de Brouilly. Drink some straightaway for fruit. Keep some for six months or so out of curiosity.

A pleasing recent development has been the emergence of groups of growers selling their wines under a common umbrella. Three excellent associations are the Eventail des Vignerons Producteurs (imported by Winecellars; Haynes, Hanson & Clark; Thomas Peatling and Eldridge Pope), Harmonie des Terroirs (Alex Findlater) and the snappily-titled GIE de Roche-Cours (Julian Baker). The general standard of their wines is high. Try the 1989 Beaujolais from Jean-Paul Brun of Harmonie des Terroirs for a reminder of how real Gamay should taste.

Two years after Regnié was elevated to the tenth cru, there seems no prospect of an eleventh. 'We've already got too many,' says Robert Felizzato of Champclos. 'it's hard enough to sell Chénas, Côte de Brouilly and Juliénas as it is.' Regnié, too, has had its problems. Half of the 1988 vintage was sold off as Beaujolais-Villages, according to one source. At the same time Regnié, which used to make up ten per cent of the *appellation*, has pushed up the price of Beaujolais-Villages. Terribly complicated. It almost makes you long for the simplicity of Beaujolais Nouveau day.   **Tim Atkin**

GRAPES & FLAVOURS

CHARDONNAY Chardonnay does in fact make some white Beaujolais, and it's usually quite good. Grown in the north, it has a stony dryness rather closer in style to the northern wines of Chablis. In the south it is much closer in style to the fatter, softer, sunny wines you'd expect in southern Burgundy.

GAMAY The Gamay grape produces pretty dull or tart stuff in most other areas. But somehow, on these granite slopes, it manages to give one of the juiciest, most gulpable, gurgling wines the world has to offer. The Gamay has no pretensions. Ideally Beaujolais is simple, cherry-sharp, with candy-like fruit, sometimes with hints of raspberry or strawberry. The wines from the *crus* go further than this, but in the main the similarity they share through the Gamay grape is more important than the differences in the places they come from. All but the wines of the top villages should be drunk as young as you can find them, although years like 1985, '87, '88 and '89 have produced wines at *cru* levels that are now ageing well. 1988s still need another year or two for the best wines.

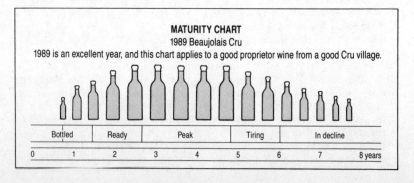

MATURITY CHART
1989 Beaujolais Cru
1989 is an excellent year, and this chart applies to a good proprietor wine from a good Cru village.

Bottled	Ready	Peak	Tiring	In decline

| 0 | 1 | 2 | 3 | 4 | 5 | 6 | 7 | 8 years |

WINES & WINE REGIONS

BEAUJOLAIS, AC This covers *all* the basic wines, the produce of the flatter, southern part of Beaujolais, stretching down towards Lyon. Most of the best is now sold as Nouveau. Run-of-the-mill Beaujolais, apart from Nouveau, is likely to be pretty thin stuff, or beefed up illegally with something altogether different. In fact, since you're allowed to re-label Nouveau as 'Beaujolais', some of the best wine in the new year (much appreciated by those who scoffed at Nouveau) will be none other than re-labelled Nouveau. Good producers include *Blaise, Carron, Charmet, Château de la Plume, co-op at Bully, Duboeuf Bouteille Cristal, Garlon, Labruyère*.

BEAUJOLAIS BLANC, AC To be honest, Beaujolais Blanc is usually quite expensive and in its rather firm, stony-dry way is rarely as enjoyable as a good Mâcon-Villages. Most of the examples we see come from the north, often bordering on St-Véran in the Mâconnais, so despite being rather closed in, you expect it to blossom sometime – but it doesn't. I'd plant Gamay instead if I were them. *Charmet* is the most interesting producer, but his vineyards are in the south. *Tête* is good.

BEAUJOLAIS ROSÉ, AC I never thought I'd waste space on this apology for a wine – but a couple of years ago I came across an absolute stunner from *M Bernard* of Leynes – one of the best pinks I'd had all year. The *co-op* at *Bois d'Oingt* have also shown they can make exciting rosé.

BEAUJOLAIS NOUVEAU (or **PRIMEUR**), **AC** The new vintage wine of Beaujolais, released in the same year as the grapes are gathered, at midnight on the third Wednesday in November. It is usually the best of the simple wine, and will normally improve for several months in bottle, but in good Nouveau vintages like 1988, '85 and '83 it can improve for years. I always keep a bottle or two to fool my wine-buff friends – and it always does – they're usually in the Côte de Beaune at about £12 a bottle. I'm sniggering in the kitchen.

BEAUJOLAIS SUPÉRIEUR, AC Superior means that the basic alcoholic degree is higher. It doesn't ensure a better wine, and is rarely seen on the label.

BEAUJOLAIS-VILLAGES, AC Thirty-five villages can use this title. They're mostly in the north of the region and reckoned to make better than average wines, with some justification because there are quite major soil differences that account for the demarcation of Beaujolais and Beaujolais-Villages. The wines are certainly better than basic Beaujolais, a little fuller and deeper, and the cherry-sharp fruit of the Gamay is usually more marked. However, look for a wine bottled in the region, and preferably from a single vineyard, because an anonymous blend of Beaujolais-Villages may simply mean a heftier version of an ordinary Beaujolais. *Noël Aucoeur, Domaine de la Brasse, Domaine de la Chapelle de Vatre (Sarrau), Château des Vergers, de Flammerécourt, André Large, Château des Loges, Jean-Charles Pivot, Jean-Luc Tissier*, and *Trichard* are good local producers, but most domaines are bottled by one of the merchants in the region, even though there is an increasing, and welcome, tendency to label the wine with its domaine title.

BROUILLY, AC Southernmost and largest of the Beaujolais *crus*, Brouilly has the flattest of the *cru* vineyards, and usually makes one of the lightest *cru* wines. There is some variation in style between the more northerly villages and those in the south where granite produces a deeper, fuller wine, but in general Brouilly rarely improves much with keeping. In fact, it makes a very good Nouveau! A few properties make a bigger wine to age – but even then, nine months to a year is quite enough. Good properties include *Château de la Chaize, Domaine Crêt des Garanches, Château de Fouilloux, Hospices de Belleville, Château de Pierreux, Domaine de Combillaty (Duboeuf)* and *Domaine de Garanches, Château de Nevers. Château des Tours*, although lovely young, can age much longer.

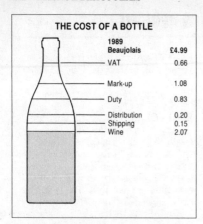

THE COST OF A BOTTLE

1989 Beaujolais	£4.99
VAT	0.66
Mark-up	1.08
Duty	0.83
Distribution	0.20
Shipping	0.15
Wine	2.07

CHÉNAS, AC This second-smallest *cru*, from between St-Amour and Moulin-à-Vent, makes strong, dark wines, sometimes a bit tough, that can be drunk a year after the harvest, or aged to take on a Pinot Noir-like flavour. Not very popular so usually good value. Look out for the wines of *Louis Champagnon, Charvet, Château de Chénas, Domaines des Brureaux, Domaine Chassignon, Domaine de la Combe Remont (Duboeuf), Pierre Perrachon, Emile Robin.*

CHIROUBLES, AC Another *cru* for early drinking, grown on hillsides south-west of Fleurie, towards the southern end of the Beaujolais *crus*. The wines are naturally light, similar to Beaujolais-Villages in weight, but with a perfumed, cherry fragrance that makes Chiroubles France's favourite Beaujolais *cru*. Good producers include *René Brouillard, Cheysson, Château Javernand, Château de Raousset, Jean-Pierre Desvignes, Duboeuf, Méziat* and *Georges Passot.*

CÔTE DE BROUILLY, AC The slopes of the hill in the centre of the Brouilly area make fuller, stronger-tasting *cru* wines than straight Brouilly, since they come largely from exposed slopes and have lapped up the sun. Best producers include: *Château Thivin, Conroy, Claude Geoffray, Jean Sanvers, Lucien Verger.*

CRU The ten *crus* or growths (Fleurie, Moulin-à-Vent, Brouilly, Chénas, Côte de Brouilly, Chiroubles, Juliénas, St-Amour, Morgon, Regnié) are the top villages in the steeply hilly, northern part of the Beaujolais region. They *should* all have definable characteristics, but the produce of different vineyards and growers is too often blended to a characterless mean by merchants based anywhere in France. Always buy either a single estate wine, or one from a good local merchant like *Chanut Frères, Duboeuf, Dépagneux, Ferraud, Sarrau, Thomas la Chevalière, Trenel.*

FLEURIE, AC Often the most delicious of the *crus*, gentle and round, its sweet cherry and chocolate fruit just held firm by a touch of tannin and acid. This is the most popular of all the *crus* and I used to be prepared to pay the price, but now the wine has to be *very* special for me to shell out the extra. Look out for *Château de Fleurie (Loron), Chauvet, Chignard, Colonge, Domaine de la Grand, Grand Pré (Sarrau), Domaine de la Presle, Domaine des Quatre Vents, Duboeuf's la Madone, Bernard Paul, Verpoix* and the local co-op.

JULIÉNAS, AC Towards the north end of the Beaujolais region, Juliénas *can* provide big wine, with more tannin and acidity, but many of the best more closely resemble the mixture of fresh red fruits and soft, chocolaty warmth that makes for good Fleurie. It can age, but it's better young. Good ones include *Château du Bois de la Salle, Domaine des Bucherats, Château des Capitans, Château de Juliénas, Domaine de la Dîme* and *Domaine de la Vieille Eglise.* Also good: the wines of *Pelletier* and *Duboeuf's* selections.

MORGON, AC The wines of this southern *cru* village can be some of the great glories of Beaujolais. They can start out thick and dark, and age to a sumptuous, chocolaty, plummy depth with an amazing smell of Kirsch cherries, not unlike Côte de Nuits Burgundy, and yet still Beaujolais. *Jacky Janodet* usually makes a big, intense Morgon. Look out also for *Aucoeur, Château de Pizay, Descombes, Desvignes, Domaine de la Chanaise, Domaine de Ruyère, Lapierre, Félix Longepierre* and *Georges Vincent.*

MOULIN-À-VENT, AC Enter the really heavy brigade. These *cru* wines should be solid and strong, and should age very well for three to five years, sometimes longer, especially from years like 1985 and '88. The best have a big, plummy, slightly Burgundian style, and the toughness of a young Moulin-à-Vent doesn't give you much option but to wait. It rarely resembles anyone's view of straight Beaujolais – it takes itself far too seriously – but quite a few of the 1988s are already extremely good. *Louis Champagnon* makes a very good one, as do *Brugne, Charvet, Château des Jacques, Château du Moulin-à-Vent, Château Portier, Domaine de la Tour de Bief, Jacky Janodet, Raymond Siffert* and *Héritiers Maillard* (formerly *Héritiers Tagent*). *Duboeuf* is experimenting with new oak barrel-ageing – with considerable success.

REGNIÉ, AC Since the 1988 vintage Beaujolais' tenth *cru*. Makes wine quite similar to Brouilly in ripe vintages but a bit weedy when the sun doesn't shine. Isn't too expensive I suppose. *Duboeuf Bouteille Cristal* the best so far, and *Domaine des Buyats* was very good in 1989.

ST-AMOUR, AC Among the most perfect Beaujolais, this pink-red wine from the most northerly and one of the least spoilt villages usually has freshness and peachy perfume and good, ripe fruit all at once. It isn't that common here (though the French love it), and yet it is frequently the most reliable and most enjoyable *cru*. Sadly, the news has leaked out and prices are leaping up. Look out for *Château de St-Amour, Domaine des Billards (Loron), Domaine des Ducs, Domaine du Paradis, André Poitevin, Francis Saillant.*

BEAUJOLAIS VINTAGES

With most Beaujolais the rule is, drink it as young as possible. Only the top wines from the best villages will benefit much from ageing, although Nouveau can benefit from a month or two's rest.

1989 Along with other vineyard areas of France, and indeed Europe, the 1989 vintage in Beaujolais was one of the earliest ever. Picking of the grapes, which had been sunning themselves under a blazing sky all summer, started on 3 September. The heat meant that colour was unusually deep, but along with this the aromas were much more pungently fruity than expected after the hot and dusty summer season. Dry weather meant there were few problems with rot or mildew, and the crop came in in healthy condition.

The bad news is that prices have increased substantially, especially for Beaujolais-Villages. You never know, this may be the year when Fleurie finally loses its grip on the UK, and *crus* like Chénas and Côte de Brouilly may come to the fore. Georges Duboeuf reckons that the moment is right for Morgon and Moulin-à-Vent, but in terms of value for money those bottles of 1989 Chénas and Côte de Brouilly look like being the better bet. At the time of writing, many of the 1989s have retreated into their shell - by the time you read this they should be re-emerging.

1988 There's no doubt that 1988 was a lovely year in Beaujolais. There is a marvellous quality of luscious, clear, ripe fruit about the best wines. Even the Nouveaus were terrific. I remember a string of delicious Beaujolais-Villages. And some delightful St-Amour and Brouilly. Pressure on supply meant overproduction in some quarters, though. So I'm going to say – 1988 is an exceptional year: just try and make sure you grab hold of the good examples.

1987 Many are still drinking well, although this was a vintage best enjoyed in its youth. Some of the sturdier *crus* produced wines with the class and stamina to survive – Moulin-à-Vent can be delicious. But the lighter wines are fading already.

1986 Started mean and few remaining bottles will excite anyone.

1985 No vintage has ever given me so much sheer pleasure as 1985 with its riot of fruit and spice. Many of the wines are still excellent – but they're changing suits, growing up, becoming serious and adult. Many will be delicious, but the days when they made you dance with delight are now over. It was fun, though.

CHAMPAGNE

The only good news out of Champagne in the past year has been the size and quality of the 1989 vintage. Champagne, it can never be said too often, comes from the most northerly fine wine vineyard in the world and it's a miracle that any grapes, let alone that notoriously difficult beast the Pinot Noir, achieve any alcoholic strength worth measuring. In the summer of 1989 it – and the Pinot Meunier and the Chardonnay – emphatically did ripen as they have not done for a generation or more. Even in 1989 the Champenois did not need to worry about the lack of acidity which posed a problem in other French vineyards that year.

Moreover, because the vintage started so early, and the weather remained hot for so long, the Champenois benefitted from that rarest of phenomena, a harvest several weeks after the first, in which they gathered 'second crop' grapes, the ones which are normally left to rot, green and unloved, on the vine. In volume terms the harvest should present the world's Champagne lovers with stocks of 275 million bottles, 26 million bottles more than we all drank last year, which should help to refill the region's sadly depleted reserves.

Great harvest, great vintage. But that's it, I'm afraid. We who drink the wine are going to suffer, immediately from substantial price rises, and, in the longer term, from some shading of quality, both resulting from a nasty outbreak of civil war in the Champagne region. This erupted in early 1990 as a result of the breakdown of the elaborate contract system, renewable every six years, which has ruled in Champagne since 1959. Since then prices of the grapes have soared, but sales have rocketed too, showing a five-fold increase in 1989.

SATISFACTION GUARANTEED?

The growers are now guaranteed £1.40 or more for every pound of grapes, however mixed the condition of the bunches they have to sell. So in an average year an acre of vines brings in a gross income of around £6000 – and most growers have at least five acres. Nevertheless they have become greedy, selling less than half their grapes to the world-famous firms on whom the drink's reputation depends. And increasing numbers have been boosting their income by sending their grapes to the local co-ops, getting finished bottles back in return and palming them off to French buyers as all their own work. And if they couldn't be bothered to work on the Sabbath when the customers motored out from Paris, they left the wines with the co-ops, who sold them, usually young, green and acid, to bargain-hunting buyers for French supermarkets.

The quality charter discussed in last year's *Webster's* was supposed to put a stop to this particular deception. In future, if they want to put the magic letters RM – *récoltant-manipulant* – on a bottle, growers will have to make the wine themselves; otherwise they will be confined to using the letters RC, indicating a grower whose wine has been made by a co-operative. But this gesture is laughable: the letters are small, their meaning unknown to the majority of buyers; they will help only the minority who know the reality behind the brand.

To be fair the charter did tighten up on growing techniques by requiring more severe pruning, defining picking dates more precisely, ensuring that more grapes go into each bottle than before and taxing heavily the infamous trade of *vin sur lattes*, Champagne already in bottle and sold to unscrupulous merchants who rely on the *dosage* – the final dose of old wine and sugar inserted just before the wine is sold – to give it their own 'style'.

The crucial element in the contract was how many grapes the growers were prepared to commit to the established Champagne houses, instead of making their own wine or sending the grapes to the local co-operative. Over the years the proportion had fallen to just under half of the total: but this time, instead of accepting the minimal fall in the percentage resulting from the ballot, the houses refused to endorse the contract. Yves Benard, the mild-mannered and polite young man who, as head of Moët, is the uncrowned king of Champagne, led his colleagues into declaring that they would prefer a free and open market.

After a lot of gesturing and hot air the two sides settled on a new agreement, the details to be decided before the 1990 harvest, the prices to be decided by the market. At a guess, prices of the cheapest Champagne will rise by about a tenth, but any superior blend, especially a Blanc de Blancs, will cost up to a fifth more as a result – although the better firms have at least three years' worth of sales in stock and so the increases may not be too sudden.

At the same time the big firms continued to press, among other improvements, for the elimination of the *deuxièmes tailles*, juice extracted from the third pressing of the grapes which invariably produces poor Champagne. They have also got the growers to agree that the hundreds of wine presses in the region, many of them elderly, are to be inspected and brought up to scratch or replaced within the next few years. This will greatly improve the wine since the grapes will be pressed more evenly, and the juice will be cleaner.

But the agreement had one ominous sign for future quality. The ten-year planting programme, agreed in the early 1980s after three disastrously short harvests, provided 5000 more hectares, a near-20 per cent increase in the area planted with vines. But, inevitably, these hectares of vineyard were in marginal areas, mostly in the Aube, nearer Chablis and Burgundy then Reims, an area where the most widely-planted variety, the Pinot Noir, produces a very smoky, overripe-loganberry style of wine, not to everyone's taste.

The other major new plantations were in the Aisne and the west of the Marne Valley, a region dominated by the Pinot Meunier. Purists would say that this is a bad sign since the variety has suffered badly from one of Champagne's least-justified snobberies (after all, Krug uses up to 20 per cent of Pinot Meunier). But if it is well vinified – as it is by Mercier, who make a delicious NV Brut containing up to half of Pinot Meunier – it should not hurt Champagne's reputation.

Mercier have also shown the way in the firms' counter-attack against the enormous Co-operative Unions which have come to dominate the French home market. After doing a deal with the biggest, the Centre Vinicole Champenois at Chouilly, to make wine specially for the firm, Mercier's oenologists have moved in to improve the CV's formerly uninspiring wines.

But any long-term improvement in the general quality of the cheaper Champagnes will have to wait, not only for the elimination of the *deuxièmes tailles* and the replacement of older presses, but also for a lengthier stay – of a minimum of two years – in bottle. Only then will the Champenois be able to look at competing fizzes, many of them wines they themselves are making all over the world, notably in California and Australia, from proper Champagne grapes – and say, sincerely, that Champagne is worth the increasing premiums the growers are forcing everyone to charge. **NICHOLAS FAITH**

GRAPES & FLAVOURS

CHARDONNAY The grape of white Burgundy fame here produces a lighter, fresher juice, and the resulting Champagnes are certainly the most perfumed and honeyed. They have been criticized for lacking depth and ageing potential. Not true. Good Blancs de Blancs have a superb, exciting flavour that is positively improved by ageing, especially those from the southern end of the Côte des Blancs.

PINOT NOIR The grape that makes all the finest red Burgundies also makes white Champagne. Pinot Noir has enough difficulty in ripening in Burgundy, and further north in Champagne it almost never attains any great depth and strength of colour or alcohol, which is fair enough since the general idea here is to produce a *white* wine. Very careful pressing of the grapes in enormous square vertical presses is the best way to draw off the juice with as little colour as possible, and the rest of the reddish tinge generally precipitates out naturally during fermentation. Even so, the black grape juice does have a fairly big feel to it, and a Champagne relying largely on Pinot Noir is certain to be heavier and take longer to mature.

PINOT MEUNIER The other black grape, making a softer, fruitier style of wine, important for producing easy wines for drinking young, and crucial for toning down the assertive flavours of Pinot Noir.

WINES & WINE STYLES

BLANC DE BLANCS An increasingly common style from Chardonnay grapes. Usually fresh and bright with a soothing, creamy texture. Many de luxe Champagnes are now labelled Blanc de Blancs, but they rarely have the added nuances the conspicuously increased price would suggest. Best producers: *Avize* co-op, *Billecart-Salmon, Henriot, Lassalle, Pol Roger, Louis Roederer, Dom Ruinart, Sézanne* co-op, *Taittinger Comtes de Champagne*.

BLANC DE NOIRS This rare style is made 100 per cent from black grapes. The wine is white, usually rather solid, but can be impressive if aged long enough. The *Pierre Vaudon* brand from the Avize co-op is excellent, and inexpensive. *Barancourt* is more expensive, and fairly beefy stuff. *Bruno Paillard* is usually good.

BRUT Very dry.

BUYER'S OWN BRAND (BOB) A wine blended to a buyer's specification, or more probably, to a buyer's price limit. The grapes are of lesser quality, the wines usually younger, and they should be notably cheaper. The following are remarkably consistent: *Maison Royale (Victoria Wine), Sainsbury, Tesco, Waitrose. Marks & Spencer* is less consistent, but can be best of all.

CM In the small print at the bottom of the label, this means *co-opérative-manipulant* and shows that the wine comes from a co-operative.

COTEAUX CHAMPENOIS Still wines, red or white. Overpriced, rather acid. A village name, such as Cramant (white) or Bouzy (red) may appear. *Alain Vesselle*'s Bouzy is one of the few exciting reds.

CRÉMANT A Champagne with only half the normal amount of fizz. If the base wine is good, that's still enough. Best producers: *Besserat de Bellefon, Alfred Gratien, Abel Lepitre, Mumm Crémant de Cramant.*

DE LUXE/CUVÉE DE PRESTIGE/ CUVÉE DE LUXE A special, highly prized, highly priced blend, usually vintage. Some great wines and some gaudy coat-tailers. Most come in silly bottles, and are not worth the money, but a few really do deliver. In general offered for sale and drunk *far* too young. Most need ten years to shine. Best producers: *Bollinger RD, Dom Pérignon, Dom Ruinart, Heidsieck Diamant Bleu, Krug Grande Cuvée, Laurent Perrier Grand Siècle, Pol Roger Cuvée Sir Winston Churchill, Roederer Cristal, Taittinger Comtes de Champagne.*

The price guides for this section begin on page 298.

DEMI-SEC Medium sweet. Rarely very nice, but *Louis Roederer* is outstanding, and *Mercier* is surprisingly fresh and floral.

DOUX Sweet. Even more rarely very nice, but *Louis Roederer* is still outstanding.

EXTRA DRY Confusingly, this is less dry than 'Brut', but drier than 'Sec'.

GRANDE MARQUE Ambiguous term meaning literally 'great brand'. It's a self-styled grouping of, at the last count, 28 Champagne houses, including the 15 or so best known. The term *should* be synonymous with quality, denoting houses using more expensive grapes, older reserve wines, and more rigid selection of vats. But the pressure to grab increasing shares of the market has been taking its toll on stocks of reserve wines, with some of the 'lesser' houses coming into their own.

MA In the code at the bottom of the label, this means *marque d'acheteur*, implying a subsidiary brand or a secondary label. Any Champagne selling for a quid less than you expect is likely to be one of these.

NM In the code at the bottom of the label, this means *négociant-manipulant* (merchant-handler) and shows that the wine was bottle-fermented by the Champagne house on the label.

NON-DOSAGE Most Champagne has a little sweetness – a 'dosage' – added just before the final cork. A few Champagnes are sold bone-dry and will have names like Brut Zero, implying a totally dry wine. Best are *Jeanmaire, Laurent Perrier, Piper-Heidsieck*.

NON-VINTAGE The ordinary, most basic blend. Many houses used to pride themselves on providing a continuous house style through the judicious blending of various vintages. Some would even occasionally go to the extent of not declaring a vintage in a good year if they wanted to use the wine to keep up the standard of their non-vintage. Sadly, this happens far less nowadays. Although a little older reserve wine is added to smooth out the edges when the blend is being put together, most non-vintages are now released 'ready' for drinking, heavily dependent on a single year's harvest of perhaps two or three years' age and some producers will offer wine not much more than 18 months old. The current blends are based on excellent vintages but are often released much too young to justify fully the scary prices. Best are *Alfred Gratien, Billecart-Salmon, Charles Heidsieck, Duval-Leroy, Henriot, Lanson, Laurent Perrier, Mercier, Bruno Paillard, Pol Roger, Louis Roederer, Veuve Clicquot.* All improve greatly if laid down for even a few months between buying and drinking.

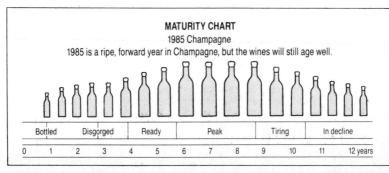

MATURITY CHART
1985 Champagne
1985 is a ripe, forward year in Champagne, but the wines will still age well.

Bottled	Disgorged	Ready	Peak	Tiring	In decline

| 0 | 1 | 2 | 3 | 4 | 5 | 6 | 7 | 8 | 9 | 10 | 11 | 12 years |

RC A new designation indicating *récoltant–co-opérateur* – for a grower selling wine produced at a co-operative. Too many small growers had been pretending they'd made base wine into Champagne themselves, when in fact they'd just sent it to the co-op. The RC designation should put a stop to that practice.

RÉCEMMENT DÉGORGÉ A term used for Champagnes that have been left in the cellars, drawing flavour from their yeast deposits, for much longer than usual before disgorging. The wines can happily rest for 20 to 30 years on the lees but are usually released after seven to ten years. *Bollinger RD* is the most famous; wines also from *Deutz, Alfred Gratien* and *Laurent Perrier*.

RICH The sweetest Champagne.

RM Indicates that the wine comes from a single grower, a *récoltant-manipulant*, literally harvester-handler. Until 1989, if he belonged to a co-operative, it is more than likely that he'd have sent all his grapes there, had them fermented in a great vat along with the grapes of hundreds of other producers, then taken back the bottles he wanted to sell over his farm gate either complete with bubbles or ready for champenization at home. Only around a tenth of the growers calling themselves *récoltants-manipulants* ferment their own wine at home, although they account for most of the wine labelled RM. RM should now indicate a grower

who's done the lot himself. Some good results come from *Bara, Beerens, Bonnaire, Brice, Fliniaux, Michel Gonet, André Jacquart, Lassalle, Albert Lebrun, Leclerc-Briant, Legras, Vesselle*.

ROSÉ Traditionally, the pink colour is gained by a careful and short maceration of the black Pinot Noir and Pinot Meunier skins with the juice. Other producers add a little red Bouzy wine to white Champagne before bottling. Ideally rosés are aromatic, fruity wines, with a delicious cherry or strawberry flavour. Sadly, many rosés are virtually indistinguishable from their white stablemates. Most should be drunk young to capture what character they *do* have. Best producers: *Besserat de Bellefon, Boizel, Alfred Gratien, Lassalle, Laurent Perrier, Moët et Chandon, Taittinger Comtes de Champagne. Krug rosé* is in a class of its own, and so it should be.

SEC Literally 'dry', but actually medium dry.

SR Société de Récoltant. Another new label designation, for a company created by growers who are from the same family.

VINTAGE Wine of a single, good quality year, generally fuller, than non-vintage, but almost without exception nowadays released too young. Best producers of vintage: *Billecart-Salmon, Bollinger, Alfred Gratien, Joseph Perrier, Pol Roger, Louis Roederer, Veuve Clicquot*.

CLASSIFICATIONS

The classification system in Champagne is based on vineyards. The approved areas for vineyards are strictly demarcated and the vineyard land graded according to suitability for black and white grapes, going from 100 per cent for the finest *grand cru* villages through 90–99 per cent for the 41 *premier cru* villages and on to 80 per cent for the least favoured.

If the basic price is 20 francs per kilo of grapes, a 100 per cent village grower receives the full 20 francs. An 80 per cent grower will receive only 80 per cent – 16 francs – and so on, it's all quite simple. The whole system is now less rigorous than it was 50 years ago, when percentages ranged from 50 to 100.

Champagne houses boast about how high their 'average percentage' of grapes is. Some Champagne labels will say either '100 per cent Grand Cru' or 'Premier Cru' and a village name, Avize, for example, if the wine comes from one single top village.

Hardly surprisingly, no one ever bothers to declare on the label percentages in the 80s or lower 90s, but in actual fact many of the best value Champagnes on the UK market come from these so-called 'lowly' villages.

CHAMPAGNE HOUSE PROFILES

BOLLINGER ★★★(★) Like Krug, produces 'English-style' Champagnes, warm, rich, oaky. Reputation slightly marred in recent years because the wines were released too young, and it showed. Sensibly makes vintage Champagnes only in best years and keeps a percentage on the lees until just before sale (hence the name RD, *Récemment Dégorgé*, for their luxury cuvée). Also *Vieilles Vignes*.

DEUTZ & GELDERMANN ★★★ Much underrated. Basic NV well-matured, balanced, fruity; warm, biscuity Blanc de Blancs. Its prestige wine Cuvée William Deutz, not disappointing exactly, just not substantially better than the basic blend.

KRUG ★★★★★ The classic heavy, serious Champagne. Grande Cuvée, oak-fermented is outstandingly good, and naturally weightier than any competitor. Expensive rosé has an incomparable Pinot Noir cherry-fruitiness. Even more expensive Clos de Mesnil is a delicate, single vineyard Blanc de Blancs.

LANSON ★★★(★) Until recently had (well-deserved) reputation for excessive acidity. Now maturing wine longer, providing light, quaffable Champagne.

LAURENT PERRIER ★★★★ Possibly the most reliable of all the non-vintage blends. Excellent, reasonably-priced rosé. Prestige brand Grand Siècle is (sensibly) blend of several vintages. Good value.

MOËT & CHANDON ★★(★) Brut Imperial infuriatingly unreliable – sometimes as good as any NV, at other times hardly tasting like Champagne at all. Vintage Moët usually shows well but is increasingly released far too young. Most famous wine Dom Pérignon.

MUMM ★(★) Traditionally rich wine, but all too frequently the least impressive of the famous names. Delicate, creamy Crémant from south-facing slopes in Cramant. I wish some of the Crémant's class would rub off on the NV and vintage.

PIPER HEIDSIECK ★★(★) The leanest of all the standard brands but becoming full and toasty with a bit of age. New prestige cuvée Champagne Rare much-praised. The sugarless Brut Sauvage is simply too mouth-tightening for many, but give it time – five years softens it up.

PERRIER-JOUËT ★★★ Reputedly the brand most respected by the winemakers, who drink it if they can't get their own. Best known for Belle Époque in Champagne's prettiest bottle, all flowery elegance, echoed in fresh, slightly unripe-cherry feel of the wine.

POL ROGER ★★★★ Model family firm, producer of Churchill's favourite fizz. Used to be heavy, overwhelmingly Pinotish, now all delicate, spring-flowery freshness, quality reflected in delicious Blanc de Blancs. NV, vintage, Blanc de Blancs and Cuvée Sir Winston Churchill all top class.

POMMERY ★★ Despite ownership changes, Pommery is still rather too bland. The wine can be exciting, when it tries.

LOUIS ROEDERER ★★★★(★) Most profitable drinks firm in the world. Most famous for Cristal, invented to satisfy sweet tooths of Russian Tsars. Now the most natural of all the prestige cuvées, reflecting the quality of individual vintages. Cristal is made (in small quantities) even in theoretically bad years – like 1974 and 1977 – when its almost vegetal sweetness comes through. NV usually one of the best despite needing more maturity. Good Demi-sec and Doux.

TAITTINGER ★★★(★) Splendidly light, modern, Chardonnayish style, carried through in its model Blanc de Blancs, Comtes de Champagne.

VEUVE CLICQUOT ★★★★ For a century and a half greatly loved by the British. The NV still has the rich, warm style first made famous by the formidable Madame Veuve Clicquot-Ponsardin. Prestige cuvée La Grande Dame almost chocolate-rich.

CHAMPAGNE VINTAGES

A vintage table for Champagne is not straightforward since so much Champagne is blended without vintage designation. Also, vintage wines released and sold very young, while good for laying down, are unlikely to give any more pleasure than good non-vintage for immediate consumption. Most Champagne can do with ageing; vintage Champagne demands it. Historically, a vintage was 'declared' by Champagne houses after an exceptional year, and then released at perhaps six to seven years old when reasonably mature. Recently there has been a trend for some vintage wine to appear almost every year, and at only four to five years old. Moët is often guilty of infanticide and released its 1985, in particular, far too young. Their excellent '79 is still only just coming into its own yet most of it has already been drunk. Interestingly enough some of the 1982s, released at only six years old were immediately delicious.

1989 For once an enormous, much-hyped vintage is turning out to be as good as the Champenois thought it would be. But inevitably, they'll be releasing the wines, vintage and NV alike, far too young.

1988 The harvest in this northernmost part of France started on 19 September in 1988 – weeks before supposedly warmer areas further south. But in fact the vines had flowered incredibly early – around 12 June – and the grapes *were* ripe. The young wine looks very promising, and in ten years' time there could be some memorable bottles of 1988 vintage.

1987 I can say precisely one thing in favour of the 1987 Champagne harvest – there's lots of it; it's the third biggest vintage ever. Well, hang on, there's another thing in its favour – 1987 produced some of the blandest, least memorable wine I can ever remember tasting. Now let's hope this means that no-one in their right mind will release it as vintage-dated wine. What they should do is to use the low-acid, somewhat characterless, base wine to make lots of pleasant, fairly-priced non-vintage Champagne.

1986 Not bad – useful wines of reasonable quality, but the yield was rather spoiled by rot which knocked off about 20 to 25 per cent of the grapes. Mostly good for blending into non-vintage brands, but the way the Champagne hounds are all rushing headlong into the more expensive styles, you're sure to see 1986 vintage labels peeking out in a few years.

1985 Well, after all the gloom and despondency when the Champagne guys were wringing their bejewelled hands and crying 'no wine, no wine', there is in fact a fair amount of wine and first tastes show it to be good to excellent in quality. Look for fine vintage wine in five years' time if it is still around.

1984 This was a very feeble vintage. Anyone who produced a vintage 1984 could probably turn water into wine. The one exception was Waitrose – who found a producer making his wine in fresh new wood.

1983 The second of the back-to-back record-breaking vintages which sent fizz prices plunging in the UK and – I hope the Champenois noticed – dramatically increased the amount of Champagne we all drank. 1983 wines are mostly now current and they are extremely good, a little leaner than 1982, but excellent, high-quality fizz. They're just too young, that's all! It looks as though the inexorable march towards vintages being released at only five years old, as against seven to eight when they're actually ready to drink, is not just an unhappy flash in the pan. Accountants of the world, rejoice. Wine lovers, despair.

1982 Not so long ago I castigated houses like Bollinger and Veuve Clicquot for wantonly releasing their '82s at only five years old. Eight years old used to be the rule, and even the '79 was almost seven years old on release. Well, the '82s which swamped the market were sheer bliss. They *were* ready at five years old – in fact the Bollinger '82 tasted readier to drink than their NV! That doesn't mean that they won't be better in two years' time. If you've got some, do keep a bottle for a couple of years, to see the difference.

1981/1980 These were tiny vintages, little seen with a vintage label, but some '81s aren't bad.

1979 This is an excellent vintage, the beautifully soft and balanced wines only now hitting peak form.

RHÔNE

With peaks in 1983, '85 and '88, plus the very fine vintages of '82 and '86, the '89 crop crowned a decade of success in the Rhône. Jean-Pierre Perrin of Château de Beaucastel is delighted. 'I don't understand how we were able to make balanced wines ... a few vines suffered, but in general 1989 was a miracle ... a little miracle,' he said earlier this year. According to Marcel Guigal of Côte-Rôtie, 1984 is the only hiatus in an otherwise brilliant series of vintages. 'We have been very spoilt', he adds.

In a drought year like 1989 it was by no means obvious that good wine would be produced. There have been complaints of lack of acidity in the rare white wines of Condrieu, and Guigal points to some Hermitage growers who picked underripe, fearing a deluge of rain in September. Michel Chapoutier reported vines where the heat had stopped the sap rising to the bunches. For him 1989 was a vintage where the good producer made good wines – skill was rewarded. For those who had abandoned traditional vine husbandry, the results could have been completely different.

Down south at Châteauneuf-du-Pape there was no rain in 1989 from 15 May to the night of 2–3 September. Jean-Pierre Perrin's only explanation for the quality of the resulting wines lies in the heavy rainfall in March and April which had created reserves for the long, hot summer. A little rain fell over towards Vaison-la-Romaine, benefitting the Côtes du Rhône villages of Gigondas, Rasteau and Beaumes-de-Venise.

SUPPLY AND DEMAND

With another excellent vintage safely tucked away in vat, tun and barrel, the choice facing growers now is whether to maintain prices or to bump them up *à la bordelaise*. Last year we saw further evidence of the escalation of prices for Guigal's Côte-Rôtie *crus*: La Mouline, La Landonne and the new *cru*, la Turque. Except in the case of La Landonne, the quantities made of these wines are so minuscule that their astronomic prices bear little relation to the real world of the Côtes du Rhône. So far at least, the interest shown by millionaires in one or two single *cru* Côte-Rôties has yet to alter the good value image of, say, the villages of the south. Furthermore, there are still bargains to be had in Côte-Rôtie, Hermitage, Cornas and Châteauneuf-du-Pape. At Hermitage the '89 whites are particularly good, strongly scented, full of fruit and deep in flavour.

Last year, Oz attributed the price rises in the Rhône to the 'Parker effect'. Certainly the American critic's 100 per cent scoring of two of Guigal's '83 wines must have shown the way forward for the Rhône market in the USA, but many of the price rises post-1983 were also a reflection of the fact that only small quantities of wine were available. To some extent the last two vintages must have stabilized the situation. Château de Beaucastel keeps price rises down to below annual interest rates. Jaboulet still adheres to a policy of setting the price by the quality of the vintage. For example, the lightweight '87 opened at 60 francs a bottle from the cellars, while the '88 opened at 100 francs, the same price as the '85. Jaboulet's Côte-Rôtie '89 opened at 10 francs cheaper than the '88. If only his pricing philosophy were adhered to in all wine regions.

The Parker effect has been felt in other ways. Robert Parker's trendification of the Rhône valley has not made it a quiet place to visit. Every half-way decent winery is permanently besieged by his fellow countrymen with copies of the famous guide tucked under their elbows. Gérard Chave, who received Parker's highest accolade, responded by installing a television camera at his front door so that he could vet his constant callers. Even that has proved insufficient: recently a restaurateur friend who was lunching with Chave in his garden, was appalled to see an American enthusiast descending the back wall to the winery, completely undeterred by attempts to keep him from the winemaker and his vastly oversubscribed stocks.

Fortunately Gérard Chave does have a little more Hermitage to sell as a result of his acquisition of the Irish milord, Terence Gray's, vineyard at L'Hermite. Up in Côte-Rôtie, rumours that Marcel Guigal had produced a new *cuvée* in honour of his late father were scotched at source. On the other hand, the world (or at least a very rich part of it) has now seen the first two vintages of La Turque. The British allocation was ten cases, which importers French Wine Farmers distributed to their ten best customers. With 12 bottles apiece, don't expect to see much of this precious stock reaching your local wine merchant.

CUTTING YOUR CÔTE

Quality is improving throughout the region. One of the benefits of receiving a little more money for their wines has been investment in new materials. New oak barrels are no longer a rarity in the Northern Rhône. The old wisdom that the big Syrah grape doesn't require the flavours of new oak is being challenged by a growing number of winemakers. Excellent Côte-Rôties are now being made by the Jamet brothers (look out for the '88 when it hits the market), Gilles Barge, Marius Gentaz, Jasmin and Vidal-Fleury. In Hermitage, Chapoutier has improved immeasurably in the past few years.

Delas too is making highly attractive wines at competitive prices. Look out for Desmeure's accessible style, or if you're looking for something to put away for a godchild, try Sorrel's blockbusters. In Cornas, Jean Lionnet has joined the leaders: Clape, Michel, de Barjac and Noël Verset.

In the south, increasing amounts of Syrah are being added to the vats of Clos des Papes in Châteauneuf with stunning results. Both Château de Beaucastel and Vieux Télégraphe continue to hold their positions, but there are interesting wines being shipped from the Domaine Roger Sabon and the Clos de l'Oratoire. Try, in particular, Sabon's Cuvée Prestige 1986. In Gigondas, the top flight includes the wonderful Domaine des Pallières and Roger Meffre's inspired Domaine St-Gayan.

From where I sit writing in mid-summer, things are looking good for the 1990 vintage, at least as far as quantity is concerned. The winter was mild, with a slightly worrying absence of rain. The frosts which rampaged through various French vineyards at the beginning of April spared the Rhône, though at one point, Marcel Guigal tells me, it was touch and go at Côte-Rôtie until the south wind arrived, Seventh Cavalry-like, to blow away the freezing air. The danger of further frosts has now passed and the bud-burst took place in perfectly healthy conditions. So far there has been no report of *coulure* or *millérandage* – uneven flower or berry setting which would diminish the potential size of the crop. Keep your fingers crossed. Who knows, we might be in for the vintage of the century? Miracles do happen.   GILES MACDONOGH

RED WINES

Northern Rhône reds are really the different manifestations of a single grape variety – the Syrah. It is virtually the only red grape grown in the north, and certainly the only one tolerated for the various *appellations contrôlées*. Syrah can range from light, juicy and simple in the more basic St-Joseph and Crozes-Hermitage offerings, to something rich, extravagant and wonderfully challenging in the top wines of Hermitage, Côte-Rôtie and Cornas.

Southern Rhône reds are usually made from a range of grape varieties, all chosen to complement each other, yet none – except the Syrah and very occasionally the Grenache – able to produce wine of dramatic individuality on its own, and that means basic fruit flavours across the whole area are very similar. These are usually raspberry-strawberry, often attractively spicy, slightly dusty, and sometimes livened up with some blackcurrant sweetness or wild herb dryness. The introduction of *macération carbonique* – the Beaujolais-type method of vinification – in the Rhône has meant that many wines, even at the cheapest level, can have a deliciously drinkable fruit; but again, a certain uniformity of style is imposed from top to bottom.

GRAPES & FLAVOURS

CARIGNAN This is a much-maligned grape because in the far south it produces tough, raw wines in big volumes which frequently form the bulk of France's red contribution to the wine lake. Old vines can produce big, strong, but very tasty wines that age well.

CINSAUT Another gentle grape, giving acidity and freshness but little fruit to the reds and rosés of the southern Rhône.

GRENACHE The most important red grape in the southern Rhône, because it gives loads of alcoholic strength, lots of volume, and a gentle, juicy, spicy fruit perked up by a whiff of pepper, ideal for rosés and easy-going reds. So what's the problem? Well, it keeps failing to flower properly. In years like 1983 and 1984 its flowers never set and the crop was decimated. On the other hand, a little *coulure* or *millérandage* could have been an advantage in years like 1982, when it virtually flooded the valley.

MOURVÈDRE An old-fashioned, highly flavoured wine, low in alcohol, which doesn't usually ripen fully (its home base is Bandol, right on the Mediterranean). But it

has an excellent, rather berryish taste, and a strong whiff of tobacco spice that is making it increasingly popular with the more imaginative growers.

SYRAH Wine-making in the northern Rhône is dominated by this one red grape variety. Along with the Cabernet Sauvignon, Bordeaux's great grape, the Syrah makes the blackest, most startling, pungent red wine in France, and, although it is grown elsewhere, it is here that it is at its most brilliant. From Hermitage and Cornas, it rasps with tannin and tar and woodsmoke, backed by the deep, ungainly sweetness of black treacle. But give it five or ten years, and those raw fumes will have become sweet, pungent, full of raspberries, brambles and *cassis*.

Syrah is less prevalent than the Grenache in the southern Rhône, but as more is planted, the standard of southern Rhône reds is sure to rise.

VIOGNIER This aromatic white grape can be used as up to 20 per cent of the blend of red Côte-Rôtie to add fragrance and it really does: Côte-Rôtie made purely of Syrah lacks the haunting beauty of one blended with Viognier.

WINES & WINE REGIONS

CHÂTEAUNEUF-DU-PAPE, AC The largest of the ACs of the Côtes du Rhône, spreading over 3100 hectares north of Avignon, this can be quite delicious, deep, dusty red, almost sweet and fat, low in acidity, but kept appetizing by just enough back-room tannin. *Can* be. It can also be fruit-pastilly and pointless, or dark, tough and stringy. Thirteen different red and white grape varieties are permitted, and the resulting flavour is usually slightly indistinct, varying, too, from one property to another. The occasional 'super-vintage' like 1978 gives wines that can stay stunning for ten years and more. Experts reckon that perhaps one-third of the growers make good wine, and that as much as two-thirds of the wine sold on the world market exceeds the *appellation contrôlée* yields. So it makes sense always to go for a domaine wine and certainly not to buy one bottled away from the region of production. Good, full-bodied Châteauneufs include: *Château de Beaucastel, Château Rayas* and *Clos du Mont-Olivet, Château Fortia, Château St-André, La Nerte, Chante Cigale, Clos des Papes, Chante-Perdrix, Le Vieux Doujon, la Jacquinotte* and in a slightly lighter style, *Font de Michelle, Font du Loup, Clos du Mont Olivet, Brunel, Quiot, Domaine du Grand Tinel, Domaine de Mont-Redon* and *Domaine du Vieux Télégraphe*.

CORNAS, AC Black and tarry tooth-stainers, from the right bank of the Rhône, opposite Valence. Usually rather hefty, jammy even, and lacking some of the fresh fruit that makes Hermitage so remarkable, yet at ten years old this is impressive wine. There have been quite big price rises in recent years, but then quality seems to improve year by year, too. Really excellent blockbusters are made by *Auguste Clape* and *Verset*. It's also worth looking out for the wines of *de Barjac, Colombo, Delas, Juge, Lionnet* and *Michel*.

COTEAUX DU TRICASTIN, AC Constantly improving spicy, fruity reds from this large *appellation* east of the Rhône. Good value. Best producers: *Domaine de Grangeneuve, Tour d'Elyssas* (especially their 100 per cent Syrah), *Producteurs Réunis Ardéchois* (co-op).

CÔTE-RÔTIE, AC By the judicious admixture of juice from the white Viognier grape, this most northerly *appellation* of the Rhône valley is one of France's most perfumed and fragrant reds when properly made. But the *appellation* has been extended on to the flat plateau above the traditional 'roasted slope', and unless something is done to differentiate 'slopes' wines from plateau wines, the reputation of this highly prized, highly priced vineyard will be in tatters. At best, from a few individual producers such as *Gentaz-Dervieux, Jamet, Guigal* and *Jasmin*, Côte-Rôtie is a rare and delicious wine. Look out also for the wines of *Gilles and Pierre Barge, Bernard Burgaud, Champet, Albert Dervieux-Thaize, René Rostaing, Vidal-Fleury* and *Delas Cuvée Seigneur de Maugiron*.

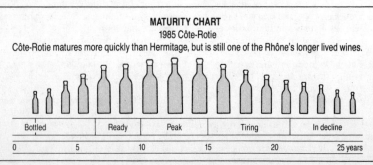

MATURITY CHART
1985 Côte-Rotie
Côte-Rotie matures more quickly than Hermitage, but is still one of the Rhône's longer lived wines.

Bottled	Ready	Peak	Tiring	In decline
0	5	10	15	20	25 years

CÔTES DU LUBÉRON, AC Upgraded from VDQS in 1987, Lubéron makes some pretty decent reds, usually rather light, but capable of stronger personality. The Val Joanis rosé is one of the best in the south. Good producers: *Château de Canorgue, Château de l'Isolette, Mas du Peyroulet, Val Joanis* (also seen under own label as *Domaines Chancel* or *Domaine de la Panisse), Vieille Ferme.*

CÔTES DU RHÔNE, AC This huge *appellation* covers 80 per cent of all the wines of the Rhône valley. It spreads out on both sides of the valley from Vienne to Avignon. Well-made basic Côtes du Rhônes are quite delicious when young, tremendously fresh and fruity, like a rather softer version of Beaujolais. Or they can be fierce, black, grape-skins-and-alcohol monsters. Since the label gives no clue, it's trial and error, or merchants' recommendations. *Coudoulet de Beaucastel* (formerly Cru de Coudoulet) is a particularly beefy version from the family who own Beaucastel, and many of the weightiest are made by Châteauneuf or Northern Rhône producers, *Guigal*, for instance. *Château du Grand Moulas* is spicy and attractive, with plenty of body. Also good: *Caves C.N. Jaume, Château de Deurre, Château de Fonsalette, Château de Goudray, Château de Ruth, Clos du Père Clément, Domaine de Bel Air, Domaine de la Cantharide, Domaine de St-Estève, Domaine des Aussellons.*

CÔTES DU RHÔNE-VILLAGES, AC One of the best areas to search for good, full reds that can also age, combining the rather earthy, dusty southern heat with a good deal of spicy, raspberryish fruit. They come from specific higher quality villages, 17 of which can add their own names on the label, including Vacqueyras, Cairanne, Chusclan, St-Gervais, Valréas, Beaumes-de-Venise and Rasteau. The local co-ops produce remarkably consistent wines, frequently now labelled under the village name. Good examples of single-grower wines are (Laudun) *Domaine Pelaquié*; (Rasteau) *Cave des Vignerons, Domaine de Grangeneuve*; (Sablet) *Jean-Pierre Cartier, Château de Trignon, Domaine de Boisson, Domaine St-Antoine, Domaine de*

Verquière; (Cairanne) *Domaine de l'Ameillaud, Domaine Brusset, Domaine l'Oratoire St-Martin, Domaine de la Présidente, Domaine Rabasse-Charavin;* (St-Gervais) *Domaine Ste-Anne;* (Séguret) *Domaine Courançonne, Domaine de Cabasse;* (Valréas) *Roger Combe, Domaine des Grands Devers, Le Val des Rois;* (Vacqueyras) *Château de Montmirail, Clos des Cazaux, Domaine la Fourmone, Domaine des Lambertins, Le Sang des Cailloux.*

CÔTES DU VENTOUX, AC Rather good area just to the east of the Rhône producing lots of fresh, juicy wine, of which the red is the best. Can occasionally be quite special as in the juicy *Domaine des Anges* and the heftier wines of *Jaboulet* and *Pascal* as well as *Vieille Ferme* and *Vieux Lazaret.*

CROZES-HERMITAGE, AC A large *appellation* on the left bank, north and south of the town of Tain l'Hermitage, providing a lot of fairly strong and slightly tough and smoky Hermitage-type wine which at its best has a lovely juicy fruit as well. *Jaboulet's Thalabert* brand is outstanding and good wine is made by *Desmeures, Ferraton, Graillot* and *Tardy & Ange.* The large Tain co-op is also finally producing some decent stuff.

GIGONDAS, AC Red and rosé wine from the village of Gigondas, west of Orange. While not the most immediately attractive of reds – a bit ragged at the edges – Gigondas is nonetheless a remarkably consistent, big, plummy, rather solid wine. *Domaine de St-Gayan* is very good, as are *Château de Montmirail, Château du Trignon, Clos des Cazeaux, Domaine les Gouberts, Domaine de Longue-Toque, Domaine l'Oustau Fauquet, Domaine les Pallières, Domaine Raspail-Ay.*

HERMITAGE, AC One of France's burliest and grandest wines from a small, precipitous vineyard area spread around

The price guides for this section begin on page 304.

the slopes of the hill of Hermitage, near the town of Tain l'Hermitage. Strong and fierily tough when young, it matures to a rich, brooding magnificence. There is always a stern, vaguely medicinal or smoky edge to red Hermitage, but also an unmatchable depth of raspberry and blackcurrant fruit. Although a reasonable number of people produce an Hermitage of sorts, there have traditionally been only two stars, the low-key but marvellously good *Chave*, who produces small amounts of impeccable wine, and the ebullient, publicity-conscious, export-orientated *Paul Jaboulet Aîné*, who produces larger amounts of more variable wine. Other good producers: *Delas Cuvée Marquise de la Tourette, Desmeure, B. Faurie, Guigal, Sorrel, Ferraton* and *Fayolle*.

LIRAC, AC An excellent and often underrated area just south-west of Châteauneuf whose wines it can frequently equal. The reds are packed with fruit, often tinged with a not unwelcome mineral edge. The rosés are remarkably fresh for so far south. And they're cheap. Whites can be first-class if caught young enough. Best producers: *Domaine de Château St-Roch, Domaine des Causses et St-Eymes, Domaine la Fermade, Domaine les Garrigues, Domaine de la Tour.*

ST-JOSEPH, AC Almost smooth and sweet by comparison with their tougher neighbours, these reds, especially those from the hillsides of the long stretch along the right bank of the river, between Condrieu and Cornas, can be fairly big, fine wines, stacked with blackcurrant in a good year. There has been some expansion of the *appellation* wine into unsuitable terrain, but the quality is still mostly high, and though there have recently been hefty price rises, the wines *were* undervalued. *Chave, Coursodon, Florentin, Gripa, Grippat, Jaboulet* and *Trollat* are leading producers. The co-operative at *St-Désirat Champagne* is the chief producer of 'Beaujolais-type' St-Joseph which may not be traditional, but is a lovely drink.

TAVEL, AC The AC only applies to one colour of wine – pink! The wines are quite expensive, certainly tasty, but too big and

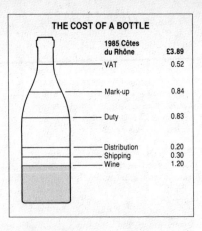

THE COST OF A BOTTLE

1985 Côtes du Rhône	£3.89
VAT	0.52
Mark-up	0.84
Duty	0.83
Distribution	0.20
Shipping	0.30
Wine	1.20

alcoholic to be very refreshing. It can be made with any of the Côtes du Rhône grape varieties, but generally it's Grenache-dominated, with a little Cinsaut. Best producers: *Château d'Aqueria, Château de Trinquevedel, Domaine de la Forcadière, Domaine de la Génestière.*

VIN DE PAYS DES COLLINES RHODANIENNES An expanding and usually impressive northern Rhône area, particularly good for inexpensive, strongly flavoured Syrah reds, though Gamay can also be good.

VIN DE PAYS DES COTEAUX DE L'ARDÈCHE This straggly, upland Rhône *département* puts into a nutshell what the *vins de pays* should be trying to achieve. Not content with the usual mishmash of southern grapes, a mixture of good, go-ahead co-ops and outside influences decided to plant varieties to make wine that would *sell*: delicious Beaujolais Nouveau-style Gamay, first class Syrah, good Cabernet, and they've planted Sauvignon Blanc, Pinot Noir – and Chardonnay. *Louis Latour*, one of the largest sellers of Burgundian Chardonnay, has inspired much of the Chardonnay planting here for his Chardonnay de l'Ardèche. 60 local growers have planted Chardonnay and are contracted to Latour. That's good news. But the news that the local co-ops are already producing higher quality wines at far lower prices – without his help – is much better!

WHITE WINES

The two main styles of northern Rhône white could hardly be more different. The wines based on Marsanne and Roussanne – Hermitage, Crozes-Hermitage, St-Joseph and St-Péray – are in general weighty, strong, initially lacking in perfume and charm, but capable of a great, opulent, Lord Mayor-like, broad richness, given the decade or so they need to mature. Some modern versions, like those of Jaboulet, are less ambitious but ready within the year. The wines based on the Viognier are heavenly – totally different in style, bursting with the fruit flavours of apricots and pears and a mad, heady perfume like flower gardens in spring. Very special.

The interest in Southern Rhône whites is fairly recent because it had always been assumed, with justification, that white wine from the region's non-aromatic grapes, produced on parched vineyards in the baking summer heat, could not possibly be anything but dull and flabby and fruitless. Now that many leading producers have invested in refrigerated equipment, and adopted cool fermentation techniques, it is quite remarkable what delicious, soft, scented flavours are beginning to appear. The vintage of 1989 was particularly good and should make for some exciting drinking in two or three years.

GRAPES & FLAVOURS

CLAIRETTE Makes sparkling Clairette de Die, but is a bit dull unless livened up with the aromatic Muscat. In the south it makes rather big, strong whites, occasionally creamy, but more often dull and nutty. Needs careful handling and early drinking.

GRENACHE BLANC A widely planted variety in the southern Rhône producing appley wines with a strong whiff of aniseed. Good, but soft, so drink young.

MARSANNE The dominant of the two grapes that go to make white Hermitage and Crozes-Hermitage, as well as white St-Joseph and St-Péray. Its wine is big and weighty but with a rather good, rich, sweet scent. Further south it makes big, burly wine, fat, lanoliny, but capable of rich exotic peach and toffee flavours, too. A good quality producer.

MUSCAT Used to great effect blended with Clairette to make the sparkling Clairette de Die Tradition, but more famous for Muscat de Beaumes de Venise.

ROUSSANNE An altogether more delicate and fragrant grape than the Marsanne, but it is prone to disease and also a low yielder, so it is increasingly losing ground to Marsanne. Found chiefly in Hermitage and St-Péray in the northern Rhône, though it also produces light, fragrant wines further south in Châteauneuf-du-Pape.

UGNI BLANC Boring workhorse grape planted all over the south to produce basic gulping stuff.

VIOGNIER The grape of Condrieu and Château Grillet. It has one of the most memorable flavours of any white grape because it manages to blend the rich, musky scent of an overripe apricot with the breeze-blown perfume of springtime orchard flowers. Autumn and spring in one glass. The wine is made dry, but it is so rich you hardly believe it! The rarest of the world's great grapes, though interest in planting it is growing.

WINES & WINE REGIONS

CHÂTEAU GRILLET, AC A single property in the far north-west of the northern Rhône, and the smallest individual *appellation contrôlée* in France at only three hectares, excepting a couple of Vosne-Romanée *grands crus* in Burgundy. This wine should have that magic reek of orchard fruit and harvest bloom about it. Sometimes it does.

CHÂTEAUNEUF-DU-PAPE BLANC, AC Only three per cent of the AC is white, but the wines can be outstandingly perfumed and fragrant with a delicious nip of acidity, leaving you wondering how on earth such aromatic wines could come from such a hot, arid region. Magic, that's what; or it might be such delights as Roussanne, Picpoul and Picardan varieties adding something to the base of Grenache Blanc, Clairette and Bourboulenc. Most likely, the

reason is that across the world there are special slashes of earth and microclimates that produce wonderful wines in the most unlikely places – and this is one of them. Although the wine can age OK, you lose that perfumed rush of springtime madness after a year. Best producers: *Beaucastel* (especially their pure Roussanne *Vieille Vigne* cuvée), *Clefs d'Or, Clos des Papes, Font de Michelle, Nalys, Rayas, Vieux Télégraphe*.

CLAIRETTE DE DIE BRUT, AC Adequate fizz from the Clairette grape grown in the beautiful Drôme valley, east of the Rhône.

CLAIRETTE DE DIE TRADITION, AC Delicious, light, off-dry, grapy fizz made half from Clairette, half from Muscat grapes.

RHÔNE VINTAGES

1989 Now being compared favourably with 1988, but 1989 wasn't a vintage which produced wines of uniform quality. Drought affected much of the region meaning that young vines were badly stressed, often depriving the ripening grapes of nutrients and sap. This may have inspired some growers in Hermitage to pick too early, before the bunches had properly ripened. Place your trust in good winemakers and knowledgeable wine merchants.

1988 There is certainly *some* great 1988 wine. But only some. And what there is is likely to be slow-maturing, dense-flavoured wine for the long haul. But while the best winemakers in Côte-Rôtie, Hermitage and Châteauneuf-du-Pape made some stunning stuff, there is a fair amount of wine around which is far too tannic for its own good. The standard in the southern Côtes du Rhône-Villages is high, and the wines show a lot of fruit to go with their tannic structure.

1987 White Châteauneuf was actually rather good, but the red isn't special. Ordinary Côtes du Rhône reds *can* be delicious, though. Northern Rhônes can be good from dedicated growers.

1986 A rather joyless vintage for reds, as in most of the rest of France. Some reasonable Châteauneuf and Hermitage but the ambitious Côtes du Rhône properties made some of the best wines. Whites were good, and some still will be.

1985 Brilliant Côte-Rôtie, St-Joseph and Cornas. Hermitage could have been as good if its leading producers had tried a bit harder. Châteauneuf is delicious and juicy.

1983 Outstanding dark, rich, complex Hermitage and very good Côte-Rôtie, but don't drink them yet. Southern reds are good, but the failure of the Grenache crop left some of them a bit tough.

1982 Good, rather simple northern reds, soft southern reds. Good for current drinking.

1981 Nothing special in the north, but very good Châteauneuf now at its peak.

1980 Underrated but high quality in north and south.

1978 Fantastic north *and* south. The best vintage since 1961. Drink now — if you can find any.

CONDRIEU, AC From a small vineyard area at the northern end of the Northern Rhône, this is wonderful white wine when properly made, with apricot scent that leaps out of the glass, and an exciting balance between succulent fruit and gentle, nipping acidity. But its sudden popularity has led to considerable replanting, sometimes by people primarily interested in high prices rather than high quality. The potential quality is so stunning, however, that hopefully the *arrivistes* will realize that the real product is worth striving for. The potential vineyard area is 200 hectares, but there are still only just over 20 planted, so there's very little wine; and it's expensive, though less than half the price of Château Grillet. A recent departure has been the release of *cépage* Viognier wine (the grape used in Château Grillet), which will show you why we get so excited about Viognier – at half the Condrieu price. (Yapp have one.) Very good producers include *Château du Rozay, Delas, Dumazet, Guigal, Jean Pinchon* and *Georges Vernay.*

COTEAUX DU TRICASTIN, AC Fresh, fruity and quite full-flavoured southerly whites, not as exciting as the reds. *Producteurs Réunis Ardéchois* are probably the best bet.

CÔTES DU LUBÉRON, AC Usually pleasant and light southern wine but little more, though recent innovations have started to produce much more fragrant, interesting styles at such properties as *Château de l'Isolette, Mas du Peyroulet, Val Joanis* and *Vieille Ferme.*

CÔTES DU RHÔNE BLANC, AC; CÔTES DU RHÔNE-VILLAGES BLANC, AC Increasingly fresh, fruity and gulpable especially from the villages of Laudun and Chusclan. *Domaine Pelaquié* at Laudun is the leading estate, and *Domaine Ste-Anne* at St-Gervais is good.

CROZES-HERMITAGE, AC Generally a rather dull, strong northern Rhône white, but there are good ones from *Desmeure, Fayolle, Jaboulet* and *Pradelle.*

HERMITAGE, AC Often a bit heavy and dull, but curiously it ages tremendously well to a soft, rich nuttiness. Some of the finest is made by *Chapoutier, Chave, Desmeure, Ferraton, Grippat* and *Sorrel.*

LIRAC, AC The whites can be some of the best in the south if caught young. Can resemble a less exotic Châteauneuf-du-Pape. Less exotic flavour; less exotic price.

ST-JOSEPH, AC Northern Rhône *appellation*, not as interesting for white as for red, although some fairly pleasant, nutty wine is made. *Grippat* is good. *Florentin* makes a remarkable intense, earthy old-style headbanging white quite unlike any other.

ST-PÉRAY, AC Made in the southern bit of the Northern Rhône, this was once France's most famous sparkling wine after Champagne. Not any more. It tends to be rather stolid and short of freshness. And the still whites are just dull. The occasional better bottle will come from *Chaboud, Clape, Grippat, Juge* or *Voge.*

FORTIFIED WINES

MUSCAT DE BEAUMES DE VENISE, AC This Côtes du Rhône village is the only place in the Rhône to grow the Muscat grape. The golden sweet wine – a *vin doux naturel* – has become a real fad drink, but for once the fad is a good one, because it's supremely delicious! Grapy, fresh, rich but not cloying. Look for *Domaine de Coyeux, Domaine Durban, Jaboulet* and the *Beaumes de Venise* co-op.

RASTEAU, AC The Côtes du Rhône village of Rasteau also makes a few big, port-like fortified wines – *vins doux naturels* – both red and off-white. Young ones can have a delightful raspberry scent from the Grenache Noir. The whites are made from Grenache Blanc and can be frankly unpleasant. Production is pretty small. Try *Domaine de la Soumade, Co-opérative de Rasteau.*

LOIRE

We're so used to hearing hyperbole from French winemakers that, when a truly outstanding vintage comes along, the temptation is to yawn, roll the eyeballs and ask 'Not another one, surely?'. But take it from me, 1989 was an exceptional vintage in the Loire. As one grower in Chinon put it, ecstatically contemplating the condition of his grapes last September, 'Vintages of the century are easy. We produce one of those every few years. This is a vintage of the millennium'.

Well, was it? Was 1989 really better than 1947, 1959, 1976 and 1985? To be honest, I'm not sure we should worry. There were some tremendously ripe wines made last year, a vintage of abundant sunshine, so my advice is to go out and buy them. Loire wines are rarely short of acidity, as anyone who has tried to drink Chenin Blanc in its raw youth will appreciate, but in 1989 there was plenty of balancing fruit and natural alcohol.

The wines, then, are full and aromatic. If there is a question mark against the vintage, it concerns longevity. Some of the Sauvignon Blancs, in particular, are wines to drink now rather than in two years. The Gamays are ready too. The Cabernet Franc, on the other hand, produced wines with lush fruit and ripe tannins that should also age. Some are showing beautifully already; others from top producers like Charles Joguet, Couly-Dutheil and Olga Raffault in Chinon, Pierre-Jacques Druet and Pierre Breton in Bourgueil, François Roussier in Anjou or Joël Taluau in St-Nicolas de Bourgueil, have got the concentration and depth to stay the course. It really is time we started regarding Loire Cabernets as something more than charming summer tipples.

If some of the reds are a revelation, they are arguably surpassed by the region's sweet wines. I have never been a great fan of Chenin Blanc, but this year I have been converted. The drier styles, for once, have enough fresh, appley fruit to handle the acidity. And the sweeter wines – such as Vouvray, Coteaux du Layon and Coteaux de l'Aubance – have a wonderful, honeyed, peachy richness to them. Vincent Ogereau's Coteaux du Layon and Jean-Yves Lebreton's Coteaux de l'Aubance are two of the most enjoyable wines I've tasted this year. They are also comparatively cheap.

Another exciting development in the Loire is the emergence of talented young winemakers like Pascal Cailleau at the Domaine de Sauveroy in Anjou, Pierre-Jacques Druet in Bourgueil and Christophe Daviau at the Domaine de Bablut in Brissac. As in Burgundy, the new generation is travelling more, tasting foreign wines, and questioning wine-making shibboleths. Stainless steel, shorter macerations of grape skins with juice, temperature control, and, in some cases, new *barriques* are coming in; chestnut casks and concrete vats are passing them in the opposite direction.

The Loire is one of the great treasure troves of wine. There is, as they say of the January sales, something for everyone. The wines are generally cheap, well-made and drinkable, which is more than you can say for a country like Chile – the current obsession of the fashion-conscious wine drinker. Occasionally, of course, they are a lot more complex. If you've never thought of drinking a lesser-known wine from the Loire, this is the vintage with which to start.   TIM ATKIN

WHITE GRAPES & FLAVOURS

CHARDONNAY Increasingly widespread in the Loire and producing lean, light but tangy results in Haut-Poitou, in Anjou as Vin de Pays du Jardin de la France and in Orléans as Vin de l'Orléanais (where it's called Auvernat: *Clos St-Fiacre* is absolutely delicious). It also occurs in Muscadet (*Le Chouan* and *Domaine Couillaud* are found in the UK) and is allowed in Anjou Blanc up to 15 per cent to add character and softness.

CHASSELAS Makes adequate but dull wine at Pouilly-sur-Loire; it's actually best as a table grape, in a fruit salad.

CHENIN BLANC A grape that cries out for sun and ripens (if that's the word) at least a fortnight after the other varieties. It may be Anjou's chief variety, but it's so unpopular that the authorities judge a grape type's right to earn a 'premium' rating by gauging how soon *before* the Chenin it ripens. Latest experiments with allowing the skins to steep in the juice before fermentation, and the quiet addition of a bit of Chardonnay, are beginning to produce outstanding peachy whites which make brilliant summer drinking.

It also performs superbly on the Loire in a few warm and misty microclimates (especially Quarts de Chaume and Bonnezeaux), where, with hot, south-facing slopes, and a river to provide dampening autumn mists, noble rot strikes the Chenin with enough frequency to make it worthwhile going through all the pain and passion of producing great sweet wine, with steely acidity and honeyed, ripe-apple fruit. These wines can seem curiously disappointing when they're young, but fine sweet Chenin manages to put on weight and become sweeter and sweeter for perhaps 20 years before bursting out into a richness as exciting as all but the very best German or Bordeaux sweet white. And it will stay there for many years more.

MELON DE BOURGOGNE The grape of Muscadet, light and neutral. It's good at producing fresh, surprisingly soft, slightly peppery, dry white wine with a salty tang, generally for drinking young, though a good domaine-bottled *sur lie* can mature surprisingly well.

SAUVIGNON BLANC The grape of Sancerre, and the main white grape of Touraine, with a whole range of fresh, green, tangy flavours that might remind you of anything from asparagus through gooseberries to nettles and fresh-cut grass, and there's sometimes even a whiff of newly roasted coffee. The wines are usually quite tart – but thirst-quenching rather than gum-searing – and have loadsafruit.

WHITE WINES & WINE REGIONS

ANJOU BLANC SEC, AC France's cheapest AC dry white made from the hard-to-ripen Chenin Blanc, grown anywhere in the large Anjou area upriver from the Muscadet region, often tart, sulphured and sour. But it *can* be good, steely and honeyed, especially from Savennières with its two tiny special ACs, Coulée-de-Serrant and La Roche aux Moines, and from an increasing number of growers such as *Domaine Richou* who are beginning to mix Chardonnay with their Chenin, for extra flavour, fruit and body. They are allowed to plant their white vineyards with up to 20 per cent Chardonnay or Sauvignon Blanc. Some have planted a little bit more on the side, and it's no bad thing. Other good producers are *Baranger, Château de Valliennes, Jaudeau.*

BONNEZEAUX, AC One of the most unfairly forgotten great sweet wines of France. After a long period of decline, this small AC centred round Thouarcé inside the larger Coteaux du Layon is on the up again. The vineyard area has grown from 42 hectares in 1975 to 157 hectares in 1985 and prices for the lovely noble-rot-affected sweet wines are rising fast. So much the better; they were far too cheap before, and if you don't make it profitable for the growers to indulge themselves in the passion and commitment necessary to make great sweet wine, they'll give up and plant apples. Look out especially for the outstanding Bonnezeaux of *Jacques Boivin* of *Château de Fesles* as well as *Goizil*, *Renou* and *Denéchère*.

COTEAUX DE L'AUBANCE, AC A

rambling *appellation* south of Anjou giving pleasant semi-sweet whites at a pretty low price. *Gérard Chauvin* at *Domaine des Rochettes*, *Jean-Yves Lebreton* and *Domaine Richou* make excellent Coteaux de l'Aubance.

COTEAUX DU LAYON, AC A large

appellation along the steep banks of the Layon river producing varying qualities of sweet white wine, at its best rich and tasty with a taut, cutting acidity that allows the wine to age for a long time. *Château de la Guimonière*, *Château de la Roulerie*, *Domaine Ambinois*, *Domaine du Petit Val*, *Domaine des Quarres*, *Domaine de la Soucherie* and *Ogereau* are worth seeking out and reasonably priced.

CRÉMANT DE LOIRE, AC Sparkling

wine AC intended to denote higher quality but not used to any great extent by Loire winemakers. Compared with Saumur AC fizz, the yield must be lower (50 rather than 60 hectolitres per hectare), the juice extract less (you must use 150kg of grapes as against 130kg to make one hectolitre of juice), and the wine must lie on its lees after second fermentation for 12 months rather than 9. The product is usually softer and more enjoyable than the frequently harsh products of Saumur, but the merchants have built up their brands on the name Saumur and don't seem inclined to put much effort into Crémant de Loire. Laudable exceptions are the first-rate house of *Gratien & Meyer*, *St-Cyr-en-Bourg* co-op, and the small *Cave des Liards*.

The price guides for this section begin on page 313.

GROS PLANT, VDQS Gros Plant rejoices

in being one of the rawest wines in France, and the prosperity of dentists in the Nantes area is thanks in no small measure to the local inhabitants' predilection for the stuff. That said, it *does* go amazingly well with seafood and is one of the wines that seems to suit oysters. *Bossard* manages to produce an example with a soft honeyed flavour. The dentists must be furious.

HAUT-POITOU, AC Produced in an

isolated area well to the south of the main Loire vineyards. Chardonnay and Sauvignon from the *Cave Co-opérative du Haut-Poitou* are good but tending to the lean side.

MENETOU-SALON, AC Small but

expanding AC to the west of Sancerre making pretty good Sauvignons (and some fair reds and rosés). The *Vignerons Jacques Coeur* co-operative group, which spends most of its time organizing cereal farmers, is very important here and produces about half the Sauvignon wine. It's usually pretty tasty. *Alain Gogué*, *Henri Pellé*, *Jean-Max Roger* and *Jean Teiller* also make good wine. Prices are keen, and always lower than Sancerre.

MONTLOUIS, AC Chenin area to the

south of Vouvray. Makes very similar wines, but frequently more robust – though that, when it comes to the Chenin grape, isn't always such a good thing. The wines of *Dominique Moyer*, *Domaine des Liards* and *Jean-Pierre Trouvé* are good, but too many Montlouis are short on fruit and long on sulphur.

MUSCADET, AC Simple, light and

neutral wine from the Nantes area of southern Brittany, near the Atlantic. Straight Muscadet, without any further regional title, is usually flat and boring. But at least it will never be heavy – the Muscadet *appellations* are the only ones in France to impose a *maximum* alcohol level (12.3 per cent)!

MUSCADET DE SÈVRE-ET-MAINE,

AC The biggest Muscadet area, around the Sèvre and Maine rivers, making the most but also the best wine. A good one may taste slightly nutty, peppery or salty, even honeyed, sometimes with a creaminess from being left on the lees, sometimes a chewy apricot-skin taste and sometimes with a slight prickle. It should always have a lemony acidity, and should feel light. Buy domaine-bottled wine only, and check the address at the bottom, looking out especially for *St-Fiacre* and *Le Pallet*, two of the best villages.

MUSCADET DES COTEAUX DE LA LOIRE, AC A small area along the banks of the Loire east of Nantes. In quality, it's somewhere between Muscadet and Muscadet de Sèvre-et-Maine.

MUSCADET SUR LIE This is the most important thing to look out for on a Muscadet label – even though not all producers use the term honestly. The 'lie' is the lees or yeast sediment left behind after fermentation. Winemakers in most parts of the world transfer their wine into a clean cask or vat soon after fermentation, leaving the lees behind. But the Muscadet tradition is to leave the new wine undisturbed on the lees until bottling. This does two things for the taste: the wine picks up yeasty, salty flavours, and it keeps its fresh, young, prickly character. Some producers are demanding that the term *sur lie* should only be allowed for domaine-bottled wines, while others tell them not to be so boringly pernickety, and why not shut up and let the large merchants get on with making decent profits out of mediocre Muscadet. I still say – only buy *sur lie* Muscadet labelled *mise en bouteille à la propriété / château / domaine*. You'll get some dud bottles, but it will be a sign of support for the good growers. Some merchants, such as *Sauvion*, have portable bottling lines, and bottle properly *sur lie* at the grower's cellar. Their *Château du Cléray* and the *Découvertes* range of single domaines are particularly good. *Guy Bossard* makes good organic Muscadet de Sèvre-et-Maine *sur lie*, and of an expanding range of enjoyable single domaine wines, these are particularly good: *Domaine de Coursay-Villages, Domaine de la Montaine, Château de Chasseloir, Clos de la Sénaigerie, Domaine du 'Perd-son-pain'. Chéreau-Carré* and both *Michel* and

Donatien Bahuaud's single domaine wines are generally top-notch, if expensive, and *Bonhomme* and *Guilbaud* sell a fair range of wines.

POUILLY-FUMÉ, AC Just over the river from Sancerre and very similar. The wines are said to smell of gunflint because of their smokiness. Being of a non-violent disposition, I find this difficult to prove, but perhaps it's the Sauvignon's occasional pungent coffee smell they mean. Top growers are *Bailly, Blanchet, Château de Tracy, André Dezat, Didier Dagueneau, André Figeat, Guyot* and the too-expensive *de Ladoucette*.

POUILLY-SUR-LOIRE, AC Made from the dull Chasselas grape which makes good eating but not memorable drinking. Rarely seen outside the area, but *Hervé Seguin* makes a fair example you might see.

QUARTS DE CHAUME, AC A tiny 40-hectare AC in the Layon valley with a perfect microclimate for nobly-rotted sweet wines. They are rare and expensive, not quite as sweet as top Sauternes, but they can be even more intense, with a high acid stalking the rich apricot and honey fruit. *Jean Baumard* makes superb wine; also look for *Château de Bellerive* and *Château de l'Echarderie*.

QUINCY, AC Fairly pungent Sauvignon Blanc wines grown west of Sancerre. *Denis Jaumier, Pierre Mardon, Jacques Rouzé* and the co-op *Jacques Coeur* make good examples.

REUILLY, AC Light, fragrant Sauvignon Blanc wines from near Quincy, west of Sancerre. *Henri Beurdin* and *Gérard Cordier* are the important growers. (There is also some tasty red and rosé.)

SANCERRE, AC Green, smoky, tangy wine from the Sauvignon Blanc grape grown at the eastern end of the Loire. Drunk young when it's at its best, it should be superfresh and fruity, with a flavour and fragrance like gooseberries or fresh-cut grass, and a brilliant balance between sharpness and ripe, round body. But all too often it smells sulphurous or meaty, and tastes simply flabby. As usual in the Loire, look for single-domaine wines – especially those of *Henri Bourgeois, Château de Thauvenay, Clos du Chêne Marchand, Francis & Paul Cotat, Christian Daulny, Pierre & Alain Dézat, Alain Gueneau, Michel Naudet, Henri Natter, Bernard Noël-Reverdy, Jean-Max Roger, Pierre Riffault, Christian Salmon, Jean Vacheron* and *Jean Vatan*.

SAUMUR, AC Champagne-method wine made from Chenin grapes, sometimes with the welcome addition of Chardonnay, Sauvignon or even Cabernet Franc, any of which can give a bit more roundness to the acid Chenin. Well-made sparkling Saumur (including a little rosé) is lively and appley but too many are just too rough to revel with. Best producers: *Ackerman Laurance, Bouvet-Ladubay, Gratien & Meyer*, and *Langlois-Château*.

SAUMUR BLANC, AC White, usually ultra-dry, though it can occasionally be sweet, similar to Anjou Blanc. Best from the *St-Cyr-en-Bourg* co-op.

SAVENNIÈRES, AC Some of the steeliest, longest-living, diamond-dry white wines in the world come from this tiny Anjou *appellation* just west of Angers. One vineyard, Savennières Coulée-de-Serrant, has its own AC within Savennières, and *Madame Joly*'s wines from the *Clos de la Coulée-de-Serrant* are extremely fine. Look out also for the wines of *Yves Soulez* from the *Château de Chamboreau, Domaine de la Bizolière* and the *Domaine aux Moines*.

THOUARSAIS, VDQS Almost forgotten VDQS to the south of Saumur, where *Michel Gigon* makes very attractive, grassy-fresh reds and whites.

TOURAINE, AC Everybody sees Touraine Sauvignon, with some justification, as a Sancerre substitute. The *Confrérie des Vignerons de Oisly-et-Thésée* sell to half the British wine trade, and their wines are good, as are *Château de l'Aulée, Domaine de la Charmoise, Domaine des Corbillières, Domaine Joël Delaunay, Domaine Octavie* and *Gérald Angier*.

VIN DE PAYS DU JARDIN DE LA FRANCE The general title for *vin de pays* throughout the Loire valley. Usually light and unmemorable, though pleasant, but the results can be impressive, especially when based on Sauvignon and Chardonnay. *Biotteau's Château d'Avrille Chardonnay*, and *Domaine des Hauts de Saulière's Chardonnay* have lovely fruit.

VOUVRAY, AC Sparkling wine and still whites ranging from the tangily dry to the liquorously sweet, though usually caught in the middle. In fact Vouvray is best at producing the off-dry demi-sec style, and from a good producer this Chenin wine, initially all searing acidity and rasping dryness, over a number of years develops a delicious, deep, nutty, honey-and-cream, slightly exotically fruity wine. Sadly, most commercial Vouvray is poor. Good producers are: *Bertier-Pichot, Brédif, Bourillon Dorléans, Château Moncontour, Foreau, Huet* and *Prince Poniatowski*.

RED & ROSÉ GRAPES & FLAVOURS

CABERNET SAUVIGNON This doesn't always ripen too well in the Loire, but even so it is planted a fair bit to add some firm backbone to the wines. It is really at its best in the ripest years.

CABERNET FRANC The great quality grape of Anjou and Touraine. All the best reds are based on Cabernet Franc, and the styles go from the palest, most fleeting of reds to deep, strong, proud wines of great character and considerable longevity.

GAMAY This rarely achieves the lovely, juicy glugginess of Beaujolais, but when it is made by a careful modern winemaker it can have a fair amount of fruit, though it always has a tough edge.

PINOT NOIR In Sancerre and the neighbouring villages, this can sometimes produce a lovely, light, cherry-fragrant wine that will be either a rosé or a light red. But really interesting examples are rare in the Loire.

RED & ROSÉ WINES & WINE REGIONS

ANJOU ROUGE CABERNET, AC Until a few years ago Anjou Rouge was a byword for raw, rasping red fit to drive a chap to Liebfraumilch. But an increasing amount of excellent red is now made, light and dry from the co-ops, up to spicy, strong and capable of considerable maturity from the best domaines. The top wines can rival Bourgueil in quality. Best producers: *Château d'Avrille, Château de Chamboureau (Soulez), Clos de Coulaine, Domaine de la Petite Croix, Domaine du Petit Val, Domaine des Rochettes (Chauvin), Logis de la Giraudière (Baumard), Richou, Roussier.*

ANJOU ROUGE GAMAY, AC Rarely more than adequate, but in the hands of someone like *Richou*, the 'rooty' character is replaced by a fresh, creamy fruit that is sharp and soft all at once, and *very* good. *Domaine des Quarres* is also worth a bottle or two.

ANJOU-VILLAGES, AC A new AC for red wine from the 46 best villages in Anjou, declared in October 1987. Only Cabernet Franc and Cabernet Sauvignon may be used, and the basic permitted yields are the same as for Anjou Rouge. Some will be labelled 'Anjou-Villages Val-de-Loire' – an optional extra. 1987 wasn't the greatest year to start out with, but the signs are hopeful and in 1988 the improvements should begin to be obvious.

BOURGUEIL, AC Along with Chinon and St-Nicolas de Bourgueil, the best reds of the Loire come from this AC in Touraine. They are usually quite light and very dry, and when they are young they can taste a bit harsh and edgy, but give them a few years and they will have a piercing blackcurrant fruitiness, sharp and thirst-quenching. They can age remarkably well, and should end up at ten years or so resembling a particularly pure claret. Good producers include *Audebert* (estate wines), *Breton, Caslot-Galbrun, Caslot-Jamet, Chasle, Domaine des Forges, Domaine des Raguenières (Maître et Viémont), Druet, Lamé-Delille-Boucard.*

CABERNET D'ANJOU, AC (Rosé) There is a reasonable chance of a pleasant drink here, because the Cabernets – mostly Cabernet Franc, but often with some Cabernet Sauvignon in there too – do give pretty tasty wine, and it is usually made a good deal less sweet than simple Rosé d'Anjou. Various estates make it well – *Domaine Baranger, Domaine de Richou, Domaine de Hardières, Château de Valliennes.*

CHINON, AC From a good producer in a ripe year (1982, '83, '85, '88, '89), Chinon, an AC within the Touraine AC, is the most delicious of all Loire reds. It gets straight into its stride, exhibiting from the start a great gush of blackcurrant and raspberry with the acid strongly evident just as it would be in fresh-picked fruit. There's an earthiness too, but it is soft and strangely cooling in its effect, and after a few years it seems to dissolve into the clear, mouthwatering fruit of the vine. Domaine wines are *far* better than *négociant* wines, which can be rather thin and insipid. Best producers: *Baudry, Couly-Dutheil, Raymond Desbourdes, Domaine du Colombier, Domaine du Roucée, Domaine de la Tour, Druet, Gatien Ferrand, René Gouron, Charles Joguet, Le Logis de la Bouchardière, Pierre Manzagol, Jean François Olek, Olga Raffault, Raymond Raffault.*

HAUT-POITOU, AC Fairly 'green' but reasonably enjoyable reds from the Loire hinterland, usually made from Gamay.

ROSÉ D'ANJOU, AC The omnipresent and frequently omnihorrid French rosé. It is based on a pretty feeble grape, the Groslot, and suffers in the main from lack of fruit and excess of sulphur. A few producers like the co-op at *Brissac* can make it fresh and bright.

ROSÉ DE LOIRE, AC A rosé from Anjou or Touraine. It was intended to cater for the move in public taste to drier wines. However, the public decided it was tired of rosé in general and switched to dry white!

SANCERRE ROUGE, AC In general a much overrated wine from the Pinot Noir, but just occasionally you can find a fleeting cherry-ripe fragrance and lingering sweetness of strawberries that can even survive a year or two in bottle. If it weren't for the silly price it would be a good wine for a whimsical state of mind. Efforts to make the wine in new oak barrels haven't impressed me very much yet but it may well improve. *Pierre and André Dezat* are my favourites.

SAUMUR ROUGE, AC Usually very light and dry Cabernet Franc from 38 villages round Saumur, but despite the lightness, the fruit is often very marked and attractively blackcurranty. The co-op at *St-Cyr-en-Bourg* is good.

SAUMUR-CHAMPIGNY, AC Cabernet red from the best villages in the Saumur region. Deeper and more exciting than straight Saumur, the fruit is a marvellous reeking blackcurrant, appetizing and satisfying at the same time. *Domaine Filliatreau* makes an 'old vines' wine which is outstanding. Other good producers: *Château de Chaintres, Château du Hureau, Domaine Dubois, Domaine Lavigne, Domaine Sauzay-Legrand, Denis Duveau.*

ST-NICOLAS DE BOURGUEIL, AC These Cabernet reds from an AC within Touraine AC are supposed to be lighter and more forward than nearby Bourgueils but, though I've found them lighter, I also think they are earthier and less fruity. They can be good, but I'd stick to warm years if I were you. The wines of *Claude Ammeux, Jean-Paul Mabileau* and *Joël Taluau* seem best for consistency and style.

TOURAINE, AC The reds aren't usually very exciting, being rather green and stalky on the whole. They are often Gamay-based but may be made from a variety of grapes, including Cabernet. The *Domaine de la Charmoise (Marionet)*, and the co-op of *Oisly-et-Thésée* produce quite good Gamays.

VIN DE PAYS DES MARCHES DE BRETAGNE These wines from the mouth of the Loire are usually fairly flimsy numbers, but a good grower can use the denomination to produce something unusual and exciting. *Guy Bossard*, for instance, a leading Muscadet producer, makes an amazingly fragrant and fruity red from the Cabernet Franc which I've managed to clock as high-class Chinon in blind tasting!

LOIRE VINTAGES

Loire vintages are *very* important, and can be radically different along the river length. In poor vintages, Muscadet is most likely to be OK, while in hot vintages Sauvignon goes dull, but the Chenin finally ripens. The red grapes need the warm years.

1989 A truly exceptional year in the Loire, particularly for sweet whites which are utterly gorgeous, made from Chenin Blanc, now being compared with the legendary 1947s. Red grapes everywhere reached full ripeness. Care is needed with the dry whites though; some lack acidity and are heavy as a result. Oddity of the year: the sweet, botrytis-affected Sancerre in new oak spotted in at least two cellars in the area!

1988 The Sancerres and Pouilly-Fumés were delicious early and are developing well. The Touraine reds and whites were all ripe for once, and the market is full of lovely juicy wine. Muscadet was first class and the wines are still enjoyable, especially the *sur lie*.

1987 Some excellent Muscadet (still drinking well), and despite vintage time rain, a surprising number of good, soft reds. The best Sancerres and Pouilly-Fumés are dry but very true to type.

1986 A good Muscadet year, though the wines need drinking up, an average Anjou one, and – at last – a tremendous success in Sancerre and Pouilly-Fumé whose best cuvées are still excellent.

1985 Tremendously ripe up and down the valley. Touraine made lovely reds, and Anjou made marvellous wines, lots of exciting reds and very fine Chenin whites – both sweet and dry.

ALSACE

As a literary critic might put it, Alsace presents a problem of interpretation. Historically, the region has been pampered successively by Germans and French, French and Germans so that the Alsatians are used to being spoilt, coddled and fought over. These days the Alsatians will tell you they are French (which of course they are), and that their language is a 'French patois' (which of course it isn't – it's a German dialect).

Of course Francophiles will tell you that Alsace is typically French. For them Germany starts at the Rhine. The truth is that culturally, Germany starts at the Vosges and Alsace is in it (next time you are in Germany, look at the posters advertising holidays in *Elsass*, where Germans will feel 'at home'). Alsatian food demonstrates how good German food can be when you refine it. It is the best of German food, and not even Vienna can match it.

The same problem of interpretation prevents a reasonable evaluation of the wines. Yields are distinctly German. 'What do you do', they ask you, wringing their hands, 'when you prune right back and you still get 100 hl/ha? Throw the extra grapes away?'. Nonsense, you make wine. If you have a *grand cru* vineyard (where the maximum is 60) you declassify. You can sell more that way.

All that may seem a trifle harsh, and it should be emphasized at this point that Alsace wines are good, and some of them outstanding. Ignore the cheap Edelzwickers (blends of different grapes) so beloved of tourists and go for varietal wines: Riesling, Sylvaner, Pinot Blanc, Pinot Gris, dry Muscat and Gewürztraminer. With the possible exception of Sylvaner (though there *are* good Sylvaners, with weight), they are all big, recognizable flavours. Perfect wines to cut your teeth on.

Unlike most of the German wines made from the same grapes across the border in Baden, virtually all Alsatian wine is dry and high in alcohol. They make excellent food wines. In the region they will drink white wines with meat without question, and a good Alsatian Riesling is wonderful with the local chickens in cream sauces (*poulet au Riesling*, for example). The dry Muscat is a magnificent complement to asparagus (also grown locally – on both sides of the Rhine), while a late-picked Pinot Gris can be just about the best possible flavour to cut through the richness of *foie gras*.

MATURITY CHART
1985 Alsace Gewürztraminer
Some Gewürztraminer is now made soft and flowery for early drinking, but 1985 is a particularly good year. Vendange Tardive wines will age more slowly.

Bottled	Ready	Peak	Tiring	In decline

| 0 | 1 | 2 | 3 | 4 | 5 | 6 | 7 | 8 | 9 | 10 | 11 | 12 | 13 | 14 | 15 years |

After the war Alsace developed a poor reputation in France for being the *vin des comptoirs*, the bog-standard plonk of the French bar. Wine of this sort is still being made, but, mercifully, rather less than before. The younger generation of growers, of which Marc Kreydenweiss and André Ostertag are the most quoted examples, are increasingly interested in new techniques which bring surprising flavours to the wine. Ostertag, in particular, is experimenting with new oak on his Pinot Gris. Some would say that he has gone overboard. Time will tell.

Among the better, more conservative growers, Schlumberger is distinguished by the extreme modesty of its yields (45 hl/ha!). Madame Beydon-Schlumberger believes that the region 'is still paying the bill for the mistakes of the post-war years', when the French market was flooded with cheap Alsace wines. Some of the problems were ironed out 15 years ago when it was decided to ship all Alsace wines in bottle. But too much Alsace wine still comes from the plain, where quality wine cannot be produced, and not from the steep and difficult slopes of the foothills of the Vosges, where the wines of breed are born. Although the quantity of Klevner and Chasselas is diminishing, there is still enough about to provide pretty basic Alsace, should any buyer wish to go out and look for it. Madame Schlumberger thinks that there are probably no more than 50 decent houses in the region.

Of course the new Germanic names on the more expensive wines are a problem for those trying to sell the wines here. Virtually overnight we had to get used to about five times as many *grands crus* as exist in the Côte d'Or. Moreover, wily Alsatians have taken to putting the vineyard names on the labels, which has the effect of making a far less noble wine look like a *grand cru*. The only thing you can do is to study the label carefully for the words 'Alsace Grand Cru' or memorize the names of the better slopes and growers. It may be hard work, but it is worth the effort of interpretation.   GILES MACDONOGH

GRAPES & FLAVOURS

In Alsace wines are generally labelled according to their grape type. Only the cheaper wines (labelled Edelzwicker or Vin d'Alsace) are blends of several grapes. For this reason, recommended producers are listed here under the name of the appropriate grape.

CHASSELAS In a local tavern, fresh from the last vintage, Chasselas can be nice enough. It used to be the backbone for basic blends but Pinot Blanc and Sylvaner usually fill this role nowadays.

EDELZWICKER or VIN D'ALSACE
A blend of the less interesting grape varieties, in particular Chasselas, Pinot Blanc and Sylvaner. Usually it is fresh and nothing more. Just occasionally, it is spicy, and then much more enjoyable. Look for *Dopff & Irion, Rolly Gassmann, Klipfel, Maurice Schoech*. Some of the supermarket own-label Vin d'Alsace wines are good.

GEWÜRZTRAMINER It is sometimes difficult to believe that these wines are dry, because they can be so fat and full of spice. But, with a few exceptions, dry they are, yet big, very ripe, and with all kinds of remarkable, exotic fruit tastes – lychees, mangoes, peaches – and if you're lucky, finishing off with a rasping twist, just like the perfumed tang of black pepper straight from the pepper mill. Best producers: *Becker, Beyer, Caves de Turckheim, Dopff au Moulin, Domaine Ostertag, Théo Faller, Heywang, Klipfel, Kreydenweiss, Muré, Schlumberger, Trimbach, Zind-Humbrecht* and *Sainsbury's* and *Tesco's* own-labels.

MUSCAT Light, fragrant, wonderfully grapy. Imagine crushing a fistful of green grapes fresh from the market and gulping the juice as it runs through your fingers. That's how fresh and grapy a good Muscat is! Best producers: *Théo Cattin, Dirler, Dopff & Irion, Gisselbrecht, Hugel, Trimbach, Zind-Humbrecht.*

PINOT BLANC This is taking over from Sylvaner as the basis for Alsace's bright and breezy young whites. It's a much better grape, giving clean, rather appley wine, light, acidic, sometimes creamy, sometimes with a whiff of honey. Best producers: *Becker, Blanck, Gisselbrecht, Heim, Hugel, Humbrecht, Kreydenweiss, Rieffel, Scherer, Sparr, Trimbach, Zind-Humbrecht.*

PINOT GRIS Still known locally as the Tokay, even though the EC now insists on the title Tokay-Pinot Gris. These are mouth-filling, musky and sumptuously honeyed at best. Even the lighter Tokays have a lusciousness lingering behind the basically dry fruit. The best – especially from *grand cru* vineyards – can age well too. Best producers: *Becker, Caves de Turckheim, Éguisheim co-op, Théo Faller, Gisselbrecht, Hugel, Klipfel, Kreydenweiss, Kuentz-Bas, Trimbach, Zind-Humbrecht.*

PINOT NOIR The Burgundy grape here makes light reds and rosés. It often achieves quite an attractive perfume and a light, strawberryish flavour, which can be worth seeking out. A number of producers – *Muré, Hugel, Caves de Turckheim, Deiss* – are oak-ageing Pinot, and the wines can be delicious. Also good: *Cattin, Éguisheim co-op, Zind-Humbrecht.*

RIESLING This is the grape that produces the great, juicy-sweet wines of Germany. In Alsace, it is usually startlingly dry – as austere and steely as any wine in France. The best wines also have more than a hint of honey. As it ages, it goes 'petrolly' in a surprisingly delicious way. Best producers: *Becker, Deiss, Domaine Ostertag, Dopff & Irion, Théo Faller, Louis Gisselbrecht, Hugel, Klipfel, Kreydenweiss, Kuentz-Bas, Schaller, Trimbach, Zind-Humbrecht.*

SYLVANER Light, slightly tart and slightly earthy. It sometimes achieves rather more class than this, but usually tastes a bit empty and one-dimensional. If you leave it too long, it begins to taste of tomatoes. Best producers: *Beyer, Gisselbrecht, Schlumberger, Seltz, Zind-Humbrecht.*

ALSACE VINTAGES

1989 The exceptional weather produced an abundant harvest of very good quality, perhaps not as superb as first reported. The crop was brought in in unusually hot weather and cellars without temperature-control facilities had difficulty handling fermentation. Wines are already showing lively fruit and there will be some exceptional wines in spite of the difficulties, especially from *grand cru* sites and better producers.

1988 Just as pickers were sharpening up their secateurs, down came the rains. Those who rushed out and picked under leaking skies made pleasant, but hardly inspiring wine. Growers of greater faith waited and the result was some very good wine, though not as spectacular as 1985 or 1983. Tokay-Pinot Gris and Riesling were the most successful varieties.

1987 Not great, but better than first thought. Good single vineyard wines.

1986 These always tasted a bit dilute and maturity hasn't done a great deal to liven them up. Even so, those who waited into the late autumn managed to make some fairly good Vendange Tardive and even Sélection de Grains Nobles, enriched by some late, late botrytis.

1985 An absolute corker of a vintage. Not as overripe and fabled as 1983, but across the board even better – wonderful wines to drink now but they will keep.

1983 A great year, but only at the top level. These top quality wines are brilliant – rich, ripe and bursting with character, and they will still keep for several years yet.

CLASSIFICATIONS

ALSACE, AC This is the simple *appellation* for the whole region, normally used in conjunction with a grape name. Thus: 'Riesling – Appellation Alsace Contrôlée'.

CRÉMANT D'ALSACE, AC White fizz, made in the same way as Champagne, but mainly from Pinot Blanc. The few who use a touch of Riesling make more interesting, flowery-fragrant versions and there are one or two good 100 per cent Rieslings worth trying. Look for wines from *Baron de Hoen, Dopff & Irion, Gisselbrecht, Kreydenweiss, Schaller, Wolfberger*.

GRAND CRU Twenty-five historically excellent vineyards were classified as *grand cru* in 1983, and must meet stricter regulations than ordinary Alsace: they can only be planted with Riesling, Tokay-Pinot Gris, Gewürztraminer or Muscat, and notably lower (but still high) yields apply. They are recognized by the words

Perhaps the best value white wines in France
Louis Gisselbrecht is a charming family team producing award winning wines.
Available from leading Wine Merchants in London and throughout the country

For details or stockists
please contact Sole UK Agents

Thorman Hunt & Co Ltd
Wine Shippers
4 Pratt Walk,
Lambeth, London SE11 6AR
Telephone   071-735 6511
Telex   8953098 THOHUN
Fax   071-735 9799

Appellation Alsace Grand Cru Contrôlée on the label. A further 24 vineyards were given permission in 1985 to add the words *grand cru* to the name of the vineyard on the label, and their AC is, illogically, *Appellation Alsace Controlée, Grand Cru*. Yes, confusing. But these 24 are not yet fully fledged *grands crus*. In theory, any of them should be several rungs above ordinary Alsace, and first signs are that the *grand cru* classification is providing the spur needed to inspire growers to strive for quality not quantity.

RÉSERVE Descriptions such as 'Réserve', 'Réserve Personnelle' and 'Réserve Exceptionnelle' have been used in Alsace for generations to describe a grower's or merchant's best wines.

SÉLECTION DE GRAINS NOBLES The higher of the two 'super-ripe' legal descriptions in the Germanic mould based on the very high sugar content in the grapes. It only applies to wines from Riesling, Tokay-Pinot Gris, Muscat and Gewürztraminer and corresponds to a German Beerenauslese.

SIGILLE A 'Sigille' label – a band with a red paper seal – means that blind tasting by a jury has confirmed the wine as a fine example of its type.

SPÉCIAL Terms such as 'Cuvée Spéciale' or 'Sélection Spéciale' usually apply to a producer's best wines.

VENDANGE TARDIVE The first of the 'super-ripe' categories, made from late-picked grapes. Only applies to wines from Riesling, Tokay-Pinot Gris, Muscat and Gewürztraminer. They are usually dry, though they are occasionally sweetish – the label, I'm afraid, is unlikely to say. The quality is in general extremely high.

The price guides for this section begin on page 320.

SOUTH-WEST FRANCE

T he south-west of France is the most interesting area for regional wines, partly because there are various areas using the Bordeaux mixtures of grapes (Cabernet Sauvignon, Cabernet Franc, Merlot and Malbec for reds, Sauvignon and Sémillon for whites) with generally tasty results. However, the most *exciting* flavours are from wines, often of considerable historic importance, which have somehow fallen out of the mainstream and in some cases only narrowly avoided extinction. These are made from such weird and wonderful grapes as Fer-Servadou, Négrette, Petit Manseng, Tannat, Ruffiac, L'En de l'El and Baroque. When lovingly produced, the flavours can be as mysterious and beguiling as the names themselves – though I haven't yet quite worked out what a Baroque wine is supposed to *taste* like.

RED & ROSÉ WINES

BÉARN Red and rosé from the far south-west. The reds are predominantly from Tannat, but with other local varieties and both Cabernets thrown in. They are basically undistinguished wines but the Jurançon star Domaine Cauhapé makes quite a good red, and you could also try those of the *Vinicole de Bellocq* co-op, or the co-op at Crouseilles.

BERGERAC, AC An eastward extension of the St-Émilion vineyards, Bergerac is a kind of Bordeaux understudy, but it performs with more mixed results. The rosés are often extremely good, deep in colour, dry and full of fruit, but the reds are more exciting, because Bergerac can produce the fruit and bite of a good, simple Bordeaux without the rough edges. Like St-Émilion, it relies on the Merlot grape, with help from the Cabernet Sauvignon, Cabernet Franc and Malbec, but the Bergerac reds are less substantial than St-Émilions. Sadly, most British merchants are cutting the prices just too much for the potential of the area to be seen, so that what we get here is frequently tough, meaty, medicinal and charmless. Bergerac Rouge is usually at its best at between one and four years old, depending on vintage and style. The wines of *Château la Jaubertie* are very good and they've recently produced a wood-aged 'Reserve' which looks promising. *Château le Barradis* is also very good, and *Château*

Court-les-Mûts makes a delicious rosé and a good red. Most of the wines in the UK originate at the large central co-op, and whether they're any good or not depends on whether someone was prepared to pay a few extra centimes for a better vat.

BUZET, AC Used to be labelled Côtes de Buzet. The most exciting of the claret look-alikes from a region that was historically considered part of Bordeaux, a little way to the south-east. Made from Bordeaux grapes with the Cabernet flavour predominant, they can combine a rich blackcurrant sweetness with an arresting grassy greenness. They are for drinking at between one and five years old, depending on vintage and style. Look out for the wines of *Château Sauvagnères*, as well as those of the co-operative, which dominates the area and produces a wood-aged *Cuvée Napoléon* and a *Château de Gueyze* that is pretty special. The co-op has what is a real rarity in the modern wine world – its own cooper. Almost all the wine spends at least a couple of months in wood – and this contributes massively to Buzet's serious-but-soft appeal.

CAHORS, AC Of all the south-western country wines, Cahors is the most exciting. It's grown on both banks of the River Lot in the region of Quercy, practically due east of Bordeaux (though hotter, because it's well away from the influence of the sea). It's made chiefly (at least 70 per cent) from the Auxerrois (Bordeaux's Malbec), the rest being made up of varying proportions of Merlot, Tannat and Jurançon.

Two hundred years ago, it was one of France's most famous wines, and the 'Black Wine of Cahors' is still held up as an example of how it used to be done. It isn't done like that any more. The wine was made black by the simple expedient of giving the grapes a quick crushing and then, literally, boiling the must. Just as boiling gets the stain out of a shirt, so it gets the tannin and colour out of a grape skin. Fruit? Er, no, but strength (it was sometimes even fortified) and stability and massive ageing potential – yes. Without fruit, it's difficult to know what age was expected to do.

Adopting modern wine-making methods has added some lovely sweet fruit to the still dark, but now less aggressively tannic wines of Cahors. There's a clear whiff of fine wine about some of the big, firm products of private growers. With age, they are often almost honeyed and raisiny, with a plummy fruit that gets deeper, spicier and darker, often resembling tobacco and prunes. But another sort of Cahors has sprung up, too, lighter and less inspired, for drinking young. It can sometimes be very good. The raw materials for these lighter wines are quite different. Whereas the best, traditional vineyard land of Cahors is up in the hills, most grapes are now grown in easier vineyards on the valley slopes. One third of the wine comes from the co-op, *Côtes d'Olt*, which, after a pusillanimous, fruitless start, is beginning to produce some very good, lightish but proper-tasting wine with real individual style. Best properties are: *Château de Cayrou, Château de Chambert, Château de Haute-Serre, Château St-Didier, Château de Treilles, Clos la Coutale, Clos de Gamot, Clos Triguedina, Domaine du Cèdre, Domaine Eugénie, Domaine de Gaudou, Domaine de Paillas* and *Domaine de Quattre*.

The price guides for this section begin on page 325.

CÔTES DE BERGERAC, AC This is to Bergerac what Bordeaux Supérieur is to Bordeaux: from the same region, but with a slightly higher minimum alcohol level. It should be better than basic Bergerac, and often is, but most of the wines we see are still labelled as basic Bergerac, although the excellent Château Court-les-Mûts now uses the AC.

CÔTES DE DURAS, AC Light, grassy claret look-alikes. *Château de Pilar* and *Le Seigneuret* from the co-op are quite good and cheap. The co-op also does a Beaujolais-type *macération carbonique cuvée* which is good quaffing stuff.

CÔTES DU FRONTONNAIS, AC This small area north of Toulouse and just south-west of Gaillac makes red wines largely from the local Négrette grape, along with Cabernet Sauvignon and Cabernet Franc. (Malbec, Syrah, Cinsaut and Gamay are also allowed.) At their best they are unbelievably soft for red wine, silky and plummy, sometimes with more than a hint of raspberry and liquorice. The distinctive Négrette grape is wonderfully juicy and tasty and there are now some 100 per cent Négrette *cuvées* from Bellevue-la-Forêt and Flotis which are almost succulently soft. Good Côtes du Frontonnais reds are great value. *Domaine de Baudare, Château Bellevue-la-Forêt, Château Flotis, Château Montauriol* and *Château la Palme* are among the best.

CÔTES DU MARMANDAIS, VDQS Simple, soft, fruity wines for drinking young, made from the two Cabernets, Merlot, Fer and Abouriou, a little way west of Cahors and not far to the east of Bordeaux. A few wines are made for more serious ageing, but it doesn't suit them.

GAILLAC, AC From south-east of Cahors, this is one of the best known of the south-west wines. There are two styles: Duras plus Fer-Servadou and Syrah, or Duras plus Merlot and Cabernet. Mostly, this is co-op land, but the growers who care can make remarkable red wine. *Domaine Jean Cros* makes an especially delicious one. Other good producers: *Lastours, Mas Pignou, Labarthe, Larroze*.

IROULÉGUY, AC A small AC in the Basque country on the border with Spain. The co-op dominates production which is predominantly a roughish red based on the Tannat grape though the presence of Cabernet in the vineyards is increasing.

MADIRAN, AC Grown near the Armagnac region, midway between Bordeaux and the Spanish border, Madiran is often likened to claret, but only rarely shows anything approaching the finesse and excitement of Bordeaux. It is generally made about half from the Tannat grape, along with the two Cabernets and occasionally the Fer, with a minimum ageing period in wood of 20 months. It is often rather astringent, and can be toughly tannic. Experts say you have to age it – and I'm having a go with a few. (So watch this space.) Good ones include *Château d'Arricau-Bordes, Château Aydie, Château Montus* (whose wines aged in new wood are the only Madirans I really like), *Château Peyros, Domaine de Boucassé, Domaine du Crampilh* and *Domaine Laplace.*

PÉCHARMANT, AC The best red wine of Bergerac from the best slope of the region, east of Bordeaux, this is very good dry red that can take considerable ageing, but is deliciously full of quick-drinking blackcurrant fruit when young. Unlike Bergerac, Pécharmant doesn't cut its prices, and shows what could be achieved in other nearby regions if we paid a proper price. There is a strong, but uninspired co-op. *Château de Tiregand* is very good indeed, but *Domaine du Haut-Pécharmant* is even better, resembling a top-line Médoc.

WHITE WINES

BERGERAC SEC, AC A Bordeaux Blanc Sec look-alike from a large region to the east of Bordeaux, where the important grapes are Sémillon and Sauvignon. *Château Court-les-Mûts* and *Château de Panisseau* make good examples, but increasingly the star is *Château la Jaubertie* where tremendous flavour and panache are being extracted from Sauvignon, Sémillon and Muscadelle; this last now being made into a 100 per cent varietal.

BLANQUETTE DE LIMOUX, AC This sparkling wine from near Carcassonne claims to be the original French fizz, pre-dating even Champagne. It's mostly made from the Mauzac grape, which has a very green-apple kind of bite, but this is often softened up (and improved) by Chardonnay and Chenin Blanc. Most of it comes from the local co-op and the quality is always good, but never as good as Champagne – regardless of who pre-dates whom. *Domaine de Martinolles* is a good producer.

CÔTES DE DURAS, AC Fairly good Sauvignon-based white that can be as fresh as good Bordeaux Blanc, but just a little chubbier. *Château de Conti Le Seigneuret* from the co-operative is good.

GAILLAC, AC North-east of Toulouse and south of Cahors, Gaillac makes more white wine than red. It can be *moelleux* (medium sweet), *perlé* (very faintly bubbly) or dry; the dry is usually a little terse, though it can have a quite big apple-and-liquorice fruit if you're lucky. The sparkling wines can sometimes be superb: peppery, honeyed, apricotty and appley all at the same time. From producers such as *Boissel-Rhodes* or *Cros*, they are very good value. Other producers to look out for are *Château Larroze, Domaine du Bosc Long* and *Domaine de Labarthe.* The co-op at *Labastide de Lévis* is the dominant force in the area and the new director is forcing distinct improvements on the wines. One to look out for.

JURANÇON, AC Sweet, medium or dry (though never *very* sweet or *totally* dry) wine from the Pyrenean foothills. Based on the Petit Manseng, Gros Manseng and Courbu, the dry wines are usually rather nutty and dull, but the sweet wines are not excessively sweet, honeyed, raisiny and peachy, yet keeping a lick of acidity to stop them cloying. New oak is starting to appear in some cellars. Most wine is from the local co-op which has always been undistinguished, so always plump for a grower's wine if you can. The best are *Château Jolys, Clos Cancaillaü* (sweet), *Clos de la Vierge* (dry), *Cru Lamouroux* (sweet), *Clos Uroulat* (sweet), *Domaine de Cauhapé* (the best).

MONBAZILLAC, AC From east of Bordeaux, south of Bergerac, this is one of the most famous names in the world of sweet wine, but the general standard has been debased to an over-sulphured, artificially sweetened mediocrity. The occasional true Monbazillac is a fine sweet wine, rich and honeyed, even unctuous, yet never of the standard of a top Sauternes – more like a good Loupiac or Ste-Croix-du-Mont. Unlike in Sauternes, there are very few quality-conscious single properties prepared to make the real thing. Ones worth seeking out include *Château du Treuil de Nailhac* and *Clos Fontindoule*; and the *Château de Monbazillac* and *Château Septy* of the local co-op can be good.

MONTRAVEL, AC Dry to sweet white wine from the Dordogne just ten kilometres east of St-Émilion. The wine is frequently sold as Côtes de Bergerac.

PACHERENC DU VIC-BILH, AC One of France's most esoteric whites, at its best dry and pear-skin-perfumed, sometimes rich and sweet, grown in the Madiran area near Armagnac. Look out for *Domaine Boucassé* and *Domaine du Crampilh*.

VIN DE PAYS CHARENTAIS As Cognac production declines, table wine production increases, and the Charente produces some good, grassy-fresh whites with fairly sharp acidity, although sometimes the acidity gets the better of the fruit.

VIN DE PAYS DES CÔTES DE GASCOGNE The table wine of Armagnac, and the rising star of this corner of France. The Ugni Blanc is the major grape, in more abundant supply since the drop in Armagnac sales, and the Colombard adds a definite touch of class. They're trying out the Gros Manseng and Chardonnay too – which should be interesting. The co-operative of *Plaimont* supplies most of those on sale in Britain at very reasonable prices, but variable quality. However, the mood of change sweeping the south-western co-ops is evident here too and after a shaky phase they are producing some delicious stuff. There are several labels available from the *Grassa* family estates – notably *Domaine de Planterieu* and *Domaine de Tariquet*, which are very good, full, dry and acid even. Usually an A1 bargain buy. Also good: *Domaine St-Lannes, San Guilhem*.

SOUTH-EAST FRANCE

The method of vinification is generally more important than the grape variety in the far south, since most of the traditional varieties used are pretty neutral. The whites are dominated by the dull Clairette, Macabeo and Ugni Blanc, sometimes livened up with Grenache Blanc, Rolle, Sauvignon, Sémillon, even Chardonnay. Cold fermentation to preserve freshness and brief maceration of the skins with the juice prior to fermentation are two ways of producing, at the very least, acceptably neutral whites to drink young and cold. Reds and rosés are largely made from Carignan, Grenache and Cinsaut, but increasingly Syrah, Mourvèdre and Cabernet are adding style and character to the wines. Avoidance of excessive ageing in wood is crucial here, and the employment of the Beaujolais-style of fermentation – *macération carbonique* – has dramatically increased the freshness and fruitiness of the wines, seeming to suit Carignan especially well. There are a few estates making a point of employing Syrah and Cabernet, and making the wines in small oak barrels as in Bordeaux. This is the other optimistic direction being taken by the south, and early results are impressive.

RED & ROSÉ WINES

BANDOL, AC Expensive, but without doubt one of the best Provence reds. These terraced vineyards above Toulon are the heartland of the excellent Mourvèdre, which is the dominant grape, along with Grenache, Cinsaut and Syrah, and makes gorgeous, dark, spicy, soft wine, with sweet fruit to match the herby, tobacco edge. Most reds need five years' ageing. The rosé is also excellent, showing the soft, spicy style of the red. Best estates include *Château Ste-Anne, Château Vannières, Domaine de la Bastide Blanche, Domaine du Cagueloup, Domaine de Pibarnon, Domaine Ray-Jane, Domaine Tempier, Domaine Terrebrune, Mas de la Rouvière, Moulin des Costes.*

BELLET, AC The reds from fragmented vineyards behind Nice can be pretty dire, but there are a few good examples, deeply coloured with blackberry-like fruit. *Château de Crémat* can be delicious and *Château de Bellet* isn't bad, though the population of Nice deny the existence of the AC altogether.

CASSIS, AC A gorgeous, mini-wine region between Bandol and Marseille, making the best whites of the Riviera, surprisingly fresh and fruity for an area so far south, and stylish rosés. Don't try the reds; they're guaranteed to bring you back to earth with a bump.

COLLIOURE, AC Startling, big, intense reds from the ancient vineyards cramped in between the Pyrenees and the Mediterranean, just north of the Spanish border. You can get *Domaine de la Rectorie* and *Domaine du Mas Blanc* in the UK – if you like that sort of thing.

CORBIÈRES, AC Coarsely fruity, peppery red based on Carignan, Grenache, Cinsaut and others from the welter of mountains stretching from Narbonne towards Spain. The region is wild, untamed, and exciting – and it looks as though the wines are beginning to match the scenery. Good wines are emerging from *Château des Colombes, Château de*

Montrabech and *Château des Ollieux.* There is increasing use of *macération carbonique (à la Beaujolaise)* and the results, particularly from some of the co-ops like *Mont Tauch* and *Embrès et Castelmaure*, are very encouraging – the peppery bite is still there, but the fruit is enhanced to a really juicy level. New oak is starting to appear here and there too. Other good producers: *St Auréol, La Baronne, Fontsainte, Villemajou, La Voulte-Gasparets.*

COSTIÈRES DE NÎMES, AC Quite good rosés, and rather meaty, smoky reds from a large area between Nîmes and Montpellier. I must say I always find the meatiness dominates the fruit, and I'd rather it were the other way round. Until 1989 this AC was called Costières du Gard.

COTEAUX D'AIX-EN-PROVENCE, AC Mostly reds and rosés grown to the south and east of Aix. Recently upgraded from VDQS to AC. An increase in Cabernet and Syrah and a commitment to careful selection and new oak are pushing some of the wines into the top class in a rush. The reds range from very light, strawberry-fruited wines, to drink at a great rate and without fuss, to such properties as *Château Vignelaure*, a remarkable Cabernet-based wine that achieves a Provençal-Bordeaux style. Most wines aren't expensive and worth watching. Other producers to look out for are *Château de Beaulieu, Domaine de la Crémade, Domaine de Paradis, Domaine du Château Bas, Château de Fonscolombe.*

COTEAUX DES BAUX-EN-PROVENCE, AC For some obscure local political reason Coteaux des Baux-en-Provence only enjoys its recently awarded AC as a subregion of Coteaux d'Aix-en-Provence, though its wines are different –

The price guides for this section begin on page 328.

and better. This is a wild, rock-cluttered moonscape of a region, with many of the vineyards literally blasted from the rock. The results are a sensation; as well as producing some very good, soft, fruity whites and some delicious rosés, the reds are the best in the whole of the Mediterranean region. Based on Syrah, Mourvèdre and Grenache they have an absurdly drinkable deep, ripe, raspberry juicy fruit. The finest property, *Domaine de Trévallon*, can make reds as exciting as almost any in France. Cabernet Sauvignon and Syrah are used to produce fine wine, still juicily ripe but humming with potential and class. In the lunatic way of French officialdom, this is now relegated to *vin de pays* because of the lack of Grenache in the vineyard, but you may still see some wines as AC on the UK market. If Trévallon continue to have trouble, perhaps they should plant some Grenache – and make rosé out of it. Best wines: *Domaine de Trévallon, Mas du Cellier, Mas de Gourgonnier, Terres Blanches*.

COTEAUX DU LANGUEDOC, AC

Usually a pretty solid red. A whole series of former VDQS regions have been re-defined as Coteaux du Languedoc *crus*: Cabrières, La Clape, La Méjanelle, Montpeyroux, Picpoul-de-Pinet, Pic-St-Loup, Quatourze, St-Christol, St-Drézéry, St-Georges-d'Orques, St-Saturnin, Vérargues. ACs Faugères and St-Chinian now come under the Coteaux du Languedoc AC umbrella too. We'll be seeing some good value from these because there is a sense of excitement in quite a few spots, like the *St-Georges-d'Orques co-op* where they're starting to use new wood, and at the *Prieuré de St-Jean de Bébian* where the owner says he has the same soil as Châteauneuf-du-Pape and so he's planted all 13 of the Châteauneuf grape varieties! Look forward to a flood of fresh, fruity wines at affordable prices as better grapes are planted and bad vineyards disappear.

COTEAUX VAROIS, VDQS

Large region recently upgraded to VDQS. Slightly better than basic reds and rosés, particularly where Syrah and Cabernet are used. A few good estates now appearing – especially *St-Jean de Villecroze*.

CÔTES DE PROVENCE, AC

Sprawling, catch-all *appellation* that still provides a lot of very mediocre wine. However, when a grower decides he can do better than provide swill for the sunseekers at St Trop, these scented southern hills can be induced to provide excellent rosé, good, fruity red and fair white. Only a few single-domaine wines are worth seeking out: *Château de Pampelonne, Château St-Maurs, Commanderie de la Peyrassol, Domaine de la Bernarde, Domaine des Féraud, Domaine Gavoty* and *Domaine de Rimauresq. Domaines Ott* is good, though expensive. The wines of *Les Vignerons de la Presqu'Île de St-Tropez* are widely available and good.

CÔTES DU ROUSSILLON, AC

Good, fruity reds, just touched by the hot dust of the south. The Carignan is the dominant grape, mixed with Cinsaut, Grenache and Syrah. The Beaujolais method of *macération carbonique* is increasingly used for reds to draw out the really juicy fruit. Mostly good value, as are the rosés.

CÔTES DU ROUSSILLON-VILLAGES, AC

Usually better than the basic *appellation*, coming from communes higher up in the foothills of the Pyrenees. That juicy fruit and dust cocktail can be quite delicious in the best selections of the large co-op group *Vignerons Catalans* from villages like Caramany, Cassagne and Rassiguères. Other good producers are *Cazes Frères, Château Corneilla* and *Château de Jau*. The best two villages have their own separate ACs, Côtes du Roussillon-Villages Caramany and Côtes du Roussillon-Villages Latour de France.

FAUGÈRES

Big, beefy wine, but soft with it. Something of a fad in France, so prices have risen, but the quality is there. A few bottles with Faugères AC are still around but newer Faugères is now sold as a *cru* of Coteaux du Languedoc. Try *Gilbert Alquier, Château de Grezan, Château Haut-Fabrègues, Domaine de Fraisse*.

FITOU, AC

Traditionally a fine, rich, old-style red based on at least 70 per cent Carignan grapes, from an *appellation* between Corbières and the plain running south to Perpignan. Sainsbury's began Fitou's phenomenal rise in the UK market, after which it became so widely available that quality couldn't hold up. In fact, Fitou's importer had orders at one point for twice as much as the AC could produce! So Fitou's off the boil now, but as things calm down, quality should return to what is a thoroughly good chunky red at best. If you feel like checking on progress, try the single domaine *Château des Nouvelles*.

MINERVOIS, AC The most forward-looking red of the Aude department, from a hilly region north-west of Narbonne. Usually lighter than its southern neighbour Corbières, with lots of raspberry fruit and pepper, mainly from the Carignan grape. Again the use of *macération carbonique* has transformed these wines and, at their low price levels, made them a very good buy. Most of this type is made at the co-ops but good properties now experimenting with deeper, wood-aged wines include: *Château Fabas, Château de Gourgazaud, Château de Paraza, Château Villerambert-Julien, Domaine Maris* and *Domaine de Ste-Eulalie*.

PALETTE, AC A tiny *appellation* hidden in the pine forests near Aix-en-Provence, distinguished rather than delicious, where the wines are usually pretty hard and resiny and need time to develop more attractive flavours. *Château Simone* is virtually the only producer.

ST-CHINIAN, AC A *cru* of AC Coteaux du Languedoc, making spicy, sturdy reds of the old school, once again beginning to blossom as more producers employ *macération carbonique* to draw out the fruity flavours from the grapes. *Cave de Berlou, Caves de Roquebrun, Château Cazals-Vieil* and *Château Coujan* look good. *Domaine Guiraud-Boyer* is good for rosé.

VIN DE CORSE, AC The overall regional *appellation* for Corsican AC wines, to which the local names are added. These are: Figari, Sartène, Porto-Vecchio, Coteaux du Cap Corse and Calvi. Ajaccio and Patrimonio can use their own ACs. Grenache, Cinsaut, Carignan and other

Webster's is an annual publication. We welcome your suggestions for next year's edition.

grape varieties typical of southern France are common, but it is the indigenous varieties Nielluccio and Sciacarello which give Corsican wines a distinctive character. The best wines have a warm, spicy perfumed quality and are generally fairly solid, but the overall standard is still pretty rustic. (White wines from the local Vermentino grape can be good when picked early.) If you want to taste the style, try the wines of *Cantone, Clos d'Alzetto, Clos Capitoro, Domaine Martini, Domaine Peraldi, Domaine du Petit Fournil* and *Domaine de Torraccia*.

VIN DE PAYS DE L'HÉRAULT One of the areas where all the good guys are experimenting furiously with grape varieties and wine-making styles. Very good 'ordinary' *vins de pays* include *Domaine du Chapître*, made at the institute of oenology at Montpellier, *Domaine de St-Macaire*, and the innovative wines of Pierre Besinet, marketed here as *Domaine du Bosc* and *Domaine Cante-Cigale*. *Mas de Daumas Gassac* is a weird and wonderful one-off using a variety of grapes, but primarily Cabernet Sauvignon, to produce strong, concentrated reds that some have called the 'Lafite of Languedoc'. I'd say Rhône myself.

VIN DE PAYS DE MONTCAUME Good reds from around Bandol. The *Bunan* family make a good Cabernet Sauvignon.

VIN DE PAYS DES BOUCHES DU RHÔNE Large departmental *vin de pays* producing torrents of reasonably decent reds and rosés.

VIN DE PAYS DES SABLES DU GOLFE DU LION Sandy coastal region to the west of the Rhône delta, and the only *vin de pays* to be delineated by its soil, not by administrative boundary. Mostly producing fairly light wines of all colours. However, the *Listel* operation, based out in the foggy sands of the wild Camargue, produces an astonishing range of wines of every sort, shape and persuasion. It is one of France's foremost experimental wineries, and suggestions that they should upgrade to VDQS are dismissed, since this would hinder their at present untrammelled experimentation, such as growing grapes in a salty swamp!

VIN DE PAYS DU GARD Produces interesting reds and whites from classic 'northern' grapes. It is the smallest of the 'big three' departmental *vins de pays* in the Midi, producing about 30 million bottles. The reds and the rosés are often supposed to have something of a Rhône quality. Most are light and spicy with a gamey earthiness. The rosés are often better.

WHITE WINES

BELLET, AC One of the few pockets of 'special' wines within the Côtes de Provence, just behind Nice. It is a highly unusual, nutty white, expensive and popular with the Nice glitterati. On present experience, they can keep most of them. But the characterful *Château de Crémat* and *Château de Bellet* can be worth seeking out, and the latter improves with bottle age.

BANDOL, AC White Bandol can be the best white of Provence, with a remarkable aniseed-and-apples freshness. Best properties include *Château des Vannières, Domaine de la Bastide Blanche* and *Domaine de la Laidière*.

CASSIS, AC No, not the blackcurrant liqueur, though Cassis (AC) and Cassis (Crème de) would mix to a good summer drink. This one is a very good but expensive white from a small, dauntingly

beautiful vineyard tucked into the bluffs by the Mediterranean between Marseille and Toulon. The grapes are a blend of Clairette, Ugni Blanc and Marsanne (rare this far south), sometimes with a little Sauvignon Blanc. Its cool freshness and fruit is a rare find on this coast, though it has low acidity and needs to be drunk young. Look out for *Domaine du Paternel* and *Clos Ste-Magdeleine*.

CLAIRETTE DE BELLEGARDE, AC Small AC between Arles and Nîmes making dry, still white wine from 100 per cent Clairette grapes. Unmemorable, a dull old workhorse.

CLAIRETTE DU LANGUEDOC, AC Heavy, alcoholic whites, dry or semi-sweet, mercifully used, for the most part, as a base for French vermouth. Signs of improvement from *Domaine de la Condemine Bertrand*.

FORTIFIED WINES

BANYULS, AC (*Vin doux naturel*) Based on at least 50 per cent Grenache, these wines are red or tawny and sweet or dryish, but always a hefty, slightly grapy mouthful whatever the style. Try *Domaine de la Rectorie* or *Domaine du Mas Blanc*.

MAURY, AC (*Vin doux naturel*) 100 per cent Grenache AC for red or rosé wines, quite light and fresh when young but often purposely oxidized to a rather sweet-sour, burnt caramel flavour. This is called *rancio* and is done in other ACs too. *Mas Amiel* is the best (and the 15-year-old is worth looking out for).

MUSCAT DE FRONTIGNAN, AC (*Vin doux naturel*) The best-known of the fortified Muscats and, although it is rich and raisiny, it lacks, rather surprisingly, any great aroma. The fresher, more fragrant style of *Château de la Peyrade* is a step in the right direction.

MUSCAT DE RIVESALTES, AC (*Vin doux naturel*) Similar to Frontignan, but headier, fatter and developing with age a rather pungent sweetness not unlike cooked marmalade. It's not the trendiest of styles, so some Muscat is being made as a dry white – which is rather good.

JURA

T he Jura certainly doesn't like to be told what it should plant and how it should make its wines, because some of the most fearsome and entirely unique flavours in French wine are lurking in those high, damp mountain valleys east of Burgundy and bordering on Switzerland. And although there *are* grapes like Pinot Noir and Chardonnay planted, these international superstars are definitely subordinated to the proud, pug-faced local varieties. Above all, it is the red Trousseau (which sounds bridally innocuous but would strike terror into the hearts of most suitors I know) and the white Savagnin – whose flavours stain the mind as they strip your teeth of enamel – which hold sway. Approach these two at your peril. But, having said that – they *are* there, they *are* original, so you must try them at some time, just don't expect to like them, that's all! The Savagnin reaches its awesome apogee through a miasma of sweet-sour sensations in the infamous *vin jaune*. It is fierce, sherry-like stuff. But again, so long as you're sitting down, with the wind behind you and a good life insurance policy, you *have* to try it at least once.

WINES & WINE REGIONS

ARBOIS, AC The general *appellation* for wines of all types from the northern part of the Jura around the town of Arbois. Reds are mostly Trousseau and thuddingly full of flavour. Savagnin weaves its demonic spells on the whites, though Chardonnay is sometimes used to soften it. Interestingly there are some attractive light reds and rosés from Pinot Noir or Poulsard which seem positively out of place, they are so delicate. *Henri Maire* is the biggest producer, but the best wines come from the village of Pupillin, where the *co-op* produces delicious Chardonnay and a fizz.

CÔTES DE JURA, AC These are the wines, of all colours, from the centre and south of the Jura. They are virtually indistinguishable from Arbois wines, though they are sometimes a little less disturbing in their weirdness.

L'ÉTOILE, AC Small area in the south producing whites from Savagnin and Chardonnay and, occasionally, from the red Poulsard, vinified without the colour-giving skins. Also *vins jaunes* from Savagnin.

VIN JAUNE The kind of wine of which more than a small glass makes you grateful it is as rare as it is. It grows the same yeasty *flor* as dry sherry, but whereas dry sherry has to be drunk young, this monster thrives on ageing, and its startlingly, painfully intense flavours just get more and more evident as it matures. No one seems to know how long it can live, because the wine is virtually indestructible, and as long as the cork is healthy, should last as long as any man.

Château-Chalon AC – the 'Montrachet' of *vin jaune*! Well, that's what they think, anyway. This is the most prized – and pricy – of the *vins jaunes*, and is difficult to find even in the region. *Vins jaunes* are always sold in small 62cl *clavelin* bottles, which, naturally, the EC tried to ban as being non-conformist. That left me in two minds. I felt that 75cl of *vin jaune* would be just too much for any man to handle, and indeed 37.5cl might be more like it. But I was blowed if I was going to stand by and watch the EC destroy yet another great original in the stultifying name of conformity. The EC backed down – they probably tasted the wine – and the 62cl *clavelin* lives yet! Actually there *is* a reason for the 62cl size, in that 100 litres of wine, kept in barrels for six years without being topped up, would reduce to 62 litres. Which would yield 100 bottles. So they can order their bottles in nice round numbers!

SAVOIE

I've decided that I've been unfair to Savoie wines in the past. I've talked about them being feather-light, ethereal as melting snow, pure as the mountain streams that gambol skittishly ... you know the kind of thing. Well, there *is* a mountainy freshness about the wines, certainly, but it's more of the bracing, breeze on your brow and only another mile to climb, kind of high altitude effect, because the majority of Savoie wines are *not* ethereal, and not really even feather-light. I suspect that that was how I *wanted* the wines to be. What the wines do have is fruit flavours honed and sharpened by a clean, cutting acidity, making them taste as though they've had a squirt of fresh lemon just before bottling. This is particularly evident in the whites, usually based on the Altesse and Jacquère grapes, and at their best in the southern area down towards Chambéry. Only the wispy wines from Crépy fall short of this standard. The reds are mostly pale but with a fairly insistent flavour from Gamay or Pinot Noir, and the local Mondeuse grape is a star, producing big, plummy, smoky wines not all that different from the Syrah.

WINES & WINE REGIONS

BUGEY, VDQS This little VDQS half-way between Savoie and Beaujolais is a rising star for its deliciously crisp Chardonnays, although it also uses the other Savoyard grapes for whites and reds. It is one of the most refreshing, zippy Chardonnays in France, and, not surprisingly, has become a 'fad' wine with some of the local Michelin-starred restaurants. At least that means the growers will make enough money to keep producing it.

CRÉPY, AC The least interesting Savoie region to the south of Lake Geneva, where the Chasselas produces an even flimsier version of the Swiss Fendant, if that's possible. Drink it very young, very fast, or not at all.

ROUSSETTE DE SAVOIE, AC This can be the fullest and softest of the Savoie whites. It can come from a blend of Altesse and Chardonnay or 100 per cent Altesse (also called Roussette) when it comes from one of the better villages like Frangy or Monterminod. Even at its basic level, it's good, crisp, strong-tasting white.

SEYSSEL, AC and **SEYSSEL MOUSSEUX, AC** The Roussette (sometimes blended with Molette) makes quite full, flower-scented but sharp-edged whites in this commune of the Haute-Savoie. Sparkling Seyssel is also good and, after a few years off the UK market, this light but pepper-pungent fizz is back again from *Varichon et Clerc*.

VIN DE SAVOIE, AC Vin de Savoie covers the whole Savoie area, but produces the most interesting results in the south. These alpine vineyards are some of the most beautiful in France and produce fresh, snappy wines. The white, from the Jacquère or the Chardonnay, can be excellent, dry, biting, but with lots of tasty fruit. Avoid ageing them for too long. The reds from Pinot Noir are subtly delicious, while the Mondeuse produces some real beefy beauties when the vintage is hot enough. A *cru* name is often tacked on to the best wines. Ones to look out for are Abymes, Apremont, Chignin, Cruet and Montmélian, with Chautagne and Arbin quite important for reds.

VINS DE PAYS

Country wine. That's what it says, that's what it means. This ancient-sounding title was in fact coined only in 1973, but is already one of the most important parts of French viticulture. It sprang out of France's concern to overcome the curse of the south – overproduction and lousy quality – exacerbated by EC policy which, in the late 1970s and early 1980s managed to beef up members' wine production by a billion litres! In typical EC manner, they managed to achieve this just as the consumption of wine began to drop like a lead weight in the two major markets – France and Italy.

Vins de pays used to be loosely defined as 'wines of simple origin'. Then in 1973, the table wine producers were approached with the idea that if they limited their yields, cut out some of their worst grapes (Aramon and Alicante Bouschet, for instance, which give impressive colour but zero taste), and followed some fundamental rules in vinification, ageing and bottling, they could climb out of the rut of mass-produced hooch, put their own name on the label, and develop the personal incentive to improve quality.

All of which means that *vin de pays* is like a more lax *appellation contrôlée*. The yields allowed are higher, between 80 and 90 hectolitres per hectare, and alcoholic strength required will be fairly low, between nine and ten degrees, although this will usually be exceeded. The grape varieties must be 'recommended', but grapes like the Carignan, discouraged for some ACs, are the backbone of southern country reds.

In some ways, *vin de pays* has potentially tighter controls than many ACs. The wine must be approved by an 'official' tasting panel to get its label; and the levels of wine preserving sulphur and volatile acidity are closely controlled. Also, in areas where the AC enshrines some rather dull grapes, *vin de pays* frequently allows for planting of more attractive grape varieties, such as Sauvignon, Chardonnay, Cabernet or Merlot, which the AC doesn't allow.

Vins de pays come in three categories.

VINS DE PAYS RÉGIONAUX There are three of these, which between them cover a major portion of France's vineyards. Vin de Pays du Jardin de la France covers the whole Loire basin across almost to Chablis and down to the Charente. Vin de Pays du Comté Tolosan is for the South-West, starting just below Bordeaux, and covering Bergerac, Cahors, the Tarn and down to the Pyrenees, but not including the Aude and Pyrénées Orientales. Vin de Pays d'Oc covers the Rhône, Provence and the Midi right down to the Spanish border.

VINS DE PAYS DÉPARTEMENTAUX These are also large groupings, and each one is defined by the boundaries of the *département*. So, for instance, any wine of *vin de pays* quality grown in the *département* of Vaucluse will qualify for the title 'Vin de Pays du Vaucluse'.

VINS DE PAYS DE ZONE These are the tightest-controlled of the categories, and can apply to actual communes or at least carefully defined localities. The allowed yield is lower and there may be more control on things like grape varieties. So, for example, we could have a Vin de Pays de la Vallée du Paradis which is in the Aude and therefore could be sold as Vin de Pays de l'Aude, and the Aude is in the Pays d'Oc, so, as a third option the wine also qualifies for the widest, least demanding description, Vin de Pays d'Oc.

GERMANY

U nderstanding the wines of Germany used to be so simple. All you had to do was remember the difference between the 11 wine regions identified on the label, memorize a few dozen of the 2600 Einzellagen (single vineyards), recall the numerous grape varieties planted (many of them unsavoury hybrids), succumb to the fiction that the higher the quality grade (such as Kabinett or Spätlese) the better the wine, note the distinction between dry and half-dry, and remember which producers (including about a dozen in the Mosel all named Prüm) make the best wine. Then you had to learn how to disentangle Gothic script, and you were all set.

The good news for 1991 is that German wine producers are coming to terms with the absurdities of their system, and there is a determined effort to continue the improvement in quality that has been discernible at the upper end of the market. The bad news is that this quiet revolution in German wine production and marketing will, at least in the immediate future, lead to more confusion for the wine drinker. Still, most of the recent trends are to be welcomed.

Many estates are turning away from the laborious identification of individual vineyard sites on the label, arguing that it is preferable to make a handful of high-quality blends from a variety of sites rather than persist with single-vineyard wines. Some growers work both sides of the fence. Dirk Richter of the Mosel estate of Max Ferd Richter produces a range of excellent Mosels, and a relatively inexpensive blend called, quite simply, Dr Richter's Riesling. More and more estates, including the superb Rheingau producer Langwerth von Simmern are adopting a similar strategy.

Other larger estates and importers, such as Scholl & Hillebrand, Sichel, and Deinhard, all with access to grapes from a variety of sources, have for some time been marketing wines simply identified by grape variety and style, such as Riesling Dry or Silvaner Dry.

These trends have been established for a few years. What is more recent is the determination of some of the best estates in Germany to buck the system altogether. The most wretched quality level among German wines is *Tafelwein*, and yet that is how the radical winemaker Armin Diel sells his wines. He has abandoned the notion of single-vineyard wines and instead concocts blends of different grape varieties which are aged in new *barriques*. The marketing is as sophisticated as the wine, and the evident aim is to produce wines for the international market. Georg Messer of the Rheinpfalz produces dry varietal wines in snazzy designer bottles at prices that might make even a Burgundian blush. Whether the quality is equal to the marketing wizardry only time will tell. Top Italian estates were clearly right to ignore constricting DOC regulations and produce fine wines as *vini da tavola*, so there is no reason why the Germans, following their own styles, should not succeed just as well.

The new wave of German red wines, mostly Spätburgunder (Pinot Noir), is also generally sold as mere Tafelwein because of its supposed lack of 'typicity'. Until a few years ago, German reds were anaemic, thanks to officially sanctioned vinification methods that ignored the need to extract flavour and tannin from the grapes, by limiting fermentation on the grape skins to a couple of days. Now growers such as Lingenfelder, Heger, Kessler and Becker, among others, are adopting Burgundian methods, observing that in certain sites climatic conditions are directly comparable to the Côte d'Or. These new-wave winemakers aim for fermentation on the skins that continues for about two weeks. Lingenfelder and others have have obtained alcoholic levels of 13 degrees without chaptalization, which is more than most Burgundians can claim. Some of these winemakers are using French oak *barriques*, and in the case of Kessler, new *barriques*. In my experience, the results are patchy at best, but there is no doubt that the quality of German Spätburgunder from the Pfalz and from Baden is improving.

Pinot Noir is not the only trendy grape variety. While the more northerly German wine regions still achieve their most dazzling results from the noble Riesling grape, warmer regions look to varieties such as Chardonnay and Pinot Gris (Grauburgunder), experimenting with *barriques*, minimal yields, and complete dryness, sometimes resulting in wines with awesomely high alcohol levels – I recently tasted two German Pinot Gris wines with over 15 per cent! The grapefruity Scheurebe is also making a comeback, largely thanks to the crusading efforts of Rainer Lingenfelder in the Rheinpfalz.

The innovation, the internationalization, of the iconoclasts of German wine-making, notably Messer, Diel and the wildly experimental Bernd Philippi of the

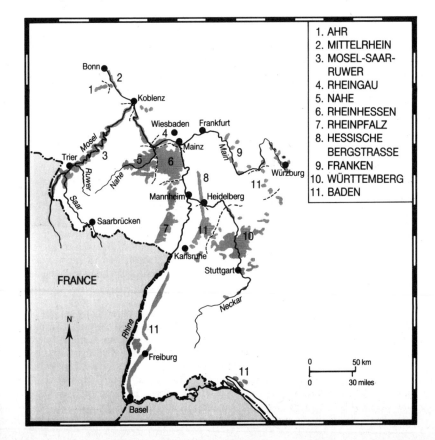

1. AHR
2. MITTELRHEIN
3. MOSEL-SAAR-RUWER
4. RHEINGAU
5. NAHE
6. RHEINHESSEN
7. RHEINPFALZ
8. HESSISCHE BERGSTRASSE
9. FRANKEN
10. WÜRTTEMBERG
11. BADEN

Koehler-Ruprecht estate in the Rheinpfalz, must be welcomed, if only because their wines are of outstanding quality, whatever arguments are made against them on the grounds that they lack 'typicity'. Philippi has even made dry red wines of Beerenauslese quality, ice wines from Pinot Noir, and a Trockenbeerenauslese aged in new *barriques*! Some of these wines are superb, others fairly dreadful; they are produced as curiosities, as experiments, in order to test the limits.

All the same, I am not at all sure that I want to see a large number of winemakers following the example of Philippi and Diel. Some bottles of Diel's dry Pinot Gris are slumbering in my cellar, but they are greatly outnumbered by traditionally made Rieslings from the greatest estates of the Saar, the Mosel, the Rheingau. If innovations become fads and more producers plant Chardonnay and invest in *barriques* then we shall all be the losers. German Riesling is unique and should not be scorned.

These developments affect the top German wines. Although the finest, compared with the top growths of France and the most fashionable wines of Italy and California, remain relatively inexpensive, few of us can afford to drink them on a regular basis. And sadly, the prospects for radical improvement at the everyday drinking level look less rosy. The German wine laws of 1971 did regulate traditional estate wine-making to some degree, despite the abuses it has always been possible to perpetrate. At the less exalted end of the market, however, there has always been something of a free-for-all. Producers have been permitted to blend different grape varieties from different regions, to add unfermented grape juice by the truckload, and to engage in what can only be regarded as industrial wine-making in order to churn out tanker-loads of watery, sugary, cut-price blends.

YIELDING TO PRESSURE

The German wine authorities now hope to remedy the situation, beginning with the 1990 vintage, by imposing greater control over one hitherto unregulated area: yields. If your one-hectare vineyard customarily produces 60 hectolitres of wine, and you change your pruning and harvesting practices in order to squeeze 150 hectolitres from the same vines, quality is bound to suffer. The French routinely regulate yields (30-65 hl/ha in the best wine regions), and now the Germans are following suit. Unfortunately the new regulations will do no more than legitimize already excessive yields. One example: Mosel growers may produce no more than 120 hl/ha of Riesling and 130 of Müller-Thurgau. If growers find this restriction too confining, they are permitted to 'carry over' excess production to make up for any shortfalls in subsequent vintages. If this is the wine authorities' idea of a joke, it's not very funny, and we, as wine drinkers, are being conned.

The authorities, one must assume, have enacted these regulations not out of concern for the wine lover, but because of the crisis in which German growers find themselves. Throughout the Mosel and the Rheinhessen, for example, large areas under vine, including many excellent sites, are for sale. The Von Buhl and Dr Weil estates are now under Japanese control. Price wars have led to minuscule profit margins, the destruction of the reputation of German wines, and a plunge in quality that is proving hard to reverse. The new regulations are too little, too late, and will do next to nothing to improve quality. After all, any half-decent estate or co-operative already insists on yields far lower than those now legalized. And so while the outlook for great (and increasingly expensive) German wine has never been better, the prospects for sound, sensibly priced fruity wines for everyday drinking remain bleak.

But there are still bargains to be found, especially among modest QbA and Kabinett wines from good estates. British supermarkets, notably Tesco, have taken the trouble to seek out good wines both from famous estates and from enterprising top-quality co-operatives and have evidently had the muscle to negotiate favourable prices. Moving slightly upmarket, you can find a splendid range of Mosel and Saar wines, mostly at under £7.50, from Dr Richter and Schloss Saarstein at Bibendum. Other excellent ranges can be found on the lists of merchants such as Berry Bros and Justerini & Brooks. But the strength of other markets, and the revival of a German gastronomy that seeks to match the finest native wines, is making German estates even less dependent than formerly on UK custom. If in the 1990s we are to find fewer and fewer great German wines on our retailers' shelves, we will have to share the blame. **STEPHEN BROOK**

CLASSIFICATIONS

The German classification system is based on sugar levels, and therefore potential alcohol, of the grapes when they are picked. The main categories are as follows:

DEUTSCHER TAFELWEIN Ordinary German table wine of supposedly tolerable quality; low natural strength, sugared at fermentation to increase alcohol, no specific vineyard origin. Deutscher Tafelwein must be 100 per cent German. From a good source, like the major supermarkets, it can be better than many QbAs, but other wines labelled 'Tafelwein' may also bear the ignominious title 'Wein aus verschiedenen Ländern der EG', (wine from different countries of the EC). Avoid them – they will be some of the least pleasant vinous experiences you have ever had the misfortune to suffer. Most honest merchants who do sell an 'EC Tafelwein' have now given up the Germanic pretence and call it 'Table Wine', which is an improvement *outside* the bottle anyway.

LANDWEIN German *vin de pays*, slightly up-market and drier table wine from one of 20 designated areas. It can be *Trocken* (dry) or *Halbtrocken* (half-dry).

QbA (Qualitätswein bestimmter Anbaugebiete) Literally 'quality wine from designated regions' – one of 11 specific areas: Ahr, Hessische Bergstrasse, Mittelrhein, Nahe, Rheingau, Rheinhessen, Rheinpfalz, Franken,

Württemberg, Baden, Mosel-Saar-Ruwer. QbAs cover a multitude of sins, from the most boring of Bereich Niersteins to products of prestigious single vineyards, where growers set standards far above those required by the law. These wines can be brimming with class and outstanding value for money.

QmP (Qualitätswein mit Prädikat) Quality wine with special attributes, classified in ascending order according to the sweetness of the grapes: Kabinett, Spätlese, Auslese, Beerenauslese, Eiswein, Trockenbeeren-auslese. In each category, up to and including Beerenauslese, the sugar content of the wine may range from virtually non-existent to positively luscious. Drier wines may be either Trocken (dry) or Halbtrocken (half-dry).

KABINETT Made from ripe grapes from a normal harvest. Usually lighter in alcohol than ordinary QbA, and often delicious.

Webster's is an annual publication. We welcome your suggestions for next year's edition.

SPÄTLESE From late-picked (and therefore riper) grapes. Often moderately sweet in style, though there is now an increasing tendency to produce a slightly drier version.

AUSLESE From selected bunches of especially ripe, sometimes late-picked grapes. Although Auslesen are often sweet and occasionally have an added richness from grapes affected by noble rot, many are now fermented to dryness.

BEERENAUSLESE (BA) From specially selected single grapes. Not quite so overripe as Trockenbeerenauslese, but almost always affected by 'noble rot', a fungus that feeds on the water in grapes, thus concentrating sugar and acidity. Beerenauslese from new, non-Riesling grapes can be a little disappointing and one-dimensional. The Huxelrebe, for instance, takes to noble rot so easily that you can make a BA before you've even picked Riesling. But any Riesling BA, and many a Scheurebe or Silvaner BA, will be truly astonishing experiences.

EISWEIN Just that – 'ice wine' – often picked before dawn in the depths of winter when the grapes are actually frozen pellets of ice in a sludgy fruit concentrate. The frozen fruit is dashed to the winery by the frost-bitten pickers; once there, quick and careful pressing removes just the slimy-sweet concentrate; the water, in its icy state, stays separate. Eiswein always has a high level of acidity and needs to be matured for at least seven years in bottle after the vintage.

TROCKENBEERENAUSLESE (TBA) 'Shrivelled berries gathered late.' That's a very pedestrian translation of one of the world's great taste sensations. To qualify for the TBA description, wines have to reach a ripeness of 21.5 degrees potential alcohol (21.1 in Baden), and some of the greatest reach a remarkable potential of 30 degrees or more. Anything much over 15 degrees in potential strength begins to stifle the yeasts – so much so that frequently fermentation hardly gets going at all, and a year later the liquid may have five to six degrees of actual alcohol but 15 to 20 degrees of unconverted sweetness (sugar unfermented to alcohol). A top Sauternes might be picked with 22 degrees potential alcohol, but end up with about 13 degrees or more, the rest remaining as unfermented sugar, so that TBAs are usually among the sweetest wines in the world. However, the general tendency is to produce a slightly drier, more alcoholic style. Few growers try to make TBAs because of the risk and the cost. Remember that the vines are producing a glass of wine each instead of a bottle, and picking is slow, labour-intensive and expensive – and the weather can so easily ruin it all anyway. That's why TBAs are expensive – usually starting at £30 to £40 a bottle ex-cellars. But, even at those prices, a grower won't make money on them; it's his pride, not his accountant's insistence that makes him do it. And the wines can age for as long as most of us will last.

The price guides for this section begin on page 333.

GRAPES & FLAVOURS

RIESLING I would say about 98 per cent of all the most exciting wines in Germany are made from the Riesling grape. It generally grows on the best slopes in the best villages, and its slow ripening and reasonably restrained yield produce an entire spectrum of flavours: from steely, slaty, and dry as sun-bleached bones through a range of deliciously scented fruits – apples, peaches, apricots, even lychees – more or less sweet according to the ripeness of the grapes and the intentions of the winemaker, and finally arriving at the great sweet wines, which can be blinding in their rich, honeyed concentration of peaches, pineapples, mangoes, even raisins ... with an acidity like a streak of fresh green lime that makes these wonderful wines the most appetizing of all great sweet wines (and allows the best to live for 50 years or more).

MÜLLER-THURGAU The most widely planted German grape, this is a 'cross' propagated in 1882 as a way of getting Riesling character but with big yields and early ripening. Well, frankly that's like saying, 'Hey, I've just found a way to turn this plastic bowl into a gold chalice'. You can't do it. Müller now does the workhorse job all over Germany, producing soft, flowery, grapy wines when ripe – and rather grassy, sharp wines when not. When the yields are kept right down, Müller can achieve the flavour of a good Silvaner.

SILVANER This was the German workhorse before Müller-Thurgau. At its worst it's a broad, earthy wine – dull, fat and vegetal. But on some sites in the Rheinhessen, Franken and the Nahe it is impressive – broad, yes, but powerful, too, developing a honeyed weight which means the slightly earthy, even tomatoey edge to the fruit balances rather than dominates.

ELBLING One of the original German grapes – maybe *the* original, but it doesn't have a lot to say for itself. It produces rather hollow, slight wine. It's still grown on the Mosel, where it's used either for fizz, or to pad out things like Mosel Tafelwein.

KERNER Another competitor in the 'Riesling-without-the-heartache' stakes. This was recently hailed as 'Riesling in type, but with bigger yields, and earlier ripening.' Is it? Of course not. It does ripen quickly, but the wine ages quickly, too, though with some peachy style.

MORIO-MUSKAT A pungent creation in the German battle to dominate the rump-end of the medium-sweet market. A few too many drops of this could turn a Sancerre into a Muscat de Beaumes de Venise, and, although it's still grown, use of its pungent muskily grapy wine is restricted.

RULÄNDER The French Pinot Gris. It produces two styles of wine in Germany. The first is strong, rather broad-shouldered, with a bite of kasbah spice and a big splash of honey. The second, sold as Grauburgunder, is firm and dry and can make exciting drinking.

SCHEUREBE A tricky grape. When it's unripe, it can pucker your mouth with a combination of raw grapefruit and cat's pee. But properly ripe, it is transformed. The grapefruit is still there, but now it's a fresh-cut pink one from Florida sprinkled with caster sugar. There's honey too, lashings of it, and a crackling, peppery fire which, in the Rheinhessen, Rheinpfalz and even in the Rheingau, produces dry wines as well as sweeter, sometimes outstanding Auslese and Beerenauslese.

SPÄTBURGUNDER The Pinot Noir produces a more thrilling display, with a bit more sun, further south in Burgundy. In Germany they have tended in the past to let it make gently fruity, slightly sweet, vaguely red wines. Now growers like *Becker* in the Rheingau, *Lingenfelder* in the Pfalz, *Karl-Heinz Johner* (ex Lamberhurst) in Baden and *Meyer-Näkel* in the Ahr are doing more exciting things. Their wines have good colour, tannin, are completely dry and often have a spell in oak. What's more, they reach (and pass) 13 degrees of alcohol without any added sugar at all. Eat your heart out Burgundy.

WINES & WINE REGIONS

AHR Ironically, this small area contrives to celebrate its northernmost position by being famous for red wines, though the flavour and the colour are pretty light, and its Rieslings are in fact more interesting. The *Staatliche Weinbaudomäne* is the best producer of old-style Spätburgunder. *Meyer-Näkel* represents the new school.

BADEN In the distant, balmy south of the country, free from some of the northern problems of climate, Baden makes some red and a lovely rosé in the hills near Freiburg, where they mix white Ruländer (the Pinot Gris or Tokay of Alsace) with red Pinot Noir. Ruländer by itself, as a white wine, can be really special – often as good as the fine examples from Alsace, only an hour's drive away over the Rhine. In Baden, even in ordinary vintages, it produces absurdly good, honeyed wine. Gewürztraminer is often dense and spicy, and even grapes like Müller-Thurgau and Silvaner can get quite interesting. There's only a little Riesling, but it's good and Spätburgunder is definitely on top. Some very good value wines come from small co-operative cellars, while production is dominated by the vast *Zentralkellerei*.

DEUTSCHER SEKT Often a sure route to intestinal distress and sulphur-led hangover, though Deinhard regularly manages to express the lovely, lean grapiness of the Riesling in its brands, of which *Lila* is particularly good. Now more and more private estates are making a Riesling Sekt. Not cheap, but quality is generally high.

FRANKEN (Franconia) This eastern region, actually part of Bavaria, is dry wine country. Even Spätlesen and Auslesen, while fairly big and beefy, are often basically dry. The slightly earthy, slightly vegetal, dryish Franken wines in their flagon-shaped 'Bocksbeutel' bottles are usually based on solid Silvaner or Müller-Thurgau and with strong Bavarian support, their prices are higher than for the Rhine or Mosel equivalent. The quality is, happily, good, but you can often get something much more interesting from elsewhere in Europe for a good deal less money. The best producers are Church and State – the *Juliusspital* and *Bürgerspital* charities and the *Staatlicher Hofkeller* – all in Würzburg, though *Johann Ruck* and *Hans Wirsching* at Iphofen are also good. The *Castell'sches Domänenamt* and *Rudolf Fürst* at Bürgstadt merit a detour.

HALBTROCKEN Half-dry. The general run of German wines goes from slightly sweet to very sweet, and this 'half-dry' classification was created primarily to satisfy the Germans' own desire for dry wine in the French style. The trouble is it's a lot easier to ripen a grape in France, so first efforts were mean and unbalanced. The 1985 vintage showed that producers were learning how to preserve the fruit flavour without oversweetening. At Kabinett and Spätlese level there are at last some quite good wines – but they're *not* cheap.

HESSISCHE BERGSTRASSE A tiny Rhine side-valley running down to Heidelberg, where, presumably, most of its wine is drunk – because it never gets over here. The central town of Bensheim has one of the highest average temperatures of any wine region in Germany, so the wine is worth seeking out. In general the Rieslings are of good quality, bright, fresh and fruity. The *Staatsweingut Bergstrasse* is the best producer.

LIEBFRAUMILCH Liebfraumilch is a brilliant invention, an innocuous, grapy liquid, usually from the Rheinhessen or Rheinpfalz, that has dramatically fulfilled a need in the UK and US markets: as the perfect 'beginner's wine', it has broken through the class barriers and mystique of wine-drinking. In a way, the rest of German wine has let Liebfraumilch down, because if Liebfraumilch is the base, you should be able to move on to a variety of other experiences – yet many of the supposedly superior QbAs and even some Kabinetts, for all their high-falutin' names, are *less* satisfying than a properly made young Liebfraumilch.

MITTELRHEIN The Rhine gorge at its most beautiful, providing all the label ideas for castles clinging to cliffs high above the boats and river-front cafés. It really is like that, and the tourists sensibly flock there in enormous numbers, and just as sensibly drink almost all of its wine. If you do see a bottle, try it, because it's almost all Riesling on those slaty slopes.

MOSEL-SAAR-RUWER When they are based on the Riesling grape, and when they come from one of the numerous steep, slaty, south-facing sites nestled into the folds of the river, or strung out for mile upon mile along the soaring, broad-shouldered valley sides, these northerly wines are unlike any others in the world. They can achieve a thrilling, orchard-fresh, spring flowers flavour, allied to an alcohol level so low

that it leaves your head clear enough, glass after glass, to revel in the flavours of the fruit. Most Mosel wine comes from the river valley itself, but two small tributaries have been incorporated in the general designation: the Saar and the Ruwer, making even lighter, sometimes sharper, sometimes more ethereal wines.

Some of the best wines come from the *Bischöfliches Konvikt, Bischöfliches Priesterseminar, Wegeler-Deinhard, Dr Loosen St Johannishof, Friedrich Wilhelm Gymnasium, Hohe Domkirche, Geltz-Zilliken, Fritz Haag, von Kesselstatt, Müller-Scharzhof, J.J. Prüm, Lauerburg, Mönchhof, Prüm-Studert, M.F. Richter, Schloss Saarstein, von Schubert, Bert Simon, Thanisch, Van Volxem, Vereinigte Hospitien, Weins-Prüm* and the *Staatliche Weinbaudomänen* based in Trier.

REGIONAL DEFINITIONS

German wine is classified according to ripeness of grapes and also according to provenance. The country is divided into 11 wine regions (alphabetically listed on these pages – Rheingau, Rheinhessen, etc); inside these regions, there are three groupings.

Bereich This is a collection of villages and vineyard sites, supposedly of similar style, and grouped under a single name – generally that of the most famous village. So 'Bereich Nierstein' means 'a wine from the general region of Nierstein'. I'm afraid it does *not* mean that the wine need bear the remotest resemblance to a good wine from the village of Nierstein – it could come from any one of 50 or more villages that have the right to the name 'Bereich Nierstein' regardless of quality. Bereich wines are pretty basic.

Grosslage A group of vineyards supposedly all of similar type, and based on one or more villages. The objective was to try and make some sense of the thousands of obscure vineyard names which obfuscated the German wine scene prior to the revamp of the German Wine Law in 1971. But it doesn't work. Among the 152 designated names, there are a few good Grosslagen that group closely related vineyards together under a single name – like Honigberg, which groups the vineyards of Winkel in the Rheingau, or Badstube which covers the best sites in Bernkastel. In these Grosslagen, a blend of several different vineyard sites will produce a wine of considerable quality and identifiable local character. However, most Grosslagen debase the whole idea of a 'vineyard' identity. Taken to absurd limits, Germany's most famous Grosslage is Niersteiner Gutes Domtal. Gutes Domtal was originally a vineyard of 34 hectares in Nierstein – and not terribly special at that. The Niersteiner Gutes Domtal Grosslage covers 1300 hectares, spread over 15 villages, almost all of which share no quality traits with Nierstein whatsoever! But, ridiculously, unless you manage to memorize all the Grosslage names, there is *no* way of telling from the label which is a Grosslage and which is an Einzellage, or genuine single vineyard.

Einzellage This is a real 'single' vineyard wine, corresponding to a 'Cru' in Burgundy or Alsace. There are about 2600 of these, ranging from a mere half hectare to 250 hectares. All the best wines in Germany are from Einzellagen, though only a distressingly small proportion have real style or individuality. Some growers are using Einzellage names less, and emphasizing their estate and vine variety names more.

NAHE Important side-valley off the Rhine, snaking south from Bingen. Many of Germany's best Kabinett and Spätlese wines come from its middle slopes, wines with a grapy taste balanced by quite high acidity, and something slightly mineral too. Away from this centre of quality, the wines are, sadly, less reliable. Top producers include *Weingut Ökonomierat August Anheuser, Weingut Paul Anheuser*, another branch of the same family, *Crusius, Hermann Dönnhoff, Schloss Plettenberg, Diel*, and, a long mouthful to build up a thirst, the *Verwaltung der Staatlichen Weinbaudomänen Niederhausen-Schlossböckelheim*.

RHEINGAU This famous fine wine area spreads north and east of Bingen. It is here, in the best vineyards, that the Riesling makes its most remarkable wines – given a long, warm ripening period and a caring winemaker. The Rheingau contains more world-famous villages than any other German vineyard area, and even its lesser villages are well aware of their region's prestige. It seems a shame to grow the lesser grapes here at all, because the Riesling picks up the minerally dryness, the tangy acidity and a delicious, grapy fruitiness, varying from apple-fresh in a good Kabinett to almost unbearably honeyed in a great Trockenbeerenauslese. Even the Kabinetts have body and ripeness. Top Rheingau producers include: *Aschrott, Balthasar Ress, J.B. Becker* (who also makes a very good red), *G. Breuer, Diefenhardt'sches Weingut, Wegeler-Deinhard, Krayer, Langwerth, Knyphausen, von Mumm, Nägler, Schloss Groenesteyn, Schloss Johannisberg, Schloss Reinhartshausen, Schloss Schönborn, Schloss Vollrads, von Simmern, Sohlbach, Staatsweingut Eltville* and *Dr Weil*.

RHEINHESSEN The Rhine turns south at Wiesbaden and flows down the side of the Rheinhessen, which, despite having one village as famous as any in the world – Nierstein – is packed with unknown backwoods names. Single-vineyard wines from Nierstein and its unsung neighbours Nackenheim, Oppenheim and Bodenheim can be superb, softer than Rheingaus, but still beautifully balanced, flowery and grapy. Otherwise, we're in the land of Liebfraumilch and Bereich Nierstein and a great deal of Rheinhessen wine ends up anonymously in one of these two blends. Bereich means district, and poor old Nierstein has had to lend its name to a mass of flabby up-country wines that have nothing to do with the river-front specials of the village itself. The village, rightly, feels aggrieved, because its own reputation – traditionally sky-high – is seriously compromised by the flood of sugared mouthwash that oozes out under the Bereich name. It is only the propagation of pungent new grape types that gives most of these overproduced wines any character at all. But even this is a distortion of Rheinhessen's previous reputation, which was built on light, flowery wines, notably from Silvaner grapes. Yet since 1964, the percentage of Silvaner has dropped from 47 to 13 per cent of the whole area under vine. Top producers include *Balbach, Carl Koch Erben, Gunderloch-Usinger, Guntrum, Heyl zu Herrnsheim, Schloss Westerhaus, Senfter, Gustav Adolf Schmidt* and *Villa Sachsen*.

RHEINPFALZ Sometimes known in English as the Palatinate, this has two distinct halves. The northern half clusters round some extremely good villages, in particular Forst, Wachenheim, Deidesheim and Ruppertsberg. There's lots of Riesling, and the wine has a big, spicy, fiery fruit, rather exotic in a tropical-fruit-salad way, but with the lovely, clear Riesling bite. Scheurebe is also fierily excellent. In general, this isn't true of the southern portion, the Südliche Weinstrasse, although a few young, outstanding winemakers are causing a stir in hitherto unknown villages near 'the Southern Wine Road'. The best wines come from sloping vineyards where members of the Pinot family of grapes making up to nearly 16 per cent alcohol – naturally – can be found! Down on the plain much Liebfraumilch is produced, and it's normally a bit tastier than the Rheinhessen equivalent. Some of the finest Rheinpfalz wines come from *Basserman-Jordan, von Buhl, Bürklin-Wolf, Wegeler-Deinhard, Koehler-Ruprecht, Müller-Catoir, Pfeffingen, Rebholz, Siegrist* and *Weingut Lingenfelder*. There are some good, true-to-type wines from co-operatives such as the *Forster Winzerverein*, the *Niederkirchen Winzerverein* and the large *Rhodt U. Rietburg*.

SCHAUMWEIN Basic German fizz. I just find it difficult to work out how they manage to make it so incredibly unrefreshing and aggressive.

SEKT Supposedly the superior form of Schaumwein, but really there's little difference between most of them, since they rely on appallingly foul foreign imports for their base wine – unless the label says 'Deutscher Sekt'. Ugh!

TROCKEN Dry. The driest German wines. Back in the early 1970s these were painfully, searingly horrid creatures, but things have been improving, and at Spätlese level in particular there are some positively attractive (though pricy) wines, and 1988s and 1989s have even kept some fruit! Dry Auslesen can be outstanding if you can track any down.

WÜRTTEMBERG We don't see much Württemberg wine here in the UK. In fact, nobody sees much of it, except the Württembergers, because it's almost all drunk on the spot. Württemberg's claim to fame – if fame is the right word – is for vaguely red wines, particularly from the Trollinger grape. They're usually pretty unspecial in a smoky, slightly sweet way.

VINTAGES

1989 The vintage to prove the exception – that big can still be beautiful – where there is style to go with the body, as the second largest vintage of the decade showed. The wine everywhere was good and sometimes great, with quick-off-the-mark Riesling grapes producing luscious TbA as early as *27 September* on the Bürklin-Wolf estate in the Rheinpfalz! Growers who restricted yields, picked from mature vines, and survived a very dry August and September, made concentrated and powerful wines. Keep the good dry ones for 1993; the sweeter styles need longer to develop.

1988 Wonderful, wonderful wines. Lovely fresh acidity, a beautiful clear, thrilling fruit and remarkable array of *personalities* – you really can see the differences between vineyard sites.

1987 A lovely, dry, not entirely ripe vintage which produced lots of QbA wines from top vineyards which are absolutely delicious.

1986 Not very ripe, not very clean, not very exciting. Some fair wines, nothing outstanding.

1985 Very attractive, fresh-fruited wines, without the sheer zinging class of '88, but still drinking well.

1983 Some examples this year have seemed a bit dull. Better estates should provide good drinking for some years yet.

1976 There are still wines around from this super-rich, super-ripe vintage – and they're not always too expensive.

WINERY PROFILES

FRIEDRICH-WILHELM-GYMNASIUM
★★★★(★) (Mosel-Saar-Ruwer) Large Trier
estate consisting of vineyards given to the
school where Karl Marx was educated. The
wines are textbook Mosel – flowery-
scented, fresh and racy.

**FÜRSTLICH CASTELL'SCHES
DOMÄNENAMT** ★★★★ (Franconia)
Princely estate in the Steigerwald hills
which produces excellent Müller-Thurgau,
Silvaner, Riesling and as a speciality in top
years, wonderfully concentrated Rieslaner.

SCHLOSS VOLLRADS ★★(★)
(Rheingau) The Rheingau's most beautiful
private estate. Very clean, steely, rather
austere wines which can be overdone in
less ripe vintages. Vollrads Beeren- and
Trockenbeerenauslesen of top years are
some of the world's greatest dessert wines.

STAATLICHE WEINBAUDOMÄNE
★★★★★ (Nahe) The State Domaine at
Niederhausen is one of the great white
wine estates of the world, producing
Rieslings which combine Mosel-like flowery
fragrance with a special mineral intensity.
Prices are very reasonable, considering the
very good quality.

VON SCHUBERT ★★★★★ (Mosel-Saar-
Ruwer) Exquisitely delicate, fragrant
Rieslings are grown on the slopes above the
Maximin-Grünhaus, a former monastic
property on the tiny Ruwer. The best
vineyard at the top of the hill is called
Abtsberg, because the wine was reserved
for the abbot: the scarcely less good middle
slope, whose wine was served to the monks,
is called Bruderberg. Superlative at every
level of quality.

WEGELER-DEINHARD ★★★★(★)
(Mosel-Saar-Ruwer) Koblenz-based shipper
with substantial holdings in Rheingau and
Rheinpfalz as well as Ruwer and Mosel,
where it shares the famous Bernkasteler
Doctor vineyard. Wines from all three
estates are impeccably made, clean, fresh
and racy: BAs and TBAs can be delicious
too. Good new Heritage range.

WEINGUT BALTHASAR RESS
★★★★(★) (Rheingau) Stefan Ress's
beautifully fresh, clean Riesling wines have
performed consistently well in blind
tastings. Highly successful at both
traditional-style Spätlese and Auslese
(some wonderful '83s) and medium-dry
wines under the Charta group label.

WEINGUT G. BREUER ★★★ (Rheingau)
Has improved by leaps and bounds since
Bernhard Breuer took over in 1975. The
best wines from the Rüdesheimer Berg
vineyards – especially Rüdesheimer Berg
Schlossberg – are ripe and concentrated.

WEINGUT DR BÜRKLIN-WOLF ★★★★
(Rheinpfalz) Bürklin's wines have an
aristocratic elegance which sometimes
suggests the Rheingau. Their top
Wachenheim wines, from flat vineyards,
disprove the theory that great German
wines must come from steep slopes.

WEINGUT LOUIS GUNTRUM ★★★(★)
(Rheinhessen) Guntrum wines are always
reliable: top Rieslings and Silvaners from
Oppenheimer Sackträger are impressively
powerful, with a touch of earthiness.

WEINGUT HEYL ZU HERRNSHEIM
★★★★(★) (Rheinhessen) Scandalously
underrated in Britain, producing
magnificent, traditional-style Riesling
Spätlese, ripe yet beautifully balanced,
from the red slate vineyards of Nierstein.

WEINGUT LINGENFELDER ★★★(★)
(Rheinpfalz) Dynamic small estate in
northern Pfalz, producing excellent
Riesling and Scheurebe, both dry and
'traditional', as well as remarkably deep-
coloured, full-bodied red Spatburgunder.

WEINGUT J.J. PRÜM ★★★★(★) (Mosel-
Saar-Ruwer) Legendary estate with large
holding in the great Wehlener Sonnenuhr
vineyard. These are wines for the long
haul: often prickly with carbon dioxide
when young, and high in acidity, they
develop a marvellous peachy richness with
time. Wonderful stuff.

ITALY

After an era of sometimes frantic change, Italy's wine industry leaders at last seem determined to reduce production and improve quality, while making wine laws and labels more comprehensible.

The government took steps in 1990 to bring production closer in line with EC standards through long-delayed reforms of the wine laws and a broadened system of controls. Moves by the Ministry of Agriculture and the National DOC Committee were prompted in part by the growing realization that wine lovers outside Italy are confused by the disorderly array of wines emanating from the country. One result is that DOC and DOCG, Italy's AC equivalents, have been ridiculed outside Italy by critics who find it odd that so many of the nation's fine wines are categorized as simple *vini da tavola* (table wines).

The national viticultural programme, established in late 1990, aims to increase the proportion of wine of controlled name and origin (DOC or DOCG) from 11 per cent to about 20 per cent of the total in coming years – though that would still leave Italy below the EC average of 30 per cent. Another 40 per cent of the total is to come under the new category of *vini tipici* (equivalent to the French *vins de pays*) to cover a significant portion of what have been categorized up to now as *vini da tavola*.

Among a series of planned revisions, perhaps the most important step toward building prestige for the top wines would be official recognition of individual vineyards within the DOC/DOCG zones. Already many Italian wines carry vineyard names on their labels, but their authenticity relies on producers' integrity alone. Under the proposed system, which seems likely to begin with the Barolo and Barbaresco DOCG zones of Piedmont, individual vineyards could be officially placed at the peak of wine categories.

The base of the pyramid would be table wines, or eventually *vini tipici*, from geographical areas covering entire regions (such as Piemonte or Toscana) or provinces (Verona or Siena) or else large vineyard areas such as Tuscany's Maremma or Piedmont's Langhe hills. The next step up the scale would be existing DOC zones, of which there are about 230, and then DOCG zones, of which there are now eight. Communes or certain areas in the DOC or DOCG zones may now be cited on labels. Production in approved vineyards would be validated through annual crop controls so that names could appear on labels as the highest level of status.

Another change being considered by the DOC Committee is the recognition of important wines with special niches of their own within the system. This would mean that a prominent table wine, such as Tuscany's Sassicaia, would earn its own appellation. It remains to be seen how the many other so-called Super Tuscan and other key table wines might be categorized. But there seems to be little doubt that wines of proven class will be recognized officially.

A recent decree by the Ministry of Agriculture requires all DOC wines to be subjected to taste examinations to certify that they are true to type and meet a reasonable quality standard. Previously, all DOC wines were subject to chemical analysis, but taste tests had been optional, often carried out by producers' consortiums for the right to carry a seal. All DOCG wines have been subject to approval by tasting commissions from the start. The process has been credited

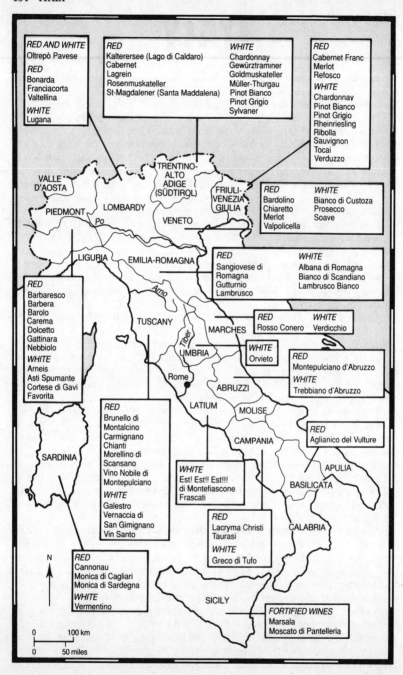

RED AND WHITE
Oltrepò Pavese

RED
Bonarda
Franciacorta
Valtellina

WHITE
Lugana

RED
Kalterersee (Lago di Caldaro)
Cabernet
Lagrein
Rosenmuskateller
St-Magdalener (Santa Maddalena)

WHITE
Chardonnay
Gewürztraminer
Goldmuskateller
Müller-Thurgau
Pinot Bianco
Pinot Grigio
Sylvaner

RED
Cabernet Franc
Merlot
Refosco

WHITE
Chardonnay
Pinot Bianco
Pinot Grigio
Rheinriesling
Ribolla
Sauvignon
Tocai
Verduzzo

RED
Bardolino
Chiaretto
Merlot
Valpolicella

WHITE
Bianco di Custoza
Prosecco
Soave

RED
Sangiovese di
Romagna
Gutturnio
Lambrusco

WHITE
Albana di Romagna
Bianco di Scandiano
Lambrusco Bianco

RED
Rosso Conero

WHITE
Verdicchio

WHITE
Orvieto

RED
Montepulciano d'Abruzzo

WHITE
Trebbiano d'Abruzzo

RED
Barbaresco
Barbera
Barolo
Carema
Dolcetto
Gattinara
Nebbiolo

WHITE
Arneis
Asti Spumante
Cortese di Gavi
Favorita

RED
Brunello di
Montalcino
Carmignano
Chianti
Morellino di
Scansano
Vino Nobile di
Montepulciano

WHITE
Galestro
Vernaccia di
San Gimignano
Vin Santo

WHITE
Est! Est!! Est!!!
di Montefiascone
Frascati

RED
Lacryma Christi
Taurasi

WHITE
Greco di Tufo

RED
Aglianico del Vulture

RED
Cannonau
Monica di Cagliari
Monica di Sardegna

WHITE
Vermentino

FORTIFIED WINES
Marsala
Moscato di Pantelleria

VALLE
D'AOSTA

TRENTINO-
ALTO
ADIGE
(SÜDTIROL)

FRIULI-
VENEZIA
GIULIA

PIEDMONT

LOMBARDY

VENETO

Po

LIGURIA

EMILIA-ROMAGNA

Arno

TUSCANY

MARCHES

Tiber

UMBRIA

Orvieto

Rome

ABRUZZI

LATIUM

MOLISE

CAMPANIA

APULIA

BASILICATA

CALABRIA

SARDINIA

N

SICILY

0   100 km

0   50 miles

with reducing the quantities of two controversial guaranteed wines – Chianti and Albana di Romagna – and improving their quality standards.

There is also a movement in favour of replacing the G in DOCG with an S (for selected) on the grounds that the state is not qualified to offer a commercial guarantee. Standards would be made even more rigid for wines to qualify as 'selected', but it has to be admitted that it would be difficult to change the existing terminology. The number of wines covered by DOCG increased from six to eight this year with the addition of Carmignano in Tuscany and Torgiano Rosso Riserva in Umbria. Piedmont's Gattinara, Latium's Frascati and Umbria's Orvieto are among other wines expected to join the guaranteed list soon.

At last, Italy's officials seem aware of the need to make the country's wine laws credible, thereby upgrading its image.　　　　　　　**BURTON ANDERSON**

RED WINES

Whereas France has been – and is – the model for all the New World exploits, and although grapes like Cabernet Sauvignon and Pinot Noir *are* important in Italy, the true glories of Italy are unimitated anywhere else. Red wines from Nebbiolo, Dolcetto, Montepulciano, Lagrein, Sangiovese, Aglianico, Sagrantino and many others are unique expressions of a wine culture which has been too inward-looking for too long. But the jewels are coming out of the woodwork – a mixed metaphor which I think is entirely apt for the strange delights I'm now lapping up with such zeal.

GRAPES & FLAVOURS

AGLIANICO A very late-ripening grape of Greek origin, grown in the south of Italy. At its most impressive in Aglianico del Vulture (Basilicata) and Taurasi (Campania).

BARBERA The most prolific grape of Piedmont in the north-west. Traditionally the wines have high acidity, a slightly resiny edge and yet a sweet-sour, raisiny taste or even a brown-sugar sweetness. However, Barbera doesn't have to make this traditional style of wine. There has been some excitement in Piedmont over Barbera wines made 'Beaujolais style' by carbonic maceration, fermenting whole grapes to keep in all the fruit and aromas, while keeping out much of the tough astringency. Experiments with *barrique*-ageing it are even more encouraging, and wines like *Bertini's Alto Mango* are outstandingly richly flavoured reds. Also look for *Michele Chiarlo* and *Tesco's Valle del Sole*.

BONARDA Low acid, rich, plummy reds, often with a liquoricy, chocolaty streak, and sometimes a slight spritz. Most common in Emilia-Romagna (Colli Piacentini) and Oltrepò Pavese (where it is also known as Croatina). Often blended with Barbera to good effect under the title Gutturnio.

CABERNET SAUVIGNON A contentious grape in Italy, not because of quality, but because of *tipicità* – typicity. Many traditionalists are distressed at how this world-class grape is usurping the place of indigenous varieties in the vineyard and also dominating any grape with which it is blended. In fact there has been Cabernet Sauvignon in Italy for well over a century, and it has produced wine of memorable fruit and perfume in Tuscany for a very long time, but, following the surge in popularity – and price – of top red Bordeaux as well as the new Australian and US classics, Italians have planted Cabernet Sauvignon in a rush. This is most evident in Tuscany, where Cabernet has added greatly to the fruit of many wines and, aged in small oak barrels, is producing wines of irresistible fruit and potential world class. Sassicaia has spawned a host of imitators. There are Chiantis around with a dollop of Cabernet in too, though the trend seems already to have peaked.

CABERNET FRANC Fairly widely planted in the north-east of Italy, especially in Alto Adige, Trentino, Veneto and Friuli. It can make gorgeous grassy, yet juicy-fruited reds – unnervingly easy to drink very young, but also capable of a good few years' ageing. At six to ten years old, they can be very special, in an earthy, soft way.

DOLCETTO Makes good, brash, fruity, purple wine of the same name in Piedmont, ideally full yet soft, slightly chocolaty and spicy, and wonderfully refreshing when young. Try and get hold of some of the exciting 1989s – *now*.

LAGREIN Local grape of the Alto Adige (Südtirol) and Trentino, making delicious, dark reds, strongly plum-sweet when they're young, ageing slowly to a smoky, creamy softness. It also makes one of Italy's best rosés, called Lagrein Kretzer.

MERLOT Widely planted in the north-east. Often good in Friuli; provides enormous amounts of jug wine in the Veneto. *Mecvini* is experimenting with Merlot-Cabernet Sauvignon blends in the Marches, but classic Cabernet-Merlot is still not all that common. In Tuscany, *Avignonesi* and *Castello di Ama* are achieving promising results with the grape.

MONTEPULCIANO One of Italy's most underrated grapes because, while it has toughness, it also has masses of plummy, herby fruit. *Banfi* in Montalcino have high hopes for it. It's also grown along the Adriatic coast, from the Marches to Puglia.

NEBBIOLO The big, tough grape of the north-west, making – unblended – the famous Barolos and Barbarescos as well as less famous names such as Gattinara, Ghemme, Carema, Spanna and plain Nebbiolo. This is a surly, fierce grape,

producing wines that are dark, chewy, harsh and unyielding behind a shield of cold-tea-tannin and acidity for the first few years of their life; but which then blossom out into a remarkable shower of flavours, a richness full of chocolate, raisins, prunes, and an austere perfume of tobacco and pine and herbs. Well, the best wines do this anyway. In the past, sloppy wine-making has been all too evident in the wines available here. But our wine buyers are more willing now to fork out for the best, and in 1985 modern wine-making principles allied with a really beautiful vintage produced some truly stunning wines. There are good 1986s and '87s around too. The Swiss, the Germans and the Americans liked the '85s so much that the prices are pretty high. A few growers (*Elio Altare, Clerico, Conterno Fantino* and *Voerzio*) are producing some superb *vini da tavola* by ageing their wines in *barrique*, or blending them with Barbera, or both.

SANGIOVESE Too much is often asked of this Chianti mainstay. It is extremely good at providing purple-fresh, slightly rasping, herby wines, full of thirst-quenching, acid fruit, to be drunk young. It's not always so successful at providing the weight and personality needed for more 'serious' wines. This is mainly because the recommended clone for the 1970s replanting scheme was a high-yielding one, rather than the native Tuscan variety. You can make decent quaffing wines from the high-yielders, but wines of real class and substance are only made on estates with the Tuscan clone. There is a spirited attempt under way in the Chianti Classico region to isolate and propagate the best clones in replanting and grafting schemes in the vineyards. These make a deeper, plummier wine and are contributing hugely to the improved quality of Tuscan reds.

SCHIAVA Quaffable, light reds with almost no tannin and a unique taste that veers between smoked ham and strawberry yoghurt. An Alto Adige (Südtirol) grape, though also grown in Trentino, Schiava is at its best in the wines of Kalterersee Auslese (Lago di Caldaro Scelto) and Santa Maddalena. The locals call it by its German name, Vernatsch.

WINES & WINE REGIONS

AGLIANICO DEL VULTURE, DOC
(Basilicata) High up the side of gaunt
Monte Vulture, in the wilds of Basilicata
(Italy's 'instep'), the Aglianico grape finds
sufficiently cool conditions to make a
superb, thick-flavoured red wine. The
colour isn't particularly deep, but the
tremendous almond paste and chocolate
fruit are matched by a tough, dusty feel
and quite high acidity. What's more, it's *not*
very expensive. Good producers:
Paternoster, Fratelli d'Angelo. D'Angelo's
new *barriqued Canneto d'Angelo* is good.

ALTO ADIGE Also called Südtirol as the
majority of the population is German-
speaking. Although the UK drinks
primarily white Alto Adige wines, the
attractive light reds made of the
Vernatsch/Schiava grape – especially
Kalterersee and St Magdalener – have
until recently been the most famous
offerings, because the Swiss, Austrians and
Germans were keen on them. However,
Cabernet, Pinot Nero, Lagrein and the tea-
rose-scented Rosenmuskateller all make
Alto Adige reds – and rosés – with a lot
more stuffing to them.

BARBARESCO, DOCG (Piedmont)
Toughness and tannin are the hallmarks of
the Nebbiolo, Barbaresco's only grape
variety, and they often overshadow the
finer points of this wine which can reach a
delicious soft, strawberryish maturity,
edged with smoke and herbs and pine, as
long as the surprisingly delicate fruit
doesn't give out under pressure from the
Nebbiolo's remorseless tannin. Most wine
is of *normale* quality – and only needs two
years' ageing, one of which must be in
wood. A Riserva has to age for three years
before release, and Riserva Speciale for
four. Traditionally, this has been in large
old wooden barrels, which doesn't help in
the battle to emphasize the Nebbiolo's
fruit, so an increasing number of producers
are doing part of this ageing either in
stainless steel or in bottle to preserve that
fruit, which can have more nuances and
glints of brilliance than any other Italian
grape. Top producers include *Castello di*

*Neive, Cigliuti, Giuseppe Cortese, Gaja,
Bruno Giacosa, Marchesi di Gresy,
Moresco, Pasquero, Pelissero, Pertinace,
Pio Cesare, Produttori del Barbaresco,
Roagna* and *Scarpa.*

BARBERA, some **DOC** (Piedmont and
elsewhere) Barbera is Italy's most widely
planted red vine, and makes a good, gutsy
red, usually with a resinous, herby bite, an
insistent, high acidity, and a fairly
forthright dry raisin sort of fruit. It is best
in Piedmont, where it has four DOCs,
Barbera d'Alba, Barbera d'Asti, Barbera
del Monferrato and Rubino di Cantavenna,
and in Lombardy under the Oltrepò Pavese
DOC; also common in Puglia, and found in
Emilia-Romagna, Liguria, Campania,
Sicily and Sardinia.

BARDOLINO, DOC (Veneto) An
increasing number of pale pinky reds with
a frail wispy cherry fruit and a slight bitter
snap to the finish are appearing from the
banks of Lake Garda, along with some
lovely Chiaretto rosés and some excellent,
very fresh-fruited Novello wines. There are
also a few fuller, rounder wines like
Boscaini's Le Canne which can take some
ageing. As quality has risen, so have the
prices though. Other good producers:
*Arvedi d'Emilei, Guerrieri-Rizzardi,
Lenotti, Masi* (especially *Fresco* and *La
Vegrona*), *Portalupi* and *Le Vigne di San
Pietro.*

BAROLO, DOCG (Piedmont) Praise be;
I'm slowly becoming a Barolo fan! Yet only
five years ago I wouldn't have found *any*
examples I liked.
    The raw material is still the muscular,
brooding, unrepentant Nebbiolo grape, a
monstrously difficult character that has
had to be dragged squealing and roaring
into the latter half of the twentieth century.
But an increasing number of growers are
attempting to emphasize the fruit of the
grape rather than the raw, rough tannins
of skin and cask and not only will these
wines be enjoyable younger – in five years
rather than 20 – they will actually *age
better* because you can't age a wine without

balance, and balance is also what makes a wine enjoyable reasonably young. There. That's my heresy for the day.

It would be easy to say only expensive Barolo is any good, but the efforts of Tesco, Sainsbury and Oddbins show that, as always, good buyers *can* find good bargains. Because despite being a difficult grape to grow and a difficult wine to vinify and mature properly, the Nebbiolo does have a remarkable, deep, sweet, plum and woodsmoke richness, sometimes even blackcurrants and raspberry pips, often a dark, wild maelstrom of chocolate and prunes and tobacco. If you bend the laws by shortening fermentation to extract less tannin, by ageing in stainless steel, or by bottling early, there are some magical experiences to be had. The first releases of 'modern' 1983 are a triumphant vindication of this philosophy. The 1984s from good producers who ruthlessly cut out poor grapes are drier, but delicious. I'm sticking with '83 and '84 for the moment until the hefty '85s start coming around. Some are already displaying delicious perfume, and in the wines from the best sites there's certainly masses of sweet, supple fruit to stand up to the tannin. The best wines come from *Altare, Ascheri,* *Borgogno, Bovio, Cavallotto, Ceretto, Chiarlo, Clerico, Aldo* and *Giacomo Conterno, Cordero di Montezemolo, Fontanafredda* (only their *cru* wines), *Bruno Giacosa, Giuseppe Mascarello, Migliorini, Pio Cesare, Prunotto, Ratti, Sandrone, Scarpa, Scavino, Vajra, Vietti* and *Voerzio.*

BONARDA (Lombardy) Delicious, young, plummy, fruity red with a dark chocolate bitter twist from Lombardy and Emilia in the central north. *Castello di Luzzano* is very good.

BREGANZE, DOC (Veneto) Little-known but excellent claret-like red from near Vicenza. There's Pinot Nero, Merlot and Cabernet (Sauvignon and Franc) and these Bordeaux grapes produce a most attractive grassy, blackcurranty red, with the slightest touch of cedar. Very good. *Maculan* age theirs in new wood, which is even more exciting.

BRUNELLO DI MONTALCINO, DOCG (Tuscany) A big, strong neighbour of Chianti – traditionally better known for its ridiculous prices than for exciting flavours – slowly coming to terms with a modern

---

CLASSIFICATIONS

Only 10 to 12 per cent of the massive Italian wine harvest is regulated in any way at present, and the regulations that do exist are treated in a fairly cavalier manner by many growers. At the same time producers, rebelling against the constraints imposed on their originality and initiative, have often chosen to operate outside the regulations and classify their – frequently exceptional – wine simply as *vino da tavola*, the lowest grade. This situation looks set to change, with up to 60 per cent of Italy's wines becoming subject to the law, and wines like Sassicaia in line for their own appellation, but for the time being the following are the main categories:

Vino da Tavola This is currently applied to absolutely basic stuff but also to 'maverick' wines of the highest class such as Sassicaia or Gaja's Piedmontese Chardonnay. In future, wines like these last will probably have their own appellation.

Vino Tipico This will apply to table wines with some reference to place, and maybe grape type, but which do not qualify for DOC.

Denominazione di Origine Controllata (DOC) This applies to wines from specified grape varieties, grown in delimited zones, then vinified and aged by prescribed methods to certain standards. Nearly all of Italy's traditionally well-known wines are DOC, but more get added every year. In future, the wines will also undergo a tasting test (as DOCG wines do now).

Denominazione di Origine Controllata e Garantita (DOCG) The top tier – a tighter form of DOC with more stringent restrictions on grape types, yields, methods of vinification, ageing and a tasting panel. First efforts were feeble, but a run of good vintages in 1982, '83, '85, '86 and '88 gave the producers lots of fine material to work with. The revised DOCG should give due recognition to particularly good vineyard sites in future.

cosmopolitan world where people are prepared to pay high prices, but demand the excellence that should go with them. Indeed, an increasing amount of the best Brunello wine is being siphoned off to provide the backbone for various non-DOC *barrique*-aged, super-trendy super-blends. The reason why the wine is usually disappointing is that it has lost its fruit during the interminable three and a half years' wood ageing required by the regulations. I can't wait until it comes down to three. In the right hands, however, in a good, clean cellar, the fruit can hold out against oxidation, or indeed – with a bending of the rules – it can be preserved by earlier bottling, or storage in steel, and then the wine can achieve a remarkable combination of flavours: raisins, blackberries, pepper, acidity, tannin with, hopefully, a haunting sandalwood perfume, and all bound together by an austere richness resembling liquorice and fierce black chocolate. As such, I'll admit it can be great wine. But such wines are still the minority while scary prices are the norm. The best wines come from *Altesino*, followed by *Campogiovanni, Caparzo, Casanova, Il Casello, Col d'Orcia, Costanti, Fattoria dei Barbi, Pertimali, Il Poggione, Talenti* and *Val di Suga*. *Biondi Santi* is the most famous and the most expensive producer. I haven't yet had a bottle that remotely justified the cost.

CAREMA, DOC (Piedmont) The most refined in bouquet and taste of the Nebbiolo wines from a tiny mountainous zone close to Val d'Aosta. *Luigi Ferrando* is the best producer, especially his 'black label', but almost all are good – and need five to six years to be at their best.

CARMIGNANO, DOCG (Tuscany) Although the advent of Cabernet Sauvignon in Tuscany is often talked of as an entirely recent phenomenon, Carmignano – a small enclave inside the Chianti zone to the west of Florence – has been bringing excitement to its wine by adding in 10 to 15 per cent Cabernet Sauvignon since the nineteenth century. The soft, clear blackcurranty fruit of the Cabernet makes a delicious blend with the stark flavours of the Sangiovese – the

majority grape. There is also some good rosé and some *vin santo*. The zone rose to DOCG status in 1990. *Capezzana* is the original estate and the only one regularly seen over here. Their '83 and '85 Riservas are special.

CHIANTI, DOCG (Tuscany) The first few times I had real Chianti, fizzy-fresh, purple-proud, with an invigorating, rasping fruit, I thought it was the most perfect of jug wines I'd ever had. It still can be. But after DOC arrived in 1963, there was a period when demand for Italian wine exceeded supply, vineyards expanded all over the place, and the wine industry attracted a lot of investors who cared only about profit and knew nothing of wine. Chianti, and especially Chianti Classico suffered more than its fair share of these fair weather investors.

But Chianti might have stood more chance if the chief grape, the Sangiovese, had not been debased, first by the planting of inferior, high-yielding clones, and second by the admixture of an excessive amount of white juice in with the red. Along with the traditional Malvasia, the habit had developed of mixing in the dull white Trebbiano to 'soften' the flavour. 'Deaden', more like. Growers could at one time legally mix in almost one-third white grapes in their Chianti – and the inevitable result was wines that simply faded before they even made it into bottle.

Thankfully DOCG regulations limit the proportion of white grapes to between two and five per cent. This seems to have stemmed the flow of thin Chianti we used to suffer and own-labels from companies like Asda can be very good.

Another important development in the Chianti region has been the emergence of Cabernet Sauvignon as a component of red wines. Although not really permissible for more than ten per cent of the total, the variety is so brilliantly suited to Tuscany that even five per cent can transform a blend. A number of growers include Cabernet in their Riserva blends to delicious effect, although as clonal selection of better Sangiovese develops, there may come a day when this addition is no longer necessary. The Chianti Classico Consorzio has set in train an operation called 'Chianti

Classico 2000' which is intended to ensure that all the mistakes committed in the rushed expansion of the 1970s don't occur again, and as replanting takes place only top clones of Sangiovese and Canaiolo are used. By 2000 we may well be classing Chianti Classico at least, as one of the world's great red wines.

The Chianti region is divided into seven regions as follows: Classico, Colli Aretini, Colli Fiorentini, Colli Senesi, Colline Pisane, Montalbano and Rufina. Classico and Rufina are almost always marked on the label, but the majority of wines from the other zones are simply labelled 'Chianti'.

In recent years growers have become increasingly interested in mapping out the different vineyard zones in this sprawling region, to give them a clearer view of which are the particularly good sites. Vineyard names are already starting to appear on the label.

CHIANTI STYLES There are two basic styles. The first is the sharp young red that used to come in wicker flasks and just occasionally still does. This starts out quite purple-red, but quickly takes on a slightly orange tinge and is sometimes slightly prickly, with a rather attractive taste, almost a tiny bit sour, but backed up by good, raisiny-sweet fruit, a rather stark, peppery bite and tobacco-like spice. This style is traditionally made by the 'governo' method, which involves adding – just after fermentation – a small quantity of grapes dried on racks, or concentrated must, together with a dried yeast culture, so that the wine re-ferments. Apart from imparting a prickle, this leaves the wine softer, rounder and more instantly appealing, but it also removes some of the colour and tannin and makes it age more quickly. So this is wine for drinking young.

The second type is usually several years old and, before the advent of DOCG, was likely to be light red fading to orange with a taste both acid and tannic – the acidity having an almost lemony, searing quality. In the bad old days, most Chiantis of more than four years old had all the acidity and tannin they needed, but the only fruit on show was a fistful of old raisins and a curious, unwelcome whiff of

tomatoes. Nowadays there are enough exceptions around to reckon that they are becoming the rule. The Chiantis of top estates, especially in fine vintages such as 1985, 1986 and 1988 are gaining a range of slightly raw strawberry, raspberry and blackcurrant flavours backed up by a herby, tobaccoey spice and a grapeskinsy roughness that makes the wine demanding but exciting. Top estates include *Amorosa, Badia a Coltibuono, Castellare, Castello di Ama, Castello di Fonterutoli, Castello dei Rampolla, Castello di San Polo in Rosso, Castell'in Villa, Castello di Volpaia, Felsina Berardenga, Fontodi, Montesodi* and *Nipozzano (Frescobaldi) Isole e Olena, Le Masse di San Leolino, Pagliarese, Peppoli (Antinori), Poggio Reale, Riecine, Selvapiana, San Felice, Vecchie Terre di Montefili, Vignale* and *Villa di Vetrice*.

DOLCETTO, some **DOC** (Piedmont) At its best, delicious, full but soft, fresh, and dramatically fruity red for gulping down fast and young. Wonderful ones come from *Altare, Ascheri, Gaja, Cogno-Marcarini, Aldo Conterno, Giacomo Conterno, Mascarello, Oddero, Pasquero, Prunotto, Sandrone, Vajra, Vietti, Viticoltori dell'Acquese* and *Voerzio*.

FRANCIACORTA ROSSO, DOC (Lombardy) Raw but tasty blackcurranty wine from east of Milan. The *Contessa Maggi* is particularly good – as is *Bellavista: Ca' del Bosco* and *Longhi De' Carli* are also good.

FRIULI Six different zones (of which Grave del Friuli DOC is by far the most important quantitatively) stretching from the flatlands just north of Venice to the Yugoslav borders. The wines are characterized by vibrant fruit. In particular, the 'international' grapes, Cabernet Franc and Merlot, have an absolutely delicious, juicy stab of flavour; and Refosco has a memorable flavour in the tar-and-plums mould – yet sharpened up with a grassy acidity. Good Cabernet from *Ca' Ronesca* and *Russiz Superiore. La Fattoria* and *Collavini* make excellent Cabernet and Merlot too and *Pintar* in the Collio area makes good Cabernet Franc. *Borgo Conventi*'s reds are very good.

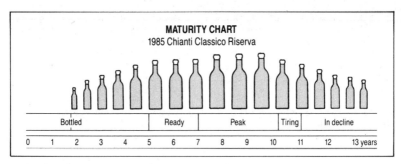

MATURITY CHART
1985 Chianti Classico Riserva

| Bottled | Ready | Peak | Tiring | In decline |

| 0 | 1 | 2 | 3 | 4 | 5 | 6 | 7 | 8 | 9 | 10 | 11 | 12 | 13 years |

GATTINARA, DOC (Piedmont) Good Nebbiolo-based red from the Vercelli hills in Piedmont, softer and quicker to mature than Barbaresco or Barolo, but also less potentially thrilling. *Dessilani* and *Travaglini* are important producers.

KALTERERSEE/LAGO DI CALDARO, DOC (Alto Adige) Good, light, soft red with an unbelievable flavour of home-made strawberry jam and woodsmoke, made from the Schiava (Vernatsch) grape in the Alto Adige. It is best as a young gulper. With higher (11 per cent) alcohol, it may be called Auslese or Scelto to indicate later-picked grapes. Best producers: *Gries* co-op, *Lageder, Muri-Gries, Hans Rottensteiner, St Michael-Eppan* co-op, *Tiefenbrunner* and *Walch*.

LAGREIN DUNKEL, some **DOC** (Alto Adige) Dark, chewy red from the Alto Adige (Südtirol) with a remarkable depth of flavour for the product of a high mountain valley. These intense wines have a tarry roughness jostling with chocolate-smooth ripe fruit, the flavour being a very successful mix between the strong, chunky style of many Italian reds and the fresher, brighter tastes of France. Best producers: *Gries* co-op, *Lageder, Muri-Gries, Niedermayr* and *Tiefenbrunner* are particularly good. *Tiefenbrunner* also makes an outstanding pink Lagrein Kretzer.

LAMBRUSCO, some **DOC** (Emilia-Romagna) Good Lambrusco – lightly fizzy, low in alcohol, red or white, dry to vaguely sweet – should *always* have a sharp, almost rasping acid bite to it. Real Lambrusco with a DOC, from Sorbara,

Santa Croce or Castelvetro, is anything but feeble and is an exciting palate-tingling accompaniment to rough-and-ready Italian food. But most Lambrusco is not DOC and is softened for fear of offending consumers. *Cavicchioli* is one of the few 'proper' ones that braves the UK shelves.

MONTEPULCIANO D'ABRUZZO, DOC (Abruzzi) Made on the east coast opposite Rome from the gutsy Montepulciano grape, a good Montepulciano d'Abruzzo manages to be citrus-fresh and plummily rich, juicy yet tannic, ripe yet with a tantalizing sour bite. Fine wines are made by producers such as *Mezzanotte* and *Pepe*, while the standard of co-ops such as *Casal Thaulero* and *Tollo* is remarkably high. Other good names include *Colle Secco, Illuminati Invecchiato* and *Valentini*. Prices are *not* high, except for the unique Valentini and, as one of Italy's most consistent wines, this rather forgotten, well-rounded red offers very good value.

OLTREPÒ PAVESE, some **DOC** (Lombardy) The leading DOC of Lombardy covering reds, rosés, dry whites, sweet whites, fizz – just about anything really. Almost the only wines we see are the sparklers, usually Champagne-method, and based on Pinot Grigio/Nero/Bianco – but often not sold with the DOC. In fact, only 17 per cent of Oltrepò Pavese uses the DOC, since most of it is drunk in nearby Milan, where regularity of supply is more prized than fancy letters on the label. We see a little red – ideally based on Barbera and Bonarda, which is thoroughly good, substantial stuff, big, soft and full of fruit though if you drink it in Milan, don't be surprised to find it's fizzy.

POMINO, DOC (Tuscany) A DOC for red, white and the dessert wine *vin santo* in the Rufina area of Chianti. The red, based on Sangiovese with Canaiolo, Cabernet and Merlot, is rich, soft and velvety. It can age well becoming increasingly spicy. Only producer: *Marchesi de' Frescobaldi*.

REFOSCO, some **DOC** (Friuli) Native Friuli grape producing dark, smoky reds with some plum sweetness too. Good, when not too tough. *Dri* is the best I know.

ROSSO CONERO, DOC (Marches) A very good, sturdy red from the Marches, on the east coast opposite Florence and Siena. Combining the tasty Montepulciano grape and up to 15 per cent Sangiovese, Rosso Conero frequently blends herb and fruit flavours with a slight prickle because, as in Chianti, the *governo* method is much practised here; sometimes with some oak barrel ageing to add extra richness. Look for wines of *Bianchi, Garofoli, Marchetti* and *Mecvini*.

ROSSO DI MONTALCINO, DOC (Tuscany) DOC introduced in 1984 as an alternative for producers of Brunello who didn't want to age all that wine for Brunello's statutory four years, or who, like the top châteaux of Bordeaux, wanted to make a 'second wine'. Softer, more approachable and cheaper than Brunello.

ROSSO DI MONTEPULCIANO, DOC (Tuscany) New DOC, starting from the 1989 vintage. This will be to Vino Nobile what Rosso di Montalcino is to Brunello, for the 'second wines' of Montepulciano.

SPANNA (Piedmont) A Nebbiolo-based wine with a lovely raisin and chocolate flavour in the old style. Even cheap 'trattoria' Spannas are usually a good bet.

TAURASI, DOC (Campania) Remarkable, plummy yet bitingly austere red grown inland from Naples. To be honest, I'm *not* totally convinced, and am still waiting for a really exciting follow-up to the remarkable 1968. Recent releases just haven't had the fruit or, as with the 1983, are impossibly tannic. *Mastroberardino* is the chief producer.

TORGIANO, DOC and **DOCG** (Umbria) A region south-east of Perugia whose fame has been entirely created by *Lungarotti*. The reds are strong, plummy, sometimes overbearing wines, usually carrying the tradename Rubesco. Single vineyard Monticchio and San Giorgio Cabernet Sauvignon are exciting. In 1990 Torgiano Rosso Riserva wines gained DOCG status. Whites are clean and good, while the Chardonnay Miralduolo Riserva is dry, carefully oaked and classy. They also make a good *flor*-affected sherry-type wine called Solleone.

TRENTINO, DOC Just south of the Alto Adige (Südtirol), making reds either from local varieties such as Lagrein, Teroldego and Marzemino or from international grapes like Cabernet, Merlot and Pinot Noir. Too often they are light, with their attractive fruit hopelessly diluted by overcropping, which is a pity, because some lovely Cabernets and Chardonnays in particular have come from good producers. Good producers: *Conti Martini Foradori (Teroldego), Istituto di San Michele, Gonzaga, Guerrieri, Pojer e Sandri, de Tarczal (Marzemino), Zeni.*

VALPOLICELLA, DOC (Veneto) Over the years, the amount of rubbish the DOC rules have somehow passed as typical and fit to drink from this north-eastern region leaves one aghast. Made from a variety of local grapes, but especially the Corvina, Rondinella and Molinara, Valpolicella *should* have delicious, light, cherry-fruit, and a bitter almond twist to the finish – just a bit fuller and deeper than nearby Bardolino with a hint more sourness. However, it's virtually a forlorn quest searching for these flavours. It's worth going for a Classico or a single-vineyard wine, but avoid Superiore – technically these have a higher natural alcohol, but all it seems to mean is that the wine has been aged for a minimum of a year. These are wines you must drink young! Producers

The price guides for this section begin on page 341.

who can oblige with good flavours are *Allegrini, Boscaini, Guerrieri-Rizzardi, Masi, Quintarelli, Le Ragose, Santi, Tedeschi* and *Zenato*.

There are now a few single-vineyard wines appearing, like *Masi's Serègo Alighieri*, which are a street ahead of the 'generic' stuff and *Bolla* make a juicy *'Jago'*, which is good. The wines are more expensive but if you want to understand what once made Valpolicella great, a single-vineyard wine may show you. You might also try wine made by what some producers vow is the only method to make real traditional Valpol – the *ripasso* method. New Valpolicella is pumped over the skins and lees of Recioto or Amarone, starting a small re-fermentation and adding an exciting sweet-sour dimension to the wine. *Masi* and *Quintarelli* do this well.

But the wine which can really show you greatness is the weird and wonderful Amarone della Valpolicella. *Amaro* means bitter, and this huge wine, made from half-shrivelled Valpolicella grapes, *is* bitter, but it also has a brilliant array of flavours – sweet grape skins, chocolate, plums and woodsmoke – which all sound sweet and exotic and, up to a point, they are ... but the stroke of genius comes with a penetrating bruised sourness which pervades the wine and shocks you with its forthrightness. It's always at least twice the price of simple Valpolicella, which makes it good value for a remarkable wine. If the label simply says 'Recioto della Valpolicella', the wine will be sweeter and may still be excellent but a little less strangely special. Fine examples from *Allegrini, Bertani, Masi, Quintarelli, Le Ragose, Tedeschi* and *Tramanal*.

VALTELLINA, DOC (Lombardy) Nebbiolo wine from along the Swiss border, north-east of Milan. I find it a little stringy, but someone must drink it because it has the largest output of Nebbiolo of any DOC.

VINO NOBILE DI MONTEPULCIANO, DOCG (Tuscany) A neighbour of Chianti, with the same characteristics, but magnified. Usually, this means more pepper, acid and tannin at a higher price; but increasingly fine Vino Nobile is surfacing with a marvellously dry fragrance almost reminiscent of sandalwood, backed up by good Sangiovese spice, and a strong plum-skins-and-cherries fruit. Many of the wines are likely to be expensive flops, so don't go out of your way to look for them, but the following producers should be OK and better: *Avignonesi, Boscarelli, La Calonica, di Casale, Fassati, Fognano, Poliziano* and *Trerose*.

CENTRAL ITALY VINTAGES

1989 The spring was good, but in the summer the sun stopped shining, the rains came and the maturation of the grapes slowed to a snail's pace. The sun returned in the first week of October. Producers who had the courage to interrupt the harvest and wait for another week will have made the best wines. Careful selection and early bottling should provide some good Chianti for early drinking.

1988 'Condition of grapes absolutely bloody marvellous ... Wow! Anyone who can't make good wines this year ought to give up wine-making completely!' Better than '85? Many think so. Reds in particular looking exciting.

1987 It looked like being very good until the rains came. Even so, reasonable reds such as Carmignano and nice young Chiantis.

1986 Some people are now rating 1986 Chianti Riserva more highly than the 1985s. Those who broke the law in Montalcino and bottled early will have produced the best wines.

1985 Hardly a drop of rain from the Lords Test to the end of the season in September, so some of the wines are positively rich, but with the new wave of wine-making philosophies sweeping Tuscany – *this* vintage shows what DOCG is made of. Chianti Riservas now appearing and looking good.

1983 In Chianti, the best '83s have aged very well. They are better balanced than the '82s, and are drinking well now.

WHITE WINES

It isn't more than five years since I used to write in my tasting notes, 'dull, sulphured, oxidized, dead – typical Italian'. An entire nation's wines dismissed in the irritated flourish of my pen. Thank goodness it would be impossible to make such a generalization today. The revolution in white-wine-making has taken three forms. First, new, refrigerated, high-tech methods of wine-making are now commonplace. In a warm climate like Italy's they are fundamentally important if the fruit character of the grape is to be preserved – although they can lead to an *over*-emphasis on neutrality and cleanness. While Trebbiano rules the vineyards, the potential for *exciting* wines *is* limited, but if we at least get cleanness and reliability, we have a base to move on from when plantations of better grape varieties mature.

Second, there has been a welcome resurgence of interest in traditional Italian varieties. Grapes like Arneis in Piedmont, Grechetto in Umbria, Tocai and Ribolla in Friuli ... exciting individualistic native varieties that are now being given the praise and attention they deserve.

Third, there is the French influence, most marked in the onward march of Chardonnay, particularly when combined with barrel-fermentation and maturation in new oak. The wines already show world-class potential. And the results from such grapes as Sauvignon, Pinot Grigio and Pinot Bianco (all of French origin) are giving a lead for the rest to follow.

GRAPES & FLAVOURS

CHARDONNAY Italy was a *very* late starter in the Chardonnay stakes. While the rest of the world was involved in a scramble for any wine labelled Chardonnay, Italy was still – and indeed *is* still in some places – denying Chardonnay DOC status. It is now clear that some excellent Chardonnay can be produced, particularly in Alto Adige, Trentino, Veneto and Tuscany. The typical Italian style is unoaked, lean, rather floral and sharply balanced from Alto Adige, a little leaner and more neutral from elsewhere. However, there is some exciting, creamy, spicy wine being made – especially by the Tuscan tyros. Names to look for are *Avignonesi, Banfi, Caparzo, Capezzana, Gaja, Lageder, Lungarotti, Portico dei Leoni, Ruffino, Tiefenbrunner, Vallania*.

GARGANEGA The principal grape of Soave. Well, shall I say it *should* be the major grape, because it is supposed to make up the majority of the blend in Soave, and when well made it does have a particularly refreshing character, soft, yet green-apple fresh both at once. However, it has to compete with Trebbiano Toscano in cheaper blends, and often loses. Good producers use Trebbiano di Soave, which is a much better idea.

GEWÜRZTRAMINER Although this grape is supposed to have originated in the Alto Adige (Südtirol) village of Tramin, most of the plantations there now are of the red Traminer – rather than the spicier, more memorable Gewürztraminer of Alsace fame. Gewürztraminer can be a lovely drink, needing some time in bottle to develop a perfume that is mildly sinful rather than devilish.

GRECHETTO A central Italian grape with a delicious, nutty, aniseed character that adds dramatically to Trebbiano-dominated blends in central Italy (Orvieto benefits significantly), as well as occasionally surfacing triumphantly under its own colours in Umbria.

MALVASIA This name and the related Malvoisie seems to apply to a whole range of grapes, some not related at all. However, Malvasia is most consistently found in central Italy – particularly Tuscany, Umbria and Latium – where it gives a full, creamy nuttiness to various dry whites like Frascati. It is also used to produce brilliant, rich dessert wines with the density of thick brown-sugar syrup and raisins, especially in Sardinia and the island of Lipari north of Sicily.

MOSCATO The Alto Adige (Südtirol) grows various varieties of Muscat, including the delicious Goldmuskateller and Rosenmuskateller, making dry wines to equal the Muscats of Alsace and sweet wines of unrivalled fragrance. However Moscato's greatest achievements are in Piedmont, where Asti Spumante is a delicious, grapy, sweetish fizz and Moscato Naturale is a wonderful heartily-perfumed sweet wine, full of the fragrance of grapes, honey, orchard-fresh apples and unsmoked cigars! Usually drunk young, *Ivaldi*'s Passito from Strevi can age beautifully. It can make fine dessert wines, too, as on Pantelleria, south of Sicily.

MÜLLER-THURGAU A soft, perfumy workhorse grape in Germany, but on the high, steep Alpine vineyards of the Alto Adige it produces glacier-fresh flavours; not bad in Trentino and Friuli either.

PINOT BIANCO Produces some of its purest, snow-fresh, honeyed flavours in the Alto Adige (Südtirol), up by the Austrian border, and can do very well in Friuli where the best are buttery and mouthfilling.

RHEINRIESLING or RIESLING RENANO The true German Riesling is grown up by the Austrian border in the Alto Adige (Südtirol), producing marvellously refreshing, sharp, green, steely dry wines – as good as most Mosel or Rhine Kabinetts in Germany. It can also be OK as a slightly fatter wine in Friuli and Lombardy. The Riesling Italico, nothing to do with real Riesling, is none other than the dreaded Olasz/Laski/Welsch Riesling, which so despoils Riesling's reputation across Eastern Europe.

SAUVIGNON BLANC Quite common in northern Italy as well as providing some acid bite to far-southern blends like Sicily's Regaleali. It can be spicy, grassy and refreshing, particularly in the Alto Adige and Friuli. Volpaia have started making one in Chianti Classico land and there are rumours of more Tuscan Sauvignon to come from established producers.

SYLVANER Grown very high in the northern valleys of the Alto Adige, towards the Austrian border, at its best this can be chillingly dry, lemon-crisp and quite delicious. But there are fat, muddy examples around.

TREBBIANO Unfortunately for Italy's white wine production, the widely-planted Trebbiano Toscano is a wretched thing, extremely easy to grow, regularly producing enormous quantities of grapes with frightening efficiency. It is responsible for an awful lot of fruitless, oxidized, sulphured blaagh-ness. However, attempts to pick it early and vinify it sharp and fresh are having some effect, and at least its use in red, yes *red* Chianti is now severely restricted. In the Veneto they have a different clone, Trebbiano di Soave, which is a much better variety altogether. Lugana is one 100 per cent Trebbiano DOC of character (*Zenato's* is widely available and good). Abruzzi has a different strain again that may actually be Bombino masquerading as Trebbiano – what an idea! – which *can* be extremely tasty from producers like *Tenuta del Priore, Pepe* and *Valentini*. I wish they'd send a few cuttings to Emilia-Romagna, Tuscany, Latium ...

VERNACCIA There are several types of Vernaccia – including some red varieties – but usually we just see two. Vernaccia di Oristano in Sardinia is a sort of Italian version of sherry, best dry – when it has a marvellous mix of floral scents, nutty weight and taunting sourness – but also medium and sweet. Vernaccia di San Gimignano *can* be Tuscany's best traditional white – full, golden, rather peppery but with a softness of hazelnuts and angelica. *Fagiuoli, Teruzzi & Puthod*, and *Sainsbury's* own-label show what can be done.

WINES & WINE REGIONS

ALBANA DI ROMAGNA, DOCG
(Emilia-Romagna) I resent putting DOCG
against this patently uninspiring white,
which some not particularly cynical people
say was awarded DOCG *a* because they
were the first to apply, *b* because they *had*
to have a white DOCG and all the other
contenders were too frightful to
contemplate and *c* because the local
politicos in Bologna have a lot of clout.
What's the wine like? Well, it's dry – or
sweet; still – or slightly fizzy, or very fizzy;
you see what I mean. These days it's far
less likely to be oxidized than before and,
at its best, the dry version can be delicately
scented and fruity with an almondy finish.
It's still a wine for quaffing, that's all. The
only really decent producer is *Fattoria
Paradiso*.

ALTO ADIGE, various **DOC** The locals up
here by the Austrian border answer more
warmly to *grüss Gott* than to *buon giorno*
so this area is often referred to as Südtirol
in deference. Indeed, wines from these
dizzily steep mountainsides are much more
in the German than in the Italian
tradition. Though 80 per cent of the wines
are red, this is one of Italy's most
successful white wine regions, making a
higher percentage of DOCs than any other
area. The wines are light, dry and
intensely fresh, with spice and plenty of
fruit – qualities that become progressively
rarer as you head south into the heart of
Italy. They could be a lot better if yields
weren't so high, but I always get faced with
the same question – if I halve my yield, will
you pay double? Answer: well, no. The best
wines come from *Tiefenbrunner* who
specializes in an uplifting, aromatic
German style, with Riesling, Sylvaner,
Müller-Thurgau and Gewürztraminer,
which carries over into his Pinot Bianco
and Chardonnay; and *Lageder* who makes
fuller, rounder wines. Both of these are
now experimenting with oak-barrel
maturation – to good effect. Good wines
also come from *Hofstätter, Schloss
Schwanburg, Walch* and the co-ops of
Terlan, Schreckbichl and *St Michael-
Eppan*.

ARNEIS (Piedmont) Stunning, apples-
pears-and-liquorice-flavoured wines from
an ancient white grape of the same name,
with high prices to match – but since
there's a very definite feel of ripe white
Burgundy about the best of them, that's not
such a turn-off. Unfortunately Arneis has
become trendy so a number of wines may
bear the name and not bear much
resemblance to my description. A really
excellent one is *Arneis di Montebertotto,
Castello di Neive* – intense yet subtle.
Bruno Giacosa's delicious version even has
a taste of hops! *Deltetto, Malvirà* and *Vietti*
are very good.

ASTI SPUMANTE, DOC (Piedmont) It's
difficult to believe that this frothy, crunchy,
fruit-bursting sweet fizzy wine is made
next door to the beetle-browed Nebbiolo
giants like Barolo and Barbaresco. Indeed,
some producers make both! It's wine
snobbery that defeats this wine, because it
is absurdly delicious, with a magical, grapy
freshness, and it's ultra-reliable – a poor
Asti is difficult to find. It should be drunk
very young and so should always be bought
from a high-turnover store. Of the big boys,
Fontanafredda, Martini and *Riccadonna*
are always good, as are *Vignaioli di Santo
Stefano* and *Duca d'Asti*.

BIANCO DI CUSTOZA, DOC (Veneto)
Thought of as a Soave look-alike, but
recent improvements in Soave make me
wonder if Soave hasn't decided to style
itself a Bianco di Custoza look-alike! It
contains both Tocai and Garganega, as well
as Trebbiano, which explains some of its
success. But the lack of commercial
pressure to produce any old liquid at the
lowest possible price must be as important.
*Gorgo, Portalupi, Santa Sofia, Tedeschi, Le
Tende* and *Le Vigne di San Pietro* make
good examples.

CORTESE DI GAVI, DOC (Piedmont)
Frankly, if we're going to be seduced into
paying over the odds for a white wine like
Gavi that has improbably little to say for
itself, we might as well go for the less
vaunted versions, which are usually

NORTH-WEST ITALY VINTAGES

North-west vintages are difficult to generalize about because it isn't always easy to catch them at their best, and a good year for Nebbiolo may not have been a good one for Dolcetto. And vice versa. Also, styles of wine-making may vary from one producer to the next. In general, Dolcetto needs drinking in its youth, Barbera can last but is often at its best young, when the fruit is most vibrant, and although there are Barolo and Barbaresco wines which you can drink after five years or so, the best last for 20 years or more. Whites should be drunk as young as possible.

1989 Unlike the rest of Italy, Piedmont basked in glorious sunshine in 1989. Dolcetto looks even better than it has in the last five (excellent) vintages, Barbera promises great things too. Nebbiolo came in early at remarkable levels of ripeness. Some feel this could be the best vintage of the decade for the wines of the north-west.

1988 Dolcetto and Barbera look really good, a little tough to start with perhaps, but the concentration and fruit are there. Nebbiolo got caught by the rain, but the good growers left the vineyards to dry out and picked healthy ripe grapes.

1987 Very good for early varieties like Dolcetto and the whites, but the rains came at the wrong moment for Nebbiolo so Barolo and Barbaresco will be patchy.

1986 Barbaresco and Barolo are overshadowed by '85's greatness but quality is good.

1985 An exciting vintage when more and more growers decided to emphasize fruit and perfume in their wines. We will see some truly great '85s eventually.

1983 First releases of Barolo show a remarkable forward juicy fruit. Not a classic vintage, but a very attractive one.

1982 Excellent, big ripe reds – which do have the fruit to age – when the winemakers and the regulations let them.

1978 Loads of fruit and lots of deep, dark structure. Traditionalists' delight for those who are prepared to wait.

---

labelled Cortese di Gavi. Cortese is the grape, Gavi is the area in south-east Piedmont. The wine is dry and sharp, like a Sauvignon without the tang, and fairly full, like a Chardonnay without the class. Add those two together and we should have a refreshing, straight-up gulper at a pocket-easy price. Fat chance of that, with restaurant chic in Italy cooing over Gavi. The only ones I've enjoyed at a reasonable price have been the fresh *Deltetto*, and the atypical but exciting oaked *Gavi Fior di Rovere* from *Chiarlo*.

ERBALUCE DI CALUSO, DOC

(Piedmont) This is half the price of Gavi, and has a soft, creamy flavour as well as encouragingly dry acidity. Clean-living, plumped-out, affordable white. Drink it. *Boratto* and *Ferrando* make good ones and *Boratto* also makes a rich, sweet but refreshing *Caluso Passito*.

EST! EST!! EST!!! DI MONTEFIASCONE, DOC (Latium)

Usually an overpriced fiasco, this white from near Rome should have a gentle angelica-and-almond-paste sort of fruit, but is usually bland and flat. The local co-op is now producing wonderful dry wine, reeking of fresh hops, apricot skins and pepper. I don't know if it's supposed to taste like that, but it's so good I'm not going to enquire for risk of upsetting the boat.

FIANO DI AVELLINO, DOC (Campania)

After numerous attempts to stomach this inexplicably famous wine from near Naples I have made a dramatic breakthrough. I got hold of a bottle of the single-vineyard *Fiano di Avellino Vignadora* from *Mastroberardino* and found it had a brilliant spring flowers perfume and a flavour of honey, peaches and pear skins. But it may have been a flash in the pan.

FRASCATI, DOC (Latium) True Frascati remains a mirage for almost everybody, since most of it is spoilt by pasteurization before sale. It is made from Malvasia and Trebbiano grapes and should have a lovely, fresh, nutty feel, with an unusual but very attractive tang of slightly sour cream. By the time it gets to the UK even the half-decent ones seem to have developed an undue ration of sour cream and not enough nuts. *Fontana Candida*'s special releases and *Colli di Catone* – with a frosty bottle and enough Malvasia to swamp the Trebbiano – can be good. Colli di Catone's *cru Colle Gaio* is very special.

FRIULI, some **DOC** Some very good, fruity and fresh whites come from this region up by the Yugoslav border in the north-east. There's better-than-average Pinot Bianco, good Pinot Grigio, Chardonnay, better Gewürztraminer, Müller-Thurgau, Riesling Renano, Ribolla and Sauvignon, and the brilliantly nutty and aromatic white Tocai, all made with the intention of capturing the fresh fruit of the varietal for quick, happy-faced drinking. With prices generally in the middle range to upper range, Friuli wines are not cheap, but are good value, especially from independent producers such as *Abbazia di Rosazzo, Attems, Borgo Conventi, Caccese, Ca' Ronesca, Collavini, Dri, EnoFriulia, Gravner, Jermann, Livio Felluga, Pintar, Plozner, Puiatti, Ronchi di Cialla, Ronco del Gnemiz, Schiopetto, Venica, Villa Russiz* and *Volpe Pasini*. *Collavini* is the best of the big producers, but is getting pricy too. The almost mythical Picolit sweet wine is beautifully made by *Al Rusignul* – the *only* producer I've ever found who took this difficult grape variety seriously.

GALESTRO, DOC (Tuscany) Created to mop up the excess Trebbiano and Malvasia no longer being used in red Chianti. Low in alcohol with sharp, lemony, greengage flavours in a high-tech style.

GAVI, DOC (Piedmont) (See *Cortese di Gavi*.) Grossly overpriced, clean, fresh, appley white from Piedmont. If it's labelled 'Cortese di Gavi' there's just a chance you'll get it cheaper. If it's labelled Gavi dei Gavi – multiply the number you thought of by two and add the price of your train fare home: Waterloo-to-Woking for some of the more sensible wine shops, King's Cross-to-Edinburgh for the more poncy restaurants.

GRECO DI TUFO, DOC (Campania) Chewy, lemon-and-liquoricy white from near Naples, always marked by its dryness – rarely by anything else except a silly price tag.

LACRYMA CHRISTI DEL VESUVIO, DOC (Campania) The most famous wine of Campania and Naples. It can be red or white, dry or sweet: I'm told *Mastroberardino's* is good, but otherwise, if you find a half-decent one, let me know.

MOSCATO D'ASTI, DOC (Piedmont) Celestial mouthwash! Sweet, slightly fizzy wine that captures all the crunchy green freshness of a fistful of ripe table-grapes, while adding spiciness and richness, too. Especially heavenly ones come from *Ascheri, Dogliotti, Bruno Giacosa, I Vignaioli di Santo Stefano, Michele Chiarlo, Rivetti* and *Vietti. Gallo d'Oro* is the most widely available in the UK.

ORVIETO, DOC (Umbria) Umbria's most famous wine, grown bang in the centre of Italy, has shaken off its old, semi-sweet, yellow-gold image and emerged less dowdy and, if anything, rather slick and anonymous – but just right to benefit from the boom in light white wines. It used to have a slightly sweet, rich, smoky, honeyed flavour, which came mostly from the Grechetto and Malvasia grapes. Its modern, pale, very dry style owes more to the feckless Trebbiano. I must say I'm looking forward to Orvieto getting back to its golden days and there are signs that good producers are starting to make this happen. *Scambia* is making lovely, peach-perfumed wines and the wines from *Palazzone* are even better. *Decugnano dei Barbi* is good too, while exciting wines, full, fragrant, soft and honeyed, are coming from the big *Bigi* company, whose *Cru Torricella Secco* and *Cru Orzalume Abboccato* (medium-sweet) are exceptional and not expensive. *Antinori* makes a typical over-modern, under-flavoured dry, though their medium is delicious, and a new *vino da tavola* mix of Chardonnay, Grechetto, Malvasia and Trebbiano called *Cervaro della Sala* is outstanding. Their sweet, unctuous, noble-rot affected *Muffato della Sala* is a delicious mouthful.

PROSECCO, some **DOC** (Veneto) Either still or sparkling, a lovely fresh, bouncy, light white, often off-dry, at its best from the neighbourhoods of Conegliano and Valdobbiadene. *Sainsbury's* does a very typical easy-going crowd-pleaser and other good ones come from *Canevel, Carpené Malvolti* and *Le Case Bianche*.

SOAVE, DOC (Veneto) Soave is at last beginning to turn away from the tasteless, fruitless, profitless mass-market bargain basement to show itself off as an attractive, soft, fairly-priced white. The turn-around in the last few years has been quite amazing. More often than not nowadays an own-label Soave from a good retailer will be pleasant, soft, slightly nutty, even ' creamy. What a welcome addition to the dry white wine market! Drink the wines as young as possible. Big producers *Tadiello, Pasqua, Bertani* and *Zenato* are supplying a lot of the decent basic stuff. On a higher level *Anselmi's* is outstanding and *Pieropan's*, especially the single-vineyard wines *La Rocca* and *Calvarino*, are very good, if expensive. The *Monte Carbonare* from *Suavia* is another exciting addition. Other good ones come from *Boscaini, Zenato, Costalunga*, the *Castellare* vineyard of *Bolla*, the *Monteforti* of *Santi*, the *Capitel Foscarino* of *Anselmi* and the *Costalta* of the local co-op. *Anselmi* also makes a *Recioto di Soave dei Capitelli*

which is shockingly good in its sweet-sour way, and *Pieropan's* unoaked *Recioto* is even more exciting, redolent of apricots.

TOCAI, DOC (Friuli) Full, aromatic, sometimes copper-tinged, sometimes clear as water, the Tocai grape makes lovely, mildly-floral and softly nutty, honeyed wines throughout Friuli, as well as some increasingly good wines in Veneto and Lombardy. Best producers: *Abbazia di Rosazzo, Borgo Conventi, Cà Bolani, Caccese, Collavini, Lazzarini, Livio Felluga, Maculan, Schiopetto, Villa Russiz, Volpe Pasini*.

TRENTINO, DOC This northern region, below Alto Adige, is capable of making some of Italy's best Pinot Bianco and Chardonnay, as well as some interesting whites from varieties such as Riesling and Müller-Thurgau and excellent dry Muscat. But until they stop grossly over-producing we're never going to see the potential and it might help if they stopped sending some of their best cuvées up to the Alto Adige as well. The tastiest come from the more mountainous bit north of the town of Trento. Look especially for the wines of *Conti Martini, Gaierhof, Istituto di San Michele, Mandelli, Pojer e Sandri, Spagnolli* and *Zeni*. Trentino also makes sparkling wines from Pinot Bianco and Chardonnay, the best being *Ferrari* and *Equipe 5*, and some pretty fair Vino Santo comes from *Pisoni* and *Simoncelli*.

VERDICCHIO, DOC (Marches) Of Italy's numerous white wines, only Soave produces more white wine than Verdicchio. The wine is made from the grape of the

---

NORTH-EAST ITALY VINTAGES

1989 Cool growing season temperatures meant more aroma in the whites, but a lack of concentration in the reds.

1988 Quantity reduced, but tremendous quality, in particular for reds. There *was* some hail, however – which won't affect the good producers who made careful selections.

1987 A small vintage in most areas, and not a humdinger for reds, but whites were generally good.

1986 Good, balanced vintage, but too much overproduction for it to be exciting. Superb for Amarone and not bad for Ripasso Valpolicella.

1985 Very good reds, now drinking well. Whites are on their way out.

same name (with a little Trebbiano and Malvasia) on the east coast opposite Florence and Siena. The wines are reliable rather than exciting – usually extremely dry with a lean, clean feel and a nuttiness and streak of dry honey, sharpened by slightly green acidity. Occasionally you find fatter styles, since there is sometimes a bit of noble rot in the vineyards and *Fazi-Battaglia's* single vineyard *vino da tavola Le Moie* shows the potential quality the area could produce. There is also a sparkling Verdicchio. The two leading areas are Verdicchio dei Castelli di Jesi and Verdicchio di Matelica. The rarer Matelica wines have more flavour. Good producers: *Brunori, Bucci, Fabrini, Fazi-Battaglia, Garofoli, Mecvini, Monte Schiavo, Umani Ronchi* and *Zaccagnini*.

VERDUZZO, DOC (Friuli and Veneto) Usually a soft, nutty, surprisingly low acid, yet unmistakably refreshing light white. It also makes a lovely, gentle fizz, and in Friuli Colli Orientali some of Italy's greatest sweet wines, in particular *Dri's Verduzzo di Ramandolo* and *Abbazia di Rosazzo's Amabile*.

VERNACCIA DI SAN GIMIGNANO, DOC (Tuscany) This can be a marvellously full, nutty, honeyed wine, slightly lanoliny in the mouth and sometimes with a hint of pepper. These are the good versions. Too much Vernaccia has had all the guts stripped out of it in the headlong pursuit of bland neutrality. *Frigeni, Fagiuoli, Falchini, Teruzzi & Puthod* and *La Torre* show what can be done.

FORTIFIED WINES

The best known Italian fortified wine is Marsala from Sicily. The good examples may be sweet or dryish and have a nutty, smoky character which can be delicious. The off-shore island of Pantelleria produces Moscato which can be even better. Sardinia is strong on fortified wines, particularly from the Cannonau (or Grenache) grape. In general, however, the rich, dessert wines of Italy are made from overripe or even raisined grapes, without fortification. I suppose you could say I've missed out the most important fortified wine of all - vermouth, but if you can think of anything interesting to say ...

MARSALA This Sicilian wine has, at its best, a delicious, deep brown-sugar sweetness allied to a cutting, lip-tingling acidity that makes it surprisingly refreshing for a fortified dessert wine. The rare Marsala Vergine is also good – very dry, lacking the tremendous concentration of deep, brown texture that makes an old *oloroso seco* sherry or a Sercial Madeira so exciting, but definitely going along the same track. *De Bartoli* outclasses all the rest, and even makes an intense, beautifully aged, but *unfortified* non-DOC range called *Vecchio Samperi*. He also does a wine called *Josephine Dore* in the style of *fino* sherry.

MOSCATO PASSITO DI PANTELLERIA From an island closer to Tunisia than Sicily, a big, heavy wine with a great wodge of rich Muscat fruit and a

good slap of alcoholic strength. Rare, but seek it out. *De Bartoli* is best.

VIN SANTO Holy Wine? Well, I wouldn't be too pleased with these if I were the Almighty because too much *vin santo* is vaguely raisiny and very dull. It *should* have all kinds of splendid, rich fruit flavours – apricots, apples, the richness of ripe grape skins, the chewiness of toffee, smoke and liquorice. But it's sadly rare and only *Isole e Olena* has provided me with this thrill so far. If you can't get a bottle of that try *La Calonica* or *Avignonesi* in Tuscany or *Adanti* in Umbria.

The price guides for this section begin on page 341.

VINI DA TAVOLA

If I want to find out how exciting the wines can be from the Tuscan hills, I'll buy a bottle of Sammarco, or Tignanello, Pèppoli, Balifico or Vinattieri. Barolo is *the* famous name of Piedmont, but I may learn more about the region's capabilities if I get a bottle of Barilot or Vigna Arborina. I'm tired of feeble Valpolicella, but if I get a bottle of Catullo or Le Sassine, *they* might show me why the region used once to be famous.

Yet all these wines have one thing in common – they don't qualify for the DOC or DOCG of the area concerned. That none of these wines – and numerous other exciting taste experiences – like Spanna, Arneis, Moscato di Strevi, Torcolato, Anghelu Ruju, Cuccanea – is currently entitled to the DOC is a heavy indictment of Italian wine regulations. No-one doubts that when the laws were drawn up in 1963 there was a desperate need for them, since Italian wine was rapidly sliding into an abyss of chaos and self-interest. However, there were so few winemakers left who clung to a quality-first approach that, when it came to formulating the rules, they were easily outnumbered by those who neither cared about nor, in many cases, understood the true potential of their wines. Local politics triumphed over a quality-first attitude, and laziness over imagination. Permitted yields were far too high; the best grape varieties were often hopelessly diluted with inferior, more productive varieties; and an insistence on historic wine-making practices allowed no flexibility towards new techniques and methods.

The only option for the small but determined band of winemakers who cared passionately about quality, was to confront the DOC regulations head-on and say, 'If you force mediocrity on us with your wretched laws then we shall operate outside the law'. Luckily, there were a few cosmopolitan winemakers in Italy who had seen the international trends and were reacting. Led by Angelo Gaja in Piedmont and Antinori in Tuscany, French oak barrels were brought in, Chardonnay and Cabernet Sauvignon were planted, or trucked in if they couldn't be grown, DOC laws were completely disregarded, and care and money were lavished on handcrafted wines outside the DOC.

Although the movement away from tradition in Piedmont has been slower, the Tuscans have grasped their salvation with both hands. Antinori's Tignanello shows that these careful techniques can make great wine out of Cabernet-Sangiovese blends, and several of the best 'super' *vini da tavola* are from a blend of these two grapes. And these in turn have given rise to a movement determined to make great wine solely from Sangiovese producing wines far more exciting than most traditional Chianti wines.

They call them the 'Super-Tuscans'. That sounds like an all-conquering American football team based entirely on six-foot-four expatriate Florentines. Well, all-conquering they may well turn out to be because nowhere else in Europe is there such a sense of excitement and innovation as in the Tuscan hills. The vineyard sites here are superb. The chief grape variety, Sangiovese, has a character quite different from that found anywhere else in the world, and Cabernet Sauvignon is totally different in flavour here when compared with Cabernet in Bordeaux, California or Australia. Money and imagination are being poured into a new breed of Tuscan wines, determined to achieve high quality *and* high price, a combination which the DOCG Chianti wines are finding it most difficult to arrive at. These wines are often impressive and capable of long life.

As Burton Anderson explains at the begining of this chapter, there are moves afoot to give the whole system an overhaul, and incorporate wines like Tignanello in the official wine laws – at an appropriately elevated level. If, in future editions of *Webster's*, the pages on *vini da tavola* shrink to 'recommended older vintages', I can only say, jolly good thing too.

Italy's total wine production in 1989 was just over 60 million hectolitres, the third straight year that the crop was down from the average of 75 million hectolitres that was the norm in the earlier part of the decade. The EC had supported programmes for uprooting vines in undesirable areas, so that was a factor in the drop, but in 1989 adverse weather conditions and drought were as much to blame as anything. All the same, high production figures are likely to become more and more unusual as the new viticultural programme takes effect, with emphasis on rewarding growers for reduced yields. DOC producers have been warned that requests to raise yields are likely to be refused in future.

SANGIOVESE AND CABERNET SAUVIGNON

ALTE D'ALTESI A 70 per cent Sangiovese and 30 per cent Cabernet Sauvignon blend from Altesino. Aged for about a year in new *barrique*, the first vintage was 1985. The '86 has great depth of colour and fruit, with a hint of oak and blackcurrants, concentrated but firm and very elegant.

BALIFICO Volpaia's 'special', a blend of two-thirds Sangiovese and one-third Cabernet Sauvignon aged for 16 months in French barrels. An exciting, exotic, oaky-rich wine, tasting rather French in its youth but sure to become more Tuscan as it ages.

CA' DEL PAZZO Brunello and Cabernet from Caparzo in Montalcino. Long-lived, powerful wine behind a juicy blackcurrant and vanilla oak exterior.

GRIFI Avignonesi's Sangiovese/Cabernet Franc blend. It has a cedary perfume and a spicy richness of fruit but lacks the class of their Vino Nobile. The '85 is the best yet.

SAMMARCO Castello dei Rampolla's blend of 75 per cent Cabernet Sauvignon, 25 per cent Sangiovese. Magnificently blackcurranty, Sammarco is built to last. The '85 is massive

TIGNANELLO The prototype of the super-Tuscans. First produced in 1971 by Antinori, when it was a blend of

Sangiovese and Canaiolo with about two per cent Malvasia, it is now about 80 per cent Sangiovese and 20 per cent Cabernet Sauvignon. Vintages in the late 1970s were superb and set standards that the others could only aspire to. 1982 is rather dull, but '85 seems back on form although at a fiendish price.

CABERNET SAUVIGNON

GHIAIE DELLA FURBA Made at Villa di Capezzana from roughly equal proportions of Cabernet Sauvignon, Cabernet Franc and Merlot, it is becoming more convincing with each vintage. 1981 is at its blackcurrant peak now. The '83 is even better, and the '85 is one of Tuscany's finest reds in this excellent vintage.

SASSICAIA 100 per cent Cabernet Sauvignon wine from Bolgheri, south-east of Livorno, it has an intensely varietal Cabernet character but a higher acidity and slightly leaner profile than most New World Cabernets. It needs about eight to ten years to begin to show at its best; '68 was the first vintage, and remains, with '72 and '82, one of the best, but '85 is also supremely good.

SOLAIA Piero Antinori's attempt to match Sassicaia. A blend of 80 per cent Cabernet Sauvignon and 20 per cent Sangiovese. Sassicaia beats it for sheer beauty of flavour but Solaia does have tremendous rich fruit and a truly Tuscan bitterness to balance.

TAVERNELLE Villa Banfi's 100 per cent Cabernet from young vines on their estate at Montalcino. It has good style and varietal character. But the tannin and oak are not yet matched by richness of fruit. As the vineyard matures, so should the wine.

SANGIOVESE

CEPPARELLO Very fruity rich wine from Isole e Olena, the oak blending in beautifully, making this one of the leaders of the super-Sangioveses.

COLTASSALA Castello di Volpaia's Sangiovese/Mammolo blend, leaner and less rich than most; lovely, austere wine, needing time to soften and blossom.

FLACCIANELLO DELLA PIEVE Fontodi's Sangiovese, aged in *barrique* and with a little *governo* used. It has a cedary, tightly grained fruit, evident but not dominant oak and elegance. A little more concentration would be good.

FONTALLORO 100 per cent Sangiovese from Felsina Berardenga, fatter and richer than the Flaccianello, with a spicy rather than a cedary oak character, which takes a long time to come out of its tannic shell.

IL SODACCIO 85 per cent Sangiovese and 15 per cent Canaiolo wine from Monte Vertine. It could have been a Chianti, but was too oaky when young to be approved. Very elegant style for young drinking.

I SODI DI SAN NICCOLÒ Interesting slightly sweet and soft wine made at Castellare using the traditional but rare Malvasia Nera with Sangiovese.

LE PERGOLE TORTE From Monte Vertine, the first of the 100 per cent Sangiovese, *barrique*-aged wines. Its success paved the way for others to follow. It is intensely tannic and oaky when young, and needs at least five years before it begins to open up.

PALAZZO ALTESI 100 per cent Brunello, aged for about 14 months in new *barrique* at the Altesino estate in Montalcino, packed with a delicious fruit and oakiness, and though it needs five years to show its full splendour, its brilliant blackberry fruit makes it drinkable much younger.

SANGIOVETO Made from carefully selected old vines (about 40 years old) at Badia a Coltibuono in Chianti Classico. Yields are minute (15 to 20 hectolitres per hectare) giving wine of tremendous concentration. Austere when young: should age superbly.

VINATTIERI ROSSO *Barrique*-aged blend of Sangiovese from Chianti Classico and Brunello, getting better each vintage, with the 1985 showing the superb rich Sangiovese fruit and sweet oak that epitomizes the best of the 'New Classics' in Tuscany.

TUSCAN WINERY PROFILES

MONTALCINO

ALTESINO Resurrected by Milanese money in the 1970s and now making excellent Brunello di Montalcino, Palazzo Altesi, a Sangiovese, partially vinified by carbonic maceration, and Alte d'Altesi, 70 per cent Cabernet Sauvignon and 30 per cent Sangiovese.

BANFI Oenologist Ezio Rivella's space-age winery in the hills of Montalcino, created with the money of the Mariani brothers, who brought Lambrusco to the USA. Wines include: Brunello di Montalcino, Pinot Grigio, Fontanelle Chardonnay, Tavernelle

Cabernet Sauvignon; Castello Banfi, a blend of Pinot Noir, Cabernet Sauvignon and Sangiovese, and Moscadello Liquoroso. New versions of Pinot Noir and Syrah are due to be released in the near future. The Banfi Spumante is one of Italy's best.

BIONDI SANTI A legendary family making a fabulously priced, but not necessarily legendary wine; however there are indications that quality is improving again, with some modernization in the cellars of their Il Greppo estate. 1988 saw their celebration of the centenary of Brunello di Montalcino.

CAPARZO is one of the new wave of Montalcino estates; investment from Milan has turned it into a serious wine producer of not only Brunello and Rosso di Montalcino, but also oak-fermented Chardonnay, called Le Grance and Ca' del Pazzo, a barrel-aged blend of Cabernet Sauvignon and Sangiovese.

FATTORIA DEI BARBI is owned by one of the old Montalcinese families, the Colombinis. Traditional methods produce serious Brunello and Rosso di Montalcino, as well as Brusco dei Barbi, and a single-vineyard wine, Vigna Fiore.

MONTEPULCIANO

AVIGNONESI An old Montepulciano family, but a relative newcomer to the ranks of serious producers of Vino Nobile, also two excellent Chardonnays: Terre di Cortona, without oak, and Il Marzocco, oak-fermented and aged wine of considerable depth. I Grifi is a barrel-aged blend of Prugnolo and Cabernet Franc.

FASSATI are traditional producers of Vino Nobile di Montepulciano now undergoing gentle modernization; they are linked in ownership with Fazi Battaglia in Verdicchio and also make Chianti Colli Senesi.

CARMIGNANO

TENUTA DI CAPEZZANA Most important producers of Carmignano, a tiny DOCG in the hills of Chianti Montalbano to the west of Florence, they also make good Chianti, a pink Vin Ruspo, a leafy Chardonnay, Barco Reale, a Sangiovese and Cabernet Sauvignon blend and the outstanding Ghiaie della Furba, from Cabernet and Merlot.

VERNACCIA DI SAN GIMIGNANO

TERUZZI & PUTHOD Commonly acknowledged to be the best producers of Vernaccia di San Gimignano. Finest of all is the oak-aged Terre di Tufo. Also Chianti Colli Senesi and Galestro.

CHIANTI

ANTINORI are indisputably one of the great names of Chianti, boasting 600 years of wine-making. Not only do they make excellent Chianti Classico from their estates Peppoli and Badia a Passignano, but they initiated the moves towards modern wine-making in Tuscany, with the development of wines like Tignanello, which is the archetypal *barrique*-aged Sangiovese, Cabernet blend. Their Orvieto estate, Castello della Sala, is the source of exciting experiments with white grapes. Champagne-method wine is also produced. Created a new company with Whitbread as majority shareholders in 1988.

BADIA A COLTIBUONO A twelfth-century abbey that now belongs to the Stucchi family, and with the help of expert oenologist, Maurizio Castelli, they make excellent Chianti, as well as a pure Sangiovese, called Sangioveto.

CASTELLO DI AMA Excellent single-vineyard Chianti Classico: San Lorenzo, La Casuccia, Bellavista; also a Merlot that had critics raving in 1990. Promising Chardonnay and Pinot Grigio.

FELSINA BERARDENGA Winery very much on the up. Vigneto Rancia is a single-vineyard Chianti, I Sistri a *barrique*-aged Chardonnay. Fontalloro is a Sangiovese, aged in *barrique* for 12 months.

FRESCOBALDI The best Frescobaldi estate is Castello di Nipozzano, with a special selection Montesodi, from Chianti Rufina. They are also the producers of some excellent Pomino, including an oak-aged white, Il Benefizio. They manage the Castelgiocondo estate near Montalcino, where they make Brunello and a good white wine under the new Predicato label. Mormoreto is a fine, Cabernet-style red.

ISOLE E OLENA is rapidly increasing a reputation for fine Chianti Classico. Also Cepparello, a rich concentrated Sangiovese wine, made from the oldest vines of the estate; outstanding *vin santo* and a superb Syrah.

RICASOLI As well as sound Chianti, Brolio makes a host of other Tuscan wines.

RUFFINO One of the largest producers of Chianti. Riserva Ducale is their best wine.

PIEDMONT WINERY PROFILES

ELIO ALTARE (Barolo, La Morra) New wave producer – wines of firm structure and plentiful tannin behind positive, perfumed fruit. Highly successful 1984 Barolo. Very good Barbera and Dolcetto and *barrique*-aged Barbera Vigna Larigi and Nebbiolo Vigna Arborina.

GIACOMO ASCHERI (Barolo, Bra) Run by son Matteo since father's (Giacomo) death in 1988. Despite being sited outside the Barolo zone, most of production is from own vineyards. Barolo predominates, a lightweight, fruit-forward style that is ideal beginners' Barolo and remarkable value. Barbera d'Alba and Dolcetto d'Alba in same mould. Moscato d'Asti is one of the best; delicately grapy and fresh.

BRAIDA DI GIACOMO BOLOGNA (Rochetta Tanaro) One of the earliest to see the potential of Barbera in *barrique*: his *cru* Bricco dell'Uccellone continues to impress with depth, balance and richness. Has now added an equally impressive Bricco della Bigotta. Unoaked, youthful Barbera, La Monella. Good Moscato d'Asti and sweetish Brachetto d'Acqui.

CASTELLO DI NEIVE (Barbaresco, Neive) Impeccable, finely crafted Barbaresco of elegance from Santo Stefano. *Barriqued* Barbera from *crus* Messoirano and Santo Stefano and firm, classic Dolcetto from three different sites topped by Basarin. Revelatory Arneis.

CERETTO Known for both Barolo and Barbaresco. Wines like Barolo Bricco Rocche Bricco Rocche (sic) and Barbaresco Bricco Asili have legendary reputations. Other Barolo vineyards are Brunate, Prapo and Zonchera, with Faset from Barbaresco. Lightweight Barbera and Dolcetto. Arneis called Blangé is disappointing.

Webster's is an annual publication. We welcome your suggestions for next year's edition.

CLERICO (Barolo, Monforte) Top-notch producer using *barrique* to fine effect. Arte is a *barriqued* Nebbiolo/Barbera blend. Two *crus*, Bricotto Bussia and Ciabot Mentin Ginestra, excellent Dolcetto and Barbera.

ALDO CONTERNO (Barolo, Monforte) Great Barolo, traditionally made, slow to mature but well worth the wait. Bussia Soprana is very special, Cicala and Colonello quite remarkable. Gran Bussia is made from specially selected grapes in the best years only. Il Favot (*barrique*-aged Nebbiolo), powerful Barbera, Dolcetto and Freisa also noteworthy.

GIACOMO CONTERNO (Barolo, Serralunga) Staunchly traditional wines, big and powerful. Monfortino, his top wine, is a special selection. Chunky Barbera d'Alba. Dolcetto d'Alba and Freisa complete the range.

CARLO DELTETTO (Roero, Canale) Excellent Favorita and very good Arneis, both understated yet intriguing. Reliable Roero. Good Gavi.

LUIGI FERRANDO (Carema) The byword for high quality, elegant Carema. Normal label white; black label produced for wines of particularly high quality. Also produces Erbaluce di Caluso and Caluso Passito.

FONTANAFREDDA (Barolo, Serralunga) Eight separate Barolo sites identified (La Rosa, Gallaretto, San Pietro, La Villa, Gattinera, Lazzarito, Bianco, La Delizia). Plus one for Barbera d'Alba (Raimondo) and Dolcetto di Diano d'Alba (La Lepre). Asti Spumante of very good quality; dry Contessa Rosa (Brut, Pas Dosé and Rosé plus *cru* Gattinera).

ANGELO GAJA (Barbaresco, Barbaresco) Uses *barriques* for most of his wines, including all Barbarescos: straight and selected, Costa Russi, Sori San Lorenzo, Sori Tildin. In vanguard of Piedmontese Cabernet (Darmagi) and Chardonnay (Gaia and Rey) production. Two Barberas (straight and *cru* Vignarey), two Dolcettos (straight and *cru* Vignabajla), Freisa and Nebbiolo also produced. Quality exceptional, prices exceptional. Bought Barolo vineyards in Serralunga in '88.

BRUNO GIACOSA (Barbaresco, Neive) Traditional wines of, at their best, mind-blowing quality, especially Barbaresco *cru* Santo Stefano. Produces Barolo and Barbaresco plus most of the other major varieties. Wines are quite outstanding: rich, concentrated without being overbearing yet elegant in finish. Also a white Arneis and a highly rated sparkler.

MARCHESI DI GRESY (Barbaresco, Barbaresco) The leading site, Martinenga, produces Barbaresco, two *crus* – Camp Gros and Gaiun, and a non-wood aged Nebbiolo called Martinenga. Emphasis firmly on elegance. Fine '85s.

GIUSEPPE MASCARELLO (Barolo, Castiglione Falletto) Outstanding *cru* Monprivato at Castiglione Falletto. From other zones, *crus* Villero and Dardi. Barbera d'Alba Ginestra and Dolcetto d'Alba Gagliassi are notable. Excellent '84 Barolo a triumph in a difficult year.

PAOLO CORDERO DI MONTEZEMOLO (Barolo, La Morra) Wines retaining plentiful weight and structure. Standard bearer is *cru* Monfalletto from La Morra; for some the holy of the holies. *Cru* Enrico VI is from Castiglione Falletto, refined, elegant and perfumed. Barbera, Dolcetto etc also produced.

FRATELLI ODDERO (Barolo, La Morra) Medium-large estate producing Barolo, Barbera, Dolcetto etc from own vineyards in prime sites in the area and Barbaresco from bought-in grapes. Somewhat lightweight wines but good roundness, balance and style and without doubt very good value.

PIO CESARE (Barolo, Alba) Full spread of Barolo, Barbaresco, Nebbiolo d'Alba, Dolcetto, Barbera, Grignolino and Gavi. Wines are gaining elegance, losing a bit of punch but also gaining harmony and

balance. Experimentation with *barriques* is in progress; modern thinking has also espoused Nebbio (young-drinking Nebbiolo), Piodilei (*barriqued* Chardonnay).

PRODUTTORI DEL BARBARESCO (Barbaresco, Barbaresco) A co-op of impeccable standards with wines well above the level normally associated with even the best of other co-ops. Grapes carefully selected, those from nine *crus* kept separate, of which Asili, Rabayà, Moccagatta, Ovello excel, depending on year. Copy book Barbaresco: the 1985 was very good indeed, the '82 a classic wine which will last well into the '90s.

RENATO RATTI (Barolo, La Morra) One of the greats. Wines made by nephew Massimo Martinelli since Ratti's death in 1988. All the wines are full of excitement and strongly perfumed, recalling the style of the past, which gives them the credentials to develop wonderfully. Excellent Barolo, from Marcenasco, Marcenasco-Conca, Marcenasco-Rocche; highly prized Dolcetto (*normale* and *cru* Campetto Colombè).

GIUSEPPE RIVETTI (Asti, Castagnole Lanze) Smallish quantities of magical Moscato d'Asti which, not surprisingly, sell out in a flash.

VIETTI (Barolo, Castiglione Falletto) Wines go from strength to strength. Classically perfect examples of their type, not lacking the necessary punch of acidity and tannin, but with elegance and classy style. Barolo (straight plus *crus* Briacca, Rocche, Villero) and Barbaresco (normale plus *crus* Masseria, Rabajà) are intensely complex wines. Dolcetto and Barbera also very good. Also one of the top Moscato d'Astis. Highly enjoyable Arneis.

ROBERTO VOERZIO (Barolo, La Morra) Ultra-modern approach. Attractive and fine wines, full of fruit and perfume, made with great skill, giving Roberto (not to be confused with brother Gianni) the reputation as an up and coming great. Produces Barolo, Dolcetto d'Alba, Barbera d'Alba, Freisa, Nebbiolo d'Alba.

SPAIN

The weekend of 9 June last summer was reserved in my diary for a wine weekend, at which I was to lecture on Spanish wines. But in the end, I spent the weekend weeding the asparagus patch and writing overdue articles. Only one couple had booked.

Interest in Spanish wines is not exactly running at an all-time high. By far the brightest Spanish performer at the moment is *cava*, the Spanish Champagne-method fizz, with UK sales up about a third last year. Imports of bulk still wine are down by about a third, but still wines imported in bottle are up by about 15 per cent. All the same, no clear conclusions can be reliably drawn from this confused picture, as these swings in consumption have happened before and been reversed soon afterwards. The one thing that is certain is that *cava* sales are fizzing – and that probably has a lot to do with rising prices in Champagne.

We are drinking better Spanish wines and paying more for them, but then, we have to, following steep price rises over the last couple of years after two bad harvests. However, Spanish wine prices have stabilized following a decently sized 1989 vintage, while prices of competing French and Italian wines have risen steeply. The weakness of the pound has meant that Spanish prices have risen, but not anything like as much as they have in France and Italy. Still, Allan Cheesman, in charge of drinks at Sainsbury's, has a theory that we've stopped

buying cheap Spanish wines because the last 10p price rise this year has tipped the cheapest Spanish wines just over the £2 barrier. If last year a bottle of French *vin de pays* cost £1.99 and a bottle of cheap Spanish £1.79, the Spanish won hands down. Now the *vin de pays* costs £2.39, the Spanish £2.09, but they're both over the psychological £2 hump, and we're tending to go for the French wine.

It's not only the cheaper Spanish wines that have been throwing up price barriers, either. Prices of many of Spain's finest wines have been soaring, too. As well as the particularly bad 1988 harvest, there is another crucial factor, the domestic market. Spain is booming. Their admission to the EC has created wealth, and that money has spawned 'el yuppi'. Rioja and, even more so, Ribera del Duero wines have never seen such domestic demand. What's more, successful entrepreneurs have money to invest, and they like buying *bodegas*. Owning your own winery is a prestigious jewel in the corporate crown, and there's no point in going for anything less than the best. To a Spaniard, that means Rioja or Ribera del Duero. Grapes are in short supply in Ribera del Duero, so Rioja is the target.

Only the last time I was in Rioja, my advice was sought (through a Spanish friend) on the quality of the wines from a small, family-owned *bodega*. My friend knew a Basque businessman who was looking for a Rioja *bodega* to buy – money no object – and had set his sights on one that was, very discreetly, for sale. The three of us paid the place a visit, but the wines weren't up to much and the setting wasn't right for the showpiece the Basque entrepreneur had in mind. So he dropped the idea of buying that *bodega*, though I'm sure he went on looking.

INTERNATIONAL INVESTMENT

A group of Scandinavians has actually succeeded in buying a *bodega* in the Ribera del Duero. It used to be a co-op, and they have bought the buildings and machinery, and rented 50 hectares (124 acres) of vineyard for 25 years – buying vineyard land in Ribera del Duero is well-nigh impossible. The first wines made at Monte Vega look promising, especially a 1985 *reserva*, but they probably wouldn't have taken the plunge had there not been so much interest in Ribera del Duero wines in Spain and, of course, in the USA. The attitude to Ribera del Duero wines in the States has not been the same since Robert Parker, America's current wine guru, compared the wines of Viña Pesquera, at that time a little-known *bodega*, with those of Château Pétrus. No wonder the price of grapes has risen in recent years.

One Spanish importer I talked to thinks the problem is simple. Even with the large investments in Rioja and Ribera del Duero, there aren't enough Spanish companies making wines in the fresh, fruity style that appeals to markets outside Spain. The Spanish themselves, or most of them at least, still prefer wines made in a 'traditional', barrel- and bottle-aged style, and that's what most companies try to achieve in their top wines. A visit I made to a winemaker in Navarra early last year confirmed this for me beyond doubt. He was making excellent wines, taking immense care in the vineyard and cellar, but then leaving his wines in barrel and bottle until all the freshness and fruitiness had long gone before releasing them for sale. I asked him why, and he replied that the Spanish market attached great importance to *reserva* and *gran reserva* labels, and, since he sold more wine in Spain than anywhere else, he had to mature his wines accordingly. He thought it was rather peculiar of me to suggest that other markets didn't attach the same importance to such names.

His young wine, though, illustrated what improvements are being and have been achieved in the wines of Navarra. With a research programme largely funded by the provincial government that is second to none, Navarra winemakers have benefitted from an attitude that is both innovative and sensibly subsidized. Much of the thrust of this programme has been directed at improving the mix of grape varieties grown in Navarra's vineyards, and this has taken a few years to work through to the wines on our shelves. However, the results are really starting to appear now, and most Navarra wines are worth trying. The mix of Tempranillo (and some Cabernet Sauvignon) replacing Garnacha in the vineyards, and investment in modern, stainless steel equipment in the cellars has worked wonders, and made Navarra the most rapidly improving wine area in Spain.

But here as everywhere, the only way to be sure of getting good wine is to know who the good producers are. Sadly, the Denominación de Origen (DO) symbol is becoming even less of a guarantee of quality than it used to be. Of those awarded over the last year, El Bierzo, up in the mountains between Galicia and León, makes no wines aspiring to real quality, most of Conca de Barberá's wine is white and disappears straight into the maw of the huge Catalan *cava* companies, and Calatayud's coarse, alcoholic brews have no business up alongside the likes of Ribera del Duero, Rioja and Navarra. The most recent addition is Txacoli (Chacoli in Spanish), the sharp white wine virtually unobtainable outside its Basque homeland, and rumour has it that the next may be Binisalem in Majorca, an area with only two producers of anything approaching quality wine, whose wines are of totally different styles.

While on wine denominations, the excursion into *vinos de la tierra* seems to have been a waste of time. No one takes any notice of it in Spain: you'll search far and wide to see *vino de la tierra* on the label of a bottle. The EC offered Spain the possibility of creating a category of superior table wines, the Spanish bureaucrats jumped at the chance, and now almost every plot of vines in Spain can call itself either DO or *vino de la tierra*. First there were 11, declared in 1986, four of which have now been promoted to DO, then came another 21 in 1988. Names such as Belchite, Alto Jiloca and Pozohondo are unlikely ever to appear on a wine label.   **CHARLES METCALFE**

CLASSIFICATIONS

Spain has the largest acreage of vineyards in the world, and a relatively small number of demarcated regions, which are called *Denominación de Origen* (DO for short). This is because, so far, the kind of historical subdivisions which make up all the individual ACs in France, *within* a general *appellation* have not taken place. So regions like Rioja or Penedés, although they have lots of microclimates, still only have one legally defined title. The DO is based, like the French system of *appellation contrôlée*, on suitable terrain, permitted grape varieties, restricted yields and approved methods of vinification but, because the areas covered are so vast, the regulations are somewhat 'general' and not too demanding, with the exception of a fairly comprehensive ban on irrigation which, especially in the arid central regions, naturally restricts yields to extraordinarily low levels.

Spain now has its own official equivalent of *vins de pays*, a category which has proliferated since the country joined the EC, but few of the *vinos de la tierra* would make the grade in France.

RED & ROSÉ WINES

It has to be said that when it comes to wine, Spain is plodding rather than sprinting into the 1990s, but movement is positively in a forward direction, even if it is slow. Spanish growers are used to grape varieties which can stand warmth, searing heat even, or drought, or desert, or lack of attention from flowering to harvest, and there's been comparatively little experimentation with new wine-making technology, new ways with old grapes or even old ways with new grapes. Producers like Torres, or Jean León, people with an eye to the international market but with feet firmly planted in Spain, can be counted in handfuls, not thousands.

As a result, Spain still has numerous native grape varieties carpeting the country, some of which may yet produce more interesting wine than dark, tannic jam-juice, once we get a chance to find out. To date, evidence of class in Spanish wine-making has come from Rioja, Ribera del Duero, and parts of Catalonia, all in the northern part of the country. There are interesting wines emerging from Toro, some lovely soft wines from Valdepeñas, chunky offerings from Navarra and León. Navarra in particular has made great strides recently, thanks to the input of the government's viticulture research station there. But wines which push Spain centre-stage, apart from Gran Coronas Black Label, Pesquera or Vega Sicilia, are still few and far between.

GRAPES & FLAVOURS

CARIÑENA A high-yielding grape (the Carignan of Southern France) producing extremely dark and prodigiously tannic wine. It has its own DO, Cariñena, south of Zaragoza, where it is thought the variety was first propagated, but the zone is now dominated by Garnacha and Bobal. Most Cariñena is grown in Catalonia and is useful primarily as a beefy blender. It is also a minority grape in Rioja under the name Mazuelo. With its high tannin and acidity, and its aroma of ripe fruit, plums and cherries, it complements the Tempranillo so well – adding to its ageing potential – that, each vintage, the Rioja *bodegas* fight over the small quantities available from growers.

GARNACHA This is Spain's – and the world's – most planted red grape variety. It grows everywhere, except Andalucía, and makes big, broad, alcoholic, sometimes peppery or spicy wines. The French, who know it as Grenache, moan about its lack of colour; but here in Spain, where burning heat and drought naturally restrict its yield, there's more dark skin in proportion

to pale juice, and the wines turn out darker. They don't last well, but they can be delicious drunk young, whether as red, or fresh, spicy rosé. In Navarra the presence of Garnacha is gradually giving way to Tempranillo and Cabernet.

GRACIANO This high quality red grape of Rioja and Navarra has all but died out because its yields are so low as to be unprofitable, but some *bodegas* still use it to add a fresh, grassy, savoury aroma and good colour.

MONASTRELL Spain's second most planted red variety, used to add body and guts to many Catalonian Tempranillo blends. Produces good crops of dark, tasty, alcoholic reds and rosés right down the eastern seaboard in Alicante, Jumilla, Almansa, Yecla and Valencia – usually dry and stolid but sometimes made sweet

TEMPRANILLO This fine red grape of Rioja and Navarra crops up all over Spain except in the hot south, but with a different name in practically every region. It's called the Cencibel up on the central plains of La Mancha and Valdepeñas, Ull de Llebre (hare's eye) in Penedés, Tinto Fino in the Ribera del Duero, while elsewhere it may be Tinto de Madrid, Tinto de Toro, Tinto del País ... It is so highly thought of that it is being introduced into new areas (Cariñena, Somontano, the Rioja Baja ...) and its plantations are being extended elsewhere. The wines have a spicy, herby, tobacco-like character, along with plenty of sweet strawberry or sour cherry fruit, good, firm acidity and a bit of tannin. Tempranillo makes very good, vibrantly fruity wines for gulping down young, as well as more robust wines for longer ageing – and its flavours harmonize brilliantly with oak. Often blended with other grapes, especially the fatter Garnacha, it contributes firmness and finesse.

WINES & WINE REGIONS

ALICANTE, DO Heavy, rather earthy reds made in south-east Spain from the Monastrell grape; useful blending wines.

ALMANSA, DO Falling between the high La Mancha plain and the near coastal plains of Alicante and Valencia, up-and-coming Almansa produces strong spicy reds from Monastrell and Garnacha, and even better reds from Tempranillo. *Bodegas Piqueras* make very good wines under the *Castillo de Almansa* and *Marius* labels.

AMPURDÁN-COSTA BRAVA, DO This part of Catalonia, right up in the north-east, is a major supplier to the Costa Brava beaches. Seventy per cent is rosé, catering to the sun-freaks, but it also produces some 'Vi Novell', supposedly after the fresh, fruity style of Beaujolais Nouveau.

CALATAYUD, DO A new DO south-east of Zaragoza. Reds are made from Garnacha, Mazuelo, Tempranillo and Monastrell, and must reach 12 degrees to get their DO. General quality benefits from the presence of the Calatayud Viticultural Station.

CAMPO DE BORJA, DO A new DO in the heart of Aragón between Navarra and Cariñena. Hefty alcoholic reds made from Cariñena and Garnacha, now making way for lighter reds and very good rosés. *Bodegas Bordejé, the Borja co-op* and the *Santo Cristo co-op* all look promising.

CARIÑENA, DO A lot of basic red from Cariñena, south-east of Rioja, finds its way as common *tinto* into Spain's bars, but the best co-operatives (they make most of the wine) produce pleasant, full, soft reds. The main grape is the fat, jammy Garnacha, though a certain amount of Tempranillo firms up the better reds. White and rosé can be pleasant, but are mostly dull. The reds of the *Bodegas San Valero* co-operative are well made, sold here as *Don Mendo* and *Monte Ducay*.

COSTERS DEL SEGRE, DO A virtual one-producer DO (Raimat) in the Catalan province of Lérida. It's desert country, but has been extensively irrigated to grow cereals, fruit crops and, in places, vines, despite the fact that irrigation is officially banned both in Spain and the EC generally. But all over the EC, wine producers make good use of two let-out clauses: if your vineyard can be considered 'experimental', or if you can claim extraordinary local conditions, you can turn on the tap. Well, thank goodness the owners of the fine Lérida estate of *Raimat* knew how to get round the regulations, because their wines, both white and red, are some of Spain's most attractive. The reds – particularly *Raimat Abadia*, based on Cabernet Sauvignon, Tempranillo and Garnacha and aged in oak – are consistently good. The *Raimat Cabernet Sauvignon* is also very good; blended with a little Merlot and Tempranillo, it is ripe but light, blackcurranty-oaky wine. The *Raimat Tempranillo* isn't so different either, for that matter.

The price guides for this section begin on page 355.

EL BIERZO, DO A New DO in the cool mountains around Ponferrada, making rasping reds from the Mencia grape.

JUMILLA, DO Usually a palate-buster of a red from super-ripe Monastrell grapes grown in the dust bowls of Murcia. Much of it is sold in bulk for beefing up blends elsewhere. However, French investment is now creating a new fresh-flavoured red style. The *Condestable* brands, *Castillo de Jumilla* and *Con Sello*, are quite good and gentle as is the ripe, plummy *Taja* from French merchants Mahler-Besse. The *San Isidro* co-op is the biggest in Spain.

LA MANCHA Vast area south of Madrid. Only ten per cent red and most of this is pale semi-red plonk for the bars of Madrid. The wines *can* be highly enjoyable easy-going reds, yet so far only *Vinicola de Castilla* and the 1000-hectare estate of *Cueva del Granero* are proving this with any regularity. *Arboles de Castillejo* from *Bodegas Torres Filoso* is a 100 per cent Tempranillo well worth a try.

MENTRIDA, DO Strong, sturdy reds produced in central Spain – bang in the middle, in fact.

NAVARRA, DO This large region immediately north of Rioja grows the same grape varieties, though with more Garnacha. Things are set to improve though, because the officially-funded experimental winery here, EVENA, is one of the most impressive in Europe, and their influence is already noticeable in the wines. As Garnacha gives way to plantings of Tempranillo and Cabernet, we can look forward to some sounder drinking.

Much Navarra wine is made in co-operatives, then generally sold to *bodegas* for blending, and it's cheering to see how fast methods and equipment in the co-operatives are improving. The best wine so far by a street is the single estate *Magaña*, where grape vines include Cabernet and Merlot, not really DO-permitted varieties, but thank goodness Magaña use them. Other wineries which are potentially good are *Chivite* and *Bodegas Cenalsa*, who also use the label *Agramont*. *Monte Ory*, *Bodegas Ochoa* and *Señorio de Sarría*

wines are now much fresher and better than they were. *Vinicola Navarra* make old-fashioned, oaky reds worth trying – look for *Castillo de Tiebas*.

PENEDÉS, DO Catalonia's leading wine region. There is more *will* here to make good wines in commercial quantities to sell at a profitable but not silly margin than anywhere else in Spain due to that good old Catalan industriousness – and the investment the wealth of the region makes possible. Mostly, however, the usual Spanish problem of indifferent grape varieties causes most of the reds to be rather solid and unrefreshingly overripe. But there are high spots. *Jean León's Cabernet Sauvignon* is one – a superbly weighty, impressively long-lasting red, though sadly lighter since 1980. *Torres* is another, from the rich, rather too sweetly oaky basic reds, right up to the exciting Cabernet-Sauvignon-based *Gran Coronas Black Label,* now called *Mas La Plana.* Other names to look out for are *Cavas Hill, Ferret i Mateu, Masia Bach, Mont Marçal.*

PRIORATO, DO You need 13.5 degrees here to get your DO! Cool, mountainous region, abutting the west of Tarragona. The reds from Garnacha and Cariñena are renowned – rich and full-bodied in style, and *Scala Dei* and *de Muller* are worth trying.

RIBERA DEL DUERO, DO 'Ribera' means river bank, and this fine red wine region spreads out over the broad river valley of the Duero (Portugal's Douro) and the smaller, broad, pine-clad valleys behind. The Tinto Fino grape (alias Tempranillo) is by far the predominant variety, sometimes mixed with Garnacha for drinking young, but used alone for the bigger reds. There's a growing interest in Cabernet for blending into the better wines, too. The wines we see most of are from the *Bodega Ribera Duero* co-operative at Peñafiel, where a change of winemaker has signalled improvements. The *joven* (young) reds show the tremendous soft fruit style of the region.

Vega Sicilia is the famous name, a large estate that has grown Cabernet, Merlot and Malbec to blend in with its Tinto Fino

As you travel, it soon becomes clear that Spain offers an opportunity to sample some very good wines in perfect settings. The bars and cafes not only provide refuge from the sun, but a wide selection of cool, fragrant white wines and rosados.

IN THE SEARCH FOR THE REAL SPAIN, THE WINES ARE ONE OF THE GREATEST REWARDS.

At lunch, in the cobbled squares and courtyard gardens, the lighter reds are good company for local dishes, and always make easy drinking.

Dinner, usually calls for one of Spain's full-bodied oak-aged red wines. Wherever you go, you'll find a wine from Spain for every occasion.

THE SPAIN JUST WAITING TO BE TASTED.

WINES FROM SPAIN, 66 CHILTERN STREET, LONDON W1M 1PR

since early this century. These frighteningly expensive wines taste like a mix between very good Rioja and grand old-style Piedmont wines, with great depth and concentration. Actually the second wine, *Valbuena*, is often more enjoyable: still rich, but with less wood ageing – and less of an assault on the wallet. Two other *bodegas* that have sprung into prominence in the last few years offer lovely, rich, oaked reds at, sadly, rapidly sky-rocketing prices – a disease that seems to be afflicting this DO at the moment. Watch out for the unctuous, ripe, but over-oaky *Tinto Pesquera* from *Bodegas Alejandro Fernandez*, whose 1986 is the best of recent vintages, and the delicious *Viña Pedrosa* from *Bodegas Hermanos Perez Pasqua*. Look out also for *Bodegas Victor Balbas* and the co-op of *Ribera Duero* (go for the young, fruity reds not the more dubious *reservas*). *Bodegas Peñalba Lopez* are so far not reaching their potential.

RIOJA, DO Above all, classic red Riojas taste of oak and in particular – vanilla sweetness. Oak – and in particular American oak, the type preferred in Rioja – is full of vanilla, and wine leaches it out, taking up its buttery-vanilla-toffee aromas and flavours. The actual fruit content of Rioja is usually rather light, sometimes peppery, but more often matching the buttery richness with a kind of strawberry jam sweetness.

Practically all the Rioja on sale in this country comes from the firms who make or buy in wine of varying styles from three distinct parts of the region and different grape varieties, blending and ageing them

to a 'house style'. Some use more of the more elegant Tempranillo grape, some more of the fatter, riper Garnacha, perhaps adding a little of the two minority grapes, Graciano and Mazuelo. The Rioja Alavesa region makes lighter, more delicate, perfumed wines; Rioja Alta produces wines that are firmer, leaner, slower to show their character – but slower to lose it too; while the lower, hotter Rioja Baja grows mostly Garnacha, which gets super-ripe and usually rather lumpish. Nowadays there's a distressing tendency among some *bodegas* to use less and less oak, and there are an increasing number of wines with no oak at all. This all results in boring wines, which are by no means cheap.

Best bets are from *Bodegas Riojanas, Campo Viejo, El Coto, Cune, Faustino, Lopez de Heredia, Marqués de Cáceres, Marqués de Murrieta, Martínez Bujanda, Montecillo, Muga, Olarra* and *La Rioja Alta*.

There is little credence given, as yet, to the 'estate' mentality, but it will come, as quality expectations rise and the over-achievers of the area determine to set an individual stamp on their wines. It's already worth trying to search out the wines from *Contino* and *Remelluri*.

SOMONTANO, DO A newly demarcated region lying in the foothills of the Pyrenees, in the province of Huesca north of Zaragoza. It uses a clutch of grape varieties to make lightly perfumed, attractive reds, whites and rosés, and I've even tasted some pretty good fizz. The *Co-operativa de Sobrarbe* under the Camporocal label is encouraging.

MATURITY CHART

1982 Rioja Reserva

In general, Reservas are ready to drink when they are released, though they may stay at their peak for some years.

Bottled		Ready	Peak		Tiring		In decline

0	1	2	3	4	5	6	7	8	9	10	11	12	13 years

TARRAGONA, DO The largest DO in Catalonia and lying to the south of Penedés. Originally known for its high-strength dessert wines; now making fairly undistinguished and unimpressive reds, whites and rosés.

TERRA ALTA, DO Hefty, sometimes coarse red from west of Tarragona. Rather better at producing altar wine – *de Muller* is the world's biggest supplier.

TORO, DO Newish DO by the Portuguese border to the west of Ribera del Duero and Rueda, capable of making excellent, inexpensive, beefy, tannic but richly fruity reds from the Tinto de Toro – yet another alias for the Tempranillo. So far, the only really good wines are being made by *Bodegas Fariña*, whose *Gran Colegiata*, aged French-style in small oak barrels, is already making waves over here.

UTIEL-REQUENA, DO An extension of the central plateau to the west of Valencia. The reds, made from the Bobal grape, are robust and rather hot and southern in style. The rosés *can* be better – delicate and fragrant.

VALDEPEÑAS, DO Till recently the home of soft, unmemorable reds, Valdepeñas – down in the south of the central plateau – has latterly much improved its wine-making and equipment. Many of these potentially rich, fruity wines are sadly emasculated by a generous dollop of white Airén wine; they are then unable to stand up to the ageing that's nevertheless inflicted upon them. However, the best firms selling wine for export tend to make their top reds exclusively from the Cencibel (alias Tempranillo) grape, so that they can turn out deep and herby with good strawberry-like fruit – and excellent value at extremely low prices, even in the case of *gran reservas* with a decade's ageing. One or two *bodegas* age their best growths in oak but this is a rare practice. Look out for the succulently soft reds, aged in new oak, of *Señorio de los Llanos*, good wines under the brand name *Viña Albalí* from *Bodegas Felix Solis* and the young, fruity reds of *Marqués de Castañega* and *Casa de la Viña*.

RIOJA CLASSIFICATIONS

Rioja is divided into three geographical sub-regions: Rioja Alta, Rioja Alavesa and Rioja Baja: most wines will be a blend from all three. The wine's age, indicated on the label, falls into one of four categories.

Sin crianza Without ageing, or with less than one year in wood; wine sold in its first or second year.

Vino de crianza With a minimum of 12 months in wood and some months in bottle; cannot be sold before its third year. Whites will have had a minimum of six months in cask before bottling.

Reserva Selected wine from a good harvest with a minimum of 36 months' ageing, in cask and bottle, of which 12 months minimum in cask. It cannot leave the *bodega* until the fifth year after the vintage. Whites at least six months in cask, and 24 months' ageing in total.

Gran Reserva Wine from an excellent vintage (supposedly) that will stand up to lengthy ageing: 24 months minimum in cask and 36 months in bottle, or vice-versa. Cannot leave the *bodega* until the sixth year after the vintage. Whites wines have at least six months in cask and 48 months' ageing in total.

VALENCIA, DO Large quantities of red, white and rosé wines of no great distinction are made on this coastal plain of the Levante by a handful of producers. The wine is typical easy drinking, the sort of thing that's fine for the beach. Some low-priced reds from *Schenk* and *Gandia Pla* can be good and the sweet Moscatels can be extremely tasty.

YECLA, DO Sandwiched between Jumilla and Alicante, this dry region makes fairly full-bodied reds and more dubious whites. *La Purisima co-op* is the chief label we see.

Webster's is an annual publication. We welcome your suggestions for next year's edition.

WHITE WINES

Spanish white wines have one major problem – Spanish grapes. Because the country is hot and far south, most of the grape types which go into the classic white table wine styles – Chardonnay, Sauvignon, Sémillon, Riesling – would ripen, then overripen, far too quickly for any character to have had time to form. It is relevant that innovators, like Miguel Torres in Penedés, who want to grow these sorts of varieties, have to push high into the hills where grapes have never been grown before to get the slow, cool-ripening conditions such grapes need. Results of his efforts are impressive – but it really is cold up there. I've been in his hill vineyards in October and at midday it's still too cool to take your coat off.

Elsewhere, there is a pallid procession of sallow, neutral grapes. Airén carpets La Mancha south of Madrid. Viura (or Macabeo), Xarel-lo and Parellada do the donkey work in much of the rest of the north, while Pedro Ximenez and Palomino slog it out in the south. None of these varieties makes interesting table wine.

There are two saving graces. First, there are a few native grapes with real character. In Galicia, in the north-east, the Treixadura, Godello, Loureiro and Albariño have very interesting flavours, although they are too often spoilt in the wine-making. A little south and east, the Verdejo grape gives very dry, nutty wine with a hint of Sauvignon greenness, good and crisp when young. And in the Levante, especially around Valencia, there is Muscat, although early experiments to produce a dry wine which was crisp and delicious seem to be faltering for want of a market. But that's just about it.

Which brings us to the second point. Miguel Torres in Penedés has shown that, even with a variety as dull as Parellada, ultra-modern techniques can draw out the frail, shy fruit and produce a very decent, lemon-sharp, dry, summer gulper (his Viña Sol); and the same lessons – pre-fermentation skin contact, cool fermentation, stainless steel, sterile storage – have been learnt and applied by go-ahead winemakers in all parts of Spain.

GRAPES & FLAVOURS

AIRÉN This plain and simple white grape hardly deserves its prominence, but it nevertheless tops the list of the grape varieties of the *world*! It's by no means tops in flavour, nor even in the volume it produces, but it covers far, far more land than any other grape on earth. It holds sway over Spain's massive central plateau, where the summers are baking hot, irrigation is banned, and the vines are widely spaced to survive on the arid soils. As a result, the Airén must be a front-runner for another record in the viticultural world – the *smallest* producer per hectare. Traditionally, these grapes have yielded tired, alcoholic, yellow plonk to service the bars of Madrid. But new, cool wine-making methods have transformed part of the production into some of the most refreshing basic white wine yet produced in Spain, with a delicious, light, apple, liquorice and lemon flavour. That said, the vast majority is still more of that same dull old hooch.

GARNACHA BLANCA A relation of the red Garnacha, and widely grown in the north-eastern quarter of Spain. Like the red version, it makes wines high in alcohol, low in acidity and with a tendency to oxidize, so they are usually blended in with wines of higher acidity, such as the Viura. However, it is an important variety used in the white wines of Navarra. Good growers are grubbing it up, but its high yields keep it popular.

MALVASÍA This interesting, aromatic, flavourful grape is difficult to handle in Spain because it tends to produce wines of low acidity that turn yellow and oxidize rapidly unless extreme care is taken. It is also low-yielding and prone to rot, so many growers in its traditional homelands of Rioja and Navarra have been ousting Malvasía in favour of the more productive but less interestingly flavoured Viura. Only five per cent of Rioja is now planted with Malvasia. When well made, Malvasía wine is full-bodied, fairly strongly scented, spicy or musky, often with a hint of apricots, and sometimes slightly nutty. It blends well with Viura, which ups its acidity, but one of the reasons for the recent decline of real quality in wooded white Riojas is that more and more of them are now based solely on Viura, which can't meld in the oaky softness as successfully as Malvasía. Ten years ago, good white *reservas* really *did* taste like white Burgundy – because of the high proportion of Malvasía in the blend. Still flying the flag are the excellent *Marqués de Murrieta* and *Cune's Monopole*.

MOSCATEL There is a great deal of Muscat of Alexandria (Moscatel) in Spain, mostly grown in the south, where it overripens and shrivels and makes big, rich fortified wines. Valencia can make some extremely good, grapy, sweet white from it and *Torres* makes a good, off-dry, aromatic version mixed with Gewürztraminer in Penedés, as does *de Muller* in Tarragona.

PARELLADA Touted as the provider of all the perfume and finesse in Catalonia's whites and in *cava* sparkling wine; but frankly Parellada doesn't have much to say for itself, except in the hands of the best producers, such as *Torres*, whose *Viña Sol* is simply sharp, refreshing, lemony wine. The versions of *Ferret i Mateu* and *Miret* are also worth trying.

VERDEJO This native of Rueda on the River Duero is one of Spain's more interesting white grapes. Nowadays it's used more for table wines than for Rueda's traditional fortified wines, and makes a soft, creamy, very slightly nutty white, sometimes a touch honeyed, with good, green acidity, and less alcohol than Viura wines grown nearby. It isn't exactly a world-beater, but in terms of a Spanish white it does pretty well. It can also make very good sparkling wine.

VIURA The main white grape of Rioja, made nowadays apple-fresh and clean and, at best, rather neutral-flavoured, at worst, sharp and grapefruity. It achieves similar mixed results, under the name Macabeo, in Catalonia (where it also forms part of the *cava* sparkling wine blend). Made in this light, modern style, it's a wine for gulping down young, in its first year. But blended with the Malvasía grape, topped up with a slug of acidity and left to age in oak barrels, the Viura used to make some wonderful, rich, almost Burgundy-like white Riojas. But it can't do it without help from the Malvasía.

XAREL-LO One of the three main white grapes of Catalonia, heavier, more alcoholic and even less aromatic than the barely aromatic Parellada and Macabeo, with which it is generally blended. Some producers of *cava* and still wines like to use it to give extra body and alcohol, while others scorn it as coarse. It still accounts for a third of all white plantings in Penedés. In Alella, it's known as the Pansá Blanca.

WINES & WINE REGIONS

ALELLA, DO Catalonian wine region north of Barcelona, gradually disappearing under the suburban sprawl, whose best wine is from the impressive firm of *Marqués de Alella*. The vines are found on granitic slopes somewhat sheltered from the prevailing easterly wind. Their best-known wine is the off-dry, very fruity Marqués de Alella. Also look out for their light, pineapple-fresh *Chardonnay* and appley *Marqués de Alella Seco*, as well as their sparkling *Parxet*, which beats most of the famous *cavas* hands down with its fresh, greengagey flavour.

CAVA, DO The Spanish name for Champagne-method wine. Around 95 per cent of it comes from Catalonia in the east, not far from Barcelona, and indeed the authorities there have been given the task of supervising the new *cava Denominación de Origen* for the whole of Spain. Various other small vineyard enclaves have been granted the DO, odd little patches of Rioja and Aragon for instance. The DO was granted to regions or villages that already had a tradition of making *cava*, and one or two more recent sparklers will now have to take the term *cava* off their labels.

An absolutely delicious, fresh, fruity and nutty one in just such a position comes from *Bodegas Castilla la Vieja* in Rueda, worth looking out for in Spain, though not available here. The *cava* authorities admit it's one of Spain's best, but it doesn't fit their rules! Raimat make a 100 per cent Chardonnay which was superb but is now suffering from super-heated demand.

Rioja *cava* suffers from the same ills as that of Catalonia – the Riojan base wines from Viura, like the Catalan from Parellada, Xarel-lo and Macabeo (Viura), are not long-keepers, and their fruit often fails to stand up to a year's ageing in bottle (let alone the three years to which many *cava* wines are treated). The famous sparklers of Catalonia generally end up with a rather dull, earthy, peppery taste, often aggravated by the use of extra-matured wine in the final topping-up liqueur after the bottles have been disgorged.

Some Catalan companies are now starting to turn out fresher, less earthy *cavas* by better wine-making and less excessive ageing, and where available by including some Chardonnay in the blends. *Cavas Hill, Codorníu, Juve y Camps, Mont Marçal* and *Rovellats* look hopeful, though there's a distressing trend to raise prices with the use of Chardonnay. But most producers are stuck with their grape varieties, none of which will ever be renowned for its perfume or fruit. Most appetizing of the Catalan brands are *Cavas Hill Reserva Oro Brut Natur, Codorniú Première Cuvée Brut, Mont Marçal Cava Nature* and *Chardonnay, Parxet, Raimat, Segura Viudas, Costers del Segre* and *Rovellats*.

CONCA DE BARBERÁ, DO A region next to Penedés making fairly ordinary whites and rosés.

CONDADO DE HUELVA, DO Faces Jerez across the Guadalquivir river in Andalucia and has broadly similar climate and soils. Apart from some sweet, fortified wines, it produces young whites from Zalema and Palomino grapes; these are mostly drunk locally at no loss to export markets.

COSTERS DEL SEGRE, DO Raimat, virtually the only vineyard in the area, makes light, lemony, gently oaked *Raimat Chardonnay*, as well as a good sparkler, *Raimat Chardonnay Blanc de Blancs*, which is Spain's best fizz when demand isn't outstripping supply, though the price has gone up and it's no longer the bargain it once was.

LA MANCHA, DO Long dismissed as the most mediocre kind of base-wine producer, Spain's enormous central plateau of La Mancha – producing 40 per cent of all Spain's wine – is now bringing in cool fermentation methods for the whites and sterile, cool fermentation for the reds, and is already drawing out quite unexpected fresh flavours from both – and still at a pretty rock-bottom price. The traditional, typical wines were light yellow in colour, thanks to creeping oxidation, but this has changed. Some of the ones we see here now are the new style, either bland, but fresh and fruity, or else quite surprisingly young and bright-eyed. But you have to catch them *very* young. Best are *Casa la Teja, Castillo de Alhambra, Lazarillo, Senorio de Guadianeja, Viña Santa Elena, Yuntero, Zaragon.*

NAVARRA, DO Most Navarra white is a dull reflection of mediocre white Rioja, hardly helped by the fact that vintages on sale in this country are rarely the latest. However, a few are fresh, zippy, fairly neutral-flavoured, but adequate light summer gulpers. The most recent vintage from *Chivite* and *Bodegas Cenalsa* (Agramont and Campo Nuevo) or *Ochoa* might inspire you momentarily. Successful experiments with Chardonnay promise more exciting wines in the future.

PENEDÉS, DO The general run of Penedés whites is either flabby and fruitless or lemony, spare and characterless. This uninspiring state of affairs arises because the three main grapes – Macabeo, Xarel-lo and Parellada – *all* lack personality. There are exceptions to the rule, especially *Torres*, whose resident genius, Miguel Torres, manages to extract a lean, lemony, sharply refreshing flavour from his Parellada. Other good whites from local varieties come from *Cavas Hill, Ferret i Mateu* and *Mont Marçal*. As well as the local varieties, Torres and *Masia Bach* have successful plantations of Riesling, Chenin, Chardonnay, Sauvignon, and what have you; and *Jean León* makes a delicious oaky, pineappley Chardonnay. Of the new varieties only Chardonnay is officially permitted in wines labelled 'Penedés'.

RIAS BAIXAS, DO Three separate districts make up this DO on the Galician coast north of Portugal. The Val de Salnes zone around Cambados makes whites almost exclusively from Albariño grapes – fresh and fragrant when well made. *Martin Codax* is good. Further south, Condado de Tea and O Rosal make Albariño-dominated wines, sometimes with a dash of Loureiro and Treixadura. As the wines become more fashionable in Spain, the prices are unfortunately rising. *Bodegas Morgadio, Santiago Ruiz, Granja Fillaboa* and *Lagar de Cervera* are all good.

RIBEIRO, DO Since this Galician area was granted DO status, a zone once known for flabby dry whites has been benefitting from investment in vineyard and bodega. Fresh white wines from Treixadura and Torrontes are a distinct improvement on the old regime, though as in nearby Rias Baixas, demand is causing prices to rise.

RIOJA, DO White Rioja *can* be tremendously buttery and rich, slightly Burgundian in style. This was how white Rioja used to be made, from a blend of Viura and the richer, more interesting Malvasía, aged for several years in oak. Some were awful, tired and flat; some were wonderful. The style is now on the wane, though *Marqués de Murrieta* still make an excellent example, and so, with rather less

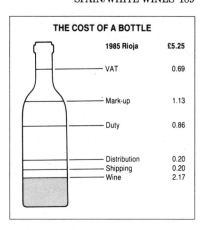

THE COST OF A BOTTLE

1985 Rioja	£5.25
VAT	0.69
Mark-up	1.13
Duty	0.86
Distribution	0.20
Shipping	0.20
Wine	2.17

oak, do *Cune* with their Monopole and *Bodegas Riojanas* with their Monte Reál. *Lopez de Heredia* make an old-fashioned style.

The best examples of new-wave white Rioja are zip-full of sharp, fresh, breath-catching raw fruit, with the acid attack of unsugared grapefruit. Always look for the latest vintage, because these wines soon become dull.

RUEDA, DO This predominantly white wine region lies north-west of Madrid, by the river Duero shortly before it crosses over into Portugal. Rueda used to be famous, or notorious rather, for its heavy, oxidized, sherry-type wines made from the Palomino grape of Jerez – high on alcohol, low on fruit and freshness. But production of these *vinos generosos* is now really limited to a couple of *bodegas*, and the rest of the region has switched over to light table wines, picked early and fresh and fermented in cool, modern style. They have a natural advantage here in their local grape, the Verdejo, which makes soft, full, nutty wines, sometimes padded out with uninteresting Palomino, or sharpened up with a little of the more acid Viura. Most are sold for drinking young, but there are occasional oaked versions, too. 'Rueda Superior' once had to spend a spell in oak, but the regulations have recently been changed, and 'Superior' now simply means that the wine has a high proportion of Verdejo. The most interesting Rueda is new arrival *Marqués de Griñon*, made and bottled for the Griñon estate by *Bodegas Castilla La Vieja*. Other fair wines come from the Rueda transplant of the major Rioja producer *Marqués de Riscal*; their basic white is pleasant, clean, grassy-fresh, but try the *Reserva Limousin Rueda Superior*, with its oak softness balancing the green nuttiness of Verdejo, and the soft and flowery-grassy *Sauvignon Rueda Superior*. Other good *bodegas* include *Alvarez y Diez*, who are making good wines without any sulphur, *Martinsancho* and *Vinos Sanz*. The *La Seca co-op* makes good, clean dry whites.

VALDEORRAS, DO Of the three Galician DOs, Valdeorras seems to have made the least progress. Few wines travel further than the local bars and cafés. Only *Bodegas Jesus Najareno*, using the best Galician varieties like Torrontes, Treixadura and Godello, shows promise.

FORTIFIED WINES

For the third year running, the Trophy for Fortified Wines at the 1990 WINE International Challenge was won by a sherry. Against fortified competition from the rest of the world – ports, Madeiras, Malagas, Australian Liqueur Muscats among them – Matusalem, the magnificent *oloroso* from Gonzalez Byass, triumphed for the second year running.

But wines like Matusalem hardly conform to the popular image of sherry. Many people, assaulted on all sides by 'sherries' from Cyprus, South Africa, and (shamefully) Britain, don't even realize that 'real sherry comes only from Spain,' as the Spanish advertising slogan puts it. Even *real* Spanish sherry has been so relentlessly cheapened in price and stature that most people wouldn't actually recognize Matusalem, or any of the other fine sherries on sale (dry *amontillados,* dry *olorosos* or *palos cortados*) as being *sherry* at all.

And that's the problem. As one leading member of the wine trade who used to import sherry put it: 'Almost every mistake that could have been made has been made. RUMASA (the huge Spanish banking and industrial company that was declared bankrupt and expropriated by the Spanish government in 1983) started the rot, and we all followed suit'. What he was referring to was the lowering of prices (to maintain 'market share') to which RUMASA had to resort in the last years before the company foundered. What RUMASA started became accepted as the norm for almost all sherry brands, and, through the 1980s, sherry gained its cheap, downmarket image, and quality plummetted.

The result has been disastrous. Brand has warred against brand – to 'maintain market share' – and the reputation of sherry as one of the world's finest wines has been all but lost. And that's a tragedy, for sherry can be wonderful, from the crisp, tangy glass of bone-dry fino served chilled before a meal to the rich *oloroso*, scented with raisins and walnuts, as a digestif. Good sherry is also remarkable value. Even the best rarely cost more than £12 a bottle, and that's with the higher rate of duty that applies to fortified wines: extraordinary for the top performers of one of the world's classic wines.

However, prospects do seem to be brightening. More of the top sherry companies are letting us buy some of their older and rarer wines. Domecq have recently launched three excellent sherries: 51-1A, a dry *amontillado*, Sibarita, a fragrant *palo cortado*, and Venerable, a luscious, aged Pedro Ximenez. These join the exalted ranks of the Gonzalez Byass trio (Amontillado del Duque, Matusalem and Apostoles) and some delicious old 'bone-dry' wines from Sandeman.

Maybe, as one sherry shipper put it, sherry is 'going to sell itself as wine' again (and not just watch all the brands chasing each other's tails). Certainly, in Jerez, hard decisions are having to be taken, about pulling up vineyards and coping with increasing local unemployment. The only way up for sherry is to re-establish its position as one of the world's great wines. But, while the quality of *fino*, the standard-bearer of sherry's reputation, is so variable (as a comprehensive tasting of wines available in Britain showed it to be last year) there is still a long way to go. Certain wines (such as Tio Pepe, Tio Mateo, Don Zoilo, Carta Blanca, Inocente and Pando) are as reliable as ever, but, generally speaking, if you're after a crisp, dry, tangy glass of sherry, it will pay you to be very choosy. **KATHRYN MCWHIRTER**

GRAPES & FLAVOURS

MOSCATEL Almost all Spanish Moscatel is the second-line Muscat of Alexandria rather than the top-quality Muscat à Petits Grains. Even so, it makes a lot of good wine – mostly rich and brown in Málaga, or fresh and grapy in Valencia. It is planted in Jerez to provide sweetening for cream sherries. The fact that Moscatel is often detectable in medium and dry sherries reflects no glory on the producers concerned.

PALOMINO This is the dominant grape of the sherry region, making up 100 per cent of the dry sherries, and an increasing proportion of the others. Although it produces a great style of fortified wine it is not considered to be a great grape, though it thrives in Jerez. It plays a minor role in Montilla-Moriles. As a table wine grape, it produces dull, fat stuff but reacts brilliantly to the *flor* yeast which imparts to sherry that characteristic bone-dry, stark-sour perfume.

PEDRO XIMÉNEZ In decline in Jerez, where it used to be the chief component of sweet sherries, and still makes a startlingly rich wine essence for flavouring called 'PX'. However, it constitutes 95 per cent of the nearby Montilla-Moriles vineyards, as well as providing richness in Málaga; otherwise used extensively for rather dull dry white table wines in the south.

WINES & WINE REGIONS

MÁLAGA, DO We don't see much Málaga here – in fact no one sees much of it anywhere because Malaga's wine industry, beset by encroaching tourism and its voracious lust for land, is in a state of disintegration right now. However, in the last century, Málaga was very popular and the wines are still worth a peep. They are generally full, brown and sweet in a raisiny, but not gooey, way and slightly smoky too. There is some dry Málaga, but you'll have to take a long weekend on the Costa del Sol to see much of that. Solera 1885 from *Scholtz Hermanos* is intense, raisiny stuff while *Lagrima 10 Años* is outstanding sweet wine – and neither are expensive. *Bodega Lopez Hermanos* also make good wine.

MONTILLA-MORILES, DO Montilla wines are usually thought of as lower-priced – and lower-strength – sherry look-alikes. This is a reasonable generalization, on the evidence of the wines we see over here. However, there is a great deal of fine wine made in Montilla-Moriles – the problem is getting any UK retailer to ship it. In general the dry wines, from Pedro Ximenez grapes which are grown here in preference to the Palomino, do not quite have the bite of a really good sherry, but many of the mediums and sweets can outshine all but the best. I only wish we saw these instead of the cheap dross that saturates our market. *Tesco's Moriles* isn't bad and well worth trying as an alternative.

SHERRY (JEREZ-XÉRÈS-SHERRY, DO)

There are two basic sherry styles, *fino* and *oloroso*, each with sub-divisions. *Fino*, from Jerez or Puerto de Santa Maria, should be pale and dry, with a quite unnerving dry austerity. The austere tang comes from a layer of natural yeast, called *flor*, that forms on the surface of the wine in the barrels. The lightest, freshest wines are selected for *fino*, and they are fortified to a lower degree than the heavier *oloroso* wines. *Fino* is usually drunk cool and fresh, often as an aperitif.

Manzanilla is a form of *fino* matured by the sea at Sanlúcar de Barrameda. It can be almost savoury dry, and you might even imagine a definite whiff of sea salt – if you're lucky to catch it young enough. The best *finos* and *manzanillas* come from *Barbadillo, Caballero, Diez-Merito, Don Zoilo, Garvey, La Guita, Hidalgo, La Ina, Inocente, Lustau, La Riva, Sanchez Romate, Tio Pepe*. Good Puerto *fino* comes from *Burdon*.

All these can be exciting but on the UK market there is a desperate problem with freshness, and even good quality brands can suffer from tired-out tastes. Lesser brands and most own-labels are usually an absolute disgrace (*Sainsbury's* half-bottles are an exception), softened, sweetened, plumped out so that they certainly don't resemble proper *fino* sherry, and whatever it is they *do* resemble, I don't want it down my throat. There is now a move to reduce dry sherry strengths from the traditional 17.5 per cent to 16.5 or even 15.5 per cent. They argue that this produces finer wine, and with modern wine-making technology producing such clean, healthy wine, the extra alcoholic strength isn't needed to preserve the wine. I'm not so sure – it seems to dilute it instead.

Real *amontillado* also started life as *fino*. It's a *fino* aged in cask until the *flor* dies and the wine deepens and darkens to a tantalizing, nutty dryness. In the natural state, as drunk in Spain, it is *completely* dry, and a proper *amontillado* will usually say *seco*, dry, on the label. But we've adulterated the word in English. Mostly, we use it to mean a downmarket, bland, vaguely medium drink of no style or interest. Most brands sold in Britain probably have little or no real *amontillado* in them at all. But look out for sherries labelled *almacenista*, unblended from the cellars of small stockholders, because these can be wonderful, characterful, dry wines with a unique flavour. Other fine ones include *Principe* and *Solear* from *Barbadillo, La Goya Manzanilla Pasada* and *Amontillado Fino Zuleta* (*Delgado Zuleta*), *Amontillado del Duque* from *Gonzalez Byass, Hidalgo Manzanilla Pasada, Sandeman Bone Dry Old Amontillado* and *Amontillado Coliseo* and *Don Tomás* from *Valdespino. Sainsbury's Oloroso* and *Palo Cortado* in halves are also very good.

Olorosos in the natural state, made from the richer, fatter wines without any *flor*, are deep and dark, packed with violent burnt flavours – and totally dry. Again, for Britain, the term has come to mean sweet sherry, and most are sweetened up with wine from Pedro Ximénez or Moscatel grapes. Though some are labelled *oloroso*, they usually come as 'Milk', 'Cream', 'Amoroso' or 'Brown'.

Pale Creams, interestingly, are not *oloroso* but sweetened (inferior) *fino*. Please excuse my misuse of 'interestingly' here, since Pale Creams are some of the most *un*interesting drinks around. For the real, dry thing, once again, look for *Lustau's almacenista olorosos*. There are just a few good, rich, concentrated sweetened *olorosos* on the market, including the fairly sweet, delicious *Matúsalem Oloroso Muy Viejo* from *Gonzalez Byass*, the *Valdespino Solera 1842* and the less sweet *Apostoles Oloroso Viejo* from *González Byass, Barbadillo Oloroso Seco, Don Zoilo, Sandeman Dry Old Oloroso, Valdespino Don Gonzalo Old Dry Oloroso, Williams & Humbert Dos Cortados Very Old Dry Oloroso*. Oddbins seem to be the people taking most interest in top quality sherries – yet none are more than £8.99, making these intense old sherries one of today's great wine bargains.

The price guides for this section begin on page 363.

HIS MASTER'S CHOICE

GONZALEZ BYASS

Henry. Dalmatian. Born 1985. Wet nose, warm heart.
Tio Pepe. Sherry. Est. 1835. Dry, fresh, best chilled.

WINERY PROFILES

ANTONIO BARBADILLO (Sanlúcar de Barrameda) ★★★★ Best of the *manzanilla bodegas* in Sanlúcar. Barbadillo co-own the ultra-modern winery with Harveys; Principe is a *manzanilla amontillada* with a tangy, nutty flavour.

CAMPO VIEJO ★★★ Although an enormous operation, the Riojas are decent and the Reservas are worth trying for soft, traditional flavours.

CODORNÍU (Penedés) ★★★ Giant *cava* company, owned by the Raventos family, making some of the most likeably reliable fizzes. Chardonnay from their Raimat estate is added to some wines such as the soft and honeyed Anna de Codorníu.

CONTINO (SOCIEDAD VINICOLA LASERNA) (Rioja) ★★★★ Excellent, single-vineyard wine made from an estate half-owned by Cune, half by private investors. Vines are predominantly Tempranillo, planted in one 45-hectare vineyard in prime Rioja Alta land. Big, plummy and spicily complex, Contino is made only as *reserva* and *gran reserva*. If you see any '82, snap it up.

CUNE (Rioja) ★★★★ Old-established, traditionally-inclined *bodega* in Haro; the initials stand for Compañía Vinícola del Norte de España. Their Blanco Viura is one of the best fresh, modern white Riojas, and their Monopole has a nice oakiness. Best of the reds are the sadly rare Imperial range of *reservas* and *gran reservas* (especially the '81). Grab any '75 or '78 Viña Real you come across.

FAUSTINO MARTÍNEZ (Rioja) ★★★ Huge, family-owned *bodega* with high-tech, modern equipment and respect for tradition. Their reds are best by far.

GONZÁLEZ BYASS (Jerez) ★★★★(★) It's unusual to find a best-seller amongst the best wines, but that's certainly true of Tio Pepe, the *fino* from this huge, family-owned company. González Byass also make an impressive top range of wines.

CAVAS HILL ★★(★) Makers of table wines as well as fresh, clean Cava Reserva Oro Brut Natur. Look out for Blanc Cru and Oro Penedés Blanco Suave whites, and Rioja-style reds, Gran Civet and Gran Toc.

JEAN LEÓN (Penedés) ★★★★(★) Jean León makes some of Spain's most 'Californian' wines, super-oaky, pineapple and honey Chardonnay, and soft, blackcurranty Cabernet Sauvignon.

LOS LLANOS ★★★ The brightest spot in Valdepeñas: wonderfully soft oak-aged reds. The '78 Gran Reserva is especially good.

LÓPEZ DE HEREDIA (Rioja) ★★★★ Rich, complex whites, Viña Tondonia and Viña Gravonia, and delicate, ethereal reds, Viña Cubillo and Viña Tondonia.

LUSTAU ★★★★★ 'Reviving Traditional Sherry Values' with their wonderful range of *almacenista* wines.

MARQUÉS DE CÁCERES (Rioja) ★★★ Enrique Forner, who started this *bodega* in the mid-70s, trained in Bordeaux. Whites are cool-fermented and fresh, and reds have less wood ageing than usual, but still keep an attractive fruity style.

MARQUÉS DE GRIÑON (Toledo) ★★★★(★) Carlos Falco, the Marqués de Griñon, makes one of Spain's best Cabernet Sauvignons in his irrigated, wire-trained vineyard aided by Professor Emile Peynaud from Bordeaux.

MARQUÉS DE MURRIETA (Rioja) ★★★★(★) A remarkable, ultra-traditional winery built into a hill just outside Logroño. Red, rosés and whites are oak-aged far longer than in any other Rioja *bodega*; the Etiqueta Blanca wines, the youngest they sell, spend at least two years in barrel, and are richly oaky, with pungent, lemony flavour. The red is soft and fruity-oaky, while the *reservas* are deep and complex. The best wines of the very top years are sold as Castillo Ygay, and sometimes sit in barrel for 30 to 40 years.

MARTÍNEZ BUJANDA (Rioja) ★★★(★) Wine is produced only from the family's own vineyards, and is very well made, from the super-fresh and lively Valdemar white to the strongly oaky Reserva and Gran Reserva Conde de Valdemar.

MONTECILLO (Rioja) ★★★★ Since 1973, Bodegas Montecillo has belonged to Osborne, the sherry company, who built a new winery to turn out an exciting, aromatic white Viña Cumbrero, a raspberry and oak red, Viña Cumbrero *crianza*, and a classic *reserva*, Viña Monty.

MUGA (Rioja) ★★★(★) Bodegas Muga has a sternly traditional image, which naturally extends to rather old-fashioned methods of wine-making. For reds, it does nothing but good, however, and the Muga *crianza* is fragrant and delicate, while the Prado Enea *reserva* or *gran reserva* is more complex, but still subtle and elegant. It's not cheap though.

VIÑA PESQUERA (Ribera del Duero) ★★★★ Prices have shot up for wine from Alejandro Fernandez's estate since American wine writer Robert Parker compared it with Château Pétrus. Viña Pesquera, made from Tinto Fino and a little Garnacha, is good but not *that* good, oaky and aromatic, with rich savoury fruit.

RAIMAT (Costers del Segre) ★★★★(★) The Raimat Chardonnay *cava* is honeyed, with grassy acidity. Abadía is an oak-enhanced blend of Cabernet, Tempranillo and Garnacha. Raimat Cabernet Sauvignon has more concentration, and will improve for ten years.

LA GRANJA REMÉLLURI (Rioja) ★★★★ Single-estate wine; the Rodriguez family have completely rebuilt the winery, installing stainless steel fermentation tanks instead of the old wooden vats, and now make a fine, meaty *reserva*, aged in barrel for two to three years.

LA RIOJA ALTA (Rioja) ★★★★★ A traditional Haro *bodega*, firm believer in long barrel-ageing: over half the wines qualify as *reservas* or *gran reservas*. Even the Viña Alberdi Crianza has a delightfully

oaky flavour. They make two styles of *reserva*, the elegant Viña Arana and the rich Viña Ardanza. In the best years, they make exceptional *gran reservas*.

RIOJANAS (Rioja) ★★★(★) One of the few still using the open *lagar* method of semi-carbonic maceration. Best reds are the *reservas*: the light, elegant, plummy Viña Albina and the richer, more concentrated Monte Reál. Their white Monte Reál Crianza is soft and peachy, with just enough oak.

MIGUEL TORRES (Penedés) ★★★★★ The best range of table wines in Spain. Viña Sol is a super-fresh modern white, fairly fizzing with fruit. Gran Viña Sol is half and half Parellada and Chardonnay, fresh and pineappley, enriched with hints of vanilla oak. Gran Viña Sol Green Label pairs the Parellada with the Sauvignon Blanc, like a richer, oakier version of Sancerre. The superstar white is Milmanda Chardonnay, with all the excitement you expect to find in expensive white Burgundy. Recent red additions are a Pinot Noir, Mas Borras, and a Merlot, Las Torres. Viña Esmeralda combines Muscat d'Alsace and Gewürztraminer. Gran Coronas Black Label is Torres' top red, pure Cabernet Sauvignon, packed with blackcurranty power, nicely tamed by oak-ageing. It now has the vineyard name, Mas La Plana, added to the label. Viña Magdala is made from equal parts of Pinot Noir and Tempranillo, Gran Sangredetoro is mainly Garnacha, and Coronas is the least exciting; savoury Tempranillo.

VALDESPINO (Jerez) ★★★★(★) A name you'll see more often in Spain than the UK, Valdespino is another family-owned *bodega* making a range of top-class, dry sherries. Their Pedro Ximénez Solera Superior is one of the few examples of sherry's great sweetening wine bottled by itself.

BODEGAS VEGA SICILIA (Ribera del Duero) ★★★★(★) Makers of Spain's most famous and expensive red wine. Vega Sicilia Unico, the top wine, is sometimes kept in barrel for as long as ten years. Younger wines, called Valbuena, offer a cheaper glimpse of Vega Sicilia's glories.

PORTUGAL

T he chief wine buyer for one of Britain's largest supermarket chains explained the problem. 'We'd like to do more with Portugal', he commented, but then went on to detail the difficulties he and his buying team had had getting information about exactly what was happening in Portugal's reorganization of her vineyard areas. Despite all the ballyhoo about 26 new regions being demarcated by 1991, there are still disputes about the exact boundaries of the regions, what grape varieties people will be able to grow in them, and general bickering about the rules by the very people who will miss out unless they present more of an export-friendly, united front to the world's wine buyers.

It is frustrating, because Portugal has so much to offer: an array of indigenous grape varieties (particularly red) second only to Italy in its range of interesting flavours; an extraordinary diversity of climates, from the lush, green pastures and kiwi fruit plantations of the north to the gently rolling hills of the Alentejo, where the green of spring quickly wilts to an exhausted brown in midsummer; and people whose charm and hospitality is only matched by their ability to cling doggedly to 'tradition' and their stubborn refusal to change their wine-making ways to suit anyone else.

No-one wants those splendid Portuguese grapes to be overrun by serried ranks of Cabernet Sauvignon and Chardonnay, but the ordinary growers of Portugal have an enduring capability to stymie the very schemes that would bring them more money for their grapes, put better machinery into their co-ops and ensure the continuing attentions of wine buyers from all over the world.

For years, the most successful Portuguese wine exporters have been the private companies like SOGRAPE, José Maria da Fonseca and João Pires, innovative, aggressive and technically up-to-date. Apart from the very few co-ops (Arruda, Torres Vedras, Borba and Reguengos de Monsaraz come to mind), who realized there was money to be made by moving with the times, the co-ops who make up the bulk of the Portuguese wine industry sat on their hands, took no risks, and watched others making the money, mumbling about the importance of traditional wine-making styles and not flogging the family jewels.

Now these very co-ops are in a position to influence the development of Portugal's wine regions, and some of them are turning bloody-minded. Witness an example. Two of Portugal's best wine companies, J.M. da Fonseca and João Pires, are based on the Setúbal peninsula, where two of the new wine regions, Arrábida and Palmela, are being shaped and discussed. At the moment, as with all 26 new regions, Arrábida and Palmela have IPR status (Indicação de Proveniencia Regulamentada – indication of controlled origin), and have a probationary VPQRD (roughly equivalent to the French VDQS) on their labels at present. In time, the hope is that these regions, by getting their local sets of rules drawn up and policed properly, will qualify for full RD (demarcated region) status.

Now, J.M. da Fonseca, with 250 hectares, happen to have the second largest area of vineyard in Palmela, and sell 55 per cent of all the wine produced in Arrábida. João Pires are smaller, but also significant in export markets. Important people to remain friendly with when drawing up the new rules, you might think. Not a bit of it. The boundary dividing Palmela from Arrábida goes straight through J.M. da Fonseca's flagship estate, Quinta da Camarate, for no good reason. Jealousy? It prevents J.M. da Fonseca from calling their Quinta da Camarate wine either Palmela or Arrábida. That went down wonderfully with the Soares Franco family who own J.M. da Fonseca, as you can imagine.

That is not the only instance of what seems like deliberate obstruction of successful companies by resentful, stick-in-the-mud co-ops. But there are positive things happening in Portugal as well. Thanks to the recent removal of a protectionist piece of legislation in Dão, the outside world will shortly have the opportunity to see whether the Dão wines are all they're cracked up to be by the Portuguese.

For years, it has been illegal to trade in Dão grapes, effectively preserving rights of wine-making in the region for the growers, or, yes, you've guessed, the co-ops. This meant that the private companies, the ones with money to spend on such things as building new wineries with modern equipment, had no way of becoming directly involved in growing grapes or making them into wine. They had to buy ready-made (and often badly made) wine from the co-ops, and could do only the blending and maturation themselves. Thanks to EC law, this has now changed. Moreover, it looks as though the very conservative Federation of Dão Wine Producers may have lost some of their power to reject red wine they considered too young, fresh and fruity – just the qualities that would have had overseas buyers queuing up for samples. So we may soon see red wines coming out of Dão unlike anything we have met before. SOGRAPE already own a 100-hectare estate, and 1990 will be the first vintage processed in the new winery they have built there.

THE WAY AHEAD

Generally, things are looking good for Portugal's red wines. In Britain, we drank less of their white (mostly Vinho Verde) last year. This was because of a disastrous 1988 vintage, when prices went up steeply, forcing the British wine drinker to reconsider his image of Vinho Verde as a light, inexpensive, summery white. Inexpensive it suddenly wasn't.

So what can be expected of the 1989 vintage? In late July and early August the countryside was relentlessly baked by the rays of a scorching sun. This led to an early vintage and picking started, in most regions, during the first week of September. The overall quality looks good, despite the heat, and will probably be above average from good producers, but as some wines will lack acidity, careful and selective buying will be needed. The upside, however, is that the '89s will help to counterbalance the awful '88s which were so poor that very few decent wines were made, with crop quantities down by as much as 60 per cent. Out-and-out bargains in Portugal are difficult to find, but we are buying more of their excellent red wines and there are more on the way.

Many of the best of the reds come from the Alentejo, which covers most of the south-eastern quarter of Portugal, and, coincidentally, has five of the new IPR regions that have been fastest to organize themselves properly for the new demarcations. Let's hope their revolutionary attitude towards reorganization and wine-making spreads through the rest of Portugal. Meanwhile, make the most of the reds from new regions like Reguengos de Monsaraz and Borba while they're still excellent value for money.   CHARLES METCALFE

WHITE WINES

Portuguese white wines are still dominated in our perception by Vinho Verde, despite a poor 1988 vintage and subsequent price rises. *Real* Vinho Verde, made dry, and very slightly spritzy from good grapes – in particular Loureiro – can be a magnificent, refreshing drink in hot summer weather.

Portugal hasn't done so well with its other white wines, and the reason is the usual one – the grapes aren't very nice and so they don't make terribly nice wine. Or perhaps we should put it the other way round – they don't make terribly nice wine so we can't tell whether the grapes are nice or not.

WINES & WINE REGIONS

BUCELAS, RD This tiny region just north of Lisbon used to boast just one producer – Caves Velhas – and one wine, a rather tired, dry white made from the Arinto grape. Now there are three producers, 70 hectares of new vines have been planted, and *Quinta do Avelar* is making a crisp, fresh white which shows the Arinto can deliver the goods.

DÃO, RD White Dão was traditionally (and mostly still is) yellow, tired and heavy. But a few companies are now making a lighter, fresher, fruitier style, and now that the co-ops are losing the upper hand with production, others look set to follow suit. White *Grão Vasco*, in particular, is pale, soft, clean and lemony-zesty – if you catch it young. Sadly, local regulations insist that the wine should be at least six months old before bottling, and even then, the official tasting panel sometimes rejects fresh, attractive samples as 'too young'!

DOURO, RD Nearly all the best table wines are red, though the Planalto white from *Sogrape*, the Mateus-makers, is full and honeyed and good, the *Quinta do Côtto* isn't bad, and *Esteva* from *Ferreira* is clean and crisp. *Quinta da Pacheca* have been experimenting with Sauvignon Blanc, Riesling and Gewürztraminer, but results

The price guides for this section begin on page 365.

aren't yet that exciting. *Quinta do Valprado* Chardonnay made by the Seagram-owned *Raposeira* fizz company near Lamego, is honeyed and mouth-filling.

SETÚBAL About to be given IPR status, this peninsula south-east of Lisbon is where Portugal's most advanced white wine-making happens. At *João Pires*, Peter Bright makes a grapy dry Muscat and an oaky Chardonnay. The California-trained Domingo Soares Franco, winemaker at *J.M. da Fonseca*, prefers local grapes, though Chardonnay gives a lemony lift to the white *Pasmados*, and *Quinta da Camarate* boasts Riesling, Gewürztraminer and Muscat.

VINHO VERDE, RD Verde here means youthful-green, immature-green, un-aged, rather than implying that the liquid is the colour of a croquet lawn. Ideally, these wines are extremely dry, positively tart, and brilliantly suited to the heavy, oily Portuguese cuisine. But we almost always get them slightly sweetened and softened, which is a pity. Although, it is in its peculiar way a classic wine style.

Most wines come from co-ops or are sold under merchants' brand names, but there is an increasing tendency for the larger, grander private producers to bottle their own. And some of the big firms are beginning to make characterful single-quinta Vinhos Verdes alongside their big brands. *Palacio da Brejoeira*, made from the Alvarinho grape, is much more alcoholic and full bodied, and expensive, for that matter, than the general run of Vinho Verde. *Casa de Cabanelas, Casa de Compostela, Casa de Sezim, Paço d'Anha, Paço de Cardido, Paço de Teixeiro, Quinta da Aveleda* (their *Grinalda* is one of the best), *Quinta do Tamariz, Solar das Bouças* and the pure Loureiro wines from the *Ponte do Lima* co-op are even better.

Vinho Verde can be made from a variety of grapes, but there's often a higher proportion of Loureiro in the single-property wines. Indeed, there's quite rightly a lot of interest in Loureiro, with its dry, apricotty, Muscatty aroma and flavour. It is more attractive than the much-praised Alvarinho, and it gives the wines a much more tangy, but fruity character. *Peter Bright's* new Vinho Verde, for example, is almost entirely Loureiro, as are the excellent *Solar das Bouças, Quinta do Tamariz* and *Casa dos Cunhas*. And *Sogrape* have planted predominantly Loureiro in their new Vinho Verde quinta at Quinta de Azevedo.

RED WINES

Portuguese red wines *can* be some of the most exciting in Europe. The country is a treasure-house of unique, indigenous grape types with flavours totally unrelated to the mainstream of the French or German classics. But most wines are vinified in a heavy-handed manner and aged too long in unsuitable concrete or old wooden vats. Paradoxically, it's in the established wine regions that ageing requirements are most heavy-handed. In areas like Ribatejo, Oeste or Alentejo, because there are no rules (except for grape variety recommendations), it's easier to bottle wine at its optimum age. The flavours of the young reds flowing out of these regions can be startling, and the price is *never* high. Now that various areas are getting demarcated status we're keeping our fingers crossed they won't be too restrictive, but we can't be sure, because trying to persuade a Portuguese winemaker that his red is *better* as young as possible and bottled without *any* ageing requirement, is one of life's more thankless tasks.

WINES & WINE REGIONS

ALENTEJO An area of great potential, where some producers are still very primitive, but more and more are well-equipped and capable of producing good wines. It's an enormous area, covering much of the southern part of the country, and there is no doubt it can produce exceptional grapes. The large *J.M. da Fonseca* company, who are the leading innovators in commercial red wine production, have invested a lot of time and energy in the region. Apart from Fonseca's blends, and the *Tinto Velho* from the *J.S. Rosado Fernandes* estate, which Fonseca now own, the best wines are from various co-ops. The reds from the *Redondo* co-op, with their big, brash grapy fruit show the potential waiting to be tapped. The upfront rich damson and raspberry fruit of the *Paço dos Infantes* from Almodovar, south of Lisbon, shows the same marvellously untamed excitement. The *Borba* co-op and *Reguengos de Monsaraz* are producing reds with wonderful fruit, and the new space-age *Herdade do Esporão* does excellent, though expensive, red as well as lovely aromatic Roupeiro white.

ALGARVE, RD The south coastal strip of the country, making undistinguished wines – mostly alcoholic reds. Rumour has it the area is to be demoted – goodness knows why it got an RD rating in the first place. Local politics? The *Lagoa co-op* is the best bet.

BAIRRADA, RD In the flat scrubland down towards the sea from the hilly Dão region, vineyards mingle with wheatfields, olive trees and meadows, and the wines frequently overshadow the more famous

Webster's is an annual
publication. We welcome
your suggestions for next
year's edition.

Dão reds. The wines are apt to be aged
rather too long in old wooden barrels, as in
Dão, but the Baga grape, the chief one in
the blend, gives a sturdy, pepper, plum-
and-blackcurrant fruit to the wine which
can often survive the over-ageing, and at
ten years old, although the resiny bite and
peppery edge are apparent, a delicious, dry
fruit is more in command. The best
Bairrada wines age extraordinarily well.
Some growers, like *Luis Pato*, are now
experimenting with blending in a dollop of
softening Cabernet Sauvignon.

Some Portuguese merchants will tell
you that their own 'Garrafeira' wines are
based on Bairrada, though the label won't
say so. That's probably true, because of the
traditional Portuguese approach to high
quality reds – buy where the grapes are
best, blend and age at your company's
cellars, and sell the 'brew' under your own
name. Since 1979, however, the Bairrada
region has been demarcated and bulk sales
have been banned, and the challenging,
rather angular, black fruit flavours of the
wines now sport a Bairrada label. *São João*
produces wine of world class. *Aliança, São
Domingos, Imperio, Sogrape* (one of the two
big Mateus plants is in Bairrada),
Vinexport and *Barroçao* are good. The best
co-op is *Cantanhede* and *Mealhada* is not
bad. Single-estate wines are emerging,
with *Luis Pato* the leader so far. He must
be good because he's already had some of
his wine turned down by the Bairrada
Região as untypical: he'd used new oak
instead of old! His 1980 is excellent.

COLARES, RD Grown in the sand dunes
on the coast near Lisbon from the doughty
but scented Ramisco grape. Almost all the
wine is vinified at the local Adega
Regional, stalks and all, aged in concrete
tanks for two to three years, then sold to
merchants for further maturation and sale.
The young wine has fabulous cherry
perfume but is *numbingly* tannic. As it
ages it gets an exciting rich pepper and

bruised plums flavour, but the 1974s are
only just ready. The Adega no longer has a
monopoly on Colares, but for the time
being only *Carvalho, Ribeiro & Ferreira*
show interest in exploiting the new
freedom.

DÃO, RD This upland eyrie, ringed by
mountains, reached by steep, exotic, forest-
choked river gorges, makes Portugal's most
famous, if not always her most appetizing
reds. They are reputed to become velvet-
smooth with age. My experience is that
they rarely achieve this and could do with
less ageing in wood and more in bottle.
They are made from a mixture of six
grapes, of which the Touriga Nacional is
the best, and they develop a strong, dry,
herby taste, almost with a pine resin bite.

Protectionist local regulations stipulate
that firms from outside the region should
not set up wineries there, but fortunately
the old rule about buying finished wine, not
grapes, from growers, has gone, so the new
winemakers are now able to work with raw
material before it has been ruined by inept
handling.

The makers of *Grão Vasco, Vinicola do
Vale do Dão*, have now bought their own
quinta, have stopped buying from the co-op
at Tazem, and will start off the decade by
supplying wine-making skills and advice to
others in the region. All of which sounds
like good news to me.

Other firms are persuading their co-op
suppliers to leave the grape stalks out of
the fermentation vats and make cleaner,
more modern wines, but there's a long way
to go. However, *São João's Porta dos
Cavaleiros* is marvellous, *Grão Vasco* is
good and will be better when they start
bottling early enough. I'd choose the
following as the other current fair bets:
*Acacio, Aliança, Caves Velhas, Dom Ferraz,
São Domingos, Rittos* and the remarkable
Asda own-label.

DOURO, RD The Douro valley is famous
for the production of port. But only a
proportion of the crop – usually about 40
per cent – is made into port, the rest being
sold as table wine. Traditionally, all the
best grapes have gone into the region's
most famous product, but a number of
private producers and now quite a few of

the port houses themselves have started making high quality table wines, based on Touriga Francesa, Touriga Nacional and Tinta Roriz, but sometimes including foreign varieties such as the Cabernet Sauvignon. The flavour can be delicious – soft and glyceriny, with a rich raspberry and peach fruit, and a dry perfume somewhere between liquorice, smoky bacon and cigar tobacco. But quality is still patchy. Early days. Look out for *Acacio, Champalimaud (Quinta do Côtto, Côtto Grande Escolha), Barca Velha, Esteva* and *Reserva Especial* from *Ferreira, Mesão Frio, Penajora, Quinta da Pacheca, Santa Marta.*

OESTE Portugal's largest wine area north of Lisbon is capable of quality, and just beginning to do something about it. Arruda makes strong, gutsy reds, Alenquer makes softer, more glyceriny wine, while the Obidos reds are drier, more acid, but good in a cedary way. Torres Vedras' reds are lighter than Arruda, with a climate more influenced by cooling Atlantic air. These four areas now have IPR status. Single-estate *Quinta de Abrigada*, with light, creamy whites, stylish damson and cherry reds is the only private estate doing much so far, though *Paulo da Silva's Beira Mar and Casal de Azenha* are both good Oeste blends.

RIBATEJO Portugal's second largest region, in the flatlands alongside the Tagus, provides the base wine for some important brands – in particular the Romeira of *Caves Velhas*, *Teobar* of *Dom Teodosio* and *Serradayres* of *Carvalho, Ribeiro & Ferreira*. The co-op at *Almeirim* markets good wine under its own name, and the *Torre Velha* brand isn't bad. The *Margaride* estate is the Ribatejo's leading estate. The wines are sold as *Dom Hermano, Margarides* and under the names of their properties, *Casal do Monteiro* and *Convento da Serra*. Patchy, but can be very good. The region is being split up into six new IPRs: Almeirim, Cartaxo, Chamusca, Santarem, Tomar and Coruche.

SETÚBAL *João Pires* and *J.M. da Fonseca* are the leading lights here, for

reds and whites. Imports like Cabernet Sauvignon and Merlot are made as varietals as well as in blends with local grapes like Periquita or Castelão Frances.

VINHO VERDE, RD Sixty per cent of all Vinho Verde produced is, surprisingly, red, made from four different native grapes, of which the Vinhão is best. The wine is wonderfully sharp, harsh even, is hardly ever seen outside the country and is losing its popularity even in Portugal. I'm virtually alone in the entire English-speaking world in regretting this. No other wine but a red Vinho Verde will do to wash down a pan of *bacalhão* (salt cod) – try it!

FORTIFIED WINES

Although the general fortified wine market worldwide is in decline, as people look for fresher, brighter flavours – and less alcohol – in their drinks, the mood in the Douro remains buoyantly optimistic. Barren land in the Cima Corgo and Douro Superior, way up the Douro river near the Spanish border, has been replanted even though there is no road anywhere near the vineyard to carry any crop to a winery! But the experts are confident about the quality potential of these hillsides where no vines have grown for a hundred years. *Webster's 2000* will no doubt be reporting on these wines as the vines reach producing maturity.

Port is the exception to this fall off in trade – it is doing well. Sadly, the profits that fuel the rise in port's fortunes are largely being generated by the proliferation of 'Late Bottled Vintage' – a label which implies a vintage style – big, strong, wonderfully rich wines – but LBVs are, in general, shallowly sweet, lack-lustre liquids which are a disgrace to the very idea of 'vintage'. There are only four I *can* recommend: Warre, Smith Woodhouse, Ramos-Pinto and Fonseca.

Fortified wine quality is in the main remarkably good – and that's including Madeira. We may be buying less, but that's not because the wines are lowering their standards. The arrival of the Symington family of port fame in Madeira bodes well for the future of the island's wine, so we may see even more of the quality and individuality Madeira is capable of in years to come.

All everyone needs now is for the weather to start behaving itself.

GRAPES & FLAVOURS

Eighteen different grape varieties are used to make red and white ports, and of these the most important in terms of quality and flavour are the Roriz, Barroca, Touriga Francesa and Touriga Nacional among the reds, and the Malvasia Dorada and Malvasia Fina in the whites. The Moscatel is chiefly grown in Setúbal just south of Lisbon, where it makes a famous, but not thrilling, sweet fortified wine.

WINES & WINE REGIONS

CARCAVELOS, RD Just when Carcavelos looked as if it was about to disappear for ever, along comes a new vineyard. *Quinta de Santa Rita* is making a good, nutty, fortified wine rather like an aged Tawny port, with the help of winemaker Peter Bright.

MADEIRA, RD Each Madeira style is supposedly based on one of four grapes, Malmsey (Malvasia), Bual, Verdelho and Sercial, though at the moment only the more expensive Madeiras really live up to their labels – the cheaper ones, up to 'five-year-olds', are almost exclusively made from the inferior Tinta Negra Mole. The EC is enforcing a rule that 85 per cent of a wine labelled with a grape variety should be made from that stated grape; as this happens the cheaper Madeiras are likely to start calling themselves, more honestly, 'Pale Dry', 'Dark Rich', etc.

But up-market, the Malmsey grape makes the sweetest style of Madeira, reeking sometimes of the finest Muscovado sugar, dark, rich and brown, but with a smoky bite and surprisingly high acidity that makes it positively refreshing after a long meal. The Bual grape is also rich and strong, but not quite so concentrated, sometimes with a faintly rubbery whiff and slightly higher acidity. The Verdelho makes a pungent, smoky, medium-sweet wine with a more obvious, gentle fruit, and the Sercial makes a most dramatic dry wine, savoury, spirity, tangy, and with a steely, piercing acidity. To taste what Madeira is all about you really have to pay for a ten-year-old, and, frankly, really good Madeira should be two or three times that age.

The recent move into Madeira by the Symington family of port fame should herald new investment – and even better wines to come.

MOSCATEL DE SETÚBAL, RD Good, but always a little spirity and never quite as perfume-sweet as one would like. It comes in a six-year-old and a 25-year-old version, and the 25-year-old does have a lot more character and less overbearing spiritiness, but the sweetness veers towards the cooked marmalade of southern French Muscats rather than the honeyed, raisined richness of the Australian versions.

PORT (DOURO, RD) The simplest and cheapest port wines available in Britain

The price guides for this section begin on page 367.

are labelled simply 'Ruby' and 'Tawny'. Ruby is usually blended from the unexceptional grapes of unexceptional vineyards to create a tangy, tough, but warmingly sweet wine to knock back uncritically. It should have a spirity rasp along with the sweetness to make it more than just sugary. Cheap Tawny at around the same price as Ruby is simply a mindless mixture of light Ruby and White ports, and is almost never as good as the Ruby would have been, left to itself.

Calling these inferior concoctions 'Tawnies' is very misleading because there's a genuine style 'Tawny', too. Proper Tawnies are kept in wooden barrels for at least five, but preferably ten or more years to let the colour leach out and a gentle fragrance and delicate flavour of nuts, brown sugar and raisins develop. Most of these more expensive Tawnies have an age on the label, which must be a multiple of 10: 10, 20, 30 or even 40 years old. Lack of age on a Tawny label – however often it says 'Fine', 'Old', etc – is a bad sign and

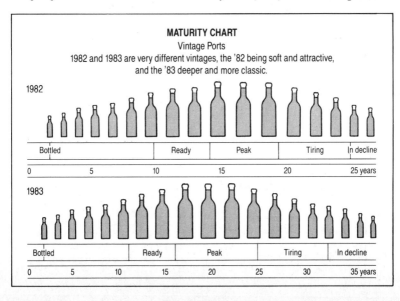

MATURITY CHART
Vintage Ports
1982 and 1983 are very different vintages, the '82 being soft and attractive, and the '83 deeper and more classic.

usually implies a cheap, Ruby-based blend, though there are some good brands like *Harvey's Director's Bin Very Superior Old Tawny*. Any age stated is the *average* age of the ports in the blend. A 10-year-old Tawny might contain some six-year-old and some 14-year-old wine. Most Tawnies reach their peak at somewhere between 10 and 15 years, and few ports can possibly improve with more than 20 years in barrel, so don't pay inflated prices for 30- and 40-year-old Tawnies. Recommended wines: *Cockburn's 10-year-old*, *Ferreira 10 and 20-year-old*, *Fonseca 10-year-old* and *20-year-old*, *Harvey's Director's Bin*, *Sainsbury's 10-year-old*.

VINTAGE PORTS are the opposite to the Tawnies, since the objective here is to make a big, impressive, concentrated mouthful, rather than anything too delicate. Vintage years are 'declared' by port shippers when the quality seems particularly good – usually about three times a decade although we managed four in the 1980s. These are matured in wooden casks for two years or so, then bottled.They should then be left to mature for at least a dozen years and sometimes twice that.

The final effect should have far more weight and richness than a Tawny of similar age, since the maturation has taken place in the almost airless and neutral confines of the glass bottle, which ages the wines far more slowly. There should also be a much more exciting, complex tangle of flavours; blackcurrant, plums, minty liquorice, pepper and herbs, cough mixture and a lot more besides. Vintage port you get animated and opinionated about, whereas Tawny is more a wine for quiet reflection.

If you want a peek at what Vintage port can be like, buy Single-Quinta wine. Single Quintas (Portuguese for 'farms') are usually from the best vineyards in the less brilliant years, but instead of being bottled and shipped after only two years or so to the cold, slow-maturing cellars of Britain, they are bottled after two years, frequently stored for up to ten years in Portugal's warmer climate, and are then shipped mature and ready to drink. They cost several pounds a bottle less than similarly mature vintage port and are usually extremely good. Fortunately, producers are getting more and more interested in making these wines.

Another good-value Vintage port look-alike is Crusted port. These are a British speciality, blends of wines from two or three different vintages, shipped in cask, then bottled slightly later than Vintage, say on average at three years old, so they retain the peppery attack of the top wines and also keep a good deal of the rich, exotic perfumed sweetness of real 'Vintage'. They are called Crusted because of the sediment that will form after three or four years in bottle. More and more houses are producing 'Crusteds' and they are often the best quality/price ratio on the market.

Two other types of port like to think of themselves as vintage style. Vintage Character and Late Bottled Vintage are bottled four to six years after the harvest, after most of the sediment has dropped out in cask. Ideally, this extra time maturing in wood should bring about an effect similar to a dozen years of bottle-ageing. Bottled at four years, and not too heavily filtered to remove all the sediment, it still can, but most Vintage Character and Late-Bottled ports are, sadly, too browbeaten into early decline and have about as much personality as a panful of potatoes. The best, labelled with the year of bottling, are from *Fonseca, Niepoort, Smith-Woodhouse, Ramos-Pinto* and *Warre*. They are delicious, high-quality products, and like Vintage, Single Quinta, and Crusted ports, they can throw a sediment in the bottle, and may need decanting.

There are two styles of White port, dry and sweet. In general, the flavour is a bit thick and alcoholic, the sweet ones even tasting slightly of rough grape skins. But there are a few good dry ones, though I've never felt any great urge to drink them anywhere except in the blinding mid-summer heat of the Douro valley when they're refreshing with a few ice-cubes and a big splash of lemonade or tonic.

Webster's is an annual publication. We welcome your suggestions for next year's edition.

PORT SHIPPER PROFILES

CALEM ★★★★ Important Portuguese shipper founded in the last century and still family owned. Calem produce excellent 10, 20, 30 and 40-year old Tawnies and good Vintage port from the spectacular Quinta da Foz at Pinhão.

CHURCHILL GRAHAM ★★★★ Established as recently as 1981, the first independent port shipper to be founded in more than 50 years. Nine years is not long in the port trade but John Graham has already established a reputation for intense, concentrated wines made to last.

COCKBURN ★★★★ Shippers of the best-selling 'Fine Old Ruby' and 'Special Reserve'. At the forefront of research into viticulture in the Upper Douro. Recent Vintage ports have been stunning.

CROFT ★★★ One of the oldest of all port shippers. Quinta da Roeda near Pinhão forms the backbone of their vintage wines, but too many wines are a little over-delicate.

DELAFORCE ★★(★) The Tawny, His Eminence's Choice, is their best-known wine.

DOW ★★★★★ Quinta do Bomfim at Pinhão produces the backbone of Dow's firm-flavoured, long-living Vintage ports. Bomfim has recently been launched as a lesser vintage, single-quinta wine.

FERREIRA ★★★★ One of the best Portuguese-owned shippers, making elegant early-maturing Vintage ports and two superb Tawnies; 10-year-old Quinta do Porto and 20-year-old Duque de Bragança. Bought by Sogrape, the Mateus Rosé company, in 1988.

FONSECA GUIMARAENS ★★★★★ Family-run shippers belonging to the Yeatman side of Taylor, Fladgate and Yeatman. Fonseca's wines are sweeter and less austere than Taylor's. The Vintage ports are often outstanding, but the quality of their commercial releases is reassuring.

GOULD CAMPBELL ★★★★ Name used mainly for Vintage ports which tend to be ripe in style and relatively quick to mature.

GRAHAM ★★★★(★) Graham's ports tend to be rich and sweet in style. Quinta dos Malvedos is their best-known property and is released as a single-quinta wine in lesser vintages.

OFFLEY FORRESTER ★★★(★) Famous for 'Boa Vista' vintage and LBV ports. Vintage wines are based almost exclusively on their own Quinta da Boa Vista and can be insubstantial. They also make excellent Tawnies sold as Baron de Forrester.

QUINTA DO NOVAL ★★★★ A beautiful quinta high above Pinhão as well as a shipper. Noval's Nacional wines, produced from a vineyard of pre-phylloxera, ungrafted vines, are legendary and fetch a stratospheric price at auction. Other Noval wines don't attempt such heights, but are usually good, if light. Noval LB is widely sold, but isn't that special; the Tawnies are much better.

RAMOS-PINTO ★★★★ Delicious Tawnies from two quintas – Ervamoira and Bom Retiro. Elegant, nutty and delicate in classic Tawny style.

REAL VINICOLA ★★(★) The largest port producer selling ports under seven different names. The wines can be good. Vintage ports generally early maturing.

SANDEMAN ★★★ Best at making good, aged Tawnies and, recently, improved, quite concentrated vintage wines.

SMITH WOODHOUSE ★★★★ Some delicious Vintage and LBV ports. Concentrated vintage wines which tend to mature early. LBV and Crusted ports are wonderfully full-flavoured.

TAYLOR, FLADGATE AND YEATMAN ★★★★(★) Very high quality range, some would say of 'first growth' level. Every wine from 'Chip Dry' white to the rich, long-lasting Vintage ports is made to high standards. All the same, some recent commercial releases have seen standards slip a little, and their Vintage port is no longer ahead of the field. Quinta de Vargellas produces some of the best lesser-vintage, single-quinta wines, well worth the hunt.

WARRE ★★★★★ The first port company in which the entrepreneurial Symington dynasty became involved. Warre produce serious wines: good LBVs, the fine 'Nimrod' Tawny and Vintage wines. Quinta da Cavadinha has recently been launched as a single-quinta wine – it is a style that is becoming increasingly popular.

PORT CLASSIFICATION

If you think that Burgundy and Bordeaux make a meal out of classifying their vineyards, just look at how rigidly port is controlled. Nothing is left to chance. The age of the vines is classified on a scale from 0 to 60 points. The level of upkeep of the vines is ruthlessly marked from –500 to +100 points. The objective is to score as many points as possible, because the authorities allow the top scorers to turn a larger proportion of their crop into port. The highest possible score would be +1680 points, while the bottom score possible would be a massively embarrassing –3430. They'd have to be very bad to get anywhere near that. The classification, based on points scored, is from A to F, and controls how many litres of juice per 1000 vines can be turned into port. The rest has to go as table wine, which gives a smaller return, so there is considerable incentive for the growers to score high points.

THE VINEYARD CALCULATION

Productivity (Ranging from about 500 litres per 1000 vines to about 2000 litres; the lower the yield the higher the points scored.)
Worst: 0 points   Best: +80 points
Altitude (Ranging from a highest allowable altitude of 650 metres to a lowest of 150 metres.)
Worst: –900 points   Best: +150 points
Soil (Scored according to type. Schist scores best, granite worst.)
Worst: –350 points   Best: +100 points
Geographical position (Predetermined locations score different marks.)
Worst: –50 points   Best: +600 points
Upkeep of vineyard (Good housekeeping awards for various factors.)
Worst: –500 points   Best: +100 points
Variety and quality of grapes
Worst: –300 points   Best: +150 points
Gradient (From 1-in-6 to 1-in-30 – the steeper the better.)
Worst: –100 points   Best: +100 points
Shelter
Worst: 0   Best: +70 points

Age of vines (With 5-year-olds scoring 30; up to 25-year-olds scoring 60.)
Worst: 0   Best: +60 points
Distance root to root (The distance from the end of one vine's root to the start of the next root – too close is frowned upon.)
Worst: –50 points   Best: +50 points
Nature of land
Worst: –600 points   Best: +100 points
Aspect
Worst: –30 points   Best: +100 points

THE TOTAL
The experts then add up all these points and classify the vineyards according to score, allowing each group to make a certain number of litres of wine per 1000 vines, as follows:

A (1201 points or more)	600 litres
B (1001–1200 points)	600 litres
C (801–1000 points)	590 litres
D (601–800 points)	580 litres
E (401–600 points)	580 litres
F (400 points or less)	260 litres

PORT VINTAGES

Vintage port takes a long time to reach the smooth, mellow peak that induces leather-chaired slumber. Young Vintage port can be a brilliant, fiery, intensely sweet, show-stopper of a wine. If you hanker for that pepper, cough-mixture and plum brandy full frontal attack, go ahead and down a 1977 or a 1980 – but cancel any early appointments the next morning.

1985 A tremendously ripe and healthy crop of grapes – along with the rest of Europe. A unanimous 'declaration' of a vintage is not that common, but 1985 was declared a 'vintage' year by every important shipper. The prices are high, but the quality is exceptionally good. The wines don't quite have the solidity of the 1983s but they make up for this with a juicy ripeness of fruit and unusually precocious signs of fragrant perfumes to come. Although *Taylor* isn't as outstanding as usual, several perennial under-achievers like *Croft* and *Offley* are very good, *Cockburn* is very attractive, and *Fonseca* is rich and lush. However, my favourites are *Graham, Warre, Dow, Gould Campbell* and *Churchill Graham*. The price makes me nervous; but the wine's seductive in the extreme, so...

1983 Marvellous wine, strong and aggressive to taste at the moment, but with a deep, brooding sweetness which is all ripe, clean fruit. This won't be one of the most fragrant vintages, but it will be a sturdy classic in a dozen years' time.

1982 Perfectly nice but lacking the brilliance of a really good year. The wines have a slightly concocted sweetness about them, and lack the hidden depth which great Vintage port needs to reveal as it matures. Good, not great.

1980 A good vintage, though excessively expensive when first offered. Although they were consequently unpopular, the wines are developing a delicious, drier than usual style. It should be starting to soften now, and will peak about 1995.

1977 Brilliant wine which has hardly begun to mature. The flavour is a marvellous mixture of great fruit sweetness and intense spice and herb fragrance. Still extremely youthful, these wines will rock you back on your heels if you drink them now, but maybe you like that sort of thing.

1975 These in general don't have the stuffing that a true vintage style demands, but some are surprisingly gaining weight and richness and are excellent for drinking now. *Noval, Taylor, Dow, Warre* and *Graham* need no apologies. Most of the others do.

1970 Lovely stuff, but, curiously, only cautiously praised. Fainthearts, take up your corkscrews! This is exceptional, balanced port, already good to drink, very sweet, and ripe with a fascinating citrus flash of freshness. It'll last for ages but it's delicious already. All the top houses are really special – led by *Fonseca, Taylor, Warre, Graham* and *Dow*, but lesser houses like *Calem* and *Santos Junior* are also excellent.

1966 They didn't rate this at first, but they do now. It's gained body and oomph and is now approaching its best. Doesn't *quite* have the super-ripe balance of the '70 or the startling, memorable character of the '63, but a very good year. *Fonseca* is the star at the moment.

1963 They call it the 'classic' year, and one can see why. It's big, deep, and spicy, with a remarkable concentration of flavours based on any really ripe red or black fruit you can think of washed in an essence of liquorice, mint and herbs. One or two have lost a surprising amount of colour recently, but in the main it's so good that if you decide to see in the millennium with a bottle of *Fonseca, Taylor, Graham, Dow* or *Cockburn* ... get my address from the *Webster's* office!

UNITED STATES

Until very recently when you talked about American wines, you were really talking about California wines. You were aware, in an academic kind of way, that wine was made on other parts of the North American continent, but it wasn't really necessary to pay much attention.

No longer true. Without a doubt, this was the year that American wines from non-California producers fairly began to come into their own. I tasted a sparkling wine from New Mexico, a Gruet non-vintage Brut, that would rank near the top of any tasting of New World sparkling wines. I've tasted at least two Chardonnays from the eastern US that are the equal of anything coming from California: Prince Michel 1988 Barrel Select Virginia Chardonnay, and a Bridgehampton 1988 Estate Reserve Chardonnay from Long Island, New York. Texas, Arizona, Idaho, Missouri, Georgia and North Carolina, among others, are also coming up with the odd bottle of first-rate wine.

In the north-west, the wines of Washington State just keep getting better and better. What has surprised many is the excellent quality of the Washington red wines, especially Merlot and Cabernet Sauvignon – all share an intense varietal fruit character which is simply astonishing. If I were just beginning to stock a cellar of American wines now, I would look first at Washington, beginning with the friendly giant, Chateau Ste Michelle.

Oregon continues to be something of a disappointment, though. The 1987 Oregon Pinot Noirs were a fairly uninteresting lot, despite all the pre-release publicity. Perhaps growers should take a closer look at the potential for Riesling and Chardonnay and not pin all their hopes on one obviously bewildered grape.

Not that California is letting the side down. Releases of 1985 and 1986 California Cabernets are showing remarkable quality, though some of the prices are silly. Heitz Martha's Vineyard 1985? $65 ex-cellars. Caymus '85 Select? $50. Yet there are outstanding Cabernets on the market for under $15 in California. To mention only a few: Alexander Valley Vineyards 1986; Franciscan 1986, Oakville bottling; Iron Horse 1986 Cabernets; Charles Krug 1985 Cabernet (a fantastic bargain in California at $9); Louis Martini 1986 North Coast Cabernet; Mont St John 1985 Napa Cabernet, and Raymond 1986 Napa Cabernet.

Many of these excellent value, high quality bottles are from wineries which are out of the trendy loop. They may be well-established, well-respected names to many, but have simply never become darlings of the wine press.

A very welcome mini-trend of the past year has been the introduction of a few light red wines made for immediate drinking. Notable was Fetzer's experimental Red Zinfandel, a partial carbonic-maceration wine (that is, made like Beaujolais) with attractive berry fruit. Served slightly chilled, it is a great wine for picnics, pasta and drinking by the pool. Let's hope it becomes a major trend — it may even attract new wine drinkers into the fold.

Perhaps in response to health fears or the crackdown on drinking and driving, non-alcoholic wines enjoyed a boom in the US this year, with J. Lohr's Ariel brand and St Regis from Vintners International both finding growing acceptance for their wines. Ariel has just introduced a barrel-fermented Chardonnay and a Champagne-method Blanc de Blancs. The price for this non-alcoholic bubbly is $20. Enough to drive anyone to drink. **LARRY WALKER**

WHITE GRAPES & FLAVOURS

CHARDONNAY California's Central Coast — Santa Barbara and San Luis Obispo — are challenging Napa and Sonoma as top Chardonnay country. After a disappointing 1987, the '88s are crammed with excellent fruit and show great balance and style. Sometimes with Chardonnay, especially from the Central Coast, you find a positive fruit salad of flavours with figs, peaches and lychees all fighting for prominence. Napa and Sonoma wines are drier, less overtly fruity.

With the dollar remaining weak, you should stock up on these while you can. You *can* age Napa and Sonoma wines, but the majority don't improve much after three to four years — although *Acacia, Chalone, Cuvaison, Flora Springs, Mondavi's Reserve, Newton, Saintsbury* and *Sonoma-Cutrer* will last well. Good producers: *Acacia, Belvedere (Bacigalupi* and *Winery Lake) Beringer, Buena Vista, Chalone, Christian Brothers Reserve, Clos du Bois, Cuvaison, Domaine Wolther, Dry Creek, Edna Valley, Far Niente, Fetzer, Flora Springs, Franciscan, Glen Ellen, Grand Cru, Grgich Hills, Girard, Groth, Inglenook Reserve, Jekel, Jordan, Kendall-Jackson, Kistler Estate, Long, Matanzas Creek, Meridian, Mondavi, Chateau Montelena, Monticello, Mount Eden, Newton, Phelps, Rombauer, Saintsbury, Simi, Signorello, Sonoma-Cutrer, Talbott, Trefethen, ZD* (California); *Adams, Bethel Heights, Rex Hill, Shafer, Tualatin, Tyee* (Oregon); *Covey Rise, Rose Creek* (Idaho); *Arbor Crest, Blackwood Canyon, Chinook, Cold Creek, Covey Run, Salishan, Chateau St Michelle, Hogue Cellars, Woodward Canyon* (Washington); *Bridgehampton, Lenz, Hargrave, Pindar, Wagner, West Park* (NY); *Piedmont, Prince Michel* (Virginia).

CHENIN BLANC For so long a rather soft and seedy workhorse grape, California Chenin is now going back to its high-acid French roots, but taking a honeyed ripeness with it. Good producers: *Callaways Sweet Nancy, Christian Brothers, Dry Creek, Hacienda, J. Lohr, Parducci* (California), *Salishan* (Washington), *Llano Estacado* (Texas).

FRENCH COLOMBARD This is the most widely planted wine grape in California. *Chalone* make a very good dry version, and *Llano Estacado* in Texas do it quite well.

GEWÜRZTRAMINER Rarely a great success in California as a dry wine because too often the grapes are picked when overripe, leading to bitterness in the finished wine. With the help of cold fermentation techniques, good dry Gewürztraminers have emerged this year from *Adler Fels, Gundlach-Bundschu* and *Rutherford Hill*. For the best sweet stuff, *Mark West* and *De Loach*.

RIESLING Called White Riesling or Johannisberg Riesling. Never very successful in California, probably because it was grown in areas that were just too hot for it. Still, some dry Rieslings from cooler areas have been successful recently. *Jekel* and *Ventana* (Monterey), and *Storr's* (Santa Cruz) are excellent. *Trefethen* and *Navarro* also make good versions. Sweet Rieslings have always been successful, especially from *Buena Vista, Chateau St Jean, Firestone, Kenwood, Phelps, Mark West* (California); *Arbor Crest, Chateau Ste Michelle, Hogue Cellars, Kiona, Steward* (Washington); *Heron Hill, Wiemer* (NY), *Texas, Fall Creek* (Texas).

SAUVIGNON BLANC also called **FUMÉ BLANC**. This grape suffers from a chaotic identity crisis. Since the true, rather herbaceous style of classic Sauvignon doesn't seem very popular with the American public, winemakers tend either to strip it of all its grassy flavour or overripen it to a fat, faintly honeyed style. Good producers: *Belvedere 'Discovery', Byron, Chateau St Jean, Dry Creek, Fetzer 'Valley Oaks', Geyser Peak, Hanna, Inglenook, Lake Springs, de Lorimier, Mondavi, Monticello, Newton, Preston, William Wheeler* (California); *Arbor Crest, Chinook, Hogue Cellars* (Washington); *Hargrave* (NY). Sweet wines (Semillon/Sauvignon): *Kalin Cuvée d'Or, Merlion, Phelps Delice du Semillon* (California).

RED GRAPES & FLAVOURS

CABERNET SAUVIGNON Increasingly impressive wines as winemakers learn how to deal with Cabernet's strong, big-boned flavours. We're now getting back to the gorgeous, rich mixture of blackcurrant, mint and eucalyptus wrapped in warm, vanilla oak, but supported by tannic toughness, which puts California Cabernet in a world class and I say — welcome back. Good producers: *Alexander Valley, Belvedere ('Discovery' series and Robert Young), Beringer (Knight's Valley and Reserve), Buena Vista, Burgess, Cain, Caymus, Chateau Montelena, Chimney Rock, Clos du Bois, Clos Pegase, Conn Creek, Cuvaison, Diamond Creek, Dry Creek, Duckhorn, Dunn, Estancia, Fetzer (Lake County), Flora Springs, Franciscan, Girard, Grace Family, Groth, Heitz, Johnson-Turnbull, Jordan, La Jota (Howell Mountain), Kistler Estate, Laurel Glen, Long, Martini, Mayacamas, Mondavi, Monticello (Corley), Mount Eden, Newton, Phelps (Backus or Eisele), Ridge, Silverado, Silver Oak, Simi, Shafer, Spottswoode, Stag's Leap, William Hill, Whitehall Lane, ZD* (California); *Arbor Crest, Chateau Ste Michelle, Quilceda Creek* (Washington); *Hargrave* (NY); *Allegro* (Pennsylvania); *Byrd* (Maryland); *Pheasant Ridge, Sanchez Creek* (Texas); *Rose Creek* (Idaho).

A number of wineries are now producing wines based on Cabernet Sauvignon, but with more than the legal limit of other Bordeaux varieties (usually Cabernet Franc and Merlot) blended in. Many of these 'Proprietaries' are excellent. Best producers: *Cain 5, Carmenet, Dominus, Flora Springs, Inglenook Claret, Mount Veeder Red Table wine, Opus One, Prince Michel* (Virginia), *Rubicon, Rombauer Meilleur du Chais, Sterling Reserve.*

MERLOT There's now a fair amount of Merlot on the West Coast, ideally for use in blending, but some wineries make a successful varietal (often with a little Cabernet added back) and Merlot is fast becoming the 'hot' varietal on the West Coast. With its Bordeaux pedigree, but soft, round, creamy plum flavours, I can

see why. *Cosentino, Cuvaison, Clos du Bois, Clos du Val, Duckhorn, Franciscan, Geyser Peak, Keenan, Markham, Matanzas Creek, Newton, Pine Ridge, St Francis, Santa Cruz Mountain, Shafer, Sterling Estate, Silverado, Stag's Leap, Whitehall Lane* (California). *Chinook, Covey Run, Hogue Cellars* (Washington).

PETITE SIRAH Not the same as the great Syrah red grape of the Rhône or the Shiraz of Australia. It produces big, stark, dry, almost tarry wines — impressive, certainly, but usually lacking real style. *Bonny Doon, Duxoup, Edmunds St John, McDowell Valley, Kendall-Jackson, Edmeades, Preston, Phelps, Qupé, Thackrey, Sierra Vista, Solano* and *Zaca Mesa* all have plantings of the real Syrah, and are making wines ranging from good to superb. Brim full of potential.

PINOT NOIR Burgundy's red grape has met with indifferent success in the US. Although there were great hopes for Oregon Pinot Noir, based on a few vintages, recent wines have been disappointing. Results from California have also been sketchy, but consistently good wines now come regularly from several different regions, notably the lower Russian River Valley in Sonoma county, Carneros in Sonoma-Napa and cooler parts of Central Coast. Good producers: *Acacia, Bay Cellars, Calera, Chalone, Dehlinger, Mondavi, Saintsbury, Sanford, Schug (Beckstoffer), Sea Ridge, Trefethen, Zaca Mesa, ZD* (California); *Adelsheim, Bethel Heights, Eyrie, Knudsen Erath, Ponzi, Rex Hill, Sokol Blosser* (Oregon); *Salishan* (Washington).

ZINFANDEL 'Zin' makes a whole gamut of styles, from pink (called white), to light, cherryish and almost Beaujolais-like, to deep, strong and peppery. There are signs of a welcome renewed interest in full-flavoured reds, and the following are good producers: *Cuvaison, Fetzer, Guenoc, Heitz, Kendall-Jackson, Montevina, Nalle, Phelps, Quivira, Ravenswood, Ridge, Stevenot, Storybook.*

WINE REGIONS

AMADOR COUNTY (California) The home of Zinfandel. This small area northeast of San Francisco in the Sierra Foothills produces superb, massively flavoured Zinfandels from old vines.

CENTRAL VALLEY An umbrella name for the San Joaquin and Sacramento River Valleys. Most Central Valley fruit comes from the San Joaquin Valley between Bakersfield and Stockton.

CARNEROS (California) At the southern end of the Napa and Sonoma Valleys, this is a fairly cool area, the temperatures kept low by the sea breezes which regularly flow in from San Francisco Bay. Some fine Chardonnay and Pinot Noir.

IDAHO (Pacific North-West) A recent entrant into the wine-growing stakes, but already producing some very good Riesling and Gewürztraminer from the *Sainte Chapelle* winery. Also starting to produce good Chardonnay grapes, the best of which are *Covey Rise* and *Rose Creek*.

MENDOCINO COUNTY (California) This area still has an attractive, vaguely 'frontier' feel about it since the logging industry is as yet more in evidence than the wine industry. Most valleys stretch up the Russian River Valley north of Sonoma County. The climate is hot, but with very cool nights and wineries like *Fetzer* and *Parducci* make tasty Chardonnay, Cabernet Sauvignon and Zinfandel. Anderson Valley is a cool area towards the Pacific shore where pioneers *Husch* and *Navarro* have done well with Chardonnay and Gewürztraminer, but it is as a top source for sparkling wine grapes that Anderson is most important: *Roederer Estates'* first release of fizz is very good and the *Handley Cellars Brut* is one of the best in California.

The price guides for this section begin on page 372.

MONTEREY COUNTY (California) Subregions of the large Salinas Valley include Arroyo Seco, Carmel Valley, Chalone, Greenfield, The Pinnacles and King City. Although efforts were made to produce good reds, most tasted distinctly of capsicum/green pepper and the area is now best for Chardonnay, Chenin, Sauvignon Blanc, Riesling and Gewürztraminer. *Chalone* is an exception, with fine Pinot Noir. On the coast side, the small Carmel Valley manages to produce Cabernet Sauvignon without green pepper.

NAPA VALLEY (California) Subregions are Calistoga, Carneros, Chiles Valley, Mount Veeder, Oakville, Pope Valley, Rutherford, St Helena, Spring Mountain, Stag's Leap and Yountville. This is the heart of California's wine industry, and most of the famous wineries are based here. Napa can produce all types of wines, but excels at making impressive, excitingly flavoured ones that are proud to be big. Chardonnay is best of the whites, though some believe that in the next century or so, the classic red Cabernet Sauvignon will dominate the Napa.

NEW YORK STATE The second biggest grape-growing state, but until recently regarded as a bit of a joke, because most of its wines were based on the *labrusca* species — which makes pretty weird-tasting grape juice, let alone table wine! Well, there are now small, but increasing amounts of delicious wine being made. With the exception of *Hargrave*, who have managed some decent Cabernet Sauvignon, it is white wine country and Long Island, with its gentle, temperate climate, is producing Chardonnay, Sauvignon and Riesling to very high standards. The Hudson River is also showing an increasing ability to make good Chardonnay, and the Finger Lakes region now produces some very attractive Chardonnay, Riesling and even Gewürztraminer. Good producers: *Bridgehampton, Glenora, Gold Seal, Hargrave, Lenz, Pindar, Le Rêve, Vinifera Cellars, Wagner, West Park, Wiemer.*

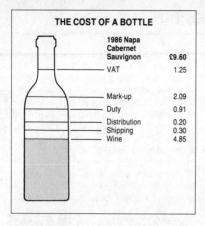

THE COST OF A BOTTLE

1986 Napa Cabernet Sauvignon	£9.60
VAT	1.25
Mark-up	2.09
Duty	0.91
Distribution	0.20
Shipping	0.30
Wine	4.85

NEW MEXICO This surprising wine-growing district, based on irrigated dry desert in the south-west, is turning out some remarkable Chardonnay, Sauvignon Blanc and sparkling wines. *Devalmont Vineyards (Gruet)* and *Anderson Valley Vineyards* are two of the best.

OREGON (Pacific North-West) Regarded as having great potential with so far scattered results. The Chardonnay has been a little hard and withdrawn, the Pinot Noir promising at times but lacking the lush fruit of California and the brilliant, velvety balance of Burgundy.

SAN LUIS OBISPO (California) Edna Valley subregion in the southern area is developing quite a reputation for cool-climate whites, in particular Chardonnay. Warmer northern subregions Shandon and Paso Robles are known for Cabernet Sauvignon and Zinfandel.

SANTA BARBARA COUNTY (California) Subregions are Santa Maria and Santa Ynez. Coastal area just north-west of Los Angeles. Surprisingly, given its southerly latitude, this is a cool zone, because of the influence of sea breezes, and the Santa Maria subregion is only just warm enough to ripen Chardonnay and Pinot Noir. The slightly warmer Santa Ynez Valley has a reputation for such grapes as Pinot Noir, Chardonnay and Riesling as well as Sauvignon Blanc and Merlot, which is quite often justified.

SANTA CRUZ MOUNTAINS (California) Just south of San Francisco, this is a wine-making rather than wine-growing region since most of the two dozen wineries use grapes grown outside the region, although some of the older, historic vineyards are being replanted. Some, like *David Bruce, Bonny Doon, Congress Springs, Mount Eden, Ridge* and *Santa Cruz Mountain Vineyards* are of the highest order.

SONOMA COUNTY (California) This area has for far too long been lost in the shade of the Napa Valley. On the west coast, people are beginning to realize that Sonoma's Chardonnay need not take a back seat to anyone. The Sonoma Valley, running down to the Bay, is the great historic subregion, but many of the county's exceptional vineyards are in the most northerly Russian River drainage area, in particular, Alexander Valley, Chalk Hill, Dry Creek, Knight's Valley, and the Russian River Valley itself (with its subregion Green Valley). In general, the Cabernet Sauvignon and Chardonnay are the best wines, usually a little fruitier and softer than their Napa equivalents.

TEXAS Wine is booming in Texas and the quality isn't at all bad — rather big and beefy as you would expect from the Lone Star State. Chardonnay and Cabernet look good and some 'Emerald Riesling' is worth trying and their blush wines are excellent. Fall Creek do a Riesling/Cabernet blend! Recent economic downturn means Texan wine has been offering good value here. The best wineries are *Llano Estacado, Fall Creek, Pheasant Ridge* and *Sanchez Creek*.

VIRGINIA Some fairly decent wines are now being made by *Piedmont* and *Meredyth* vineyards near Middleburg.

WASHINGTON STATE A table grape state until a decade or so ago, Washington wines are now world class, with incredibly fruity and intense Cabernets and Merlots as well as excellent Chardonnay and Riesling. However, Washington vintages may vary considerably because of the effects of spring frosts. Especially good: *Chateau Ste Michelle, Columbia Winery, Covey Run and Hogue Cellars*.

WINERY PROFILES

ACACIA ★★★(★) (Carneros, Napa) Since its first crush in '79, Acacia has confirmed Carneros as California's closest equivalent to Burgundy with its attractive, often underplayed Chardonnays, and enviably stylish raspberry-filled Pinot Noirs. Go for vineyard wines: Marino Chardonnay (only planted in 1980 so its best wines are yet to come), Madonna and St Clair Pinot, and Winery Lake for both.

BERINGER ★★★★ (Napa) Good all-round performers but increasingly showing top form on Reserve bottlings. Private Reserve Cabernet Sauvignon is generally rich and spicy; from Knight's Valley lighter, softer, for early drinking. Chardonnay is oaky, late-harvest Riesling attractive, and there is a basketful of other eggs to choose from, including Fumé Blanc, Gewürztraminer and botrytized Semillon.

BONNY DOON ★★★ (Santa Cruz) Wild man of wine Randall Grahm is the leading California spokesman for the 'meridional wines' of the Rhône, northern Spain and northern Italy. But he's not just wild; his wines have real class with supple, pleasing fruit in blends like Le Cigare Volant and Clos du Gilroy.

BUENA VISTA ★★★ (Sonoma) One of California's oldest wineries, founded in 1857 just outside Sonoma, is the site of Agoston Haraszthy's pioneering wine-making. It buckled under the combined weight of phylloxera and the 1906 'quake (wine is still buried in the hand-dug caves); was re-established in 1943; and has been German-owned since 1979, with a new winery and 1100 acres of vineyard in Carneros. The accent is on fruit, the style light and approachable. Fumé Blanc is intensely fruity, Cabernet Sauvignon very easy to drink. The quality/price ratio is very good.

CALERA ★★★★ (San Benito) Pinot Noir in non-Burgundian style — more opulent, extrovert, louder. Selleck Vineyard is the most forward, Reed slower to develop, and Jensen the most accomplished.

CHALONE ★★★★(★) (Monterey) Exemplary, quality-conscious winery up in the dry limestone hills overlooking the Salinas Valley. Pinot Noir is the pinnacle, often compared favourably with Burgundy: 1984, '80 and '78 stand out. Barrel-fermented Chardonnays are big, buttery and powerful, and Pinot Blanc looks like it has a future.

CHATEAU ST JEAN ★★★(★) (Sonoma) Good Cabernet Sauvignon is made at this Suntory-owned property, but whites dominate in both quality and quantity. Late-harvest Riesling, rich and luscious, is the apogee. Gewürztraminer is the perihelion (!!: Ed). The new sparkling wine venture is showing great promise, but Fumé Blancs are distinctive, and single-vineyard Chardonnays can be as fat as a Sumo wrestler.

CHATEAU STE MICHELLE ★★★★ (Washington) This pioneering winery has been in top form with the last few vintages of Cabernet Sauvignon and Merlot. Also a winner for Chardonnay and Riesling. Intensely fruity wines.

CLOS DU BOIS ★★★ (Sonoma) Winery extracting the last ounce of character from vineyards only a couple of miles apart in Dry Creek and Alexander Valley. Dry Creek (DC) is the cooler of the two, producing racier, more austere wines; Alexander Valley (AV) makes them fruitier, more forward. Most effort goes into Chardonnay, and it shows; Calcaire Chardonnay (AV) is creamy textured, big and classy; the Flintwood (DC) is toasty, peppery, lean and stylish; the '87s are very good. Sauvignon Blanc shows similar contrasts; Cabernet Sauvignon is soft, herby, pastelly, delicious. Marlstone is an easy-drinking claret-style blend.

CUVAISON ★★★(★) (Napa) Good, forward-looking winery making more interesting reds than whites. Can make exceptional Merlot and good Cabernet and Zinfandel. Reserve Chardonnay far superior to normal release.

DEHLINGER ★★★★ (Sonoma) Makes some of the best Pinot Noir in California in the cool, lower Russian River Valley, only a few miles from the Pacific. Good Cabernet Sauvignon too.

DRY CREEK ★★★ (Sonoma) Tip-top Fumé Blanc is the speciality, delightfully herby in youth, but lasting longer than most. Chardonnay and Chenin Blanc are attractively fruity if less exciting; Cabernet is dry and slightly grassy, but extremely good all the same.

FETZER ★★★★ (Mendocino) Outstanding value winery across the board, from good Cabernets through a range of individually styled Zinfandels and a first-rate Petite Sirah, to straightforward Riesling and Gewürztraminer, and two Chardonnays: a crisp and fresh Sundial, and a richly toasty Barrel Select. New range of Reserve wines excellent. An outperformer at every level.

GALLO ★★ (Central Valley) The biggest winery in the world and still growing — it turns out a quarter of a million *cases* of consistent, cheap wine every working day. Attempts at top quality are lacking.

HEITZ ★★★★ (Napa) In the early days Martha's Vineyard was a wine right for its era, the epitome of excellence among Napa Cabernets, at a time when California was becoming a force that could compete with the best from Bordeaux. Its dark, minty, spicy, cedary, cigar-boxy style, and ability to age, the perfect marriage of fruit and oak, provided a focal point, an ideal to which all other Napa makers aspired. Nowadays aspirations in California are changing; ever-flexible, the maker of the late '80s is aiming for more 'complexity' in the form of Merlot, or Cabernet Franc or some such. Martha's hasn't yet seen this.

IRON HORSE ★★★(★) (Sonoma) Half the production is sparkling, and extremely good it is too; lip-smacking, zippily-crisp clean fruit flavours set the tone for all the wines, including Sauvignon Blanc and Chardonnay. The Cabernet Sauvignon is lean and promises long life. A new blend of red wine called Cabernets (sic — it's both Franc and Sauvignon) is stunning.

JORDAN ★★★★ (Sonoma) In an industry where imitating the French has long been considered normal, Jordan takes the biscuit. A flagrantly Bordeaux-style Cabernet Sauvignon and a Meursault-like Chardonnay are the aims. The actual results are not really very French, but extremely lush and delicious. Very consistent from year to year, in quality *and* high price.

LOUIS MARTINI ★★★★ (Napa) Old guard Napa winery has always been a well-kept secret for lovers of great California Cabernet. Blended from different regions, the wine is drinkable young and ages beautifully. It's a bargain to boot! New vineyard-selection wines promise even more excitement in the future.

MAYACAMAS ★★★★(★) (Napa) A brace of the region's best wines, Cabernet and Chardonnay are distinctively and concentratedly fruity, the ultimate in tortoise wines; they dawdle along but eventually reach the winning post in front of many a flash hare.

ROBERT MONDAVI ★★★★(★) (Napa) Robert Mondavi has been in the game for 24 years with his own winery, yet tireless innovation continues at every turn; impressive, sometimes outstanding quality right through the range. His barrel-fermented Fumé Blanc has become a standard. Lovers of fruit should drink it young. Regular Chardonnays are oaked just enough to balance the fruit, but the Reserves are far finer, and the same applies to straight and Reserve Cabernets (with long-term success in years such as '71, '75, '78). He is winning the Pinot Noir battle; and his Reserves are some of California's best Pinots. He turns out very respectable house red and white, plus a lovely Moscato d'Oro, like Asti without the fizz. All that and some excellent botrytised Sauvignon too. On a different note, he began, with Opus One, the vogue for high-priced Franco-Californian joint ventures in the Bordeaux style.

NEWTON ★★★★ (Napa) A young winery making elegant Chardonnays, primarily from Carneros fruit. However, their great strength is in reds, especially Cabernet and Merlot grown on steep slopes above St Helena, which are impeccable examples of restrained, long-lasting, positively Bordeaux styles.

PHELPS ★★★(★) (Napa) Distinctive redwood winery making successful Johannisberg Riesling in two styles, an attractive, off-dry Early Harvest, and superb Late Harvest combining botrytis, great concentration, and a gloriously light touch in a golden Californian classic. Cabernet Sauvignon is the second biggest success, in particular, the intense, concentrated Backus or Eisele Vineyard wines and the Bordeaux-style blend Insignia. Syrah is very Rhône-like in good years.

RIDGE ★★★★(★) (Santa Clara) At best, sensational intense, long-lived classic reds using grapes trucked-in from Napa, Sonoma, Santa Cruz, San Luis Obispo. Copybook Zinfandels come from Geyserville and Lytton Springs, from Paso Robles and (along with Petite Sirah) York Creek; 1986 is a crack recent vintage. But Cabernets thrill most: Montebello vineyard next door is rich, dark, concentrated, Rip van Winkle stuff. In fact the best mature Cabernet I've had all year, from anywhere (France included) is the peerless Montebello 1972. 1972? Yes, even in duff years like 1972, they have a touch of magic down there.

SCHRAMSBERG ★★★★(★) (Napa) The best sparkling wine in California. The vintage-dated wines age beautifully. Non-vintage Blanc de Blancs have lovely fruit and deep flavour.

SONOMA-CUTRER ★★★★★ (Sonoma) William Bonetti's varietal obsession, which began in the '60s when he made Chardonnays for Krug, embraces three Russian River vineyards, all distinct and showing tremendous quality. Russian River Ranches is the most forwardly fruity and approachable but the least thrilling. 1987 is back on form after a dull patch. Cutrer is from the lowest yielding vines, and is stunningly rich and full, mainstream Californian; Les Pierres in Sonoma Valley is severely classical; made to last.

STAG'S LEAP WINE CELLARS ★★★★(★) (Napa) Cabernet, the undisputed star, shot straight into orbit in the mid-'70s and has withstood comparison with the best anywhere ever since. Cask 23, once a world-beater, has hit a rocky patch. (Many feel the 1985 is overpriced at $75.) Straight Stag's Leap Vineyard is only marginally less wonderful. Now making remarkably good Chardonnay as well as an extremely attractive off-dry Riesling.

TREFETHEN ★★★(★) (Napa) In a decade and a half the Trefethen family have secured a place in the First Division with Cabernet and Chardonnay. Cabernet Sauvignon from the valley floor is attractively fleshy, from the hillside is more structured; blended together, who needs Merlot? The ripest Chardonnay gets three months in French oak, the rest goes in stainless steel, and the assemblage is as fresh as a pippin when young but, in a good vintage, actually needs a few years to show its class. Trefethen Eshcol red and white are outstandingly good wines at keen value-for-money prices.

AUSTRALIA

E veryone else blames the greenhouse effect, so why shouldn't I? For the weather conditions during the 1989 vintage in Australia were bizarre at best, abysmal at worst. As always, a few good – indeed very good – wines were made, and the overall quantity (an all-time high of 563,000 tonnes producing 495 million litres) meant more wine around for everyone.

One year later – May 1990 – saw the conclusion of one of the most perfect (and again, largest) vintages imaginable in almost all parts of Australia: only the Hunter Valley (severely) and the Lower Great Southern region of Western Australia (to a lesser degree) were affected by rain. Elsewhere very big crops of grapes reached high sugar levels in perfect dry and warm weather, free from disease or any other problems.

Yet just as there is plenty of wine, Australians themselves seem to be drinking less, exports are weakening and there is no question the industry is in the grip of a wild boom-bust, roller coaster ride. Grape prices reached ridiculous heights in 1988 and 1989; they fell sharply in 1990 and it is anyone's guess where they will end in 1991.

In this unstable situation, it has become fashionable to predict the end of Chardonnay. Over the past few years production of this variety has doubled, and is set to double again. By the time you read these words, the unthinkable will have happened: 100 per cent vintage Chardonnay will be available in two-litre and four-litre boxes at the equivalent of two to three dollars a bottle.

The mere fact that Chardonnay has fallen from a ridiculous price pedestal should not obscure the fact that in Australia – as in so many parts of the world – it produces wines of tremendous flavour, complexity and diversity of style – and of quality. Australian Chardonnay can be restrained and elegant or outrageously seductive, with soft, mouthfilling peaches and cream fruit and a warm (alcohol-derived) finish. Australian makers have not gone down the American track of 'food wines', wines which are deliberately toned down (with the exception of ferociously tannic Napa Valley Cabernets) so as not to compete for attention at the meal table.

The world is likely to have increasing opportunities to give its verdict on which country has got it right: as a result of the mega-merger in early 1990 of Penfolds and Lindemans, a huge group has been formed with the ability – and the will – to tackle the important markets of the world. Curiously, it is Penfolds which continues to antagonize the French by using controlled names such as Beaujolais and Champagne for their wines, and the outcome of legal cases in Australia and New Zealand will be watched with interest. Quite why Penfolds apparently wishes to create barriers against entry into the post-1992 EC is not easy to fathom, particularly in a climate which is fostering greater discipline (and truth) in all aspects of wine labelling.

Thomas Hardy, owners of Chateau Reynella and Houghton among other labels, have gone down an altogether different track, purchasing two distribution companies in the United Kingdom, a vineyard and winery in the French Midi, and – most spectacularly – the Tuscan producers Ricasoli in Italy. This will give the company a substantial European presence if and when the barriers go up to outsiders in a few years' time.

It may also give Thomas Hardy the means to compete with Penfolds: certainly the other large companies in Australia are all under pressure, and further mergers are quite certain to follow. This will lead to even greater polarization between the very big and the very small: the top ten company groups will end up producing 90 per cent of all Australian wine, the next 600 companies the remaining ten per cent.

As a result competition at all levels is intense. No longer is the new small winery given an armchair ride just because it is new, any more than the older small winery can afford to rest on its laurels. Poor wines are still made, but not many; most of the small producers are aware of the necessity of blending technical perfection with individuality, packaging the wine with flair and marketing it with energy. Fortunately the English trade is astute and well-informed, and few of the overpriced wines which one can find in Australia make their way to the UK. **JAMES HALLIDAY**

WHITE GRAPES & FLAVOURS

CHARDONNAY Several leading winemakers admit they haven't yet mastered the variety – but that merely whets the taste-buds because already some of the wines are world-class. Oak barrel ageing – and, increasingly, fermentation in the barrel – is universally practised in any but the cheapest Chardonnay.

Often the wine is a shockingly bright gold-yellow colour, and the fruit generally rich but not too lush; a suggestion of ripe apples, maybe melons, figs or even pineapples, but with a savoury toastiness from the charred wooden barrels. The one major criticism is that acidity levels need to be adjusted upwards in some of the very warm regions and this is not always done subtly enough, leaving a slight lemon-peel citric flavour. The wines mature quickly – even top examples can be at their peak after only two years – but they don't fade too fast. Leading producers: *Basedow* (SA), *Blewitt Springs, Coldstream Hills* (Yarra), *Dalwhinnie* (Victoria), *Evans Family* (Hunter Valley), *Richard Hamilton* (McLaren Vale), *Lake's Folly* (Hunter Valley), *Leeuwin Estate* (Margaret River), *Lillydale* (Yarra), *Mountadam* (SA) *Moss Wood* (Margaret River), *Orlando RF, Peterson* (Hunter Valley), *Rosemount Show Reserve* and *Roxburgh* (Hunter Valley), *Rouge Homme* (SA), *St Hilary* (Barossa), *St Huberts* (Yarra), *St Leonards* (NE Victoria), *Simon Whitlam* (Hunter Valley), *Wolf Blass* (SA), *Yalumba* (Coonawarra), and many, many others.

GEWÜRZTRAMINER Known as Traminer, this is quite widely planted, mostly in South Australia and New South Wales. Blowsy and spicy, it is frequently mixed with Riesling to produce a good, tasty, commercial blend. In cool parts of Victoria, it can make sublimely scented, delicate wine. *Delatite* and *Lillydale* are two excellent producers, but the best yet is from *Brown Bros'* new high altitude vineyard at Whitlands. In South Australia *Orlando* do well with the variety in the Eden Valley.

MARSANNE In Central Victoria, both *Chateau Tahbilk* and *Mitchelton* have made big, broad, ripe wines from this grape.

MUSCAT There are two types of Australian Muscat: first, the 'bladder pack' Fruity Gordo, which translated into English comes out as 'bag-in-box' Muscat of Alexandria – fruity, sweetish, swigging wine, from the heavy-cropping lowish-quality grape of the same name in the irrigated vineyards along the Murray River; second, Liqueur Muscat, made from the Brown Muscat, a strain of the top quality Muscat à Petits Grains, grown in North-East Victoria. It is a sensation: dark, treacly even, with a perfume of strawberry and orange peel and honeyed raisins. Best producers: *All Saints, Bailey's, Bullers, Campbells, Chambers, Morris* and *Stanton & Killeen.*

RIESLING The true German Riesling is always called Rhine Riesling in Australia, where it ranks as the most widely planted noble white grape. Particularly dominant in the Barossa Valley of South Australia – largely because this was settled by Germans – where it makes a very different style of wine, usually off-dry, with a good appley fruit and a decent lick of lemony acidity.

Australia also produces some of the world's greatest dry Riesling – a steely, slaty wine, full, but flecked with limey acidity, which after a few years develops strong, petrolly aromas. This comes from the hills above Adelaide and the Barossa – at Springton, Eden Valley, Clare (especially good) and Pewsey Vale. The Coonawarra, Western Australia and cool-climate areas of Victoria make equally exciting dry Riesling. There are also some sweet, botrytis-affected Rieslings, rich but fiercely concentrated, from the Barossa and Adelaide Hills. Top producers: *Leo Buring, Orlando, Yalumba/Hill-Smith* (Barossa), *Leconfield, Wynns* (Coonawarra), *Petaluma* (with Clare fruit), *Jim Barry, Enterprise, Mitchell, Pike* (Clare), *Brown Bros (Whitlands), Delatite, Diamond Valley, Lillydale* (Victoria).

SAUVIGNON BLANC Sauvignon Blanc has caught on in a big way – mostly in South Australia, with one or two bright spots in Victoria. It overripens quickly, though, becoming oily, flat and fruitless. Nonetheless, there is some good stuff from *Jim Barry* (Clare), *Hardy's Signature Collection, Lindeman* (Padthaway), *Hill-Smith* (Adelaide Hills), *Middlebrook, Primo Estate* and *Wirra Wirra* (McLaren Vale), all in South Australia; *Taltarni* and *Tisdall* in Victoria and *Cullens* in Western Australia. Sometimes Sauvignon Blanc wine is called Fumé Blanc, as in California.

SEMILLON At its finest in Australia. An excellent blender – fattening up the rather lean flavours of Sauvignon, and broadening a less than top-line Chardonnay. By itself, the greatest examples are from the Hunter Valley and Western Australia, where it starts slowly, building up gradually into a magnificent strong white full of mineral, petrol, toasted nut, herb and honey flavours. South Australia is making some increasingly good Semillon, in a less majestic, more modern style – soft, fat fruit fleshed out by oak. Top producers: *Lindeman, McWilliams, Peterson, Rothbury, Sutherland, Tyrrell* (NSW), *Tim Adams, Basedow, Hamilton, Hardy's, Hill-Smith, Mount Horrocks, Penfolds, Yalumba* (SA), *Brown Bros* (Victoria), *Cape Mentelle, Chateau Xanadu, Moss Wood, Sandstone* (WA). It also makes a sweet, noble-rot-affected wine: *De Bortoli, Rothbury, Rosemount* (NSW), *Basedow* (SA).

RED GRAPES & FLAVOURS

CABERNET SAUVIGNON A top quality variety in Australia, but can be grown superbly well even at the most basic level in the irrigated riverlands where high yields produce a very attractive, gently blackcurranty wine. Blackcurrant is the key to Australian Cabernet, and it is at its most splendid in Western Australia, South Australia's Southern Vales and cooler regions of Victoria, and at its most delicately balanced in South Australia's Coonawarra. Top producers: *Bailey's, Brown Bros Koombahla, Chateau Le Amon, Chateau Tahbilk, Coldstream Hills, Crittenden's Dromana, Delatite, Mount Langi-Ghiran, Seppelt's Drumborg, Seville Estate, St Huberts, Tisdall Mount Helen,* *Yarra Yering* (Victoria), *Cape Mentelle, Leeuwin Estate, Moss Wood, Vasse Felix* (WA), *Bowen, Chateau Reynella, Elderton, Jeffrey Grosset, Katnook, Leconfield, Lindeman's St George, Geoff Merrill, Orlando, Penfolds, Petaluma, Pike, Pirramimma, Rosemount, Shottesbrooke, Wirra Wirra Estate, Wolf Blass, Wynns Coonawarra* (SA), *Brokenwood, Lake's Folly, Peterson, Saxonvale* (NSW) *Moorilla Estate, Pipers Brook* (Tasmania), *Robinson Family* (Queensland).

PINOT NOIR As in the rest of the world, a thoroughly troublesome variety. However, there are signs that a distinctly Australian flavour is starting to emerge which is quite different from the overworked Burgundian model. At its best, it is remarkably perfumed, almost with a Turkish Delight sweetness, and has big, soft, rather glyceriny flavours of plum and cherry, mint, and even honey. We may not see *many* great Australian Pinot Noirs, but those that we do see will be among the finest in the world. Top producers: *Moss Wood* (WA), *Leeuwin* (WA), *Coldstream Hills, Delatite, Mount Mary, St Huberts, Yarra Burn, Yarra Yering* (Victoria), *Rothbury, Tyrrells* (NSW), *Pipers Brook* (TAS).

SHIRAZ This marvellous grape (the Syrah of France) can make sensational wine in Australia, and yet is generally used as a bulk-producing makeweight. Yet even at its most basic level, it will produce juicy, chunky reds in enormous quantities. When it is not overcropped – and is vinified carefully – the results can be supreme. Often blended with Cabernet Sauvignon to provide a richness of texture the slightly angular Cabernet might otherwise lack. *Penfold's* great *Grange Hermitage* shows just how successful this blend can be. Other good examples are *Drayton* and *Lindeman's Coonawarra Limestone Ridge*. By itself, Shiraz has a brilliant array of flavours from impressively deep, leathery wines, full of dark chocolate, liquorice and prunes intensity to a rich, spicy, plums and coconut, blackcurrant, raspberries and cream lusciousness that is most unusual in a dry red wine – and absolutely delicious! Top producers: *Bailey's, Best's, Cathcart Ridge, Chateau Le Amon, Chateau Tahbilk, Dalwhinnie, Heathcote, Montara, Mount Langi-Ghiran, Redbank Mountain Creek, St Leonards Wahgunyah, Watervale, Wynns Ovens Valley, Yarra Yering* (Victoria), *Cape Mentelle, Evans & Tate Gnangara, Plantagenet* (WA), *Tim Adams, Basedow, Bowen, Coriole, Lindeman, Penfolds, Rosemount, Orlando* (SA), *Drayton, Montrose, Rothbury, Tyrrell* (NSW).

WINES & WINE REGIONS

ADELAIDE HILLS (South Australia) An ill-defined, but top quality, high altitude wine zone east of Adelaide. First-class vineyards specializing in cool-climate whites include *Orlando's Steingarten, Mountadam* and *Yalumba's Heggies* and *Pewsey Vale*. Also *Petaluma*, a top-rate winery, whose *'Croser'* sparkling wine is one of Australia's best.

BAROSSA VALLEY (South Australia) This large zone north of Adelaide is one of Australia'a best-known wine areas. Various of the greatest Australian wine companies are established there – *Basedow, Leo Buring, Hill-Smith, Orlando, Penfolds, Seppelt, Tollana, Wolf Blass* and *Yalumba*. They process a gigantic amount of fruit, but 75 per cent of it comes from outside the Barossa Valley. (In Australia trucking grapes, juice or wine hundreds of miles for blending purposes is quite usual and not at all frowned on – so long as you tell people you're doing it.)

BENDIGO (Victoria) This great 19th-century wine region, totally destroyed by phylloxera, has been re-planted since 1969 and now produces much excellent Cabernet Sauvignon, good Shiraz and even some Pinot Noir. *Balgownie* is the leading property, with *Chateau Le Amon, Craiglee, Harcourt Valley, Heathcote, Mount Ida, Passing Clouds* and *Yellowglen* also important.

CENTRAL VICTORIA Goulburn Valley is the most important vineyard area, with *Chateau Tahbilk* producing big old-style Shiraz and Cabernet, and some interesting white Marsanne, *Tisdall* making outstandingly fruity Cabernet Sauvignon, Chardonnay and Sauvignon Blanc, and *Mitchelton* also good. The *Delatite* vineyards at Mansfield produce delicately delicious whites and remarkably intense reds in cool-climate conditions.

CLARE VALLEY (South Australia) A warm area well to the north of Adelaide, first planted to red grapes, but now making more fine wine from whites, in particular a deftly fragrant style of Rhine Riesling and a soft but attractively grassy style of

Sauvignon; Chardonnay also exhibits a gentle, attractive style. Best exponents are *Jim Barry, Enterprise, Horrocks, Mitchells* and *Pike* but many Barossa wineries use Clare fruit, and *Petaluma* and *Lindeman* have well-established vineyards there. *Taylor's Chateau Clare*, *Tim Adams* and *Jeffrey Grosset* produce the best reds.

COONAWARRA (South Australia) Perhaps the most famous of all Australia's fine wine regions, excelling at Bordeaux-style Cabernet Sauvignon. It is one of the most carefully defined wine zones. Incredibly fertile and already planted to the hilt, this streak of red soil is about 14.5km long and between 1.5km and 200 metres wide. Cabernet Sauvignon is the dominant variety, characterized by a soft, blackcurrany fruit turning cedary with age. Shiraz is good, as are Merlot and Malbec. Whites are less important, but there are some beautifully stylish Rhine Rieslings and Chardonnays. Best producers: *Bowen Estate, Brand's Laira, Hardy/Chateau Reynella, Haselgrove, Hollick, Katnook, Krondorf, Leconfield, Limestone Ridge, Lindeman (St George), Orlando, Petaluma, Penfolds, Rosemount, Seppelt* and *Wynns*.

GEELONG (Victoria) The best wines are dark, intensely flavoured Cabernets from vineyards like *Idyll* and *Bannockburn*, Pinot Noir from *Prince Albert*, and interesting whites from *Idyll*.

GLENROWAN (Victoria) Famous for two things: first the *Ovens Valley Shiraz* which *Wynns* (of South Australia) make into one of Australia's best commercial reds, and second, the great wines produced by *Bailey's* – torrid, palate-blasting reds from Cabernet Sauvignon and Shiraz (here called Hermitage) and, more importantly, Liqueur Muscats. These are intensely sweet, seeming to distil the very essence of the overripe brown Muscat grape, as well as adding an exotic tangle of orange and honey of blackcurrants, blackberries and strawberries. At Milawa, *Brown Brothers* make a wide range of good table wines and fortifieds, but their best wines are from the Koombahla vineyard in King Valley, and the high altitude Whitlands site.

GREAT WESTERN (Victoria) Historic area round Ararat, best known as the producer of base wine for Australia's celebrated sparkler – *Seppelt's Great Western* – but more exciting for the quality of its reds. Great Western Shiraz is outstanding, succulently soft and plummy, full of chocolate, coconut and cream flavours as at *Cathcart Ridge*, or dry, liquoricy and with an impressive pepperiness as at *Mount Langi-Ghiran*. *Best's*, *Montara* and *Seppelt* are other top producers. There is also good Cabernet Sauvignon from *Mount Langi-Ghiran* and 'Vintage Port' from *Montara*.

HUNTER VALLEY (New South Wales) Leading NSW wine region, making great wines. Hunter reds are traditionally based on Shiraz (Hermitage) and whites on Semillon. Both can age better than almost any other Australian wines. The Shiraz used to be notorious for a 'sweaty saddle' sulphurous flavour when young which

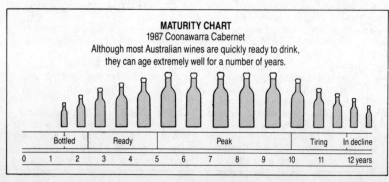

MATURITY CHART
1987 Coonawarra Cabernet
Although most Australian wines are quickly ready to drink, they can age extremely well for a number of years.

Bottled	Ready	Peak	Tiring	In decline

| 0 | 1 | 2 | 3 | 4 | 5 | 6 | 7 | 8 | 9 | 10 | 11 | 12 years |

disappeared with time to give a gentle, buttery, smoky flavour. The Semillon often ages even better, starting out rather tart and lifeless but over 10 to 15 years developing a luscious, honeyed nuttiness, tempered by a vaguely old-Riesling, oily, herby character. Nowadays riper Semillon grapes are giving a more immediately attractive style. Cabernet and Chardonnay are both successful here. Pinot Noir, especially from *Rothbury* and *Tyrrell* can be very fine, and there's even some good Traminer and sweet, botrytis-affected Semillon.

The valley is in two halves. Upper Hunter is a recent, irrigated development, dominated by *Rosemount*, but *Arrowfield* can also be good. The region is basically a white wine producer, but Cabernet Sauvignon has fared much better than Shiraz. Lower Hunter is the traditional quality area. Best producers: *Allandale, Brokenwood, Evans Family, Hungerford Hill, Lake's Folly, Lindeman, McWilliams, Peterson, Rothbury Estate, Saxonvale, Sutherland, Tyrrell, Simon Whitlam.*

LOWER GREAT SOUTHERN (Western Australia) A vast, rambling area dotted with vineyards of considerable promise, especially in the zone round Mount Barker. *Alkoomi, Chateau Barker, Forest Hill, Plantagenet* and *Redmond* are good. The whites are fragrant and appetizing, but the reds are more exciting, with particularly spicy, tobaccoey Cabernet Sauvignons. An increasing number of out-of-state wineries are buying these grapes and trucking them cast to be made into wine.

MARGARET RIVER (Western Australia) There has been an astonishing number of superb wines from this area. Foremost among them are *Cape Mentelle, Cullens, Leeuwin Estate, Moss Wood, Sandalford, Redgate* and *Vasse Felix*. At their best, the Margaret River Cabernets exhibit magnificent fruit with a streak of grassy acidity and are as good as top-line Classed Growths in Bordeaux. Pinot Noir also does well sometimes. Chardonnay is increasingly barrel-fermented and shows enormously rich flavours, balanced by acidity and toasty oak. Semillon is frequently now made in an apple-fresh, but weighty style – though old-style Semillons age superbly. There is also some port-style wine and *Happ's* have planted traditional Portuguese varieties which are interesting.

MCLAREN VALE (South Australia) Important area just south of Adelaide. Originally known for thick, heavy red styles, the region has recently begun to make beautifully balanced reds and whites of positively cool-climate style. Great Cabernet, Shiraz and Chardonnay have already been produced, and much fine Sauvignon and Semillon, too, from recent vintages. Good producers: *Blewitt Springs, Coriole, Hardy's, Richard Hamilton, Geoff Merrill, Middlebrook, Pirramimma, Reynella, Shottesbrooke, Wirra Wirra, Woodstock.*

MUDGEE (New South Wales) Capable of producing good table wines owing to a very late spring and cold nights. Though established as a red wine area, based on

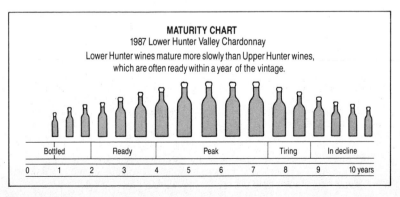

MATURITY CHART
1987 Lower Hunter Valley Chardonnay
Lower Hunter wines mature more slowly than Upper Hunter wines, which are often ready within a year of the vintage.

| Bottled | Ready | Peak | Tiring | In decline |

| 0 | 1 | 2 | 3 | 4 | 5 | 6 | 7 | 8 | 9 | 10 years |

Shiraz (*Montrose* does an outstanding example) the best reds have been deep, tarry, plummy Cabernets. However, the Chardonnay is the most successful variety, usually made in a rich, soft style, full of fruit-salad flavours. Good producers: *Craigmoor, Huntington, Miramar, Montrose.*

MURRUMBIDGEE IRRIGATION AREA (New South Wales) Known as the MIA, this vast irrigated area centred round Griffith provides between 15 and 20 per cent of the total Australian crop. Most of this is bulk wine blended up by various companies in various states, but the dominant *McWilliams* make some attractive wines, as do *de Bortoli*, including an ultra-sweet Sauternes-style Semillon.

PADTHAWAY (South Australia) An increasingly important producer of high quality wines, in particular white, and notably Rhine Riesling, Chardonnay and Sauvignon Blanc. Established only in the 1960s when pressure on land in Coonawarra forced major wineries to look elsewhere. Padthaway/Keppoch was chosen because it also had some of the 'terra rosa' soil which makes Coonawarra so special. Much base material for sparkling wine is from this region, and there is some exceedingly good sweet Riesling. Best producers: *Hardy's, Lindeman, Seppelt*; other major producers such as *Orlando* also use the grapes.

'PORT' Shiraz and other Rhône-type grapes are often used to make exceptionally high-quality 'port'. The 'Vintage ports' are wonderful. Top producers: *Montara, Penfolds, Seppelt, Stanton & Killeen, Yalumba.*

PYRENEES (Victoria) Area north-west of Melbourne. It has produced many very dry reds from Shiraz and Cabernet and whites, primarily from Sauvignon. Top producers are *Redbank, Taltarni* and *Warrenmang*, and for sparkling wine, *Chateau Remy* and *Taltarni.*

RIVERLAND (South Australia) The grape basket of Australia – a vast irrigation project on the river Murray providing 38

per cent of the national crop. Dominated by the highly efficient co-ops of *Berri* and *Renmano* as well as the *Angoves* company, it produces enormous quantities of bag-in-box reds and whites of a consistently good quality. But also fresh, fruity Rhine Riesling, Chardonnay, Sauvignon, Colombard, Chenin, Cabernet Sauvignon and Shiraz.

RUTHERGLEN (Victoria) The centre of the great fortified wine tradition. The table wines are generally dull, except for some consistently fine wines from *St Leonards*. The fortified wines, either as *solera*-method 'sherries', as 'Vintage ports', or as intense, brown sugar-sweet Tokays, are all memorable. The true heights are achieved by the Liqueur Muscats, unbearably rich but irresistible with it. Good producers: *Bullers, Campbells, Chambers, Morris, Rosewood, Stanton & Killeen.*

SPARKLING WINES These have changed out of all recognition in the last three years. Along with Pinot Noir, quality sparkling wine seems to be a Holy Grail here as elsewhere. Leading the pack are *Croser, Yalumba D* and the *Ian Wilson* fizz. At the cheaper end, there are the clean and fruity *Seaview, Angas Brut* and *Orlando Charrington*; going upmarket a bit *Seppelt's Chardonnay, Yellowglen* and *Fareham Estate* are good.

SWAN VALLEY (Western Australia) One of the hottest wine regions in the world, it made its reputation on big, richly flavoured reds and whites, but even the most famous of these, *Houghton's Supreme*, is now much lighter and fresher than it used to be. Good producers: *Bassendean, Evans and Tate, Houghton, Moondah Brook, Sandalford.*

TASMANIA So far only tiny amounts of wine are made, but the quality is exciting. There are some remarkable Cabernets from *Heemskerk, Moorilla Estate* and *Pipers Brook* and the Pinot Noirs from these producers are better than most of the mainland versions.

YARRA VALLEY (Victoria) There is a distinct possibility that the Yarra Valley is about to emerge as Victoria's table wine

"Quietly Sensational"

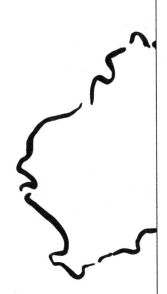

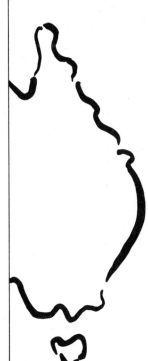

producing superstar. It is cooler than any other mainland Australian area, with a variety of soil types suitable for different grapes' needs. The area's successes are equally divided between red and white, but most excitement has been generated by the 'Bordeaux blend' of Cabernet Sauvignon, Cabernet Franc and Merlot. Pinot Noir looks exciting. Whites, too; the scented flavours of Gewürztraminer, Rhine Riesling and Chardonnay are a revelation. Good producers: *Coldstream Hills, Diamond Valley, Lillydale, Mount Mary, Seville Estate* (who also make great sweet wine), *St Huberts, Yarra Burn, Yarra Yering, Yeringberg*.

WINERY PROFILES

BAILEY'S OF GLENROWAN ★★★★(★) (Victoria) Greatest of Australia's fortified winemakers in north-east Victoria, with their 'Founder' Liqueur Muscat an unbearably delicious concentration of sweet dark Muscat flavours. Also make splendidly impenetrable Cabernet and Shiraz of top line quality. Now extending vineyard holdings, planting in rows suitable for machine-picking, increasing yield per hectare. I hope the quality can hold up.

BAROSSA VALLEY ESTATES ★★★(★) (South Australia) Recently formed group in the south of Barossa Valley owned by Berri-Renmano. Specializing in high quality cheap wine, they provide the bulk of Oddbins' basic range.

JIM BARRY ★★★★ (South Australia) Clare Valley winery concentrating on white wine and producing outstanding Rhine Riesling, Sauvignon Blanc and Chardonnay. First sightings of Cabernet are good too.

BERRI-RENMANO ★★★ (South Australia) Enormous co-op in the irrigated Murray River hinterland producing remarkably high quality wine. Most cheap own-label Aussie wines will be from here but they also do their own bottling and the Chairman's Selection Chardonnay and Cabernet are high class.

WOLF BLASS ★★★★ (South Australia) Large winery with an uncanny knack of producing exactly what the public likes. Its wines are marked by tremendous fruit and carefully judged enrichment with oak. Good Riesling and outstanding Cabernet and Chardonnay with three different styles – yellow, grey or black label.

DE BORTOLI ★★★ (New South Wales) Shot to fame with an astonishing sweet 1982 botrytis Semillon. This Murrumbidgee Irrigation Area winery has since put together a string of well-priced basics. Now setting up another operation in Yarra Valley.

BROWN BROTHERS ★★★(★) (Victoria) Large family firm producing an enormous range of wine at a high quality level. From a variety of vineyards, the best of which are the cool climate Koombahla and the even-cooler climate Whitlands, come many exciting wines, in particular the Muscats, Semillons, Chardonnays, Koombahla Cabernet Sauvignon and Whitlands Gewürztraminer and Riesling.

CAPE MENTELLE ★★★★ (Western Australia) Important Margaret River winery owned by David Hohnen – who also owns New Zealand's buzz winery Cloudy Bay. Excellent Cabernet and variations on the Semillon/Sauvignon theme as well as Shiraz – and Zinfandel, of all things.

CHATEAU TAHBILK ★★★★ (Victoria) One of Victoria's historic landmarks in the Goulburn Valley and a winery still making great red wines in an unashamedly traditional way.

COLDSTREAM HILLS ★★★★(★) (Victoria) James Halliday, Australia's foremost wine writer, decided he'd better practise what he preached. World class Pinot Noir in the offing, exciting Chardonnay.

DELATITE ★★★★(★) (Victoria) 'A magic piece of dirt, it could grow anything' is how the owners describe the Delatite vineyard north of Melbourne. I'd agree. The wines have an individuality of fruit combined with superb wine-making which puts them straight in the top class. Dry Riesling is delicious, sweet Riesling superb, while their handling of Gewürztraminer, Pinot Noir, Cabernet and Shiraz is brilliant.

HARDY ★★★(★) (South Australia) Maintains an impressive quality level across their entire range. Particularly good Padthaway Fumé Blanc and Chardonnay, and delicious McLaren Vale Cabernet. Also controls Chateau Reynella, a high quality producer of Cabernet and Chardonnay.

HENSCHKE ★★★★★ (South Australia) Old red vines, some of them 80 years old, yield deep, dark, curranty wines of top class. Whites equally stunning – Riesling, Semillon and Chardonnay.

HILL-SMITH/YALUMBA ★★★★ (South Australia) A large Barossa Valley company producing good wines under the Yalumba and Hill Smith labels, and exceptional ones under the Signature, Heggies and Pewsey Vale Vineyard labels, where dry and sweet Rieslings are some of the finest in Australia. Yalumba D is very good fizz.

LAKE'S FOLLY ★★★★ (New South Wales) Tiny Hunter Valley winery. Making highly idiosyncratic Cabernet and Chardonnay which with age turn into very exciting wines.

LEEUWIN ESTATE ★★★★ (Western Australia) Ultra-high profile estate with ultra-high prices for exciting Chardonnay and Pinot Noir, rich, leather and blackcurrant flavoured Cabernet Sauvignon and good Riesling and Sauvignon Blanc.

LINDEMAN ★★★★★ (New South Wales) Remarkable company based in Sydney but with big interests in South Australia and Victoria too. The quality of the basic varietal wines, in particular the Bin 50 Shiraz and the Bin 45 Cabernet and Chardonnay, is exceptional, while the old-style Hunter Valley wines, and the releases from Padthaway and Coonawarra, are some of Australia's finest. New, vineyard-

designated Coonawarra reds (Limestone Ridge and St George) are tiptop as well as superb Bordeaux blend – Pyrus.

MCWILLIAMS ★★(★) (New South Wales) Old fashioned giant now rapidly improving its quality. Though traditionally a Hunter company, much McWilliams wine now comes from Griffith in the MIA and blends like the Hillside Colombard/Chardonnay show what can be achieved from fairly basic fruit.

MILDARA ★★★ (South Australia) Based in the irrigated Murray River hinterland, but with large holdings in Coonawarra. Quality is erratic, though price is fair. They also own Yellowglen and Balgownie in Victoria, Krondorf in SA and Morton Estate in New Zealand.

MOSS WOOD ★★★★★ (Western Australia) Superbly original wines from Margaret River. Semillon, with and without wood-ageing, is some of the best in Australia. Pinot Noir is daring and delicious, Chardonnay less daring but just as delicious, Cabernet rich and structured.

MOUNT LANGI-GHIRAN ★★★★ (Victoria) New Great Western winery already making superbly-styled dry, intense, challenging Shiraz and deep, long-lasting Cabernet.

MOUNT MARY ★★★★ (Victoria) Finely structured Cabernet and a Pinot Noir improving with age. Tiny production, much sought after.

ORLANDO ★★★(★) (South Australia) Barossa winery with commendable ability to offer fine quality at every price level. Their boxed wine is outstanding, their RF Cabernet, Chardonnay and Riesling are usually the best in the price bracket, and their top of the line St-Helga Riesling, St-Hilary Chardonnay and St-Hugo Cabernet are amongst Australia's finest.

The price guides for this section begin on page 377.

PENFOLDS ★★★★★ (South Australia)
The greatest red winemakers in Australia, and now working well in whites too. Although based in Adelaide they have big holdings all over the state. Their basic reds and whites are clean and tasty, their varietal wines packed with flavour, and their special selection reds, culminating in the deservedly legendary Grange Hermitage, are superlative, massively structured reds of world class. If you can't afford Grange, try Bin 28, Bin 128 or Bin 707. Bin 820 is even better but they won't let us have any.

PETALUMA ★★★★ (South Australia) The baby of Brian Croser, who has taught many of Australia's top young winemakers, is slowly hitting its stride. Some of his Rieslings, sweet and dry, have been tip-top, his Chardonnays less so, and his Cabernets are improving with each vintage. Now also producing 'Croser' sparkling wine, which is absolutely delicious.

PIPERS BROOK ★★★★ (Tasmania) Top quality winery in north of Tasmania run by the highly-qualified Andrew Pirie. The objective is to produce classic French-style wine and the Cabernet Sauvignon, Pinot Noir and Chardonnay are outstanding.

ROSEMOUNT ★★★★ (New South Wales) The company which did more than any other to help Australia take the UK market by storm with its Chardonnay, Fumé Blanc and Cabernet. Fumé and Cabernet are no longer of the quality they were, though Chardonnay is on the way back and the single vineyard Roxburgh Chardonnay is impressive. Worldwide, the Chardonnays have set new standards for affordable, quality wine. We are seeing some surprising Pinot Noir, some excellent Semillon and outstanding sweet wine, as well as the gluggable Diamond Reserve range.

ROTHBURY ★★★★ (New South Wales) One of the leading Hunter companies founded by the indomitable Len Evans. Its wines went through a bad patch a few years ago, but are now back on form with classic flavours. The Chardonnay and Semillon are now some of the Hunter's best and Pinot Noir and Shiraz increasingly good.

ST HUBERTS ★★★★ (Victoria) One of the original Yarra Valley vineyards near Melbourne, now triumphantly returned to the top class. Equally brilliant with whites and reds; the Chardonnay and Cabernet Sauvignon are exceptional.

SEPPELT ★★★★ (Victoria) Leading makers of quality sparkling wine from traditional Champagne grapes, peaking with Salinger. Also good, fruity, easy-drinking styles.

TALTARNI ★★★(★) (Victoria) Central Victoria winery which makes a remarkable bone-dry, grassy-sharp Fumé Blanc and fine Cabernet and Shiraz which are tannic and tough for the best part of a decade before softening into classy, if austere reds. If that all sounds more French than Australian – well, the winemaker grew up at Château Lafite in Bordeaux.

TISDALL ★★★ (Victoria) Goulburn winery making fresh, easy-to-drink reds and whites and cool-climate, quality classics from their Mount Helen grapes.

TYRRELL ★★★(★) (New South Wales) Famous, eccentrically brilliant Hunter winery which makes a lot of its living selling 'port' and 'blackberry nip' to tourists through the front door while making some great classic wines out the back. There has never been a more excitingly different Australian Chardonnay than the Vat 47 of the early '80s, and for years Tyrrell was the only Australian who could make great Pinot Noir. Vat 1 Semillon is also excellent, as is his 'plonk' – Long Flat Red and White.

WYNNS ★★★★(★) (South Australia) Coonawarra company whose quality has remained remarkably high. Spot-on Riesling, big, oaky Chardonnay and perfect, refined Cabernet and Shiraz. Wynn's Ovens Valley Shiraz is a lot less refined, but just as good.

YARRA YERING ★★★★★ (Victoria) Wonderful Yarra Valley winery, which labels its Cabernet-based wine Dry Red No.1 and its Shiraz-based wine Dry Red No.2: exceptional, powerful yet fragrant reds. Fine Chardonnay and Pinot Noir.

NEW ZEALAND

The big news from New Zealand since last year's *Webster's* is an outbreak of the vine enemy phylloxera in the vineyards of Marlborough in the north of South Island. Marlborough is where the likes of Montana, Corbans, Hunter's and Cloudy Bay have vineyards and where a large proportion of the vines are not grafted on to resistant rootstocks.

Phylloxera doesn't affect the flavour or quality of the wines, just the quantity, because it reduces vine vigour. In New Zealand's climate, where vines are often over-leafy and even keep growing after the grapes have been picked, the growers can afford a little time to consider future strategy.

On the plus side, the recent trend of high-quality vintages in New Zealand just keeps on going. After a splendid, if short, 1988 harvest, the 1989 is being described as the best ever. There was certainly no lack of sugar in the grapes. In Canterbury one of the Riesling/Müller-Thurgau blends hit record sugar levels for the southern hemisphere; the concentration was the equivalent of a German Trockenbeerenauslese!

The quality overall from 1990 is turning out to be extremely good and quantity was high too – good news after complaints in this spot last year that there was still not enough Kiwi wine to go round. The grapes ripened so well that some of the wines may have balance problems to be solved as a result of low acidity, but some of the richest wines ever have come out of that harvest and there is tremendous colour in the reds. John Buck of Te Mata has said they should be drunk early; they are very forward but will be short-lived.

On the style front, the latest intelligence is the growing enthusiasm among winemakers for a move away from the grassy/gooseberry intensity of Sauvignon Blanc and other whites towards something approaching a 'tropical flavour'. Attractively spicy, peppery elements have been more evident in wines from the past couple of vintages, drawing favourable reaction for breadth and complexity.

Luckily, the very best stuff comes to our shores. Every year there are more superb Sauvignon Blancs and Chardonnays to jostle into the crowd. New Zealand reds are achieving top quality; sumptuous Pinot Noirs are coming out of St Helena in Canterbury and Martinborough in the Wairarapa, and fragrant Cabernet combinations from St Nesbit and Matua Valley around Auckland.

You should look out, too, for the half-bottles of Late Harvest Muscat and Riesling dessert wines. They are quite startlingly good and underline how grossly overpriced their French counterparts are. Those from Redwood Valley in Nelson and Giesen in Canterbury are worth the hunt.   GORDON BROWN

WHITE GRAPES & FLAVOURS

CHARDONNAY New Zealand's vineyards are only a dolphin's leap from the South Pole, and the cool ripening period gives the Chardonnay a light style, but with intense, high-acid flavours – a penetrating fruit bowl of apple, peach, pineapple and pear – softened out by new oak barrels into some of the most original Chardonnays the New World has yet produced. Hawke's Bay already makes classic wines and is being followed by Marlborough and Nelson in the South Island, and the small Wairarapa area just across the straits near Wellington. Gisborne produces a softer, less intense Chardonnay. Top wines include *Babich, Cloudy Bay, Collards* (especially *Tolaga* and *Rothesay*), *Cooks* (Hawke's Bay and Gisborne), *Coopers Creek, Delegat's, Hunters, Kumeu River, Matawhero, Matua Valley,* (*Judd, Yates* and *Egan Estates*), *Morton Estate, Nobilo* (*Dixon Estate* and *Te Karaka*), *de Redcliffe, Selaks, Te Mata, Vidals, Villa Maria.*

CHENIN BLANC This difficult Loire grape is at its most versatile in New Zealand, ranging from stone-dry to rich. Best with some sweetness back-blended in from unfermented grape juice; it could make fine wines in the Vouvray style, but is usually too overcropped. *Collards* is good; *Cooks* and *Matawhero* not bad.

GEWÜRZTRAMINER At its best, a world-beater. It can produce a remarkably pungent wine, reeking of fresh ground black pepper, mangoes, lychees, yet remaining dry and refreshing. Gisborne is a particularly good region and *Matawhero* can be outstanding. Good producers: *Cooper's Creek, Morton Estate, Nobilo, Pacific Wines, Villa Maria.*

MÜLLER-THURGAU The dominant grape in New Zealand. When well made, as, for instance, by *Montana* in the South Island, it has an excellent, flowering currant, green tang, or, from *Nobilo* in the North Island, the same grapiness as many Rheinhessen wines in Germany, but with fresher acidity and fruitiness. Also good: *Collards, Cooks, Delegat's, Matawhero, Matua Valley* and *Totara.*

RIESLING A lot of Rhine Riesling (as the New Zealanders call it) is made up into fairly bland blends, but there are some

outstanding wines, either in the bone-dry Alsace style, or occasionally big, rich and sweet. *Corbans Stoneleigh* is good, as are *Babich, Collards, Coopers Creek, Delegat's, Matua Valley, Millton, Seifried* and *Selaks Brigham Creek. Montana* is lean but OK while *Giesen* in the Canterbury area may produce the most classic dry Riesling yet. *Delegat's, Ngatarawa, St Helena* and *Seifried* have produced stunningly rich late-harvest examples. In fact New Zealand could well become one of the great sweet wine countries – witness the outstanding success of *Corbans Private Bin Noble Rhine Riesling.*

SAUVIGNON BLANC Half-a-dozen New Zealand Sauvignons top the world rankings already. The best, such as *Montana Marlborough Sauvignon* from the new South Island plantings, or *Selaks* from Hawke's Bay, bring a depth of nettly, almost asparagus and gooseberry fruit to a style zinging with fresh, sharp balance yet rounded off with honey and spice. Recent attempts to modify the grassy style and introduce complexity are proving successful. Also excellent: Cape Mentelle's much-vaunted *Cloudy Bay, Babich, Brookfields, Coopers Creek, Corban's Stoneleigh, Delegat's, Hunter's, Montana's Brancott Estate, Morton Estate, Selaks, Vidal, Villa Maria.*

SEMILLON Steering away from the heavy, oily Australian tradition towards something much fresher, like the grassy *Vidal* or the classic beeswax and sweet apples flavour of *Villa Maria, Montana* and *Delegat's.* It is increasingly, and successfully, blended with Sauvignon or Chardonnay as in *Babich 'Fumé Vert'* and *Semillon/Chardonnay, Delegat's Semillon/Chardonnay* and *Mission Semillon/Sauvignon.*

RED GRAPES & FLAVOURS

CABERNET SAUVIGNON The Cabernets, weedy and green in the early days, are certainly still dry, but the fruit has developed into a piercing, fresh, grassy, blackcurrant-and-nettles style about as pure as you can get. *Cooks* Hawke's Bay

Cabernet is usually grassy, soft and delicious but there are also many single estates producing outstanding wine. Each vintage shows improvements. Top wineries for Cabernet include the great *Te Mata, Antipodean, Cloudy Bay* (from 1987),

Cook's Fernhill, Goldwater, Kumeu River, Montana, Matua Valley, Neudorf, Ngatarawa, St Nesbit, Selaks, Vidal and *Villa Maria.*

MERLOT Planted primarily for blending with Cabernet (the *Te Mata* Coleraine is classic), but also made into single varietals. *San Marino*'s Kumeu River is full, peppery and plummy.

PINOTAGE A curious grape making a light, smoky, marshmallow and raspberry wine – but usually dried out.

PINOT NOIR Not generally successful so far, with the shining exception of *St Helena* in South Island and the newish *Martinborough* winery near Wellington. Also makes excellent perfumed white – *Matua Valley*'s is first-rate.

WINES & WINE REGIONS

GISBORNE (North Island) They call Gisborne 'carafe' country, because it's a positive grape basket of a region, planted with one-third of the nation's vines. Above all, it is the home of Müller-Thurgau, which can yield 20 to 25 tons per hectare on the Poverty Bay alluvial flats. In general, the wine is light but good, but there are exceptions. Matawhero is a high-quality sub area, as are Tolaga and Tikitiki further north. From these areas, Chenin and Gewürztraminer and, increasingly, award-winning Chardonnay, can be excellent. Reds on the whole are less exciting in Gisborne, although *Delegat's* have produced some good Cabernet.

HAWKE'S BAY (North Island) Potentially New Zealand's greatest wine region because it is becoming evident that, as well as fine whites, there is the possibility of great reds being made. Indeed, the deep gravel banks, allied to its being one of the country's sunniest areas, mean that there is enormous potential for Cabernet and Merlot to produce top quality claret-type reds. I believe that if *any* of the world's regions is ever going to produce the flavour equivalent of a Médoc Classed Growth it will be Hawke's Bay, but in the meantime the joyous originality of the fruit flavours is as shocking as it is delightful. Good producers: *Brookfield's, Cooks, Matua Valley, Ngatarawa, Vidal, Villa Maria* and, above all, *Te Mata.*

MARLBOROUGH (South Island) Now one of the biggest vineyard regions in the country – and still growing. The strengths – thanks to a long, slow ripening period – have always been white wines:

outstanding Rhine Riesling, Chardonnay, and especially Sauvignon. Reds are improving dramatically.

OTHER NORTH ISLAND Northland doesn't have much, excepting the *Antipodean* vineyard at Warkworth. North of Auckland, at Waimauku (with *Matua Valley* and *Collards*), Huapai (*Nobilo*) and Kumeu (*Kumeu Valley* and *Selaks*) there are excellent reds and whites. West of Auckland at Henderson the top producers include *Babich, Collards, Delegat's* who produce award-winning white wines, and *Pacific*. South of Auckland is the impressive *Villa Maria* as well as *St Nesbit* and *de Redcliffe*, and at Te Kauwhata, the *Cooks/Corbans* operation. On Waiheke Island, *Goldwater Estate* is already producing excellent wine, and Terry Dunleavy of the New Zealand Wine Institute has bought land there to plant with vines. *Morton Estate* on Bay of Plenty is already established as one of New Zealand's best.

OTHER SOUTH ISLAND Nelson to the east of Marlborough is a minor area, but has good performers in *Neudorf* which returned its first vintage in 1981 and *Seifried*, the largest Nelson winery. Canterbury is dominated by the excellent *St Helena*, though other plantings are maturing fast, and *Giesen* and *Larcomb* look set to produce exciting wines.

The price guides for this section begin on page 384.

WINERY PROFILES

BABICH ★★★ Leading Henderson winery producing the entire range of wine styles including fresh Fumé Vert made from Semillon, oaky Irongate Chardonnay and a grassy Cabernet Sauvignon made from Hawke's Bay grapes.

CLOUDY BAY ★★★★★ Highest profile of the small South Island wineries owned by Cape Mentelle of Western Australia. The excellent Sauvignon, fattened out with a little Semillon, sells out within days of release. Chardonnay and, eventually, Cabernet may be even better.

CORBANS ★★★(★) Includes Cooks and McWilliams. Some excellent special bottlings under the Stoneleigh label, as well as straightforward varietals. Cooks Fernhill is a rich Cabernet Sauvignon, Longridge very attractive Chardonnay.

DELEGAT'S ★★★★ A white wine specialist near Auckland, using primarily Hawke's Bay and Gisborne fruit. Excellent Sauvignon, Chardonnay and sweet wine; highly promising Cabernet Sauvignon.

HUNTER'S ★★★(★) Up-and-coming South Island winery making intensely flavoured Sauvignon, Fumé Blanc and Chardonnay with a very particular style of their own.

KUMEU RIVER ★★★★ Imaginative, progressive winery just north of Auckland experimenting with considerable success with different grape growing, vinification and maturation methods. Merlot/Cabernet, Sauvignon and Chardonnay increasingly exciting.

MARTINBOROUGH ★★★★ New and exciting operation in the far south of the North Island making lovely Riesling, Sauvignon and Müller Thurgau and outstanding Pinot Noir.

MATUA VALLEY ★★★★(★) High quality winery producing superb single-estate Chardonnays and exciting Cabernet reds. However it also produces delicious Riesling, lovely Gewürztraminer and some

of the country's best Müller-Thurgau, as well as making sensible use of the problematic Pinot Noir by turning it into a very decent white.

MONTANA ★★★(★) Marlborough Sauvignon Blanc from Montana is regularly one of New Zealand's best. Latest releases of Cabernet are also very much on the up. Newest arrival in the UK is Lindauer fizz, made with the help of Champagne house Deutz.

MORTON ESTATE ★★★★ Exceptional winery east of Auckland, so far concentrating on whites with award-winning Sauvignon, Chardonnay and Gewürztraminer. Winemaker John Hancock is planning his assault on red wine territory and in the meantime makes top quality Champagne-method fizz.

NGATARAWA ★★★ Newish Hawke's Bay winery likely to make great red wine and sweet wines in the near future, as well as fine Chardonnay.

ST HELENA ★★★(★) Shot to prominence with its world-famous 1982 Pinot Noir. Perhaps inevitably, it's taken a while to match that peak again – but the last few vintages have been superb.

SELAKS ★★★(★) Excellent producer of bone-dry wines from north of Auckland. They also make spot-on Sauvignon, and a Sauvignon/Semillon, a 3:2 blend, which is delicious young but even better after two years.

TE MATA ★★★★★ Te Mata Coleraine is the most consistently impressive and most sought-after of all New Zealand reds. Te Mata Awatea is also a fine red and the new Elston Chardonnay, distinctly 'Burgundian' in style, is rich and powerful.

VILLA MARIA ★★★★ Vidal and Villa Maria Reserve Bin wines from Sauvignon to Merlot. Rich, juicy Chardonnays and classic Cabernet are encouraging. Prices are very fair.

UNITED KINGDOM

One way or another 1989 was a strange year in the UK. London saw rioting in the heart of the West End. An earthquake shook the country from Wales outwards. Even the most un-sports-conscious of citizens cannot have failed to hear that the England cricket team won a Test in the West Indies. But of all these extraordinary events, the most outlandish by far for wine-lovers was that after a decade of harvests buffeted and disrupted by cool weather, hurricanes, mildew and storm damage, the sun shone on the vineyards of England and Wales and drew out an abundant crop of marvellously healthy grapes. The 1989 harvest will produce over four million bottles of wine.

The wines, in the main, are delicious to boot and the best will age well. We held a tasting of them in the *Webster's* offices in the summer of 1990 (see the feature on page 7 for Oz Clarke's full report on the event). Fruity and fragrant drinking, with lively but never sharp acidity, in spite of all that warm weather from Cornwall to Kent. The tasting inspired some pondering. What if we really do have Global Warming on our hands? Should we perhaps be planting Cabernet Sauvignon instead of Seibel? Or, if that's going too far, what about the grapes of Champagne, France's most northerly wine-growing district? Pinot Noir, Pinot Meunier and Chardonnay? If the average air temperature rises by between 1.5 and 4.5 degrees, central England would acquire a climate similar to that in the Gironde valley by the year 2050, government research tells us.

In other words, we need to be planting our sparkling wine grapes *now*, preferably on chalk if we intend to follow French models. Fortunately, there are areas of southern England with the same type of chalk as in Champagne, so we could be carrying out comparative tastings of South Downs versus the Vallée de la Marne just as soon as the vines reach full producing maturity.

Then why stop there? As we wait for the weather to get warm enough to start planting Shiraz, we could plant other grapes for sparkling wine. Crémant de Chiddingly. Prosecco di Pulborough. Cuckfield Cava!

Just in case you are starting to think that this is all a little excessive, let me just remind you of one or two things about UK wine. For a start, although our vineyards are relatively immature by European standards, this doesn't mean that vine growing here is a new notion. The Romans were keen on a drop of wine and so were the Normans. The Domesday Book records some 40 vineyards, some of which were around ten acres in size and not all attached to monastic properties. By 1270 vine planting was spreading thanks in no small part to warmer temperatures. It's happened before, you see. By the 1300s techniques like sweetening the grape juice to improve alcohol levels (and hence the wine's ability to keep) were understood and adopted. Imagine what twentieth century technology could achieve!

Besides, dreams of Kentish fizz are not only whimsical moments of fantasy confined to wine tasters enjoying the results from 1989. The professionals also do their share of crystal-ball-gazing. David Carr Taylor has Pinot Noir on his estate in Sussex, Bernard Theobald in Berkshire has too. In Surrey, a 250-acre estate has been planted with Pinot Noir, Chardonnay and other grapes. Are they all mad? Maybe to be a winemaker you have to be a gambler too.   **FIONA WILD**

WHITE WINES

BACCHUS A German crossing of Riesling and Sylvaner with Müller-Thurgau, and a classic example of why many of these new German crossings are suited to England. In Germany, it usually produces fat, blowsy, marmalade-Muscatty flavours. In England, it is more likely to produce a sharp wine, with strong flavours of gooseberry, whitecurrant and elderflower as well as something of orange rind. *Nutbourne Manor* make a particularly good version.

FABER A crossing of Pinot Blanc and Müller-Thurgau, making fragrant wines with good acidity. One of the few varieties where you can actually taste Riesling characteristics.

HUXELREBE A German cross of Gutedel with Courtillier Musqué. In Germany it beetles to overripeness in no time at all and the wine is usually rich, flat and grapy. In England it's generally the exact opposite, renowned for a strong grapefruit pith taste and a greenish bite. For this reason it is often softened up by blending. *Headcorn's* version is almost as light and delicate as a German Mosel; *Lamberhurst* make a pleasantly full-bodied version; *Staple St James* and *Pilton Manor* a more grapefruity, smoky example. *Astley* mix it with Müller-Thurgau in their delicious Huxelvaner while *Three Choirs* actually late-pick it and try to make a sweetie.

KERNER A bright, new German crossing of Riesling and Trollinger that is producing good results. *Astley* in Worcester make one rather like a light Mosel.

MADELEINE ANGEVINE Basically this is a table grape, but it performs quite well in England, where its somewhat 'fruit-juicy' character is matched by good acidity, either in the very green but refreshing elderflower perfumed style of *Astley* 1985 and '86, or the more honeyed but apple-pips green style of *Hooksway* 1984.

MÜLLER-THURGAU This is one of the original German crosses – from Riesling and Sylvaner in 1882 – and is the English

vineyard workhorse, taking up over one-third of the acreage. Consequently, there is a fair amount of dull Müller about, which usually needs beefing up with something more aromatic. In Somerset, *Wootton's* is very good. *Bruisyard St Peter* in Suffolk make an uncompromisingly dry and very Sauvignon-sharp example, even with a touch of smokiness. *Breaky Bottom* from Sussex is another uncompromising winery whose excellent dry Müller often needs five or six years to become gentle and honeyed. Müller can sometimes acquire a dry but peachy flavour – especially in Kent, at *St Nicholas of Ash, Staple St James* and *Tenterden*, or at *St George's* in Sussex. And it can make very attractive, slightly sweet wine (through the addition of *Süssreserve* – unfermented grape juice – just before bottling) sometimes with a mango, honeyish taste – as at *Lamberhurst* in Kent, *Rowney* in Hertfordshire and *Pulham* in Norfolk.

ORTEGA A German cross making fat, rich, grapy wine mostly in the Mosel, of all places, but better suited to England. *Biddenden*, in particular, makes a delicious, slightly sweet, but tremendously fruity elderflower and apricot-tasting example. Since it is an excellent 'improver' of neutral varieties, it is rarely seen on its own.

REICHENSTEINER A real 'EC' grape since it is a crossing of French Madeleine Angevine, German Müller-Thurgau and Italian Calabrese! Does this multi-coloured background make it an exciting, tempestuous grape? Sadly, it's rather more of a Brussels bureaucrat clone. At ten per cent of UK acreage it's the second commonest variety. It's usually pretty dull made dry – although *Carr Taylor's* '86 and '87 were bitingly good with loads of elderflower fruit – but made slightly sweet like *St George's* '86, it can develop a pleasant, smoky, quince and peaches taste which ages surprisingly well. *Carr Taylor* are using Kerner and Reichensteiner for their Champagne-method fizz, which gets better and better as the years go by.

SCHEUREBE Silvaner crossed with Riesling, capable of producing good quality, grapefruity, curranty wines in good years.

SCHÖNBURGER Now this is a *good* grape, pink in colour – from its Pinot Noir x Chasselas Rosé x Hamburg Muscat parentage. It makes a positively 'fat' wine by English standards, with something of the boudoir perfumes of the Gewürztraminer, a fruit flavour of pears and lychees and good acidity. Because of its flowery, super-scented style it needs expert wine-making, otherwise it can end up tasting like a bathroom detergent. The best examples are made by leading winemakers like *Lamberhurst, Wootton* and *Carr Taylor*.

SEYVAL BLANC A French hybrid vine with just under ten per cent of UK acreage. *Breaky Bottom* are the most successful with it – dry and Sauvignon-like when young, smooth and honeyed like Burgundy after four to five years – but it is generally best blended with something more exotic like Schönburger or Huxelrebe, or made sweetish by *Süssreserve. Three Choirs*

blend it successfully with Reichensteiner and *Adgestone* with Reichensteiner and Müller to produce big, soft but non-aromatic wines, while *Tenterden* really show what it's capable of by making a very good oaked Reserve!

OTHER WHITES Numerous other varieties are being tried. Of these, the most interesting are Gewürztraminer at *Barton Manor* on the Isle of Wight where it was planted in plastic tunnels in 1984 and Ehrenfelser, aged in a 4000-litre oak barrel, at *Penshurst*. There are also some preliminary efforts with Chardonnay – the new, 250-acre *Denbies Estate* in Surrey planted theirs in 1986 with a view to sparkling wine production.

RED & ROSÉ WINES

CABERNET SAUVIGNON It's not just my solitary vine in SW6! Real vineyards do exist in Guernsey; I've seen them!

PINOT NOIR There are now over 20 hectares of the great Burgundy grape planted! So far, full reds have been difficult to achieve, but Kent has several patches making very good rosé – *Chiddingstone* blend it with Pinot Meunier to make a delicious version redolent of eucalyptus; *Bodiam Castle* make a tasty rosé blended with Blauburger, as well as an excellent dry, honeyed Blanc de Pinot Noir white; and *Tenterden's* blend with Dunkelfelder produces a gently honeyed, smoky mango-flavoured pink. Some estates are now planting Pinot Noir with sparkling wine in mind.

SEIBEL *Beaulieu* make a first-class rosé from Seibel like a lighter, fruitier Provence style. Other producers use Seibel as a component in red and rosé blends.

OTHER WINE REGIONS

ARGENTINA

Despite some reasonably encouraging noises from the large group of Masters of Wine who visited South America in 1989, the vision of supplies of drinkable plonk at a very fair price now seems to be fading back into the future. It *is* a pity, because if Argentina can ever get itself organized, it will probably be better suited than Chile to providing the large quantities of juicy, easy-going reds and whites which could be a most welcome addition to our market in a time of rising European wine prices. Tighter controls are needed over yields in particular, but winery standards generally need to improve too. Should they get their act together, there could be some interesting drinking, not just from European varieties, but also from the native white Torrontes grape.

AUSTRIA

Having tried various Austrian wines over the last few years, I'm afraid I have to report that I actually preferred quite a few of the wine styles we saw 'pre-antifreeze' or even 'during-antifreeze'. Grüner Veltliner in particular used to have a rather attractive coarse pepperiness. Riesling, Müller-Thurgau and Traminer all showed real varietal style, drier than German equivalents but with a rounder, riper feel too. I don't find much evidence of this now. Somehow they seem to have been inveigled into the Trocken trap which is obsessing German winemakers, and they've started producing the tart, bodiless gum-numbing wines which are the scourge of Germany's export attempts. Why? Misguided attempts to be fashionable, perhaps. One Austrian wine expert said, when I was quietly moaning about it all, 'Ach, you must age them'. Well, most of the wines were *too* old at 18 months old or less, and the genuinely mature wines – 1986 and earlier – simply lacked the fruit to age. All this and a bevy of new Germanic names doesn't bode well for Austria's revival on the UK market.

Austria's only really good value wines are still the fabled dessert wines, made around the steamy Neusiedlersee, where noble rot comes round regularly every year. The Sauternes and Rheingau growers would give several sets of eye teeth for such a climate. Austrian sweet wines are tremendously rich, yet not so excitingly balanced by fine acidity as their German equivalents since their climate is hotter. But they're a snip.

BRAZIL

Most Brazilian wine is sold to the Brazilians, and much of it is made from *Vitis labrusca* rather than the better quality *Vitis vinifera* grape varieties. Since the 1970s, interest from overseas companies like Moët & Chandon and Rémy Martin has encouraged moves towards vinifera, and we may in the future see more interesting wines emerging. The wine industry battles with a high-humidity climate, and work is under way to identify which grapes would do best in the conditions. *Palomas* is the only Brazilian wine you're likely to see here.

BULGARIA

I think a few figures might be in order here to show just how much Bulgaria has achieved in the last few years. In 1985 we drank 390,000 cases, and by 1989 the figure was 1.5 million cases, plus 1.4 million litres in bulk. In 1980 imports of Bulgarian wine didn't even merit a percentage point! Good flavours, good value.

All this heady success has meant that quality has been under strain. The straightforward Cabernet Sauvignon isn't the gorgeously obvious essence of blackcurrants it once was – it hasn't been for several years. The Reserve wines kick off each new vintage with a blare of trumpets. But they're such good value that stocks are quickly exhausted, and the replacements never seem quite as good, despite identical labels. Each year I taste the entire range of Bulgarian wines, and find few stand out. It's as if the wine-making has reached a plateau from which it's difficult to take a step upwards. Yet the vineyards are there, if someone can find the willpower.

CANADA

Remarkably, Canada now has an *appellation contrôlée* system. Ontario has managed to form a Vintners' Quality Alliance which seems determined to pursue strict varietal, origin and minimum ripeness objectives. Canada's climate has always bedevilled attempts to create significant amounts of decent wine on a regular basis and, until the 1980s, the Niagara Peninsula was still thought of as a hybrid heaven at best. Yet the new VQA *appellation* for Niagara Peninsula stipulates 100 per cent *Vitis vinifera* wines. Well, fellahs, if you think you can make it stick where the rest of the New World has so far failed – you go right ahead and I offer my full support. You're going to need it now that that free-trade agreement with the USA is getting moving, because they've got a serious glut of jug wine building up as their neo-prohibitionist movement takes hold. If you don't strike out for quality you could just get drowned in the flood.

CHILE

Once poised for discovery by wine drinkers in the UK and sold (oversold?) to readers as 'the new Australia', Chile in the first year of the new decade managed one step forward and two steps back. The presence of excessive sorbitol in a number of Chilean wines, both white and red, brought the South American country's wine industry into the limelight in April 1990. Chilean wines were removed from the shelves and disappeared entirely from view for some months, even ones which weren't implicated at all. Unlike other wine scandals, this one seems to have flared and flashed but to have left very little trace.

A lot of this is probably due to the fact that sorbitol is harmless. It has a sweetening, softening effect on wine and can smooth over any rough edges. It occurs naturally in wine, and up to 0.7g/l is perfectly acceptable, but you are not allowed to *add* it to any wine which is going to be sold in the EC. A few years ago Tyrrells winery in Australia's Hunter Valley was faced with similar charges.

The Chilean wineries responsible – Santa Rita, San Pedro and Viña Linderos – sell their wines under different labels such as Viña Carmen or Santa Helena, but you don't need to memorize a list, because since 1 January 1990 it has been illegal for any wine to leave Chile with excess sorbitol, and the wines are now accompanied by certificates declaring their fitness for consumption.

Did you notice the date? January 1990? When did the news break? April 1990? Yes, it's thank you, Ministry of Agriculture Fisheries and Food again. The excess sorbitol was identified by the state liquor importing company in Norway in 1989. The Chileans were informed, and the new certification procedure instigated. MAFF were informed in February. Importers, retailers, wine buyers and wine drinkers were told the news in April.

The market could be a very important one for Chile, so if there is to be a silver lining to all this, it could be a heightened awareness in South America of what the European market demands and expects. Wine producers like Torres obviously need no assistance, but in other wineries the march of progress has been uneven. Yet this phylloxera-free paradise could produce marvellous wines. Growers are now learning to limit irrigation, and stop watering altogether at five to six weeks before harvest, improving flavour and concentration; skills with new oak are being acquired and the benefits of cool fermentation temperatures are becoming more evident.

Perhaps next year it'll be one step back and two steps forward?

CYPRUS

With the increasing unfashionability of their chief product, Cyprus sherry, Cyprus's winemakers fight against the island's climate, terrain and traditions – and even the tourist trade – in their attempt to make a fresher, more modern style of wine. The vineyards are up in the baking-hot mountains, an hour and more's drive up from the coast along part winding and narrow, now partly modernized roads. That wouldn't be much of a problem if the wineries were up there, too. But all four of Cyprus's big wineries (who make practically all the wine) are down on the coast near Limassol. Back up in the mountains, the workforce has become thin on the ground since the tourist boom began. At harvest time young people are slaving away down in the seaside hotels, restaurants and bars, leaving their mothers and grannies to pick the grapes, while the men, as usual, drink coffee all day outside the village *cafeneon*, taking the odd day off now and then to drive the grape truck down to Limassol. If the truck is only half full after a day's picking, it will sit around the village all night, then up in the vineyards all the next day to complete its load. Then down it bounces to the winery and even *then* the queues of lorries outside the winery gate are sometimes so long that they may have up to a day's wait.

Cypriot winemakers are well aware that to make *good* wine, you need to pick the grapes at their peak and press them as quickly as possible. They're now managing to bring in *a bit* of the harvest in good condition and make a small amount of fresh, modern wine, but we're seeing little of it here as yet.

Keo have been working on a low alcohol, cool-fermented, pressurized-fermentation wine made from local white grape Xinisteri, and remarkably fragrant. The excellent government research institute at Limassol is working hard to improve the raw materials, too. Most of the grapes are unfortunately of the non-aromatic, rather neutral southern sort, but there is some good Muscat, both sweet and dry, some marvellous Syrah, and a few others.

GREECE

Greece suffers from many of the same problems as Cyprus – overripe grapes that take their time getting to the wineries, and then often fairly primitive wine-making. But there are a few wineries turning out some reasonable wines, and a couple of categories, Mavrodaphne sweet red dessert wine and Samos Muscats, that the Greeks seem to get right more often than the rest – big, sweet, brutish stuff, but often quite well made.

Of Greece's 'lighter', dry wines, reasonably good ones come from *Château Carras* – their *Côtes de Meliton* and raisiny-blackcurranty *Château Carras*, made from the red Bordeaux grape mix. For something rather cheaper and good value, the dry reds from *Tsantali* are the only really good ones available and their Mavrodaphne and Muscat are the best on the market.

If you have a taste for pine trees (I confess I do), Retsina is probably the safest choice amongst the rest of Greek wines. Sainsbury's own label is good, with a bit more resin than the rest, and *Tsantali* and *Metaxa* are OK. This year Wizard Wine Warehouses have some good value drinking from Greece: the peppery, dry red *Kouros Nemea*, a lovely grapy *Kourtakis Samos Muscat* and quite the best, freshest Retsina (from *Kourtakis*) I've tasted.

HUNGARY

Hungary is a curious mixture. It has one of the UK's most successful wine brands – Bull's Blood. It has one of the world's most fabled sweet wines – Tokay. And yet it led the charge with the vaguely sweet, foggy-day reds and flabby innocuous own-label whites which now adorn every supermarket shelf. This is a pity, because Hungary has as fine a wine tradition as any country in Europe. There was a time when Bull's Blood was so good that you could take it to any wine buff's table and be applauded. Now, each bottle seems different from the last.

Tokay is a different story because the taste that marks this out is oxidation. But don't expect the honey sweetness of Sauternes, or the grapy richness of a Muscatel. This is rasping, fiery wine, with its personality dragged out of a hectic Magyar past. But it does look as though things are changing at last. There is no longer a state monopoly on exports. Now any company of a decent size can apply for an export licence and four different companies were showing at the London Wine Trade Fair in 1989. A Gold Medal in the 1989 International Wine Challenge for Hungarian Merlot should have given them a boost.

INDIA

A self-made millionaire decided that he was going to make Champagne at whatever cost. Of course, he didn't make Champagne – he made sparkling wine in India – but he did call on the services of a Champagne house, Piper Heidsieck, to help him. The result, made from Chardonnay and Ugni Blanc in the Satiyadri hills east of Bombay, does the Champagne house no discredit, although the price is a bit high: supermarkets sell their own-label Champagnes more cheaply.

ISRAEL

Israel has been making wine since Baron Edmond de Rothschild planted vines there in the 1880s. But it is only in the last few years that any really interesting wines have been made. Previously most of the vineyards had been sited in the hot coastal regions. But in the late 1960s a professor from the University of Davis at California, visiting a kibbutz in the Golan Heights, realized that the volcanic soils would be ideal wine-growing territory. Lack of rain could be a problem, but there were already plenty of reservoirs and, most importantly, it was so high above sea level (up to 3000 feet) that temperatures throughout the summer seldom exceeded 25°C, *and* dropped back significantly at night.

In war-torn Israel it took until 1977 for the planting programme to begin and another nine years before the first Cabernet Sauvignon – under the name Gamla – and the Sauvignon Blanc – called Yarden – were released commercially. But the quality of both is excellent. Other grape varieties coming into production on the 400 acres so far planted include Semillon, Chenin Blanc, Colombard, Riesling, Chardonnay, Pinot Noir and Merlot.

LEBANON

The Middle East is the cradle of the grape, and we are able to taste fine modern day equivalents of those first wine efforts largely through the astonishing bravery of the Hochar family, and in particular Serge Hochar, who makes the wine of *Château Musar*. Much of the bitterest fighting between Lebanese factions has been in the Bekaa valley, precisely where Hochar has the 50-year-old vineyard which forms the basis for the Musar wine.

By means of astonishing ingenuity and fearlessness, Hochar has managed to produce a vintage every year. His luck almost ran out in 1984, his grape trucks held hostage by virtually every political faction. Since 1982 the civil war front line has cut right across the road between his vineyards and his winery, and in 1984, only one truck managed to get past the Israeli soldiers. It took six days to make the journey. By that time his super-ripe Cabernet and Cinsaut grapes were a seething, fermenting mass and the vintage was a virtual write-off. In 1982 it was only due to the confusion following the Israeli invasion that his trucks could zig-zag backwards and forwards across the lines with the precious harvest of grapes. And in 1983 the American gunboats enforced a truce just long enough for Hochar to whip up his pickers, put all the truck drivers on a bonus, and bring in the vintage. The weather wasn't that good in 1988, but 1989 produced a smallish harvest of rather good quality.

LUXEMBOURG

Luxembourg's vineyards flank the Mosel upstream from Germany. The wines are similar in style – light and delicate, sometimes a little neutral – but they don't age like the best German Mosels. Müller-Thurgau (here called Rivaner) accounts for half the area under wine, white Elbling, Riesling and Auxerrois are also quite important. Gewürztraminer and Pinot Gris are less important in terms of acreage, but they make some of the more interesting wines, the one gently spicy, the other fuller and slightly honeyed.

NORTH AFRICA

Because of their years of French rule – and despite the Muslim stricture on alcohol – Algeria, Tunisia and Morocco have a long-established tradition of wine-making. Originally most of the wine found its way into French blending vats, where it did a very good job beefing up insipid local brews. But since the departure of the French in the 1960s and the tightening up of control by the EEC in the '70s, outlets have been closed, and the North African countries have rather lost the incentive to make good wine. Algeria, the largest producer of the three, makes reasonable, rather solid red wines in the Coteaux de Mascara, but nothing else of much interest, and Tunisia's wines are generally oxidized. Morocco, however, is capable of producing better results helped by its proximity to the Atlantic. Tarik, a Southern Rhône-like blend of Cinsaut, Carignan and Grenache, is a fat, soupy red, while Sidi Brahim is a good varietal Cinsaut.

ROMANIA

Romania's vineyards do have great potential, indeed many say the best in the whole of what we used to call the Eastern bloc. And when one of our major supermarket buyers looks wistfully eastwards and says Eastern Europe is where she feels the next surge of growth in our market is coming from, it's Romania and Hungary she's thinking of. The appearance of a good Pinot Noir at Sainsbury's and the occasional sighting – at Thos Peatling, and Irvine Robertson Wines for a start – of the luscious 1979 Pietroasele Edelbeerenauslese – are signs that Romania, along with Hungary and Bulgaria, *is* preparing to play an increasingly important role in our wine boom. With 290,000 hectares of vineyard to play with, Romania could easily conquer our shelves as Bulgaria did.

RUSSIA

Although Hugh Johnson's *The Story of Wine* series on Channel 4 kicked off with some history in Georgia, the idea of modern Russian wine is not one that many take very seriously. An exploratory trip made a few years ago by a group of UK wine buyers concluded that though there's plenty of good raw material, and good sites exist, there's a great deal of progress needed on quality control before Russian wine can compete for space on our shelves.

In 1990 Russian wine hit the headlines however, when the Russian Imperial Cellar from Massandra on the Black Sea, came up for auction at Sotheby's. The cellar, built for Tsar Nicholas II between 1894 and 1897, housed sweet and fortified wines modelled on Western styles of wine like port and sherry. A grand total of 13,000 bottles taking in vintages from 1830 to 1945 went on sale, including nineteenth century Muscats.

Apart from awakening interest in European fortified wine producers, who may be able to sell their wines to Russia in future, the auction highlighted the fact that the Russian winemakers were clearly able to recreate fine fortified wine styles from local grapes and conditions. Spanish sherry was sent to Russia so that they had models to copy. David Molyneux-Berry of Sotheby's described some of the Crimean Muscats as 'amongst the finest sweet wines in the world'. Makes you pause, doesn't it?

SOUTH AFRICA

If there is a group of winemakers who profess to strive for change and progress in the restrictive atmosphere of the apartheid system, it is the Cape Independent Winemakers' Guild, which includes the highly articulate anti-apartheid campaigner Tim Hamilton-Russell and the doggedly courageous Boer breakaway Jan Boland Coetzee of Vriesenhof as well as others. I've tasted the whole range of their wines, and I wish I could be more enthusiastic about the general standard, but I can't. There were good wines – Neil Ellis's Sauvignon Blanc, Overgaauw's Sylvaner (!), Kanonkop's Pinotage, Hamilton-Russell's Pinot Noir. But if these are the cream of South African talent – and tastings of the Berghelder group of Winemakers don't reveal any shooting stars of a higher quality than these – then the standard really isn't high enough yet to make *my* heart beat faster. As the liberalization policies of President de Klerk start to work, perhaps the cross-fertilization of ideas that distinguishes other New World wine regions will occur. Whether it will be enough to make up for years of isolation from the rest of the wine-making world remains to be seen.

SWITZERLAND

The quality of Swiss wine can be high, but in a way which we are not keen to pay for – light, snow-fresh whites, wines with gentle perfume and a spritzy acid bite. Swiss wines in the UK are usually of the ski-resort brand-name Fendant type. There are some fine *grand cru* estates, making a fascinating variety of whites and some reds. They're well worth seeking out *in situ*, but not over here.

TURKEY

Turkey's history of viticulture is rather more impressive than the end product – the wine itself. Although only three per cent of the total – huge – grape crop is made into wine, wine-making can be traced back some 4000 years – plenty of time in which to count the 1172 different grape varieties currently registered as being cultivated. The authorities are now desperately trying to modernize the industry, but it is uphill work. Agriculture in general is very backward and there is inevitably a distinct lack of commitment to wine in a Muslim population. Producers tend to blend in grapes from other regions and vintage dates are treated in a very cavalier fashion – bottles of so-called 1929 red still crop up surprisingly regularly.

Four regions account for over 90 per cent of production with Thrace, in the north-west along the shores of the Sea of Marmara, the most important, followed by the Central North, Aegean, Central South and the rest of Marmara. It's hard positively to *recommend* Turkish wines or even any individual grape varieties, but Buzbag (red), Villa Doluca and Doluca (red and whites), Hosbag (red), Villa Dona (red and white) are brand names to consider.

YUGOSLAVIA

A few years ago Yugoslav Cabernet Sauvignon was the *first* of the varietal wines to sell well here. It was big, rather soupy stuff, but with loads of fruit, the blackcurrant mixed up with a strong, meaty, roasted taste. But as soon as others threatened to get in on the act, Yugoslavia seemed to give up the ghost.

Cabernets now tend to be coarse and raw, tasting of grapeskins and harsh, overpressed fruit. The Merlot is much more encouraging; usually soft, slightly honeyed wine. Vranač, too, has a distinct style: tough, but with lots of fruit.

In UK market terms the Yugoslav red production could disappear and hardly anyone would notice, because 95 per cent of Yugoslav sales in the UK are white. And of that, 70 per cent is a single brand – the ubiquitous Lutomer Laski Rizling. Although the wine has never been that brilliant, it became a household name, and in the 1970s was notching up annual sales increases of over 20 per cent. My first ever mouthful of white wine was Lutomer – what else? In 1978 Yugoslav Rizling accounted for over six per cent of the UK market but since then it has gradually lost out to Germany in the battle for the light, fruity sector. Figures for the 1980s show a genteel though respectable gradual decline, but through all this Lutomer remains a remarkably strong brand, and it is own-label Laski Rizling and the tiny band of more interesting Traminers and Sauvignons which have unfortunately been on the slide. With the present political turmoil in Eastern Europe there seems to be little likelihood of Yugoslavia increasing its share of the UK market just yet.

ZIMBABWE

An enterprising Leeds wine merchant, Vinceremos, imports a range of wines from Zimbabwe. You have to admire their temerity, which is not to say that the wines are bad, but they're a mixed bunch under the gloriously irrelevant brand name of Flame Lily. The grapes are grown over 4000 feet above sea level, and the wines are bottled at the *Mukuyu Winery* for a *négociant* firm called Philips Central Cellars of Harare. If you're feeling brave, try the Premium Dry White but just remember, when I had to blind taste it on TV I said it was Scottish! The dry white and red are an 'experience'.

PRICE GUIDES

I suppose it could cross your mind that you don't need price guides – perish the thought, because if nobody wants a Price Guide I shall be back to doing pantomime at Northampton rep by next Christmas. But does that mean that you don't feel the need to know where you're likely to find the best price for your favourite wine? That you don't want to find out what alternatives you can expect for the amount of money you wish to spend? That you don't want to know if you're on to a super bargain? Surely not!

On expensive wines the price differences are often dramatic. On cheaper wines, the differences may be small but they're still worth knowing about. And our specially recommended wines may well be in limited distribution: it's of crucial importance to find out *where* the wines are stocked, as well as what the price differences are. By using these price guides judiciously, you should be able to drink *better* and more *cheaply* during the coming year.

● All prices are *per bottle inclusive of VAT*, unless otherwise stated. Remember that many merchants sell only by the case, and that price should be affected positively if you buy a case or more.

● Wines are listed in price bands and by vintage. Price bands run from the lowest to the highest. Vintages run from the most recent to the oldest. Within these categories the wines are listed in alphabetical order to help you find a particular wine more easily.

● Within the price bands, stockists are listed in brackets after each entry in ascending order of price. Occasionally, the same wine will fall into more than one price band, but before you get too agitated about variations in price, remember that wine warehouses, for example, often come out much cheaper because you have to buy by the case, they do not deliver, they do not have smart high street premises, and so on. Equally, there's no getting away from the fact that the price of a given wine sometimes varies wildly for no good reason.

● The claret prices are a special case. Specific prices are shown in ascending order by vintage. There *are* some dramatic price variations here – some are to do with keen pricing and the reverse; more often they will be because claret is now (for better or for worse) an investment medium and responsive to market pressures. A merchant buying wine *en primeur* in Bordeaux on Monday *afternoon* may pay 25 per cent more than the going rate that morning! Replacement stocks over the years will vary in cost and currency movements will also be a factor. So – for the sake of clarity – the prices we list were valid in the late spring/early summer of 1990.

● In the claret guide, all châteaux are listed alphabetically regardless of class. When a wine is quoted EC or IB, it means that the wine is offered on an *en primeur* basis (in Bordeaux or at the châteaux) or in bond (in the UK). All EC and IB prices are per dozen. The EC price simply includes the price of the wine in the bottle and excludes shipping, duties and taxes such as VAT. The EC price is usually payable when the wine is offered in the summer following the vintage. The other costs (including VAT on both invoices) become payable when the wine is shipped. The *crus classés* and better *bourgeois* are shipped two years later, and the *petits châteaux* and the lesser *bourgeois* after a year. You should check the exact terms of sale with your merchant who will give you a projection of the final 'duty paid delivered' price at current rates of shipping, duty and VAT.

● Where merchants sell only by the case we have divided by 12 the VAT-inclusive price of a single case.

● When clubs (e.g. Les Amis du Vin) have both member and non-member prices we have used the *non-member* prices.

● Stars (★) denote wines that the editors consider particularly good value for money *in their class*.

● To get the most out of the lists in the book, please remember that *Webster's* is a price GUIDE not a price LIST. An invaluable reference whenever you are ordering or buying wine, it is not meant to replace up-to-date merchants' lists. What it *does* do, however, is give you a unique opportunity to compare prices; to develop a sense of what you can reasonably expect to pay for any given wine; to spot a bargain; to work out exactly what you can afford – *and to find it*.

MERCHANT CODES

The following list of abbreviations enables you to identify the merchants from whose lists the wines in the price guides were selected. For more detailed information on each merchant, see the Merchant Directory on page 440.

AD	Adnams	BOT	Bottoms Up
AI	James Aitken & Son	BR	Broad Street Wine Company
ALL	H. Allen Smith	BY	Anthony Byrne
AMI	Les Amis du Vin (also Cullen's)	BYR	D. Byrne
AN	André Simon Wines	CAP	Cape Province Wines
AS	Ashley Scott	CB	Corney & Barrow
ASD	ASDA	CH	Chaplin & Son
ASK	Askham Wines	CHA	Châteaux Wines
AUG	Augustus Barnett	DAV	Davisons
AUS	Australian Wine Centre	DI	Direct Wine Shipments
AV	Averys	DOM	Domaine Direct
BAR	Barnes Wine Shop	EL	Eldridge, Pope & Co
BE	Bedford Fine Wines	ELL	Ellis, Son & Vidler
BEK	Berkmann Wine Cellars	FIZ	Fine Wines of New Zealand
BER	Berry Bros & Rudd	GI	Grape Ideas
BIB	Bibendum	GIL	M. & W. Gilbey
BL	Blayneys	GRE	Peter Green
BO	Booths Fine Wines	HA	John Harvey & Sons
BOD	Bordeaux Direct	HAC	Harcourt Fine Wines
BOR	Borg Castel	HAG	Gerard Harris

HAH	Haynes Hanson & Clark		RES	La Réserve
HAU	Haughton Fine Wines		SAF	Safeway
HAW	Roger Harris Wines		SAI	Sainsbury
HAY	Richard Harvey Wines		STA	Stapylton Fletcher
HE	Douglas Henn-Macrae		TAN	Tanners
HIC	Hicks & Don		TES	Tesco
HIG	High Breck Vintages		THR	Thresher
HOG	J.E. Hogg		UP	Upper Crust
HUN	Hungerford Wine Company		TW	T. & W. Wines
IR	Irvine Robertson Wines		UN	Unwins Wine Merchants
KA	J.C. Karn		VA	Valvona & Crolla
LA	Laymont & Shaw		VIC	Victoria Wine Company
LAY	Lay & Wheeler		VIG	La Vigneronne
LO	London Wine		VIN	Vintage Wines
LOR	Lorne House Vintners		WAI	Waitrose
MAJ	Majestic Wine Warehouses		WCL	Winecellars
MAR	Marks & Spencer		WHI	Whitesides of Clitheroe
MOR	J. Moreno Wines		WIC	Wine Club
MV	Morris & Verdin		WIL	Willoughbys
NI	James Nicholson		WIW	Wines of Westhorpe
OD	Oddbins		WIZ	Wizard Wine
OL	Old Street Wine Company		WRI	Wright Wine Company
PD	Peter Dominic		WS	Wine Society
PE	Thos Peatling		WW	Windrush Wines
PIP	Christopher Piper Wines		WY	Peter Wylie
RAE	Raeburn Fine Wines		YAP	Yapp Brothers
REI	Reid Wines		YF	Yorkshire Fine Wines

RED BORDEAUX

d'Agassac *cru bourgeois supérieur Haut-Médoc*
1985 £6.95 (WAI) £7.09 (PE) £7.50 (LAY)

Amiral-de-Beychevelle *St-Julien*
★**1989 EC** £82.20 (PIP)
1986 £13.85 (AI)
1985 £12.30 (WRI)

Andron-Blanquet *cru grand bourgeois exceptionnel St-Éstèphe*
1983 £8.38 (PIP)
1982 £7.98 (OL)

l'Angélus *grand cru classé St-Émilion*
1988 EC £125.00 (WW)
1983 £17.50 (AD)

d'Angludet *cru bourgeois supérieur exceptionnel Margaux*
1989 EC £87.00 (HUN) £88.40 (HAH) £90.00 (HAY)
1988 EC £67.00 (BE)
1987 £6.90 (AD) £7.90 (TAN) £8.65 (WS)
1986 £8.29 (WIL) £9.75 (DAV) £10.83 (TAN) £11.30 (BE)
1986 EC £63.00 (HAG)
1985 £10.10 (BEK) £11.30 (BE) £11.61 (PIP)
1983 £13.80 (BE)
1982 £11.80 (GI)
1971 £17.83 (REI)

des Annereaux *Lalande-de-Pomerol*
1986 £6.89 (CH)
1985 £6.55 (BYR) £7.95 (BAR)
1983 £7.95 (WCL) £7.96 (IR) £8.43 (CB)

Arnauld *cru bourgeois Haut-Médoc*
1987 £5.39 (WHI)
1985 £6.98 (BIB) £8.75 (BO) £8.95 (VIG)
1983 £9.30 (ALL)

d'Arricaud *Graves*
1985 £6.50 (HAY) £6.95 (RAE)
1984 £4.99 (WIL)
1982 £7.50 (BIB)

All châteaux are listed alphabetically regardless of class.

---

l'Arrosée *grand cru classé St-Émilion*
1988 EC £118.00 (BIB)
1987 £12.00 (HUN) £15.27 (BY)
1985 £19.50 (HUN)
1983 £15.30 (BEK)

Ausone *1er grand cru classé St-Émilion*
1987 £26.80 (AD)
1986 £43.70 (AD)
1985 £52.20 (AD) £75.10 (AN)
1983 £52.00 (AD)
1982 £84.00 (UN)

Bahans-Haut-Brion *Graves*
1989 EC £112.00 (RAE)
1985 £13.95 (WIZ) £22.23 (CB)
1982 £16.37 (CB)

Baret *Pessac-Léognan*
1988 £6.90 (HIG)
1986 £7.47 (HIG)
1985 £8.05 (HIG)

Batailley *5ème cru classé Pauillac*
1989 EC £86.20 (HAH)
1988 £9.20 (HIG)
1986 £11.25 (DAV)
1985 £11.50 (HIG) £12.25 (BER) £13.75 (DAV)
1984 £8.62 (HIG) £8.93 (HA)
1983 £11.63 (HAH) £12.50 (WY) £14.50 (DI) £16.20 (HA)
1982 £12.46 (BIB) £14.95 (DAV) £17.39 (AV)
1981 £10.50 (HOG) £14.00 (WY) £15.75 (DAV)
1979 £15.00 (UN) £17.75 (DAV)
1979 jeroboam £115.00 (WY)
1978 £15.81 (BIB) £19.75 (DAV)
1975 £19.75 (DAV)
1975 imperial £175.95 (EL)
1974 £16.50 (BOR)
1970 £20.99 (BO)
1966 £31.00 (WY)
1961 £50.00 (VIG) £57.00 (WY)

Beau-Séjour-Bécot *1er grand cru classé St-Émilion*
1988 EC £115.00 (WW) £129.00 (ASK)
1983 £14.49 (BO)
1981 £14.49 (BO)

Beau-Site-Haut-Vignoble *cru bourgeois St-Éstèphe*
1982 £6.76 (IR)

Beau-Site *cru grand bourgeois exceptionnel St-Éstèphe*
1986 £4.25 (AS)
1985 £7.25 (DAV) £7.47 (HIG)
1984 £6.32 (HIG)
1982 £7.25 (DAV)

Beaumont *cru grand bourgeois Haut-Médoc*
1987 £5.95 (ALL)
1986 £6.03 (BEK) £6.90 (ALL) £7.25 (DAV, OL)
1985 £6.65 (AI) £6.75 (GRE) £6.90 (EL, LAY)
   £6.99 (BYR) £7.25 (DAV) £7.84 (HA)
   £9.00 (WRI)
1983 £8.60 (WRI)

Belair *1er grand cru classé St-Émilion*
1989 EC £187.15 (HAH)
1988 EC £160.00 (WW)
1986 £21.60 (HUN)
1985 £17.25 (LAY) £19.50 (AD)

de Bel-Air *Lalande-de-Pomerol*
1985 £7.75 (DAV)
1982 £8.05 (WY) £8.49 (BO)

Belgrave *5ème cru classé Haut-Médoc*
1985 £10.45 (NI)
1982 £7.99 (WHI)
1979 £9.75 (GRE)
1970 £25.30 (TW)

Bel-Orme-Tronquoy-de-Lalande *cru bourgeois Haut-Médoc*
1983 £5.85 (DAV)
1982 £6.50 (DAV)

Beychevelle *4ème cru classé St-Julien*

1989 IB £180.00 (PIP)
1989 EC £175.00 (HIC) £176.00 (HUN)
   £179.25 (HAH)
1988 £17.25 (HIG)
1988 EC £122.00 (BIB) £160.00 (HUN)

1986 £16.99 (BO)
1986 magnum £35.68 (BY)
1985 £17.39 (AV) £18.45 (AUG) £20.05 (AN)
   £24.10 (TAN) £26.65 (VIC)
1985 magnum £42.14 (BY)
1984 £12.64 (AV) £15.34 (BY) £15.50 (GI)
   £17.95 (AUG)
1983 £15.90 (GI) £17.69 (WHI) £17.70 (TAN)
   £179.00 (VIG)
1982 £19.55 (HAG) £21.15 (AI) £21.93 (BY)
   £22.34 (TAN) £25.45 (WIL) £26.35 (PE)
1981 £19.78 (CH) £23.50 (PIP)
1978 £22.04 (BIB) £23.50 (ALL)
1976 £25.40 (BIB) £27.35 (OL)
1976 magnum £50.80 (BIB)
1975 £29.50 (GI) £29.75 (OL) £37.50 (VIC)
1975 magnum £35.75 (HAG)
1970 £40.00 (WY) £45.00 (RES, GI)
1966 £52.71 (BIB) £56.46 (YF) £57.00 (WY)
1961 £109.00 (WY)

Blaignan *cru bourgeois Médoc*
1986 £5.45 (THR)
1985 £5.45 (THR) £5.85 (WIL)
1984 £4.09 (WIL)
1983 £5.19 (WIL)

le Bon-Pasteur *Pomerol*
1989 EC £143.00 (HUN)
1987 £12.64 (BY)
1986 £15.00 (HUN)
1985 £14.29 (BYR) £19.00 (HUN)
1983 £13.05 (HAH)

la Bonnelle *St-Émilion*
1985 £7.49 (LO) £7.65 (WCL)

le Boscq *cru bourgeois St-Éstèphe*
1985 £6.09 (PE)
1983 £5.45 (PE)
1981 £6.80 (CHA)

Bourgneuf-Vayron *Pomerol*
1985 £15.00 (HUN)
1979 £12.72 (BEK) £14.98 (PIP)

Bouscaut *cru classé Pessac-Léognan*
1989 EC £85.00 (RAE)
1986 £9.60 (RAE)
1985 £9.80 (RAE)

Boyd-Cantenac *3ème cru classé Margaux*
1986 £10.35 (ASK)
1985 £16.99 (WIL)
1983 £12.94 (WW)

Branaire-Ducru *4ème cru classé St-Julien*
1985 £14.45 (BYR) £16.48 (HIG) £16.99 (BO) £17.50 (DI)
1983 £13.99 (BOT) £15.80 (NI) £17.15 (PD)
1982 £19.85 (HAG) £22.00 (WY)
1978 £18.00 (WY) £19.50 (LAY) £20.38 (TAN)
1978 double magnum £103.50 (WY)
1976 £24.73 (TAN)
1966 £49.99 (PE)

Brane-Cantenac *2ème cru classé Margaux*
1988 EC £92.00 (BIB)
1986 £12.69 (BYR) £17.00 (HAG)
1985 £15.79 (BYR) £16.77 (BIB)
1984 £12.99 (BO) £14.50 (GI)
1983 £12.49 (HOG) £17.25 (WHI)
1982 £16.62 (BY) £17.50 (GI)
1982 magnum £40.00 (ALL)
1980 £11.49 (BO)
1979 £12.95 (UP) £18.50 (OL)
1978 £17.00 (HOG) £19.55 (WY) £19.90 (OL)
1978 magnum £38.50 (GI)
1971 £22.88 (TW)
1970 £20.15 (PE) £31.00 (WY) £31.75 (OL)
1966 £43.50 (WY)
1964 £25.00 (VIG)
1961 £55.78 (REI) £57.50 (BIB) £72.00 (WY)

du Breuil *cru bourgeois Haut-Médoc*
1987 £7.60 (WRI)
1981 £6.65 (WS)

Cabannieux *Graves*
1989 EC £47.00 (HUN)
1986 £5.70 (WW) £6.69 (WHI)

Cadet-Piola *grand cru classé St-Émilion*
1988 EC £92.00 (BIB) £113.00 (HUN)

Calon-Ségur *3ème cru classé St-Éstèphe*
1989 EC £152.00 (HUN)
1988 EC £130.00 (WW)
1986 £13.59 (WIL) £14.49 (BYR)
1985 £16.29 (BIB) £17.50 (HUN)
1983 £21.50 (UN)
1982 £24.00 (UN) £25.88 (EL)
1978 £23.00 (EL)
1970 £25.00 (HAG) £38.00 (WY) £42.00 (BE)
1961 £66.00 (WY)

de Camensac *5ème cru classé Haut-Médoc*
1986 £8.95 (DI)

1985 £8.49 (TES) £8.50 (AI) £9.38 (TAN) £9.50 (LOR) £10.89 (OL)
1983 £9.50 (LOR) £11.00 (HA) £11.11 (YF)
1982 £11.15 (WRI) £14.50 (HAH)
1979 £12.14 (HA)
1976 £16.68 (REI)
1975 £16.50 (GI)

Canon *1er grand cru classé St-Émilion*
1989 EC £238.00 (HUN)
1988 EC £195.00 (WW)
1987 £13.95 (RAE)
1986 £19.95 (RAE) £21.95 (BYR)
1985 £26.50 (HUN)
1983 £20.25 (BYR) £26.80 (GI)
1982 £30.00 (UP)
1979 £20.80 (BE)
1970 £32.75 (REI)

Canon-la-Gaffelière *grand cru classé St-Émilion*
1989 EC £118.00 (RAE)
1985 £10.93 (REI) £11.13 (BY) £11.49 (BYR) £12.94 (EL)
1982 £11.75 (BO)
1979 £16.70 (WRI)

Cantemerle *5ème cru classé Haut-Médoc*
1987 £9.99 (OD)
★**1985** £12.65 (BIB) £13.99 (BO) £14.99 (PE)
1984 £8.00 (UP) £10.95 (BYR) £13.00 (TAN)
1982 £12.50 (HOG)
1981 £11.00 (HOG) £11.15 (AI) £13.75 (OL) £14.55 (REI) £17.55 (PE)
1980 £13.09 (PE)
1979 £14.00 (WY) £14.50 (NI) £15.00 (UN)
1978 £13.71 (HOG) £15.00 (WY) £18.49 (BO)
1975 £15.70 (NI)
1967 £20.00 (VIG)
1966 £25.00 (RES) £38.00 (WY)

Cantenac-Brown *3ème cru classé Margaux*
1989 EC £119.00 (HUN)
1982 £21.50 (WRI)
1970 £32.77 (TW)

> *Please remember that* **Webster's** *is a price GUIDE and not a price LIST. It is not meant to replace up-to-date merchants' lists.*

Carbonnieux *cru classé Pessac-Léognan*
1986 £7.28 (ASK)
1975 £13.98 (BER)

de Cardaillan *Graves*
1986 £5.25 (DAV)
1984 £4.99 (DAV)
1982 £5.65 (DAV) £7.00 (HIC)
1980 £5.19 (WIL)

la Cardonne *cru grand bourgeois Médoc*
1985 £4.85 (HOG) £6.35 (BYR) £10.23 (PIP)
1982 £5.75 (ASD) £7.00 (HIC)

Caronne-Ste-Gemme *cru grand
bourgeois exceptionnel Haut-Médoc*
1985 £6.19 (BYR) £6.50 (REI) £6.85 (AI)
£6.90 (EL) £7.45 (PE)
1983 £6.15 (BO) £6.55 (BYR) £6.59 (WHI)
£7.75 (LOR) £8.25 (WCL)
1982 £9.45 (WS)
1979 £7.99 (BO)

du Castéra *cru bourgeois Médoc*
1986 £5.49 (AUG)
1982 £6.49 (BO)

Certan-de-May *Pomerol*
1985 £34.75 (LAY) £49.50 (HUN)
1981 £31.50 (LAY) £34.75 (ALL)

Chasse-Spleen *cru grand bourgeois
exceptionnel Moulis*
1989 EC £112.00 (HUN) £114.70 (HAH)
1988 IB £103.15 (CHA)
1988 EC £95.00 (VIG) £99.96 (LAY)
1987 £8.23 (TAN) £9.18 (CHA)
1986 £9.79 (BYR) £12.65 (TAN) £12.75 (AI)
£13.59 (WIL)
★**1985** £11.19 (BYR) £11.30 (BE) £11.50 (BIB)
£11.95 (RES) £11.99 (BOT) £12.95 (ALL)
1985 magnum £23.00 (BIB)
1984 £7.60 (MV) £7.69 (BYR)
1983 £10.49 (BO)
1982 £14.50 (AI) £19.99 (PE)
1981 £12.50 (AI)
1978 £13.90 (BIB) £18.50 (RES)

Chauvin *grand cru classé St-Émilion*
1989 EC £87.00 (RAE)
1987 EC £65.00 (RAE)
1979 £9.95 (RAE)

Cheret-Pitres *Graves*
1985 £4.80 (STA) £7.38 (CHA)

Cheval-Blanc *1er grand cru classé St-
Émilion*
1988 EC £390.00 (HUN)
1987 IB £290.00 (CB)
1986 £39.75 (DAV)
1986 EC £375.00 (BIB)
1985 £45.00 (HAY) £46.50 (DAV) £57.00 (RES)
£60.10 (AN) £65.00 (HUN)
1984 £23.15 (CB) £37.15 (BER)
1983 £44.50 (DAV) £48.00 (WS) £49.80 (GI)
1982 £55.00 (UP) £62.00 (VIC) £65.00 (ALL,
GI) £69.00 (WY) £69.50 (AD) £74.50 (UN)
£79.50 (DAV) £88.65 (WIL)
1981 £37.70 (HAG) £40.39 (AV) £41.45 (BER)
£45.00 (GI) £46.50 (DAV) £51.00 (NI)
£53.30 (VIN) £60.10 (AN)
1979 £41.45 (BYR) £42.00 (HAG) £45.00 (WY)
£67.50 (DAV)
1978 £59.42 (BIB) £60.00 (BER) £67.00 (GI)
1978 magnum £118.83 (BIB)
1976 £59.90 (BIB)
1975 £72.50 (DAV) £79.50 (GI) £80.00 (RES)
1970 £115.00 (DAV)
1964 £110.00 (OL)
1962 £80.00 (WY)
1961 £333.00 (WY)
1959 £147.00 (WY)
1949 £316.00 (WY)
1945 £425.00 (WY)

Chicane *Graves*
1986 £6.64 (TAN)
1985 £4.79 (BYR)
1983 £6.90 (AD)

Cissac *cru grand bourgeois exceptionnel
Haut-Médoc*
1989 EC £67.00 (HUN) £68.30 (HAH) £69.00
(HIC) £70.00 (HAY)
1988 EC £51.00 (BIB) £58.30 (WW) £60.00
(HIC) £61.44 (TAN) £61.92 (LAY) £62.00
(HAY) £69.00 (ASK)
1986 £7.95 (DI) £11.30 (TAN)
1985 £7.85 (NI) £8.62 (HIG) £8.63 (EL)
1984 £6.87 (IR) £7.18 (HIG)
1983 £10.63 (BEK) £11.50 (HUN) £11.81 (TAN)
£11.95 (LAY) £11.96 (YF) £12.41 (PIP)
£14.06 (VIN)
1982 £10.99 (BYR) £11.55 (PE) £13.75 (WRI)
£26.34 (EL)
1981 £10.15 (EL) £10.49 (CH)
1981 magnum £20.70 (EL)
1979 £12.75 (BIB) £12.89 (YF) £12.95 (WRI)
1975 £17.31 (EL)
1970 £23.86 (EL) £28.84 (YF)

Citran *cru grand bourgeois exceptionnel Haut-Médoc*
★**1985** £6.09 (PE) £6.99 (BYR)
1983 £6.95 (WHI)

la Clare *cru bourgeois Médoc*
1986 £5.75 (GRE)
1985 £4.79 (HOG) £6.40 (IR)

Clerc-Milon *5ème cru classé Pauillac*
1988 EC £107.00 (HUN)
1985 £12.48 (REI) £13.95 (AUG) £16.79 (WIL)
1984 £9.25 (BO) £14.49 (WIL)
1983 £14.95 (AUG)
1982 £15.21 (HOG) £17.35 (WIL)
1949 £59.00 (VIG)

Clos des Jacobins *grand cru classé St-Émilion*
1983 £12.65 (WIL)
1980 £17.50 (UP)
1977 £10.15 (PE) £12.50 (UP)

Clos du Clocher *Pomerol*
1987 £8.69 (BIB) £10.55 (BIB)
1986 £12.70 (HUN)

Clos du Marquis *St-Julien*
1989 EC £97.00 (HUN)
1987 £9.44 (BY)
1986 £8.49 (WIZ) £9.45 (DAV)
★**1985** £9.10 (BIB) £12.45 (THR)
1984 £7.85 (BEK, VIC) £8.99 (BYR) £10.81 (BY)
1983 £10.69 (VIC) £11.95 (RES) £12.25 (LAY) £12.99 (NI)

Clos Fourtet *1er grand cru classé St-Émilion*
1983 £23.85 (PIP)
1982 £15.95 (WIL) £18.25 (BOT)
1960 £14.95 (VIG)

Clos René *Pomerol*
1985 £16.04 (TW)
1975 £15.90 (HOG) £19.90 (GI)

la Clotte *grand cru classé St-Émilion*
1986 £12.22 (CB)
1985 £13.95 (CB)

Connétable Talbot *St-Julien*
1985 £9.75 (DAV) £9.99 (PE)
1984 £7.85 (UN) £8.65 (WIL) £9.37 (HIC)
1983 £9.50 (UP) £9.95 (ASD) £10.25 (PE)

la Conseillante *Pomerol*
1987 £20.45 (WHI)
1981 £28.90 (CB)
1978 £23.48 (BIB) £25.00 (AD)
1970 £42.00 (GI)

Cos d'Estournel *2ème cru classé St-Éstèphe*

1989 EC £245.00 (HUN)
1988 EC £145.00 (BIB)
1986 £23.99 (BO)
1986 EC £150.00 (HAG)
1985 £20.25 (BYR) £21.60 (AN)
1985 magnum £41.69 (BY)
1984 £11.99 (OD) £12.65 (ELL) £13.41 (CB) £14.15 (PE) £14.55 (BYR) £15.81 (BIB) £15.95 (GI) £17.58 (BER) £20.09 (WIL)
1984 double magnum £65.00 (GI)
1984 jeroboam £190.00 (GI)
1983 £17.80 (HOG) £18.80 (NI) £19.60 (AN) £20.78 (CH) £20.79 (BY) £21.50 (GI) £23.00 (BER) £23.50 (ALL) £25.13 (TAN) £27.65 (AUG) £27.75 (CB)
1983 magnum £45.00 (LAY)
1982 £32.89 (BYR) £39.75 (DAV)
1981 £23.15 (CB)
1978 £28.80 (LAY)
1975 double magnum £138.00 (EL)
1975 jeroboam £230.00 (EL)
1971 double magnum £99.00 (GI)
1970 £45.00 (RES) £50.68 (TAN)
1961 £86.50 (BAR)
1959 £145.00 (RES)
1928 £184.00 (REI)

Cos Labory *5ème cru classé St-Éstèphe*
1985 £11.20 (TAN) £13.15 (PIP)
1983 £8.99 (PE) £10.54 (PIP)
1971 £17.50 (GI)

Coufran *cru grand bourgeois Haut-Médoc*
1981 £8.25 (BEK) £8.60 (YF) £9.80 (AI)
1979 £10.75 (GRE)

le Couvent *grand cru St-Émilion*
1986 £6.95 (PD) £6.99 (BOT)

Couvent-des-Jacobins *grand cru classé St-Émilion*
1982 £17.50 (PIP)
1980 £9.99 (WIL)

le Crock *cru grand bourgeois exceptionnel St-Éstèphe*
1989 EC £65.00 (RAE)
1988 EC £50.00 (BIB)
1986 £8.70 (RAE) £8.97 (HA)
1985 £7.95 (RAE) £8.09 (PE)

la Croix-de-Gay *Pomerol*
1985 £11.02 (BIB)
1983 £12.75 (BIB)
1982 £16.77 (BY) £16.99 (BO)
1981 £11.26 (HOG)

Curé-Bon-la-Madeleine *grand cru classé St-Émilion*
1986 £11.75 (OL)
1983 £14.25 (OL)
1982 £15.50 (OL)

Dauzac *5ème cru classé Margaux*
1988 EC £84.00 (WW)
1982 £15.22 (CB)

Deyrem-Valentin *cru bourgeois Margaux*
1989 EC £75.00 (RAE)
1987 EC £52.00 (RAE)
1986 £7.95 (RAE)
1985 £7.95 (RAE) £9.65 (PE)
1984 £7.50 (RAE)
1979 magnum £18.21 (BIB) £19.90 (RAE)
1975 magnum £29.70 (RAE)

Domaine de Chevalier *cru classé Pessac-Léognan*
1989 EC £246.00 (HUN)
1986 £22.19 (BYR) £25.97 (WW)
1985 £23.96 (BIB) £26.50 (HUN)
1984 £14.38 (BIB) £15.69 (BYR) £15.95 (RAE)
£16.08 (BY) £21.60 (AN)
1983 £18.29 (BYR) £20.75 (WHI) £22.25 (BO)
£22.30 (AD) £25.43 (PIP)
1982 £24.44 (BIB) £25.60 (BE) £32.75 (AD)
£36.80 (TW)
1979 £24.00 (RES)
1978 £25.99 (BYR) £37.50 (BAR)
1975 £28.00 (BE) £33.50 (GI)
1966 £42.50 (DAV)

Domaine de l'Église *Pomerol*
1988 £10.73 (HIG)
1986 £12.75 (DAV)
1985 £13.95 (DAV)
1983 £11.50 (HIG) £13.75 (DAV)
1980 £9.39 (HIG)
1962 £21.62 (TW)

Domaine de Fontarney *Margaux*
1983 £6.79 (HOG)
1981 £8.00 (IR)

Domaine de Gaillat *Graves*
1985 £5.19 (BYR)
1983 £6.75 (ALL) £6.90 (AD) £7.95 (RES)

Domaine la Grave *Graves*
★**1989 EC** £71.20 (HAH)
1988 £7.18 (HIG)

la Dominique *grand cru classé St-Émilion*
1989 EC £143.00 (HUN)
1985 £13.00 (MV) £13.99 (BYR)
1983 £11.68 (BY) £12.19 (BYR)

Ducru-Beaucaillou *2ème cru classé St-Julien*

1989 EC £259.00 (HUN)
1988 £23.00 (HIG)
1988 EC £210.00 (HAY)
1986 £24.00 (HAG) £24.30 (CB)
1986 EC £205.00 (BIB)
1985 £28.27 (BIB) £33.53 (EL)
1984 £15.10 (CB) £15.87 (ELL) £17.15 (PE)
£21.11 (EL) £22.80 (BER) £24.89 (WIL)
1983 £24.96 (LAY) £25.00 (ALL) £25.30 (AD)
£27.75 (CB) £30.15 (BER) £195.00 (VIG)
1983 magnum £54.80 (HUN)
1983 imperial £402.50 (HUN)
1982 £30.00 (BER)
1981 £22.50 (GRE) £22.60 (BER) £23.73 (CB)
£24.75 (DAV)

1979 £18.00 (HOG) £25.95 (DAV) £26.48 (BEK)
£28.00 (PE) £32.35 (AN)
1978 £35.00 (UP)
1976 £45.00 (RES)
1975 £23.00 (HAG) £35.91 (BY) £45.00 (GRE)
1975 double magnum £138.00 (EL)
1975 jeroboam £230.00 (EL)
1971 £29.50 (GRE)
1970 £48.00 (GI) £54.15 (BIB) £70.00 (RES)
1962 £50.79 (BIB)
1961 £98.50 (OL) £126.50 (REI) £135.00 (RES)
1959 £115.00 (WY)
1949 £65.00 (VIG)

Duhart-Milon-Rothschild *4ème cru
classé Pauillac*
1989 EC £142.00 (HUN)
1986 £18.00 (HAG)
1983 £11.59 (BYR) £13.50 (OL)
1982 £14.75 (BO)

l'Église-Clinet *Pomerol*
1989 EC £150.00 (RAE) £168.00 (HUN)
1983 £15.01 (TAN)
1962 £31.63 (REI)

l'Enclos *Pomerol*
1989 EC £96.96 (PIP)
1985 £12.29 (BYR) £15.00 (CB)
1980 £10.09 (WIL) £10.87 (PIP)
1979 £13.25 (BO)

l'Ermitage de Chasse-Spleen *Haut-
Médoc*
1987 £7.60 (AN)
1986 £6.49 (THR)

l'Étoile *Graves*
1985 £5.45 (PE)
1984 £4.15 (PE)

l'Évangile *Pomerol*
1984 £20.31 (CB)
1976 £37.95 (TW)
1952 £59.00 (VIG)

Ferrande *Graves*
1986 £6.00 (LOR) £6.74 (BEK) £7.99 (PIP)

Feytit-Clinet *Pomerol*
1989 EC £108.90 (HAH)
1987 £8.35 (AD)
1986 £11.60 (AD)
1985 £13.50 (AD) £14.46 (TAN)
1970 £20.00 (VIG)

Les Fiefs-de-Lagrange *St-Julien*
1989 EC £70.75 (HAH)
1986 £10.35 (OL) £10.99 (THR)
★**1985** £7.95 (LAY)

de Fieuzal *cru classé Pessac-Léognan*
1989 EC £120.00 (HUN) £124.50 (HAH)
1988 EC £108.84 (TAN)
★**1985** £10.93 (REI) £12.55 (PE) £12.89 (BYR)
£13.00 (HUN) £13.75 (BO) £15.05 (AD)
1984 £7.99 (PE) £9.25 (BO) £12.40 (BER)
1983 £9.99 (PE)
1982 £16.99 (PIP) £19.99 (PE)
1981 £10.75 (BO)

Figeac *1er grand cru classé St-Émilion*

CHATEAU - FIGEAC
SAINT EMILION PREMIER GRAND CRÙ CLASSÉ
St ÉMILION
1981
MIS EN BOUTEILLES AU CHÂTEAU
PRODUCE OF FRANCE

1989 EC £248.00 (HIC) £256.00 (HUN)
1985 £29.95 (THR)
1985 EC £227.00 (HAG)
1984 £15.15 (AV)
1983 £19.99 (GRE) £21.50 (THR)
1982 £29.50 (GI) £30.35 (PIP) £32.00 (VIC)
1981 £21.95 (BYR)
1970 £55.58 (BIB)

la Fleur-du-Gazin *Pomerol*
1985 £13.50 (LAY)
1983 £13.25 (AD)

la Fleur-Pétrus *Pomerol*
1988 IB £230.00 (CB)
1988 EC £237.00 (LAY)
1981 £25.45 (CB)

Fombrauge *grand cru St-Émilion*
1989 EC £63.00 (HUN)
1988 £69.00 (HUN)
1987 £7.92 (PIP)
1986 £8.66 (BY) £8.93 (HA) £10.10 (HUN)
1985 £10.75 (BY) £10.90 (GRE) £11.04 (HA)
1984 £7.29 (AUG) £7.34 (HA) £8.39 (CH)
1984 magnum £17.09 (CH)
1983 £4.65 (CH) £8.29 (AUG) £10.75 (WHI)
1983 magnum £17.09 (CH)

Fonbadet *cru bourgeois supérieur*
Pauillac
1986 £10.70 (HUN)
1983 £9.90 (HOG)

Fonplégade *grand cru classé St-Émilion*
1985 £11.50 (ALL) £13.19 (WIL)

Fonroque *grand cru classé St-Émilion*
1985 £18.00 (HUN)
1983 £8.99 (BYR) £9.15 (HOG) £12.05 (HAH)

les Forts-de-Latour *Pauillac*
1984 £11.67 (HA) £14.94 (YF)
1983 £15.00 (HA) £15.45 (SAI) £17.95 (DI)
1982 £25.00 (HA)
1979 £15.50 (WAI) £17.50 (HA) £21.08 (BIB)
1978 £28.88 (HA)
1976 £26.40 (HA)
1975 £23.48 (BIB) £24.00 (HA) £24.15 (PE)
  £25.00 (RAE) £25.55 (AD)
1974 £14.50 (HA)
1970 £37.38 (REI) £43.20 (HA)

le Fougueyrat *grand cru St-Émilion*
1986 £7.45 (STA)
1985 £6.29 (WIL)

Fourcas-Dupré *cru grand bourgeois*
exceptionnel Listrac
1986 £6.75 (BO)
1983 £7.96 (PIP)
1975 £12.45 (BAR)

Fourcas-Hosten *cru grand bourgeois*
exceptionnel Listrac
1988 £7.47 (HIG)
1986 £7.95 (DI) £8.62 (HIG)
1985 £8.29 (BYR) £8.62 (HIG) £8.75 (BO)
  £8.95 (DI) £9.50 (AI)
1984 £7.95 (DI)
1982 £9.40 (HAG) £9.75 (BAR)
1949 £75.00 (REI)

Fourney *grand cru St-Émilion*
1985 £9.15 (WIL)
1983 £9.25 (WIL)
1982 £10.29 (WIL)
1978 £14.09 (WIL)

la Gaffelière *1er grand cru classé St-Émilion*
1985 £22.25 (WIL)
1983 £19.55 (WIL)
1978 £56.35 (WIL)

> Stars (★) indicate wines
> selected by the editors as
> particularly good value

1975 £19.00 (HOG)
1970 £23.50 (HOG)
1952 £45.00 (VIG)

la Garde *Pessac-Léognan*
1985 £6.49 (BO)
1983 £5.99 (BO) £6.89 (WIL) £12.77 (VIN)
★**1982** £8.29 (WIL)
1981 £6.75 (BO) £8.15 (WHI)

Gazin *Pomerol*
1989 EC £156.00 (HIC) £161.65 (HAH)
  £165.00 (HUN)
1988 EC £125.88 (LAY)
1985 £16.05 (AN) £17.46 (EL)
1985 EC £124.00 (HAG)
1978 £19.50 (GI)
1961 £46.00 (TW)
1947 £92.00 (REI)
1937 £50.00 (VIG)

Giscours *3ème cru classé Margaux*
1989 EC £138.00 (BE)
1988 EC £121.56 (TAN)
1984 £11.65 (CB)
1983 £16.25 (BOT) £16.75 (UP) £18.55 (CB)
  £19.95 (PD)
1982 £16.75 (UP) £17.25 (BIB) £23.28 (TAN)
1981 £16.50 (UP)
1979 £19.13 (CB)
1975 £27.79 (BIB)
1970 £37.38 (RIB) £38.95 (OL) £42.00 (BE)
1970 magnum £78.00 (WY)
1966 £40.25 (TW)
1961 £78.00 (WY)

du Glana *cru grand bourgeois*
exceptionnel St-Julien
1984 £8.95 (BER)
1961 £29.50 (UP)

Gloria *cru bourgeois St-Julien*
1986 £9.50 (LOR)
1985 £8.19 (VIC) £11.75 (ALL) £13.95 (GRE)
1985 EC £76.00 (HAG)
1983 £11.50 (UN) £13.59 (WIL) £15.24 (CHA)
1982 £17.25 (BIB)
1966 £30.65 (HAG)

Grand-Lartigue *St-Émilion*
1986 £6.99 (PE) £7.98 (BIB)
1985 £7.95 (RAE)
1983 £8.69 (PE)

Grand-Mayne *grand cru classé St-Émilion*
1985 £11.56 (BEK) £13.79 (BYR)

Grand-Pontet *grand cru classé St-Émilion*
1988 EC £83.52 (LAY)
1986 £9.30 (HOG)
1985 £11.30 (LAY)

Grand-Puy-Ducasse *5ème cru classé Pauillac*
1986 £8.89 (BYR) £10.25 (LOR)
1985 £12.89 (WIL) £15.49 (BO)
1984 £7.95 (SAI)
1983 £11.42 (BOR)
1979 £11.95 (OL) £14.50 (WRI)
1978 £16.70 (WRI)

Grand-Puy-Lacoste *5ème cru classé Pauillac*
1989 EC £135.00 (RAE) £142.00 (HUN)
1988 EC £124.44 (LAY)
1986 £14.95 (DAV) £17.00 (HAG)
1984 £10.25 (PE) £10.38 (AV) £11.20 (GI)
1983 £13.78 (HOG) £14.80 (NI) £16.19 (BYR)
        £16.25 (BYR) £16.35 (WHI) £18.95 (OL)
1982 £17.94 (WW)
1979 £25.00 (RES)
1975 £23.51 (LAY)
1970 £32.78 (REI) £33.35 (EL)
1967 £20.00 (VIG)

Grangeneuve de Figeac *grand cru St-Émilion*
1987 £7.99 (THR)
1985 £7.99 (TES)

la Grave-Trigant-de-Boisset *Pomerol*
1985 £23.50 (HUN)
1980 £11.76 (HA)
1978 £18.98 (REI)

Gressier-Grand-Poujeaux *cru bourgeois supérieur Moulis*
1989 EC £69.00 (HUN)
1983 £6.99 (BYR) £10.40 (WRI)
1982 £10.95 (WRI)
1981 £8.42 (BEK) £10.31 (PIP)
1979 £8.70 (MV) £8.95 (ALL) £11.00 (WRI)

Greysac *cru grand bourgeois Médoc*
1986 £5.59 (BOT, PD) £5.99 (OD)
1985 £6.09 (BYR) £7.15 (PE)

Gruaud-Larose *2ème cru classé St-Julien*
1989 EC £225.00 (HUN)
1988 EC £140.00 (BIB)
1986 £15.99 (BO) £16.65 (BY) £21.00 (HAG)
1986 EC £200.00 (BIB)
1985 £15.95 (BYR) £16.29 (BIB) £18.25 (DAV)
1984 £13.15 (PE) £17.02 (BER) £17.89 (WIL)
1983 £16.99 (PE) £18.00 (WY) £18.25 (DAV)
        £23.25 (BER) £23.85 (WIL)
1982 £19.90 (HAG) £20.49 (BO) £21.08 (CB)
        £23.00 (BIB) £25.15 (PE) £27.06 (TAN)
1981 £17.97 (BIB) £18.15 (PE) £20.13 (TAN)
1981 magnum £36.30 (PE)
1980 £11.75 (BO)
1979 £16.99 (BL) £22.88 (TW) £25.15 (PE)
1978 £23.00 (EL) £24.41 (CB) £26.15 (PE)
1978 magnum £57.50 (TW)
1977 £9.99 (WHI) £13.50 (UP) £17.39 (VIN)
1976 £23.00 (TAN)
1975 £23.15 (CB) £32.42 (TAN)
1975 ½ bottle £14.95 (BAR)
1970 £31.00 (GRE) £37.50 (OL) £38.50 (NI)
        £40.00 (WY) £46.56 (TAN)
1966 £49.50 (BAR) £52.00 (WY)
1961 £78.99 (BO)
1959 £42.00 (GI)
1949 £161.00 (WY)

la Gurgue *cru bourgeois supérieur Margaux*
1986 £7.15 (BYR) £9.90 (AI)
1983 £10.25 (AI)

Hanteillan *cru grand bourgeois Haut-Médoc*
1989 EC £42.70 (HAH) £46.00 (HUN)
1987 £6.25 (PIP)
1986 £5.85 (WIL) £5.99 (BO) £8.07 (PIP)
1985 £6.09 (PE) £6.49 (BO)

Haut-Badon *grand cru St-Émilion*
1986 £7.95 (VIG)

Haut-Bages-Avérous *cru bourgeois Pauillac*
1989 EC £95.00 (HUN)
1987 £9.63 (BY)
1986 £10.95 (MAJ) £12.75 (THR) £13.11 (BY)
1985 £11.49 (VIC) £14.49 (BY)
1984 £9.81 (BY)
1979 £15.84 (BY)

Haut-Bages-Libéral *5ème cru classé*
Pauillac
1989 EC £85.00 (HUN)
★**1988 EC** £96.00 (WW)
1986 £9.99 (BYR) £11.00 (LOR) £12.00 (HIC)
1985 £10.95 (BYR) £12.29 (AI)
1983 £11.69 (BYR) £12.90 (AI)
1982 £13.80 (BE) £15.95 (WCL)
1979 imperial £155.00 (WY)
1975 £19.50 (BAR)

Haut-Bailly *cru classé Pessac-Léognan*
1989 EC £123.00 (RAE) £130.00 (HUN)
1988 EC £92.00 (BIB) £112.00 (HAY)
1985 £13.50 (LAY) £15.00 (HAY) £15.05 (AD)
£18.70 (EL)
1985 EC £110.00 (HAG)
1984 £9.10 (BIB) £13.96 (BY)
1983 £11.49 (AUG)
1983 IB £80.00 (HAG)
1982 £11.99 (PE)

Haut-Batailley *5ème cru classé Pauillac*
1986 £13.59 (WIL)
1986 EC £76.00 (HAG)
1985 £11.59 (BYR) £13.85 (WCL)
1984 £10.95 (IR)
1983 £11.74 (ASK) £12.99 (BOT) £16.15 (PD)
1983 IB £89.00 (HAG)
1982 £15.49 (BO) £15.90 (GI)
1966 £29.75 (BIB)

Haut-Bergey *Pessac-Léognan*
1981 £9.95 (RAE) £11.15 (PE)
1979 £9.85 (RAE) £11.95 (BIB)

Haut-Brion *1er cru classé Pessac-Léognan*

CHATEAU HAUT BRION 1984

1989 EC £456.30 (HAH)
1988 EC £308.00 (BIB) £350.00 (HUN)
1986 £38.56 (BY) £39.00 (DI)
1986 EC £340.00 (BIB)
1985 £42.90 (HUN) £44.50 (DAV) £57.00 (RES)
£58.99 (BO) £60.10 (AN)

1984 £26.15 (PE) £26.39 (BYR) £32.50 (GI)
1983 £37.85 (BIB) £39.99 (PE) £41.62 (HOG)
£42.50 (ALL) £44.50 (DAV) £46.00 (GI)
£46.00 (ELL) £55.10 (AN)
1982 £61.25 (WHI) £62.00 (WY) £62.29 (BIB)
£63.00 (GI) £68.00 (VIC) £76.00 (DAV)
1981 £41.00 (UN) £42.15 (BER) £53.00 (NI)
1980 £23.50 (GI) £31.95 (OL)
1979 £41.86 (BY)
1978 £46.00 (BIB) £56.00 (BER) £57.00 (UN)
£59.99 (PE) £62.00 (GI) £79.00 (VIC)
1978 magnum £92.00 (BIB)
1976 £49.50 (GI) £62.00 (RES) £69.00 (TW)
1971 £44.85 (HAG) £54.00 (BER)
1970 £80.50 (BIB) £84.00 (WY) £95.00 (UP)
1967 £45.00 (OL) £75.00 (WY)
1966 £110.00 (DAV)
1964 £59.50 (BL) £69.58 (HA)
1962 £63.25 (REI)
1960 £46.00 (UP)
1959 £180.00 (RES)
1955 £104.00 (WY) £160.00 (RES)
1952 £110.00 (GI)
1949 £316.00 (WY)
1945 £327.75 (REI) £391.00 (WY)

Haut-Marbuzet *cru grand bourgeois*
exceptionnel St-Éstèphe
1985 £10.79 (BYR) £10.99 (BO) £11.50 (UP)
1985 ½ bottle £5.79 (BYR)
1985 magnum £21.49 (BYR)
1984 £11.20 (WRI)
1983 ½ bottle £5.19 (BYR)

Haut-Sarpe *grand cru classé St-Émilion*
1983 £10.19 (BYR)
1966 £16.68 (REI)

Hortevie *cru bourgeois St-Julien*
1985 £7.95 (PE)
1982 £6.99 (PE)
1981 £6.39 (PE)

d'Issan *3ème cru classé Margaux*
1989 EC £118.00 (HUN)
1988 IB £115.70 (CHA)
1988 EC £88.00 (BIB)
1986 £13.80 (HIG)
1985 £10.93 (REI) £14.99 (BYR) £15.56 (BER)
1984 £9.55 (GI) £9.85 (BYR) £11.24 (BY, CHA)
1983 £14.45 (BYR) £16.35 (NI) £17.99 (BO)
1983 IB £123.00 (HAG)
1982 £10.75 (HAG) £14.38 (BIB) £16.35 (NI)
1981 £20.48 (BY)
1966 £27.60 (BIB)

Jalousie-Beaulieu *Bordeaux supérieur*
1989 EC £28.00 (HUN)
1988 EC £26.00 (HUN)

Kirwan *3ème cru classé Margaux*
1989 EC £96.50 (OL)
1985 £12.95 (BYR) £12.99 (BO)
1984 £11.13 (IR) £13.50 (DI)
1983 £15.95 (DI) £16.39 (TW)
1982 £14.99 (BO)
1981 £15.40 (AI) £16.95 (DI)

Labégorce *cru bourgeois supérieur Margaux*
1985 £8.50 (NI)
1982 £10.15 (WHI)

Labégorce-Zédé *cru bourgeois supérieur Margaux*
1989 EC £88.80 (PIP) £89.00 (HUN) £91.10 (HAH)
1988 EC £62.00 (BIB)
1986 £8.65 (RAE) £9.75 (DAV)
1985 £8.79 (PE) £9.10 (BIB) £9.29 (BYR) £10.25 (BY)
1984 £5.79 (CB) £5.99 (PE) £6.95 (GI) £7.19 (BIB)
1983 £9.93 (HOG) £10.20 (BOR)

Lacoste-Borie *Pauillac*
1986 £8.25 (DAV)
1985 £8.75 (DAV) £9.20 (EL)
1984 £7.33 (BY)
1983 £9.40 (AD)

Laffitte-Carcasset *cru bourgeois St-Éstèphe*
1985 £6.29 (TES)
1983 £7.25 (WHI) £8.94 (IR) £11.62 (VIN)

Lafite-Rothschild *1er cru classé Pauillac*

1987 £37.72 (BY)
1986 £15.95 (DI)
1985 £35.25 (BOT)
1984 £26.65 (AV) £30.15 (PE) £40.25 (BYR)

1983 £40.39 (AV) £51.75 (EL)
1982 £57.99 (BO) £74.27 (BIB) £75.00 (UP)
1981 £32.99 (BO) £51.59 (WHI) £52.41 (IR) £55.43 (BY) £57.50 (HAG) £59.00 (GI)
1980 £39.99 (PE)
1980 magnum £60.75 (GI)
1979 £64.50 (DAV)
1978 £63.50 (BER) £69.65 (HAG) £84.00 (GI) £90.28 (TAN)
1976 £80.00 (WY)
1975 £108.00 (GI)
1973 magnum £81.80 (HAG)
1970 £95.00 (WY) £97.00 (RES) £115.00 (TW) £122.00 (GI)
1966 £127.00 (WY) £129.50 (GI) £150.25 (PE)
1964 £58.00 (WY)
1962 £69.00 (WY) £100.25 (PE)
1961 £325.00 (RES) £328.00 (WY) £350.00 (PE)
1955 £115.00 (UP) £155.00 (WY)
1953 £225.00 (RES) £230.00 (REI)
1953 ½ bottle £103.50 (EL)
1949 £506.00 (WY)
1949 ½ bottle £161.00 (EL)
1948 £150.00 (WY)
1948 ½ bottle £63.00 (WY)
1947 £290.00 (GI)
1919 £431.25 (TW)

Lafon-Rochet *4ème cru classé St-Éstèphe*
1989 EC £88.90 (HAH)
1987 £7.29 (TES)
1986 £9.75 (LOR)
1983 £8.59 (BYR) £8.90 (HOG)
1982 £10.20 (HOG)
1978 £9.90 (HOG)

Lagrange *Pomerol*
1988 EC £100.00 (HUN)
1986 £11.29 (BYR)
1985 £15.00 (HUN)
1957 £30.00 (VIG)

Lagrange *3ème cru classé St-Julien*
1989 EC £125.00 (HUN)
1986 £19.95 (THR)
1985 £10.93 (REI) £15.40 (HUN)
1984 £9.45 (BYR)
1983 £10.58 (HOG) £13.16 (BEK) £15.07 (PIP)
1982 £12.00 (HOG) £14.50 (UN) £16.10 (HAH)
1981 £18.15 (PE)
1979 £15.00 (UN)
1978 £18.00 (WY) £19.99 (PE)
1970 £14.99 (BL)
1966 £38.52 (TW)

la Lagune *3ème cru classé Haut-Médoc*
1989 EC £112.00 (RAE) £121.90 (HAH)
£122.00 (HUN) £125.00 (HIC)
1988 £12.65 (HIG)
1988 EC £83.00 (BIB) £99.00 (VIG) £105.00
(WW) £112.56 (LAY) £121.00 (ASK)
1986 £12.19 (BYR) £12.79 (AV) £13.75 (DAV)
£14.00 (LOR) £14.37 (HIG) £15.00 (HAG)
1985 £12.95 (BYR) £16.50 (DAV) £18.70 (EL)
1984 £9.10 (BIB) £11.64 (ASK) £12.00 (MV)
1983 £13.75 (HOG) £14.50 (GRE) £14.96 (BY)
£15.00 (ALL) £15.95 (DAV) £16.45 (BER)
£16.55 (BE) £17.77 (TAN) £19.90 (OL)
1982 £19.95 (BYR) £20.00 (VIG) £20.13 (ASK)
£20.21 (BY) £20.95 (GI) £21.75 (DAV)
1982 magnum £40.85 (ALL)
1981 £16.29 (BIB) £17.75 (DAV) £18.55 (CB)
£20.70 (HAH)
1979 £20.50 (DAV)
1978 £22.80 (GI) £24.50 (DAV) £27.69 (HA)
£28.50 (BE) £30.27 (YF)
1975 £23.00 (HOG) £24.50 (LAY) £24.95 (DAV)
£27.00 (BER)
1975 magnum £57.50 (EL)
1970 £35.50 (LAY) £42.00 (BE)
1966 £37.39 (REI)

Lalande d'Auvion *Médoc*
1989 EC £34.54 (HIC)
1985 £5.98 (TAN)

Lalande-Borie *cru bourgeois supérieur St-Julien*
1989 EC £84.00 (HUN)
1986 £9.35 (CB)
1985 £9.75 (BIB) £10.47 (HA) £10.59 (WIL)
1984 £6.05 (CB)
1983 £10.40 (LAY)

Lamothe-Cissac *cru grand bourgeois Haut-Médoc*
1985 £7.25 (DI)
1984 £5.65 (CH)

Lanessan *cru bourgeois supérieur Haut-Médoc*
1989 EC £62.00 (HUN)
1988 EC £47.00 (BIB)
1986 £7.95 (DI) £10.00 (HAG)
1985 £8.75 (BIB) £9.78 (EL) £10.75 (ALL)
1985 EC £59.40 (HAG)
1983 £9.65 (PD) £9.95 (NI)
1982 £14.56 (PIP)
1981 £10.24 (CHA)
1979 £10.75 (OL)

EC (ex-cellar) price per dozen, excl shipping, duty and VAT. IB (in bond) price per dozen, excl duty and VAT. All other prices, per bottle incl VAT.

Langoa-Barton *3ème cru classé St-Julien*
★**1989 EC** £113.00 (HUN) £116.70 (HAH)
1988 EC £97.80 (TAN)
1987 £9.43 (TAN)
1987 IB £85.00 (CB)
1986 £10.50 (NI) £11.15 (CB)
1985 £13.89 (BYR)
1984 £8.20 (CB) £9.29 (CH) £9.75 (BE)
£10.69 (TES)
1983 £14.75 (BER)
1981 £18.15 (PE)
1981 magnum £32.06 (HA)
1980 magnum £26.54 (HA)
1979 magnum £31.92 (HA)
1978 £20.00 (WY) £20.13 (BIB)
1976 £15.50 (REI)
1975 £19.65 (BIB)

Larmande *grand cru classé St-Émilion*
1989 EC £119.00 (HUN) £124.60 (HAH)
1986 £9.99 (BYR)
1985 £10.25 (BYR) £10.93 (REI)
1983 £9.79 (BYR)

Larose-Trintaudon *grand bourgeois St-Laurent*
1985 £7.79 (WCL)
1983 £7.72 (BEK) £8.99 (PIP)
1982 £7.75 (LOR) £8.25 (WCL) £9.50 (OL)
1978 £10.75 (ALL) £10.98 (OL) £11.45 (BAR)

Laroze *grand cru classé St-Émilion*
1986 £10.92 (HIG)
1985 £11.50 (HIG)
1982 £11.98 (WW)

Larrivet-Haut-Brion *Pessac-Léognan*
1985 £8.05 (REI) £11.50 (DI)

Lartigue-de-Brochon *cru bourgeois Haut-Médoc*
1988 EC £36.00 (BIB)
1986 £6.70 (RAE)
1985 £6.95 (RAE)
1983 £5.29 (WIL)

Lascombes *2ème cru classé Margaux*
1989 IB £114.60 (PIP)
1985 £13.75 (BO)
1983 £12.09 (PE) £13.80 (HOG)
1982 £16.95 (AUG)
1981 £15.35 (AUG)
1979 £15.50 (WAI)
1978 £21.30 (PE)

Latour *1er cru classé Pauillac*

1988 EC £370.00 (HUN)
1987 £23.75 (HA) £25.00 (RAE)
1986 £37.55 (HA) £39.75 (DAV) £43.85 (CB)
1985 £47.50 (HAY) £52.08 (HA)
1984 £22.85 (AV) £24.30 (CB) £27.15 (PE)
    £28.59 (BYR) £28.96 (HA) £40.10 (BER)
1983 £39.95 (LAY) £41.64 (HOG) £49.68 (HA)
1983 magnum £101.00 (HA)
1982 £62.29 (BIB) £75.00 (VIC) £78.50 (UN)
    £80.00 (RES) £100.00 (HA)
1981 £41.00 (UN) £45.50 (DAV) £47.10 (BER)
    £49.50 (GI) £50.00 (ALL) £51.72 (HA)
    £55.50 (PE) £59.95 (THR) £66.70 (TW)
1980 £33.00 (HA) £34.40 (CH) £36.35 (BY)
1979 £47.80 (HA) £59.00 (GRE) £62.50 (DAV)
1979 double magnum £212.00 (WY)
1978 £59.00 (HOG) £64.00 (HAG) £65.00 (OL)
    £68.35 (HA) £69.00 (WY) £69.50 (GI)
    £74.50 (DAV) £76.79 (BY)
1978 double magnum £339.25 (TW)
1977 £28.00 (OL) £31.15 (HA)
1976 £51.75 (EL)
1975 £79.00 (RES) £92.50 (DAV)
1973 £46.50 (HA)
1970 £99.99 (PE) £100.00 (WY) £120.00 (DAV)
1966 £97.75 (REI) £103.50 (EL) £115.25 (PE)
    £120.00 (ALL) £138.00 (WY)
1962 £86.31 (EL) £150.00 (RES)
1961 £240.00 (UP) £350.00 (PE)
1959 £180.00 (GI) £276.00 (WY)
1952 £155.00 (WY)
1940 £143.75 (REI)
1929 £460.00 (REI)

Latour-à-Pomerol *Pomerol*
1988 IB £230.00 (CB)
1988 EC £237.00 (LAY)
1985 £28.90 (CB)
1983 £22.49 (LAY)
1981 £22.00 (CB)

Léoville-Barton *2ème cru classé St-Julien*
★**1989 EC** £129.00 (RAE) £129.85 (HAH)
    £130.00 (HAY) £132.00 (HUN)
1988 EC £118.68 (LAY)
1987 £10.45 (TAN)
1987 IB £93.00 (CB)
1986 £12.46 (HOG) £12.59 (WIL) £13.39 (BYR)
    £14.29 (CB) £14.75 (DAV)
1985 £14.25 (LOR) £15.29 (BYR) £17.30 (BE)
    £17.50 (DAV)
1985 IB £125.00 (WY)
1984 £8.20 (CB) £10.35 (BYR) £10.50 (BE)
    £11.90 (BY) £12.00 (WS) £14.39 (WIL)
1983 £14.39 (WIL) £15.09 (AV) £15.47 (TAN)
    £15.89 (WHI) £16.50 (DAV) £16.89 (BYR)
    £16.95 (BER)
1982 £19.62 (BY) £19.65 (BIB) £19.69 (BYR)
    £19.95 (GI) £24.75 (BO) £24.75 (DAV)
1981 £13.90 (BIB) £17.90 (AD) £18.50 (DAV)
1980 magnum £28.84 (HA)
1979 £21.50 (DAV) £22.00 (WY)
1978 £23.48 (BIB) £23.95 (LAY) £25.95 (DAV)
1976 £25.01 (TAN)
1975 £28.80 (BER)
1971 £25.00 (VIG)
1970 £30.00 (UP) £40.00 (WY)
1969 £19.75 (UP)
1966 £33.54 (BIB)
1964 £30.00 (VIG)
1961 £86.00 (UN)
1961 magnum £190.00 (WY)

Léoville-Las-Cases *2ème cru classé St-Julien*
1989 EC £265.00 (HUN)
1985 £24.96 (LAY) £28.27 (BIB) £39.50 (THR)
1985 EC £260.00 (HAG)
1985 imperial £488.75 (HUN)
1984 £16.25 (CB) £17.15 (PE) £19.64 (BY)
    £23.10 (BER)
1983 £19.95 (LAY) £23.14 (AV) £25.00 (ALL)
    £25.30 (AD) £27.50 (GI) £27.75 (CB)
    £31.85 (BER)
1982 £30.80 (GI) £55.00 (PE)
1981 £21.15 (BYR) £21.93 (BY) £23.50 (GI)
    £23.60 (AD) £24.30 (HAG)
1980 £20.88 (CB)

1979 £23.96 (BIB) £25.90 (GI)
1978 £31.15 (BIB) £33.00 (GI) £37.38 (TAN)
1978 jeroboam £145.00 (GI)
1978 imperial £298.00 (GI)
1976 £32.00 (HA) £35.00 (OL)
1976 imperial £310.00 (GI)
1975 £38.33 (TAN)
1973 £17.16 (BOR)
1970 £40.00 (WS) £45.00 (VIG) £46.00 (GI, WY) £55.00 (RES) £58.65 (TAN)
1970 magnum £80.81 (BIB)
1966 £57.50 (EL)
1961 £132.00 (WY) £165.00 (RES)
1959 £59.00 (VIG)
1949 £270.00 (RES)

Léoville-Poyferré *2ème cru classé St-Julien*
1989 EC £141.00 (RAE) £147.00 (HUN)
1988 EC £110.00 (RAE)
1987 £10.85 (RAE)
1986 £12.69 (BYR)
1986 imperial EC £239.20 (HUN)
1985 £12.65 (REI) £16.60 (AN) £19.32 (EL)
1985 imperial EC £213.90 (HUN)
1983 £12.06 (HOG) £12.95 (AUG) £13.85 (WIL) £14.49 (BYR) £14.50 (GI) £16.85 (BER)
1982 £18.83 (BY) £18.85 (BYR) £19.95 (GI)
1981 £15.50 (GI)
1979 £16.50 (UN) £35.00 (VIG)
1978 £17.29 (BL) £22.49 (BO) £24.50 (VIC)
1976 £22.43 (TW)
1975 £24.75 (LAY)
1975 imperial £212.75 (EL)
1970 £28.27 (BIB)
1967 £20.00 (VIG)
1966 £31.00 (HAG)
1962 £32.50 (BIB)

Lestage *Listrac*
1985 £5.99 (BYR)
1983 £7.95 (ALL)
1982 £5.67 (HOG) £7.23 (HA)

Liversan *cru bourgeois supérieur Haut-Médoc*
1988 £5.75 (NI)
1987 £6.75 (OD)
1986 £7.15 (WIL) £7.50 (NI)
1985 £7.35 (WIL) £8.13 (EL) £8.71 (PIP)
1983 £7.29 (WIL) £8.25 (CH)

Loudenne *cru bourgeois Médoc*
1983 £5.99 (HOG)
1981 £5.99 (HOG)

la Louvière *Pessac-Léognan*
1989 EC £90.00 (HUN) £93.20 (HAH)
1987 £7.29 (THR)
1985 £8.99 (BOT) £9.95 (PD)
1984 £5.95 (WAI) £7.30 (NI)
1983 £12.25 (UP)

Lynch-Bages *5ème cru classé Pauillac*

1989 EC £218.00 (HUN, HIC)
1988 EC £132.00 (BIB) £179.40 (LAY)
1987 £15.01 (BY)
1986 £17.95 (BYR)
1985 £14.95 (VIC) £17.45 (AUG) £18.95 (DAV) £19.75 (BOT) £22.75 (REI) £26.06 (EL) £29.95 (THR) £34.89 (WIL)
1984 £11.99 (AV) £12.80 (CB) £12.95 (DAV) £12.99 (BO) £13.15 (PE) £13.75 (BYR) £14.95 (AUG) £15.95 (BER) £16.50 (GI) £17.07 (BY) £20.09 (WIL)
1983 £15.25 (GRE) £17.33 (BY) £17.50 (WHI) £18.19 (BYR) £18.92 (BER) £18.95 (DAV) £19.90 (OL) £20.95 (THR) £24.15 (TW)
1982 £21.39 (BYR) £22.52 (BIB) £24.00 (BER) £24.30 (CB) £24.80 (GI) £29.75 (DAV)
1981 £15.00 (HOG) £17.95 (WIZ) £21.50 (DAV) £22.25 (BO) £22.90 (OL)
1980 £17.33 (PIP)
1979 £21.56 (BIB) £22.75 (DAV) £23.50 (UN) £23.75 (BO) £25.15 (PE)
1978 £22.95 (GRE) £23.15 (CB) £24.41 (HAG) £26.00 (WY) £28.75 (OL)
1975 £26.35 (BIB) £36.50 (DAV)
1970 £45.00 (GI)
1966 £52.75 (DAV) £58.00 (WY)
1961 £126.00 (WY)
1959 £75.00 (OL)
1953 £59.00 (VIG)

Magdelaine *1er grand cru classé St-Émilion*
1988 IB £170.00 (CB)
1986 £18.55 (CB)
1985 £22.00 (CB)
1983 £21.49 (LAY)

1982 £25.45 (CB)
1981 £23.15 (CB)
1980 £11.50 (WY)
1959 £45.00 (VIG)
1957 £35.00 (VIG)
1955 £49.00 (VIG)

Malartic-Lagravière *cru classé Pessac-Léognan*
1987 £7.99 (OD)
1985 £11.50 (DI)
1983 £10.35 (AI)
1982 £13.51 (REI)

Malescasse *cru bourgeois Haut-Médoc*
1989 EC £52.60 (HIC)
1986 £6.70 (HIG)
1983 £6.55 (WHI)
1980 £6.35 (BYR)

Malescot-St-Exupéry *3ème cru classé Margaux*
1987 £12.95 (VIG)
1986 £11.99 (OD)
1985 £13.99 (OD) £14.25 (BO) £16.19 (IR)
1984 £9.79 (BOT)
1983 IB £90.00 (HAG)
1982 £11.98 (BIB) £15.39 (WHI) £17.49 (BO)
1980 £14.95 (VIG)
1980 magnum £29.90 (VIG)
1979 £14.60 (HAG)
1978 £15.50 (BOR)
1975 £20.85 (WRI) £21.92 (YF)
1966 £23.00 (BIB)
1961 £53.75 (OL)

de Marbuzet *grand bourgeois exceptionnel Médoc*
★**1989 EC** £93.20 (HAH)
1988 EC £84.10 (AN)

Margaux *1er cru classé Margaux*
1988 EC £420.00 (LAY)
1987 IB £58.00 (CB)
1985 £46.25 (BOT) £47.96 (LAY) £51.00 (GRE) £60.10 (AN)
1984 £24.12 (AV) £26.15 (PE) £28.59 (BYR) £33.00 (GI) £39.12 (BER) £40.31 (BY)
1983 £44.50 (DAV) £48.40 (ASK) £52.97 (BYR) £56.00 (WY)
1980 magnum £49.40 (GI)
1982 £60.00 (ALL) £60.10 (AN) £64.69 (BIB) £65.00 (UP, GRE) £69.00 (GI)
1981 £44.00 (UN) £45.20 (BER) £45.50 (DAV, BE) £49.50 (GI) £50.00 (ALL)

1978 £68.52 (BIB)
1971 magnum £112.10 (BER)
1970 £66.70 (WY) £71.88 (BIB) £90.00 (UP)
1966 £109.00 (WY)
1959 £130.00 (REI) £155.00 (GI)
1957 £191.00 (GI)
1953 £322.00 (WY)
1949 £402.00 (WY)
1947 £276.00 (REI)
1945 £431.00 (WY)
1943 £110.00 (GI)
1928 £563.00 (WY)

Marquis d'Alesme-Becker *3ème cru classé Margaux*
1985 £9.50 (NI)
1982 £10.00 (HOG)

Marquis-de-Terme *4ème cru classé Margaux*
1989 EC £99.00 (HUN)
1987 £8.99 (TES)
1986 £11.44 (ELL)
1983 £10.52 (HOG)
1982 £13.60 (ALL)
1929 £115.00 (WY)

Maucaillou *cru bourgeois Moulis*
1988 £7.08 (NI)
1986 £7.85 (WIL)
1985 £8.95 (WHI) £10.95 (NI)
1984 £8.50 (NI) £8.95 (SAI)
1983 £9.75 (DAV)
1982 £9.99 (WHI) £10.25 (DAV)
1981 £9.69 (CH)

Meyney *cru grand bourgeois exceptionnel St-Estèphe*
1989 EC £100.00 (HUN)
1986 £11.95 (AI)
1985 £9.99 (PE) £71.50 (HAG)
1984 £7.59 (PE) £8.25 (SAI)
1983 £8.78 (HOG) £12.35 (PE) £12.75 (AI)
1982 £9.75 (DAV) £10.38 (HOG) £11.29 (PE) £11.45 (WHI) £12.45 (BYR) £12.69 (WIL) £15.09 (AV) £15.50 (HAG)
1978 £16.95 (BAR)
1975 £21.50 (BAR)
1975 magnum £44.50 (BAR)
1966 double magnum £161.00 (WY)
1961 magnum £71.83 (HAG)

la Mission-Haut-Brion *cru classé Pessac-Léognan*
1989 EC £375.00 (RAE)

1986 £32.60 (ASK)
1986 EC £398.00 (BIB)
1984 £17.74 (AV) £25.79 (BYR) £29.15 (BER)
1983 £24.00 (BIB) £25.00 (MAJ) £32.50 (GRE)
£35.69 (HOG) £44.00 (GI) £47.00 (PE)
1982 £52.00 (DAV) £63.00 (GI)
1982 IB £540.00 (WY)
1981 £36.50 (DAV) £36.65 (BER) £41.16 (PIP)
1980 £24.08 (BY) £39.50 (TW)
1979 £35.00 (GI) £37.50 (DAV) £41.00 (BER)
1978 £46.00 (BER) £51.95 (DAV) £63.00 (WY)
1977 £26.50 (BER)
1976 £38.95 (OL) £43.60 (BER) £46.00 (WY)
1975 £125.00 (DAV)
1971 magnum £129.00 (VIG)
1970 £172.64 (AV)
1966 £115.00 (WY)
1961 £281.75 (WY)

Monbousquet *grand cru St-Émilion*
1986 £8.75 (UP) £9.60 (GRE)
1985 £6.85 (BYR)
1983 £10.52 (YF)

Monbrison *cru grand bourgeois exceptionnel Margaux*

1989 EC £121.20 (HAH) £122.00 (HUN)
1986 £12.20 (HUN)
1985 £10.85 (HA)

Monlot-Capet *St-Émilion*
1988 EC £58.92 (LAY)
1986 £7.96 (PIP)
1985 £8.60 (AD) £9.66 (TAN)

Montgrand-Milon *Pauillac*
1986 £8.39 (AUG)
1983 £9.40 (AI)

Montrose *2ème cru classé St-Éstèphe*
★**1989 EC** £167.00 (HUN) £168.00 (HIC)
£173.85 (HAH)
1988 EC £150.84 (TAN)
1986 £13.99 (BYR) £17.99 (BO)
1985 £24.05 (AN)
1984 £11.95 (BYR)
1983 £14.90 (GI) £14.95 (GRE) £16.24 (AV)
£22.50 (VIC)
1982 £17.25 (HAG) £17.95 (BYR) £18.00 (LOR)
£19.62 (BY) £23.50 (DAV, GI) £28.15
(WIL)
1981 £18.93 (TAN) £18.96 (PIP) £20.32 (HAG)
1979 £19.50 (UN) £23.00 (WY)
1978 £19.90 (GI) £19.99 (BO) £24.50 (LAY)
1975 double magnum £103.50 (EL)
1975 jeroboam £149.50 (EL)
1972 £11.45 (BER)
1970 £33.99 (BO) £42.00 (GI) £80.50 (EL)
1961 £55.00 (VIG) £78.00 (GI)
1959 £49.40 (VIG)
1955 £49.50 (VIG)
1937 £59.00 (VIG)

Moulin-des-Carruades *Pauillac*
1981 £19.95 (WHI) £20.00 (UP)

Moulin-du-Cadet *grand cru classé St-Émilion*
1985 £13.10 (AD) £13.75 (TAN)

Moulinet *Pomerol*
1986 £10.19 (WIL)
1985 £10.95 (AUG) £11.20 (MV) £13.43 (CB)
£14.59 (WIL)
1983 £8.43 (CB)
1973 £17.94 (TW)

Mouton-Baronne-Philippe *5ème cru classé Pauillac*
1989 EC £108.00 (HUN)
1988 EC £124.00 (HUN)
1986 £11.99 (OD)
1985 £12.48 (REI) £13.99 (BYR) £16.54 (EL)
£17.19 (WIL)
1983 £11.75 (BO) £15.95 (AUG)
1981 £13.95 (WIZ) £19.75 (BO)
1978 £20.00 (UP)
1975 £16.00 (HOG) £19.95 (BAR)

Mouton-Rothschild *1er cru classé Pauillac*
1988 £35.42 (NI)
1986 £46.15 (CB) £80.00 (RES)
1986 ½ bottle £25.50 (VIG)

1986 magnum £100.00 (VIG)
1985 £60.10 (AN) £61.90 (EL) £67.59 (WIL)
1985 imperial £793.50 (HUN)
1984 £23.99 (OD) £26.15 (PE) £27.49 (BYR)
£29.99 (ASD) £33.80 (HAH) £34.27 (BY)
£39.20 (BER) £44.99 (WIL) £48.45 (CB)
1983 £35.95 (AUG) £38.00 (WY) £40.49 (BO)
£41.64 (HOG) £44.50 (DAV) £50.75
(WIL)
1983 magnum £80.00 (WY)
1982 £75.00 (GI) £115.00 (DAV)
1981 £38.26 (HOG) £42.96 (BY) £45.50 (DAV)
£49.99 (WHI) £53.00 (GI) £54.00 (PE)
£56.18 (VIN) £65.00 (AN, VIG)
1981 double magnum £201.00 (WY)
1980 £39.99 (PE)
1980 ½ bottle £29.32 (TW)
1979 £36.90 (HOG) £45.50 (GI) £49.99 (PE)
£62.50 (DAV)
1978 £59.00 (HOG, HAG) £63.75 (BER) £67.50
(UP) £68.00 (UN) £68.50 (HUN) £69.50
(GI) £75.50 (DAV) £79.50 (VIC)
1978 double magnum £328.00 (WY)
1976 £63.25 (BIB) £63.80 (VIC) £95.00 (RES)
1976 magnum £63.64 (HAG)
1975 £84.00 (GI)
1971 double magnum £334.00 (WY)
1970 £84.33 (BIB) £99.99 (PE) £101.00 (WY)
£109.39 (AV) £120.00 (DAV)
1967 £46.00 (WY) £47.44 (BIB)
1966 £124.50 (GI) £126.00 (WY)
1964 £98.00 (WY)
1962 £90.00 (GI)
1959 £250.00 (GI) £345.00 (WY) £375.00
(RES)
1955 £110.00 (RES)
1948 magnum £713.00 (WY)
1939 £402.50 (WY)
1905 £320.00 (UP)

_Merchants stocking
each wine are listed after
each entry in ascending
order of price. However,
prices do fluctuate (there
are special offers and
discounts as well as
price increases) so
remember to use
Webster's as a price
GUIDE not a price LIST._

Nenin *Pomerol*
1986 £10.50 (WAI)
1985 £12.29 (BYR)
1982 £15.53 (BY)
1959 £92.00 (WY)
1949 £127.00 (WY)

Notton *Margaux*
1987 £6.75 (RAE)
1986 £8.98 (OL)
1985 £7.99 (VIC)

d'Olivier *cru classé Pessac-Léognan*
1985 £11.49 (WIL)
1983 £11.15 (WIL)
1982 £10.99 (WIL)

les Ormes-de-Pez *cru grand bourgeois
St-Éstèphe*
1987 £9.81 (BY)
1986 £9.43 (ELL) £14.33 (BY)
1985 £7.91 (BIB) £9.55 (PE) £10.95 (ALL)
£11.50 (EL) £17.34 (BY)
1985 IB £66.00 (HAG)
1984 £6.75 (DAV) £6.95 (BYR) £7.05 (CB)
1983 £10.19 (BYR) £10.90 (UN) £11.29 (AI)
£11.85 (BEK)
1983 IB £72.00 (HAG)
1982 £13.99 (PE) £17.34 (BY)
1981 £14.94 (PIP) £15.65 (BY)
1979 £12.99 (BO)

les Ormes-Sorbet *cru grand bourgeois
Médoc*
1985 £9.75 (VIC)
1984 £5.38 (BER) £5.95 (VIG)
1983 £5.60 (BER) £7.95 (DAV)

Palmer *3ème cru classé Margaux*
1989 EC £248.00 (HIC) £254.90 (HAH)
£260.00 (HAY)
1988 EC £200.00 (HAY) £205.80 (TAN)
£210.00 (BE)
1987 £13.75 (AD) £16.99 (BO) £17.30 (BE)
1986 £23.91 (ELL) £23.95 (DI) £25.00 (HAG)
£28.50 (BE)
1986 EC £178.00 (HAG)
1985 £23.00 (AD) £23.96 (BIB) £26.75 (LOR)
£28.50 (BE) £31.60 (AN) £31.95 (DI)
£34.39 (BYR)
1984 £14.15 (PE) £15.07 (TAN) £16.29 (BIB)
£18.80 (BE) £20.05 (BER) £21.85 (EL)
1983 £32.00 (RES) £32.90 (BER) £35.00 (GI)
£38.50 (BE)

1982 £34.18 (BY) £35.50 (GI) £36.20 (BER) £38.20 (BE) £43.00 (PE)
1981 £26.35 (BIB) £28.50 (LAY) £28.89 (AV)
1979 £29.00 (GI) £36.50 (BE)
1978 £40.31 (EL) £46.50 (BE) £48.00 (WY) £49.50 (GI)
1978 magnum £82.42 (BIB)
1976 £38.33 (HA) £38.70 (EL) £39.50 (OL)
1976 magnum £73.50 (GI)
1975 £52.00 (BE) £55.26 (EL)
1974 £42.50 (BAR)
1970 £70.00 (WS) £70.99 (BO) £74.80 (EL) £80.00 (BE) £95.00 (WY) £99.00 (RES)
1964 £57.50 (REI)
1962 £69.06 (EL)
1959 £185.00 (RES)
1953 £172.50 (EL) £225.00 (RES)
1953 magnum £345.00 (EL)
1952 £98.90 (REI)
1947 £172.50 (EL)
1934 £85.00 (VIG)

Pape-Clément *cru classé Pessac-Léognan*
1989 EC £164.00 (RAE) £178.00 (HUN)
1987 £15.05 (AN)
1986 £16.08 (BY)
1985 £17.25 (REI)
1982 £19.25 (BY) £21.99 (AV)
1970 £35.00 (GI) £37.00 (WY) £38.00 (RES)

la Parde-de-Haut-Bailly *Pessac-Léognan*
1985 £6.99 (RAE) £8.59 (PE)

Patache d'Aux *cru grand bourgeois Médoc*
1986 £5.59 (PE) £5.69 (TES) £5.85 (WIL) £5.99 (BO)
1985 £5.75 (BYR) £6.20 (HA) £6.39 (WHI) £7.55 (WCL) £7.61 (PIP) £7.85 (WRI)
1983 £6.39 (WIL)

Pavie *1er grand cru classé St-Émilion*
1989 EC £170.00 (RAE)
1988 EC £118.00 (BIB)
1987 EC £110.00 (RAE)
1986 £14.95 (RAE)
1985 £15.09 (AV) £15.33 (REI) £18.00 (VIC)
1984 £10.54 (BIB)
1983 magnum £39.29 (BIB)
1982 £22.00 (VIC) £24.45 (WIL) £25.00 (UN)
1978 £19.45 (BL)
1966 £55.11 (YF)
1937 £59.00 (VIG)

Pavie-Decesse *grand cru classé St-Émilion*
1986 £9.50 (RAE) £11.95 (VIG)
1985 £14.75 (PE)

Pavillon-Rouge-du-Château Margaux *Margaux*

1987 £14.90 (BY)
1986 £14.75 (DAV) £16.99 (TES)
1985 £13.95 (ASD) £16.49 (OD)
1983 £14.99 (OD) £18.55 (BYR) £19.90 (AD)
1982 £16.99 (OD)

Pédesclaux *5ème cru classé Pauillac*
1987 £8.28 (PIP)
1986 £9.50 (DI)

Petit-Village *Pomerol*
1989 EC £256.00 (HUN)
1979 £20.64 (REI)
1953 £45.00 (VIG)

Pétrus *Pomerol*
1985 £196.00 (HUN)
1983 £180.00 (GI)
1981 £145.99 (BO) £200.00 (DAV)
1980 £130.00 (DAV)
1978 £169.00 (GI)
1976 £287.50 (BIB)
1970 £339.25 (TW)
1967 £172.56 (EL)
1955 ½ bottle £253.00 (TW)

de Pez *cru bourgeois supérieur St-Éstèphe*
1989 EC £105.00 (HIC)
1986 £9.65 (BOT) £9.95 (PD)
1984 £7.05 (CB) £13.79 (BO)
1983 £9.35 (HOG) £11.25 (UP)

Phélan-Ségur *cru grand bourgeois exceptionnel St-Éstèphe*
1986 £8.75 (LOR)
1982 £9.60 (HOG)
1981 £14.75 (BO)
1973 £12.89 (YF)

Pichon *Haut-Médoc*
1985 £9.48 (BR)
1983 £10.35 (BR)

Pichon-Baron *2ème cru classé Pauillac*
1987 £8.56 (BY)
1985 £17.59 (BYR)
1983 £15.25 (WIL) £15.75 (BYR) £15.95 (BER)
1982 £19.52 (BEK) £23.67 (PIP) £29.99 (PE)
1981 £17.03 (PIP)
1966 £37.00 (WY) £45.00 (DI)
1955 £47.50 (VIG) £66.13 (REI)
1952 £45.00 (VIG)

Pichon-Lalande *2ème cru classé Pauillac*
1989 EC £225.00 (HUN)
1988 EC £210.00 (HAY)
1987 £15.23 (TAN)
1985 £24.92 (BIB) £27.60 (AD) £29.00 (VIC)
1985 imperial £454.25 (HUN)
1984 £15.25 (PE) £16.95 (WIZ) £18.40 (BYR)
   £18.90 (GI) £21.38 (BY)
1983 £18.69 (NI) £24.29 (BYR) £25.30 (AD)
   £28.00 (WY) £30.12 (TAN) £31.45 (AUG)
1982 £38.00 (VIC) £39.99 (PE)
1981 £23.50 (LAY) £23.96 (BIB) £24.88 (CB)
   £24.90 (GI) £27.20 (BE) £32.95 (BAR)
1979 £25.40 (GI)
1978 £33.00 (GI)
1975 £38.00 (GI) £40.00 (BE)
1971 £31.25 (AI)

Pique-Caillou *Graves*
1988 EC £46.00 (BIB)
1985 £7.95 (BAR) £7.98 (BIB)

Plagnac *cru bourgeois Médoc*
1986 £7.45 (ALL) £7.65 (WHI)
1985 £5.10 (BER) £5.35 (BYR) £5.75 (PE)
1984 £6.99 (UN)
1983 £6.69 (PE)
1978 £8.99 (BO)

la Pointe *Pomerol*
1989 EC £104.00 (HIC)
1983 £11.00 (HAY)
1981 £16.04 (TW)

Pontet-Canet *5ème cru classé Pauillac*
1986 £9.99 (BYR)
1985 £11.48 (ELL) £14.93 (EL)
1983 £10.45 (BYR) £10.49 (HOG) £10.99 (WHI)
1982 £10.50 (HOG) £14.38 (BIB)
1978 £17.99 (PE)
1967 £18.50 (VIG)

Potensac *cru grand bourgeois Médoc*
1989 EC £55.00 (RAE) £58.00 (HUN) £60.00
   (HAY)
★**1988 EC** £45.00 (BIB) £53.90 (WW) £55.00
   (HAY) £57.00 (HUN) £59.00 (VIG) £65.00
   (ASK) £66.10 (AN)
1987 £7.10 (AN)
1986 £7.75 (HAY) £9.16 (CHA) £9.95 (VIG)
1985 £7.75 (BYR) £8.09 (PE) £8.50 (BIB)
1985 EC £60.00 (HAG)
1983 £10.00 (HAY) £10.58 (CHA) £12.45 (BAR)
1983 IB £85.00 (HAG)
1981 £9.50 (BIB)
1978 £19.49 (BOD)

Poujeaux *cru grand bourgeois*
exceptionnel Moulis
1986 £9.95 (VIG)
1985 £8.15 (BIB) £9.95 (ALL) £9.99 (MAJ)
1983 £9.90 (BEK) £11.29 (CHA) £11.41 (PIP)
1982 £10.54 (BIB)

Prieur de Meyney *St-Éstèphe*
1987 £7.95 (UN)
1985 £6.55 (BYR)
1983 £7.95 (WRI, LAY) £8.25 (PE)
1982 £8.25 (PE)

le Prieuré *grand cru classé St-Émilion*
1985 £13.10 (AD)

Prieuré-Lichine *4ème cru classé*
Margaux

1989 EC £120.00 (HUN)
1988 IB £101.25 (CHA)
1988 EC £108.10 (AN)
1986 £13.55 (AN)
1985 £11.98 (BIB) £14.75 (BO) £14.99 (PE)
   £19.95 (DAV)

1984 £8.99 (BO) £12.89 (WIL)
1983 £12.75 (BO) £13.95 (CB) £14.19 (BYR)
1982 £14.99 (BO) £21.29 (PE)
1975 £13.25 (BO) £16.00 (HOG)

du Puy *Montagne-St-Émilion*
1988 £5.15 (STA)
1985 £4.49 (WIL)

Puy-Blanquet *grand cru St-Émilion*
1989 EC £62.00 (HUN)
1988 EC £54.84 (TAN)
1985 £11.12 (TAN)
1982 £8.85 (HAH)
1973 £15.84 (BOR)

Rahoul *Graves*
1985 £9.99 (BOD)
1983 £9.26 (BY)
★**1982** £10.19 (BY)

Ramage-la-Bâtisse *cru bourgeois Haut-Médoc*
1987 £7.15 (AS) £8.69 (WCL)
1985 £7.59 (THR) £7.64 (HA) £7.95 (UP) £8.05 (BYR) £8.36 (BOR) £8.79 (WCL)
1983 £5.93 (HOG) £6.99 (IR) £7.50 (UP)
1982 £6.50 (AS)

Rausan-Ségla *2ème cru classé Margaux*
1987 £21.55 (WHI)
1986 £18.15 (WIL)
1985 £14.85 (PE) £15.89 (BYR) £15.99 (BO) £16.79 (WIL) £17.90 (BE)
1983 £17.25 (BOT) £26.29 (WIL)
1981 £12.89 (WHI) £19.45 (WRI)
1966 £45.42 (TW)
1961 £50.00 (VIG)
1959 £43.98 (REI)
1955 £45.00 (VIG)
1952 £45.00 (VIG)
1934 £59.00 (VIG)

Rauzan-Gassies *2ème cru classé Margaux*
1986 £13.75 (DAV)
1985 £11.98 (BIB) £14.75 (DAV)
1983 £15.25 (DAV)
1952 £40.00 (VIG)

Réserve de la Comtesse *Pauillac*
1986 £10.25 (LAY)
1985 £10.95 (LAY) £11.75 (PE)
1984 £9.99 (BYR) £10.95 (NI) £12.27 (BY)
1983 £12.23 (CB)
1982 £15.54 (PIP)

Respide *Graves*
1985 £4.25 (GRE) £4.60 (AI)

Reysson *cru bourgeois Haut-Médoc*
1985 £5.95 (PE)
1983 £4.55 (BYR)

de Roquetaillade-la-Grange *Graves*
1986 £5.82 (BE)
1985 £5.49 (DAV) £6.70 (MV)

St-Bonnet *cru bourgeois Médoc*
1986 £6.25 (WRI)
1985 £5.89 (BYR)
1983 £6.07 (IR) £6.50 (BE) £7.80 (WRI)
1982 £9.00 (WRI)

St-Pierre *4ème cru classé St-Julien*
1987 £11.52 (BY)
1985 £16.30 (AD)
1982 £16.95 (LAY) £19.55 (AD)
1981 £15.81 (REI)
1979 £12.95 (RAE) £15.93 (REI) £17.95 (BAR)

de Sales *Pomerol*
1985 IB £95.00 (WY)
1983 £14.94 (BEK) £17.08 (PIP)
1971 £25.00 (VIG)

Sarget de Gruaud-Larose *St-Julien*
1986 £10.99 (WHI)
1985 £10.75 (DAV)
1984 £8.75 (WAI) £9.20 (HAG) £9.85 (UP)
1983 £9.75 (ASD) £10.65 (AUG) £10.95 (LAY) £12.49 (PE) £12.75 (HAG)

Sénéjac *cru bourgeois supérieur Haut-Médoc*
1989 EC £52.90 (HAH)
1988 EC £38.00 (MV) £46.20 (WW)
1987 £6.50 (WW)
1985 £6.60 (BE) £7.25 (LOR)

la Serre *grand cru classé St-Émilion*
1989 EC £87.00 (RAE)
1988 EC £65.00 (BIB)
1986 £9.15 (PE)
1985 £10.50 (HAY)
1985 EC £90.00 (HAG)
1982 £11.99 (PE) £16.55 (HAG)

Siran *cru bourgeois supérieur Margaux*
1989 EC £90.36 (PIP)
1985 £12.49 (BYR)
1982 £13.99 (BO) £17.37 (PIP)

1982 magnum £28.99 (BO)
1981 £18.53 (PIP)
1967 £14.95 (VIG)

Smith-Haut-Lafitte *cru classé Pessac-Léognan*
1985 £9.14 (REI) £9.99 (BOT) £10.25 (BO)
    £11.39 (WHI) £11.60 (PD) £13.05 (WIL)
1983 £13.95 (WIL)
1982 £10.76 (YF) £12.75 (DAV) £13.05 (HAG)
    £17.34 (IR)
1981 £11.69 (WHI) £12.50 (UP) £15.10 (VIN)
1979 £12.75 (BO)
1978 £18.99 (WHI)
1952 £40.00 (VIG)
1949 £59.00 (VIG)

Sociando-Mallet *cru grand bourgeois Haut-Médoc*
1989 EC £95.00 (RAE) £110.00 (HAY) £112.00
    (HUN)
1988 EC £70.00 (BIB) £85.00 (HAY) £97.00
    (HUN)
1987 £6.99 (RAE)
1986 £7.99 (PE)
1985 £12.03 (BEK) £13.25 (BYR) £14.08 (PIP)
1984 £7.50 (BIB)
1983 £11.98 (BIB)

Soutard *grand cru classé St-Émilion*
1988 EC £105.00 (WW)
1987 £10.54 (ASK) £12.95 (WW)
1986 £13.89 (WW)
1983 £10.35 (BIB) £11.98 (WW) £12.94 (ASK)
1982 £11.50 (BIB) £12.45 (WW)
1959 £35.00 (VIG)

du Tailhas *Pomerol*
1986 £9.39 (BOT)
1982 £12.45 (HAH)

Taillefer *Pomerol*
1985 £10.39 (WIL) £11.65 (CB)
1983 £8.55 (CB)

Talbot *4ème cru classé St-Julien*
1989 EC £175.00 (HUN)
1988 EC £130.40 (LAY)

1987 £12.75 (TAN)
1986 £14.99 (OD) £18.00 (HAG)
1985 £13.25 (VIC) £15.33 (BIB) £15.49 (BO)
    £16.95 (BL) £17.95 (BER)
1985 magnum £30.67 (BIB)
1984 £11.15 (PE) £11.95 (BYR) £16.09 (WIL)
1983 £14.45 (BER) £14.99 (PE, BOT) £15.99
    (BL) £17.50 (DAV) £20.54 (WIL)
1982 £18.99 (BO) £19.15 (PE) £19.69 (AV)
    £20.95 (BYR) £21.00 (WS) £22.75 (DAV)
1981 £16.44 (HA) £17.25 (BIB) £17.49 (CH)
    £17.50 (OL) £17.55 (PE) £18.50 (DAV)
    £18.95 (HAG) £19.99 (TAN) £22.49 (WIL)
1979 £18.99 (BL) £20.15 (PE) £21.50 (DAV)
1978 £22.50 (HAG) £26.50 (DAV)
1975 £26.50 (DAV) £31.85 (WIL)
1971 £21.89 (OL) £31.14 (TAN)
1970 £23.91 (BIB) £34.50 (WY) £44.28 (TAN)
1966 double magnum £230.00 (WY)
1960 £35.00 (VIG)

les Templiers *Lalande-de-Pomerol*
1988 EC £53.00 (HIC)
1987 £7.13 (HA)
1985 £7.48 (WW)

Terre Rouge *Médoc*
1985 £5.25 (DAV) £6.04 (REI) £6.70 (TAN)

Terrey-Gros-Caillou *St-Julien*
1989 EC £75.00 (HUN)
1983 £8.20 (CB)

du Tertre *5ème cru classé Margaux*
1983 £13.55 (BYR)
1981 £14.60 (HA) £15.25 (ALL)

Tertre-Daugay *grand cru classé St-Émilion*
1985 £11.19 (WIL)
1983 £11.30 (WIL)
1981 £14.29 (WIL)
1979 £14.39 (WIL)

le Tertre Rôteboeuf *grand cru St-Émilion*
1988 EC £105.00 (WW) £122.88 (LAY)
1987 £9.58 (WW) £10.54 (ASK) £10.67 (IR)
1986 £10.66 (IR) £15.90 (WW)
1985 £15.90 (WW)
1983 £11.98 (WW)

la Tour-de-Bessan *Margaux*
1986 £8.15 (WIL)
1984 £5.65 (WIL)

Webster's is an annual publication. We welcome your suggestions for next year's edition.

la Tour-de-By *cru grand bourgeois Médoc*
1988 £6.70 (HIG)
1987 £5.93 (TAN)
1986 £6.55 (STA) £6.99 (PE)
1986 EC £43.50 (HAG)
1985 £6.59 (AUG) £7.09 (PE) £7.95 (GRE)
    £8.05 (HIG) £8.14 (PIP)

la Tour-de-Mons *cru bourgeois supérieur Margaux*
1987 £9.30 (AN)
1986 £8.75 (BYR)
1985 £8.39 (ASK)
1983 £7.22 (HOG)
1975 £17.50 (BAR)
1971 £16.39 (REI)

la Tour-du-Haut-Moulin *Haut-Médoc*
1989 EC £60.00 (HUN)
1988 EC £53.00 (HIC)
1986 £7.60 (LAY)
1985 £6.45 (BYR)
1981 £7.95 (WW) £8.05 (ASK) £9.10 (AN)

la Tour-du-Mirail *cru bourgeois Haut-Médoc*
1985 £7.60 (AD)
1979 £8.98 (CH)

Tour-du-Moulin *Haut-Médoc*
1985 £5.49 (IR)
1983 £4.25 (BYR)

la Tour-du-Pin-Figeac *grand cru classé St-Émilion*
1985 £11.19 (WIL) £12.50 (DI)
1970 £19.75 (WHI)

la Tour-St-Bonnet *cru bourgeois Médoc*
1986 £4.95 (RAE) £5.25 (DAV) £5.35 (BYR)
    £5.85 (BEK) £5.94 (CH) £5.99 (PE)
1985 £5.49 (DAV) £5.89 (BYR) £6.15 (WHI)
    £7.40 (WRI)
1983 £5.18 (HOG) £5.89 (GRE) £7.88 (REI)
1982 £7.85 (OL) £8.00 (LOR)

Tourteau-Chollet *Graves*
1985 £5.45 (SAI) £5.49 (DI)
1983 £6.75 (AS) £6.98 (BR)

Tronquoy-Lalande *cru grand bourgeois St-Éstèphe*
1985 £7.57 (EL) £7.70 (LOR)
1981 £8.97 (OL)
1978 £10.95 (BL)

Troplong-Mondot *grand cru classé St-Émilion*
1989 EC £107.00 (HUN)
1986 £11.25 (DAV)
1975 £11.65 (BER)

Trotanoy *Pomerol*
1988 EC £319.44 (LAY)
1983 £34.95 (VIG)
1981 £43.00 (GI)
1979 £38.33 (BIB)
1975 jeroboam £638.25 (TW)

Trottevieille *1er grand cru classé St-Émilion*
1988 £15.33 (HIG)
1983 £15.25 (DAV)

Verdignan *grand bourgeois Médoc*
1983 £7.46 (BEK)
1982 £10.97 (YF)
1978 £9.95 (BO) £10.50 (ALL)

Vieux-Château-Certan *Pomerol*

1988 EC £225.00 (WW)
1987 £18.95 (RAE)
1987 magnum £16.10 (BIB)
1986 £28.95 (WW)
1985 £26.35 (BIB) £36.00 (HUN)
1983 £18.50 (RAE) £19.19 (BYR) £23.50 (BER)
1983 magnum £43.13 (BIB)
1982 £28.50 (VIG) £29.99 (PE) £32.90 (GI)
1978 £30.15 (PE)

Villegeorge *cru grand bourgeois exceptionnel Haut-Médoc*
1989 EC £70.00 (RAE)
1986 £6.99 (PE) £8.50 (RAE)
1985 £8.50 (RAE)

Villeneuve de Cantemerle *Haut-Médoc*
1986 £7.99 (BO)
1985 £7.29 (WHI)

PETITS CHÂTEAUX

de Barbe *Côtes de Bourg*
1985 £4.35 (DAV) £5.21 (CB)

Beauguérit *Côtes de Bourg*
1986 £4.92 (BR)
1985 £4.25 (GRE)

Bédats-Bois-Montet *1ères Côtes de Bordeaux*
1986 £3.90 (LOR)
1985 £3.95 (LOR)

de Belcier *Côtes de Francs*
1987 £5.09 (WCL) £5.20 (BR)
1986 £5.25 (DAV)
1985 £4.46 (ASK) £5.06 (BOR)

Bertin *Montagne-St-Émilion*
1985 £5.67 (CB)

Bessan *1ères Côtes de Bordeaux*
1986 £5.35 (PE)

Bonnet *Bordeaux supérieur*
1986 £5.50 (UP)

du Bousquet *Côtes de Bourg*
1986 £4.25 (SAI)

Calon *Montagne-St-Émilion*
1981 £9.35 (AN)

Canteloup *1ères Côtes de Blaye*
1987 £3.85 (SAF)
1986 £3.99 (GRE)
1985 £3.49 (BYR)

Cardeneau *Fronsac*
1985 £6.79 (BYR)

la Croix-des-Moines *Lalande-de-Pomerol*
1985 £6.99 (AUG)
1983 £9.05 (AN)

de la Croix-Millorit *Côtes de Bourg*
1983 £5.37 (BEK)

Dalem *Fronsac*
1988 EC £53.00 (HUN)

de la Dauphine *Fronsac*
1989 EC £55.00 (HUN)

1987 £6.50 (WW)
1987 IB £52.00 (CB)
1986 £6.70 (MV)

de la Duchesse *Fronsac*
1983 £4.95 (BYR) £5.45 (PE)

l'Escadre *Côtes de Blaye*
1989 EC £23.85 (HIC)
1983 £4.25 (HOG)

le Gardera *1ères Côtes de Bordeaux*
1987 £3.99 (WAI) £4.45 (ASD) £5.39 (WCL)
1986 £4.75 (PE) £4.79 (AUG)
1985 £4.99 (PE)
1983 £5.49 (BO)

Grand-Mazerolles *1ères Côtes de Blaye*
1985 £5.25 (PE)

Grand-Mouëys *1ères Côtes de Bordeaux*
1986 £4.29 (WCL)

du Grand-Pierre *Côtes de Blaye*
1986 £3.49 (ASD)

Haut-Gillet *Montagne-St-Émilion*
1983 £4.99 (BYR)

de Haut-Sociondo *1ères Côtes de Blaye*
1983 £3.79 (BL) £4.90 (HAG)

du Juge *1ères Côtes de Bordeaux*
1988 £4.29 (AUG)

Lagrange Monbadon *Côtes de Castillon*
1985 £3.99 (WAI)

Lamothe *1ères Côtes de Bordeaux*
1985 £4.49 (BO) £5.32 (VIN)

Lavergne *Bordeaux supérieur Côtes de Castillon*
1986 £3.85 (WIL) £4.10 (STA)

du Lyonnat *Lussac-St-Émilion*
1985 £6.29 (BYR) £6.89 (WCL) £7.21 (HIC)
1983 £7.42 (REI)

Macquin-St-Georges *St-Georges-St-Émilion*
1986 £4.75 (MAJ) £5.25 (DAV) £5.62 (TAN)

Mazeris *Fronsac*
1988 EC £48.00 (MV)
1986 £8.66 (CB)
1985 £8.95 (LAY) £11.07 (CB)

de Méaume *Bordeaux*
1987 £4.25 (MAJ)
1986 £4.49 (HA)
★**1985** £5.24 (CB)
1984 £4.18 (CB)

Mendoce *Côtes de Bourg*
1985 £4.25 (DAV)

Mirefleurs *1ères Côtes de Bordeaux*
1986 £3.65 (SAI)

Montaiguillon *Montagne-St-Émilion*
1986 £5.92 (BEK)

Nodez *Côtes de Bourg*
1985 £3.95 (BYR)

Péconnet *Bordeaux supérieur*
1985 £4.45 (PE)

Pérenne *1ères Côtes de Blaye*
1988 £4.43 (BEK)
1985 £5.30 (HA)

les Petits Arnauds *Côtes de Blaye*
1983 £4.19 (CH) £4.49 (BL)

Peyrabon *Bordeaux supérieur*
1985 £5.95 (PE) £6.36 (PIP)

Pitray *Côtes de Castillon*
1986 £4.51 (IR) £4.59 (PE) £5.89 (REI) £5.98
  (BIB)
1985 £4.50 (WS)

Plaisance *Montagne-St-Émilion*
1987 £5.95 (PD)
1986 £5.09 (IR) £6.06 (BEK)
1982 £10.09 (PIP)

de Prade *Bordeaux supérieur*
1989 EC £41.20 (HAH)
1986 £4.25 (WAI) £5.35 (WHI)
1985 £5.25 (BO)

Puygueraud *Côtes de Francs*
★**1989 EC** £55.00 (HUN)
1988 EC £53.00 (HUN)
1986 £5.95 (VIG)

Reynier *Bordeaux supérieur*
1986 £4.74 (CH)

Richotey *Fronsac*
1986 £4.29 (MAJ)
1985 £4.75 (RAE)

la Rivière *Fronsac*
1989 EC £55.00 (BE)
1988 EC £59.60 (BE)
1987 £7.30 (BE)
1986 £8.30 (BE)
1985 £9.10 (BE) £9.95 (VIG) £11.73 (TW)

Roquevieille *Côtes de Castillon*
1983 £6.11 (VIN)

Rouet *Fronsac*
1986 £5.59 (PE)
1985 £5.85 (BER) £6.50 (HAY) £6.65 (RAE, PE)

Rousset *Côtes de Bourg*
1985 £3.39 (WIL)
1982 £5.65 (HA) £5.79 (CB)

Tanesse *1ères Côtes de Bordeaux*
1985 £4.89 (WHI) £5.49 (PE)
  Bordeaux supérieur Côtes de Castillon
1986 £4.46 (YF) £5.08 (HA)

Thieuley *Bordeaux*
1988 £4.60 (HAY)
1986 £3.59 (WIZ) £5.10 (HUN)
1985 £5.09 (CB)

Timberlay *Bordeaux supérieur*
1987 £4.29 (AUG)
1986 £4.25 (DAV)

Toumalin *Canon-Fronsac*
1985 EC £43.00 (HAG)

la Tour-Puymiraud *Bordeaux*
1985 £3.97 (BEK)

Toutigeac *Bordeaux*
1986 £3.35 (TES)

la Valade *Fronsac*
1983 £4.80 (BER)

Villars *Fronsac*
1988 EC £42.00 (MV)
1986 £6.25 (LOR)
1985 £6.99 (DAV) £8.49 (UN)

WHITE BORDEAUX

DRY

──────── Under £4.00 ────────

Non-vintage
Asda Bordeaux Blanc (ASD)
1989
Moulin de Launay (AD)
Tertre de Launay (HAH)
★Thieuley (WIZ)
la Tuilerie (AUG)
1988
Asda Sauvignon de Bordeaux (ASD)
Moulin de Launay (AV, TAN)
Senilhac (WAI)
Thieuley (WIZ)
Trois Mouline Sauvignon (PE)
la Tuilerie (BOT)
1987
Cabannes (ASK)
Tertre de Launay (DAV)

──────── £4.00 to £4.99 ────────

1989
Bonnet (NI, EL)
la Rose St-Germain (AN)
Thieuley (MAJ, AD, HIC, HAH)
de Vergnes (AN)
1988
Bonnet (THR)
Coucheroy (THR)
Pichon-Bellevue (NI)
de Rochmorin (WAI)
Roquetaillade-la-Grange (SAF)
Thieuley (HAY)
Trois Mouline Sauvignon (TAN, AV)
la Tuilerie (MAJ)
1987
Reynon (TAN)
★Sirius (THR)
1986
Coutet Sec (AUG)
de l'Étoile (TAN)
Sirius (EL)

──────── £5.00 to £6.99 ────────

1988
Archambeau (BEK)
Bonnet (UP)
Cruzeau (ASD, EL)
★de Landiras (HAY)
Montalivet (AD)
Reynon (CB)

1987
Cabannieux (ASK)
Carbonnieux (WHI)
Château Talbot Caillou Blanc (BYR)
Grand Vin Sec du Château Doisy-Daëne
    (TAN)
Loudenne (BOT, PD)
la Louvière (WIZ)
Petit Mouta (AN)
Sirius (HAG)
Thieuley (MAJ)
1986
d'Arricaud (PE, RAE)
Coutet Sec (GRE, BYR)
Montalivet (TAN)
Sirius (BE)

──────── £7.00 to £8.99 ────────

1989
Reynon Vieilles Vignes (CB)
1988
Château Talbot Caillou Blanc (HAG, WHI,
    PE)
Couhins-Lurton (OD)
Grand Vin Sec du Château Doisy-Daëne
    (AD)
la Louvière (OD)
Rahoul (BAR)
1987
Constantin (CB)
Couhins-Lurton (PE, BIB)
Montalivet (REI)
1986
Bouscaut (RAE)
Carbonnieux (PE)
Constantin (BY)
la Louvière (CB, THR)
la Tour Martillac (OD)

──────── £9.00 to £11.99 ────────

1988
Carbonnieux (HAH)
Couhins-Lurton (RAE, AD, REI)
de Landiras (WIC)
Latour-Martillac (NI)
Smith-Haut-Lafitte (OD)
1987
Carbonnieux (HA)
Couhins-Lurton (TAN)
Rahoul (HA)
1986
Carbonnieux (TAN)

Olivier (WIL)
Rahoul (BOD)
1983
Carbonnieux (REI)
1982
Carbonnieux (WY)
1981
Rieussec 'R' (WY)
1978
la Louvière (WS)

─────── £12.00 to £14.99 ───────
1986
Carbonnieux (AV, AN)
1982
Smith-Haut-Lafitte (UP)

─────── £16.00 to £18.99 ───────
1987
de Fieuzal (BEK)
'L' de la Louvière (AD)
Pavillon Blanc du Château Margaux (LAY)
Rieussec 'R' (BY)
1986
de Fieuzal (BER)
1959
Malartic-Lagravière (REI)
1940
Pavillon Blanc du Château Margaux (RAE)

─────── £20.00 to £30.00 ───────
1988
Larrivet-Haut-Brion (HA)
1987
Bouscaut (RAE)
Laville-Haut-Brion (BEK)
Pavillon Blanc du Château Margaux (AN)

─────── £35.00 to £49.99 ───────
1983
Domaine de Chevalier (BER)

Haut-Brion Blanc (WY)
Laville-Haut-Brion (AV)
1982
Laville-Haut-Brion (EL)
1981
Domaine de Chevalier (TW)
1979
Laville-Haut-Brion (EL)
1953
la Tour-Léognan (VIG)

─────── £50.00 to £75.00 ───────
1983
Domaine de Chevalier (TAN)
Haut-Brion Blanc (EL, TW)
Laville-Haut-Brion (BER)
1982
Domaine de Chevalier (TW)
Haut-Brion Blanc (WY)
1967
Laville-Haut-Brion (VIG)

─────── c. £92.00 ───────
1978
Haut-Brion Blanc (WY)
1949
Carbonnieux (WY)

SWEET

─────── Under £4.00 ───────
Non-vintage
Asda 1ères Côtes de Bordeaux (ASD)
Asda Bordeaux Blanc Sweet (ASD)
1988
★de Berbec (OD)
la Garenne (NI)
Grolet (WIZ)
1986
Bastor-Lamontagne ½ bottle (WAI)
de Berbec (WAI, WIZ)
de Ricaud ½ bottle (OD)

─────── £4.00 to £4.99 ───────
1988
Bastor-Lamontagne ½ bottle (OD)
Grand Vignot (UN)
1987
de Berbec (SAF)
1986
des Arroucats (DAV)
Bastor-Lamontagne ½ bottle (HAY)
de Berbec (WCL, SAF, THR)
Laurette (GRE)
Loupiac Gaudiet (BOT, PD)

1983
des Tours (MV)
1981
Bastor-Lamontagne ½ bottle (WCL)

——————— **£5.00 to £6.99** ———————
1988
des Arroucats (CB, HAH)
de Berbec (HIC)
Domaine de Noble (BIB)
du Tich (PE, BIB)
1987
Clos St-Georges (SAI)
des Tours (HA)
1986
de Berbec (ALL, HAY)
Domaine de Noble (BIB)
Fayau (GRE)
Loupiac Gaudiet (HAH)
la Nère (BL)
des Tours (HIC)
1985
Terford (HAG)
du Tich (RAE)
1983
Doisy-Dubroca ½ bottle (WCL)
★Liot (ALL)
1982
★Coutet ½ bottle (HA)
Lousteau-Vieil (VIG)
Nairac ½ bottle (BYR)
1981
Filhot (OL)

——————— **£7.00 to £8.99** ———————
1988
Lousteau-Vieil (HAU)
1987
Guiteronde (BOT)
Mayne des Carmes (OD)
1986
Liot (HAY)
Lousteau-Vieil (PIP, UP)
de Malle (PE)
1983
Coutet ½ bottle (BAR)
Doisy-Dubroca (WAI)
la Tour Blanche (HOG)
1982
★Coutet ½ bottle (BYR, EL)
Rayne-Vigneau ½ bottle (DI)
1981
Filhot (REI)
1975
d'Arricaud (RAE)

——————— **£9.00 to £11.99** ———————
1987
Bastor-Lamontagne (IR, CH)
1986
Bastor-Lamontagne (IR)
★Broustet (REI)
Cantegril (TAN)
Doisy-Dubroca (HAH)
Liot (BER, MV)
Rabaud-Promis (RAE)
Rayne-Vigneau (AD)
Rieussec ½ bottle (MV)
Romer du Hayot (BOT, PIP)
de Veyres (EL)
1983
d'Arche (HIC)
Climens ½ bottle (REI, RAE)
Rayne-Vigneau (HOG)
Suduiraut ½ bottle (OL)
1981
Guiraud ½ bottle (WRI)
Lafaurie-Peyraguey (HOG)
1980
Suduiraut (HAG)
1979
Coutet ½ bottle (VIG, WY)
Filhot (HAG)
Romer du Hayot (HOG)
1975
Lousteau-Vieil (HAU)
1974
Climens ½ bottle (RAE)

——————— **£12.00 to £14.99** ———————
1987
Rabaud-Promis (AD)
1986
Broustet (PIP)
la Chartreuse (EL)
Rabaud-Promis (PE)
St-Amand (HIC)
1983
Filhot (HAG, BYR)
Lamothe-Guignard (REI, LAY, BE)
Rayne-Vigneau (RES, WY)
Rieussec ½ bottle (WHI, DAV)
la Tour Blanche (ALL, BL)
1982
Nairac (BYR)
Rieussec (DAV)
1981
Doisy-Daëne (AD)
Rieussec (DAV)
1978
Broustet (YF)

1977
Lafaurie-Peyraguey (WHI)
1974
Nairac (TW)

─────── £15.00 to £19.99 ───────

1986
d'Arche (TAN)
Climens (PE)
Coutet (AD)
Doisy-Védrines (HA)
Rieussec (OD, BYR)
Suduiraut (CB)
1985
Filhot (DAV)
1983
d'Arche (YF)
Climens (HA)
Coutet (HAG, VIC, BYR, GRE, BE, TAN, AD, WHI)
Filhot (AN, DAV)
Guiraud (BAR)
de Malle (PIP, DAV)
Sigalas-Rabaud (WS)
Suduiraut (HAG, BAR, TAN)
la Tour Blanche (AD)
1982
Climens (TAN)
Rieussec (VIC)
1981
Rieussec (AN, ALL)
1980
Lafaurie-Peyraguey (PE)

1978
la Chartreuse (YF)
1975
Lafaurie-Peyraguey (YF)
1970
Doisy-Védrines (WY)
de Malle (HA)

─────── £20.00 to £29.99 ───────

1986
Climens (CB)
Guiraud (WHI)
Rieussec (MV, CB)

1983
Climens (ELL, BAR, MV)
Coutet (PIP, HA)
Lafaurie-Peyraguey (BYR, BAR)
Rieussec (DAV)
Suduiraut (WHI, EL, CB)
1982
Suduiraut (TAN, PIP)
1980
de Fargues (WS)
Guiraud (WRI)
Raymond Lafon (VIG)
Rieussec (UN)
1979
Climens (RES)
1975
Lafaurie-Peyraguey (REI)
Rayne-Vigneau (CB)
1973
Climens (RES)
1971
Sigalas-Rabaud (HA)
Suau (HA)

─────── £30.00 to £39.99 ───────

1983
Lafaurie-Peyraguey (WIL)
Rieussec (RES)
1980
de Fargues (RES)
1979
de Fargues (VIG)
1976
Climens (RES)
Filhot (BAR)
1971
Coutet (RES)
1970
Climens (VIG)

─────── £40.00 to £49.99 ───────

1981
d'Yquem ½ bottle (RES)
1975
Nairac (VIG)
1971
Climens (RES)
1962
Gilette (MV)
1935
la Tour Blanche (WY)

─────── £50.00 to £59.99 ───────

1981
d'Yquem ½ bottle (HA)

1980
d'Yquem ½ bottle (HAG)
1979
d'Yquem (UN)
1967
Guiraud (WY)
1962
Gilette (WHI)
1961
Coutet (WY)
Gilette Crème de Tête (MV)
1933
Rayne-Vigneau (WY)
1923
la Tour Blanche (VIG)

──────── £60.00 to £74.99 ────────
1981
d'Yquem (WRI)
1979
Raymond Lafon (VIG)
1961
Climens (WY)
1955
Rieussec (DI)
1918
Rabaud-Promis (VIG)

──────── £75.00 to £90.00 ────────
1985
d'Yquem ½ bottle (TW)
1981
d'Yquem (RES)
1961
Gilette Crème de Tête (TW)
1939
Filhot (WY)
1926
Lafaurie-Peyraguey (WY)
1923
la Tour Blanche (WY)

──────── £95.00 to £115.00 ────────
1985
d'Yquem (LAY)
1983
d'Yquem (CB)
1982
d'Yquem (WIL)
1981
d'Yquem (UN, YG)
1959
Rieussec (WY)
1955
Gilette Crème de Tête (TW)

1939
Rayne-Vigneau (WY)
1926
Rayne-Vigneau (WY)

──────── £125.00 to £149.99 ────────
1983
d'Yquem (DAV)
1982
d'Yquem (HA)
1938
Gilette Crème de Tête (TW)
1914
Suduiraut (WY)

──────── £150.00 to £175.00 ────────
1983
d'Yquem (AN, HA)
1967
de Fargues (WY)
1929
Filhot (WY)
Coutet (WY)

──────── £195.00 to £215.00 ────────
1983
d'Yquem (WIL)
1961
d'Yquem (RES)
1949
Gilette Crème de Tête (TW)

──────── c. £276.00 ────────
1948
d'Yquem (TW)

──────── £350.00 to £375.00 ────────
1967
d'Yquem (WY, RES)
1959
d'Yquem (VIG)
1955
d'Yquem (RES)

──────── c. £460.00 ────────
1949
d'Yquem (REI)

> *In each price band wines*
> *are listed in vintage*
> *order. Within each*
> *vintage they are listed in*
> *A-Z order.*

BASIC BURGUNDY

RED

──────── Under £5.00 ────────

Non-vintage
Asda Bourgogne Rouge (ASD)
Sainsbury's Burgundy Pinot Noir (SAI)
Tesco Bourgogne Rouge (TES)
1987
Bourgogne Pinot Noir Cave de Buxy (WAI)
1986
Bourgogne Pinot Noir Cave de Buxy (OD)
1982
Bourgogne Passe-Tout-Grain, Lejeune
(RAE)

──────── £5.00 to £5.99 ────────

1988
★Bourgogne Pinot Noir Fûts de Chêne,
Cave de Buxy (PIP)
Bourgogne Rouge Faiveley (DI)
1987
Bourgogne Passe-Tout-Grain, Jayer (RAE,
BIB)
Bourgogne Passe-Tout-Grain, Rion (MV)
1986
Bourgogne Passe-Tout-Grain, Jayer (BIB)
Bourgogne Passe-Tout-Grain, Lejeune (BIB)
Bourgogne Pinot Noir Cave de Buxy (WCL)
Bourgogne Rouge Boisson-Vadot (BEK)
Bourgogne Rouge Faiveley (DI)
1984
Bourgogne Rouge Tasteviné, Bichot (UN)

──────── £6.00 to £6.99 ────────

1988
Bourgogne la Digoine Villaine (AD)
Bourgogne Passe-Tout-Grain, Jayer (RAE)
1986
Bourgogne la Digoine Villaine (AD)
Bourgogne Passe-Tout-Grain, Vallet (BOR)
Bourgogne Pinot Noir Jadot (VIC)
Bourgogne Pinot Noir Machard de
Gramont (AN)
Bourgogne Rouge Rossignol (BEK)

WHITE

──────── Under £5.00 ────────

Non-vintage
Sainsbury's Burgundy Chardonnay (SAI)
1989
Bourgogne Aligoté Cave de Buxy (WAI)

1988
Bourgogne Aligoté Duboeuf (BEK)
1987
Bourgogne Aligoté Cave de Buxy (HOG)
Bourgogne Blanc Jadot (BYR)
Bourgogne Blanc Ropiteau (HOG)
1986
★Bourgogne Aligoté Sorin-Defrance (BYR)

──────── £5.00 to £5.99 ────────

1989
Bourgogne Aligoté Duboeuf (BY)
Bourgogne Aligoté Larousse (AN)
1988
Bourgogne Aligoté Rollin (BIB)
★Bourgogne Chardonnay Domaine
Ste-Claire, Brocard (THR, BEK)
1987
Bourgogne Aligoté Diconne (BEK)
Bourgogne Aligoté Tabit (PE)
Bourgogne Blanc les Clous, Villaine (AD)
Bourgogne Clos de Chenoves (GI)
1986
Bourgogne Aligoté Rollin (RAE)
Bourgogne Aligoté Tollot-Beaut (BY)
Bourgogne Aligoté Vallet (UP)
★Bourgogne Chardonnay Georges Blanc (BR)

──────── £6.00 to £8.99 ────────

1988
Bourgogne Blanc Clerc (BY)
Bourgogne Chardonnay Drouhin (BR)
Bourgogne Chardonnay Jadot (THR)
1987
Bourgogne Aligoté Rion (UP)
1986
Bourgogne Blanc Clerc (BYR)

SPARKLING

──────── Under £7.00 ────────

Non-vintage
Crémant de Bourgogne, Cave de Lugny
(HAH)
Sainsbury's Crémant de Bourgogne (SAI)
★Sainsbury's Crémant de Bourgogne Rosé
(SAI)
1986
Crémant de Bourgogne, Cave de Viré (DAV,
MAJ, THR)
Crémant de Bourgogne Rosé, Cave de
Bailly (WAI)

CÔTE D'OR

RED

──────── **Under £6.00** ────────

1988
Hautes-Côtes de Beaune, Caves des
    Hautes-Côtes (DI)
1987
Hautes-Côtes de Beaune, Caves des
    Hautes-Côtes (WAI)
Marsannay Raisin Social (WAI)
1986
Côte de Beaune-Villages Labouré-Roi (SAF)
Hautes-Côtes de Beaune, Caves des
    Hautes-Côtes (OD)
1985
Hautes-Côtes de Beaune, Caves des
    Hautes-Côtes (GI)
Hautes-Côtes de Nuits, Caves des Hautes-
    Côtes (TES, SAI)
Marsannay Ropiteau (SAF)

──────── **£6.00 to £6.99** ────────

1987
Côte de Beaune-Villages Viénot (IR)
1986
Beaune Labouré-Roi (SAF)
Côte de Beaune-Villages Viénot (IR)
1985
Hautes-Côtes de Beaune, Georges Blanc
    (BR)

──────── **£7.00 to £7.99** ────────

1988
Côte de Beaune-Villages Drouhin (NI)
1987
Hautes-Côtes de Beaune, Mazilly (MV)
1986
Hautes-Côtes de Beaune, Mazilly (UP)
Hautes-Côtes de Nuits, Michel Gros (BY)
Savigny-lès-Beaune Boisset (PD, BOT)
★St-Aubin Prudhon (BIB)
1985
Hautes-Côtes de Nuits, Michel Gros (WW)
St-Aubin Bachelet (RAE)

──────── **£8.00 to £8.99** ────────

1988
Côte de Beaune la Grande Châtelaine,
    Lescure (PIP)
Monthélie Jaffelin (OD)
Santenay la Maladière, Jaffelin (OD)
St-Aubin les Frionnes, Prudhon (TAN)

1987
Hautes-Côtes de Nuits, Michel Gros (BY)
1986
Chassagne-Montrachet Lamy (PE)
Chorey-lès-Beaune Tollot-Beaut (LAY, BEK,
    DOM)
Côte de Beaune la Grande Châtelaine,
    Lescure (WIL)
Hautes-Côtes de Nuits, Michel Gros (ASK)
Hautes-Côtes de Nuits, Verdet (HAU)
Pernand-Vergelesses Rollin (RAE, BIB)
St-Aubin les Argillières, Lamy-Pillot (BAR)
1985
Côte de Beaune la Grande Châtelaine,
    Lescure (WIL)
Hautes-Côtes de Nuits, Michel Gros (BY)
St-Aubin Bachelet (BIB)
1984
Pernand-Vergelesses Rollin (RAE)
1983
Chassagne-Montrachet Bachelet (RAE)
Pernand-Vergelesses Rollin (PE, GI)

──────── **£9.00 to £9.99** ────────

1988
Chassagne-Montrachet Henri Germain
    (TAN)
Santenay Drouhin (NI)
1987
Chorey-lès-Beaune Tollot-Beaut (BY)
Monthélie Monthélie-Douhairet (MV)
Santenay la Maladière, Girardin (BEK)
1986
Auxey-Duresses Roulot (HAY)
Chassagne-Montrachet Raoul Clerget (YF)
Chorey-lès-Beaune Tollot-Beaut (BY)
Fixin Gelin (ASK)
Gevrey-Chambertin Labouré-Roi (SAF)
Santenay la Comme, Girardin (WW)
Savigny Capron Manieux (MV)
Savigny-lès-Beaune Bize (LAY)
1985
Beaune Viénot (HA)
Santenay Drouhin (NI)
Savigny-lès-Beaune Girard-Vollot (MV)
Savigny-lès-Beaune Latour (VIC, WHI)
St-Aubin les Frionnes, Prudhon (PE)
1984
Monthélie Château de Monthélie,
    Suremain (BEK)
Santenay les Gravières, Domaine de la
    Pousse d'Or (BY)

Savigny-lès-Beaune Champs-Chevrey, Tollot-Beaut (HAY)

Savigny-lès-Beaune Marconnets, Bize (DOM)

1982

Morey-St-Denis Clos des Ormes, Lignier (PE)

★Savigny-lès-Beaune les Vergelesses, Bize (PE)

1981

Chambolle-Musigny Chanson (TAN)

───── £10.00 to £10.99 ─────

1988

Monthélie Garaudet (PIP)

1987

Chassagne-Montrachet Gagnard-Delagrange (BY)

Fixin les Hervelets, Gelin (OD)

Meursault Latour-Giraud (REI)

Monthélie Monthélie-Douhairet (WCL)

Savigny-lès-Beaune les Guettes, Machard de Gramont (TAN)

Savigny-lès-Beaune Pavelot (DOM)

1986

Chassagne-Montrachet Gagnard-Delagrange (BY)

Chassagne-Montrachet Henri Germain (AD)

Chorey-lès-Beaune Tollot-Beaut (AI)

Savigny-lès-Beaune Champs-Chevrey, Tollot-Beaut (BEK)

Savigny Peuillets, Capron Manieux (MV)

1985

Beaune Teurons, Chanson (BYR)

Monthélie Monthélie-Douhairet (UP)

St-Aubin les Castets, Lamy (PE)

Santenay Latour (AI, WHI)

Savigny-lès-Beaune les Lavières, Chandon de Briailles (BYR)

1983

Beaune Bressandes, Chanson (BYR)

Beaune Grèves, Moillard (BO)

Chambolle-Musigny Lignier (PE)

Savigny-lès-Beaune Chauvenet (PE)

Savigny-lès-Beaune Latour (GI)

1982

Beaune Roulot (HAY)

Santenay la Comme, Lequin-Roussot (HAY)

Volnay Champans, Prieur (GI)

1980

Morey-St-Denis Monts Luisants, Moillard (BYR)

1976

Morey-St-Denis Boisset (GI)

───── £11.00 to £11.99 ─────

1987

Beaune Grèves, Albert Morey (BEK)

Chassagne-Montrachet Gagnard-Delagrange (WHI)

Santenay Grand Clos Rousseau, Albert Morey (BEK)

Santenay les Gravières, Domaine de la Pousse d'Or (BY)

Savigny Peuillets, Capron Manieux (MV)

Vosne-Romanée les Violettes, Georges Clerget (BY)

1986

Chambolle-Musigny Faiveley (BYR)

Chassagne-Montrachet Latour (AI)

Gevrey-Chambertin Trapet (BY)

Morey-St-Denis Tortochot (WW)

Pommard les Cras, Belland (LOR)

Santenay Clos Tavannes, Domaine de la Pousse d'Or (DOM)

Savigny-lès-Beaune les Lavières, Tollot-Beaut (PE)

Vougeot Clos de la Perrière, Bertagna (TAN)

1985

Beaune Montée Rouge, Voarick (WRI)

Beaune Teurons, Jadot (BYR)

Gevrey-Chambertin Faiveley (AI)

Nuits-St-Georges Rodet (ASD)

Pernand-Vergelesses Dubreuil-Fontaine (BEK)

1984

Gevrey-Chambertin Leclerc (HAY)

Gevrey-Chambertin Rodet (WHI)

Savigny-lès-Beaune Champs-Chevrey, Tollot-Beaut (PE)

Vosne-Romanée Mongeard-Mugneret (DOM)

1983

Aloxe-Corton Voarick (LAY)

Savigny-lès-Beaune Latour (WIL)

Savigny-lès-Beaune les Guettes, Bize (RAE)

Savigny Peuillets, Vollot (MV)

MOREY-SAINT-DENIS
Monts Luisants
Appellation Morey-Saint-Denis Contrôlée
Product of France

Propriétaire : Madame Prevot
Mis en bouteille par MOILLARD●
Négociant-Éleveur à Nuits-Saint-Georges (Côte-d'Or) France

1982

Beaune Teurons, Rossignol (CHA)

Nuits-St-Georges Viénot (OL)

1981

Beaune 1er Cru, Domaine du Château de
  Meursault (BO)

Morey-St-Denis Monts Luisants, Moillard
  (CH)

1979

Meursault les Forges, Prieur-Brunet (WIL)

─────── £12.00 to £12.99 ───────

1988

Chassagne-Montrachet Gagnard-
  Delagrange (BY)

1987

Chassagne-Montrachet Gagnard-
  Delagrange (AN)

Gevrey-Chambertin Armand Rousseau
  (TAN)

Gevrey-Chambertin Rossignol (BEK)

Gevrey-Chambertin Roty (LAY)

Gevrey-Chambertin Trapet (BY)

1986

Aloxe-Corton Rollin (RAE)

Beaune Bressandes, Henri Germain (TAN)

Beaune Chouacheux, Lescure (PIP)

Chambolle-Musigny Noëllat (BEK)

Côte de Nuits-Villages Jayer-Gilles (AD)

Gevrey-Chambertin Domaine des Varoilles
  (AUG)

Gevrey-Chambertin Faiveley (DI)

Meursault Clos de la Baronne, Manuel
  (WIL)

Morey-St-Denis Domaine Taupenot-Merme
  (LOR)

Morey-St-Denis Regis Bouvier (BEK)

Nuits-St-Georges Faiveley (DI)

Santenay 1er Cru Armand Rousseau (VIG)

Vosne-Romanée Engel (BY)

1985

Beaune Clos de la Mousse, Bouchard Père
  (PD)

Beaune Clos des Fèves, Chanson (BO)

Côte de Nuits-Villages Jayer-Gilles (PE)

Gevrey-Chambertin Faiveley (HOG)

1984

Chassagne-Montrachet Clos de la
  Boudriotte, Ramonet-Prudhon (BEK)

Nuits-St-Georges Rion (MV)

Vosne-Romanée Rion (MV)

1983

Beaune Chouacheux, Lescure (ALL)

Beaune Grèves, Chanson (DI)

Nuits-St-Georges Labouré-Roi (WHI)

Nuits-St-Georges Viénot (HUN)

Savigny-lès-Beaune les Vergelesses, Bize
  (PE)

1982

Morey-St-Denis Clos de la Bussière,
  Roumier (GI)

Savigny-lès-Beaune Ampeau (CHA)

1981

Beaune Vignes Franches, Latour (BO)

1978

Beaune Marconnets, Bouchard Père (HOG)

─────── £13.00 to £13.99 ───────

1988

Savigny-lès-Beaune les Lavières, Tollot-
  Beaut (AD)

1987

Gevrey-Chambertin Armand Rousseau
  (WHI)

Morey-St-Denis Clos des Ormes, Lignier
  (BIB)

1986

Aloxe-Corton Tollot-Beaut (BEK)

Beaune Bressandes, Henri Germain (AD)

Gevrey-Chambertin Armand Rousseau
  (WS)

Gevrey-Chambertin Bachelet (MV, WCL)

Gevrey-Chambertin Chanson (TAN)

Gevrey-Chambertin Lignier (HAU)

Gevrey-Chambertin Vieille Vigne, Domaine
  des Varoilles (CHA)

Meursault Chouet-Clivet (VIG)

Morey-St-Denis 1er Cru, Faiveley (BYR)

Morey-St-Denis Clos des Ormes, Faiveley
  (GRE)

Nuits-St-Georges Gouges (RES)

Nuits-St-Georges Rion (MV)

Volnay Clos des Santenots, Prieur (IR)

Volnay Lafarge (BEK)

Vosne-Romanée les Violettes, Georges
  Clerget (BY)

Vosne-Romanée Rion (MV)

1985

Beaune du Château, Domaine du Château
  de Beaune (BAR)

Beaune Épenottes, Machard de Gramont
  (TAN)

Beaune Marconnets, Bouchard Père (BO)
Beaune Teurons, Chanson (DI)
Chambolle-Musigny Chanson (BO, DI)
Pernand-Vergelesses Dubreuil-Fontaine (PIP)
Pommard la Platière, Coche (RAE)
Savigny-lès-Beaune Latour (YF)
Savigny-lès-Beaune les Lavières, Tollot-Beaut (PE)
1984
Corton Clos du Roi, Voarick (LAY)
Morey-St-Denis Clos des Ormes, Lignier (HAY, RAE)
Nuits-St-Georges Clos de la Maréchale, Faiveley (DI)
Nuits-St-Georges les Damodes, Machard de Gramont (AN)
Nuits-St-Georges Michelot (BEK)
1983
Beaune Cent Vignes, Mounnier (MV)
Chambolle-Musigny Roumier (RAE)
Clos St-Denis Lignier (PE)
Gevrey-Chambertin Faiveley (ALL)
Nuits-St-Georges Rion (MV)
Pommard Parent (GI)
Savigny-lès-Beaune Giraud, Hospices de Beaune (ALL)
1982
Aloxe-Corton Latour (WHI)
Auxey-Duresses Ampeau (CHA)
Corton Languettas, Voarick (PE)
Gevrey-Chambertin la Combe aux Moines, Faiveley (GI)
Morey-St-Denis 1er Cru, Ponsot (PE)
Nuits-St-Georges les St-Georges, Faiveley (GI)
Savigny-lès-Beaune Ampeau (REI)
1981
Nuits-St-Georges Clos de la Maréchale, Faiveley (BYR)
Nuits-St-Georges Georges Chevillon (ELL)
1980
Pommard les Argillières, Lejeune (BIB)
1978
★Santenay Remoissenet (GRE)
1976
Beaune Marconnets, Chanson (GI)

——————— £14.00 to £14.99 ———————
1988
★Gevrey-Chambertin Trapet (BY)
1987
Chambolle-Musigny Dujac (BY)
Vosne-Romanée Jean Gros (BY)
Vosne-Romanée les Suchots, Noëllat (BEK)

1986
Beaune Clos du Roi, Tollot-Beaut (BEK)
Beaune Toussaints, Albert Morot (RES)
Morey-St-Denis Dujac (BY)
Morey-St-Denis Monts Luisants, Pernin-Rossin (RAE)
Nuits-St-Georges Michelot (DOM)
Pommard les Saucille, Boillot (BEK)
Volnay 1er Cru Lafarge (BEK)
Volnay Santenots Lafon (DOM)
Vosne-Romanée Jean Gros (BY)
1985
Beaune Bressandes, Henri Germain (AD)
Volnay Leflaive (HAH)
1984
Gevrey-Chambertin Latour (WHI)
Morey-St-Denis Clos des Ormes, Lignier (HAU)
Volnay Clos d'Audignac, Domaine de la Pousse d'Or (BY)
1983
Corton Clos du Roi, Voarick (PE)
Corton Doudet-Naudin (BER)
Corton Viénot (HAG)
Nuits-St-Georges Clos de la Maréchale, Faiveley (BYR)
Pommard Lejeune (HAY)
1982
Aloxe-Corton Latour (HAG)
Chapelle-Chambertin Trapet (BYR)
Nuits-St-Georges Desargillier (BOT)
Pommard les Épenots, Mme de Courcel (PE)
1980
Latricières-Chambertin Newman (GRE)

——————— £15.00 to £15.99 ———————
1988
Vosne-Romanée Jean Gros (BY)
1987
Gevrey-Chambertin Cazetiers, Armand Rousseau (LAY)
Pommard Clos Blanc, Machard de Gramont (TAN)
Vosne-Romanée Jean Gros (WW)
1986
Beaune Bressandes Morot (RES)
Chambolle-Musigny Beaux Bruns, Rion (MV)
Chambolle-Musigny la Come d'Orvaux, Grivot (LAY)
Gevrey-Chambertin Bachelet (UP)
Gevrey-Chambertin Clos de la Justice, Vallet (AS)
Morey-St-Denis Clos des Ormes, Lignier (HAU)

Volnay Caillerets Cuvée Carnot, Bouchard
  Père (VIC)
Volnay Lafarge (PIP)
Volnay Santenots Matrot (CB)
Vosne-Romanée Rion (UP)
1985
Beaune Clos des Fèves, Chanson (DI)
Beaune Grèves, Albert Morot (RES)
Beaune Toussaints, Albert Morot (RES)
Chambolle-Musigny Confuron (AN)
Pommard les Bertins, Lescure (PIP)
Volnay Champans, Monthélie-Douhairet
  (MV)
1984
Nuits-St-Georges les Cailles, Michelot
  (BEK)
Nuits-St-Georges les Vaucrains, Michelot
  (BEK)
Volnay Champans, de Montille (DOM)
1983
Beaune Vignes Franches, Latour (YF)
Corton-Bressandes Voarick (PE)
Gevrey-Chambertin la Combe aux Moines,
  Faiveley (BYR)
Morey-St-Denis Dujac (BYR)
Nuits-St-Georges Jadot (VIC)
Nuits-St-Georges les Damodes, Machard
  de Gramont (AD)
Nuits-St-Georges Rion (UP)
Pommard les Épenots, Mme de Courcel (PE)
1982
Charmes-Chambertin Armand Rousseau
  (BYR)
Pommard Parent (LAY)
Volnay Frémiets, Marquis d'Angerville (CB)
1981
Clos de Vougeot Moillard (DI)
Pommard Lejeune (PE)
1978
Santenay Remoissenet (AV)

────────── £16.00 to £16.99 ──────────

1988
Aloxe-Corton Machard de Gramont (TAN)
Chambolle-Musigny Roumier (TAN)
★Morey-St-Denis Clos de la Bussière,
  Roumier (TAN)
Morey-St-Denis Dujac (AD, TAN)
Nuits-St-Georges les Damodes, Lescure
  (PIP)
1987
Aloxe-Corton Tollot-Beaut (BY)
Morey-St-Denis Dujac (BY)
Nuits-St-Georges les Cailles, Michelot
  (BEK)

Volnay Santenots Boillot (WW)
Volnay Santenots Matrot (CB)
1986
Aloxe-Corton Tollot-Beaut (BY)
Beaune Clos des Ursules, Jadot (VIC)
Nuits-St-Georges les Pruliers, Gouges (RES)
Pommard Clos Blanc, Machard de
  Gramont (YF)
Volnay Lafon (AD)
Volnay les Caillerets, Domaine de la
  Pousse d'Or (DOM)
Volnay Santenots Lafon (MV, WCL)
1985
Gevrey-Chambertin Drouhin (NI)
Nuits-St-Georges Clos de la Maréchale,
  Faiveley (BYR)
Pommard Clerget (HA)
Savigny-lès-Beaune les Vergelesses, Bize
  (AD)
1984
Volnay Clos de la Bousse d'Or, Domaine de
  la Pousse d'Or (DOM)
1983
Gevrey-Chambertin Cazetiers, Clair-Daü
  (GI)
Gevrey-Chambertin Drouhin-Laroze (GI)
Morey-St-Denis Dujac (PE)
Nuits-St-Georges Clos de la Maréchale,
  Faiveley (GI)
Nuits-St-Georges les Porets, Michelot (RAE)
Pommard les Argillières, Lejeune (PE)
1982
Clos de la Roche Armand Rousseau (BYR)
Corton Viénot (OL)
Pommard Clos de la Platière, Prince
  Florent de Merode (PE)
Volnay Santenots Lafon (MV)
1981
Corton-Bressandes Dubreuil-Fontaine (PE)

────────── £17.00 to £19.99 ──────────

1987
Beaune Teurons, Jacques Germain (WHI)
Mazis-Chambertin Armand Rousseau (LAY,
  BY, TAN)
Volnay Clos d'Audignac, Domaine de la
  Pousse d'Or (BY)
Volnay les Caillerets, Domaine de la
  Pousse d'Or (YF)
1986
Aloxe-Corton Tollot-Beaut (AI)
Beaune Clos des Mouches, Drouhin (GRE)
Chambolle-Musigny la Come d'Orvaux,
  Grivot (BY)
Chapelle-Chambertin Trapet (CB)

Clos de Vougeot Domaine des Varoilles
(TAN)
Corton Perrières, Juillot (DOM)
Corton Tollot-Beaut (DOM, BEK)
Gevrey-Chambertin Clos de la Justice,
Vallet (ALL)
Latricières-Chambertin Trapet (BEK, BY)
Nuits-St-Georges Clos de la Maréchale,
Faiveley (GRE, BE)
Nuits-St-Georges Haut Pruliers, Rion (MV)
Nuits-St-Georges les Cailles, Michelot
(DOM)
Nuits-St-Georges les Chaignots, Michelot
(DOM)
Nuits-St-Georges les Porets, Michelot
(DOM)
Nuits-St-Georges les Pruliers, Grivot (LAY)
Nuits-St-Georges les Vaucrains, Michelot
(DOM)
Nuits-St-Georges Richemone, Pernin-
Rossin (RAE)
Pommard les Bertins, Lescure (WIL)
Volnay Clos des Chênes, Lafarge (BEK)
Volnay Clos des Ducs, Marquis d'Angerville
(CB)
Volnay Santenots-du-Millieu, Tête de
Cuvée, Lafon (TAN)
Vosne-Romanée les Beaumonts, Domaine
Rion (MV)

1985
Aloxe-Corton Tollot-Beaut (AI)
Beaune Teurons, Domaine du Château de
Beaune (BAR)
Chambolle-Musigny Roumier (RES)
Corton Latour (VIC)
Gevrey-Chambertin Faiveley (HAG)
Nuits-St-Georges Clos de la Maréchale,
Faiveley (AI)
Nuits-St-Georges Jadot (HA)
Nuits-St-Georges les Pruliers, Gouges (AI)
Pernand-Vergelesses Île de Vergelesses,
Chanson (BYR)
Volnay Champans, Marquis d'Angerville
(AI)
Volnay les Caillerets, Domaine de la
Pousse d'Or (BYR)
Volnay Santenots Matrot (CB)

1984
Bonnes-Mares Roumier (DOM)
Chambertin Ponsot (MV)
Charmes-Chambertin Armand Rousseau
(PE)
Corton-Bressandes Tollot-Beaut (BEK)
Échézeaux Mongeard-Mugneret (DOM, BEK,
IR)

Gevrey-Chambertin Combottes, Dujac (PE)
Mazis-Chambertin Armand Rousseau (PE)
Mazis-Chambertin Faiveley (BYR)
Volnay les Caillerets, Clos des 60 Ouvrées,
Domaine de la Pousse d'Or (PE)

1983
Beaune Clos des Ursules, Jadot (LAY, PE)
Bonnes-Mares Domaine des Varoilles (PE)
Clos de la Roche Armand Rousseau (BY)
Clos de Vougeot Moillard (BE)
Échézeaux Labouré-Roi (WHI)
Nuits-St-Georges Jadot (HA)
Pommard Clos Blanc, Machard de
Gramont (GI)
Pommard Clos de la Commaraine,
Jaboulet-Vercherre (WRI)
Volnay Clos de la Bousse d'Or, Domaine de
la Pousse d'Or (RAE)
Volnay les Caillerets, Clos des 60 Ouvrées,
Domaine de la Pousse d'Or (RAE, PE)
Vosne-Romanée les Beaumonts, Latour (GI)

1982
Beaune Clos du Roi, Ampeau (CHA)
Clos de la Roche Vieilles Vignes, Ponsot
(PE)
Clos de Vougeot Château de la Tour (HA)

Corton-Grancey Latour (HOG, HAG)
Pommard Ampeau (CHA)
Volnay Domaine de la Bousse d'Or, Potel
(PE)
Volnay Santenots Ampeau (CHA, CHA)
Vosne-Romanée les Chaumes, Arnaux (PE)

1981
Pommard Ampeau (REI)
Volnay Santenots Ampeau (HAH)

1980
Volnay Santenots Ampeau (CHA)

1979
Morey-St-Denis Bourée (WS)

1978
Échézeaux Prosper Maufoux (WRI)
Savigny-lès-Beaune Ampeau (CHA)

1971
Clos de la Roche Chanson (GI)

——————— £20.00 to £24.99 ———————

1988

Chambolle-Musigny la Come d'Orvaux, Grivot (BY)

Gevrey-Chambertin Clos des Varoilles, Domaine des Varoilles (TAN)

1987

Chambolle-Musigny la Come d'Orvaux, Grivot (BY)

Charmes-Chambertin Bachelet (MV)

Charmes-Chambertin Roty (LAY)

Clos de la Roche Armand Rousseau (BY)

Corton-Bressandes Tollot-Beaut (BY)

Latricières-Chambertin Trapet (BY)

Nuits-St-Georges Clos de Forets St-Georges, Domaine de l'Arlot (LAY, BY)

Nuits-St-Georges les Pruliers, Grivot (BY)

Ruchottes-Chambertin Armand Rousseau (DOM)

Volnay Clos de la Bousse d'Or, Domaine de la Pousse d'Or (BY)

1986

Beaune Clos des Mouches, Drouhin (BR)

Chambertin Trapet (BY)

Charmes-Chambertin Armand Rousseau (VIG)

Charmes-Chambertin Bachelet (UP)

Charmes-Chambertin Dujac (CB)

Clos de la Roche Armand Rousseau (BY, RES)

Clos de Vougeot Noëllat (BEK)

Clos St-Denis Lignier (HAU)

Corton-Bressandes Tollot-Beaut (BY)

Gevrey-Chambertin Combottes, Dujac (BY)

Latricières-Chambertin Trapet (PIP, CB)

Mazis-Chambertin Armand Rousseau (RES)

Nuits-St-Georges Vignes Rondes, Rion (UP)

Pommard Pezerolles Domaine de Montille (CB)

1985

Beaune Clos des Mouches, Drouhin (RES)

Chapelle-Chambertin Trapet (BEK, CB)

Corton Latour (WHI)

Gevrey-Chambertin Clos des Ruchottes, Armand Rousseau (BYR)

Latricières-Chambertin Trapet (CB)

Volnay Clos des Ducs, Marquis d'Angerville (GRE)

Volnay les Caillerets, Marquis d'Angerville (GRE)

Volnay Santenots Lafon (UP)

1984

Clos de la Roche Dujac (BY)

Clos St-Denis Lignier (HAU)

Corton Tollot-Beaut (HAY)

1983

Beaune Hospices de Beaune, Rolin (EL)

Bonnes-Mares Lignier (PE)

Charmes-Chambertin Dujac (CB)

Clos de la Roche Prosper Maufoux (BER)

Clos de Vougeot Château de la Tour (EL)

Clos de Vougeot Drouhin (WIZ)

Échézeaux Mongeard-Mugneret (HAG)

Gevrey-Chambertin Clos St-Jacques, Clair-Daü (GI)

Latricières-Chambertin Trapet (BY)

Mazis-Chambertin Armand Rousseau (PE)

Volnay Clos de la Bousse d'Or, Domaine de la Pousse d'Or (BY)

Vosne-Romanée les Beaumonts, Prosper Maufoux (BER)

Vosne-Romanée Mongeard-Mugneret (AD)

1982

Bonnes-Mares Lignier (PE)

Clos de Tart Mommessin (PE)

Corton Bonneau du Martray (BO)

Pommard les Épenots, Armand (UP)

Pommard les Épenots, Latour (HA)

1981

Beaune Guigone de Salins, Hospices de Beaune (EL)

Grands-Échézeaux Chanson (DI)

Musigny Clair-Daü (WY)

1979

Volnay Santenots Ampeau (CHA)

1977

Chambolle-Musigny Roumier (UP)

1976

Clos de Vougeot Grand Cru, Prieur (GI)

Vosne-Romanée les Beaumonts, Noellat (UP)

1975

Romanée-St-Vivant Domaine de la Romanée-Conti (VIN)

1967

Corton Doudet-Naudin (BOR)

——————— £25.00 to £29.99 ———————

1988

Latricières-Chambertin Trapet (BY)

Nuits-St-Georges Clos de Forets St-Georges, Domaine de l'Arlot (BY)

Nuits-St-Georges les Pruliers, Grivot (BY)

1987

Beaune les Montrevenots, Boillot (BEK)

Chambertin Trapet (BY)

Charmes-Chambertin Dujac (BY)

Échézeaux Henri Jayer (RAE)

Gevrey-Chambertin Clos St-Jacques, Armand Rousseau (BY)

1986
Bonnes-Mares Berthau (BEK)
Charmes-Chambertin Dujac (BY)
Clos de la Roche Armand Rousseau (VIG)
Corton Pougets, Jadot (VIC)
Échézeaux Georges Jayer (AD)
Échézeaux Henri Jayer (RAE)
Latricières-Chambertin Ponsot (MV)
1985
Gevrey-Chambertin Lavaux-St-Jacques,
   Maume (PE)
Nuits-St-Georges Clos des Argillières, Rion
   (UP)
1984
Chambertin Armand Rousseau (ASK)
1983
Beaune Dames Hospitalières, Hospices de
   Beaune (EL)
Chambertin Clos-de-Bèze, Chanson (DI)
Clos de la Roche Dujac (CB, BY, PE)
Clos St-Denis Dujac (CB, TAN)
Grands-Échézeaux Mongeard-Mugneret
   (RAE)
Griotte-Chambertin Drouhin (AD)
1982
Chambertin Trapet (BY)
Clos de Tart Mommessin (HA)
Clos St-Denis Dujac (PE)
Échézeaux Domaine de la Romanée-Conti
   (VIG)
1981
Clos de la Roche Dujac (PE)
Échézeaux Domaine de la Romanée-Conti
   (IR)
1979
Clos de Vougeot Ponnelle (WHI)
Mazis-Chambertin Faiveley (RES)
1978
Clos de la Roche Prosper Maufoux (BER)
1976
Corton-Grancey Latour (UP)

——————— £30.00 to £39.99 ———————
1988
Bonnes-Mares Roumier (TAN)
Chambertin Trapet (BY)
Chambolle-Musigny les Amoureuses,
   Roumier (TAN)
Charmes-Chambertin Dujac (AD)
Clos de la Roche Dujac (AD)
Clos de Vougeot Mongeard-Mugneret (AD)
1987
Chambertin Armand Rousseau (BY, WHI)
Chambertin Clos-de-Bèze, Armand
   Rousseau (BY)

Chambolle-Musigny les Amoureuses, de
   Vogüé (RES)
Clos de la Roche Dujac (BY)
Clos St-Denis Dujac (BY)
1986
Chambertin Armand Rousseau (BY, RES)
Chambertin Clos-de-Bèze, Armand
   Rousseau (TAN, RES, BY)
Clos de Vougeot Meo-Camuzet (PE)
Clos St-Denis Dujac (BY)
1985
Beaune Dames Hospitalières, Hospices de
   Beaune (EL)
Beaune Teurons, Domaine du Château de
   Beaune (BAR)
Chambertin Armand Rousseau (RES)
Chambertin Trapet (BEK, PIP)
Clos de Vougeot Arnoux (WHI)
Échézeaux Georges Jayer (PE)
1983
Bonnes-Mares Drouhin-Laroze (GI)
Chambertin Clos-de-Bèze, Armand
   Rousseau (PE)
Chambertin Clos-de-Bèze, Faiveley (AUG)
Échézeaux Mugneret (PE)
1982
Chambertin Armand Rousseau (WS)
Clos de Tart Mommessin (YF)
Échézeaux Domaine de la Romanée-Conti
   (HA)
1981
Grands-Échézeaux Domaine de la
   Romanée-Conti (IR)
1978
Griotte-Chambertin Bassot (BER)
Nuits-St-Georges Faiveley (RES)
1976
Musigny Prieur (WY)
1964
Gevrey-Chambertin Combottes, Ponnelle
   (WHI)

——————— £40.00 to £49.99 ———————
1986
Chambertin Armand Rousseau (VIG)
Clos de la Roche Ponsot (RES)
Richebourg Grand Cru Grivot (LAY)
1985
Chambertin Clos-de-Bèze, Armand
   Rousseau (PE)
1983
Clos de la Roche Ponsot (RES)
Romanée-St-Vivant les Quatres Journaux,
   Latour (GI)
Romanée-St-Vivant Voarick (YF)

1982
Musigny de Vogüé (BEK)
Romanée-St-Vivant Voarick (PE)
1978
Clos de Vougeot Faiveley (RES)
1970
Chambolle-Musigny les Amoureuses, de
   Vogüé (RES)
1965
Grands-Échézeaux Domaine de la
   Romanée-Conti (VIG)
1959
Beaune Clos des Mouches, Chanson (VIG)
Nuits-St-Georges Drouhin (VIG)

——————— **£50.00 to £59.99** ———————
1985
Chambertin Clos-de-Bèze, Faiveley (TW)
1983
Chambertin Armand Rousseau (RES)
1982
La Tâche Domaine de la Romanée-Conti
   (BEK, BO)
1976
Musigny Faiveley (TW)
1969
Échézeaux Domaine de la Romanée-Conti
   (UP)
1966
Chambolle-Musigny de Vogüé (RES)
1953
Beaune Clos des Mouches, Chanson (VIG)

——————— **£60.00 to £80.99** ———————
1985
Échézeaux Domaine de la Romanée-Conti
   (TW)
1983
Grands-Échézeaux Domaine de la
   Romanée-Conti (TW)
1982
La Tâche Domaine de la Romanée-Conti
   (HAG, VIN, TW, YF)
1978
Bonnes-Mares Drouhin-Laroze (RES)
1976
Musigny de Vogüé (UP)

——————— **£90.00 to £105.00** ———————
1985
Romanée-St-Vivant Domaine de la
   Romanée-Conti (TW)
1983
Grands-Échézeaux Domaine de la
   Romanée-Conti (YF)

1969
Échézeaux Domaine de la Romanée-Conti
   (RES)

——————— **£135.00 to £155.00** ———————
1969
La Tâche Domaine de la Romanée-Conti
   (RES)
Richebourg Domaine de la Romanée-Conti
   (RES)
1961
La Tâche Domaine de la Romanée-Conti
   (UP)
1955
Musigny de Vogüé (REI)

——————— **c. £213.00** ———————
1953
La Tâche Domaine de la Romanée-Conti
   (REI)

WHITE

——————— **Under £9.00** ———————
1988
St-Aubin la Pucelle, Roux (WS)
★St-Aubin Les Charmois, Leflaive (AD)
1987
Santenay Blanc Lequin-Roussot (RAE)
1986
Hautes-Côtes de Nuit, Max (BAR)

——————— **£9.00 to £9.99** ———————
1988
Côte de Beaune la Grande Chatelaine,
   Lescure (PIP)
Meursault Jobard (HAU)
St-Aubin Prudhon (BIB, HAY)
St-Romain Clos Sous le Château, Jean
   Germain (TAN)
1987
Pernand-Vergelesses Chanson (TAN)
St-Aubin Drouhin (NI)
St-Aubin Prudhon (BIB)
1983
Pernand-Vergelesses Rollin (GI)

——————— **£10.00 to £11.99** ———————
1988
Auxey-Duresses Labouré-Roi (PIP)
Monthélie le Champ Fulliot, Garaudet (PIP)
Pernand-Vergelesses Capron Manieux (MV)
St-Aubin 1er Cru Leflaive (WCL)
St-Aubin Charmois, Jean-Marc Morey
   (BEK)

St-Aubin Clos de la Pucelle, Lamy-Pillot
(BY)
St-Romain Labouré-Roi (PIP)
Santenay Blanc Lequin-Roussot (PIP)
1987
Auxey-Duresses Diconne (BEK)
Pernand-Vergelesses Laleure-Piot (DOM)
Pernand-Vergelesses Rollin (PE, RAE)
St-Aubin Clos de la Pucelle, Lamy-Pillot
(BY)
St-Aubin Frionnes, Lamy (LAY)
St-Aubin La Chatenière, Roux Pere et Fils
(DOM)
St-Aubin la Chatenière, Dupard (BAR)
1986
Auxey-Duresses Battault (BAR)
Chassagne-Montrachet Labouré-Roi (SAF)
Meursault Labouré-Roi (SAF)
Meursault Latour Giraud (REI)
Pernand-Vergelesses Rollin (RAE)
St-Romain Prieur-Brunet (EL)
1985
★Auxey-Duresses Duc de Magenta (IR)

─────────── £12.00 to £13.99 ───────────
1988
Meursault Boisson-Vadot (BEK)
Pernand-Vergelesses Rollin (BIB)
1987
Chassagne-Montrachet Albert Morey (BEK)
Meursault Jaffelin (OD)
Meursault Jean Germain (TAN)
Meursault Matrot (CB)
Pernand-Vergelesses Vallet (BOR)
Puligny-Champgains Chapelle (WCL)
Puligny-Montrachet Bouchard Père (BOT)
St-Aubin Albert Morey (DAV)
1986
Clos du Château de Meursault Bourgogne
Chardonnay (BAR)
Meursault Charmes, Rodet (ASD)
Meursault Chevalier Brunet (EL)
Meursault Latour (HOG)
Meursault les Narvaux, Guillemard-
Pothier (IR)
Meursault Monatine, Rougeot (WCL)
Meursault Ropiteau (BOT)
Savigny-lès-Beaune Capron-Manieux (UP)
1985
Clos du Château de Meursault Bourgogne
Chardonnay (VIN)
Meursault l'Ormeau, Coche (RAE)
1984
Meursault Chevalier Brunet (EL)
Meursault Latour (GI)

Meursault Michel Dupont (CHA)
1983
Fixin Blanc Clair (GI)
1982
Meursault Matrot (WY)

─────────── £14.00 to £15.99 ───────────
1988
Meursault Drouhin (NI)
Meursault Henri Germain (AD)
Meursault Matrot (CB)
Puligny-Montrachet Chapelle (MV)
1987
Chassagne-Montrachet les Caillerets,
Albert Morey (BEK)
Meursault les Tillets, Chouet-Clivet (VIG)
Meursault les Vireuils, Roulot (HAY)
Meursault Remoissenet (WS)
Meursault Santenots, Monthélie-Douhairet
(MV)
Puligny-Montrachet Carillon (WW, LAY, WCL)
Puligny-Montrachet Chapelle (UP)
Puligny-Montrachet Leflaive (AD)
1986
Chassagne-Montrachet Bachelet-Ramonet
(RAE)
Chassagne-Montrachet Jevillier (IR)
Chassagne-Montrachet Latour (HOG)
Meursault Blagny, Latour (HOG)
Meursault Charmes, Brunet (EL)
Meursault Clos de Mazeray, Prieur (BYR)
Meursault Genevrières Latour (HOG)
Meursault Jadot (BYR, VIC)
Meursault Jobard (RAE, MV)
Meursault Millot-Battault (AV)
Meursault Ropiteau-Mignon (PE)
Puligny-Montrachet Carillon (ASD)
Puligny-Montrachet Drouhin (NI)
Puligny-Montrachet Labouré-Roi (SAF)
Puligny-Montrachet Latour (HOG)
1985
★Chassagne-Montrachet Albert Morey (DAV)
Meursault Millot-Battault (AV)
1984
Meursault Blagny, Latour (GI)
Meursault Charmes, Barolet (ALL)

> *Please remember that*
> ***Webster's*** *is a price*
> *GUIDE and not a price*
> *LIST. It is not meant to*
> *replace up-to-date*
> *merchants' lists.*

──────── £16.00 to £19.99 ────────
1988
Chassagne-Montrachet Leflaive (AMI, HAH)
Chassagne-Montrachet Morgeot, Gagnard
  Delagrange (BY)
Chassagne-Montrachet Sauzet (TAN)
Meursault Charmes, Henri Germain (TAN)
Meursault Henri Germain (TAN)
Meursault les Meix Chavaux, Roulot (DOM)
Meursault Michelot-Buisson (BY)
Puligny-Montrachet Carillon (ASK)
Puligny-Montrachet Chartron et Trébuchet
  (OD)
Puligny-Montrachet Clerc (BY)
Puligny-Montrachet la Garenne, Thomas
  (WCL)
Puligny-Montrachet Leflaive (AD, RAE)
★Puligny-Montrachet Sauzet (AD, TAN, BY)
1987
Chassagne-Montrachet Latour (WHI)
Chassagne-Montrachet les Champs Gains,
  Albert Morey (BEK)
Chassagne-Montrachet les Embrazées,
  Albert Morey (BEK, PIP)
Chassagne-Montrachet les Vergers, Colin
  (HAY)
Meursault Blagny, Matrot (CB)
Meursault Boyer-Martenot (AN)
Meursault Charmes, Boillot (WW)
Meursault Charmes, Leflaive (DI)
Meursault Clos de la Barre, Lafon (DOM)
Meursault Clos de Mazeray, Prieur (IR)
Meursault Jobard (RAE)
Meursault Latour (WHI)
Meursault Michelot-Buisson (DOM)
Meursault Perrières, Leflaive (DI)
Meursault Perrières, Matrot (CB)
Meursault Poruzots, Jobard (BIB)
Meursault Santenots, Monthélie-Douhairet
  (UP)
Puligny-Montrachet Clavoillon, Leflaive
  (LAY)
Puligny-Montrachet Clerc (BY)
Puligny-Montrachet Clos de la Mouchère,
  Boillot (WAI, YF)
Puligny-Montrachet Leflaive (HA, LAY, DI,
  CB)
Puligny-Montrachet les Charmes,
  Thévenot-Machal (AN)
Puligny-Montrachet les Folatières,
  Boisson-Vadot (BEK)
Puligny-Montrachet les Folatières, Clerc
  (PE)
Puligny-Montrachet Sauzet (DOM, BEK, PE,
  AI)

1986
Chassagne-Montrachet la Romanée,
  Moillard (VIC)

Chassagne-Montrachet les Caillerets,
  Albert Morey (BYR)
Chassagne-Montrachet Morgeot, Henri
  Germain (TAN)
Chassagne-Montrachet Sauzet (BAR)
Meursault Clos de Mazeray, Prieur (IR)
Gevrey-Chambertin Domaine des Varoilles
  (AUG)
Meursault les Tillets, Chouet-Clivet (VIG)
Puligny-Montrachet Clavoillon, Leflaive
  (PE)
Puligny-Montrachet Clerc (PE)
Puligny-Montrachet Jean Germain (AUG)
Puligny-Montrachet Leflaive (PE)
Puligny-Montrachet les Folatières, Latour
  (HOG)
Puligny-Montrachet les Folatières, Laroche
  (BYR)
Puligny-Montrachet Sauzet (BYR, AD, BAR)
1985
Chassagne-Montrachet les Chaumes, Jean-
  Marc Morey (DAV)
Chassagne-Montrachet Roux (PE)
Meursault Charmes, Rougeot (AD)
Meursault Michelot-Buisson (AI)
Meursault Prosper Maufoux (BER)
Puligny-Montrachet Jadot (VIC)
1984
Puligny-Montrachet Clos de la Mouchère,
  Boillot (DAV)
Puligny-Montrachet les Perrières, Sauzet
  (TAN)
1982
Meursault Genevrières Latour (GI)
1975
★Meursault Charmes, Potinet-Ampeau (PE)

──────── £20.00 to £24.99 ────────
1988
Chassagne-Montrachet Morgeot, Gagnard
  Delagrange (WHI)

Puligny-Montrachet Champs Canet, Sauzet (AD, BY)
Puligny-Montrachet les Folatières, Clerc (BY, WHI)
Puligny-Montrachet les Perrières, Sauzet (TAN)
Puligny-Montrachet les Referts, Sauzet (BY)
1987
Chassagne-Montrachet Drouhin (AN)
Chassagne-Montrachet la Maltroie, Fontaine-Gagnard (AN)
Meursault Genevrières Jobard (RAE)
Puligny-Montrachet Champs Canet, Sauzet (BEK)
Puligny-Montrachet Latour (WHI)
Puligny-Montrachet Leflaive (AMI)
Puligny-Montrachet les Perrières, Sauzet (PE)
Puligny-Montrachet les Pucelles, Leflaive (LAY)
Puligny-Montrachet les Referts, Sauzet (BEK)
1986
Meursault Blagny, Jadot (THR)
Meursault Blagny, Latour (WHI)
Meursault Perrières, Matrot (CB)
Meursault Poruzots, Jobard (UP)
Puligny-Montrachet Leflaive (TW)
Puligny-Montrachet les Champs Gains, Clerc (HAG)
Puligny-Montrachet les Perrières, Leflaive (TW)
Puligny-Montrachet les Referts, Jadot (PE)
Puligny-Montrachet Sauzet (TW)
1985
Chassagne-Montrachet Morgeot, Henri Germain (AD)
Meursault Poruzots, Thevenot-Machal (AN)
Puligny-Montrachet Clos de la Mouchère, Boillot (UN)
Puligny-Montrachet Leflaive (BAR)
Puligny-Montrachet Combettes, Sauzet (TAN)
Puligny-Montrachet Folatières, Bouchard (HA)
1984
Chassagne-Montrachet Jadot (HA)
1983
Meursault les Tillets, Chouet-Clivet (VIG)
1982
Chassagne-Montrachet Clos de Chapelle, Duc de Magenta (WY)
1980
Puligny-Montrachet les Combettes, Ampeau (CHA)

——————— **£25.00 to £29.99** ———————
1988
Chassagne-Montrachet Marquis de Laguiche (BR, VIG)
Corton-Charlemagne Leflaive (AD)
Puligny-Montrachet les Combettes, Sauzet (TAN, DOM)
Puligny-Montrachet les Pucelles, Leflaive (AD)
1987
Beaune Clos des Mouches, Drouhin (RES, HAG, BR)
Corton-Charlemagne Leflaive (AMI)
Corton-Charlemagne Rollin (RAE)
1986
Puligny-Montrachet Clavoillon, Leflaive (CB, AD)
1985
Corton-Charlemagne Rollin (RAE)
Puligny-Montrachet les Combettes, Clerc (AV)
Puligny-Montrachet les Folatières, Drouhin (BER)
1984
Corton-Charlemagne Bonneau du Martray (DOM)
1982
Beaune Clos des Mouches, Drouhin (UP)
Corton-Charlemagne Bonneau du Martray (RAE)
1980
Meursault Charmes, Ampeau (CHA)
1978
Meursault Ampeau (CHA)

——————— **£30.00 to £39.99** ———————
1988
Bâtard-Montrachet Albert Morey (BEK)
Beaune Clos des Mouches, Drouhin (VIG)
Corton-Charlemagne Rollin (BIB)
Corton-Charlemagne Roumier (DOM)
1987
Bâtard-Montrachet Blain-Gagnard (DOM)
Bâtard-Montrachet Gagnard-Delagrange (HAH, BY)
Bâtard-Montrachet Leflaive (AMI)
Bienvenues-Bâtard-Montrachet Leflaive (CB)
Corton-Charlemagne Juillot (DOM)
Corton-Charlemagne Tollot-Beaut (BY)
Criots-Bâtard-Montrachet Blain-Gagnard (DOM, BIB)
1986
Bienvenues-Bâtard-Montrachet Bachelet (RAE, BIB)

Bienvenues-Bâtard-Montrachet Leflaive
(TAN)
Corton-Charlemagne Leflaive (HAH, DI)
Corton-Charlemagne Rapet (BYR)
Corton-Charlemagne Rollin (BIB)
1985
Beaune Clos des Mouches, Drouhin (BER)
Corton-Charlemagne Latour (VIC)
Corton-Charlemagne Thévenot (EL)
Puligny-Montrachet les Combettes, Sauzet
(RES)
1984
Bâtard-Montrachet Leflaive (HAY)
Corton-Charlemagne Jadot (HA)
Corton-Charlemagne Tollot-Beaut (HAY)
1983
Puligny-Montrachet les Folatières,
Drouhin (WY)
1982
Corton-Charlemagne Bonneau du Martray
(WY)

Corton-Charlemagne Roumier (UP)
1978
Puligny-Montrachet Sauzet (WY)

──────── £40.00 to £49.99 ────────
1988
Bâtard-Montrachet Gagnard-Delagrange
(BY)
Chevalier-Montrachet Leflaive (AD)
1987
Bâtard-Montrachet Leflaive (DI)
Bienvenues-Bâtard-Montrachet Bachelet-
Ramonet (VIG)
Chevalier-Montrachet Leflaive (CB)
1986
Corton-Charlemagne Latour (WHI)
Corton-Charlemagne Tollot-Beaut (BY)
1985
Bienvenues-Bâtard-Montrachet Clerc (EL)
Corton-Charlemagne Latour (WY, BER)
1984
Chevalier-Montrachet Bouchard Père (HAG)

1983
Corton-Charlemagne Ancien Domaine des
Comtes de Grancey (YF)
Corton-Charlemagne Bonneau du Martray
(BO)
Corton-Charlemagne Latour (UP, PE)
1982
Bâtard-Montrachet Sauzet (BAR)
1978
Corton-Charlemagne Dubreuil-Fontaine
(UP)

──────── £50.00 to £69.99 ────────
1986
Bienvenues-Bâtard-Montrachet Leflaive
(RES)
Chevalier-Montrachet Leflaive (PE)
1985
Bâtard-Montrachet Latour (YF)
Bâtard-Montrachet Leflaive (RES)
1983
Bâtard-Montrachet Drouhin (TW)
Chevalier-Montrachet Leflaive (REI)
1982
Bâtard-Montrachet Leflaive (RES)
1981
Corton-Charlemagne Latour (WY)

──────── £70.00 to £85.00 ────────
1988
le Montrachet Thénard (AV)
1986
le Montrachet Marquis de Laguiche (BR)
1985
le Montrachet Latour (RES)
1983
le Montrachet Thénard (REI)
1982
le Montrachet Prieur (GI)
le Montrachet Thénard (UP)

──────── c. £110.00 ────────
1982
le Montrachet Marquis de Laguiche (WY)

──────── £170.00 to £195.00 ────────
1978
le Montrachet Marquis de Laguiche (RES)
1976
le Montrachet Marquis de Laguiche (WY)

──────── c. £327.00 ────────
1981
le Montrachet Domaine de la Romanée-
Conti (TW)

CÔTE CHALONNAISE

RED

──────── Under £7.00 ────────
1988
Givry Chanson (AS)
1987
Givry Clos du Cellier aux Moines, Delorme
  (PE, WCL)
1986
Rully Faiveley (DI)
Rully Viénot (OL)
1985
Givry Voarick (WRI)

──────── £7.00 to £8.99 ────────
1988
★Rully Domaine de la Renarde, Delorme (STA)
Rully Laborbe-Juillot (DOM)
1987
Rully Cogny (AD)
1986
Givry Cellier des Moines, Thénard (HAY)
Mercurey Château de Chamirey (EL)
Mercurey Juillot (DOM)
1984
Mercurey Marechal (RAE)

──────── £9.00 to £10.99 ────────
1987
Mercurey Château de Chamirey (WHI)
1986
Mercurey les Veleys, de Launay (TAN, BY)
Mercurey Meulien (AI)
Rully Bouchard Père (BAR)
Rully Drouhin (NI)
1985
★Mercurey Domaine de la Croix,
  Jacquelet-Faiveley (AUG)
Mercurey les Berlands, Faiveley (DI)
1983
Mercurey Château de Chamirey (BER)

──────── c. £14.00 ────────
1987
Rully Drouhin (NI)

WHITE

──────── Under £7.00 ────────
1988
★Bourgogne Aligoté de Bouzeron, Villaine
  (AD, BY, TAN)
★Montagny 1er Cru, Cave de Buxy (BYR)
1987
Bourgogne Aligoté de Bouzeron, Villaine
  (CB, PE)
Givry Chofflet (PIP)
Montagny 1er Cru, Cave de Buxy (WAI, IR)
Montagny Château de Davenay, Moillard
  (SAI)
Rully Faiveley (HOG)
1986
Bourgogne Aligoté Bouzeron Ancien
  Domaine Carnot Bouchard (PE)
Givry Ragot (DOM)
Montagny 1er Cru, Cave de Buxy (HOG,
  HAY)

──────── £7.00 to £8.99 ────────
1988
Bourgogne Aligoté de Bouzeron, Villaine
  (AV)
Montagny 1er Cru Alain Roy, Cave des
  Vignerons de Mancey (BEK)
Montagny 1er Cru, Cave de Buxy (THR, PIP)
Montagny Picard, Château de Davenay (IR)
Rully Guyot-Verpiot (WRI)
Rully les St-Jacques, Chandesais (WHI)
Rully Varot, Delorme (STA)
1987
Montagny Roy (GIL)
★Rully Grésigny, Cogny (MAJ)
Rully la Chaume, Dury (THR)
1986
Mercurey Voarick (HUN)
Montagny 1er Cru, Broisset (HIG)
Montagny Arnoux (GRE)
Montagny Latour (BYR)
Rully la Chaume, Dury (GI)
1985
Givry Ragot (IR)

──────── £9.00 to £10.99 ────────
1989
Mercurey Domaine des Lambrays (BEK)
1988
Mercurey Voarick (WRI, GRE)
Montagny Latour (WHI, REI)
Rully Rabourcé, Domaine Belleville (WRI)
1987
Mercurey Clos Rochette, Faiveley (DI)
Montagny Clos de la Saule (BOD)
1986
Montagny Latour (GI, WIL, YF)

MÂCONNAIS

WHITE

──────── Under £4.00 ────────

1987
★Mâcon-Lugny les Genièvres, Latour (HAG)
Mâcon-Villages Cave Co-op. de Viré (WIZ)

──────── £4.00 to £4.99 ────────

Non-vintage
Tesco Mâcon Blanc-Villages (TES)
1989
Mâcon-Lugny Duboeuf (NI)
Mâcon-Prissé Duboeuf (NI)
Mâcon-Villages Domaine de Rochebin (MAJ)
Mâcon-Villages Duboeuf (NI)
1988
Mâcon Blanc Clos de Condemine, Luquet (LOR)
Mâcon Blanc Domaine Dussauge (SAI)
Mâcon-Lugny Duboeuf (NI)
Mâcon-Prissé Duboeuf (BEK)
★St-Véran Domaine St-Martin, Duboeuf (BEK)
St-Véran Duboeuf (BEK)
1987
Mâcon-Lugny Duboeuf (BY)
Mâcon-Prissé Duboeuf (BY)
Mâcon-Villages Loron (BO)
St-Véran Cave Co-op. Prissé (TES)

──────── £5.00 to £5.99 ────────

1989
Mâcon Blanc Domaine de la Combe (BIB)
Mâcon Chardonnay Talmard (AD)
Mâcon-Lugny Duboeuf (PIP)
Mâcon-Prissé Duboeuf (DAV)
Mâcon-Solutré Depardon (WCL)
St-Véran Depardon (WHI)
St-Véran Tissier (HIG)
1988
Mâcon Blanc Domaine de la Combe (BIB)
Mâcon-Clessé Dépagneux (BOR, UP)
Mâcon la Roche Vineuse, Merlin (MV)
Mâcon-Lugny Domaine du Prieuré (STA)
Mâcon-Lugny Duboeuf (BY)
Mâcon-Peronne Domaine de Mortier, Josserand (BIB)
Mâcon-Prissé Cave Co-op. Prissé (HAH)
Mâcon-Prissé Duboeuf (BY, BYR)
Mâcon-Villages Duboeuf (AI, BY)
Mâcon-Villages Loron (TAN)
Mâcon-Villages Rodet (WHI)

Pouilly-Loché Cave des Crus Blancs (HAW)
St-Véran Cave Co-op. Prissé (OD)
St-Véran Depardon (CHA)
St-Véran Duboeuf (THR)
St-Véran Prissé (HAH)
1987
Mâcon-Clessé Signoret (HAW)
Mâcon-Lugny Duboeuf (AI)
St-Véran Duboeuf (THR)
1984
Mâcon-Viré Château de Viré, Desbois (HOG)

──────── £6.00 to £6.99 ────────

1989
Mâcon-Lugny Duboeuf (BY)
Mâcon-Prissé Duboeuf (BY)
Mâcon-Villages Domaine d'Agenay (BR)
Mâcon-Villages Duboeuf (BY)
St-Véran Depardon (VIG)
St-Véran Domaine Deux Roches (HAH)
St-Véran Duboeuf (DAV, BY)
1988
Mâcon-Clessé Guillemot (TAN)
★Mâcon-Fuissé la Solutré, Vincent (LAY)
Mâcon la Roche-Vineuse, Lacharme (BAR)
Mâcon-Lugny les Genièvres, Latour (GI, CH, WHI)
Mâcon-Viré André Bonhomme (GI)
St-Véran Duboeuf (BY)
St-Véran Loron (WRI)
St-Véran Vincent (EL)
1987
Mâcon-Clessé Michel (DOM)
Mâcon la Roche Vineuse, Merlin (UP)
Mâcon-Peronne Domaine de Mortier, Josserand (PE)
Mâcon-Villages Latour (BER)
Pouilly-Fuissé Domaine Desroches (SAI)
Pouilly-Loché Château de Loché (THR)
St-Véran Domaine de l'Évêque, Mommessin (YF)
1986
Pouilly-Fuissé Duboeuf (WIZ)
St-Véran Domaine St-Martin, Duboeuf (BY)
St-Véran Jadot (BYR)
1985
Pouilly-Fuissé Cave Co-op. Prissé (TES)

──────── £7.00 to £7.99 ────────

1989
Pouilly-Vinzelles Mathias (PIP)
St-Véran Duboeuf (NI)

1988
Mâcon-Lugny les Genièvres, Latour (VIN, HAG, WIL, DAV)
Mâcon-Viré Goyard (RAE)
Pouilly-Fuissé Domaine Bourdon (THR)
St-Véran Corsin (AD)
St-Véran Duboeuf (NI)
St-Véran Vincent (RAE)
1987
Mâcon-Villages Domaine de Montbellet (HAY)
Pouilly-Fuissé Duboeuf (BY)
Pouilly-Fuissé Loron (BO)
Pouilly-Fuissé Vessigaud (ASD)
Pouilly-Vinzelles Château de Pouilly-Vinzelles, Loron (WRI)
St Michael Pouilly-Fuissé (MAR)
St-Véran Vincent (DOM)
1986
St-Véran Vincent (PE)

——————— £8.00 to £9.99 ———————
1989
Pouilly-Fuissé Domaine Béranger, Duboeuf (BEK, NI)
Pouilly-Fuissé Domaine de Manclare (BR)
Pouilly-Fuissé Domaine de Pouilly, Duboeuf (DAV)
Pouilly-Fuissé la Mure, Depardon (WHI)
1988
Mâcon-Clessé Domaine de la Bon Gran, Thévenet (TAN)
Mâcon Monbellet, Goyard (BIB)
Mâcon-Villages Domaine de la Bon Gran, Thévenet (AD)
Pouilly-Fuissé Dépagneux (UP)
Pouilly-Fuissé Duboeuf (BY, BYR)

Pouilly-Fuissé les Vieux Murs, Loron (WRI)
1987
Pouilly-Fuissé Duboeuf (AI)
Pouilly-Fuissé Manciat-Poncet (HAW)
1985
Mâcon-Viré Château de Viré, Desbois (BER)

——————— £10.00 to £12.99 ———————
1989
Pouilly-Fuissé Duboeuf (BY)
1988
Pouilly-Fuissé les Crays, Forest (WCL)
1987
Pouilly-Fuissé Corsin (DOM)
Pouilly-Fuissé Domaine de l'Arillière (PE)
Pouilly-Fuissé Manciat-Poncet (BAR)
1986
Pouilly-Fuissé Corsin (DOM)
Pouilly-Fuissé Domaine de l'Arillière (BYR)

——————— £13.00 to £14.99 ———————
1988
Pouilly-Fuissé Château Fuissé, Vincent (TAN)
1987
Pouilly-Fuissé Château Fuissé, Vincent (BYR)
1986
Pouilly-Fuissé Château Fuissé, Vincent (RAE, BIB)
1985
Mâcon-Villages Domaine de la Bon Gran Cuvée Special Botrytis (AD)
Pouilly-Fuissé Corsin (HAY)

——————— £16.00 to £17.99 ———————
1988
★Pouilly-Fuissé Château Fuissé Vieilles Vignes, Vincent (AD, TAN)
1987
Pouilly-Fuissé Château Fuissé Vieilles Vignes, Vincent (DOM, RAE, BYR)

——————— £18.00 to £20.00 ———————
1988
Pouilly-Fuissé Château Fuissé Vieilles Vignes, Vincent (BIB, PE)
1986
Pouilly-Fuissé Château Fuissé Vieilles Vignes, Vincent (BIB, PE)

RED

——————— Under £4.00 ———————
Non-vintage
Asda Mâcon-Supérieur Rouge (ASD)
1988
Mâcon Rouge Loron (BL, EL)

——————— £4.00 to £5.00 ———————
1986
Mâcon Rouge Loron (UN)

CHABLIS

WHITE

Under £5.00

1987
Sauvignon de St-Bris, Domaine des
  Remparts (HIG)

£5.00 to £5.99

1989
★Sauvignon de St-Bris, Brocard (HIC)
1988
★Asda Chablis (ASD)
Bourgogne St-Bris Chardonnay, Felix (ASK)
★Chablis Domaine de Biéville, Moreau (HOG)
Chardonnay Domaine des Remparts, Sorin
  (HIG)
Sauvignon de St-Bris, Goisot (GIL)
1987
Bourgogne St-Bris Chardonnay, Goisot
  (GIL)
Sauvignon de St-Bris, Defrance (HAU)

£6.00 to £6.99

1988
Chablis Bonard (ASK)
Chablis Brocard (OD)
Chablis Defaix (LOR)
Chablis Domaine de l'Églantière (RES, HUN)
Chablis Domaine de Vauroux (LAY)
Chablis Gautheron (MAJ)
Chablis Moreau (PD, BOT)
1987
Chablis Bernard Defaix (RAE)
Chablis Droin (RAE)
Sainsbury's Chablis (SAI)
Sauvignon de St-Bris, Renard (WRI)
1986
★Chablis Domaine de Colombier, Mothe
  (ASD)

£7.00 to £7.99

1989
Chablis Domaine des Manants, Brocard
  (AD)
★Chablis Legland (BIB)
1988
★Chablis Château de Maligny (BY)
Chablis Domaine de Colombier, Mothe (REI)
Chablis Domaine de Vauroux (VIN)
Chablis Domaine Pico Race (BAR)
Chablis Domaine Servin (STA, MV)
Chablis Durup (HAH, DOM)

Chablis Grossot (LAY)
Chablis Lechet, Ponsot (MAJ)
Chablis Moreau (DAV)
Chablis Pautré (HIG)
Chablis Simmonet-Febvre (CHA)
Chablis Vocoret (WCL)
1987
Chablis Domaine de Biéville, Moreau (BL)
Chablis Droin (HAY)
Chablis Fèvre (BYR)
Chablis Louis Michel (MV)
1985
Chablis Pic (VIC)
★Chablis Vaillons, Moreau (HOG)

£8.00 to £9.99

1989
Chablis Brocard (HIC)
Chablis Laroche (DI)
1988
Chablis 1er Cru Drouhin (NI)
Chablis Château de Maligny, Durup (THR)
Chablis Domaine de Vauroux (VIG)
Chablis Domaine Servin (WRI)
Chablis Droin (PIP)
Chablis Fûts de Chêne, Grossot (LAY)
Chablis Labouré Roi (WIL)

Chablis Laroche (DI, AUG)
Chablis Montmains, Laroche (VIC)
Chablis Montmains, Rottiers-Clotilde (HAG)
Chablis Vaillons, Defaix (LOR)
1987
Chablis 1er Cru Laroche (DI)
Chablis Fourchaume, Moreau (WHI)
Chablis Louis Michel (UP)
Chablis Mont de Milieu, Lacelle (BEK)
Chablis Montée de Tonnerre, Regnard
  (HOG)
★Chablis Montmains, Louis Michel (WHI)
Chablis Pic (BER)
Chablis Vaillons, Fèvre (BYR)

1986
Chablis Fourchaume, Moreau (WHI)
Chablis Montmains, Laroche (GRE)
Chablis Vaillons, Simmonet-Febvre (CHA)
1985
Chablis Bernard Defaix (PE)
1984
★Chablis Montmains, Droin (DAV)

——————— £10.00 to £11.99 ———————
1988
Chablis Drouhin (BR)
Chablis Fourchaume, Laroche (DI)
★Chablis la Forêt, René Dauvissat (TAN)
Chablis Mont de Milieu, Grossot (LAY)
Chablis Montée de Tonnerre, Droin (RAE)
Chablis Séchet, René Dauvissat (DOM)
Chablis Vaillons, Defaix (DAV)
Chablis Vaillons, Fèvre (IR)
★Chablis Vaillons, René Dauvissat (TAN, DOM)
1987
Chablis 1er Cru Laroche (AI)
Chablis Fourchaume, Domaine de Valéry (TAN)
Chablis Fourchaume, Laroche (DI)
Chablis la Forêt, Pinson (BIB)
Chablis la Forêt, Vocoret (REI)
Chablis Mont de Milieu, Pinson (WCL, MV)
Chablis Montmains, Filippi (AI)
Chablis Vaillons, Long-Depaquit (BO)
Chablis Vaulorent, Fèvre (BYR)
1986
Chablis Montée de Tonnerre, Laroche (BYR)
★Chablis Vaillons, Collet (RES)
Chablis Vaillons, Pic (BL)
Chablis Vaudeveys, Laroche (HA)
St Michael Chablis Fourchaume (MAR)

——————— £12.00 to £13.99 ———————
1988
Chablis 1er Cru Drouhin (BR)
Chablis Montmains, Domaine de Vauroux (VIN)
Chablis Vaillons, Droin (PIP)
1987
Chablis Mont de Milieu, Rémon (BOR)
Chablis Montmains, Domaine de Vauroux (VIN)
1986
Chablis Bougros, Domaine de Colombier (ASD)
1985
Chablis Fourchaume, Moreau (WRI)
Chablis Mont de Milieu, Pic (BER)
1983
★Chablis Vaillons, Laroche (BO)

——————— £14.00 to £16.99 ———————
1988
Chablis Blanchots, Servin (DAV)
★Chablis les Clos, René Dauvissat (TAN)
1987
Chablis Bougros, Domaine de Vauroux (VIN)
Chablis Fourchaume, Laroche (AI)
Chablis les Clos, Michel (REI)
Chablis Valmur, Droin (RAE, BIB, PE)
Chablis Vaudésir, Droin (BIB, RAE)
Chablis Vaudésir, Long-Depaquit (GRE)
1986
Chablis Valmur, Moreau (WHI)
Chablis Vaudésir, Droin (HAY)
1985
Chablis Fourchaume, Laroche (WRI)
Chablis les Vaudevay, Laroche (WRI)
Chablis Vaudésir, Long-Depaquit (UN)
1983
★Chablis Blanchots, Laroche (BO)

——————— £17.00 to £19.99 ———————
1988
Chablis les Clos, Droin (RAE)
Chablis les Clos, René Dauvissat (DOM)
Chablis Valmur, Droin (TAN, DOM)
1987
Chablis les Clos, Durup (THR)
Chablis Valmur, Droin (HAY)
1986
Chablis les Clos, Pinson (UP)
Chablis Vaudésir, Droin (PIP)
1985
Chablis Bougerots Laroche (WRI)
Chablis Bougros, Ancien Domaine Auffray (BEK)

——————— £20.00 to £24.99 ———————
1988
Chablis Vaudésir, Drouhin (BR)
1987
Chablis Blanchots, Laroche (DI)

——————— £25.00 to £35.00 ———————
1986
Chablis Blanchots, Laroche (UP, HA)

RED

——————— Under £7.00 ———————
1989
★Bourgogne Coulanges-la-Vineuse, Jean Deligny (BOT)
1987
★Bourgogne Irancy Ste-Claire, Brocard (BEK)

BEAUJOLAIS

RED

Under £4.00

Non-vintage
Asda Beaujolais (ASD)
Sainsbury's Beaujolais (SAI)
1989
★Beaujolais-Villages Duboeuf (WIZ)
1988
Beaujolais Loron (BL)
Beaujolais-Villages Domaine de Gentilly (HOG)
Beaujolais-Villages Domaine de la Ronze (ASD)
Beaujolais-Villages Duboeuf (THR)
St Michael Beaujolais (MAR)
Waitrose Beaujolais (WAI)
1987
Beaujolais Loron (HUN)
Beaujolais-Villages Château du Bluizard (ALL)
1986
Beaujolais-Villages Domaine St-Charles (ALL)
le Piat de Beaujolais (PD)

£4.00 to £4.49

Non-vintage
Beaujolais Loron (GRE)
1989
Beaujolais-Villages Cellier du Samsons (WAI)
1988
Beaujolais Château de Tanay (HAW)
Beaujolais Duboeuf (BYR)
Beaujolais-Villages Château de la Roche, Loron (HUN)
Beaujolais-Villages Château des Vergers (SAI)
Beaujolais-Villages Domaine Chizeaux, Fessy (ASK)
★Regnié Château de la Pierre, Loron (BL)

1987
Brouilly Grand Clos de Briante, Loron (BO)
Chénas Domaine de la Combe Remont, Duboeuf (WHI)
1986
le Piat de Beaujolais (BOT)

£4.50 to £4.99

1989
Beaujolais Cave Beaujolais de St-Verand (HAW)
Beaujolais Duboeuf (AMI, NI, PIP)
Beaujolais Loron (DI)
Beaujolais-Villages Château du Basty (OD)
Beaujolais-Villages Château du Bluizard (ALL)
Beaujolais-Villages Duboeuf (BEK, NI)
1988
Beaujolais Duboeuf (DAV, AI)
Beaujolais Loron (DI)
Beaujolais-Villages Cave des Producteurs Juliénas (HAW)
Beaujolais-Villages Château du Basty (LAY)
Beaujolais-Villages Château du Grand Vernay (HAW)
Beaujolais-Villages Colonge (BYR)
Beaujolais-Villages Duboeuf (WHI)
Beaujolais-Villages Rochette (HAY)
Côtes de Brouilly Dépagneux (VIC)
★Côtes de Brouilly Loron (BL)
Morgon Jambon (ASD)
Regnié Baudet (ALL)
Regnié Duboeuf (BEK)
Regnié Goutty (PE)
1987
Beaujolais Loron (AV)
Morgon Domaine Jean Descombes, Duboeuf (WHI)
St-Amour Domaine des Billards, Loron (BO)
1986
Morgon Domaine Jean Descombes, Duboeuf (VIC)

£5.00 to £5.49

1989
Beaujolais Blaise Carron (HAW)
Beaujolais Garlon (HAW)
Beaujolais Loron (WRI)
Beaujolais-Villages Colonge (BIB)
Beaujolais-Villages Depardon (VIG, HAH)
Beaujolais-Villages Domaine des Dîmes (GIL)

Beaujolais-Villages Duboeuf (AMI)
★Chénas Château de Chénas, Sélection
  Éventail (STA)
Chénas Domaine de la Combe Remont,
  Duboeuf (BEK)
Juliénas Duboeuf (BEK)
Juliénas les Envaux, Pelletier (EL)
Morgon le Clachet, Brun (EL)
Regnié Braillon (EL)
Regnié Duboeuf (NI)
1988
Beaujolais Cuvée Centenaire, Charmet
  (HAW)
Beaujolais-Villages Château de la Roche,
  Loron (TAN)
Beaujolais-Villages Château des Vierres,
  Duboeuf (DAV)
Beaujolais-Villages Château Lacarelle (WW)
Beaujolais-Villages Duboeuf (BY, AI)
Brouilly Château de Nevers, Duboeuf (BEK)
Brouilly Domaine Rolland (THR)
Brouilly Grand Clos de Briante, Loron
  (HUN)
Chénas Château de Chénas (HAW)
Chénas Duboeuf (BY)
Chiroubles Passot (HIG)
★Juliénas Domaine des Mouilles, Duboeuf
  (WHI)
Juliénas Duboeuf (BEK)
Juliénas les Capitains, Louis Tête (HOG)
Juliénas Monnet (HIG)
Morgon Domaine Jean Descombes,
  Duboeuf (BEK)
★Morgon les Versauds, Dépagneux (OD)
Moulin-à-Vent Loron (BYR)
Regnié Collonge (HAW)
Regnié Duboeuf (NI)
Regnié Ducroux (HAW)
Regnié Noël (HAW)
Regnié Rochette (HAY)
Regnié Roux (HAW)
1987
Chénas Château de Chénas (EL)
Juliénas Domaine de Beauvernay, Piat
  (BOT)
Juliénas Monnet (HAU)
Morgon Côte de Py, Gaget (GIL)
Morgon Domaine des Vieux Cèdres, Loron
  (CH)
Morgon Loron (UN)
St-Amour Château St-Amour (BOT)

——————— **£5.50 to £5.99** ———————
1989
Beaujolais-Villages Duboeuf (BY)

Chénas Château de Chénas (HAH)
Chiroubles Domaine de la Grosse Pierre
  (HAH)
Côtes de Brouilly l'Ecluse Verger (CHA)
Juliénas les Envaux, Pelletier (STA, CHA)
Morgon Domaine Jean Descombes,
  Duboeuf (BEK)
Morgon Duboeuf (NI)
Morgon le Clachet, Brun (HAH)
Regnié Braillon (HAH)
Regnié Château de la Tour Bourdon,
  Duboeuf (PIP)
St-Amour Château St-Amour (IR)
1988
Beaujolais-Villages Château du Basty (TAN)
Beaujolais-Villages Colonge (HIC)
Brouilly Château de la Chaize, Marquis de
  Roussy de Sales (STA)
Brouilly Duboeuf (BYR)
Brouilly Jean Lathuilière (HAW)
Chénas Léspinasse (HAW)
Chiroubles Château de Raousset (WHI)
Chiroubles Loron (PE)
Chiroubles Passot (EL)
Fleurie Château de Fleurie, Loron (BYR)
Fleurie Château de l'Abbaye, Quinson (WIZ)
Juliénas Domaine de la Vieille Église,
  Loron (DI)
Juliénas Duboeuf (BYR)
Juliénas Léspinasse (HAW)
Juliénas Loron (CH)
Morgon Domaine des Arcades (AS)
Morgon Duboeuf (BYR, NI)
★Moulin-à-Vent Domaine Bruyère (OD)
Regnié Château de Basty (LAY)
Regnié Domaine de la Chapelière (OL)
Regnié Duboeuf (BY)
St-Amour Domaine des Billards, Loron (BL)
St-Amour Duboeuf (BYR)
St-Amour Vigne de la Côte de Beddet (EL)
1987
Brouilly Château de la Chaize, Marquis de
  Roussy de Sales (STA)
Brouilly Loron (UN)
Fleurie Château de Fleurie, Loron (EL)
Juliénas Loron (UN)
Moulin-à-Vent Domaine de la Tour du Bief,
  Duboeuf (WHI)
St-Amour Domaine Aufranc (SAI)
1986
Brouilly Château de la Chaize, Marquis de
  Roussy de Sales (STA)
Moulin-à-Vent Duboeuf (VIC)
1984
St-Amour Domaine du Paradis (PE)

───────── £6.00 to £6.99 ─────────

1989

★Brouilly Château des Tours (PIP)
Brouilly Duboeuf (BY)
Brouilly Grand Clos de Briante, Loron (OD)
Brouilly Large (HAH)
Chénas Dépagneux (UP)
Chiroubles Domaine de la Grosse Pierre
  (STA, CHA)
Chiroubles Duboeuf (NI)
Chiroubles la Maison des Vignerons (AD,
  HAW)
Côtes de Brouilly Duboeuf (NI)
Côtes de Brouilly Joubert (TAN)
Juliénas Domaine de la Bottière,
  Chanut (GIL)
Juliénas Domaine de la Seigneurie (PIP)
Juliénas Domaine des Mouilles,
  Duboeuf (BY)
Juliénas Domaine Joubert (AD)
Juliénas Duboeuf (NI, BY)
★Morgon Domaine Jean Descombes,
  Duboeuf (THR, PIP)
Morgon Duboeuf (BY)
Moulin-à-Vent Duboeuf (NI)
Moulin-à-Vent le Vivier, Brugne (EL)
Regnié Château de Basty (TAN)
Regnié Château de la Pierre, Loron (WRI)

1988

Brouilly Château de Nevers, Duboeuf (DAV)
Brouilly Château des Tours (TAN)
Brouilly Duboeuf (BY)
Brouilly Geoffray (HAW)
Brouilly Michaud (MV)
Chénas Benon (HAW)
Chiroubles Château de Raousset (WIZ)
Chiroubles Duboeuf (NI, BY)
Chiroubles Loron (TAN)
Chiroubles Passot (WW)
Côtes de Brouilly Château du Grand
  Vernay (HAW)
Côtes de Brouilly Château Thivin (HAW,
  RAE)
Côtes de Brouilly Duboeuf (BY)
Fleurie Cave Co-op. de Fleurie (BOT, PD,
  HAW)
Fleurie Château de Fleurie, Loron (PE)
Fleurie Chignard (ASD)
Fleurie Collin-Bourisset (BOR)
Fleurie Colonge (BYR)
Fleurie Domaine des Quatre Vents,
  Duboeuf (BEK)
Fleurie Duboeuf (VIC)
Juliénas Aujas (HAW, LAY)
Juliénas Benon (HAW)

Juliénas Clos des Poulettes, Loron (GRE)
Juliénas Condemine (HAW)
Juliénas Domaine de la Vieille Église,
  Loron (WRI)
Juliénas Domaine du Grand Cuvage,
  Duboeuf (DAV)
Juliénas Drouhin (NI)
Juliénas Duboeuf (NI, BY)
Juliénas les Capitans, Louis Tête (BAR)
Morgon Aucoeur (HAW, AD)
Morgon Château Gaillard (BIB, RAE)
Morgon Château de Raousset, Duboeuf (BY)
★Morgon Côte de Py, Savoye (HIC)
Morgon Duboeuf (BY)
Morgon Janodet (TAN)
Morgon les Charmes, Louis Tête (BAR)
Moulin-à-Vent Domaine Labruyere (LAY)
Moulin-à-Vent Domaine Lemonon,
  Loron (CH)
Moulin-à-Vent Duboeuf (BYR, NI)
Moulin-à-Vent Janin (HAY)
Moulin-à-Vent Picolet (HAW)
Regnié Duboeuf (AI)
St-Amour Domaine des Billards, Loron (CH)
St-Amour Domaine du Paradis (BEK)
St-Amour Louis Tête (HOG)

1987

Brouilly Grand Clos de Briante, Loron (AV)
Chénas Château Bonnet (AV)
Chénas Duboeuf (AI)
Côtes de Brouilly Château Thivin (LAY)
Fleurie Domaine des Quatre Vents,
  Duboeuf (WHI)
Juliénas Domaine de la Seigneurie (AI)
Moulin-à-Vent Domaine de la Teppe,
  Chanut (IR)
Moulin-à-Vent Drouhin (RAE)
Moulin-à-Vent Loron (UN)
St-Amour Domaine des Pins, Echallier (PE)
St-Amour Duboeuf (BY)

1986

Morgon Domaine de Lathevalle,
  Mommessin (YF)
St-Amour Domaine des Billards, Loron
  (GRE)

───────── £7.00 to £7.99 ─────────

1989

Chiroubles Château de Javernand,
  Duboeuf (PIP)
Chiroubles Domaine du Moulin (WRI)
Chiroubles Duboeuf (BY)
Côtes de Brouilly Chanut (IR)
Fleurie Château de Fleurie, Loron (TAN)
Fleurie Colonge (BIB)

Fleurie Domaine de Montgénas, Sélection
   Éventail (CHA, STA)
Fleurie Duboeuf (THR)
Fleurie la Madone, Duboeuf (BEK)
Fleurie Michel Chignard (MV)
St-Amour Château St-Amour (GIL)
St-Amour Duboeuf (NI)
1988
Chiroubles Loron (UP)

Chiroubles Louis Tête (GRE)
Côtes de Brouilly Château Thivin (GRE)
Côtes de Brouilly Domaine des Brussières,
   Dépagneux (UP)
Fleurie Blanc (BL)
Fleurie Château de Fleurie, Loron (HA,
   HUN, CH, DI)
Fleurie Colonge (ALL, PE)
Fleurie Duboeuf (LAY, BY)
Fleurie Grill Midi, Duboeuf (WHI)
Fleurie la Madone, Duboeuf (WHI, DAV)
Fleurie la Roilette, Vin Dessalle (ASK)
Fleurie Loron (AV)
Morgon Janodet (MV, UP)
Moulin-à-Vent Château des Jacques (AS)
Moulin-à-Vent Château du Moulin-à-Vent
   (HAW)
Moulin-à Vent Domaine Charvet (PE)
Moulin-à-Vent Domaine de la Teppe,
   Chanut (GIL)
Moulin-à-Vent Domaine de la Tour du Bief,
   Duboeuf (THR)
Moulin-à-Vent Domaine des Rosiers,
   Duboeuf (AMI)
Moulin-à-Vent Duboeuf (BY)
St-Amour Château St-Amour (IR)
St-Amour Duboeuf (NI)
St-Amour les Berthaux, Dépagneux (UP)
St-Amour Poitevin (HIC)
St Michael Fleurie (MAR)
1987
Brouilly de Pierreux, Duboeuf (AI)
Chiroubles Duboeuf (AI)
Fleurie Colonge (ALL)

Fleurie Duboeuf (AMI)
Fleurie la Madone, Louis Tête (HOG)
Fleurie Loron (UN)
Moulin-à-Vent Domaine de la Tour du Bief,
   Duboeuf (DAV)
1986
Chénas Domaine des Vieilles Caves,
   Charvet (PE)
St-Amour Domaine des Pins, Echallier (PE)

——————— **£8.00 to £8.99** ———————
1989
Fleurie Château de Fleurie, Loron (WRI)
Fleurie Château des Deduits, Duboeuf
   (PIP, BY)
Fleurie Domaine de Montgénas, Sélection
   Éventail (VIG)
Fleurie Domaine des Quatre Vents,
   Duboeuf (BY)
Fleurie Drouhin (NI)
Moulin-à-Vent Domaine des Héritiers
   Tagent, Duboeuf (BY)
Moulin-à-Vent Duboeuf (BY)
St-Amour Domaine des Pins, Duboeuf (PIP)
St-Amour Domaine du Paradis (BY)
St-Amour Duboeuf (BY)
1988
Fleurie Château de Fleurie, Loron (AV)
Fleurie Château de Labourons (BAR)
Moulin-à-Vent Domaine Lemonon, Loron
   (WRI)
Moulin-à-Vent Duboeuf (AI)
Moulin-à-Vent Fût de Chêne, Berrod (AD)
1987
Moulin-à-Vent Drouhin (WRI)
1986
St-Amour Duboeuf (AI)

WHITE

——————— **Under £6.00** ———————
1989
Beaujolais Blanc Bully (WAI)
1987
Beaujolais Blanc Loron (DI)
1986
Beaujolais Blanc Domaine de Savy,
   Duboeuf (BY)

——————— **£6.00 to £7.99** ———————
1989
Beaujolais Blanc Château des Tours (PIP)
Beaujolais Blanc Domaine des Grands
   Vents (PIP)
Beaujolais Blanc Duboeuf (BY)

CHAMPAGNE

SPARKLING WHITE

─────── **Under £8.00** ───────
Non-vintage
Massé ½ bottle (BAR)
Moët & Chandon ½ bottle (WIZ)

─────── **£8.00 to £9.99** ───────
Non-vintage
Asda Champagne (ASD)
★Canard-Duchêne (HOG)
Moët & Chandon ½ bottle (WHI, AD, BOT,
    AUG, BO, TAN, AV, OD, AN)
Tesco Champagne (TES)
Veuve Clicquot ½ bottle (HUN, BO, AD, BAR)
★Waitrose Champagne (WAI)
1983
Moët & Chandon ½ bottle (UN)

─────── **£10.00 to £11.99** ───────
Non-vintage
Adnams Champagne (AD)
Alexandre Bonnet Prestige (LOR, HAY)
Beerens (BIB)
Blin (OD)
Bricout Carte Noire (THR)
Chantal & Cie (STA)
de Clairval (BL)
Descombes (THR)
Duchatel (UN)
Ellner (LAY)
Heidsieck Dry Monopole (SAF, OD, LO)
Jacquesson Blanc de Blancs (WIZ)
Lambert Extra Dry (PD, BOT)
Louis Kremer (BYR)
Massé (ASK, WIZ)
Mercier (WIZ, ASD, TES, LAY, VIC)
Sainsbury's Champagne (SAI)
Tanners Reserve (TAN)
★de Telmont (MAJ)
Veuve Clicquot ½ bottle (EL, AN)
1985
Lambert Blanc de Blancs (BOT)
★Sainsbury's Champagne (SAI)
1983
Waitrose Champagne (WAI)
1982
Veuve Clicquot ½ bottle (BAR)

─────── **£12.00 to £14.99** ───────
Non-vintage
Ayala (VIC, MAJ, TES)

Besserat de Bellefon Crémant (TES)
Billecart-Salmon (IR, ASK, BYR, WW)
Boizel (AUG)
Boizel Rich (AUG)
Bricout Carte Noire (BOR)
Bricout d'Or (UP)
Bruno Paillard (LOR, BEK, BYR)
Camuset Réserve (YF)
Canard-Duchêne (IR, REI, WIL, BAR)
Charles Heidsieck (BO, UN, BYR, VIC, AUG,
    MAJ)
Chiquet Blanc de Blancs (LOR)
Dagonet Cuvée Exceptionelle (ELL)
de Venoge Cordon Bleu (WHI)
Deutz (TES)
George Goulet (BYR, PIP)
Georges Gardet (HUN, UP)
Heidsieck Dry Monopole (WIL, GI, BL)
Jacquesson Blanc de Blancs (YAP)
Jacquesson Perfection (YAP)
Joseph Perrier (HIC, HAG, BYR, PE)
Joseph Perrier Cuvée Royal (TES)
Lanson (HOG, ASD, BYR, SAF, BOT, HA, UN,
    AUG, WAI, WHI, OD, PE, LAY, BL, VIC, TES,
    THR)
Laurent-Perrier (AMI, LO, OD, PE, MV, BL,
    BYR, LAY, MAJ)
★Le Mesnil Blanc de Blancs (HAY, BIB)
Massé (BAR)
Mercier (WHI, PD, BOT, PE, UN, WIL)
Moët & Chandon (HOG, UP, VIC, WAI, ASD, SAI,
    TES, WIZ, BYR, GRE, WHI)
Mumm Cordon Rouge (OD, SAF, TES, BOT,
    VIC, AUG, THR)
Perrier-Jouët (OL, OD)
Pierre Vaudon 1er Cru (HAH)
Piper Heidsieck (NI, OD, TES)
Pol Roger White Foil (HOG, BYR, BOR, ASD,
    GRE)
Pommery (OD, GRE)
St Michael Blanc de Blancs (MAR)
St Michael Blanc de Noirs (MAR)
St Michael Champagne Desroches (MAR)
Taittinger (WIZ)
Thienot (OD)
de Venoge Blanc de Blancs (BO, OL)
★Veuve Clicquot (HUN)
1985
Lambert Blanc de Blancs (PD)
Lambert Cuvée Exceptionelle (BOT)
1983
Duchatel (UN)

Duval Leroy Fleur de Champagne (TAN)
Veuve Clicquot ½ bottle (EL)
1982
Georges Gardet (UP)
Louis Kremer (BYR)
1979
Alfred Gratien ½ bottle (HAY)
Ayala (ASD)
Georges Gardet (UP)

─────── **£15.00 to £19.99** ───────
Non-vintage
Alfred Gratien (WCL, HAY)
Boizel (AV)
Bollinger (HOG, WHI, UP, WIZ, ASD, HUN, WAI,
    BYR, CB, GRE, MV, PIP, VIC, BL, REI, AUG, AI,
    BER, WRI, BE, WIL, LAY, CH, OL, AV, AD, GI,
    BOT, DAV, LO, SAF, MAJ, PE, TES, EL, HAH,
    TAN, UN, ELL, ALL, HAY, HAG)
Bricout d'Or (WCL)
Bruno Paillard Blanc de Blancs (BEK)
Charles Heidsieck (THR, AI, GI, WIL, AD)
Deutz (AN)
Heidsieck Dry Monopole (HUN)
Henriot Blanc de Blancs (VIC)
Henriot Souverain (BOT, TAN, ALL)
Joseph Perrier (TAN, VIG)
Lanson (YF, CH, PD, DAV, WRI, WIL, TAN, EL,
    VIN)
Laurent-Perrier (CB, CHA, EL, UP, THR, WIL,
    ELL, YF, ALL, GI, HAH, BIB, AN)

Louis Roederer (HOG, GI, WS, REI, HUN, MV,
    NI, GRE, UP, WRI, TAN, BER, LAY, PE, WHI, AV,
    WCL, HA, EL, YF, HAY, BIB, AD, AMI, CB, VIC,
    MAJ, HAG, THR, BAR, HAH)
Michel Gonet (WRI)
Moët & Chandon (CH, BL, WRI, LAY, AD, AMI,
    GI, SAF, PE, DAV, OL, PD, BOT, UN, AUG, EL,
    TAN, ELL, AN, AV, HAG, WIL, CB, HA, VIN)
Mumm Cordon Rouge (WIL, PD, WCL, BL, UN)
Mumm Crémant de Cramant Blanc de
    Blancs (BOT, TES, OD, PD)
Perrier-Jouët (HUN, REI, PIP, UP, BYR, BAR,
    WIL, WHI, WRI, HA, BE, VIN)

Piper Heidsieck (BYR, WIL)
Piper Heidsieck Sauvage (TES)
Pol Roger (UP, VIG)
Pol Roger White Foil (CH, TES, OD, AV, YF, HA,
    BOT, OL, WRI, ALL, WIL, UN, MAJ, HAH, VIN)
Pommery (CH, AI, AN)
★The Society's Champagne (WS)
Taittinger (BO, AI, IR, VIC, BOT, LAY, WHI, WS,
    BYR, OD, BIB, UN, WRI, PD, BAR, ALL, AN)
de Venoge Blanc de Blancs (WHI, WIL)
de Venoge Cordon Bleu Extra Dry (HA)
Veuve Clicquot (BO, HOG, ASD, AI, GI, WHI, BL,
    OD, UP, WAI, WIL, CH, REI, WCL, GRE, BYR,
    MV, LAY, MAJ, DAV, TES, AD, BOT, HAY, ELL,
    TAN, EL, VIC, UN, WRI, BER, BIB, ALL, PD, CB,
    BAR, AUG, THR, AN, HAG, PE, HAH)
1986
Moët & Chandon (TAN)
1985
Bruno Paillard (BEK)
Descombes (THR)
Ellner (LAY)
Heidsieck Dry Monopole (OD)
Lambert Cuvée Exceptionelle (PD)
Laurent-Perrier (CHA, BL, EL)
Le Mesnil Blanc de Blancs (AD, BIB)
Moët & Chandon (WHI, VIC)
Mumm Cordon Rouge (OD, WIL)
Perrier-Jouët (OD)
Piper Heidsieck (NI)
Thienot (OD)
1983
Ayala (MAJ)
Binet Blanc de Blancs (BER)
Bruno Paillard (BEK)
Bruno Paillard Blanc de Blancs (LOR)
Ellner (DAV)
George Goulet (BYR, PIP)
George Goulet Crémant Blanc de Blancs
    (OL)
Jacquesson Perfection (YAP)
Lanson (VIC, PE)
Lanson Red Label (OD)
Le Mesnil Blanc de Blancs (BIB)
Moët & Chandon (WHI, BO, WRI, PD, CH, WIL,
    AUG, UN, BOT, OD, HAG)
Pol Roger (MAJ)
de Venoge (WHI, WIL)
Veuve Clicquot (REI)
1982
Alfred Gratien (WS)
Bauget-Jouette (HIG)
Billecart-Salmon (BYR)
Billecart-Salmon Cuvée N.F. Billecart (IR,
    ASK)

Bruno Paillard (BYR)
Charles Heidsieck (BO, BYR, WIL)
George Goulet Crémant Blanc de Blancs
   (ALL, PIP)
Joseph Perrier (HIC)
Lanson Red Label (BYR)
Laurent-Perrier (CB, EL, BO)
Moët & Chandon (BYR)
Mumm Crémant de Cramant Blanc de
   Blancs (ASD)
Piper Heidsieck (NI, IR)
Piper Heidsieck Sauvage (UP)
Pol Roger (BYR, REI, GRE)
de Venoge (WHI)
Veuve Clicquot (AV, WHI, BAR)
1981
Laurent-Perrier (BYR)
1979
Bruno Paillard (BEK)
Georges Gardet (HUN, ALL)
Perrier-Jouët (UP)
de Venoge (HA)
1976
Georges Gardet (UP)
Pol Roger (GRE)
1975
★Georges Gardet (UP)

──────── **£20.00 to £24.99** ────────
Non-vintage
Louis Roederer Rich (HA)
★Moët & Chandon magnum (LAY)
1988
Bollinger (WHI)
1985
Louis Roederer (BIB)
Moët & Chandon (BL, EL, DAV, AN)
Perrier-Jouët (HIC, WIL)
1983
Billecart-Salmon Blanc de Blancs (ASK, IR,
   WW)
Billecart-Salmon Cuvée N.F. Billecart (WW)
Bollinger (BYR, WIZ, BAR, GRE, MV, BL, CB,
   WCL, OL, AMI)
Louis Roederer (BYR, WCL, TAN, MV, LAY, UP,
   CB, BIB, WIL)
Moët & Chandon (BL, PE, EL, AV)
Pommery (AN)
Taittinger (BYR, IR, WHI)
Veuve Clicquot (BL, AI, CH, GRE, OD, BIB, CB,
   THR, EL, HIC, HAH, WS, AN)
Veuve Clicquot Gold Label (LAY)
1982
Boizel (AV)
Bollinger (UP, WIZ)

Heidsieck Diamant Bleu (WIL)
Jacquesson Signature Cuvée de Prestige
   (YAP)
Laurent-Perrier (WIL)
Piper Heidsieck (WIL)
Piper Heidsieck Sauvage (WRI)
Pol Roger (UP, ALL, WIL, OD, HA, VIN)
Pol Roger Blanc de Chardonnay (REI)
Taittinger (AI, ALL)
Veuve Clicquot (BYR, BOT, WRI, VIC, HAG, UN)
Veuve Clicquot Gold Label (PD)
1981
Louis Roederer (GI)
1979
★Alfred Gratien Crémant (HAY)
1976
Bruno Paillard (BYR)
Moët & Chandon (UP)
1959
Moët & Chandon ½ bottle (VIG)

──────── **£25.00 to £29.99** ────────
Non-vintage
Dom Ruinart (TES)
Lanson magnum (AUG, LAY)
1985
Bollinger (DAV)
Deutz Blanc de Blancs (AN)
1983
Louis Roederer Blanc de Blancs (GRE)
Taittinger (WIL)
Veuve Clicquot Ponsardin Carte d'Or (PIP)
1982
Alfred Gratien (WCL)
Dom Ruinart Blanc de Blancs (WHI)
Louis Roederer (BER)
1979
Bruno Paillard (VIG, WIC, BOD)
Louis Roederer (PE)
Perrier-Jouët Belle Époque (BOR)
1969
Bruno Paillard (BEK)

──────── **£30.00 to £39.99** ────────
Non-vintage
Bollinger magnum (WIZ, BER, LAY, CH, AD)

> *Please remember that*
> ***Webster's** is a price*
> *GUIDE and not a price*
> *LIST. It is not meant to*
> *replace up-to-date*
> *merchants' lists.*

Krug Grande Cuvée (UP, IR, CB, GI)
Lanson magnum (WHI, HA, WRI)
Laurent-Perrier Cuvée Grande Siècle (HAG, CB, BL)
Laurent-Perrier magnum (CHA)
Moët & Chandon magnum (WHI, WRI, BOT, AUG, AD, AV, TAN, OD)
Perrier-Jouët Belle Époque (TES)
Perrier-Jouët magnum (BAR)
Pol Roger Cuvée Sir Winston Churchill (TES)
Pol Roger White Foil magnum (HA, WRI)
Veuve Clicquot magnum (HUN, BAR, BER, VIG)

1985
Perrier-Jouët Belle Époque (EL)

1983
George Goulet Cuvée de Centenaire (PIP)
Perrier-Jouët Belle Époque (PIP, BY, AD, EL, WHI, BE, WRI, WIL, HA)
Veuve Clicquot la Grande Dame (VIC, WIL)

1982
Charles Heidsieck Cuvée Champagne Charlie (WIL)
Dom Pérignon (WIZ)
Mumm René Lalou (OD)
Perrier-Jouët Belle Époque (HUN, UP, OD, WHI, HAG)
Pol Roger Cuvée Sir Winston Churchill (UP)
Taittinger Comtes de Champagne Blanc de Blancs (IR)

1981
Dom Ruinart Blanc de Blancs (VIC, HAH, PE)
Louis Roederer Cristal (BO, GRE)
Taittinger Comtes de Champagne Blanc de Blancs (OD, BYR)

1980
Dom Pérignon (WIZ)

1979
Bollinger Tradition RD (WIZ, BO, WCL, WIL, AD, GRE, TAN, OL, WS, CH, BOT, BAR, YF, PIP)
Perrier-Jouët Belle Époque (UP)
Piper Heidsieck (NI)
Pol Roger Cuvée Sir Winston Churchill (HA, GRE)
Salon le Mesnil (WIL)

1976
Bollinger Tradition RD (UP, BE)
Laurent-Perrier Millésime Rare (CHA)

1971
Canard-Duchêne (VIG)

───────── £40.00 to £49.99 ─────────

Non-vintage
Dom Pérignon (HOG)
Krug (MV, CH, BO, AD)
Taittinger Comtes de Champagne Blanc de Blancs (TES)

1985
Dom Pérignon (AV)

1983
Bollinger magnum (WIZ)
Dom Pérignon (VIC, BOT, LAY, BL, WHI, DAV)
Louis Roederer Cristal (GI, MV, UP, LO, WCL, TAN, EL, AD, BO, HUN, AMI, LAY, WRI, CB, BIB, OD, BER, YF, BAR, PE, MAJ)
Moët & Chandon magnum (UN)
Taittinger Comtes de Champagne Blanc de Blancs (WHI)

1982
Bollinger magnum (WIZ)
Dom Pérignon (CB, TES, OD, TAN, WIL, AMI, WHI, BY, BER, EL, HAH, PE)
Krug (LAY, UP, CB)
Taittinger (WIL)
Taittinger Comtes de Champagne Blanc de Blancs (HAH, WHI, LAY, HAG)
Veuve Clicquot magnum (BAR)

1981
Dom Pérignon (BYR)
Krug (UP, GI, MV, BAR, HAG)
Perrier-Jouët Belle Époque (VIN)
Taittinger Comtes de Champagne Blanc de Blancs (HA, WRI)

1980
Dom Pérignon (GI, UP, WRI)

1979
Bollinger RD (PIP)
Krug (IR, GRE)
Pol Roger Cuvée Sir Winston Churchill (WIL)

1973
Bollinger Tradition RD (VIN)

───────── £50.00 to £59.99 ─────────

1985
Louis Roederer Cristal (WIL, THR, AN)

1982
Deutz Cuvée de William Deutz (AN)
Dom Pérignon (VIN)
Louis Roederer Cristal (ALL)

1981
Krug (VIN)

1973
Krug (REI)

1961
Moët & Chandon (VIG)

──────── **£60.00 to £74.99** ────────
1981
Krug (WIL, TW)
1980
Krug Clos du Mesnil Blanc de Blancs (BAR, BO, UP)
1979
Krug (TW)
Krug Clos du Mesnil Blanc de Blancs (BO)
1975
Bollinger Année Rare RD (TAN)
1959
Bollinger (WY)

──────── **£75.00 to £89.99** ────────
Non-vintage
Bollinger jeroboam (LAY, TAN)
Laurent-Perrier Cuvée Grande Siècle magnum (CHA)
Pol Roger White Foil jeroboam (WRI, HA)
1982
Bollinger Vieilles Vignes Françaises, Blanc de Noirs (GRE)
Pol Roger Cuvée Sir Winston Churchill magnum (REI, AV)
1979
Pol Roger Cuvée Sir Winston Churchill magnum (BER)
1976
Krug (TW)
1975
Krug (TW)
1959
Krug (WY)

──────── **£90.00 to £105.00** ────────
Non-vintage
Lanson jeroboam (WRI)
1983
Dom Pérignon magnum (BOT)
1982
Bollinger Vieilles Vignes Françaises, Blanc de Noirs (WIL)
1981
Bollinger Vieilles Vignes Françaises, Blanc de Noirs (YF)
Krug magnum (BER)
1980
Dom Pérignon magnum (OD)
Krug Clos du Mesnil Blanc de Blancs (GRE)
1979
Bollinger Vieilles Vignes Françaises, Blanc de Noirs (TW)
Pol Roger Cuvée Sir Winston Churchill magnum (VIN)

1971
Dom Pérignon (WY)
1964
Dom Pérignon (WY)
1949
Louis Roederer (WY)

──────── **£110.00 to £135.00** ────────
Non-vintage
Pol Roger White Foil methuselah (WRI)
1982
Bollinger Vieilles Vignes Françaises, Blanc de Noirs (AN)
1980
Krug Clos du Mesnil Blanc de Blancs (WIL)
1949
Charles Heidsieck (REI)
Krug (WY)

──────── **c. £232.00** ────────
Non-vintage
Pol Roger White Foil salmanazar (WRI)

SPARKLING ROSÉ

──────── **Under £10.00** ────────
Non-vintage
★Waitrose Champagne Rosé (WAI)

──────── **£10.00 to £11.99** ────────
Non-vintage
Lambert (BOT)
★Sainsbury's Champagne Rosé (SAI)

──────── **£12.00 to £14.99** ────────
Non-vintage
Alexandre Bonnet Prestige (HAY)
Bauget-Jouette (HIG)
Jacquart (MV)
Jacquesson (YAP)
Lambert (PD)
Mercier (WHI, THR)
Pommery (AI)
Tanners Reserve (TAN)
1983
Jeanmaire (ALL)

──────── **£15.00 to £19.99** ────────
Non-vintage
Ayala (MAJ)
Billecart-Salmon (IR, ASK, BYR, WW)
Bricout (WCL)
Bruno Paillard (NI)
George Goulet (BYR)
Charles Heidsieck (WAI)

Lanson (BOT, PE, WHI, WRI, AUG, CH, HA, WIL,
    LAY, OD, PD, THR, DAV)
J. Lassalle Réserve des Grandes Années (BIB)
Laurent-Perrier (MV, WRI, CHA, BL, CB, AMI,
    ALL, LAY, REI, OD, UN, EL, BIB, ELL, BAR, LO)
Mercier (UN, OL)
Bruno Paillard (LOR, BEK, BYR)
Pommery (CH)
1985
Piper Heidsieck (NI)
1983
George Goulet (PIP)
1982
George Goulet (ALL)
Charles Heidsieck (AI)
Piper Heidsieck (NI)
1979
Piper Heidsieck (IR)

───────── **£20.00 to £29.99** ─────────
Non-vintage
Lanson (UN)
Laurent-Perrier (TAN, GRE, WIL, AN)
Louis Roederer (BO, REI, BAR, HA, WHI, BIB,
    WIL)
1985
Deutz (AN)
Moët & Chandon (WHI)
1983
Bollinger (BE, TAN, HIG, WIL)
Charles Heidsieck (WIL)
Moët & Chandon (WHI, WIL, UN)
Veuve Clicquot (AI, GRE, WIL)
1982
Pol Roger (REI, GRE, UP, CH, WRI, WIL, OD)
1981
Veuve Clicquot (BYR)

───────── **£30.00 to £39.99** ─────────
Non-vintage
Laurent-Perrier magnum (CHA)
1982
Bollinger (TW)
Perrier-Jouët Belle Époque (PIP, WHI, HAG,
    WIL)

───────── **£40.00 to £49.99** ─────────
Non-vintage
Krug (BO)
1983
Perrier-Jouët Belle Époque (TW)
Taittinger Comtes de Champagne (WIL)
1982
Dom Pérignon (HA)
Taittinger Comtes de Champagne (IR)

1981
Taittinger Comtes de Champagne (WHI)

───────── **£50.00 to £65.00** ─────────
Non-vintage
Krug (HAG)
1983
Taittinger Comtes de Champagne (BIB)
1982
Taittinger Comtes de Champagne (BIB)

───────── **£70.00 to £82.00** ─────────
Non-vintage
Krug (WHI, WIL, TW, AN)
1980
Dom Pérignon (WHI, WIL)

STILL WHITE

───────── **Under £10.00** ─────────
Non-vintage
Ruinart Coteaux Champenois Chardonnay
    (WIZ)

───────── **£12.00 to £14.50** ─────────
Non-vintage
Moët & Chandon Saran Nature Coteaux
    Champenois (AN)
Laurent-Perrier Blanc de Chardonnay
    Coteaux Champenois (CHA, WIL)
Ruinart Coteaux Champenois Chardonnay
    (VIC)

STILL RED

───────── **Under £12.50** ─────────
Non-vintage
Laurent-Perrier Pinot Franc, Cuvée de
    Pinot Noir, Coteaux Champenois (CHA)

───────── **c. £15.50** ─────────
1982
Bollinger Ay Rouge la Côte aux Enfants
    Coteaux Champenois (GRE)

NORTHERN RHÔNE

RED

──────── Under £4.00 ────────
Non-vintage
Sainsbury's Crozes-Hermitage (SAI)

──────── £4.00 to £4.99 ────────
1988
Crozes-Hermitage Delas (AUG)
St-Joseph de Vallouit (LOR)
1987
Crozes-Hermitage Delas (AUG, IR)
1986
Crozes-Hermitage Cave des Clairmonts
  (WAI)
★Crozes-Hermitage Domaine de
  Thalabert, Jaboulet (HOG)
Crozes-Hermitage Jaboulet (HOG, GI, HUN)
1985
Crozes-Hermitage Jaboulet (HOG)

──────── £5.00 to £6.99 ────────
1988
★Crozes-Hermitage Domaine de
  Thalabert, Jaboulet (OD)
Crozes-Hermitage Domaine des Entrefaux
  (PIP, BY)
Crozes-Hermitage Graillot (BY, YAP)
Crozes-Hermitage Jaboulet (OD, MAJ, WHI)

Crozes-Hermitage Domaine des
  Remizières, Desmeure (WCL)
St-Joseph de Vallouit (ALL)
★St-Joseph le Grand Pompée, Jaboulet
  (OD)
1987
Crozes-Hermitage Delas (AN)
Crozes-Hermitage Domaine des Entrefaux
  (BY)
Crozes-Hermitage Graillot (HAH, BY, WW)
1986
Crozes-Hermitage Cave des Clairmonts
  (MV, ELL)

Crozes-Hermitage Domaine de Thalabert,
  Jaboulet (HUN, LAY, VIC, MV, WS, TAN, BYR,
  GRE, ASK, HAY, HA, AD, RES)
Crozes-Hermitage Domaine des
  Clairmonts, Borja (YAP)
Crozes-Hermitage Domaine des Entrefaux
  (BY)
Crozes-Hermitage Graillot (LAY)
Crozes-Hermitage Jaboulet (AI, TAN)
Crozes-Hermitage les Meysonniers,
  Chapoutier (BYR)
Crozes-Hermitage Domaine des
  Remizières, Desmeure (PE)
St-Joseph Courbis (PIP)
St-Joseph Delas (OL)
St-Joseph le Grand Pompée, Jaboulet (HOG,
  SAI, HA, VIC, WW)
St-Joseph Réserve Personnelle, Jaboulet
  (NI, AUG)
1985
Crozes-Hermitage Domaine de Thalabert,
  Jaboulet (GI, HOG)
Crozes-Hermitage Jaboulet (LAY)
Crozes-Hermitage les Meysonniers,
  Chapoutier (GI, LAY)
Crozes-Hermitage Pascal (OL, LO, CH, DAV)
St-Joseph Cave Co-op. Agricole de St
  Désirat-Champagne (YAP)
★St-Joseph Coursodon (LAY)
1984
Crozes-Hermitage Domaine de Thalabert,
  Jaboulet (AI, REI)

──────── £7.00 to £8.99 ────────
1988
St-Joseph Grippat (YAP)
St-Joseph le Grand Pompée, Jaboulet (WHI)
1987
St-Joseph Grippat (YAP)
1986
Cornas Jaboulet (HOG, VIC)
Crozes-Hermitage Domaine de Thalabert,
  Jaboulet (WW)
Crozes-Hermitage Domaine des
  Clairmonts, Borja (HIC)
St-Joseph Réserve Personnelle, Jaboulet
  (HUN, AI)
1985
Cornas Jaboulet (HOG, HAG, BYR, ASK)
Crozes-Hermitage Domaine de Thalabert,
  Jaboulet (PE)
Crozes-Hermitage Graillot (PE)

Crozes-Hermitage les Meysonniers, Chapoutier (AD)
St-Joseph Clos de l'Arbalestrier, Florentin (HAU, PE, RAE)
St-Joseph Deschants, Chapoutier (BYR)
St-Joseph Grippat (BYR)
St-Joseph le Grand Pompée, Jaboulet (PE, HAY)
1984
Cornas de Barjac (LAY)
Cornas Jaboulet (AI)
Côte-Rôtie les Jumelles, Jaboulet (HOG)
Hermitage la Sizeranne, Chapoutier (LAY)
Hermitage Marquise de la Tourette, Delas (WIZ)
St-Joseph Clos de l'Arbalestrier, Florentin (WCL)
St-Joseph Gripa (BOD)
1983
Cornas Jaboulet (HAG)
★Crozes-Hermitage Domaine de Thalabert, Jaboulet (HOG, HAG)
Crozes-Hermitage les Meysonniers, Chapoutier (AD)

──────── £9.00 to £11.99 ────────
1988
Cornas Coteau, Michel (OL)
★Cornas de Barjac (AD)
Hermitage la Sizeranne, Chapoutier (TAN)
1987
Cornas Clape (YAP, OD)
Cornas de Barjac (HAH)
Cornas Michel (YAP)
Cornas Verset (RAE, PE)
Hermitage Sorrel (BIB)
1986
Cornas de Barjac (AD, HA)
Cornas Jaboulet (CB, GRE)
Cornas Verset (HAY, BIB)
Côte-Rôtie Boisselet (WIL)
Côte-Rôtie de Vallouit (LOR, ALL)
Hermitage Domaine des Remizières (RAE)
Hermitage Sorrel (BIB)
1985
★Cornas Michel (REI, YAP)
Côte-Rôtie Chapoutier (GI)
Côte-Rôtie Delas (BYR)
Hermitage Domaine des Remizières (WCL)
Hermitage la Sizeranne, Chapoutier (GI, BYR, GRE, LAY)
Hermitage Marquise de la Tourette, Delas (BYR)
Hermitage Sorrel (BIB)
St-Joseph Grippat (AD)

1984
Cornas de Barjac (BAR)
Côte-Rôtie les Jumelles, Jaboulet (GI)
Hermitage Domaine des Remizières (HAY, RAE, PE)
Hermitage la Chapelle, Jaboulet (HOG, LAY)
1983
Côte-Rôtie Chapoutier (HOG, GI, BO)
Côte-Rôtie Jamet (RES)
Crozes-Hermitage Domaine de Thalabert, Jaboulet (BAR)
Hermitage de Vallouit (LAY)
1982
Côte-Rôtie les Jumelles, Jaboulet (HOG)
1980
Cornas Jaboulet (LAY)
1979
★Côte-Rôtie les Jumelles, Jaboulet (HOG)

──────── £12.00 to £14.99 ────────
1988
Cornas Clape (YAP)
Cornas Michel (YAP)
Hermitage Cuvée des Miaux, Ferraton (TAN)
Hermitage la Sizeranne, Chapoutier (AD)
1987
Côte-Rôtie Barge (MV)
Côte-Rôtie Burgaud (YAP)
Côte-Rôtie Jamet (BIB, HAU)
Hermitage Grippat (YAP)
1986
Cornas Clape (YAP)
Côte-Rôtie Barge (RAE)
Côte-Rôtie Brune et Blonde, Guigal (OD)
Côte-Rôtie Champet (YAP)
Côte-Rôtie Chapoutier (BYR)
Côte-Rôtie Côte Blonde la Garde, Dervieux-Thaize (RES)
Côte-Rôtie Côte Brune, Gentaz-Dervieux (RAE)
Côte-Rôtie Gentaz-Dervieux (HAY)
Côte-Rôtie Pierre Barge (MV)
Hermitage la Chapelle, Jaboulet (HOG)
Hermitage Vidal Fleury (BYR)
1985
Cornas Cuvée Saynale, Clape (BYR)
Cornas Michel (LAY)
Côte-Rôtie Brune et Blonde, Guigal (REI)
Côte-Rôtie Chapoutier (LAY)
Hermitage Desmeure (BIB)
Hermitage Guigal (BO)
1984
Cornas de Barjac (HA)
Côte-Rôtie Champet (YAP)

Hermitage Chave (LAY)
Hermitage la Chapelle, Jaboulet (HA, TAN,
  GI, HAY, REI, AD, PE)
1983
Côte-Rôtie Chapoutier (LAY)
Hermitage Guigal (RES, OD, LAY)
Hermitage la Sizeranne, Chapoutier (WHI)
1982
Côte-Rôtie Chapoutier (LAY)
1981
Hermitage Cuvée des Miaux, Ferraton (PIP)

─────── £15.00 to £19.99 ───────
1988
Côte-Rôtie Burgaud (YAP)
Côte-Rôtie Jasmin (YAP)
Côte-Rôtie les Jumelles, Jaboulet (AD)
Hermitage Grippat (YAP)
Hermitage la Chapelle, Jaboulet (LAY, AD,
  OD)
1987
Côte-Rôtie Jasmin (YAP)
Hermitage Chave (YAP)
1986
Cornas Clape (AD)
Côte-Rôtie Guigal (TAN)
Côte-Rôtie les Jumelles, Jaboulet (HUN, CB)
Hermitage Chave (OD, YAP, BYR)
Hermitage Guigal (OD, BE)
Hermitage la Chapelle, Jaboulet (RES, MAJ,
  TAN, VIC, MV, HAY, WW, WHI)
1985
Côte-Rôtie Brune et Blonde, Guigal (MV, NI,
  HAY, BY, BAR, RES)
Hermitage Chave (OD)
Hermitage Guigal (NI, BE, BY)
Hermitage la Sizeranne, Chapoutier (DI)
1984
Côte-Rôtie Brune et Blonde, Guigal (HAY,
  BY)
Hermitage Chave (AD)
1983
Côte-Rôtie Brune et Blonde, Guigal (AD,
  HAG, HAY, RES)
Côte-Rôtie Chapoutier (AD)
Hermitage Guigal (GI, PE, AD, NI)
Hermitage Sorrel (UP)
1982
Côte-Rôtie Brune et Blonde, Guigal (RES)
Hermitage la Chapelle, Jaboulet (HAG)
1981
Côte-Rôtie Brune et Blonde, Guigal (AD)
1980
Côte-Rôtie les Jumelles, Jaboulet (HUN,
  WHI)

─────── £20.00 to £29.99 ───────
1988
Hermitage la Chapelle, Jaboulet (HAH, CB)
1986
Côte-Rôtie Jasmin (AD)
1985
Côte-Rôtie Jasmin (BYR, REI)
Hermitage la Chapelle, Jaboulet (BYR, LAY,
  HAY, AD, GI)
1983
Côte-Rôtie Brune et Blonde, Guigal (HA)
1982
Hermitage Chave (RES)
Hermitage la Chapelle, Jaboulet (LAY, CB)
1981
Hermitage Chave (REI)
1979
Hermitage la Chapelle, Jaboulet (BAR)
1978
Cornas Jaboulet (VIG)

─────── £30.00 to £45.00 ───────
1985
Hermitage la Chapelle, Jaboulet (HUN, CB)
1983
Hermitage la Chapelle, Jaboulet (AD)
1978
Côte-Rôtie Champet (VIG)

─────── c. £259.00 ───────
1961
Hermitage la Chapelle, Jaboulet (REI)

WHITE

─────── Under £7.00 ───────
1989
Crozes-Hermitage la Mule Blanche,
  Jaboulet (GRE)
1988
Crozes-Hermitage Delas (AN)
Crozes-Hermitage Domaine des Entrefaux
  (BY, PIP)
Crozes-Hermitage la Mule Blanche,
  Jaboulet (AI, TAN)
1987
Crozes-Hermitage Domaine des Entrefaux
  (BY)
Crozes-Hermitage la Mule Blanche,
  Jaboulet (HOG, HUN)
1986
Crozes-Hermitage Domaine des
  Clairmonts (YAP)
Crozes-Hermitage Domaine des Remizières
  (RAE)

──────── £7.00 to £8.99 ────────

1988
Crozes-Hermitage la Mule Blanche,
  Jaboulet (REI)
St-Joseph Courbis (PIP)
St-Joseph Grippat (YAP)
1986
Crozes-Hermitage la Mule Blanche,
  Jaboulet (HAG)
Hermitage la Tourette Delas (BYR)

──────── £9.00 to £11.99 ────────

1988
Hermitage Chante-Alouette, Chapoutier
  (TAN)
1987
Hermitage Chevalier de Stérimberg,
  Jaboulet (OD)
1986
Hermitage Chante-Alouette, Chapoutier
  (BYR, HAG, VIG)

Chante-Alouette
APPELLATION HERMITAGE CONTRÔLÉE
BOTTLED BY
M. CHAPOUTIER S.A.
NÉGOCIANTS ÉLEVEURS A TAIN L'HERMITAGE (DRÔME) FRANCE
e 75 cl

Hermitage Chevalier de Stérimberg,
  Jaboulet (GRE)
Hermitage Domaine des Remizières (RAE)
Hermitage Guigal (BO)
1985
Crozes-Hermitage la Mule Blanche,
  Jaboulet (HOG)
1984
Hermitage Chevalier de Stérimberg,
  Jaboulet (TAN)

──────── £12.00 to £15.99 ────────

1988
Hermitage Grippat (YAP)
1987
Condrieu Delas (PIP)
Hermitage Chave (YAP)
Hermitage Chevalier de Stérimberg,
  Jaboulet (WHI, VIG)
1986
Condrieu les Cepes du Nebadon,
  Paret (PE)
★Condrieu Vernay (WIL)

Hermitage Chante-Alouette, Chapoutier
  (GRE, WIL, DI)
★Hermitage Chave (EL, WS)
Hermitage Guigal (BE)
1985
Condrieu Vernay (LAY)
Hermitage Chevalier de Stérimberg,
  Jaboulet (LAY, TAN, HAG)
1984
Hermitage Chave (LAY)

──────── £16.00 to £19.99 ────────

1989
Condrieu Château du Rozay Cuvée
  Ordinaire (YAP)
Condrieu Dumazet (BIB)
Condrieu Guigal (AD, MV, WW, BE)
Condrieu Vernay (YAP, EL)
1988
Condrieu Dumazet (BIB)
Condrieu Pinchon (WW)
Condrieu Vernay (YAP, BYR)
Hermitage Chave (YAP)
Hermitage Chevalier de Stérimberg,
  Jaboulet (VIG)
1985
Hermitage Chevalier de Stérimberg,
  Jaboulet (CB)

──────── £20.00 to £24.99 ────────

1989
Condrieu Guigal (BY, TAN)
1988
Condrieu Coteau de Vernon, Vernay (YAP,
  RES)
1987
Condrieu Coteau de Vernon, Vernay (RES)
Condrieu Delas (AN)
Condrieu Guigal (REI)
1985
Condrieu Vernay (HAG)
Hermitage Chave (RES)
1982
Hermitage Chevalier de Stérimberg,
  Jaboulet (PE)

──────── £25.00 to £35.00 ────────

1987
Château Grillet (YAP)
1984
Château Grillet (REI)

──────── c. £37.50 ────────

1988
Château Grillet (YAP)

SOUTHERN RHÔNE

RED

Under £3.00

Non-vintage
Asda Coteaux du Tricastin (ASD)
Sainsbury's Côtes du Rhône-Villages (SAI)
Tesco Côtes du Rhône (TES)
1989
Vin de Pays de Vaucluse, Domaine de
l'Ameillaud (AUG)
Waitrose Côtes du Rhône (WAI)
1988
Coteaux du Tricastin Enclave des Papes
(THR)
Vin de Pays de Vaucluse, Domaine de
l'Ameillaud (AUG)
1987
Côtes du Rhône Château du Bois de la
Garde, Mousset (ASD)

£3.00 to £3.99

1989
★Côtes du Rhône Château du Grand
Moulas (AD)
Côtes du Rhône Domaine la Garrigue (CHA)
1988
Côtes du Rhône Domaine de la Renjardière
(EL)
Côtes du Rhône Loron (UP)
★Côtes du Rhône Parallèle 45, Jaboulet
(HOG)
Côtes du Rhône Puyméras (WW)
Côtes du Rhône-Villages Rasteau (OD)
Côtes du Ventoux Jaboulet (OD, HUN, MAJ,
NI)
★Côtes du Ventoux la Vieille Ferme (WHI,
BEK, MV, GRE, RES, PIP)
1987
Côtes du Rhône Loron (CH)
Côtes du Ventoux Domaine des Anges (LAY)
Côtes du Ventoux la Vieille Ferme (WHI)
Côtes du Ventoux Pascal (LO)
1986
Coteaux du Tricastin Domaine de Vieux
Micocoulier (HAG)
Côtes du Ventoux Domaine des Anges (BAR)
Vacqueyras Pascal (VIC)
1985
Côtes du Rhône Parallèle 45, Jaboulet (GI)
Côtes du Ventoux la Vieille Ferme (WCL)
★Vacqueyras Sélection Maître de Chais,
Combe (BO)

£4.00 to £4.99

1989
Côtes du Rhône Caves des Vignerons de
Vacqueyras (TAN)
Côtes du Rhône Château du Grand Moulas
(TAN)
Côtes du Rhône Domaine des Moulins (DAV)
Côtes du Rhône Parallèle 45, Jaboulet
(WHI)
Côtes du Rhône-Villages Château du
Grand Moulas (TAN)
Côtes du Rhône-Villages Ryckwaert (AD)
Côtes du Ventoux Domaine des Anges (AD,
BIB)
1988
Côtes du Rhône Château St-Estève (ELL)
Côtes du Rhône Domaine Bel-Air,
Ryckwaert (HAY)
Côtes du Rhône Domaine St-Gayan (YAP)
Côtes du Rhône Parallèle 45, Jaboulet (NI)
Côtes du Rhône Puyméras (YAP)
Côtes du Rhône Valréas, Bouchard (WS)
Côtes du Rhône-Villages Jaboulet (WHI)
★Côtes du Ventoux Domaine des Anges
(TAN)
Côtes du Ventoux Jaboulet (BYR, ASK)
Côtes du Ventoux la Vieille Ferme (UP)
Vacqueyras Caves des Vignerons des
Vacqueyras (TAN)
Vacqueyras Jaboulet (HOG, OD)
1987
Côtes du Rhône Cave de Chusclan (WIC,
BOD)
Côtes du Ventoux Domaine des Anges (BIB)
1986
Coteaux du Tricastin Domaine de Vieux
Micocoulier (STA)
Côtes du Rhône Château Redortier (PE)
Côtes du Rhône Cuvée Personnelle, Pascal
(ASK)
Côtes du Rhône Domaine Apollinaire (SAI)
Côtes du Rhône Domaine le Château (ALL)
Côtes du Rhône Jaume (WS)
Côtes du Rhône-Villages Domaine Ste-
Anne (LAY)
Côtes du Rhône-Villages Jaboulet (WHI)
Lirac la Fermade, Domaine Maby (LOR)
Lirac les Queyrades, Mejean (BER, TAN, AD,
AUG)
Vacqueyras Domaine le Sang des Cailloux
(HAY)
Vacqueyras Pascal (CH, DAV)

1985
Châteauneuf-du-Pape Brotte (WIZ)
★Côtes du Rhône Cuvée Personnelle,
Pascal (LOR, WW, GI, LO, YAP, VIN)
Côtes du Rhône Pascal (UP)
Lirac la Fermade, Domaine Maby (IR, HUN)
Vacqueyras Pascal (LO)

───────── **£5.00 to £6.99** ─────────
1988
Cairanne Rubasse-Charavin (BEK, PIP)
Côtes du Rhône-Villages Domaine Ste-
Anne (TAN, AD)
Lirac Domaine les Garrigues (AV)
Vacqueyras Domaine le Sang des Cailloux
(PIP)
Vacqueyras Jaboulet (AUG, GRE, WHI, CB)
1987
Châteauneuf-du-Pape les Arnévels (TES)
Côtes du Rhône Cru de Coudoulet (OD)
Côtes du Rhône-Villages Cairanne,
Thompson (AN)
Gigondas Côtes de la Tour, Sarrazine
(HAH)
Lirac Domaine de Castel Oualou (GRE)
Lirac Sabon (PIP)
Vacqueyras Domaine Clos des Cazaux (AN)
Vacqueyras Domaine la Garrigue (HIC)
1986
★Châteauneuf-du-Pape Domaine de Mont-
Redon (HOG)
Côtes du Rhône Cru de Coudoulet (WCL, MV)
Côtes du Rhône Domaine la Garrigue (HIC)
Côtes du Rhône Guigal (NI, OD, BE, AD, HIC,
BY, HAY)
Côtes du Rhône-Villages Domaine Ste-
Anne (HA)
Gigondas Château du Trignon (BOD)
Gigondas Domaine de St-Gens (LO)
★Gigondas Domaine du Grand Montmirail
(LOR)
Gigondas Domaine Raspail (BYR)
Gigondas Jaboulet (HOG)
Lirac la Fermade, Domaine Maby (YAP)
Lirac Sabon (WW)
Vacqueyras Jaboulet (HA)
Victoria Wine Châteauneuf-du-Pape (VIC)
1985
Châteauneuf-du-Pape Cuvée Clement-
Pascal (GI)
Châteauneuf-du-Pape Domaine Brunel
(SAI)
Côtes du Rhône Guigal (LAY, NI, MV, VIG,
BAR, ALL)
Côtes du Rhône-Villages Jaboulet (HUN, AI)

Gigondas Domaine du Grand Montmirail
(YAP, WW, ASK, DAV)
Gigondas Domaine St-Gayan, Roger Meffre
(OD)
Gigondas Guigal (NI)
Gigondas Jaboulet (GI)
Gigondas l'Oustau Fauquet, Domaine la
Fourmone (RAE)
Côtes du Rhône-Villages Rasteau Domaine
la Soumade (HAG)
Vacqueyras Domaine de la Couroulu (PE, BYR)
Vacqueyras Domaine la Fourmone, Combe
(RAE)
Vacqueyras Jaboulet (AI, AV)
Vacqueyras Pascal (YAP)
Vacqueyras Sélection Maître de Chais,
Combe (ASK)
1984
Gigondas Domaine des Bosquets, Gabriel
Meffre (HAG)
Gigondas Domaine du Grand Montmirail
(CH, VIN)
Lirac les Queyrades, Mejean (BAR)
1983
Côtes du Rhône-Villages Château la
Couranconne (RAE)
Vacqueyras Jaboulet (LAY)
1982
Côtes du Rhône Château Redortier (VIC)

───────── **£7.00 to £8.99** ─────────
1988
Châteauneuf-du-Pape Delas (AUG)
Châteauneuf-du-Pape Domaine de Mont-
Redon (MAJ)
Châteauneuf-du-Pape Domaine de Nalys
(GRE)
Châteauneuf-du-Pape Domaine du Père
Caboche (YAP)
Châteauneuf-du-Pape Domaine du Vieux
Télégraphe (AD)
Châteauneuf-du-Pape Domaine la
Roquette (PIP)
Gigondas Perrin (WCL)
1987
Châteauneuf-du-Pape Château de
Beaucastel (MV)
Châteauneuf-du-Pape Domaine de
Montpertuis (GIL)
Châteauneuf-du-Pape Domaine de Mont-
Redon (EL)
Châteauneuf-du-Pape Domaine du Vieux
Télégraphe (PIP, LAY, HAH, TAN)
Châteauneuf-du-Pape Domaine Font de
Michelle (THR)

Châteauneuf-du-Pape Domaine la
Roquette (BEK)

1986

Châteauneuf-du-Pape Chante-Cigale (ASK,
BAR)

Châteauneuf-du-Pape Château de
Beaucastel (WCL, BYR)

Châteauneuf-du-Pape Delas (AUG)

Châteauneuf-du-Pape Domaine de Nalys
(IR, WW)

Châteauneuf-du-Pape Domaine du Vieux
Télégraphe (TAN)

Châteauneuf-du-Pape les Cèdres, Jaboulet
(WHI)

Châteauneuf-du-Pape Réserve, Sabon (HIC)

Côtes du Rhône Rabasse-Charavin (BEK)

Gigondas Domaine de Gour de Chaulé (ELL)

Gigondas Domaine du Cayron (AD)

Gigondas Domaine Raspail (LAY)

Gigondas Domaine St-Gayan, Roger Meffre
(YAP)

1985

Châteauneuf-du-Pape Chante-Cigale (YAP)

★Châteauneuf-du-Pape Château de
Beaucastel (WIZ)

Châteauneuf-du-Pape Château de la Font
du Loup (HOG)

Châteauneuf-du-Pape Domaine de la
Solitude (BYR)

Châteauneuf-du-Pape Domaine du Père
Caboche (YAP)

Châteauneuf-du-Pape Domaine du Vieux
Télégraphe (AD)

Châteauneuf-du-Pape Domaine Font de
Michelle (LAY, DAV)

Châteauneuf-du-Pape les Cailloux, Brunel
(UP)

Châteauneuf-du-Pape Quiot (MAR)

Châteauneuf-du-Pape Vieux Donjon (YAP)

Gigondas Domaine les Pallières (BYR, RES,
PIP, BIB)

Gigondas Domaine St-Gayan, Roger Meffre
(YAP)

Gigondas Jaboulet (WHI, AI)

1984

Châteauneuf-du-Pape les Cèdres, Jaboulet
(AI, NI)

Châteauneuf-du-Pape Vieux Donjon (YAP)

Gigondas Domaine les Pallières (PE)

1982

Châteauneuf-du-Pape Delas (OL)

Côtes du Rhône Château de Fonsalette
(HOG)

1980

Châteauneuf-du-Pape Chante-Perdrix (BYR)

──────── **£9.00 to £11.99** ────────

1988

Châteauneuf-du-Pape Domaine Font de
Michelle (CB)

1987

Châteauneuf-du-Pape Clos des Papes, Avril
(RAE, BIB)

Châteauneuf-du-Pape Domaine du Père
Caboche (WRI)

Châteauneuf-du-Pape Domaine du Vieux
Télégraphe (HAG)

1986

Châteauneuf-du-Pape Château de
Beaucastel (OD, WHI, BER, TAN, RES, HAU)

Châteauneuf-du-Pape Château Fortia
(BYR)

Châteauneuf-du-Pape Clos des Papes, Avril
(HAY, BIB)

Châteauneuf-du-Pape Domaine de
Beaurenard (VIC)

Châteauneuf-du-Pape Domaine du Vieux
Télégraphe (BYR, REI)

1985

Châteauneuf-du-Pape Château de
Beaucastel (AD, WCL, MV)

Châteauneuf-du-Pape Clos de l'Oratoire
des Papes (BYR)

Châteauneuf-du-Pape Clos des Papes, Avril
(LAY)

Châteauneuf-du-Pape Clos Pignan,
Reynaud (HOG)

Châteauneuf-du-Pape Domaine de Mont-
Redon (BYR)

Châteauneuf-du-Pape les Cèdres, Jaboulet
(PE, GRE)

Châteauneuf-du-Pape Clos Mont Olivet
(BYR)

Côtes du Rhône Château de Fonsalette
(VIG)

1982

Châteauneuf-du-Pape Château de
Beaucastel (AD)

Châteauneuf-du-Pape les Cèdres, Jaboulet
(AI)

1981
Châteauneuf-du-Pape Domaine du Père
Caboche (UP)
Châteauneuf-du-Pape les Cèdres, Jaboulet
(GRE)
1980
Châteauneuf-du-Pape les Cèdres, Jaboulet
(HUN)

──────── £12.00 to £14.99 ────────
1986
Châteauneuf-du-Pape Château de
Beaucastel (VIG)
1985
Châteauneuf-du-Pape Château de
Beaucastel (ALL)
Châteauneuf-du-Pape la Bernardine,
Chapoutier (DI)
1983
Châteauneuf-du-Pape Château de
Beaucastel (BO, AD)
1981
Châteauneuf-du-Pape Château de
Beaucastel (BO, ASK, AD)
1980
Châteauneuf-du-Pape Château de
Beaucastel (AD)

──────── £15.00 to £19.99 ────────
1985
Châteauneuf-du-Pape Château Rayas
(HOG)
1981
Châteauneuf-du-Pape Château de
Beaucastel (RES, TAN, HAU, WCL, VIG, BAR)
1980
Châteauneuf-du-Pape Château de
Beaucastel (VIG)
1979
Châteauneuf-du-Pape Château de
Beaucastel (TAN)
Châteauneuf-du-Pape les Cèdres, Jaboulet
(WS)

──────── £20.00 to £29.99 ────────
1983
Châteauneuf-du-Pape Château Rayas (RES)
1964
Châteauneuf-du-Pape Domaine du Vieux
Télégraphe (REI)

──────── c. £37.00 ────────
1966
Châteauneuf-du-Pape la Grappe des
Papes, Jaboulet (REI)

WHITE

──────── Under £5.00 ────────
1989
Côtes du Rhône Domaine Pelaquié (BIB)
1988
Côtes du Rhône Parallèle 45, Jaboulet
(HOG)
Côtes du Rhône Puyméras (WW, YAP)
★Vin de Pays des Coteaux de l'Ardèche
Chardonnay, Latour (HOG)
1987
Lirac la Fermade, Domaine Maby (IR, BER)
1986
Lirac la Fermade, Domaine Maby (IR)

──────── £5.00 to £6.99 ────────
1989
Côtes du Rhône Domaine St-Gayan (YAP)
1988
Côtes du Rhône Guigal (NI, AD)
Lirac la Fermade, Domaine Maby (YAP)
Vin de Pays des Coteaux de l'Ardèche
Chardonnay, Latour (UP, REI)
1987
Côtes du Rhône Guigal (BE)
1984
Côtes du Rhône Guigal (BY)

──────── £7.00 to £8.99 ────────
1988
★Châteauneuf-du-Pape Domaine de Mont-
Redon (EL)
Châteauneuf-du-Pape Domaine de Nalys
(WW, IR, GRE)
1987
Châteauneuf-du-Pape les Cailloux (BYR)
Châteauneuf-du-Pape Berard (GRE)
1986
Châteauneuf-du-Pape les Cailloux (UP)

──────── £9.00 to £11.99 ────────
1989
Châteauneuf-du-Pape Domaine du Vieux
Télégraphe (AD, TAN)
1988
Châteauneuf-du-Pape Domaine de Mont-
Redon (WS)
Châteauneuf-du-Pape Domaine du Père
Caboche (YAP)
Châteauneuf-du-Pape Domaine du Vieux
Télégraphe (LAY, BYR)
1986
Côtes du Rhône Château de Fonsalette
(VIG)

────────── £12.00 to £14.99 ──────────

1988
Châteauneuf-du-Pape Château de
  Beaucastel (WCL, AD, TAN, RES)
1987
Châteauneuf-du-Pape Château de
  Beaucastel (HAU)
1982
Châteauneuf-du-Pape Liquoreux, Château
  Rayas (HOG)

────────── £15.00 to £20.99 ──────────

1988
Châteauneuf-du-Pape Château de
  Beaucastel (VIG)
Châteauneuf-du-Pape Roussanne Vieille
  Vigne, Château de Beaucastel (AD, WCL)
1987
Châteauneuf-du-Pape Roussanne Vieille
  Vigne, Château de Beaucastel (RES)
1985
Châteauneuf-du-Pape Château Rayas (VIG)

ROSÉ

────────── Under £5.00 ──────────

1989
★Lirac Domaine des Causses, Assémat
  (TAN)
Lirac Rosé la Fermade, Domaine Maby
  (YAP)
1988
Tavel Château de Trinquevedel (EL)
Tavel Domaine de la Genestière (LAY)
Tavel la Forcadière, Domaine Maby (LOR)
1987
Tavel Château de Trinquevedel (EL)
Tavel la Forcadière, Domaine Maby (HAY)
Tavel l'Espiègle, Jaboulet (HOG)

────────── £5.00 to £6.99 ──────────

1989
Tavel Domaine de la Genestière (TAN)
1988
Tavel Domaine de la Genestière (PIP)
Tavel l'Espiègle, Jaboulet (WHI, AI)

SPARKLING

────────── Under £7.50 ──────────

Non-vintage
Clairette de Die Brut Archard-Vincent
  (YAP)
Clairette de Die Tradition Demi-sec
  Archard-Vincent (YAP, HAU)

FORTIFIED

────────── Under £5.00 ──────────

Non-vintage
★Sainsbury's Beaumes-de-Venise (SAI)
1987
Muscat de Beaumes-de-Venise Domaine de
  Coyeux ½ bottle (AD)
Muscat de Beaumes-de-Venise Jaboulet
  ½ bottle (BAR)
1986
Rasteau Cave des Vignerons de Rasteau
  (BR)

────────── £5.00 to £6.99 ──────────

Non-vintage
Muscat de Beaumes-de-Venise Cave Co-op.
  de Beaumes-de-Venise (LAY, OD)
1987
Muscat de Beaumes-de-Venise Cave Co-op.
  de Beaumes-de-Venise (SAI)
1985
Muscat de Beaumes-de-Venise Domaine de
  Coyeux (MAR)

────────── £7.00 to £9.99 ──────────

Non-vintage
Muscat de Beaumes-de-Venise Cave Co-op.
  de Beaumes-de-Venise (IR, AD, PIP)
Muscat de Beaumes-de-Venise Cuvée des
  Papes (BYR)
Muscat de Beaumes-de-Venise Cuvée
  Pontificale, Pascal (LO, DAV, YAP)
Muscat de Beaumes-de-Venise la Vieille
  Ferme (WHI, BIB)
Rasteau Vin Doux Naturel, Domaine la
  Soumade (PIP)
1989
Muscat de Beaumes-de-Venise Cuvée
  Pontificale, Pascal (YAP)
1988
Muscat de Beaumes-de-Venise Domaine de
  Coyeux (OL)
Muscat de Beaumes-de-Venise Domaine de
  Durban (EL, RES, WW, PIP)
Muscat de Beaumes-de-Venise Jaboulet
  (HOG, MV, AI, GRE)
1987
Muscat de Beaumes-de-Venise Domaine de
  Coyeux (ELL)
Muscat de Beaumes-de-Venise Jaboulet
  (HOG)
1986
Muscat de Beaumes-de-Venise Perrin
  (PE)

LOIRE

DRY WHITE

─────── **Under £3.00** ───────

Non-vintage

Asda Muscadet de Sèvre-et-Maine (ASD)

Sainsbury's Anjou Blanc (SAI)

Sainsbury's Blanc de Blancs du Val de Loire Saumur (SAI)

Sainsbury's Muscadet de Sèvre-et-Maine (SAI)

Vin de Pays du Jardin de la France Chenin Blanc (IR, WIL)

Waitrose Muscadet (WAI)

1989

Saumur Cave des Vignerons de Saumur (TES)

Vin de Pays du Jardin de la France Chenin Blanc (AUG)

1988

Vin de Pays du Jardin de la France Chenin Blanc (KA)

─────── **£3.00 to £3.99** ───────

1989

Chardonnay du Haut Poitou Cave co-op (LO)

Muscadet des Coteaux de la Loire Guindon (BIB)

Muscadet les Chardonnières, Bonhomme (WW)

★Muscadet les Ormeaux, Sauvion (NI)

Muscadet sur lie Bottinardières, Luneau (RES)

★St Michael Cheverny (MAR)

St Michael Sauvignon de Touraine (MAR)

Saumur Cave des Vignerons de Saumur (ALL, YAP)

Sauvignon de Touraine Comte d'Ormont, Saget (MAJ)

★Sauvignon de Touraine Confrérie d'Oisly et Thésée (OD)

Sauvignon de Touraine Domaine de la Garrelière (AMI)

Sauvignon de Touraine Domaine Octavie, Barbeillon (MAJ)

Sauvignon du Haut Poitou, Cave co-op (AUG, MAJ, LO, STA)

Vin de Pays de Maine et Loire, Château de Putille (ALL)

★Vin de Thouarsais, Gigon (YAP)

1988

Muscadet Château de la Galissonnière, Lusseaud (PD)

Muscadet de Sèvre-et-Maine Château de la Dimerie (SAI)

Muscadet de Sèvre-et-Maine Cuvée les Ondoises, Sauvion (BEK)

Muscadet de Sèvre-et-Maine sur lie Château de la Botinière (SAF)

Muscadet de Sèvre-et-Maine sur lie Domaine des Chateliers (WAI)

Muscadet des Coteaux de la Loire Guindon (BIB)

Muscadet sur lie Domaine des Pierres Noires (HIG)

★Quincy Domaine de la Maison Blanche (ASD)

Saumur Cave des Vignerons de Saumur (ALL)

Saumur Domaine des Frogères, Joseph (KA)

Sauvignon de Touraine Domaine Guenault (LOR, WHI)

Sauvignon de Touraine Domaine Guy Mardon (VIC)

Sauvignon de Touraine Langlois-Château (HOG)

Vin de Pays de la Loire Chardonnay, Château d'Avrille (WHI)

Vouvray Château Moncontour (WAI)

Vouvray Domaine de l'Epinay (ASD)

1987

Chardonnay de Touraine, Saget (GI)

Muscadet Château de la Galissonnière, Lusseaud (PD, BOT)

Muscadet Domaine du Manoir, Poiron (GIL)

─────── **£4.00 to £4.99** ───────

1989

Azay-le-Rideau la Basse Chevrière (YAP)

Chardonnay du Haut Poitou Cave co-op (STA, AD)

Cheverny Cépage Sauvignon, Cazin (BEK)

Gros Plant sur lie, Château du Cleray (PIP)

Muscadet de Sèvre-et-Maine sur lie Bossard (BIB, RAE)

Muscadet de Sèvre-et-Maine sur lie Château de Cléray (PIP, NI)

Muscadet de Sèvre-et-Maine sur lie Château de la Jannière (STA, DAV)

Muscadet de Sèvre-et-Maine sur lie les Descouvertes, Sauvion (BEK)

Pineau de la Loire, Confrérie d'Oisly et Thésée (WS)

★St-Pourçain Cuvée Printanière, Union des Vignerons (PIP)

Saumur Cave des Vignerons de Saumur
(WIC, BOD)
Sauvignon de Touraine Confrérie d'Oisly et
Thésée (HAH)
Sauvignon de Touraine Domaine de la
Charmoise, Marionnet (BIB)
Sauvignon de Touraine Domaine de la
Garrelière (KA)
Sauvignon de Touraine Domaine de la
Preslé (PIP)
Sauvignon de Touraine Domaine de la
Renaudie (KA)
Sauvignon du Haut Poitou Cave co-op (AD)
1988
Anjou Blanc Sec Prestige, Tijou (HIG)
Azay-le-Rideau Pavy (WS)
Chardonnay du Haut Poitou Cave co-op
(HAY)
Chauvigné d'Anjou Richou-Rousseau (HAH)
Menetou-Salon Coeur (BO)
Menetou-Salon les Faucards, Rat (WHI)
Muscadet de Sèvre-et-Maine Château de la
Cassemichère (VIC)
Muscadet de Sèvre-et-Maine sur lie
Bossard (WHI, HAY)
Muscadet de Sèvre-et-Maine sur lie Carte
d'Or, Sauvion (AI)
Muscadet de Sèvre-et-Maine sur lie
Château de Chasseloir (HUN)
Muscadet de Sèvre-et-Maine sur lie
Château de Cléray (BEK, TAN, NI, BYR)
Muscadet de Sèvre-et-Maine sur lie
Château de la Ferronière (EL)
Muscadet de Sèvre-et-Maine sur lie
Château de la Ragotière Black Label
(AUG)
Muscadet sur lie Domaine les Hautes
Pierres, Gautier (HAG)
Quincy Vignerons, Duc de Berri (CH)
Saumur Blanc Château de Parnay Collé
(OL)
Saumur Blanc Domaine Langlois (HOG)
Sauvignon de Touraine Confrérie d'Oisly et
Thésée (ASK, WW)
Vouvray Château Moncontour (WHI)
1987
Menetou-Salon Coeur (HUN)
Muscadet sur lie Domaine des Moulins (AV)
1986
Montlouis Sec Deletang (RAE)
Muscadet de Sèvre-et-Maine sur lie
Château de Chasseloir (BYR)
1985
Montlouis Demi-sec Deletang (RAE)
Montlouis Sec Deletang (RAE)

1984
Vouvray Cave des Viticulteurs de Vouvray
(MAJ)
1979
Vouvray Clos Naudin, Foreau (HOG)

──────── £5.00 to £5.99 ────────
1989
Cheverny Cépage Sauvignon, Cazin (PIP)
Coteaux du Giennois Balland-Chapuis (AI)
Menetou-Salon Fournier (PIP)
Menetou-Salon la Charniviolle, Foumier
(BEK)
Menetou-Salon Pellé (LOR, IR)
Menetou-Salon Teiller (YAP)
Montlouis Domaine des Liards, Berger
(YAP)
Muscadet de Sèvre-et-Maine sur lie
Château de Chasseloir (IR)
Quincy Jaumier (YAP)
Reuilly Beurdin (AD, WCL)
1988
Menetou-Salon Domaine de Chatenoy (UP)
Menetou-Salon Morogues, le Petit Clos (OD)
Menetou-Salon Sauvignon, Rat (PE)
Muscadet de Sèvre-et-Maine sur lie
Château de la Ragotière Black Label
(VIN)
Muscadet de Sèvre-et-Maine sur lie Cuvée
de Millenaire, Marquis de Goulaine
(GRE)
Muscadet de Sèvre-et-Maine sur lie
Domaine des Hautes Noëlles (BAR)
Pouilly-Fumé les Moulins-à-Vent (WHI)
Quincy Clos des Victoires, Duc de Berri
(TAN)
Quincy Domaine de la Maison Blanche
(WCL)
Reuilly Lafond (PIP)
★Sancerre Château de Thauvenay (ASD)
Sancerre Domaine de Fort (WAI)
Saumur Blanc Domaine Langlois (DI)
Sauvignon du Haut Poitou, Cave co-op
(HIC)
★Savennières Clos du Papillon, Baumard
(EL, GRE)
Savennières Domaine de la Bizolière (YAP)
Vin de Pays du Jardin de la France Cépage
Chardonnay (VIN)
Vouvray Château Moncontour (WCL)
1987
Menetou-Salon Pellé (IR)
Menetou-Salon Roger (LAY)
Pouilly-Fumé les Loges, Saget (WIZ)
Saumur Blanc Domaine Langlois (DI)

Vouvray Jarry (YAP)

1986
Menetou-Salon Roger (BYR)
Savennières Domaine du Closel, Mme de
   Jessey (HAU)
Vouvray Château Moncontour (UN)
1985
Muscadet de Sèvre-et-Maine sur lie
   Château de Chasseloir (LOR)

──────── £6.00 to £6.99 ────────
1989
Chinon Blanc Raffault (OD)
Menetou-Salon Domaine de Chatenoy (OL,
   VIG)
Menetou-Salon Pellé (THR, MV)
Menetou-Salon Roger (TAN)
Pouilly-Fumé Bailly (WS)
Pouilly-Fumé la Loge aux Moines, Moreux
   (CB)
Pouilly-Fumé les Loges, Saget (MAJ)
Quincy Meunier (PIP)
Sancerre Daulny (LOR)
Sancerre Domaine du P'tit Roy (NI)
Sancerre la Reine Blanche (WS)
Sancerre Laporte (HUN)
Sancerre Michel Thomas (MAJ)
1988
Menetou-Salon Domaine de Chatenoy (WRI)
Menetou-Salon Pellé (GIL, THR)
Menetou-Salon Roger (HAU)
Montlouis Demi-sec Domaine des Liards,
   Berger (BAR, BAR)
Pouilly-Fumé Domaine de Petit Soumard
   (AUG)
★Pouilly-Fumé Domaine des Berthiers,
   Dagueneau (IR)
Pouilly-Fumé Domaine des Rabichattes
   (PE)
Pouilly-Fumé Jean Pabiot (STA)
★Pouilly-Fumé les Griottes, Bailly (GI, HAY)
Pouilly-Fumé les Loges, Saget (UP)
St Michael Sancerre (MAR)
★Sancerre Clos du Chêne Marchand,
   Crochet (BOT)

Sancerre Clos le Grand Chemarin, Migeon
   (BEK)
Sancerre Daulny (HAH)
Sancerre Domaine de Montigny, Natter
   (WHI)
Sancerre Domaine des Trois Piessons (THR)
Sancerre Domaine du P'tit Roy (NI)
Sancerre Paul Prieur (HA)
Savennières Château de Chamboureau,
   Soulez (YAP)
Savennières Château d'Epiré (YAP)
Savennières Domaine du Closel, Mme de
   Jessey (OL)
Vouvray le Haut Lieu, Huet (RAE)
1987
Pouilly-Fumé Redde (HOG)
Sancerre les Creux, Gitton (HIG)
Sancerre les Monts Damnés, Cotat (RAE)
Savennières Clos du Papillon, Baumard
   (BEK)
Savennières Clos du Papillon, Domaine du
   Closel (PIP)
1986
Savennières Clos du Papillon, Baumard
   (WIL)
Savennières Clos St-Yves (AV)
Vouvray Clos Naudin, Foreau (BYR)
Vouvray Domaine Peu de la Moriette (PIP)
1985
Jasnières Caves aux Tuffières, Pinon (YAP)
Savennières Clos de Coulaine (BIB)
1984
Savennières Clos de Coulaine (HA)
Vouvray le Haut Lieu, Huet (RAE)
1982
Vouvray le Mont, Huet (RAE)
1980
Vouvray Clos Naudin, Foreau (AD)

──────── £7.00 to £7.99 ────────
1989
Menetou-Salon Morogues, le Petit Clos
   (BAR)
Pouilly-Fumé Château de Tracy (TAN, LOR)
Sancerre Domaine de Montigny, Natter
   (BIB)
Sancerre Laporte (DI, PIP)
Sancerre le Chêne Marchand, Roger (TAN)
Sancerre les Tuileries, Redde (EL)
Sancerre Vacherons (UP, AD, MAJ, CH)
1988
Menetou-Salon Pellé (ALL, WIL)
Pouilly-Fumé Château de Tracy (BYR)
Pouilly-Fumé Domaine de Petit Soumard
   (ELL)

Pouilly-Fumé Domaine des Rabichattes
(RAE)
Pouilly-Fumé Domaine Thibault (BYR, NI)
Pouilly-Fumé la Charnoie, Renaud (HAH)
Pouilly-Fumé les Folatières, Gitton (ASK)
Pouilly-Fumé les Griottes, Bailly (CH)
Pouilly-Fumé les Loges, Saget (GI, TAN)
Pouilly-Fumé les Pechignolles (HIG)
Pouilly-Fumé Redde (EL)
Sancerre André Dezat (LAY)
Sancerre le Grand Chemarin, Balland (PE,
BER)
Sancerre le Paradis, Vacheron (AI)
Sancerre les Crilles, Gitton (BR)
Sancerre les Jeannettes, Bourgeois (GRE)
Savennières Clos du Papillon, Baumard
(TAN)
1987
Pouilly-Fumé Jean Pabiot (BE)
Pouilly-Fumé les Griottes, Bailly (UN)
Quincy Pierre Mardon (AN)
Sancerre Clos du Chaudenay Vieilles
Vignes, Daulny (HAH)
1986
Sancerre les Romains, Gitton (HIG)
Sancerre Vacheron (UP)
Vouvray Château de Vaudenuits (UN)
1985
★Vouvray Clos Naudin, Foreau (AD)
1984
Savennières Roche-aux-Moines, Clos de la
Bergerie (VIG)
1983
Vouvray le Haut Lieu, Huet (AV)
Vouvray le Mont, Huet (AD, PE)

──────── £8.00 to £9.99 ────────
1989
Pouilly-Fumé Château de Tracy (AD)
Pouilly-Fumé les Bascoins, Masson-
Blondelet (HAU, PIP)
Pouilly-Fumé Seguin Père et Fils (WIC)
Sancerre le Grand Chemarin, Balland (HIC)
Sancerre le Pied Renard, Laporte (DI)
1988
Pouilly-Fumé Dageneau (LAY, TAN)
Pouilly-Fumé de Ladoucette, Château du
Nozet (BYR, RES, BOT, GRE)
Pouilly-Fumé Domaine des Berthiers,
Dagueneau (OL, WRI)
Pouilly-Fumé les Champs de la Croix (AN)
Sancerre Clos de la Poussie (PE)
Sancerre Clos du Roy, Millérioux (HAG, BAR)
Sancerre le Pied Renard, Laporte (DI)
Sancerre les Galinots, Gitton (HIG)

1987
Pouilly-Fumé Château de Tracy (WHI)
Pouilly-Fumé de Ladoucette, Château du
Nozet (WHI)
Pouilly-Fumé les Bascoins, Masson-
Blondelet (HAU)
Sancerre Clos des Roches, Vacheron (AV)
Sancerre Comte Lafond, Château du Nozet
(BYR)
Savennières Roche-aux-Moines, Soulez
(YAP)
1985
Pouilly-Fumé les Roches, Saget (GI)
Vouvray Aigle Blanc, Poniatowski (VIG)
Vouvray le Haut Lieu, Huet (AD)
Vouvray le Mont, Huet (BIB)

──────── £10.00 to £14.99 ────────
1989
Pouilly-Fumé de Ladoucette, Château du
Nozet (VIC)
1988
Pouilly-Fumé de Ladoucette, Château du
Nozet (HAH, WIL, BER, AN)
Sancerre Chavignol les Monts Damnés,
Cotat (AN)
1987
Pouilly-Fumé de Ladoucette, Château du
Nozet (PD)
1986
Pouilly-Fumé Cuvée Prestige, Chatelain
(BEK, MV)
1985
Vouvray Clos Baudoin, Poniatowski (VIG)

──────── £19.00 to £27.00 ────────
1987
Pouilly-Fumé Baron de L Château du
Nozet (RES)
1986
Pouilly-Fumé Baron de L Château du
Nozet (WHI, AN)

SWEET WHITE

──────── Under £5.00 ────────
1988
Coteaux du Layon Château de la Roulerie
(YAP)
Coteaux du Layon Domaine Sauveroy (OD)
Malvoisie Guindon (YAP)
1987
Coteaux du Layon Ackerman (AI)
Coteaux du Layon Clos de Ste-Catherine,
Baumard (EL)

1986
Coteaux du Layon Château de Breuil (BOR)
Montlouis Moelleux Deletang (RAE)
1985
Montlouis Moelleux Deletang (RAE)

──────── £5.00 to £6.99 ────────
1989
Coteaux du Layon Chaume, Morin (LOR)
1988
Coteaux de l'Aubance, Richou (OL, BAR)
Coteaux du Layon Clos de Ste-Catherine,
   Baumard (EL)
1986
Coteaux du Layon Clos de Ste-Catherine,
   Baumard (LOR, BYR, GRE)
Coteaux du Layon Domaine des Saulaies
   (TAN)
Coteaux du Layon Leblanc (HAY)
Vouvray Brédif (GRE)
1985
★Coteaux du Layon Clos de Ste-Catherine,
   Baumard (HOG)
Montlouis Moelleux Domaine des Liards,
   Jean & Michel Berger (YAP)
Vouvray Château de Vaudenuits (GRE)
1984
Coteaux du Layon Château de la Roulerie
   les Aunis (YAP)
1983
Vouvray Jarry (YAP)

──────── £7.00 to £8.99 ────────
1989
Vouvray Jarry (YAP)
1988
Vouvray Domaine Peu de la Moriette (TAN)
1987
Quarts-de-Chaume Château de Bellerive
   (WS)
1986
Quarts-de-Chaume Baumard (EL, BYR, LOR)
Vouvray Domaine Peu de la Moriette (TAN,
   OL)
1985
Vouvray Moelleux Bourillon Dorléans (MV)
1983
Vouvray Clos Naudin, Foreau (HOG)
1982
★Bonnezeaux Château de Fesles (OL)

──────── £9.00 to £12.99 ────────
1989
Coteaux du Layon Château de la Roulerie
   les Aunis (YAP)

1988
Bonnezeaux Château de Fesles (TAN)
Vouvray Clos du Bourg, Huet (RAE, AD)
1986
Bonnezeaux Château de Fesles (MV)
Vouvray Clos du Bourg, Huet (RAE)
Vouvray Clos Naudin, Foreau (OL)
1985
Bonnezeaux Tête de Cuvée, Château de
   Fesle (OL)
Quarts-de-Chaume Château de
   l'Echarderie (YAP)
Vouvray Clos Naudin, Foreau (BYR, HAG)
Vouvray le Haut Lieu, Huet (BIB, AD)
1984
Quarts-de-Chaume Château de Bellerive
   (OL)
1983
Quarts-de-Chaume Baumard (GRE, BE)
Quarts-de-Chaume Château de Bellerive
   (WS)
1980
Bonnezeaux Château de Fesles (HAG)
Quarts-de-Chaume Château de Bellerive
   (OD)
1979
Quarts-de-Chaume Château de Bellerive
   (OL)

──────── £13.00 to £15.99 ────────
1979
Anjou Moulin Touchais (WRI)
1976
Anjou Moulin Touchais (WRI)
1969
Anjou Moulin Touchais (EL)
1964
Anjou Moulin Touchais (EL)
1955
Anjou Moulin Touchais (EL)

──────── £16.00 to £18.99 ────────
1989
Bonnezeaux Château de Fesles (BY)
Quarts-de-Chaume Château de
   l'Echarderie (YAP)
1988
Bonnezeaux la Chapelle, Château de
   Fesles (MV)
1976
Vouvray Clos Naudin, Foreau (AD)
1971
Quarts-de-Chaume Baumard (GRE)
1964
Vouvray Moelleux Bourillon Dorléans (MV)

─────── £26.00 to £30.99 ───────
1959
Vouvray Brédif (HAG)

─────── £38.00 to £45.00 ───────
1959
Vouvray le Haut Lieu, Huet (WS)
1955
Anjou Moulin Touchais (TW)

1947
Vouvray Moelleux Bourillon Dorléans (MV)

─────── £55.00 to £60.00 ───────
1947
Bonnezeaux Château des Gauliers, Mme
  Fourlinnie (YAP)

SPARKLING

─────── Under £5.00 ───────
Non-vintage
Ackerman Saumur Brut (AUG)
Sainsbury's Saumur (SAI)
Saumur Brut Delacote (WAI)
★Saumur Brut Gratien & Meyer (HOG)
Saumur Rosé Gratien & Meyer (HOG)

─────── £5.00 to £6.99 ───────
Non-vintage
Anjou Rosé Gratien & Meyer (BOT, PD, HAY)
Cadre Noir Saumur (WHI, CH)
Château Langlois Crémant (BL)
Crémant de Loire Brut Gratien & Meyer
  (HAY, WS)
Diane de Poitiers Cabernet Rosé (STA, AD)
★Montlouis Mousseux Brut Berger (YAP)
Montlouis Mousseux Demi-sec Berger (YAP)
Saumur Ackerman 1811 Brut (AI, BYR, DAV,
  CH)
Saumur Ackerman 1811 Rosé (AI, DAV)
Saumur Brut Saget (GI)
Saumur Langlois-Château (HOG, HAG)
Saumur Rosé Langlois-Château (BYR)
Vouvray Brut Jarry (YAP)

─────── £7.00 to £8.99 ───────
Non-vintage
Château Langlois Crémant (DI)
Crémant de Loire Brut Gratien & Meyer
  (WIL)
Saumur Brut Gratien & Meyer (WIL)
Saumur Brut Bouvet-Ladubay (WRI)
Vouvray Méthode Champenoise, Huet (RAE)

RED

─────── Under £4.00 ───────
1989
Gamay du Haut Poitou Cave co-op (STA)
Saumur Cave des Vignerons de Saumur
  (ALL)
1988
Cheverny Pinot Noir, Maison Père et Fils
  (KA)
St-Pourçain Union des Vignerons (YAP)
1987
Bourgueil Clos de la Henry, Morin (BE)
Gamay de Touraine Domaine de la
  Renaudie (KA)

─────── £4.00 to £4.99 ───────
1989
Gamay de Touraine Domaine de la
  Charmoise, Marionnet (BIB)
Vin de Thouarsais, Gigon (YAP)
1988
Bourgueil Clos de la Henry, Morin (OL, AV)
★Chinon Domaine Morin (AV)
Gamay de Touraine Domaine de la
  Charmoise, Marionnet (HAY, BIB)
1987
Anjou Rouge Tijou (HIG)
Chinon les Gravières (STA)
1986
Anjou Rouge Bolvin (MV)
★Anjou Rouge Château d'Epire (YAP)
★Chinon Domaine de Turpenay, Couly (EL)
1985
Anjou Rouge Cabernet Château de
  Chamboureau (LAY)
Anjou Rouge Château du Breuil (PIP)
★Bourgueil la Hurolaie Caslot-Galbrun
  (TES)
Chinon Domaine de la Chapellerie, Olek
  (RAE)

─────── £5.00 to £6.99 ───────
1988
Bourgueil Beauvais, Druet (BY)
Bourgueil Grand Mont, Druet (BY)

Chinon Cuvée Prestige, Gouron (KA)
Chinon l'Arpenty Desbourdes (YAP)
Chinon les Gravières (OL)
Chinon les Grezeaux, Baudry (MV)
Chinon Vieilles Vignes, Angelliaume (PIP)
Menetou-Salon Rouge, Pellé (MV)
Sancerre Domaine du P'tit Roy (NI)
Saumur-Champigny Caves des Vignerons
　de Saumur (ALL)
Saumur-Champigny Château de Targé (OL)
★Saumur-Champigny Château des
　Chaintres (TAN)
Saumur-Champigny Filliatreau (YAP, YAP)
Saumur Domaine Langlois (DI)
St-Nicolas-de-Bourgueil Clos de la Contrie,
　Ammeux (YAP)
St-Nicolas-de-Bourgueil Taluau (OD)
1987
Chinon Buisse (BYR)
Chinon Domaine Dozon (BEK)
Chinon Réserve Druet (BYR)
Saumur-Champigny Caves des Vignerons
　de Saumur (ALL)
Saumur-Champigny Couly-Dutheil (AI)
Saumur-Champigny Vieilles Vignes,
　Filliatreau (YAP)
Saumur Domaine du Langlois-Château
　(UP)
Saumur Domaine Langlois (DI)
1986
Anjou Cabernet Clos de Coulaine (PE, AD,
　BIB)
Bourgueil Beauvais, Druet (AD)
Bourgueil Domaine de Raguenières (KA)
Bourgueil Domaine des Ouches (PIP)
Chinon Couly (BER)
Chinon Couly-Dutheil (BYR)
Chinon Olga Raffault (LAY)
Chinon Réserve Druet (YAP)
St-Nicolas de Bourgueil Clos du Vigneau
　(HAY)
Sancerre Domaine du P'tit Roy (NI)
1985
Anjou Cabernet Clos de Coulaine (RAE, BIB)
Chinon Château de Ligre (HAY)
★Chinon Olga Raffault (KA)

───────── **£7.00 to £10.99** ─────────
1989
Sancerre la Bourgeoise, Henri Bourgeois
　(UP)
Sancerre les Baronnes, Saget (UP)
1988
Chinon Clos de la Dioterie, Joguet (AD)
Sancerre André Dezat (PIP)

Sancerre Domaine de Montigny, Natter
　(BIB)
1987
Bourgueil Beauvais, Druet (BY)
Sancerre Clos du Roi, Crochet (BEK)
Sancerre Domaine de Montigny, Natter
　(BIB)
Sancerre les Romains, Vacheron (GI)
Sancerre Reverdy (HAY)
1986
Bourgueil Grand Mont, Druet (YAP, BY)
Chinon Clos de l'Echo, Couly-Dutheil (OL)
1985
Bourgueil Grand Mont, Druet (MV)
1984
Bourgueil Grand Mont, Druet (BY)

ROSÉ

───────── **Under £3.00** ─────────
Non-vintage
Anjou Rosé Cellier de la Loire (LAY)
Sainsbury's Rosé d'Anjou (SAI)
Tesco Rosé d'Anjou (TES)
1989
Anjou Rosé Cellier de la Loire (IR)
1988
Anjou Rosé Cellier de la Loire (IR)
Cabernet d'Anjou Ackerman-Laurance (AI)

───────── **£3.00 to £4.99** ─────────
1989
Azay-le-Rideau la Basse Chevrière, Pavy
　(YAP)
Rosé d'Anjou Sauvion (NI)
Rosé de Cabernet du Haut Poitou Cave
　co-op (MAJ)
Vin de Pays du Jardin de la France Gris
　Fumé (AD)
1988
Vin de Thouarsais, Gigon (YAP)
1987
Coteaux d'Ancenis Guindon (YAP)
1986
Cabernet d'Anjou Domaine de Bellevue
　(HIG)

───────── **£5.00 to £7.99** ─────────
1989
Reuilly Pinot Gris Cordier (YAP)
Reuilly Pinot Noir, Beurdin (AD)
1988
Sancerre Rosé Dezat (BYR)
Sancerre Rosé Domaine de la Mercy Dieu,
　Bailly-Reverdy (LAY)

ALSACE

WHITE

──────── Under £3.50 ────────
1989
Sainsbury's Pinot Blanc (SAI)

──────── £3.50 to £3.99 ────────
Non-vintage
Gewürztraminer Tesco (TES)
1989
★Pinot Blanc Cave Co-op. de Ribeauvillé
  (AUG)
1988
Pinot Blanc Cave Co-op. de Ribeauvillé
  (AUG)
Tokay Cave Co-op. Turckheim (OD)
Victoria Wine Riesling (VIC)
★Waitrose Gewürztraminer (WAI)
1987
Muscat Réserve, Cave Co-op. Turckheim
  (OD)
Pinot Blanc Dopff & Irion (HOG)
Pinot Blanc Ziegler (GI)
Riesling Willy Gisselbrecht (WAI)
Riesling Ziegler (GI)
Sylvaner Zind-Humbrecht (BY)
1986
Sainsbury's Gewürztraminer (SAI)
Sylvaner Dopff & Irion (GRE)

──────── £4.00 to £4.49 ────────
1989
★Muscat Muré (AS)
Pinot Blanc Cave Co-op. Turckheim (UP)
Pinot Blanc Muré (AS)
Riesling Cave Co-op. de Ribeauvillé (AUG)
1988
Edelzwicker Muré (CH)
Gewürztraminer Cave Co-op. de
  Ribeauvillé (AUG)
Pinot Blanc Ingersheim (DAV)
Pinot Blanc Louis Gisselbrecht (NI)
Pinot Blanc Tradition, Cave Co-op.
  Turckheim (WCL, BR)
Pinot Gris Cave Co-op. Turckheim (VIC)
Riesling Cave Co-op. de Ribeauvillé (AUG)
Riesling Caves de Bennwihr (PE)
Sylvaner Louis Gisselbrecht (HUN)
Sylvaner Schleret (YAP)
Sylvaner Zind-Humbrecht (BY)
1987
Flambeau d'Alsace Hugel (DI)

Gewürztraminer Cave Co-op. Turckheim
  (BAR)
Gewürztraminer Dopff & Irion (HOG)
Gewürztraminer Tradition, Cave Co-op.
  Turckheim (ASK)
Pinot Blanc Dopff & Irion (EL)
Pinot Gris Cave Co-op. Turckheim (BAR)
Sylvaner Dopff & Irion (EL)
Tokay Tradition, Cave Co-op. Turckheim
  (ASK)
1986
Flambeau d'Alsace Hugel (DI)
Pinot Blanc Hugel (HOG)
Riesling Louis Gisselbrecht (BYR)
Sylvaner Dopff & Irion (BYR)
1985
Muscat Wolfberger (BOT)
Pinot Blanc Wolfberger (BOT)
★Riesling Wolfberger (BOT)
Sylvaner Wolfberger (BOT)

──────── £4.50 to £4.99 ────────
1989
Tokay Tradition Cave Co-op. Turckheim
  (UP)
1988
Gewürztraminer Cave Co-op. Turckheim
  (BO, VIC, WCL)
Gewürztraminer Caves de Bennwihr (PE)
Gewürztraminer Hugel (LAY)
Gewürztraminer Réserve Speciale,
  Gisselbrecht (NI)
★Pinot Blanc Ostertag (MV)
Pinot Blanc Tradition, Cave Co-op.
  Turckheim (VIN)
Pinot Blanc Willm (AMI)
★Riesling Blanck (AV)
Riesling Cave Co-op. Turckheim (BR)
Sylvaner Louis Gisselbrecht (PIP)
Tokay Cave Co-op. Turckheim (WCL)
1987
Muscat Louis Gisselbrecht (NI)
Pinot Blanc Schleret (YAP)
Pinot Blanc Schlumberger (LAY)
Riesling Blanck (AV)
Riesling Louis Gisselbrecht (PE)
Sylvaner Hugel (DI)
1986
Edelzwicker Rolly Gassmann (HAY)
Riesling Haut Rhin Réserve (CHA)
Riesling Seigneur d'Alsace, Dopff &
  Irion (BYR)

Sylvaner Hugel (DI)
Tokay Louis Gisselbrecht (NI)
1985
Gewürztraminer Wolfberger (BOT, PD)
Pinot Blanc Réserve Personnelle, Sipp
  (WHI)
Riesling Dopff & Irion (GRE)
Riesling Hugel (HOG)

──────── **£5.00 to £5.99** ────────
1989
Gewürztraminer Cave Co-op. Turckheim
  (UP)
Muscat Cave Co-op. Turckheim (UP)
1988
Edelzwicker Rolly Gassmann (BIB)
Gewürztraminer Ingersheim (HA, DAV)
Gewürztraminer Louis Gisselbrecht (HUN,
  PE, PIP, NI)
Gewürztraminer Réserve, Cave Co-op.
  Turckheim (WCL, BR, VIN)
Gewürztraminer Schléret (YAP)
Gewürztraminer Wiederhirn (HIG)
Muscat Froehn, Beck (BEK)
Muscat Louis Gisselbrecht (PIP, RES)
Muscat Schleret (YAP)
Muscat Tradition, Cave Co-op.
  Turckheim (BR)
Pinot Blanc Hugel (DI, HA)
Pinot Blanc les Amours, Hugel (VIN)
Pinot Blanc Schlumberger (UP)
Pinot Blanc Tradition, Hugel (HAG)
Riesling Hugel (WIL)
Riesling Réserve Cave Co-op.
  Turckheim (VIN)
Riesling Schleret (YAP)
★Riesling Zind-Humbrecht (BY)
Sylvaner Meyer (HAU)
Sylvaner Vieilles Vignes, Ostertag (MV)
Sylvaner Zind-Humbrecht (AN)
Tokay Wiederhirn (HIG)
1987
Auxerrois Rolly Gassmann (PE)
Gewürztraminer Hugel (DI)
Gewürztraminer Rimmelsberg, Beck (BEK)
Gewürztraminer Seigneur d'Alsace, Dopff
  & Irion (EL, AI)
Gewürztraminer Sipp (WHI)
Gewürztraminer Willy Gisselbrecht (OL)
Pinot Blanc Humbrecht (THR)
Pinot Blanc les Amours, Hugel (VIN)
Pinot Blanc Trimbach (UP)
Riesling Hagenschlauf, Beck (BEK)
Riesling Réserve, Schlumberger (LAY)
Riesling Trimbach (CH)

Riesling Zind-Humbrecht (BY)
Sylvaner Trimbach (UP)
Tokay Schleret (YAP)
1986
Auxerrois Rolly Gassmann (HAY)
Gewürztraminer Haut Rhin Réserve (CHA)
Gewürztraminer Lorentz (VIC)
Gewürztraminer Sipp (WHI)
Muscat Dopff & Irion (BYR)
Muscat Schleret (YAP)
Pinot Blanc Clos de Stangenberg, Heim (IR)
Pinot Blanc Sélection Trimbach (BYR)
Riesling Princes Abbés, Schlumberger
  (GRE)
Riesling Réserve, Schlumberger (VIC)
Riesling Sigille, Scherer (OD)
Riesling Trimbach (UP)
★Sporen Hugel (HOG)
Tokay Rolly Gassmann (RAE)
Tokay Sipp (OL)
1985
Gewürztraminer Hugel (HOG)
Muscat Dopff & Irion (AI)
Pinot Blanc Hugel (HAG, DI)
Pinot Gris les Maquisards, Dopff & Irion
  (HOG, GRE)
Riesling Hugel (GI, BYR)
Riesling les Murailles, Dopff & Irion (HOG)
1984
Muscat Rolly Gassmann (HAY, RAE)
1983
Riesling les Faitières (CHA)
Riesling Tradition, Kuentz-Bas (HOG)
1981
Riesling les Murailles, Dopff & Irion (HOG)

──────── **£6.00 to £6.99** ────────
1988
Auxerrois Rolly Gassmann (BIB, RAE)
Gewürztraminer Cuvée Particulière, René
  Schmidt (HAH)
Gewürztraminer Hugel (WIL)
Gewürztraminer Tradition, Kuentz-Bas
  (BER)
Muscat Zind-Humbrecht (THR, BY)
Pinot Blanc Rolly Gassmann (TAN, RAE)
Riesling Princes Abbés, Schlumberger (UP)
1987
Gewürztraminer Beyer (HAG)
Gewürztraminer les Sorcières Dopff &
  Irion (HOG)
Gewürztraminer Rolly Gassmann (RAE)
Muscat les Amandiers, Dopff &
  Irion (GRE)
Muscat Tradition, Hugel (DI)

Pinot Gris les Maquisards, Dopff & Irion
(EL)
Riesling Herrenweg, Zind-Humbrecht (BY)
Riesling Hugel (DAV, WRI)
Riesling les Murailles, Dopff & Irion (EL)
Riesling Zind-Humbrecht (AN)
Tokay Hugel (DI)
1986
Gewürztraminer les Sorcières Dopff &
Irion (GRE)

Gewürztraminer Rolly Gassmann (HAY)
Muscat Réserve, Trimbach (HAG)
Pinot Blanc Sélection Trimbach (VIG)
Riesling Clos Haüserer, Zind-Humbrecht
(BY)
Riesling Princes Abbés, Schlumberger (LAY)
Riesling Rolly Gassmann (HAY)
Tokay Hugel (DI)
Tokay Millesime, Rolly Gassmann (RAE)
Tokay Schlumberger (VIC, LAY)
1985
Gewürztraminer Hugel (BYR, BO, DI, GI)
Gewürztraminer Trimbach (HOG, CH, UP)
Muscat Tradition, Hugel (HUN)
Pinot Blanc Hugel (WRI)
Pinot Blanc Réserve, Faller (GI)
Tokay Tradition, Hugel (BYR)
1983
Gewürztraminer les Faitières (CHA)
Muscat Tradition, Hugel (WIL)

──────── £7.00 to £8.99 ────────
1988
★Gewürztraminer Herrenweg, Zind-
Humbrecht (BY, THR)
Gewürztraminer Tradition, Kuentz-
Bas (AV)
Gewürztraminer Zind-Humbrecht (AN)
Muscat Réserve, Heydt (CB)
Muscat Réserve, Trimbach (VIG)
Riesling Herrenweg, Zind-Humbrecht (BY)
1987
Gewürztraminer Altenbourg, Blanck (AD)
Gewürztraminer Bollenberg, Cattin (CB)

Gewürztraminer Hatschbourg, Cattin (CB)
Gewürztraminer Hugel (PE, DAV)
Gewürztraminer Tradition, Kuentz-
Bas (AV)
Muscat Moench Reben, Rolly Gassmann
(BIB)
Muscat Rolly Gassmann (BIB)
Riesling Beyer (HAG)
Riesling Heimbourg Cave Co-op.
Turckheim (WCL)
Riesling Rolly Gassmann (TAN)
Tokay Hatschbourg, Cattin (CB)
Tokay Rolly Gassmann (BIB)
1986
Gewürztraminer Furstentum, Blanck (AD)
Gewürztraminer Tradition, Hugel (HAG)
Gewürztraminer Trimbach (REI)
Muscat Tradition, Hugel (WRI)
Pinot Gris Schlumberger (TAN)
Riesling Altenberg de Bergheim, Koehly
(HAH)
Riesling Heissenberg (MV)
Riesling Tradition, Hugel (HAG, TAN)
Sporen Hugel (VIN)
Tokay Dopff au Moulin (BE)
Tokay Réserve, Faller (BYR)
1985
Gewürztraminer Osterberg, Sipp (CH)
Gewürztraminer Tradition, Hugel (HAG)
Muscat Altenbourg, Blanck (LAY)
Muscat de Riquewihr, Dopff au Moulin
(BYR)
Muscat Kuentz-Bas (BER)
Riesling Kappelweg, Rolly Gassmann (RAE,
HAY)
Riesling Rolly Gassmann (BIB)
Riesling Schlossberg, Blanck (AD)
Tokay Réserve Personnelle, Sipp (WHI)
1984
Riesling Brand, Zind-Humbrecht (BY)
Riesling Réserve Particulière, Faller (GI)
Tokay Réserve, Faller (GI)
1983
Gewürztraminer Réserve Personnelle,
Hugel (WIL)
Gewürztraminer Réserve, Trimbach (BYR)
Riesling Kirchberg, Sipp (WHI)
★Riesling Schlossberg, Blanck (LAY)
Tokay Réserve Personnelle, Sipp (WHI)
1981
Riesling Schoenenberg Vendange Tardive,
Dopff au Moulin (HOG)
1978
Riesling Schoenenberg Vendange Tardive,
Dopff au Moulin (HOG)

──────── £9.00 to £11.99 ────────

1988
Gewürztraminer Herrenweg, Zind-
Humbrecht (BAR)
Pinot Gris Ostertag (MV)
Riesling Muenchberg, Ostertag (MV)
1987
Riesling Altenberg de Bergheim, Koehly
(HAH)
Riesling Muenchberg, Ostertag (MV)
1986
Gewürztraminer Cuvée Exceptionnelle,
Schléret (YAP)
Gewürztraminer Réserve Rolly Gassmann
(RAE)
Riesling Muenchberg, Ostertag (VIG)
Riesling Schlossberg, Faller (BYR)
Riesling Tradition, Hugel (VIN)
1985
Gewürztraminer Kessler, Schlumberger
(BYR, BO, GRE)
Gewürztraminer Osterberg, Sipp (WHI)
Gewürztraminer Réserve Personnelle,
Hugel (DI, AV, TAN, DAV, VIN)
Gewürztraminer Seigneurs de
Ribeaupierre, Trimbach (CH, UP, LAY)
Pinot Gris Kitterlé, Schlumberger
(BYR)
Riesling Frédéric Emile, Trimbach (BYR,
GRE, LAY, HAG)
Riesling Jubilee, Hugel (AD, DI)
Riesling Kitterlé, Schlumberger (BO, BYR,
LAY, VIG, HA)
Riesling Muenchberg, Ostertag (WCL, MV)
Riesling Réserve Personnelle, Hugel (DAV,
TAN)
Riesling Tradition, Hugel (VIN)
Tokay Réserve, Rolly Gassmann (HAY)
1984
Riesling Kitterlé, Schlumberger (VIG)
1983
Gewürztraminer Hugel (HA)
Gewürztraminer Jubilee, Hugel (AD, DI)
★Gewürztraminer Osterberg, Sipp (WHI)
Gewürztraminer Réserve Personnelle,
Hugel (WRI)
Gewürztraminer Vendange Tardive, Sipp
(WHI)
Riesling Osterberg, Heydt (CB)
Riesling Tradition, Hugel (BYR)
Tokay Réserve Personnelle, Hugel (HAG)
1982
Riesling Frédéric Emile, Trimbach (UP)
1981
Riesling Frédéric Emile, Trimbach (VIG)

──────── £12.00 to £14.99 ────────

1988
Pinot Gris A360P Barriques Ostertag (MV)
1987
Gewürztraminer Rangen, Zind-Humbrecht
(BY)
Pinot Gris A360P Barriques Ostertag (MV)
1986
Gewürztraminer Kessler, Schlumberger
(UP)
Tokay Cuvée Exceptionnelle, Schleret (YAP)
1985
Gewürztraminer Kitterlé, Schlumberger
(GRE)
Riesling Kitterlé, Schlumberger (UP)
Tokay Réserve Personnelle, Hugel (REI)
1983
★Gewürztraminer Cuvée Christine,
Schlumberger (HOG)
Gewürztraminer Kitterlé, Schlumberger
(WHI)
Riesling Vendange Tardive, Dopff & Irion
(HOG)
Tokay Réserve Personnelle, Trimbach (UP)
Tokay Réserve, Rolly Gassmann (PE, RAE)
1981
Gewürztraminer Vendange Tardive, Heim
(IR)
Riesling Réserve Personnelle, Hugel (VIG)

──────── £15.00 to £19.99 ────────

1986
Gewürztraminer Hengst Vendange
Tardive, Zind-Humbrecht (THR)
Gewürztraminer Herrenweg Vendange
Tardive, Zind-Humbrecht (BY, AN)
Riesling Kitterlé, Schlumberger (VIG)
1985
Gewürztraminer Fronholz Vendange
Tardive, Ostertag (MV)
1983
Gewürztraminer Eichberg Vendange
Tardive, Dopff au Moulin (VIG)
Gewürztraminer Vendange Tardive, Dopff
& Irion (RES, HOG, GRE, EL, BYR)
Gewürztraminer Vendange Tardive, Muré
(WRI)
Gewürztraminer Vendange Tardive,
Ostertag (MV)
Pinot Gris Vendange Tardive, Dopff & Irion
(EL)
Riesling Frédéric Emile, Trimbach (VIG)
Riesling Vendange Tardive, Wiederhirn
(HIG)
Tokay Réserve Personnelle, Trimbach (VIG)

1982
Riesling Clos Ste-Hune, Trimbach (HAG)
1976
★Gewürztraminer Seigneurs de
  Ribeaupierre, Trimbach (RAE)

──────── £20.00 to £24.99 ────────
1985
Gewürztraminer Cuvée Anne Vendange
  Tardive, Rolly Gassmann (RAE)
Gewürztraminer Vendange Tardive,
  Christine Schlumberger (BO)
1983
Gewürztraminer Cuvée Anne Vendange
  Tardive, Rolly Gassmann (BIB)
Gewürztraminer Sélection de Grains
  Nobles, Dopff & Irion (HOG)
Gewürztraminer Vendange Tardive, Hugel
  (WS, BO, HAG)
Riesling Sélection de Grains Nobles, Dopff
  & Irion (HOG, EL)
Tokay Vendange Tardive, Faller (GI)

──────── £25.00 to £29.99 ────────
1986
Gewürztraminer Hengst Vendange
  Tardive, Zind-Humbrecht (BY)
1985
Gewürztraminer Cuvée Christine,
  Schlumberger (UP, REI)
Gewürztraminer Vendange Tardive, Hugel
  (VIN)
1983
Gewürztraminer Hengst Vendange
  Tardive, Zind-Humbrecht (BY)
Gewürztraminer Sélection de Grains
  Nobles, Dopff & Irion (EL)
Gewürztraminer Vendange Tardive, Hugel
  (BER)

──────── £30.00 to £39.99 ────────
1983
Gewürztraminer Cuvée Christine,
  Schlumberger (VIG)
1976
Tokay Réserve Personnelle, Trimbach (VIG)
1975
Riesling Frédéric Emile, Trimbach (VIG)

──────── £40.00 to £49.99 ────────
1983
Gewürztraminer Sélection de Grains
  Nobles, Dopff & Irion (VIG)
Tokay Sélection de Grains Nobles, Beyer
  (REI)

1976
Gewürztraminer Cuvée Christine,
  Schlumberger (VIG)
Gewürztraminer Vendange Tardive, Hugel
  (VIG)
Riesling Vendange Tardive, Hugel (VIG)

──────── c. £85.00 ────────
1976
Gewürztraminer Sélection de Grains
  Nobles, Hugel (VIG)
Tokay Sélection de Grains Nobles, Hugel
  (REI)

RED

──────── Under £7.00 ────────
1988
★Pinot Noir Louis Gisselbrecht (PIP)
1987
Pinot Noir Rolly Gassmann (BIB)
Pinot Noir Schleret (YAP)
1986
Pinot Noir Hugel (WRI)
Pinot Noir Rolly Gassmann (BIB)
1985
Pinot Noir Hugel (BYR)

──────── £7.00 to £9.99 ────────
1988
Pinot Noir Herrenweg, Zind-Humbrecht
  (BY)
Pinot Noir l'Ancienne, Cave Co-op.
  Turckheim (UP)
1985
Pinot Noir Réserve, Rolly Gassmann (RAE)
1983
Pinot Noir Réserve, Rolly Gassmann (RAE)

──────── £12.00 to £13.50 ────────
1985
Pinot Noir Hugel (BO)
Pinot Noir Réserve Personnelle, Hugel
  (DAV)
1983
Pinot Noir Réserve Personnelle, Hugel
  (WIL)

SPARKLING

──────── Under £8.00 ────────
Non-vintage
Crémant d'Alsace Dopff & Irion (EL)
Crémant d'Alsace Dopff au Moulin (GRE, LA,
  LAY)

SOUTH-WEST FRANCE

RED

─────── Under £3.00 ───────

Non-vintage
Asda Bergerac (ASD)
★Asda Fronton (ASD)
Sainsbury's Bergerac (SAI)
1989
Vin de Pays des Côtes de Gascogne,
  Producteurs Plaimont (BY)
1987
Côtes de Duras les Producteurs Réunis
  (AUG)
Côtes du Marmandais Château Marseau
  (WAI)
1986
Asda Côtes de Duras (ASD)
Côtes de Duras Seigneuret (WAI)
1985
★Cahors Carte Noire, Rigal (WIZ)

─────── £3.00 to £3.99 ───────

1989
Côtes de St-Mont, Producteurs Plaimont
  (AD)
Vin de Pays des Coteaux de l'Ardèche,
  Duboeuf (BEK)
★Vin de Pays des Coteaux de Murviel,
  Domaine de Limbardie (WS, AD)
1988
Côtes de Bergerac Château le Tour des
  Gendres (NI)
Côtes de St-Mont, Producteurs Plaimont
  (LAY, PIP)
Côtes du Frontonnais Château Bellevue-la-
  Forêt (OD, SAI, NI, AUG)
Côtes du Frontonnais Château Ferran
  (BEK)
Côtes du Frontonnais Château Flotis (HAU)
Gaillac Domaine Jean Cros (BE)
Vin de Pays des Coteaux de Murviel,
  Domaine de Limbardie (DAV)
Vin de Pays des Côtes de Gascogne,
  Producteurs Plaimont (HAU)
1987
Bergerac Château du Chayne (SAF)
Buzet Tradition les Vignerons de Buzet (PE)
Cabardès Domaine de Cannettes Hautes
  (HAY)
Côtes de St-Mont, Producteurs Plaimont
  (TAN)
Sainsbury's Buzet (SAI)

1986
Cahors Carte Noire, Rigal (BYR)
Cahors Château les Bouysses (SAI)
★Cahors Château St-Didier-Parnac, Rigal
  (OD)
★Gaillac Château Larroze (BO)
Gaillac Labastide-de-Lévis (HAY)
1985
Cahors Carte Noire, Rigal (HAY)
Cahors Château de Haute-Serre (WIZ)
Cahors Comte André de Montpezat (WIL)
★Côtes du Marmandais Cave Co-op. (HIC)
1984
Gaillac Château Larroze (CH)
1983
Cahors Côtes d'Olt (WHI)

─────── £4.00 to £4.99 ───────

1989
Gaillac Domaine Jean Cros (CH, WCL)
Gaillac Labastide-de-Lévis (WIC)
1988
Bergerac Château Boudigand (ELL)
★Bergerac Château la Jaubertie (LAY, HIG)
Cahors Château de Grezels, Rigal (AUG)
Château Montauriol Carte Blanche,
  Fronton (OD)
Côtes du Frontonnais Château Ferran (PIP)
Gaillac Château Larroze (TAN)
Gaillac Domaine Jean Cros (CH)
1987
Cahors Château de Grezels, Rigal (AUG)
Côtes de Bergerac Château Court-les-Mûts
  (BIB)
Côtes de Duras Domaine de Laulan (HUN)
Côtes du Frontonnais Château Bellevue-la-
  Forêt (HAU)
Gaillac Château Larroze (BE)
Gaillac Domaine Jean Cros (ALL, WCL)
1986
Bergerac Château la Jaubertie (NI, BYR)
Cahors Château de Cenac, Pelvillain (BYR)
Cahors Château d'Eugenie (PIP)
Cahors Château St-Didier-Parnac, Rigal
  (LAY)
Cahors Chevaliers de Lagrezette (BEK)
Cahors Domaine de Circofoul (BYR)
Côtes de Bergerac Château le Fage (GIL)
Gaillac Château Larroze (HAY, STA, ALL)
★Madiran Domaine Boucassé, Alain
  Brumont (HAU)
Madiran Domaine Floris (DI)

1985

Bergerac Château la Jaubertie (GRE)

Cahors Domaine de Circofoul (UP, GRE)

★Cahors Domaine de Gaudou (RAE)

★Pécharmant Château de Tiregand (SAI)

1984

Madiran Domaine Boucassé, Alain
Brumont (HAU)

1977

Cahors Comte André de Montpezat (WHI)

─────── **£5.00 to £5.99** ───────

1988

Bergerac Château la Jaubertie (WHI)

Côtes du Frontonnais Château Bellevue-la-
Forêt (OD)

1987

Cahors Château Lagrezette (BEK)

Cahors Clos la Coutale (WW)

Côtes de St-Mont, Château de Sabazan
(BAR)

1986

Bergerac Château la Jaubertie (CH)

Cahors Château de Haute-Serre (WS)

★Cahors Clos la Coutale (PIP)

Cahors Prieuré de Senac (THR)

Madiran Château Montus (HAU)

Pécharmant Château de Tiregand (TAN)

1985

Bergerac Château la Jaubertie (CH)

Buzet Château de Gueyze (PE)

Cahors Château de Cenac, Pelvillain
(UP)

Cahors Château de Gaudou (WCL)

★Cahors Château du Cayrou, Jouffreau
(TAN)

Cahors Domaine de Gaudou (AD)

Madiran Château de Peyros (REI)

1979

Madiran Domaine Boucassé, Alain
Brumont (HAU)

─────── **£6.00 to £6.99** ───────

1987

Madiran Château d'Aydie (PIP)

Madiran Château Montus (RAE)

1985

Bergerac Reserve Château la Jaubertie (NI)

Cahors Château Cayrou d'Albas (BIB)

─────── **£8.00 to £8.99** ───────

1985

Bergerac Château la Jaubertie (REI)

1982

Cahors Domaine de Circofoul (UP)

DRY WHITE

─────── **Under £3.00** ───────

Non-vintage

Asda Vin de Pays des Côtes de Gascogne
(ASD)

Sainsbury's Bergerac (SAI)

Sainsbury's Jurançon Sec (SAI)

St Michael Château de Beaulieu (MAR)

★St Michael Côtes de Gascogne (MAR)

St Michael Côtes de St-Mont (MAR)

Vin de Pays des Côtes de Gascogne Cépage
Colombard (IR)

Vin de Pays des Pyrénées Atlantiques Cave
Co-op. de Gan (HAY)

1989

Bergerac Sauvignon Foucaussade (SAF)

Côtes de Duras Croix du Beurrier (WAI)

Vin de Pays des Côtes de Gascogne Cépage
Colombard (EL, AUG)

Vin de Pays des Côtes de Gascogne,
Producteurs Plaimont (THR, BY)

1988

Bergerac Sauvignon Foucaussade (SAF)

Côtes de Gascogne Domaine de San de
Guilhem (HOG)

Vin de Pays des Côtes de Gascogne Cépage
Colombard (LOR, EL)

Vin de Pays des Côtes de Gascogne,
Domaine de Planterieu (WAI)

★Vin de Pays des Côtes de Gascogne,
Domaine de Tariquet (THR)

Vin de Pays des Terroirs Landais, Domaine
de Laballe (HAY, PE)

1987

Asda Côtes de Duras (ASD)

Vin de Pays des Côtes de Gascogne Cépage
Colombard (IR, DAV)

─────── **£3.00 to £3.99** ───────

1989

Bergerac Château du Chayne (SAF)

Bergerac Sec Château de Tiregand (TAN)

Côtes de Duras Sauvignon, les Vignerons
des Coteaux de Duras (BEK)

Côtes de St-Mont Producteurs Plaimont
(AD, LAY, TAN)

Vin de Pays des Côtes de Gascogne Cépage
Colombard (AD, TAN, PIP)

Vin de Pays des Côtes de Gascogne,
Domaine de Rieux (PE, AD, TAN, REI)

Vin de Pays des Côtes de Gascogne,
Domaine de Tariquet (STA)

Vin de Pays des Terroirs Landais, Domaine
de Laballe (BIB)

1988
Bergerac Château du Chayne (SAF, PIP)
Bergerac Château le Fage (GIL)
Côtes de Duras Château de Conti (CB)
Côtes de Duras Château la Pilar (IR)
Vin de Pays des Côtes de Gascogne Cépage
 Colombard (LAY, CB)
Vin de Pays des Côtes de Gascogne,
 Domaine de Rieux (CH, BER)
Vin de Pays des Côtes de Gascogne,
 Domaine de Tariquet (BAR)
Vin de Pays des Côtes de Gascogne,
 Producteurs Plaimont (ALL)
Vin de Pays des Terroirs Landais, Domaine
 de Laballe (BIB)
1986
★Gaillac Château Lastours (HAU)

──────── **£4.00 to £4.99** ────────
1989
Bergerac Château Boudigand (ELL)
Bergerac Château la Jaubertie (LAY, HIG)
Côtes de Saussignac Château Court-les-
 Mûts (BIB)
Gaillac Perlé Jean Cros (WS, STA)
Pacherenc du Vic-Bilh Domaine Damiens
 (BIB)
1988
Bergerac Château la Jaubertie (NI)
Bergerac Château la Jaubertie Cépage
 Sauvignon (NI)
Chardonnay Ryman (BYR)
Côtes de Saussignac Château Court-les-
 Mûts (BIB)
Gaillac Château Larroze (TAN)
Gaillac Perlé Jean Cros (STA)
★Jurançon Château Jolys (TAN)
Vin de Pays des Landes, Domaine du
 Comte (AN)
1987
Pacherenc du Vic-Bilh Domaine Boucassé
 (HAU)
1986
Côtes de St-Mont Producteurs Plaimont
 (HAU)
★Jurançon Sec Clos Guirouilh (BYR)

──────── **£5.00 to £5.99** ────────
1989
Bergerac Château la Jaubertie Cépage
 Sauvignon (WHI, HIG)
Bergerac Château de Grandchamp (WHI)
Domaine de la Raze Sauvignon Blanc/
 Sémillon (BOD)
Jurançon Sec Domaine Cauhapé (TAN)

1988
Jurançon Sec Clos Guirouilh (AI)
Jurançon Sec Domaine Cauhapé (NI)
1985
Bergerac Château la Jaubertie (BYR)

──────── **£6.00 to £6.99** ────────
1989
★Jurançon Sec Domaine Cauhapé (TAN)
1988
Bergerac Château la Jaubertie Cépage
 Sauvignon (REI)
Jurançon Sec Domaine Cauhapé (AD, HAU,
 VIG, MV)

──────── **£7.00 to £7.99** ────────
1989
Jurançon Sec Domaine Cauhapé (WCL)
1988
Jurançon Sec Domaine Cauhapé (BAR)

SWEET WHITE

──────── **Under £5.00** ────────
1986
Jurançon Clos Guirouilh (BYR)
Monbazillac Château la Brie (AUG)
★Monbazillac Château Septy (RES)

──────── **£5.00 to £6.99** ────────
1989
Jurançon Moelleux Château Jolys (TAN)
1986
Jurançon Cru Lamouroux (HAY)
★Jurançon Moelleux Domaine Cauhapé
 (HAU)
Monbazillac Château le Fage (GIL)
1985
Jurançon Sec Clos Guirouilh (AI)
1983
Monbazillac Château Boudigand (ELL)

──────── **£8.00 to £9.99** ────────
1988
Jurançon Moelleux Domaine Cauhapé (AD)
1987
Jurançon Moelleux Domaine Cauhapé (REI)

ROSÉ

──────── **Under £5.50** ────────
1989
★Bergerac Château la Jaubertie (WHI)
1987
Bergerac Château la Jaubertie (NI)

SOUTH-EAST FRANCE

RED

Under £3.00

Non-vintage
Asda Corbières (ASD)
Asda Côtes de Roussillon (ASD)
Asda Minervois (ASD)
Sainsbury's Corbières (SAI)
Sainsbury's Côtes du Roussillon (SAI)
Sainsbury's Minervois (SAI)
St-Chinian Rouanet (WAI)
Tesco Corbières (TES)
Tesco Vin de Pays Catalan (TES)
Vin de Pays de la Cité de Carcassonne (EL)
★Vin de Pays de l'Hérault, Domaine de St-Macaire (WAI)
1989
★Cabardès Château Ventenac (MAJ)
Côtes du Lubéron Cellier de Marrenon (LOR, BY)
Faugères Larousse (GI)
1988
Costières du Gard Château de Nages (WAI)
Coteaux du Languedoc Château de Beauregard, Bonfils (BL)
★Coteaux du Languedoc Château Flaugergues (PE)
★Fitou Caves du Mont Tauch (MAR)
Minervois Château Millegrand (EL)
Vin de Pays de l'Aude Domaine du Puget (WAI)
Vin de Pays des Coteaux de Murviel Domaine de Grezan (ASK)
Vin de Pays de l'Hérault, Domaine de Capion (PE)
1987
Faugères les Crus Faugères (WHI)
Minervois Domaine de Campon (GI)
Vin de Pays de l'Aude Cabernet Sauvignon, Foncalieu (WAI)
1986
Corbières Resplandy (BYR, GI)
Fitou Caves du Mont Tauch (GRE)
★Minervois Château de Paraza (WIZ)
Minervois Château de Pouzols (BYR)

£3.00 to £3.49

Non-vintage
Coteaux d'Aix-en-Provence Château la Coste (BYR)
Vin de Pays des Sables du Golfe du Lion, Listel (PE)

1989
Vin de Pays des Coteaux de Murviel, Domaine de Limbardie (TAN, WS, AD)
Minervois Château de Fabas (AMI)
St-Chinian Domaine des Soulié (AUG)
1988
Corbières Château de Cabriac (NI)
Corbières Château de Mandourelle (TAN)
Corbières Chatellerie de Lastours (ASK)
★Côtes du Lubéron Château Val Joanis (ASD)
Côtes du Roussillon-Villages, Caramany (BO)
Faugères Château de Grézan (UP)
Fitou Caves du Mont Tauch (HOG, AUG, NI)
Fitou Larousse (GI)
Fitou Resplandy (VIC)
★Minervois Domaine de Ste-Eulalie (DAV)
★Minervois Maris (MAJ)
St-Chinian Domaine des Soulié (AUG)
St-Chinian Rouanet (HIG)
Vin de Pays de l'Aude Domaine du Puget (CB)
Vin de Pays de Thongue Merlot, Cave Co-op. Pouzolles (LOR)
Vin de Pays d'Oc Domaine Dusseau (BER)
Vin de Pays du Gard Domaine de Valescure (BIB)
1987
Fitou Caves du Mont Tauch (AUG, NI)
1986
★Corbières Château de Cabriac (BL, EL)
Corbières Château de Mandourelle (DAV)
★Minervois Château de Fabas (STA)
Minervois Domaine la Tour Boisée (WHI)
Vin de Pays des Collines Rhodaniennes Syrah, de Vallouit (ALL)
1985
★Côtes du Roussillon Château Corneilla (EL)
Fitou Mme Claude Parmentier (VIC)
St-Chinian Gaston (VIC)

£3.50 to £3.99

1989
Coteaux d'Aix-en-Provence Château de Fonscolombe (AD)
Côtes du Vivarais Domaine de Belvezet (TAN, AD)
1988
★Corbières Château les Ollieux (HAY)
Coteaux d'Aix-en-Provence Château de Fonscolombe (BL, TAN)

★Coteaux du Languedoc Domaine de l'Abbaye de Valmagne (EL)
Côtes du Lubéron Château Val Joanis (WHI)
Fitou Caves du Mont Tauch (AMI)
Fitou Mme Claude Parmentier (BL)
Minervois Domaine de Ste-Eulalie (AD, THR)
Vin de Pays des Côtes de Thongue, Clos Ferdinand (WCL)

1987
Corbières Château les Ollieux (WCL)
Costières du Gard Château de la Tuilerie (AV)
Coteaux d'Aix-en-Provence Château de Fonscolombe (LAY)

Coteaux d'Aix-en-Provence Château de la Gaude (YAP)
Côtes de Provence Château la Gordonne (THR)
Fitou Caves du Mont Tauch (AI, AMI, BER)

1986
Cabardès Domaine St-Roch (WCL)
Corbières Château de Cabriac (RAE)
★Corbières Château la Baronne (VIC)
Côtes du Roussillon Château de Jau (OD)
Fitou Cave Pilote (WHI)
Fitou Domaine de la Boulière (DI)

1985
Fitou Domaine de la Boulière (DI)
Vin de Pays d'Oc, Domaine d'Ormesson (BYR)

──────── £4.00 to £4.99 ────────

Non-vintage
Côtes de Provence Domaine Farnet (WIL)

1989
Baron de Coussergues Merlot, Domaine de Coussergues (WIC)
Coteaux du Lyonnais, Duboeuf (PIP)
Côtes de Provence les Maîtres Vignerons de St-Tropez (PIP)

1988
Collioure Berlande (WS)
Corbières Château de Lastours (WCL)
Corbières Château les Ollieux (PE, BIB)

Coteaux des Baux-en-Provence Mas de Gourgonnier (HAU)
Côtes de Provence Cuvée Spéciale Pawlowski, Domaine des Hauts de St-Jean (YAP)
Côtes du Lubéron Château Val Joanis (ASK)
Vin de Pays d'Oc, Domaine d'Ormesson (PIP, RES)

1987
Corbières Château de Cabriac (AN)
Coteaux du Languedoc Château Pech-Celegran (BAR)
Coteaux Varois Domaine des Chaberts (HIG)
Côtes du Lubéron Château Val Joanis (BE)

1986
Corbières Château de Cabriac (UP)
Coteaux du Tricastin Domaine de Vieux Micocoulier (HIC, PE)
Minervois Château Villerambert-Julien (TAN, VIG)
Vin de Pays d'Oc Cabernet Sauvignon, Listel (WIL)
Vin de Pays du Mont Caume, Bunan (YAP)

1985
Vin de Pays des Coteaux de Murviel Domaine de Ravanes (HIC)
Vin de Pays des Sables du Golfe du Lion, Domaine du Bosquet (HAG)
Vin de Pays d'Oc, Domaine d'Ormesson (BER)

──────── £5.00 to £6.99 ────────

Non-vintage
Côtes de Provence Domaine Richeaume, Hoesch (YAP)

1988
Côtes de Provence Château de Pampelonne, les Maîtres Vignerons de St-Tropez (BEK)
Côtes du Lubéron Château de l'Isolette (PIP)

1987
Coteaux d'Aix-en-Provence les Baux, Terres Blanches (HAG)
Côtes de Provence Domaine Richeaume, Hoesch (LOR, YAP)
Mas Chichet Cabernet (BAR)

1986
★Bandol Château Vannières (DI)
★Bandol Mas de la Rouvière, Bunan (YAP)
Coteaux d'Aix-en-Provence Domaine les Bastides (PIP)
Coteaux d'Aix-en-Provence Domaine les Bastides Cuvée Speciale (WW)

1985
Bandol Château Vannières (DI)
Corbières Domaine de Villemajou (REI)
1983
Bandol Château Vannières (NI)
Coteaux d'Aix-en-Provence Domaine les
Bastides Cuvée Speciale (HAG)

─────── £7.00 to £8.99 ───────
1987
Bandol Domaine de Pibarnon (BEK)
Bandol Domaine Tempier (WW)
1986
Bandol Château Vannières (RES)
1985
Coteaux d'Aix-en-Provence Château
Vignelaure (BYR)

─────── £9.00 to £10.99 ───────
1988
Coteaux d'Aix-en-Provence les Baux
Domaine de Trévallon (YAP)
1987
Bandol Domaine Tempier Cuvée Migoua
(WW)
Bandol Domaine Tempier Cuvée Tourtine
(WW)
Coteaux d'Aix-en-Provence les Baux
Domaine de Trévallon (RES)
Côtes de Provence Domaine de Trévallon
(BYR)
★Vin de Pays de l'Hérault, Mas de Daumas
Gassac (HAG, TAN, PIP)
1986
Bandol Château Vannières (REI)
Vin de Pays de l'Hérault, Mas de Daumas
Gassac (RAE, AMI, WCL, AD)
1985
Bandol Domaine Tempier (BYR)
Bellet Château de Crémat, Bagnis (YAP)
Palette Château Simone (YAP)
1984
Bandol Domaine de Pibarnon (PIP)
Vin de Pays de l'Hérault, Mas de Daumas
Gassac (WHI, BYR)
1982
Bandol Château Vannières (UP)

─────── £11.00 to £14.99 ───────
1988
Vin de Pays de l'Hérault, Mas de Daumas
Gassac (VIG)
1987
Coteaux d'Aix-en-Provence les Baux
Domaine de Trévallon (VIG)

1986
Vin de Pays de l'Hérault, Mas de Daumas
Gassac (VIG)
1985
Vin de Pays de l'Hérault, Mas de Daumas
Gassac (HA, VIG)
1984
Vin de Pays de l'Hérault, Mas de Daumas
Gassac (VIG)

WHITE

─────── Under £3.00 ───────
Non-vintage
Tesco Vin de Pays de l'Aude (TES)
1989
Corbières les Producteurs du Mont Tauch
(AUG)

─────── £3.00 to £3.99 ───────
Non-vintage
Coteaux d'Aix-en-Provence Château la
Coste (BYR)
Vin de Pays des Sables du Golfe du Lion,
Listel Blanc (PE)
1989
★Coteaux d'Aix-en-Provence Château de
Fonscolombe (AD)
Côtes du Lubéron la Vieille Ferme (MV, RES,
GRE)
1988
Coteaux d'Aix-en-Provence Château de
Fonscolombe (TAN)

★Côtes du Lubéron Château Val Joanis
(WHI, PE)
Côtes du Lubéron la Vieille Ferme (WHI,
ASK, LAY)
Vin de Pays d'Oc Sauvignon, Listel (WIL)
Vin de Pays du Comté Tolosan, Gallory
(RAE)
1987
Coteaux d'Aix-en-Provence Château de
Fonscolombe (LAY)

1986
Vin de Pays d'Oc Chardonnay, Labouré-Roi (ALL)

──────── £4.00 to £4.99 ────────
Non-vintage
Côtes de Provence Domaine Farnet (WIL)
Côtes de Provence l'Estandon Blanc de Blancs, Bagnis (YAP)
1989
Côtes du Lubéron la Vieille Ferme (BER)
Vin de Pays de l'Hérault Marsanne, du Bosc (AD, TAN)
1988
Côtes du Lubéron Château Val Joanis (ASK)
Côtes du Lubéron la Vieille Ferme (UP)
Mauzac Sec, Cave de Blanquette de Limoux (BOD)
1986
Vin de Pays d'Oc Chardonnay, Labouré-Roi (WIL)

──────── £5.00 to £6.99 ────────
1989
Muscat à Petits Grains, Domaine de Coussergues (BOD)
1988
Bandol Mas de la Rouvière, Bunan (YAP)
Coteaux d'Aix-en-Provence les Baux Terres Blanches (WCL, HAG)

──────── £7.00 to £8.99 ────────
1988
Cassis Domaine du Paternel (WS)
1987
Palette Château Simone (YAP)

──────── £10.00 to £11.99 ────────
1989
Bellet Château de Crémat, Jean Bagnis (YAP)
1987
Côtes de Provence Clos Mireille Blanc de Blancs, Domaines Ott (HAG)
1986
Côtes de Provence Clos Mireille Blanc de Blancs, Domaines Ott (BYR, WIL)

──────── £13.00 to £17.99 ────────
1989
Vin de Pays de l'Hérault Mas de Daumas Gassac (VIG)
1988
Vin de Pays de l'Hérault Mas de Daumas Gassac (HAG)

1987
Côtes de Provence Clos Mireille Blanc de Blancs, Domaines Ott (VIG)
1986
Vin de Pays de l'Hérault Mas de Daumas Gassac (VIG)

ROSÉ

──────── Under £4.00 ────────
Non-vintage
Vin de Pays des Sables du Golfe du Lion Gris de Gris, Domaine de Jarras (PE, CH, WIL, AUG)
1989
Coteaux d'Aix-en-Provence Château de Fonscolombe (AD, TAN)
Coteaux du Languedoc Abbaye de Valmagne (RES)
1988
Côtes du Lubéron Château Val Joanis (WHI)
1987
Costières du Gard Château de la Tuilerie (AV)
Coteaux d'Aix-en-Provence Château de Fonscolombe (LAY)
1986
Coteaux Varois Domaine des Chaberts (HIG)

──────── £4.00 to £4.99 ────────
1988
Coteaux Varois Domaine de St-Jean (ELL)

──────── £5.00 to £6.99 ────────
1989
Coteaux d'Aix-en-Provence les Baux Terres Blanches (WCL, VIG)
Vin de Pays de l'Hérault, Mas de Daumas Gassac (AD)
1987
Coteaux d'Aix-en-Provence les Baux Terres Blanches (HAG)

──────── £9.00 to £12.99 ────────
1989
Côtes de Provence Château de Selle, Domaines Ott (AN)
1988
Côtes de Provence Château de Selle, Domaines Ott (HAG, VIG)
1987
Côtes de Provence Château de Selle, Domaines Ott (WHI)
Palette Château Simone (YAP)

SPARKLING

──────── **Under £5.00** ────────

Non-vintage
Blanquette de Limoux Brut (WAI, VIC)
1986
Blanquette de Limoux Brut (UN)
1985
★Blanquette de Limoux Aimery (HOG)

──────── **£5.00 to £6.99** ────────

Non-vintage
Blanquette de Limoux Brut (BYR, WRI, AV)
★Blanquette de Limoux Domaine des
  Martinolles (WIL)

1983
Blanquette de Limoux Brut (AN)

FORTIFIED

──────── **Under £8.00** ────────

Non-vintage
★Muscat de Frontignan, Château de la
  Peyrade (STA)
1986
★Vintage Rivesaltes Domaine Cazes (BAR)

──────── **c. £9.50** ────────

1988
Muscat de Rivesaltes Domaine Cazes (BAR)

JURA

WHITE

──────── **Under £5.00** ────────

Non-vintage
Bonchalaz Maire (HAG)
1988
Côtes du Jura Chardonnay, Germain
  (WHI)

──────── **£13.00 to £16.99** ────────

1982
Vin Jaune d'Arbois, d'Arlay (TAN)
1964
Vin Jaune de Gard, d'Arlay (ASK)
1976
Château-Chalon Réserve Cathérine de Rye,
  Maire (WIL)

──────── **£21.00 to £27.50** ────────

1982
Côtes du Jura Château d'Arlay Vin Jaune
  (REI)
1979
Château-Chalon Vin Jaune, Bourdy (WS)

1978
Château-Chalon Réserve Cathérine de Rye,
  Maire (VIG)

RED

──────── **Under £7.50** ────────

1986
Côtes du Jura Château d'Arlay (REI)

──────── **c. £10.00** ────────

1969
Cotes du Jura d'Arlay, Bourdy (ASK)

ROSÉ

──────── **Under £3.00** ────────

Non-vintage
Cendre Vin Gris, Maire (HAG)

OTHER FRENCH SPARKLING

──────── **Under £5.00** ────────

Non-vintage
Comte de Neufchâtel Brut (WRI)
St Michael French Sparkling (MAR)
Veuve du Vernay (SAF, WIL, SAI)

──────── **£5.00 to £5.99** ────────

Non-vintage
Kriter Brut (UN)
Veuve du Vernay (VIC, UN, THR, AUG, AV, BOT)
1988
Café de Paris Brut Blanc de Blancs (HAH)
1987
Veuve du Vernay (BL)

RHINE

Kab. = Kabinett
Spät. = Spätlese
Aus. = Auslese
BA = Beerenauslese
TBA = Trockenbeerenauslese

WHITE

--- **Under £2.00** ---

Non-vintage
Asda Liebfraumilch (ASD)
Sainsbury's Liebfraumilch (SAI)

--- **£2.00 to £2.99** ---

Non-vintage
Liebfraumilch Rudolf Müller (LAY)
Liebfraumilch Victoria Wine (VIC)
Sainsbury's Trocken QbA, Rheinhessen
(SAI)
St Michael Bereich Nierstein (MAR)
Tesco St-Johanner Abtei Kab. (TES)
Waitrose Liebfraumilch (WAI)
1988
Asda Mainzer Domherr Spät. (ASD)
Liebfraumilch Crown of Crowns (BO)
Liebfraumilch Rosentor (BOT)
Rüdesheimer Rosengarten, Rudolf Müller
(TAN)
Waitrose Bereich Nierstein (WAI)
1987
Bereich Johannisberg Riesling Kab., von
Simmern (TES)
Liebfraumilch Blue Nun (BO)
Niersteiner Gutes Domtal, Rudolf Müller
(HUN)

--- **£3.00 to £3.99** ---

Non-vintage
Liebfraumilch Black Tower (PD)
1989
Niersteiner Gutes Domtal, Rudolf Müller
(CB)
1988
Erben Kab., Langguth (AUG)
Liebfraumilch Blue Nun (WAI, WHI, BL, AUG,
DAV)
Liebfraumilch Crown of Crowns (WHI, PE)
Mainzer Domherr Kab., Deinhard (AUG)
Niersteiner Gutes Domtal, Langenbach
(THR)

Niersteiner Spiegelberg Riesling Kab.,
Rudolf Müller (TAN)
Oppenheimer Krötenbrunnen, Rudolf
Müller (CB)
1986
St Johanner Abtei Aus., Rudolf Müller
(ASD)
1985
Oppenheimer Krötenbrunnen, Deinhard
(BYR)

--- **£4.00 to £4.99** ---

1989
Mainzer Domherr Bacchus Kab., Guntrum
(PIP)
1988
Binger Scharlachberg Riesling Kab., Villa
Sachsen (TES)
Kallstadter Kobnert Spät., Huesgen (DAV)
Liebfraumilch Blue Nun (BOT, PD)
Niersteiner Spiegelberg Kab., Guntrum
(PIP, DAV)
★Schloss Böckelheimer Kupfergrube
Riesling Kab., Staatliche
Weinbaudomäne (LAY)
1987
Binger Scharlachberg Riesling Kab., Villa
Sachsen (TES)
1986
Binger Scharlachberg Riesling Kab., Villa
Sachsen (TES)
★Forster Mariengarten Riesling Kab.,
Bürklin-Wolf (LAY)
Rauenthaler Gehrn Riesling Kab.,
Staatsweingüter Eltville (LAY)
1985
★Forster Mariengarten Riesling Kab.,
Bürklin-Wolf (LAY)
Liebfraumilch Blue Nun (UN)
1983
Booser Paradiesgarten, Spee (EL)
1971
★Grünstadter Höllenpfad Müller-Thurgau
Spät., Winzerkeller Leiningerland (HE)
★Grünstadter Höllenpfad Riesling Spät.,
Winzerkeller Leiningerland (HE)

--- **£5.00 to £5.99** ---

1988
Dexheimer Doktor Spät., Guntrum (AS)
Hochheimer Hölle Riesling Kab., Aschrott
(WHI)

1987
Deidesheimer Hohenmorgen Riesling Kab.,
Basser-Jordan (RAE)
Forster Jesuitengarten Riesling Kab.,
Bassermann-Jordan (RAE)
1986
Rauenthaler Baiken Riesling Kab.,
Simmern (LAY)
Wallhäuser Muehlenberg Riesling Trocken,
Prinz zu Salm-Dalberg'sches Weingut
(HAC)
Winkeler Hasensprung Riesling Kab.,
Schönborn (BYR)
1985
★Deidesheimer Langenmorgen Riesling
Kab., Bürklin-Wolf (DI)
Johannisberger Erntebringer Riesling
Kab., Schönborn (BYR)
Kreuznacher Kahlenberg Riesling Spät.,
Paul Anheuser (BYR)
★Niersteiner Pettenthal Riesling Spät.,
Balbach (TES)
Wachenheimer Gerümpel Riesling Kab.,
Bürklin-Wolf (LAY)
1983
★Deidesheimer Herrgottsacker Riesling
Kab., Bürklin-Wolf (GRE, BYR)
Dürkheimer Feuerberg Gewürztraminer
Spät., Kloster Limburg (AI)
Johannisberger Erntebringer Riesling
Kab., Deinhard (VIG)
★Kreuznacher Narrenkappe Riesling
Spät., August Anheuser (BYR)
Rauenthaler Langenstück Riesling Spät.,
Diefenhardt (HOG)
1982
Hattenheimer Schützenhaus Riesling
Kab., Ress (WW)
Hochheimer Domdechaney Riesling Kab.,
Aschrott (BER)
1976
Grünstadter Höllenpfad Scheurebe Aus.,
Winzerkeller Leiningerland (HE)

——————— £6.00 to £6.99 ———————
1988
Forster Stift Kab., Bassermann-Jordan
(HAY)
Hochheimer Hölle Riesling Kab., Aschrott
(AV)
Niederhauser Felsensteyer Riesling Spät.,
Anheuser (TAN)
Niersteiner Holle Kab., Guntrum (DAV)
★Niersteiner Pettenthal Riesling Spät.,
Balbach (TAN)

1987
Forster Jesuitengarten Riesling Kab.,
Bassermann-Jordan (BIB)
Schloss Vollrads Grün-Silber, Matuschka-
Greiffenclau (EL)

1986
Erbacher Marcobrunnen Riesling Kab.,
Simmern (LAY)
Hochheimer Königin Victoria Berg Riesling
Kab., Deinhard (HIG)
Niederhauser Hermannsberg Riesling
Kab., Staatliche Weinbaudomäne (RAE)
Niersteiner Auflangen Riesling Kab.,
Gessert (AI)
Schloss Vollrads Grün-Gold, Matuschka-
Greiffenclau (EL)
1985
★Freinsheimer Goldberg Riesling Spät.,
Lingenfelder (UP)
Kreuznacher Hofgarten Riesling Kab.,
August Anheuser (PE)
Niederhauser Hermannsberg Riesling
Kab., Staatliche Weinbaudomäne (RAE)
Oppenheimer Herrenberg Scheurebe Spät.,
Guntrum (HA)
Schloss Böckelheimer Kupfergrube
Riesling Kab., Staatliche
Weinbaudomäne (RAE)
Wachenheimer Gerümpel Riesling Kab.,
Bürklin-Wolf (BYR)
★Wachenheimer Mandelgarten Scheurebe
Aus., Bürklin-Wolf (BYR)
1983
Forster Ungeheuer Scheurebe Spät., Buhl
(ALL)
Johannisberger Erntebringer Riesling
Kab., Deinhard (WIL)
Kiedricher Wasseros Riesling Spät.,
Sohlbach (PE)
Niederhauser Hermannsberg Riesling
Kab., Staatliche Weinbaudomäne (BAR)
Norheimer Dellchen Riesling Spät., August
Anheuser (PE)

1981
Schloss Vollrads Grün-Gold, Matuschka-
Greiffenclau (BYR)

——————— £7.00 to £7.99 ———————
1988
Johannisberg Deinhard Heritage Selection
(DAV)
Niederhauser Hermannsberg Riesling
Kab., Staatliche Weinbaudomäne (AD)
Niersteiner Oelberg Riesling Kab.,
Herrnsheim (HAC)
Oppenheimer Kreuz Riesling Spät.
Trocken, Guntrum (PIP)
Rauenthaler Baiken Riesling Kab.,
Simmern (TAN)
Schloss Vollrads Blau-Silber, Matuschka-
Greiffenclau (EL)
Wachenheimer Gerümpel Riesling Kab.,
Bürklin-Wolf (PIP)
1987
Grosskarlbacher Burweg Scheurebe Kab.,
Lingenfelder (HAC)
1986
Freinsheimer Goldberg Riesling Spät.,
Lingenfelder (HAC)
Hochheimer Königin Victoria Berg Riesling
Kab., Deinhard (HAG)
Wachenheimer Mandelgarten Scheurebe
Spät., Bürklin-Wolf (BL)
1985
Niersteiner Auflangen Riesling Spät.,
Senfter (AI)
Niersteiner Oelberg Riesling Spät., Senfter
(WHI)
Schloss Böckelheimer Kupfergrube
Riesling Kab., Staatliche
Weinbaudomäne (BYR)
Wachenheimer Gerümpel Riesling Spät.,
Bürklin-Wolf (BYR)
Wachenheimer Rechbächel Riesling Kab.,
Bürklin-Wolf (BYR)
1983
★Deidesheimer Herrgottsacker Riesling
Spät., Deinhard (HAG)
Hochheimer Hölle Riesling Spät., Aschrott
(BER)
Wachenheimer Gerümpel Riesling Spät.,
Bürklin-Wolf (HOG, AI, GRE)
1982
Wachenheimer Rechbächel Riesling Spät.,
Bürklin-Wolf (PE)
1979
Deidesheimer Grainhübel Riesling Spät.,
Bassermann-Jordan (RAE)

——————— £8.00 to £9.99 ———————
1988
Deidesheimer Hohenmorgen Riesling
Spät., Bassermann-Jordan (HAY)
Forster Mariengarten Riesling Kab.,
Bürklin-Wolf (HAC)
1987
Forster Ungeheuer Riesling Spät.,
Deinhard (TAN)
1986
Forster Jesuitengarten Riesling Spät.,
Buhl (ALL)
Freinsheimer Goldberg Scheurebe Spät.,
Lingenfelder (HAC)
Rauenthaler Baiken Riesling QbA Charta,
Verwaltung der Staatsweingueter
Eltville (HAC)
Scheurebe Trocken, Weingut Lingenfelder
(AD)
1985
Erbacher Siegelsberg Riesling Kab.,
Schloss Reinhartshausen (HAC, AN)
Forster Jesuitengarten Riesling Spät.,
Bassermann-Jordan (HAY, BIB)

Kiedricher Sandgrub Riesling Kab.,
Schloss Groenesteyn (BER)
Schloss Vollrads Blau-Gold, Matuschka-
Greiffenclau (BYR)
Schloss Vollrads Blau-Silber, Matuschka-
Greiffenclau (BYR)
1983
★Deidesheimer Herrgottsacker Riesling
Aus., Deinhard (HOG)
Dürkheimer Feuerberg Gewürztraminer
Aus., Kloster Limburg (HIC)
Erbacher Marcobrunnen Riesling Spät.,
Staatsweingüter Eltville (HOG)
Hattenheimer Schützenhaus Riesling
Spät., Ress (HAY)
Hochheimer Herrenberg Riesling Aus.,
Nagler (HOG, BYR)
★Kreuznacher Brückes Riesling Aus.,
Anheuser (PE)

Niederhauser Hermannshöhle Riesling
  Aus., Staatliche Weinbaudomäne (HOG)
Rauenthaler Baiken Riesling Spät.,
  Staatsweingüter Eltville (HOG)
Wachenheimer Gerümpel Riesling Spät.,
  Bürklin-Wolf (HAC)
Wachenheimer Rechbächel Riesling Spät.,
  Bürklin-Wolf (BYR)

1976
★Kreuznacher Narrenkappe Riesling Aus.,
  Anheuser (TES)
Schloss Böckelheimer Burgweg Riesling
  Aus., Pleitz (HE)

———————— £10.00 to £11.99 ————————
1986
Freinsheimer Goldberg Riesling Aus.,
  Weingut Lingenfelder (AN)
1985
Hochheimer Königin Victoria Berg Riesling
  Spät., Deinhard (WIL)
Niersteiner Rehbach Riesling Spät.,
  Herrnsheim (HAC)
Ruppertsberger Hoheburg Riesling Aus.,
  Bürklin-Wolf (BL)
1983
★Hattenheimer Nüssbrunnen Riesling
  Aus., Ress (WW)
Hocheimer Königin Victoria Berg Riesling
  Spät., Deinhard (WIL)
Rüdesheimer Berg Rottland Riesling Aus.,
  Ress (WW)
Wachenheimer Böhlig Riesling Aus.,
  Bürklin-Wolf (HAG)
Wachenheimer Mandelgarten Scheurebe
  Aus., Bürklin-Wolf (HAG)
1976
Erbacher Siegelsberg Riesling Spät.,
  Schloss Reinhartshausen (BER)
★Hattenheimer Wisselbrunnen Riesling
  Aus., Schloss Reinhartshausen (HAG)

> Please don't blame
> **Webster's** or the
> merchants listed if a
> wine is sold out or if the
> vintage you want is no
> longer available. Wine is
> a living entity and a
> limited commodity –
> continuity of supply
> cannot, alas, be
> guaranteed.

———————— £12.00 to £14.99 ————————
1988
Forster Kirkenstuck Aus., Bassermann-
  Jordan (HAY)
1983
Wachenheimer Böhlig Riesling Aus.,
  Bürklin-Wolf (BER)
Wachenheimer Mandelgarten Scheurebe
  Aus., Bürklin-Wolf (PE, WS)
1976
Johannisberger Hölle Riesling Aus.,
  Deinhard (BER)

———————— £15.00 to £19.99 ————————
1986
Hochheimer Kirchenstuck Riesling Aus.,
  Aschrott (WHI)
1979
Erbacher Marcobrunn Riesling Spät.,
  Staatsweingüter Eltville (HAC)
Niederhauser Steinberg Scheurebe BA,
  Staatliche Weinbaudomäne (PE)
1976
Bechtheimer Stein BA, Wissmann (WHI)

———————— £20.00 to £29.99 ————————
1976
Niersteiner Oelberg Riesling & Ruländer
  TBA, Senfter (GRE)

———————— £30.00 to £39.99 ————————
1985
Grosskarlbacher Burweg Scheurebe TBA
  ½ bottle, Lingenfelder (HAC)
1976
Binger Scharlachberg Riesling BA,
  Staatliche Weinbaudomänen (AD)
1971
Hattenheimer Wisselbrunnen Riesling
  Aus., Schloss Reinhartshausen (HAC)

———————— c. £90.00 ————————
1971
Oestricher Lenchen Riesling TBA,
  Deinhard (TAN)

RED

———————— Under £7.00 ————————
1987
Traisener Nonnengarten Portugieser
  Halbtrocken, Pleitz (HE)
1986
Mittelheimer Goldberg Spätburgunder
  Trocken, Nägler (PE)

MOSEL/FRANKEN/BADEN

Kab. = Kabinett
Spät. = Spätlese
Aus. = Auslese
BA = Beerenauslese
TBA = Trockenbeerenauslese

MOSEL WHITE

──────── **Under £3.00** ────────

Non-vintage
Sainsbury's Mosel (SAI)
Sainsbury's Piesporter Michelsberg (SAI)
Zeller Schwarze Katz Zentralkellerei (TES)
1989
Waitrose Piesporter Michelsberg (WAI)
1988
Bereich Bernkastel Riesling, Schneider
  (EL)
1987
Bereich Bernkastel Riesling, Schneider
  (EL)
Bereich Bernkastel, Rudolf Müller (HUN)
Piesporter Michelsberg Rudolf Müller
  (HUN)
Waitrose Bereich Bernkastel (WAI)
1986
Bereich Bernkastel Riesling,
  Zentralkellerei (BOT)

──────── **£3.00 to £3.99** ────────

Non-vintage
St Michael Piesporter Michelsberg (MAR)
1989
Piesporter Michelsberg Rudolf Müller (TAN,
  CB)
Piesporter Michelsberg Schneider (WHI, EL)
1988
Bereich Bernkastel, Rudolf Müller (CB)
Piesporter Michelsberg Schneider (WHI)
1987
Piesporter Michelsberg Riesling, Deinhard
  (HOG)
1986
Bernkasteler Kurfürstlay Kab., Rudolf
  Müller (CH)
1985
Asda Bernkasteler Kurfürstlay Riesling
  Spät. (ASD)
Wehlener Klosterhofgut Kab., Schneider
  (WHI)

1983
Piesporter Michelsberg Riesling, Deinhard
  (BYR)
★Wiltinger Scharzberg Riesling Kab.,
  Zentralkellerei (TES)

──────── **£4.00 to £4.99** ────────

1988
★Brauneberger Juffer Riesling Spät.,
  Deinhard (AUG)
Deinhard Green Label (WHI, AUG)
Falkensteiner Hofberg Riesling Kab.,
  F-W-Gymnasium (LOR)
Piesporter Michelsberg Rudolf Müller
  (HAH)
Saarburger Antoniusbrunnen Riesling
  Kab., Rudolf Müller (TAN)
★Trittenheimer Altärchen Riesling Kab.,
  F-W-Gymnasium (TES)
Waldracher Doctorberg Riesling Kab.,
  Hallgarten (UP)
1987
Bernkasteler Badstube Riesling,
  Lauerberg (WAI)
Deinhard Green Label (BO, WHI)
1986
Graacher Himmelreich Riesling Kab.,
  F-W-Gymnasium (LOR)
Graacher Himmelreich Riesling Kab.,
  Kesselstatt (EL)
Trittenheimer Apotheke Riesling Kab.,
  Clusserath-Weiler (HOG)
1985
Waldracher Krone Riesling Kab., Scherf
  (BYR)
1983
Oberemmeler Scharzberg Riesling QbA,
  Hövel (ASK)

──────── **£5.00 to £5.99** ────────

1989
Graacher Himmelreich Riesling Kab.,
  F-W-Gymnasium (WHI)
1988
Bernkasteler Badstube Riesling Kab.,
  Bergweiler-Prüm (MAJ)
1987
Brauneberger Juffer Riesling Kab., Richter
  (BIB)
1986
Bernkasteler Badstube Riesling Kab.,
  F-W-Gymnasium (BYR)

Graacher Himmelreich Riesling Kab.,
  F-W-Gymnasium (AD)
Josephshof Riesling Spät., Kesselstatt (NI)
Oberemmeler Hutte Riesling Kab., Hövel
  (WW, ASK)
Ockfener Geisberg Riesling Spät.,
  F-W-Gymnasium (PE)
Scharzhofberger Riesling Kab., Kesselstatt
  (EL, NI)
Trittenheimer Altärchen Riesling Kab.,
  Bischöfliches Priesterseminar (AD)

Trittenheimer Apotheke Riesling Spät.,
  Weingut Hubertushof (HE)
Wehlener Sonnenuhr Riesling Aus., Weins
  Prüm (BO)
Zeltinger Himmelreich Riesling Kab.,
  Franz Henrich (HOG)
1985
Bernkasteler Badstube Riesling Kab.,
  Deinhard (HIG)
Brauneberger Juffer Riesling Kab.,
  Kesselstatt (BY)
Falkensteiner Hofberg Riesling Kab.,
  F-W-Gymnasium (BYR)
Wehlener Sonnenuhr Riesling Kab., Weins
  Prüm (HOG)
★Wiltinger Kupp Riesling Kab.,
  Bischöfliches Priesterseminar (LAY)
★Zeltinger Sonnenuhr Riesling Spät.,
  Kesselstatt (SAI)
1983
★Trittenheimer Altärchen Riesling Spät.,
  F-W-Gymnasium (HAY)
Waldracher Krone Riesling Aus., Scherf
  (BOR, GRE)
1982
Scharzhofberger Riesling Spät., Hohe
  Domkirche (HOG)

─────── £6.00 to £6.99 ───────
1988
Ayler Kupp Riesling Spät., Bischöfliches
  Konvikt (AD)

Graacher Himmelreich Riesling Spät.,
  F-W-Gymnasium (LOR)
Trittenheimer Apotheke Riesling Spät.,
  F-W-Gymnasium (TAN)
Wehlener Sonnenuhr Riesling Spät.,
  Bergweiler-Prüm (MAJ)
1986
Erdener Treppchen Riesling Kab.,
  Bischöfliches Priesterseminar (TAN)
Wehlener Sonnenuhr Riesling Kab., Weins
  Prüm (BYR)
1985
Erdener Treppchen Riesling Spät.,
  Monchhof (BO)
★Graacher Himmelreich Riesling Spät.,
  F-W-Gymnasium (BYR, CB)
★Scharzhofberger Riesling Kab., Hövel
  (BER)
Scharzhofberger Riesling Kab., Kesselstatt
  (BY)
Scharzhofberger Riesling Spät.,
  Kesselstatt (BYR)
1983
Bernkasteler Badstube Riesling Spät.,
  Heidemanns-Bergweiler (HOG)
Erdener Treppchen Riesling Spät.,
  Bergweiler-Prüm (ALL)
Falkensteiner Hofberg Riesling Kab.,
  F-W-Gymnasium (CB)
Ockfener Bockstein Riesling Aus., Rudolf
  Müller (RAE)
Ockfener Bockstein Riesling Spät., Staat-
  Weinbaudomänen Trier (AI)
★Serriger Vogelsang Riesling Aus.,
  Staatlichen Weinbaudomänen (HOG)
1982
Oberemmeler Hutte Riesling Kab., Hövel
  (VIG)
Serriger Vogelsang Riesling Aus.,
  Staatlichen Weinbaudomänen (RAE)

─────── £7.00 to £7.99 ───────
1988
Graacher Himmelreich Riesling Aus.,
  F-W-Gymnasium (TES)
1986
Maximin-Grünhäuser Abtsberg Riesling
  Kab., Schubert (LAY)
1985
Graacher Himmelreich Riesling Spät.,
  Prüm (BO)
Scharzhofberger Riesling Kab., Egon
  Müller (LAY)
Wehlener Sonnenuhr Riesling Kab., Loosen
  (BER)

1983
Erdener Treppchen Riesling Aus.,
  Bergweiler-Prüm (ALL)
Falkensteiner Hofberg Riesling Spät.,
  F-W-Gymnasium (GRE, BO)
Ockfener Bockstein Riesling Aus., Rudolf
  Müller (LAY)
Piesporter Goldtröpfchen Riesling Aus.,
  Tobias (AI)
1982
Scharzhofberger Riesling Spät., Hohe
  Domkirche (AI)
Wehlener Sonnenuhr Riesling Kab.,
  J.J. Prüm (BYR)
1981
Kaseler Nies'chen Riesling Spät.,
  Bischöfliches Priesterseminar (PE)

――――― **£8.00 to £9.99** ―――――
1988
Bernkasteler Bratenhöfchen Riesling
  Spät., Lauerburg (BE)
★Graacher Himmelreich Riesling Aus.,
  F-W-Gymnasium (WHI)
Maximin-Grünhäuser Abtsberg Riesling
  Kab., Schubert (LAY)
Oberemmeler Hutte Riesling Aus., Hövel
  (WW)
1986
Josephshof Riesling Spät., Kesselstatt
  (BYR)
Wehlener Sonnenuhr Riesling Kab.,
  Deinhard (TAN)
Wehlener Sonnenuhr Riesling Kab.,
  J.J. Prüm (WS)
1985
Bernkasteler Badstube Riesling Spät.,
  Heidemanns-Bergweiler (GRE)
Maximin-Grünhäuser Abtsberg Riesling
  Kab., Schubert (GRE)
Maximin-Grünhäuser Herrenberg Riesling
  Kab., Schubert (BYR)
Wehlener Sonnenuhr Riesling Kab.,
  Deinhard (WIL)
1983
Bernkasteler Badstube Riesling Spät.,
  Deinhard (HAG)
Eitelsbacher Marienholz Riesling Spät.,
  Bischöfliches Konvikt (PE)
Graacher Domprobst Riesling Aus.,
  F-W-Gymnasium (LOR)
Graacher Himmelreich Riesling Aus.,
  F-W-Gymnasium (HAY)
Kaseler Nies'chen Riesling Aus.,
  Bischöfliches Priesterseminar (BYR, GRE)

Maximin-Grünhäuser Herrenberg Riesling
  Spät., Schubert (CB)
Urziger Würzgarten Riesling Aus., Prüm-
  Erben (PE)
Wehlener Sonnenuhr Riesling Aus., Weins
  Prüm (BYR)
1982
Josephshof Riesling Aus., Kesselstatt (BY)
Maximin-Grünhäuser Abtsberg Riesling
  Spät., Schubert (ALL)
1976
Wehlener Munzlay BA ½ bottle, Schneider
  (WHI)

――――― **£10.00 to £11.99** ―――――
1989
Trittenheimer Apotheke Riesling Aus.,
  F-W-Gymnasium (WHI)
1988
Erdener Prälat Riesling Aus., Bischöfliches
  Priesterseminar (TAN)
1983
Bernkasteler Graben Riesling Aus.,
  Bergweiller (PE)
Bernkasteler Schlossberg Riesling Aus.,
  P.J. Hauth (HAC)
Kaseler Nies'chen Riesling Aus.,
  Bischöfliches Priesterseminar (PE)
Ockfener Bockstein Riesling Spät., Staat-
  Weinbaudomänen Trier (AD)
Serriger Vogelsang Riesling Aus.,
  Staatlichen Weinbaudomänen (HAC, AN)

――――― **£12.00 to £14.99** ―――――
1988
Graacher Himmelreich Riesling Aus.,
  F-W-Gymnasium (TAN)
1985
Graacher Himmelreich Riesling Spät.,
  Prüm (TAN)

1983
Bernkasteler Bratenhöfchen Riesling Aus.,
  Deinhard (AD)

Bernkasteler Graben Riesling Spät.,
Deinhard (AD)
Maximin-Grünhäuser Herrenberg Riesling
Aus., Schubert (BYR, GRE)
Piesporter Goldtröpfchen Riesling Spät.,
Deinhard (TAN)
Wehlener Sonnenuhr Riesling Aus., F.W.
Prüm (PE)

───────── £15.00 to £19.99 ─────────
1988
Wehlener Abtei Eiswein, Schneider
½ bottle (WHI)
1983
Wehlener Sonnenuhr Aus., J.J. Prüm (WS)
Wehlener Sonnenuhr Riesling Aus., Weins
Prüm (WS)
1976
Canzemer Altenberg Riesling Aus.,
Bischöfliches Priesterseminar (BER)
1971
Wiltinger Kupp Riesling Aus.,
Bischöfliches Priesterseminar (HA)

───────── £20.00 to £24.99 ─────────
1983
Scharzhofberger Riesling BA, Koch (CB)

───────── £25.00 to £29.99 ─────────
1987
Mulheimer Helenkloster Riesling Eiswein,
Richter ½ bottle (BIB)
1983
Bernkasteler Doctor Riesling Aus.,
Deinhard (BER)

───────── £30.00 to £39.99 ─────────
1986
Mulheimer Helenkloster Riesling Eiswein,
Richter ½ bottle (BIB)
1983
Bernkasteler Doctor Riesling Spät.,
Deinhard (HIG)
Bernkasteler Graben Riesling Eiswein,
Deinhard ½ bottle (AD)
1976
Scharzhofberger BA, Kesselstatt (EL)
1971
Zeltinger Sonnenuhr BA, Vereinigte
Hospitien (EL)

───────── £74.00 to £86.00 ─────────
1983
Bernkasteler Graben Riesling Eiswein,
Deinhard (TAN)

1976
Serriger Würzberg TBA, Simon (BOR)

FRANKEN WHITE

───────── £5.00 to £6.99 ─────────
1985
Würzburger Stein Riesling, Juliusspital
(BYR)

───────── £7.00 to £8.99 ─────────
1988
Casteller Kirchberg Müller-Thurgau,
Fürstlich Castell'sches Domänenamt
(HAC)
Escherndorfer Lump Riesling Kab.,
Gebietswinzergenossenschaft (GRE, WHI)

BADEN WHITE

───────── Under £4.00 ─────────
Non-vintage
Baden Z.B.W. (WAI)
Sainsbury's Baden (SAI)

───────── £4.00 to £6.99 ─────────
1988
Rivaner QbA, Karl Heinz Johner (HAC)

───────── c. £10.75 ─────────
1988
Pinot Blanc, Karl Heinz Johner (HAC)

BADEN RED

───────── c. £15.50 ─────────
1987
Pinot Noir, Karl Heinz Johner (HAC)

GERMAN SPARKLING

───────── Under £4.00 ─────────
Non-vintage
Waitrose Sekt (WAI)

───────── £4.00 to £4.99 ─────────
Non-vintage
Blue Nun Sparkling Sekt (TES)
Deinhard Sparkling Moselle (HAG)
Henkell Trocken (SAF, BL, UN, AUG)

───────── £5.00 to £5.99 ─────────
Non-vintage
Henkell Rosé (AUG)
Henkell Trocken (BOT, VIC, WIL, PD, WRI, EL)

ITALY

NORTH-WEST RED

──────── Under £4.00 ────────
1987
★Franciacorta Rosso Longhi-de-Carli (ASD)
Spanna Antonio Vallana (MAJ)
1986
Barbera d'Asti Ronco (PE)
1985
★Barbera d'Alba Fontanafredda (WIZ)

──────── £4.00 to £4.99 ────────
1988
Barbera Oltrepò Pavese, Castello di
  Luzzano (GRE)
1987
Barbera d'Alba Fontanafredda (BAR)
Barbera Oltrepò Pavese, Fugazza (VA, WHI)
Gutturnio Oltrepò Pavese, Fugazza (VA)
1986
Barbera d'Alba Nicolello (AI)
Barbera Oltrepò Pavese, Fugazza (WHI)
Inferno Nino Negri (BYR, WHI)
1985
Barbera d'Asti Guasti Clemente (HOG)
Dolcetto d'Alba Mellera, Cavallotto (VA)
★Sassella Nino Negri (BYR, WHI)
1984
Barolo Aliberti (BY, PIP)
Barolo Serafino (WAI)
1983
★Barolo Fontanafredda (WIZ)

──────── £5.00 to £5.99 ────────
1988
Dolcetta d'Alba Aldo Conterno (ALL, WCL)
Dolcetto d'Alba Ascheri (WHI)
1986
★Barolo Terre del Barolo (DAV)
Nebbiolo d'Alba Pio Cesare (BYR)
1985
Barbaresco Fontanafredda (BYR)
Barbera d'Alba Pio Cesare (WIL)
Barolo Fontanafredda (SAF, VA)
Inferno Nino Negri (GRE)
1984
Barolo Oddero (CH)
1983
Barbaresco Riserva Borgogno (LAY)
Barolo Ascheri (GI)
1982
Barolo Fontanafredda (HOG)

1980
Gattinara Riserva Nervi (LAY)
Ghemme Brugo (LAY, GI)

──────── £6.00 to £6.99 ────────
1989
Barbera d'Alba Altare (WCL)
1988
Dolcetto Ceretto Rossana (VA)
★Dolcetto d'Alba Gagliassi, Mascarello
  (WCL)
1987
Barbera d'Alba Aldo Conterno (ALL, WCL)
Barbera d'Alba Pio Cesare (DI)
1986
Barbaresco Ascheri (WCL)
Barbera d'Alba Pio Cesare (DI)
Barolo Ascheri (VA, WCL)
1985
Barolo Fontanafredda (UP, WHI, AUG)
Barolo Marchesi di Barolo (VA)
1984
Barolo Bricco Boschis Riserva San
  Giuseppe, Cavallotto (OD)
1983
Barbaresco Nicolello (AI)
Barolo Nicolello (AI)
Barolo Terre del Barolo (HAH)
1982
Barolo Fontanafredda (VA, GRE, BOT)
1981
Barolo Riserva Borgogno (PE, CH)

──────── £7.00 to £7.99 ────────
1989
Dolcetto d'Alba Pio Cesare (DI)
1988
Dolcetto d'Alba Gagliassi, Mascarello (UP)
1987
Barbera San Guglielmo, Malvira (BIB)
Nebbiolo delle Langhe Vajra (WCL)
1986
Barbaresco Nicolello (NI)
Barolo Ascheri (UP, ELL)
1985
Barbera San Guglielmo, Malvira (BIB)
Barolo Fontanafredda (THR)
1984
Barolo Nicolello (NI)
1983
Barolo Nicolello (LAY)

1982
Barolo Fontanafredda (BL, BAR)
1981
Barolo Riserva Borgogno (AV)
1978
Barbaresco Marchesi di Barolo (HOG)
Barolo Marchesi di Barolo (HOG)

——————— £8.00 to £9.99 ———————
Non-vintage
Barbaresco la Spinona (UN)
1988
Freisa delle Langhe Vajra (WCL)
1987
Franciacorta Rosso Ca' del Bosco (VA)
Nebbiolo d'Alba Pio Cesare (DI)
1986
Barbaresco Sori Paytin, Pasquero (WCL)
1985
Barolo Ascheri (WCL)
1984
Barbaresco Nicolello (TAN)
Nebbiolo Il Favot, Aldo Conterno (ALL)
1983
Barbaresco Nicolello (tan)
Barolo Brunate, Cogno-Marcarini (PIP)
1982
Barbaresco Bruno Giacosa (HOG)
Barbaresco Feyles (BIB)
1981
Barolo Borgogno (EL)
Barolo Riserva Borgogno (TAN)
1979
★Barolo Riserva Speciale Maria Feyles
  (RAE)
Carema Ferrando (VA)

——————— £10.00 to £12.49 ———————
Non-vintage
Opera Prima I Paglieri (WW)
1985
Barolo Ascheri (WHI)
Barolo Pio Cesare (BYR)
Sfursat Nino Negri (GRE)
1984
Barolo Zonchera Ceretto (UP)
Barolo Zonchetta, Ceretto (TAN, HIC)
1983
Barolo Marcenasco, Renato Ratti (PE)
★Barolo Pio Cesare (WIL)
1982
Barolo Cannubi Riserva, Prunotto (BYR)
Barolo Pio Cesare (VA)
1979
Barbaresco Torregiorgi (AD)

1978
Barbaresco Masseria, Vietti (HOG)
★Barolo Bricco Boschis Riserva San
  Giuseppe, Cavallotto (HOG)
Barolo Fontanafredda (HOG)

——————— £12.50 to £14.99 ———————
1987
Barbera d'Alba Vignarey, Gaja (OD, VA)
1985
Barbaresco Marcarini, Mascarello (WS)
Barolo Bussia Soprana, Aldo Conterno
  (WCL)
1984
Barolo Monprivato, Mascarello (PE)
1983
Barolo Bruno Giacosa (RAE)
1982
Barolo Marcenasco, Renato Ratti (AD)

1980
Barolo Bussia Soprana, Aldo Conterno (AD)
1978
Barolo Fontanafredda (AI)
1974
Barolo Borgogno (VA)

——————— £15.00 to £19.99 ———————
1986
Barbaresco Gaja (OD)
Barolo Sandrone (WW)
1985
Barbaresco Marcarini, Mascarello (WCL)
Barolo Bricco Rocche Brunate, Ceretto
  (TAN)
1984
Barolo Monprivato, Mascarello (EL)
Ca' del Bosco Maurizio Zanella(VA)
1983
Ca' del Bosco Maurizio Zanella(VA)
1982
Barolo Conca, Renato Ratti (AD)
Barolo Conterno (OD)
Barolo Gattinera, Fontanafredda (VA)

1979
Barolo Monfortino, Giacomo Conterno (OD)
1978
Barolo Barale (VA)
Barolo Gattinera, Fontanafredda (BO)
Barolo Montanello, Monchiero (WCL)
1971
★Barolo Borgogno (VA)

──────── **£20.00 to £29.99** ────────
1986
Darmagi Gaja (OD)
1985
Barbaresco Gaja (WW, WCL)
Barolo Monprivato, Mascarello (WCL, WS, REI)
1984
Darmagi Gaja (VA)
1983
Darmagi Gaja (VA)
1982
Barbaresco Gaja (VA)
Barolo Lazzarito, Fontanafredda (VA)
1981
Barbaresco Gaja (HAH)
1971
Barolo Mascarello (WCL)
Barolo Pio Cesare (WCL)
1967
Barolo Ceretto (WCL)
1961
Barolo Riserva Borgogno (GRE)

──────── **£30.00 to £39.99** ────────
1986
Barbaresco Costa Russi, Gaja (OD)
Barbaresco Sori San Lorenzo, Gaja (OD)
1982
Darmagi Gaja (VA)
1979
Barbaresco Gaja (WIL)
1978
Barbaresco Gaja (WIL)
1970
Barolo Zonchetta, Ceretto (WCL)

──────── **£40.00 to £55.00** ────────
1983
Barbaresco Sori Tildin, Gaja (VA)
1978
Barbaresco Gaja (VA)
1968
Barolo Conterno (WCL)
1964
Barolo Prunotto (WCL)

1961
Barolo Pio Cesare (WCL)

──────── **c. £124.00** ────────
1961
Barbaresco Gaja (VA)

NORTH-WEST WHITE

──────── **Under £5.00** ────────
1988
Gavi Arione Vini (WHI)

──────── **£5.00 to £5.99** ────────
1989
Gavi Fontanafredda (BAR)
1988
Gavi Fontanafredda (BOT)
1987
Gavi la Raia (HAY)
1986
Lugana San Benedetto, Zenato (GI)

──────── **£6.00 to £6.99** ────────
1989
Favorita Deltetto (WCL)
Moscato d'Asti la Spinetta, Rivetti (AD)
1988
Favorita Malvira (AD)
Moscato d'Asti la Spinetta, Rivetti (HAY)

──────── **£7.00 to £8.99** ────────
1989
Arneis del Piemonte San Michel, Deltetto (WCL)
1988
Arneis Blange Ceretto (VA)
1987
Arneis Blange Ceretto (UP)
Gavi Castello di Tassarolo (TAN)

──────── **£9.00 to £11.99** ────────
1986
Pio di Lei, Pio Cesare (VA)
1985
Arneis del Montebertotto, Castello di Neive (PE)

NORTH-WEST SPARKLING

──────── **Under £4.00** ────────
Non-vintage
Asda Asti Spumante (ASD)
Gancia Spumante (HOG)
Tesco Asti Spumante (TES)

─────── £4.00 to £4.99 ───────
Non-vintage
Asti Spumante Fontanafredda (WIZ, BO)
Asti Spumante Martini (HOG, HAG, AI, WHI,
ASD, BO)
★Gancia Pinot di Pinot (VA)
Moscato d'Asti Ascheri (UP, WCL)

─────── £5.00 to £6.99 ───────
Non-vintage
Asti Spumante Fontanafredda (VA, AUG, UP,
VIG, BAR)
Asti Spumante Martini (TES, WRI, BL, BOT,
WIL, TAN, PD, UN, AUG, THR, NI, EL, DAV, VIN)
Gancia Spumante (UN)
Moscato d'Asti , Castello di Neive (VA)

─────── c. £16.40 ───────
Non-vintage
★Franciacorta Brut, Cà del Bosco (VA)

NORTH-EAST RED

─────── Under £3.00 ───────
Non-vintage
Sainsbury's Valpolicella Classico (SAI)
1989
Asda Valpolicella (ASD)
Valpolicella Tadiello (WCL)
1988
Waitrose Valpolicella Classico (WAI)
1986
Valpolicella Classico Negarine (SAI)

─────── £3.00 to £3.99 ───────
1989
Bardolino Classico Superiore Boscaini
(WHI)
Valpolicella Classico Boscaini (WHI)
1988
Bardolino Classico Superiore Boscaini
(WHI)
Teroldego Rotaliano Gaierhof (WAI)
Valpolicella Classico Boscaini (WHI)
1987
Cabernet Grave del Friuli, Collavini (VA)
Lagrein Dunkel Viticoltori Alto Adige (LAY)
Merlot Grave del Friuli Collavini (WHI)
Valpolicella Classico Superiore Tommasi
(LOR)
1986
★Bardolino Classico Superiore Masi (HOG,
BYR)
Cabernet Franc di Aquileia, Ca' Bolani
(BYR)

Valpolicella Bolla (VA)
★Valpolicella Classico Superiore Zenato
(WCL)
Valpolicella Classico Tedeschi (LAY)
1985
Cabernet Sauvignon Tiefenbrunner (BYR)
Merlot Grave del Friuli Collavini (WHI)
Valpolicella Classico Masi (AUG)
★Valpolicella Classico Superiore Masi
(HOG)

─────── £4.00 to £4.99 ───────
1989
Bardolino Portalupi (AD)
Valpolicella Classico Allegrini (WCL)
1988
Bardolino Classico Ca' Bordenis (TAN)
Valpolicella Recioto Amarone Tommasi (LA)
Valpolicella Classico Castello d'Illasi, Santi
(BAR)
Valpolicella Classico Superiore Zenato
(THR)
1987
Bardolino Classico Superiore Masi (CH)
Cabernet di Magre, Viticoltori Alto Adige
(LAY)
Cabernet Grave del Friuli, Collavini (WHI)
Lagrein Dunkel Viticoltori Alto Adige (VA)
Marzemino del Trentino Fedrigotti (VA)
Valpolicella Classico Superiore Masi (CH)
Valpolicella Classico Superiore Valverde,
Tedeschi (AD)
1986
Cabernet Franc di Aquileia, Ca' Bolani
(WIL)
Cabernet Grave del Friuli, Collavini (WHI)
Merlot di Pramaggiore Santa Margherita
(GRE)
Refosco Grave del Friuli, Villa Ronche (VA)
Valpolicella Classico Superiore Boscaini (HA)
1985
Valpolicella Bertani (VA)
1984
Valpolicella Classico Superiore Sartori (UN)
1983
Cabernet Franc di Aquileia, Ca' Bolani (EL)

─────── £5.00 to £5.99 ───────
1988
Bardolino Classico Superiore Bertani (LAY)
Teroldego Rotaliano Vigneto Pini, Zeni (VA)
1987
Cabernet Sauvignon Trentino, Santi (VIG)
Schioppettino di Gramagliano, Collavini
(VA)

1986
Cabernet Franc Conti da Schio (BIB)
Cabernet Riserva, Lageder (AUG)
Merlot Collio Collavini (VIC)
1985
Campo Fiorin Masi (VA, PIP, AUG)
Valpolicella Valpantena Bertani (LAY, WS)
1984
Valpolicella Monte Cà Paletta, Quintarelli
(RAE)
★Venegazzù della Casa Loredan-Gasparini
(BYR, WCL)

─────── £6.00 to £6.99 ───────
1988
Teroldego Rotaliano Vigneto Pini, Zeni
(TAN)
1987
Cabernet Riserva, Lageder (BY)
1986
Venegazzù della Casa Loredan-Gasparini
(VIC)
1985
Palazzo della Torre, Allegrini (VA)
Venegazzù della Casa Loredan-Gasparini
(VA)
1983
Valpolicella Recioto Amarone Sartori (WIL)
1981
Valpolicella Recioto Amarone Montresor
(HOG)

─────── £7.00 to £7.99 ───────
1986
Valpolicella Classico la Grola, Allegrini
(WCL)
1985
Campo Fiorin Masi (REI)
1984
Valpolicella Recioto Amarone Santi (TAN)
1983
Valpolicella Recioto Amarone Riserva
Tommasi (CH)
1982
Valpolicella Recioto Amarone Negrar (EL)

─────── £8.00 to £9.99 ───────
1988
Teroldego Rotaliano Conti Martini (AD)
1986
Venegazzù della Casa Loredan-Gasparini
(TAN)
1985
Ca' del Merlo, Quintarelli (WCL)
Valpolicella Recioto Amarone Bolla (VA)

Valpolicella Recioto Amarone Montresor
(VA, GRE)
Valpolicella Classico Quintarelli (WCL)
1984
Valpolicella Recioto Amarone Tedeschi (WHI)
1983
Valpolicella Recioto Amarone Sartori (HAH)
1982
Valpolicella Recioto Amarone Sartori (UN)
Venegazzù della Casa Loredan-Gasparini
(VA)

─────── £10.00 to £12.99 ───────
1986
Venegazzù della Casa Loredan-Gasparini
(BAR)
1983
Venegazzù della Casa Loredan-Gasparini
(WRI)
1981
Recioto Amarone Fieramonte, Allegrini (VA)

─────── £14.00 to £15.99 ───────
1985
Recioto Amarone Mezzanella, Masi (BYR)
1981
Recioto Amarone Mazzano, Masi (BYR)
Recioto Amarone Quintarelli (RAE)
1980
Recioto Amarone Vaio Armaron, Masi
(BYR)

─────── £16.00 to £19.99 ───────
1986
Recioto Amarone Mezzanella, Masi (PIP)
1985
Recioto Amarone Mazzano, Masi (VA)
1983
La Poja, Allegrini (WCL)
Recioto Amarone Serègo Alighieri (VA)
1980
Recioto Amarone Monte Cà Paletta,
Quintarelli (AD)

─────── c. £31.00 ───────
1983
Recioto Amarone Quintarelli (WCL)
Recioto della Valpolicella Quintarelli (WCL)

┌─────────────────────────────┐
│ *Stars (★) indicate wines* │
│ *selected by the editors as* │
│ *particularly good value* │
└─────────────────────────────┘

NORTH-EAST WHITE

──────── Under £3.00 ────────
Non-vintage
Sainsbury's Soave (SAI)
Soave Classico Lamberti (BOT)
Tesco Soave (TES)
1989
★Bianco di Custoza Pasqua (SAI)
1988
Waitrose Soave (WAI)
1987
Asda Soave (ASD)

──────── £3.00 to £3.99 ────────
Non-vintage
Soave Classico Lamberti (PD)
1989
★Asda Chardonnay Alto Adige (ASD)
Pinot Grigio Ca' Donini (VIC)
Soave Classico Boscaini (WHI)
1988
★Bianco di Custoza Tommasi (LOR)
Chardonnay Ca' Donini (AUG)
Chardonnay Mezza Corona, Trentino (VIC)
★Sauvignon di Aquileia, Ca' Bolani (BYR)
Lugana Tommasi (LOR)
Soave Classico Monte Tenda, Tedeschi (OD)
★Soave Classico Zenato (WAI)
Tocai Friulano di Aquileia, Ca' Bolani (SAI)
1987
Soave Classico Superiore Gini (HAY)
1986
★Pinot Grigio Tiefenbrunner (TES)
Soave Bolla (VA)
Soave Classico Superiore Masi (HOG)

──────── £4.00 to £4.99 ────────
Non-vintage
Chardonnay di Appiano Viticoltori Alto
   Adige (PD)
1989
Lugana di San Benedetto, Zenato (DAV)
Soave Classico Monte Tenda, Tedeschi (AD)
Soave Classico Superiore Anselmi (BY)
Tocai di San Martino, Zenato (DAV)
1988
Chardonnay di Appiano Viticoltori Alto
   Adige (LAY, BOT, VA)
Chardonnay Lageder (AUG)
Lugana di San Benedetto, Zenato (SAI)
Pinot Bianco Tiefenbrunner (VA)
Pinot Grigio Ca'vit (TAN)
Pinot Grigio Grave dei Friuli, Collavini
   (WHI, LAY, AI)

★Rheinriesling Tiefenbrunner (BYR)
Soave Classico di Monteforte Santi (WIL,
   TAN)
Soave Classico Superiore Masi (CH)
1987
Chardonnay Kettmeir (HOG)
Pinot Bianco Tiefenbrunner (WIL)
Pinot Grigio Lageder (AUG)
Soave Classico Pieropan (BO)
Tocai Grave del Friuli, Collavini (WHI, VIC)
★Venegazzù Chardonnay Loredan-
   Gasparini (WIL)
1986
Chardonnay di Appiano Viticoltori Alto
   Adige (GI)
Tocai del Collio, Felluga (BYR)
1985
Rheinriesling Tiefenbrunner (WHI)
Soave Classico Superiore Sartori (UN)

──────── £5.00 to £5.99 ────────
1989
Chardonnay Lageder (WCL)
Chardonnay Tiefenbrunner (WHI)
Lugana Ca dei Frati, Dal Cero (WCL)
Pinot Grigio Lageder (PIP, BY, WCL)
1988
Chardonnay Kettmeir (VA)
Chardonnay Tiefenbrunner (WHI, AD)
Chardonnay Vinattieri (BY)
Gewürztraminer Tiefenbrunner (VA, BYR,
   TAN)
Goldmuskateller (Moscato Giallo) Trocken,
   Tiefenbrunner (VA)
Pinot Grigio Grave dei Friuli, Collavini
   (HAH)
Pinot Grigio Lageder (BY)
Pinot Grigio Tiefenbrunner (BYR, WHI)
Soave Classico Col Baraca (AUG)
Soave Classico Superiore Anselmi (TAN)
1987
Gewürztraminer Tiefenbrunner (WIL)

Vinattieri Bianco (BIB)
1986
Gewürztraminer Trattmannhof, Viticoltori
   Alto Adige (AI)

──────── £6.00 to £7.99 ────────

1989
Chardonnay EnoFriulia (TAN)
★Chardonnay Pojer e Sandri (WCL)
Soave Classico Monte Carbonara, Tessavi
  (AD)
1988
Gewürztraminer Tiefenbrunner (AD)
Soave Classico Pieropan (OL)
1987
Pinot Grigio Volpe Pasini (WW)
Soave Classico Costalta Santa Sofia (REI)
1985
Pinot Bianco Martini (AD)

──────── £8.00 to £9.99 ────────

1989
Pinot Blanco Collio, Puiatti (WCL)
Ribolla Collio, Puiatti (WCL)
Riesling Renano Collio, Puiatti (WCL)
Sauvignon Collio, Puiatti (WCL)
1988
Pinot Grigio Collio, Felluga (VA)
Soave Recioto Pieropan (AD)
Tocai Friulano Collio, Schiopetto (BAR)
1987
Riesling Renano Collio, Schiopetto (VA)
Tocai Collio Schiopetto (VA)
1986
★Chardonnay Vinattieri (BIB)
★Torcolato Vino Liquoroso Maculan (WCL)

──────── £10.00 to £12.99 ────────

1988
Chardonnay Jermann (BAR)
Pinot Bianco Collio, Schiopetto (BAR)
1987
Chardonnay Faye, Pojer e Sandri (WCL)
Chardonnay Löwengang, Lageder (BY, WCL)
1986
Chardonnay Lageder (PIP)

──────── £14.00 to £16.99 ────────

1987
Vintage Tunina, Sermann (BAR)
1986
Torcolato Vino Liquoroso Maculan (PIP, AD)
1984
Torcolato Vino Liquoroso Maculan (VA)

──────── £18.00 to £23.99 ────────

1986
Torcolato Vino Liquoroso Maculan (REI)
1983
Bianco del Amabile, Quintarelli (RAE)

ROSÉ

──────── Under £4.00 ────────

1989
Bardolino Chiaretto, Portalupi (VA)

SPARKLING

──────── Under £6.00 ────────

Non-vintage
Prosecco di Conegliano Carpene Malvolti
  (HOG, VA, WCL)

──────── £8.00 to £11.99 ────────

Non-vintage
Berlucchi Brut (VA)
Ferrari Brut (VA)

CENTRAL RED

──────── Under £3.00 ────────

Non-vintage
Chianti Victoria Wine (VIC)
Sainsbury's Cannonau del Parteolla (SAI)
1988
Waitrose Chianti (WAI)
1986
★Chianti Classico Lamole (ASD)

──────── £3.00 to £3.99 ────────

1988
★Chianti Classico Rocca delle Macie (WAI)
★Santa Cristina, Antinori (GRE, VIC)
1987
Chianti Classico Rocca delle Macie (BO)
★Rosso di Montalcino Campo ai Sassi,
  Frescobaldi (WAI)
Santa Cristina, Antinori (HOG)
1986
Chianti Classico Aziano, Ruffino (HOG)
★Montefalco Rosso d'Arquata
  Adanti (OD)
Sainsbury's Chianti Classico (SAI)
Tesco Chianti Classico (TES)
1985
Chianti Rufina Villa di Monte (TES)
1982
Rosso Cònero Marchetti (TES)

──────── £4.00 to £4.99 ────────

Non-vintage
Chianti Classico Rocca delle Macie (BL)
1989
★Morellino di Scansano Poggio Valente
  (WCL)

1988
Chianti Classico Rocca delle Macie (WHI, AUG, DAV)
Chianti Classico San Felice (HOG)
Chianti Rufina Riserva Tenuta di Remole, Frescobaldi (AMI)
★Chianti Rufina Selvapiana (WCL)
Santa Cristina, Antinori (LAY, UP, DI)
1987
Chianti Classico Castello di San Polo in Rosso (ALL)
Chianti Classico Castello di Volpaia (NI)

Chianti Classico Castello Vicchiomaggio (VIC)
Chianti Rufina Riserva Tenuta di Remole, Frescobaldi (VA)
Chianti Rufina Selvapiana (WCL)
Montefalco Rosso d'Arquata Adanti (VA)
Rosso di Montalcino il Poggione (RAE)
Rosso di Montalcino Villa Banfi (AUG)
Santa Cristina, Antinori (LO, DI)
1986
Chianti Classico Rocca delle Macie (WHI)
Chianti Classico Viticcio Landini (LOR)
Chianti Putto, Amici-Grossi (HA)
Rosso Cònero Marchetti (VA, WCL)
Rosso Cònero San Lorenzo (GRE, UP)
1985
★Chianti Classico Riserva Villa Antinori (SAI)
Chianti Classico Riserva Villa Cerna (BYR)
Rosso Cònero San Lorenzo (VA, BO)
Vino Nobile di Montepulciano Bigi (VA)
1984
Sangiovese di Romagna Pasolini Dall'Onda (HAG)
1983
Chianti Classico Castello di San Polo in Rosso (ALL)
Chianti Classico Monsanto (RAE)

Rosso Cònero San Lorenzo (BO)
1982
Chianti Classico Riserva Brolio (WIL)
Rosso Cònero San Lorenzo (WIZ, OD)

───────── £5.00 to £5.99 ─────────
1988
Rosso di Montalcino Altesino (WCL)
Rosso di Montalcino Campo ai Sassi, Frescobaldi (AMI)
Santa Cristina, Antinori (AN)
1987
Chianti Classico Badia a Coltibuono (VA)
Chianti Classico Felsina Berardenga (WCL)
Chianti Classico Isole e Olena (WCL, HAH)
Chianti Classico San Jacopo, Vicciomaggio (UP)
1986
★Carmignano Villa Capezzana (BOT)
★Chianti Classico Castello di Volpaia (HAY)
Chianti Classico la Lellera, Matta (IR)
Chianti Classico Riserva Villa Antinori (MAJ, VA, GRE, LAY)
Chianti Classico Villa Cafaggio (MAR)
Chianti Rufina Riserva Selvapiana (WCL)
Rosso Cònero San Lorenzo (BAR)
★Vino Nobile di Montepulciano Poliziano (VA)
Vino Nobile di Montepulciano Riserva, Bigi (BYR, GRE)
Vino Nobile di Montepulciano Trerose (ASD)
1985
Chianti Classico Castello di San Polo in Rosso (BYR)
Chianti Classico Castello di Volpaia (HAG, HUN)
Chianti Classico Riserva Ducale, Ruffino (WHI)
Chianti Classico Riserva Rocca delle Macie (BYR, SAF)
Chianti Classico Riserva Villa Antinori (BYR, CB, WS)
Chianti Rufina Castello di Nipozzano (VA)
Chianti Rufina Villa di Vetrice Riserva (WCL)
Rubesco Torgiano Lungarotti (VA, SAI, UP)
Vino Nobile di Montepulciano Poliziano (AUG)
1984
Chianti Classico Castello dei Rampolla (STA)
1983
Chianti Classico Brolio (VIN)
Chianti Classico Riserva Ducale, Ruffino (WHI)

Chianti Rufina Riserva Castello di
Nipozzano (GRE, TAN)
Chianti Rufina Riserva Villa di Vetrice
(WCL)
1982
Chianti Classico Villa Antinori (HOG)
1981
Chianti Classico Brolio (BO)

─────── £6.00 to £6.99 ───────
1988
Chianti Classico Aziano, Ruffino (REI)
Chianti Classico Isole e Olena (WCL)
Rosso di Montalcino Altesino (AN)
★Rosso di Montalcino Talenti (BIB)
1987
Chianti Classico Castello Vicchiomaggio
(AI)
Chianti Classico Fontodi (WCL)
Chianti Classico Villa Cafaggio (VIG)
Ser Gioveto, Rocca della Macie (VIC, VA)
Vino Nobile di Montepulciano Poliziano
(PIP)
1986
Chianti Classico Riserva Villa Antinori (LO,
THR, DI)
Rubesco Torgiano Lungarotti (TAN)
Vino Nobile di Montepulciano Bigi (VIG)
1985
Chianti Classico Riserva la Lellera, Matta
(WHI, IR)
Chianti Classico Riserva Villa Banfi (AUG,
PIP)
Rubesco Torgiano Lungarotti (LAY, PE, HAH,
WS, DI)
Sagrantino di Montefalco, Adanti (VA)
Vino Nobile di Montepulciano Baiocchi
(WRI)
1984
Carmignano Villa Capezzana (PD)
1982
Chianti Rufina Riserva Castello di
Nipozzano (UN)
1981
★Cabernet Sauvignon di Miralduolo,
Lungarotti (LAY)

─────── £7.00 to £7.99 ───────
1987
Brusco dei Barbi Fattoria dei Barbi (VIG,
BAR)
Carmignano Ambra (WW)
1986
Chianti Classico Castello dei Rampolla (AN)
Chianti Classico Villa Antinori (TAN)

Prunaio di Viticcio Landini (LOR)
Vino Nobile di Montepulciano Garda (DAV)
Vino Nobile di Montepulciano le Casalte
(WCL)
1985
★Chianti Classico Riserva Badia a
Coltibuono (VA)
Ghiaie della Furba, Capezzana (OD)
Rubesco Torgiano Lungarotti (REI)
1984
Vino Nobile di Montepulciano Fassati (WS)
1983
Chianti Classico Riserva Badia a
Coltibuono (BYR)
Chianti Classico Riserva Ducale, Ruffino
(BOT)
1982
Chianti Classico Riserva di Fizzano, Rocca
delle Macie (VA, BL)
Chianti Classico Riserva San Polo in Rosso
(WHI)
1981
★Brunello di Montalcino Val di Suga (ASD)
Cabernet Sauvignon di Miralduolo,
Lungarotti (GRE, VA)
Chianti Classico Riserva Ducale, Ruffino
(BYR)
1980
Chianti Classico Riserva Castell'in Villa
(TAN)

─────── £8.00 to £9.99 ───────
1987
Chianti Classico Pèppoli, Antinori (LAY, DI)
1986
Chianti Classico Riserva Castello di
Volpaia (WCL)
Chianti Classico Riserva Monsanto (RAE,
BIB)
Vinattieri Rosso Secondo (BIB)
1985
Ca' del Pazzo Caparzo (VA)
Chianti Classico Castello di Cacchiano
Riserva, Millennio (WCL)
Chianti Classico Riserva di Fizzano, Rocca
delle Macie (BAR)
Chianti Classico Riserva Fontodi (WCL)
Vinattieri Rosso (BIB)
Vinattieri Rosso Secondo (BIB)
1983
Brunello di Montalcino Castelgiocondo
(GRE, VA)
★Brunello di Montalcino il Poggione (HAY,
RAE, BYR)
Carmignano Riserva Villa Capezzana (UP)

Fiorano Rosso Bon Compagni Ludovisi
   Principe di Venosa (RAE)
Sangioveto Badia a Coltibuono (BYR)
1982
Chianti Classico Riserva del Barone, Brolio
   (BYR)
1981
Cabernet Sauvignon di Miralduolo,
   Lungarotti (REI)
Chianti Classico Riserva Villa Antinori
   (LAY)
1980
Sangioveto Badia a Coltibuono (VA)
1979
Brunello di Montalcino Castelgiocondo
   (HOG)
Brunello di Montalcino Fattoria dei Barbi
   (HOG)
1978
Chianti Classico Riserva Marchese
   Antinori (AI)
1977
Brunello di Montalcino Fattoria dei Barbi
   (HOG)
1975
★Chianti Classico Riserva Badia a
   Coltibuono (REI)

──────── **£10.00 to £14.99** ────────
1988
Grosso Sanese, Il Palazzino (WW)
1987
Alte d'Altesi, Altesino (WCL)
Ghiaie della Furba, Capezzana (WCL, TAN)
Palazzo Altesi, Altesino (WCL)
1986
Balifico Castello di Volpaia (VIG, REI, WCL)
Cepparello, Isole e Olena (WCL)
Chianti Prunaio (BAR)
Coltassala Castello di Volpaia (AD, VIG, REI,
   WCL)
Grifi, Avignonesi (WCL, REI)
I Sodi di San Niccolò, Castellare (VA, OD)
Percallo San Giusto a Rentannano (WW)
Quercia Grande, Capaccia (VA)
1985
★Brunello di Montalcino il Poggione (RAE)
Brunello di Montalcino Talenti (BIB)
Ca' del Pazzo Caparzo (WHI, GRE, WCL, REI)
Carmignano Riserva Villa Capezzana (WCL)
★Cepparello, Isole e Olena (VA, UP)
★Chianti Classico Riserva Vigneto Rancia,
   Felsina Berardenga (WCL)
Chianti Rufina Montesodi, Frescobaldi (VA)
Fontalloro, Felsina Berardenga (UP)

Ghiaie della Furba, Capezzana (REI)
Grifi Avignonesi (REI)
Mormoreto Predicato di Biturica,
   Frescobaldi (AMI)
★Tignanello Antinori (SAI, VA, GRE, HUN,
   VIC)
Vinattieri Rosso Secondo (REI)
Vino Nobile di Montepulciano Avignonesi
   (AN)
1984
Brunello di Montalcino Castelgiocondo (VIC)
Brunello di Montalcino Villa Banfi (AUG,
   PIP)
1983
Brunello di Montalcino Altesino (PE)
Brunello di Montalcino Villa Banfi (WIL)
Mormoreto Predicato di Biturica,
   Frescobaldi (AD, WCL, WCL)
Tignanello Antinori (BO, BYR, WCL)
1982
Brunello di Montalcino Castelgiocondo (HA)
Brunello di Montalcino Riserva, il Poggione
   (RAE)
Chianti Classico Riserva Monsanto (RAE)
Sangioveto Badia a Coltibuono (WCL)
Tignanello Antinori (HOG)
1981
Brunello di Montalcino Fattoria dei Barbi
   (GRE)
Chianti Classico Riserva Monsanto (RAE)
Chianti Rufina Selvapiana (WCL)
1980
Brunello di Montalcino Castelgiocondo (UN)
Chianti Classico Riserva Castello
   Vicchiomaggio (WRI)
1979
Rubesco Riserva Vigna Monticchio
   Lungarotti (LAY)
Rubesco Torgiano Riserva Lungarotti (GRE,
   VA, WS, DI, AD)
Tinscvil Riserva (RAE)
1976
Chianti Classico Riserva Badia a
   Coltibuono (HAG)
1974
Chianti Classico Riserva Monsanto (RAE)

──────── **£15.00 to £19.99** ────────
1988
Syrah Isole e Olena (WCL)
1986
Cabreo Ruffino (BL, REI)
Flaccianello della Pieve, Fontodi (WCL)
Fontalloro, Felsina Berardenga (WCL)
Tignanello Antinori (THR)

1985
Brunello di Montalcino Montosoli, Altesino
(WCL)
Cabreo Predicato di Biturica Ruffino (VA)
Tignanello Antinori (HAG, HAH, TAN, UP, DI,
VIG, ALL)
1984
Sassicaia Incisa della Rocchetta (BYR)
Tignanello Antinori (YF)
1983
Tignanello Antinori (REI, GRE, LAY)

1982
Tignanello Antinori (GRE, DI)

───────── £20.00 to £24.99 ─────────
1985
Brunello di Montalcino la Casa, Caparzo
(WCL)
Le Pergole Torte, Monte Vertine (REI)
Sassicaia Incisa della Rocchetta (WCL)
1983
Sassicaia Incisa della Rocchetta (WRI)
1982
Sassicaia Incisa della Rocchetta (WIL)
1968
Chianti Rufina Selvapiana (WCL)

───────── £25.00 to £29.99 ─────────
1986
Sassicaia Incisa della Rocchetta (CB, VA,
GRE, UP, LAY, DI)
1984
Sassicaia Incisa della Rocchetta (REI, VA,
AD, DI)
1983
Sassicaia Incisa della Rocchetta (BYR)
1982
Brunello di Montalcino la Casa, Caparzo
(WCL)

1980
Brunello di Montalcino Biondi-Santi (VA)
1979
Brunello di Montalcino la Casa, Caparzo
(WCL)

───────── £30.00 to £39.99 ─────────
1985
Sammarco Castello dei Rampolla (AN)
Solaia Antinori (WCL)
1984
Sassicaia Incisa della Rocchetta (AV)
1983
Sassicaia Incisa della Rocchetta (AV)
1982
Solaia Antinori (UP)
1958
Chianti Classico Riserva Badia a
Coltibuono (REI)

───────── c. £74.00 ─────────
1977
Brunello di Montalcino Biondi-Santi (VA)

───────── £105.00 to £125.99 ─────────
1970
Brunello di Montalcino Biondi-Santi (VA)

CENTRAL WHITE

───────── Under £3.00 ─────────
Non-vintage
Sainsbury's Verdicchio dei Castelli di Jesi
(SAI)
Tesco Frascati (TES)
1989
★Sainsbury's Vermentino di Sardegna (SAI)
1987
Orvieto Abboccato le Valette (HOG)
Orvieto Secco le Valette (HOG)

───────── £3.00 to £3.99 ─────────
Non-vintage
Galestro Antinori (VIC)
Orvieto Classico Amabile Bigi (BL)
Orvieto Secco Cecchi (UN)
Sainsbury's Frascati Secco (SAI)
Verdicchio Classico Bianchi (BL)
1989
Marino Superiore Gotto d'Oro (UP)
Orvieto Classico Abboccato Antinori (GRE)
1988
Frascati Superiore Colli di Catone (OD, BYR)
Frascati Superiore Fontana Candida (SAF,
BYR)

Galestro Rocca delle Macie (BYR)
Orvieto Classico Amabile Bigi (CH, WHI)
Orvieto Classico Secco Bigi (BYR, WHI)
Verdicchio dei Castelli di Jesi Classico,
  Garofoli (SAF, BO, VIC)
Verdicchio dei Castelli di Jesi Classico,
  Umani Ronchi (VA)
1987
Frascati Superiore Fontana Candida (BO,
  WIZ)
Galestro Antinori (BYR)
Orvieto Abboccato Ruffino (HOG)
Orvieto Secco Antinori (VIC)
Orvieto Secco Ruffino (HOG)
1986
Frascati Superiore Monteporzio (HOG)
Vernaccia di San Gimignano la Torre (HOG)
1984
Verdicchio dei Castelli di Jesi Classico,
  Garofoli (GI)

──────── £4.00 to £4.99 ────────
Non-vintage
Frascati Fontana Candida (BL, PD)
Orvieto Classico Abboccato Antinori (UN)
Orvieto Secco Ruffino (UN)
1989
Bianco Villa Antinori (TES, LAY, THR, DI)
Frascati Superiore Colli di Catone (PIP,
  AUG)
Frascati Superiore Fontana Candida (UP)
Frascati Superiore Gotto d'Oro (LAY, AI,
  THR)
Galestro Antinori (VA, THR, DI)
Orvieto Classico Secco Antinori (UP, THR, DI,
  TAN)
★Vernaccia di San Gimignano San Quirico
  (THR)
1988
Bianco d'Arquata Adanti (VA)
Bianco Villa Antinori (MAJ, CB, DI)
★Castello della Sala, Antinori (BYR)
Frascati Colli di Catone (VA)
Frascati Fontana Candida (BOT)
Frascati Superiore Colli di Catone (CH, BY)
Galestro Antinori (DI)
Grechetto d'Arquata Adanti (VA, OD)
Orvieto Classico Abboccato Antinori (GRE,
  LAY, AI, DI)
Orvieto Classico Abboccato Bigi (WIL)
Orvieto Classico Secco Antinori (AI, LAY,
  ALL, DI)
Orvieto Classico Vigneto Torricella, Bigi
  (VA, AUG)
★Pomino Frescobaldi (GRE, VA)

Verdicchio dei Castelli di Jesi Classico,
  Fazi-Battaglia (WS)
Vernaccia di San Gimignano Falchini (WRI)
Vernaccia di San Gimignano la Torre (VA)
Vernaccia di San Gimignano San Quirico
  (SAI, GRE)
Vernaccia di San Gimignano Vecchione (AI)
1987
Orvieto Classico Vigneto Torricella, Bigi
  (BYR, WIL)
Verdicchio Classico Bianchi (MAJ)
Verdicchio dei Castelli di Jesi Classico,
  Garofoli (VIN)
Verdicchio dei Castelli di Jesi Classico,
  Umani Ronchi (BYR, TAN)
1986
Pomino Frescobaldi (LAY)

──────── £5.00 to £6.99 ────────
Non-vintage
Vin Santo Antinori (HOG, GRE)
1989
Galestro Antinori (AN)
Orvieto Classico Vigneto Torricella, Bigi
  (AD)
Orvieto Secco Antinori (AN)
Pomino Frescobaldi (WCL)
Vernaccia di San Gimignano Montenidoli
  (BIB)
1988
Bianco Villa Antinori (BER, HAH)
Capezzana Chardonnay (UP, WCL)
Castello della Sala, Antinori (DI)
Orvieto Classico Vigneto Torricella, Bigi
  (BAR)
Torre di Giano Lungarotti (UP)
Vernaccia di San Gimignano Bruni (WS)
1987
Chardonnay di Miralduolo, Lungarotti
  (THR)
Torre di Giano Lungarotti (VIC)
1986
Castello della Sala, Antinori (LAY, DI)
Pomino Frescobaldi (UN)
1985
Vin Santo Antinori (VA)
1983
Vin Santo Antinori (BYR)

──────── £7.00 to £8.99 ────────
1988
Borro della Sala, Antinori (TAN, AN)
1987
Frascati Colle Gaio, Colli di Catone (AUG,
  VA)

1985
Pomino il Benefizio, Frescobaldi (GRE, LAY)

──────── £9.00 to £11.99 ────────
1989
Vernaccia di San Gimignano Terre di Tufo, Teruzzi e Puthod (WCL)
1988
Chardonnay I Sistri, Felsina Berardenga (WCL)
Chardonnay Isole e Olena (WCL)
Trebianco Castello dei Rampolla (AN)
1987
Il Marzocco, Avignonesi (VA)
Pomino il Benefizio, Frescobaldi (AMI, VA, AD)
1986
Pomino il Benefizio, Frescobaldi (TAN, PIP, WCL)

──────── £12.00 to £15.99 ────────
Non-vintage
Vin Santo Antinori (REI)
1987
Cervaro della Sala, Antinori (UP)
Il Marzocco, Avignonesi (AN)
Muffato della Sala, Antinori (DI)
1986
Cervaro della Sala, Antinori (VA)
Orvieto Classico Muffa Nobile, Barberani (WCL)
1975
Vin Santo Villa di Vetrice (WCL)

CENTRAL SPARKLING

──────── Under £3.00 ────────
Non-vintage
Asda Lambrusco (ASD)
Lambrusco Amabile Luigi Gavioli (HOG, GRE, VA)
Lambrusco Bianco Ca' de Medici (WAI)
Lambrusco Bianco San Prospero (BL, AUG, TAN)
Lambrusco Ca' de Medici (WAI)
Lambrusco di Sorbara Cavicchioli (OD, BYR)
Lambrusco Grasparossa di Castelvetro (WAI)
St Michael Lambrusco (MAR)

──────── £3.00 to £3.99 ────────
Non-vintage
Lambrusco San Prospero (UP)
1987
Lambrusco Gavioli (VA)

SOUTHERN RED

──────── Under £4.00 ────────
Non-vintage
Corvo Rosso Duca di Salaparuta (BYR, WIL)
1989
Cellaro Rosso (UP)
★Montepulciano d'Abruzzo Tollo (PIP)
1988
Montepulciano d'Abruzzo Bianchi (VA)
Montepulciano d'Abruzzo Tollo (BY)
1987
Corvo Rosso Duca di Salaparuta (VA)
Monica di Sardegna, C.S. di Dolianova (WCL)
Rapitalà Rosso, Alcamo (VA)
Settesoli Rosso (VA)
1986
Corvo Rosso Duca di Salaparuta (BO)
Montepulciano d'Abruzzo Bianchi (WIZ, UP)
1985
Montepulciano d'Abruzzo Illuminati (HOG)
Montepulciano d'Abruzzo Riserva Colle Secco (VA)
1984
Settesoli Rosso (HOG)
1983
Corvo Rosso Duca di Salaparuta (HOG)

──────── £4.00 to £5.99 ────────
Non-vintage
Corvo Rosso Duca di Salaparuta (UN)
1988
Montepulciano d'Abruzzo Illuminati (GRE)
1987
Corvo Rosso Duca di Salaparuta (GRE, AI, UP, TAN)
1986
Corvo Rosso Duca di Salaparuta (THR)
1985
Aglianico del Vulture, Fratelli d'Angelo (VA)
Montepulciano d'Abruzzo Cornacchia (WCL)
Montepulciano d'Abruzzo Invecchiato, Illuminati (VA)
Regaleali Rosso (VA)
1984
Montepulciano d'Abruzzo Riserva Colle Secco (WCL, ALL)

──────── £6.00 to £8.99 ────────
1985
Montepulciano d'Abruzzo Invecchiato, Illuminati (GRE)
1977
Rosso Brindisi Patriglione, Taurino (VA)

1985
Aglianico del Vulture, Fratelli d'Angelo
(WCL, TAN)
Montepulciano d'Abruzzo Invecchiato,
Illuminati (GRE)

——————— **£9.00 to £14.99** ———————
1985
Taurasi Mastroberardino (VA)
1982
Taurasi Mastroberardino (VA)

SOUTHERN WHITE

——————— **Under £4.00** ———————
Non-vintage
Corvo Bianco Duca di Salaparuta (HOG,
BYR)
1989
Cellaro Bianco C.S. di Sambuca (UP, WCL)
1988
★Rapitalá Bianco di Alcamo (VA)
1987
Corvo Bianco Duca di Salaparuta (BO)
1986
Settesoli Bianco (HOG)
Trebbiano d'Abruzzo Illuminati (HOG)

——————— **£4.00 to £5.99** ———————
Non-vintage
Corvo Bianco Duca di Salaparuta (WIL, BOT,
UN, PD)
1989
Preludio No. 1 Torrebianco (GRE)
Sauvignon di Puglia, Vigna al Monte (GRE)
1988
Corvo Bianco Duca di Salaparuta (VA, CH,
THR, AI, UP)
Pinot Bianco di Puglia, Vigna al Monte (AI)
★Regaleali Conte Tasca d'Almerita (VA)
1987
Corvo Bianco Duca di Salaparuta (GRE,
THR, PE)
1986
Lacryma Christi del Vesuvio, Scala (WIL)
1982
★Corvo Colomba Platino Bianco (HOG)

——————— **£6.00 to £8.99** ———————
1989
Falanghina Bianco, Mustilli (WCL)
1988
Greco di Tufo Mastroberardino (VA)
Lacryma Christi del Vesuvio,
Mastroberardino (BYR)

1987
Greco di Tufo Mastroberardino (GRE)

——————— **£9.00 to £10.99** ———————
1985
Trebbiano d'Abruzzo Valentini (WCL)
1983
Trebbiano d'Abruzzo Valentini (WCL)

SOUTHERN ROSÉ

——————— **Under £4.00** ———————
1989
Cellaro Rosato C.S. di Sambuca (UP)

SOUTHERN FORTIFIED

——————— **Under £5.00** ———————
Non-vintage
★Josephine Doré de Bartoli (VA)
Moscato Passito di Pantelleria Tanit (GRE)
Marsala Superiore Garibaldi Dolce (WHI)

——————— **£6.00 to £9.99** ———————
Non-vintage
Marsala Vigna la Miccia, de Bartoli (WCL,
TAN)
Moscato Passito di Pantelleria Tanit (TAN)
Vecchio Samperi 10-year-old, de Bartoli
(WCL, VA)

——————— **£10.00 to £14.99** ———————
Non-vintage
Moscato Passito di Pantelleria Bukkuram,
de Bartoli (WCL, VA, UP)
Il Marsala 20-year-old de Bartoli (WCL)
Vecchio Samperi 10-year-old, de Bartoli
(UP)
Vecchio Samperi 20-year-old, de Bartoli
(WCL)

——————— **c. £19.75** ———————
Non-vintage
★Vecchio Samperi 30-year-old, de Bartoli
(WCL)

RIOJA

RED

────────── Under £4.00 ──────────

1986
CVNE (MAJ, BEK, BYR)
Paternina Banda Azul (CH)
Sainsbury's Rioja (SAI)
Siglo Saco (NI)
1985
Beron (RAE, PE)
Campo Viejo (BYR, MOR)
CVNE (BYR)
★Marqués de Cáceres (HOG)
Paternina Banda Azul (BYR)
Rivarey (WHI)
Siglo Saco (NI)
1984
Marqués de Cáceres (WIZ)
Paternina Banda Azul (VIC)
1983
Domecq Domain (HOG)
1981
Beronia Reserva (HOG)

────────── £4.00 to £4.99 ──────────

1989
★Las Torres Merlot (LAY)
1988
Las Torres Merlot (LAY)
Marqués de Cáceres (BYR)
1987
CVNE (LAY)
El Coto (AUG)
1986
Campo Viejo (WHI)
Carta de Plata, Berberana (GRE, BE)
Lagunilla Valle Tinto (PD)
Marqués de Cáceres (AMI)
Paternina Banda Azul (PD, AUG)
Siglo Saco (MOR, PD)
Viña Real, CVNE (BIB)
1985
Campo Viejo Reserva (WHI, BIB, AUG)
Carta de Oro, Berberana (GRE)
Carta de Plata, Berberana (MOR)
Lagunilla Valle Tinto (BOT)
Marqués de Cáceres (LO, BO, GI, HAY, WHI, MOR, WCL, AUG, LAY, GRE, DAV, ALL, TAN, BER)
Marqués de Cáceres Reserva (AI)
Reserva Bodegas Santana (ASD)
Siglo Saco (BYR, GRE)

Viña Alberdi Crianza, Rioja Alta (WAI)
Viña Alberdi, Rioja Alta (ASK)
Viña Real, Reserva, CVNE (CH, WHI, MOR)
1984
Faustino V Reserva (BYR)
Gran Condal Reserva (WAI)
Muga (WIZ)
Solar de Samaniego (MOR)
Viña Alberdi, Rioja Alta (BYR)
1983
Campo Viejo Reserva (BYR)
Carta de Oro, Berberana (MOR, UN)
CVNE 5th year (MOR)
Domecq Domain Reserva (BO, GRE, VIC, BOT)
Faustino V Reserva (BYR)
Marqués de Riscal (BYR)
Viña Pomal, Bilbainas (BYR, MOR)
1982
Berberana Reserva (BYR)
★Beronia Reserva (RAE)
Coto de Imaz Reserva (BO)
1981
Domecq Domain (UN)
★Olarra Reserva (HIC)

────────── £5.00 to £5.99 ──────────

1986
CVNE (AN, CB)
CVNE 3rd year (BOT)
Marqués de Riscal Reserva (CH)
1985
CVNE Reserva (OD, LOR)
Faustino V Reserva (MOR, WHI, WIL)
Marqués de Cáceres (VIN, LA, HAH)
Marqués de Riscal Reserva (VIC, GI, MOR)
Viña Alberdi, Rioja Alta (LA, GRE)
Viña Real, CVNE (HUN)
1984
Muga (BYR, ALL)
Viña Alberdi, Rioja Alta (HA, AI)
1983
Faustino V Reserva (GRE, WHI)
Marqués de Murrieta (ASD)
Viña Bosconia, López de Heredia (WHI)
Viña Zaco, Bilbainas (BYR)
1982
Beronia Reserva (OD)
Imperial Reserva CVNE (BYR)
Solar de Samaniego Reserva (BYR)
Viña Arana, Rioja Alta (BYR)
Viña Herminia (PD)
Tondonia Reserva, López de Heredia (BYR)

1981
St Michael Marqués del Romeral (MAR)
Siglo Gran Reserva (NI)
1980
★Paternina Gran Reserva (BYR)
Reserva Mariscol (WS)
Siglo Saco Gran Reserva (GRE)

───────── £6.00 to £6.99 ─────────
1986
Muga (LA)
1985
Berberana Reserva (ELL)
Coto de Imaz Reserva (LA)
Marqués de Riscal (GRE, LA, ELL, TAN, PE)
1984
Contino Reserva (LOR, ASK)
Marqués de Murrieta (PD, WIL, BOT)
Remelluri (TAN)
Viña Albina Reserva, Bodegas Riojanas
   (MOR)
1983
Beronia Reserva (LA)
Marqués de Riscal (UN)
1982
Beronia Reserva (BIB, LA)
★Faustino I Gran Reserva (HOG)
Faustino V (UN)
Marqués de Cáceres Reserva (BYR)
Viña Albina Gran Reserva, Bodegas
   Riojanas (BYR)
★Viña Ardanza, Rioja Alta (BYR, HOG, VIC)
Viña Real Gran Reserva, CVNE (BYR)
1981
Campo Viejo Gran Reserva (AUG)
Conde de la Salceda Gran
   Reserva (TAN)
Coto de Imaz Gran Reserva (AUG)
Faustino I Gran Reserva (ASD)
Imperial Gran Reserva CVNE (ASK)
Imperial Reserva CVNE (PIP)
Marqués de Cáceres Reserva (WHI)
Solar de Samaniego Reserva (MOR)
★Tondonia Reserva, López de Heredia (CH)
Viña Real Gran Reserva, CVNE (PIP, LOR,
   LAY)
Viña Real Reserva, CVNE (LOR, BEK)
1978
Campo Viejo Gran Reserva (GI, BYR)
Marqués de Cáceres Reserva (BO)
1975
★Berberana Gran Reserva (BYR)
Beronia Gran Reserva (BYR)
1973
Lagunilla Gran Reserva (UP)

───────── £7.00 to £7.99 ─────────
1987
Imperial Reserva CVNE (WCL)
1985
Contino Reserva (PIP)
Imperial Reserva CVNE (LOR, PIP, AD, BAR)
Marqués de Murrieta (WHI)
Remelluri (WS)
Viña Bosconia 5th year (LA)
Viña Real Reserva, CVNE (PIP, BIB)
1984
Contino Reserva (DAV, LAY, LAY, AMI, RAE)
Viña Ardanza Reserva, Rioja Alta (ASK)
1983
★Monte Real Reserva Bodegas Riojanas
   (VIG)

1982
Faustino I Gran Reserva (BO, GRE)
Lagunilla Gran Reserva (BOT)
Viña Ardanza Reserva, Rioja Alta (BEK,
   LAY)
1981
Berberana Reserva (HA)
Faustino I Reserva (MOR)
Gran Condal Gran Reserva (EL)
Imperial Gran Reserva CVNE (LAY, PIP)
Viña Arana, Rioja Alta (LA)
Viña Real Gran Reserva, CVNE (CB)
1980
Campo Viejo Gran Reserva (MOR, WHI)
Gran Reserva, Berberana (BY)
1978
Berberana Gran Reserva (GRE)
Beronia Reserva (BYR)
1975
Gran Zaco Gran Reserva (BYR)
★Viña Pomal Gran Reserva, Bilbainas
   (BYR)

───────── £8.00 to £9.99 ─────────
1985
Contino Reserva (BIB, BER)
Marqués de Murrieta (DAV, GRE, LA, BAR)

Marqués de Murrieta Gran Reserva (RAE)
Ygay, Marqués de Murrieta (LAY)
1984
Marqués de Murrieta (TAN)
Viña Tondonia, López de Heredia (LA, TAN)
1983
Viña Ardanza Reserva, Rioja Alta (AD, AV)
1982
Faustino I Gran Reserva (WHI)
Faustino V Gran Reserva (BL)
Viña Ardanza Reserva, Rioja Alta (AV, BOT,
HAY, MOR, PD, REI)
1981
Faustino I (BOT)
Faustino I Gran Reserva (UN)
Imperial Gran Reserva CVNE (AN, TAN, VIN,
VIG, MOR)
Viña Arana Reserva, Rioja Alta (AI)
1980
Viña Ardanza, Rioja Alta (AI)
1978
Campo Viejo Gran Reserva (BIB)
Gran Reserva, Berberana (BY)
Marqués de Cáceres Gran Reserva (ALL,
HAH)
Marqués de Cáceres Reserva (LAY, MOR)
Muga Prado Enea (BO)
Reserva 904 Gran Reserva Rioja Alta (BYR)
1975
Berberana Gran Reserva (MOR, GRE)
Beronia Gran Reserva (CH, LA)
Gran Reserva, Berberana (BY)
Marqués de Cáceres Gran Reserva (DI)
Monte Real Gran Reserva, Bodegas
Riojanas (MAJ, MOR)
★Reserva 904 Gran Reserva Rioja Alta
(HOG)
Viña Albina Gran Reserva, Bodegas
Riojanas (MOR)

─────── **£10.00 to £13.99** ───────
1982
Muga Prado Enea Reserva (BYR)
1981
Muga Prado Enea Reserva (ALL)
Viña Real Gran Reserva, CVNE (BER)
1978
Beronia Gran Reserva (BIB)
Muga Prado Enea Reserva (ALL)
1976
Reserva 904 Gran Reserva Rioja Alta (LAY,
LA, PE, VIG, MOR, AI, CB, REI)
1975
Reserva 904 Gran Reserva Rioja Alta (GRE,
ALL, AD)

─────── **£14.00 to £18.99** ───────
1978
Marqués de Murrieta Gran Reserva (RAE,
BO)
1976
Tondonia Gran Reserva, López de Heredia
(TAN)
1975
Marqués de Murrieta Gran Reserva (RAE,
BAR)
1973
Viña Bosconia Gran Reserva, López de
Heredia (MOR)

─────── **£25.00 to £29.99** ───────
1971
Marqués de Riscal Reserva (VIG)
Monte Real Gran Reserva, Bodegas
Riojanas (VIG)
1970
Marqués de Murrieta Gran Reserva (MOR)

─────── **£30.00 to £39.99** ───────
1968
Imperial Gran Reserva CVNE (VIG)
1964
Monte Real Gran Reserva, Bodegas
Riojanas (VIG)
Viña Real Gran Reserva, CVNE (VIG)
1961
Campo Viejo Gran Reserva (VIG)
1942
Ygay, Marqués de Murrieta (HUN)

─────── **£40.00 to £51.99** ───────
1968
Ygay, Marqués de Murrieta (AD)
1964
Marqués de Murrieta Gran Reserva (MOR)
1960
Marqués de Murrieta (TW)
1951
Viña Real Gran Reserva, CVNE (VIG)
1942
Ygay Gran Reserva, Marqués de Murrieta
(RAE, UP, AD, MOR)

WHITE

─────── **Under £4.00** ───────
Non-vintage
Tesco White Rioja (TES)
1989
Rivarey Blanco (DI)
Viura CVNE (WHI)

1988
Carta de Plata, Berberana (BYR)
El Coto (AUG)
★Marqués de Cáceres (LO, BYR, HAY)
Paternina Banda Dorada (VIC)
Sainsbury's Rioja Seco (SAI)
Siglo Saco (NI)
Viura CVNE (WHI)
1987
Añares Seco, Olarra (WAI)
Marqués de Cáceres (BO, WIZ, GI, MOR, HUN)
Muga (WIZ)
Solar de Samaniego (MOR)
1986
Marqués de Cáceres (HOG)
1985
Viña Leonora, Rioja Alta (ASK, BYR)
1984
Faustino V (BYR)

───────── £4.00 to £4.99 ─────────
Non-vintage
Faustino V (BL)
1989
Marqués de Cáceres (AD, DI, WS, HAH, DAV)
Viura CVNE (BIB)
1988
Marqués de Cáceres (AI, AUG, WCL, GRE, WHI,
  DI, AMI, TAN, BER, LA)
Muga (BYR, ALL)
1987
Carta de Plata, Berberana (MOR)
CVNE Monopole (PIP, LAY)
Siglo Saco (MOR)
1986
CVNE Monopole (BEK, THR)
1985
CVNE Monopole (HUN, MOR, PE)
Monte Real, Bodegas Riojanas (MAJ)

───────── £5.00 to £5.99 ─────────
1989
Viña Ramon Balada Xarel-lo (BIB)
1988
Faustino V (BOT)
1987
Faustino V (MOR)
1986
CVNE Monopole (BIB, CB, TAN)
Faustino V (PD)
1985
CVNE (BAR)
CVNE Reserva (PIP)
1984
CVNE Monopole (PD)

Marqués de Murrieta (UP, WAI)
1983
Marqués de Murrieta (UP)

───────── £6.00 to £7.99 ─────────
1985
Marqués de Murrieta (BYR, MOR, WHI, GRE,
  WCL, RAE)
Ygay, Marqués de Murrieta (LAY)
1984
Marqués de Murrieta (PD, BOT, WIL, ALL, VIC)
1982
Tondonia, López de Heredia (VIG)

───────── £8.00 to £10.99 ─────────
1985
Marqués de Murrieta Reserva (BO, LA, DAV)
1984
Marqués de Murrieta Reserva (AV, TAN)
Tondonia, López de Heredia (LA)
1983
Tondonia Reserva, López de Heredia (MOR)

───────── £13.00 to £17.99 ─────────
1985
Marqués de Murrieta Gran Reserva (UP,
  RAE, AD)
1976
Marqués de Murrieta Reserva (BE)

───────── c. £20.00 ─────────
1962
Marqués de Murrieta Reserva Especial (UP)

───────── c. £38.00 ─────────
1962
Ygay Gran Reserva, Marqués de Murrieta
  (MOR)

ROSÉ

───────── Under £4.00 ─────────
1988
Marqués de Cáceres Rosado (BO)
Solar de Samaniego Rosado (MOR)
1985
★Marqués de Cáceres Rosado (HOG, BYR)

───────── £4.00 to £6.50 ─────────
1988
Marqués de Cáceres Rosado (DI, ALL)
Muga Alméndora (ALL)
1985
Marqués de Murrieta Rosado (BOT, MOR,
  BYR)

OTHER SPANISH TABLE WINES

RED

──────── Under £3.00 ────────

Non-vintage
Castillo del Ebro (PD)
Condestable, Jumilla (WHI)
Sainsbury's La Mancha (SAI)
1988
Castillo de Alhambra (SAI, THR)
Condestable, Jumilla (MOR)
Monte Ory (ALL)
1987
Sainsbury's Navarra (SAI)
1986
★Gran Feudo Chivite (SAF)

Sainsbury's Valdepeñas (SAI)
1983
Viña Albali Reserva, Felix Solis (AUG)
1978
Castillo del Ebro (BOT)

──────── £3.00 to £3.99 ────────

Non-vintage
Palacio de León (HUN, MOR)
1987
Monte Ory (AD)
★Sainsbury's Toro (SAI)
Sangredetoro Tres Torres (DI)
Torres Tres Torres (WHI, GRE)
1986
Condé de Caralt (MOR)
Coronas Torres (CH, BYR, DI, WHI, GRE)
Gran Colegiata (LOR, OD)
★Raimat Abadia (BO)
★Ribera del Duero 2nd year (MOR)
Sangredetoro Tres Torres (CH, DI)
Torres Tres Torres (BYR, WIL)
1985
Colegiata (HAY, LAY, PE)
Coronas Torres (HOG, BYR, GI, DI, WIL, WHI)
Gran Colegiata (BO, HAY, HUN)

1984
Sangredetoro Tres Torres (MOR)
Torres Tres Torres (WIZ)
Viña Albali Reserva, Felix Solis (BL)
1983
Coronas Torres (ASD)
Monte Ory Crianza (ALL)
1982
★Señorio de los Llanos Gran Reserva (LAY)
Señorio de los Llanos Reserva (HOG, BYR)
1981
Señorio de los Llanos Gran Reserva (MAJ)
Señorio de los Llanos Reserva (TES, VIC,
    BAR, HAY, HIC)
1975
Castillo de Tiebas (WHI, GI, BOT)

──────── £4.00 to £4.99 ────────

1987
Coronas Torres (DAV)
Raimat Abadia (SAI)
Tempranillo Raimat (OD)
1986
Coronas Torres (LAY, PE, TAN, LA, UP, PD)
Gran Colegiata (NI, PE, AD)
Raimat Abadia (VIC, OD, BL, LA)
Sangredetoro Tres Torres (THR, PD, UP)
1985
Condé de Caralt (HA, MOR)
★Gran Sangredetoro Torres (MOR, WHI, GRE,
    BYR, DI)
Masía Bach (MOR)
Sangredetoro Tres Torres (BOT)
1984
Coronas Torres (UN, VIC, VIN)
Gran Sangredetoro Torres (RAE, CH, BYR, GI,
    DI, WHI)
Viña Magdala, Torres (DI)
1983
Marqués de Monistrol Gran Reserva (GI)
Monte Ory (VIN)
René Barbier Reserva (WHI)
★Viña Magdala, Torres (DI)
1982
Gran Colegiata (HAY, HUN)
1981
Gran Sangredetoro Torres (HOG)
Viña Magdala, Torres (MOR)
1978
Señorio de los Llanos (BOT, HA)
Señorio de los Llanos Gran Reserva (PE,
    GRE, AI, MOR, LA, WS)

──────── £5.00 to £5.99 ────────

Non-vintage
Ribera del Duero 5th year (BYR)
1989
Las Torres (BE)
1987
Tempranillo Ochoa (LOR)
1986
Gran Sangredetoro Torres (BE, LA, HIC)
Priorato Extra, Barril (WCL)
Viña Magdala, Torres (BE)
1985
Gran Colegiata Crianza (BAR)
Gran Coronas Torres (HOG, BYR, CH, MOR,
    WIL, WHI, GRE, BO, WCL)
Gran Sangredetoro Torres (AI, BE, OD, VIC)
★Raimat Cabernet Sauvignon (BYR)
1984
Gran Coronas Torres (BYR)
Gran Sangredetoro Torres (WRI, UP, THR)
Raimat Cabernet Sauvignon (GRE, VIC)
Senoro de Lazán Reserva Montesierra,
    Somontano (TAN)
Viña Magdala, Torres (WHI, GRE, BL, BE, LA)
1983
Gran Coronas Torres (WHI, RAE, GI)
Viña Magdala, Torres (WHI, BYR, CH, GI, WIL)
1982
Ochoa Reserva (LOR, AI, PE)
1978
★Castillo de Tiebas Reserva (BIB)

──────── £6.00 to £6.99 ────────

1986
Gran Coronas Torres (DAV)
1985
Gran Coronas Torres (DI, UP, BE, SAI)
Raimat Cabernet Sauvignon (LA, THR)
1984
Raimat Cabernet Sauvignon (BAR)
1983
Gran Toc Reserva, Cavas Hill (ALL)
1982
Ochoa Reserva (TAN)
Viña del Perdon, Señorio de Sarria (MOR)
1981
Gran Viña Magdala, Torres (CH, GRE, DI)

──────── £7.00 to £7.99 ────────

1985
★Marqués de Griñon Cabernet Sauvignon
    (BYR)
1984
Marqués de Griñon Cabernet Sauvignon
    (ALL)

1983
Cabernet Sauvignon Jean León (BOT)
Marqués de Griñon Cabernet Sauvignon
    (UP, BYR)
★Mauro (DAV)
1982
Marqués de Griñon Cabernet Sauvignon
    (BO)
1980
Cabernet Sauvignon Jean León (LAY)

──────── £8.00 to £9.99 ────────

1987
Pesquera Fernandez (RAE, LA)
1986
Farina Crianza Toro, Farina (TAN)
Pesquera Fernandez (AD, OD)
Ribera del Duero Crianza (TAN)
1984
Marqués de Griñon Cabernet Sauvignon
    (AD, CB, MOR, BO, HUN, GRE, WRI)
Mauro (WS)
1983
Marqués de Murrieta (PD)
Protos Ribera del Duero (DI)
1980
★Cabernet Sauvignon Jean León (HAY,
    WCL)

──────── £10.00 to £14.99 ────────

1985
Gran Coronas Black Label, Torres (GRE)
Pesquera Fernandez (BYR, CD, AD, TAN, DI)
Valbuena 3rd year (ASK)
1984
Pesquera Reserva, Fernandez (RAE, BE)
1983
Gran Coronas Black Label, Torres (HOG,
    BYR, CH, UP, WHI, RAE)
1982
Gran Coronas Black Label, Torres (WIL)
1981
Cabernet Sauvignon Jean León (MOR, AI)
1979
Cabernet Sauvignon Jean León (LA)
Valbuena 3rd year (GRE)

──────── £15.00 to £19.99 ────────

1985
Valbuena 3rd year (DI, VIG)
1984
Valbuena 3rd year (LA)
1983
Gran Coronas Black Label, Torres (WRI, LA,
    REI, AI, DI, MOR, PE)

1982
Gran Coronas Black Label, Torres (UP, DI, OD)
1981
Gran Coronas Black Label, Torres (MOR)
1978
Gran Coronas Reserva, Torres (HA)
Valbuena 5th year (GRE)
1976
Gran Coronas Black Label, Torres (UP)
1971
Gran Coronas Black Label, Torres (GRE)

──────── £20.00 to £24.99 ────────
1984
Valbuena 5th year (DI)
1983
Valbuena 5th year (LA)
1982
Valbuena 5th year (MOR)
1975
Gran Coronas Black Label, Torres (UP, MOR)

──────── £25.00 to £29.99 ────────
1985
Valbuena 5th year (VIG)
1976
Vega Sicilia Unico (ASK)
1971
Gran Coronas Black Label, Torres (MOR, UP)

──────── £30.00 to £39.99 ────────
1979
Vega Sicilia Unico (MOR, TAN, DI, HA, REI)
1976
Vega Sicilia Unico (BO, MOR, GRE)

──────── £48.00 to £64.00 ────────
1962
Vega Sicilia Unico (REI, DI, MOR)

WHITE

──────── Under £3.00 ────────
Non-vintage
Castillo de Liria (WAI)
Castillo de San Diego, Barbadillo (HOG)
★Sainsbury's Moscatel de Valencia (SAI)
Tesco Spanish Sweet White Wine (TES)
1988
Castillo de Alhambra (THR)

──────── £3.00 to £3.99 ────────
Non-vintage
Armonioso, Bodegas Los Llanos (AI, TAN)

Moscatel Valencia Castillo de Ciria (TAN)
Palacio de León Blanco Seco (MOR)
1989
San Valentin Torres (DI)
Viña Esmeralda, Torres (DI)
Viña Sol, Torres (DI, BE, AUG)
1988
Blanc Cru, Cavas Hill (ALL)
Castillo de San Diego, Barbadillo (PE)
Marqués de Gastanaga, Megia (ALL)
★Rueda Castilla la Vieja, Sanz (PE)
San Valentin Torres (DI)
Viña Sol, Torres (CH, BYR, WHI, MAJ, GRE, LAY, TES, UP, BE, PE)
Viña Vermella (BAR)
1987
Condé de Caralt (MOR)
Gran Viña Sol Torres (BYR)
Viña Esmeralda, Torres (MOR, WIZ)
Viña Sol, Torres (MOR)
1986
Colegiata (PE)
Viña Sol, Torres (HOG, WIZ)

──────── £4.00 to £4.99 ────────
1989
Gran Viña Sol Torres (BE)
Viña Esmeralda, Torres (WHI, WCL, WIL, BE, LA, DAV, ELL)
Viña Sol, Torres (LA, DAV, AN)
1988
Extrísimo Bach (AI)
Gran Viña Sol Torres (BYR, DI, GI, GRE, WHI, BE, VIC, TAN, UP, PE)
Marqués de Alella (MOR)
★Raimat Chardonnay (BO, BYR, VIC)
Viña Esmeralda, Torres (BYR, CH, WHI, GRE, VIC, AI, UP, PE, WRI, TAN, BOT)
1987
Gran Viña Sol Torres (DI, WHI, WIL, AI)
1986
Gran Viña Sol Torres (MOR)
Marqués de Riscal Blanco Rueda (MOR)
Viña Esmeralda, Torres (PD)
1984
Marqués de Riscal Blanco Rueda (WIL)
Viña Sol, Torres (VIN)

──────── £5.00 to £5.99 ────────
1988
Marqués de Griñon (PE, ALL)
Marqués de Riscal Blanco Rueda (ELL)
Raimat Chardonnay (THR, LA)
1987
Gran Viña Sol Torres (BOT, RAE, BYR)

Marqués de Griñon (MOR)
Marqués de Riscal Blanco Rueda (TAN)
1984
Gran Viña Sol Green Label, Torres (HOG)

──────── **£6.00 to £7.99** ────────
1989
Lagar de Cervera (LA)
Rias Baixas, Lagar de Cevera (AI)
1988
Gran Viña Sol Reserva, Torres (AD, WHI,
  GRE, GI, TAN, UP, LA)
1987
Gran Viña Sol Green Label, Torres (WHI,
  WIL, BOT, CH)

──────── **£11.00 to £15.99** ────────
1989
Milmanda Chardonnay Torres (DI)
1987
Chardonnay Jean León (BYR, LA)
1984
Chardonnay Jean León (GRE, MOR)

──────── **£16.00 to £20.00** ────────
1988
Chardonnay Jean León (REI)
Milmanda Chardonnay Torres (GRE, VIG,
  PE)
1987
Milmanda Chardonnay Torres (RAE, REI)

ROSÉ

──────── **Under £4.00** ────────
Non-vintage
Palacio de León Rosado (MOR)
1988
de Casta Rosado, Torres (CH, DI, BYR, BE,
  MOR)
1987
Condestable Jumilla (MOR)
1986
de Casta Rosado, Torres (WIZ)

SPARKLING

──────── **Under £5.00** ────────
Non-vintage
Castellblanch Cristal Seco (WAI, AUG)
Castellblanch Extra Seco (DI)
Condé de Caralt Brut (MOR, WIZ)
Condé de Caralt Rosado (BYR)
Jean Perico Brut (HOG)
Marqués de Monistrol Brut (BO)

Sainsbury's Cava Sparkling Wine (SAI)
Segura Viudas Brut (HOG, DI)

──────── **£5.00 to £5.99** ────────
Non-vintage
Castellblanch Brut Zero (DI)
Castellblanch Cristal Seco (BOT)
Codorníu Brut (MOR, VIC)
Condé de Caralt Blanc de Blancs (MOR)
Freixenet Brut Nature (AUG)
Freixenet Brut Rosé (WHI, LOR, PIP, WCL)
Freixenet Carta Nevada (WHI, PD, PIP, BOT)
★Freixenet Cordon Negro Brut (WHI, PE,
  PD)
Jean Perico Brut (UN)
Marqués de Monistrol Brut (UN, BL, GI, PE)
Marqués de Monistrol Rosé Brut (AUG, PE)
Marqués de Monistrol Gran Cremant (UN,
  BL)
★Raimat Chardonnay Brut (VIC)
1986
Freixenet Cordon Negro Brut (ASK, BL, TAN)
1985
Condé de Caralt Brut (MOR)
Freixenet Brut Nature (LOR, MOR)
Freixenet Cordon Negro Brut (LOR, MAJ,
  MOR, PIP, DAV, BOT, BYR)
1984
Freixenet Cordon Negro Brut (LAY)
1983
Condé de Caralt Brut (BYR)

──────── **£6.00 to £7.99** ────────
Non-vintage
Raimat Chardonnay Brut (BYR, THR)

FORTIFIED

──────── **Under £4.00** ────────
Non-vintage
Montilla Cream, Bodegas Alvear (HOG, MAJ,
  LAY)
Montilla Medium Dry, Bodegas Alvear
  (MAJ, LAY, TAN)
Montilla Pale Dry, Bodegas Alvear (HOG,
  MAJ, LAY, TAN)

──────── **£4.00 to £5.99** ────────
Non-vintage
★Málaga Solera 1885 Scholtz (WAI, LA)

──────── **£6.00 to £6.99** ────────
Non-vintage
Málaga Lagrima 10 años Scholtz (GRE, TAN)
Málaga Solera 1885 Scholtz (PE, GRE, BAR)

SHERRY

DRY

Under £4.00

Double Century Fino, Domecq (BO)
Elegante, Gonzalez Byass (HOG, AUG, PD)
Fino Bertola (HOG)
Harvey's Luncheon Dry (HOG, BO)
Lustau Fino (MAJ, DI)
★Manzanilla de Sanlúcar, Barbadillo (OD, PIP)
Waitrose Fino Sherry (WAI)

£4.00 to £4.99

Croft Delicado (HOG)
Don Zoilo Very Old Fino (BYR)
Elegante, Gonzalez Byass (BOT, WHI, UN, SAF, TES, BYR, BL, WIL)
Fino Bandera, Domingo Pérez Marín (WW)
Fino de Balbaina, Barbadillo (PE, BAR)
Fino de Sanlúcar, Barbadillo (BIB)
Fino Hidalgo (STA, NI)
Fino Quinta Osborne (BYR)
la Gitana Manzanilla, Hidalgo (HOG, WAI, STA, HAG, WW)
Harvey's Bristol Fino (WIL)
Harvey's Luncheon Dry (SAF, WHI, WRI, HA, CH, WIL, HAG, UN)

★Lustau Dry Oloroso (DI)
Lustau Palo Cortado (DI)
Manzanilla de Sanlúcar, Barbadillo (BL, IR, BAR, HOG, HAG, LA, HIC)
Manzanilla Pasada Solear, Barbadillo (PIP)
Manzanilla Pastora, Barbadillo (HAY)
Mariscal Fino, Hidalgo (TAN)
Ostra Manzanilla (LAY)
Rare Fino Solera 1914 Berisford (BYR)
San Patricio Fino, Garvey (HOG)
Tio Mateo Fino, Palomino & Vergara (HA)
Tio Pepe, Gonzalez Byass (HOG, BO)
Valdespino Fino (AS)

£5.00 to £6.99

Croft Delicado (WHI, WIL)
Don Tomas Amontillado, Valdespino (BY)
Don Zoilo Very Old Fino (BY, HAG)
Fino de Balbaina, Barbadillo (HAG, LA, CB, HIC)
Fino Especial, Hidalgo (STA, TAN)
Fino Superior Miraflores, Hidalgo (WS)
Fino Tomás Abad (WIC, BOD)
la Gitana Manzanilla, Hidalgo (HAH)
la Ina, Domecq (HOG, HAH, WHI, PD, BOT, CH, WIL, UN, DAV, AN, EL)
Inocente Fino, Valdespino (VIN, OL, BYR, AS, WS, WCL)
Jerez Cortado, Hidalgo (TAN)
La Lidia Manzanilla, Garvey (BYR)
Lustau Dry Oloroso (BAR, EL, HIG)
Lustau Fino (HUN, HIG)
Lustau Palo Cortado (HUN, BAR, HIG)
Manzanilla de Sanlúcar, Barbadillo (CB, BIB, AN)
Manzanilla Pasada Solear, Barbadillo (BO, IR, WS, LA, BIB, HIC, PE)
Oloroso Dry, Hidalgo (TAN)
Palo Cortado del Carrascal, Valdespino (OL)
Palo Cortado, Valdespino (WCL)
San Patricio Fino, Garvey (BOT, BYR, PD, HAH, HAG, WS, MAJ, AN, WRI)
Tio Diego Amontillado, Valdespino (OL)
★Tio Guillermo Amontillado, Garvey (BYR)
Tio Pepe, Gonzalez Byass (BOT, WRI, WCL, PD, OD, WHI, BL, AUG, CH, UN, SAF, TES, BYR, HAH, DAV, WIL, VIN, AN, EL)
Vino de Pasto, Lustau (LA)

£7.00 to £8.99

Don Tomas Amontillado, Valdespino (OL)
Don Zoilo Pale Dry Manzanilla (WIL, REI, BAR)
Manzanilla Pasada Solera 1914 Berisford (TW)
Oloroso Seco Barbadillo (LA, PIP)
Palo Cortado del Carrascal, Valdespino (PE)
Tio Diego Amontillado, Valdespino (WS, WCL)

£9.00 to £10.99

Amontillado de Sanlúcar Almacenista, Cuevas Jurado (BL)
Harvey's Palo Cortado (HA)
Manzanilla de Sanlúcar Almacenista, Heredos de Arqueso (BL)

Oloroso Seco, Barbadillo (HIC, BIB)
Palo Cortado, Don Beningo (BIB, HIC)
Pemartin Fino Solera 1820 (TW)
Pemartin Manzanilla Solera 1820 (TW)

MEDIUM

──────── **Under £4.00** ────────
Amontillado de Sanlúcar, Barbadillo (PIP)
Amontillado Lustau (MAJ, DI)
Amontillado Martial, Valdespino (HAH)
Concha Amontillado, Gonzalez Byass (HOG, AUG)
Double Century Amontillado (BO)
Harvey's Club Amontillado (HOG, BO)
Waitrose Amontillado Sherry (WAI)

──────── **£4.00 to £4.99** ────────
Amontillado de Sanlúcar, Barbadillo (IR, BAR, HAY, HAG, LA, HIC)
Amontillado Napoleon, Hidalgo (NI, AD, HAG)
Caballero Amontillado, Gonzalez Byass (TES, WIL)
Concha Amontillado, Gonzalez Byass (WCL, BOT, PD, WHI, SAF, TES, BL)
Dry Fly Amontillado, Findlater (BO, BYR, WIL)
Dry Sack, Williams & Humbert (HOG, AUG, WHI)
Harvey's Club Amontillado (TES, PD, WAI, CH, AUG, WHI, HA, WRI, BOT, BL, HAH, WIL, OD, HAG, DAV)
The Society's Medium Dry (WS)

──────── **£5.00 to £6.99** ────────
Amontillado de Sanlúcar, Barbadillo (BIB, AN)
Dry Fly Amontillado, Findlater (CH)
Dry Sack, Williams & Humbert (WIL, WRI, CH)
Harvey's Club Amontillado (UN, VIN, AN)
Lustau's Old East India (HOG)
Pedro Ximenez, Barbadillo (PIP)

──────── **£7.00 to £8.99** ────────
Amontillado 1914 Solera Berisford (TW)
Don Zoilo Amontillado (WIL, HAG, VIG)
Harvey's Fine Old Amontillado (HA)
★Oloroso Muy Viejo Almacenista, Lustau (HOG)
Palo Cortado, Barbadillo (PIP)
Principe Amontillado, Barbadillo (LA, BAR)
Sandeman Royal Corregidor Oloroso (HOG)
Sandeman's Royal Esmeralda (HOG)

──────── **£9.00 to £10.99** ────────
Amontillado del Duque, Gonzalez Byass (BYR, HOG, OD, REI)
★Apostoles Oloroso, Gonzalez Byass (HOG, OD)
Pemartin Amontillado Solera 1820 (TW)

──────── **£11.00 to £13.99** ────────
Amontillado del Duque, Gonzalez Byass (PE, RAE, LA, VIN)
Sandeman Royal Corregidor Oloroso (REI)

──────── **£14.00 to £24.00** ────────
Coliseo Amontillado, Valdespino (WCL, VIG)
Oloroso Extra Solera 70 years, Blázquez (AD)

SWEET

──────── **Under £4.00** ────────
Bertola Cream (HOG)
Double Century Cream (BO)
Double Century Oloroso (CH)
Oloroso Duquesa, Valdespino (ELL)
Oloroso Lustau (MAJ)

──────── **£4.00 to £4.99** ────────
Croft Original Pale Cream (HOG, BO, WAI, TES, AUG, BL, WHI, CH, UN, OD, PD)
Double Century Oloroso (WHI, UN, DAV)
Harvey's Bristol Cream (HOG, BO, OD)
Harvey's Copper Beech (BO)
The Society's Cream (WS)
Tanners Mariscal Cream (TAN)

──────── **£5.00 to £6.99** ────────
Croft Original Pale Cream (WRI, BOT, DAV, WIL, HAG, EL, VIN, SAF)
Harvey's Bristol Cream (WRI, HA, WHI, PD, BOT, TES, WIL, HAH, UN, DAV, AUG, CH, BL, HAG, VIN, AN)
Harvey's Bristol Milk (HA, CH, WIL, UN)
Sanlúcar Cream, Barbadillo (BAR)

──────── **£7.00 to £9.99** ────────
Amoroso Solera 1914 Berisford (TW)
Don Zoilo Rich Old Cream (HAG, WIL)
★Matusalem Oloroso, Gonzalez Byass (HOG, OD)

──────── **£10.00 to £13.99** ────────
Matusalem Oloroso, Gonzalez Byass (PE, RAE, LA, VIN)
Pemartin Cream Solera 1820 (TW)
Sandeman Rare Oloroso (BAR)

PORTUGUESE TABLE WINES

RED

──────── **Under £3.00** ────────

Non-vintage
★Quinta de Cardiga Ribatejo (TES)
★Sainsbury's Arruda (SAI)
Tesco Dão (TES)
1987
Bairrada Mealhada (WAI)
1986
Dão Grão Vasco (GI)
1985
★Bairrada Caves Aliança (MAJ)
Bairrada Dom Ferraz (AUG)
Dão Dom Ferraz (AUG)
★Dão Terras Altas, J.M. da Fonseca (WIZ, HUN)
1984
Coop Vinhos Arruda (OD)
★Periquita J.M. da Fonseca (WIZ)
1982
Dão Dom Ferraz (WCL)

──────── **£3.00 to £3.99** ────────

Non-vintage
Dão Vinicola Ribalonga (BOT)
1987
João Pires Meia Pipa (OD)
Periquita J.M. da Fonseca (DI)
1986
Douro Vila Regia (GI)
Douro Esteva (AUG)
Periquita J.M. da Fonseca (TAN, DI, WRI, PE, HUN)
Quinta de Santo Amaro, João Pires (WHI)
★Tinto da Anfora João Pires (OD)
1985
Bairrada Reserva Caves Aliança (AS, DI)
Bairrada Vila Regia (GI)
Dão Dom Ferraz (VIC, UN)
Dão Grão Vasco (PE, DAV)
Periquita J.M. da Fonseca (WHI)
★Quinta de Santo Amaro, João Pires (WHI, ALL)
1984
Bairrada Reserva Caves Aliança (DI)
Dão Porto dos Cavaleiros (LAY)
Tinto da Anfora João Pires (WAI)
1983
Bairrada Montanha Reserva (BAR)
Dão Grão Vasco Garrafeira (GI)
Tinto da Anfora João Pires (WIZ)

1982
★Bairrada Frei João (WRI)
Dão Dom Ferraz (VIN)
★Quinta de Camarate, J.M. da Fonseca (WHI)
1981
Colares Reserva Companhia Real Vinicola (BYR)
1980
Bairrada Frei João (GRE)
Dão Garrafeira Imperio (BOT)
Romeira Garrafeira (SAI)

──────── **£4.00 to £5.99** ────────

1987
Tinto da Anfora J.M. da Fonseca (DI)
1986
Bairrada Luis Pato (WCL)
Dão Terras Altas, J.M. da Fonseca (PIP)
★Quinta da Bacalhoa (SAI)
Quinta de Camarate, J.M. da Fonseca (DI)
1985
Dão Grão Vasco (AV)
Periquita J.M. da Fonseca (VIN)
Tinto Velho J.M. da Fonseca (BAR)
Tinto Velho Reguengos (ALL, WRI)
1984
Camarate J.M. da Fonseca (ALL, BYR, TAN, MAJ, PE, WRI, BAR)
Dão Porto dos Cavaleiros (ELL)
★Pasmados J.M. da Fonseca (ALL)

Quinta de Camarate, J.M. da Fonseca (AI)
Tinto da Anfora João Pires (BYR, ALL, AUG)
1983
Dão Porto dos Cavaleiros (HA)
Tinto da Anfora João Pires (WHI)
Tinto Velho Reguengos (BYR, TES)
1982
Bairrada Garrafeira, Montanha (UP)
Dão Grão Vasco Garrafeira (PE)
Periquita J.M. da Fonseca (VIN)

1981
Colares Reserva Companhia Real Vinicola
(WIL)
1980
Bairrada Frei João (WRI, LAY, HA)
Romeira Garrafeira (BOT)
1978
Garrafeira Caves Velhas (BOT)
Garrafeira Particular Caves Aliança (AS)
Pasmados J.M. da Fonseca (BYR)
1977
Periquita J.M. da Fonseca (BYR, ALL, GRE)
1976
Garrafeira Caves Velhas (WCL)

──────── £6.00 to £7.99 ────────
1985
Grande Escolha, Champalimaud (OD, AI)
Quinta da Cotto, Champalimaud (TAN)
1980
Garrafeira J.M. da Fonseca (AI, TAN)

WHITE

──────── Under £3.00 ────────
Non-vintage
Asda Vinho Verde (ASD)
Sainsbury's Vinho Verde (SAI)
St Michael Vinho Verde (MAR)
Vinho Verde Dom Ferraz (WAI, WCL, BOT)
Vinho Verde Gazela (GI)
1989
Bairrada Caves Aliança (SAI)
1988
★Dão Grão Vasco (GI)

──────── £3.00 to £3.99 ────────
Non-vintage
Vinho Verde Casal Garcia (AUG, PD, PE, BOT)
Vinho Verde Casalinhò (ASK, LAY, GRE, IR)
Vinho Verde Gatão (VIC, BO, BYR)
1989
Vinho Verde J.M. da Fonseca (PIP)
1988
Dão Grão Vasco (PE)
Dão Terras Altas J.M. da Fonseca (ALL,
BYR)
★João Pires Branco (WCL, OD)
Santa Marta, João Pires (ALL)
1987
Bairrada Caves Aliança (DI)
Bairrada Terra Franca (BL)
Dão Porto dos Cavaleiros (ASK)
Dão Terras Altas J.M. da Fonseca (BYR,
GRE, AI, WIL)

Dry Palmela Moscato, João Pires (ASK)
1986
Bucelas Velho Cavas Velhas (GRE)
Dão Grão Vasco (HAG)
1985
Vinho Verde Paco Teixeiro (WCL)
1982
Dão Terras Altas J.M. da Fonseca (VIN)

──────── £4.00 to £5.99 ────────
Non-vintage
Vinho Verde Arealva (UP)
Vinho Verde Aveleda (AV)
1989
Dão Terras Altas J.M. da Fonseca (PIP)
João Pires Branco (WHI, DI, PIP)
1988
Dry Palmela Moscato, João Pires (THR)
João Pires Branco (MAJ, SAI, ALL, WHI, GRE,
DI, WIL)
Palmela João Pires (AUG, VIC)
1986
★Planalto (HAG)

ROSÉ

──────── Under £4.00 ────────
Non-vintage
Mateus Rosé (ASD, HOG, WAI, SAI, BO, WRI,
TES, SAF, WHI, BYR, VIC, AUG)

──────── £4.00 to £4.99 ────────
Non-vintage
Mateus Rosé (CH, BL, DAV, EL, WIL, PE, UN,
VIN)

FORTIFIED

──────── Under £6.00 ────────
Non-vintage
Moscatel de Setúbal J.M. da Fonseca (HOG)
1986
Moscatel de Setúbal J.M. da Fonseca (ALL)
1985
★Moscatel de Setúbal J.M. da Fonseca
(WHI)

──────── £6.00 to £6.99 ────────
1981
Moscatel de Setúbal Caves Palmela (HA)

──────── £11.00 to £13.00 ────────
Non-vintage
Moscatel de Setúbal 20-year-old J.M. da
Fonseca (GRE, ALL, TAN, WIL)

PORT

Under £5.00

Non-vintage
Barros (BYR)
Cockburn's Fine Tawny (HOG)
Graham Ruby (NI)
Sandeman Fine Old Ruby (BO)
Sandeman Fine Old White (BO)
Waitrose Fine Ruby (WAI)
Waitrose Fine Tawny (WAI)

£5.00 to £5.99

Non-vintage
Cockburn's Fine Ruby (BO, WAI, WHI, TES, SAF, HA, HAG, AUG)
Cockburn's Fine Tawny (WHI, HA, HAG, UN)
Cockburn's Fine White (WHI, HA)
Cockburn's Special Reserve (HOG)
Croft Triple Crown (PD, BOT)
Delaforce Special White Port (WIL)
Quinta do Noval Old Coronation Ruby (BYR)
Sandeman Fine Old Ruby (THR)
Sandeman Fine Old White (BL)
Sandeman Tawny (THR, BL, OD)
Smith Woodhouse Fine Tawny (WCL)
Smith Woodhouse Ruby (WCL, BYR, DAV, UN)
Van Zellers Ruby (CH)
Van Zellers White (CH)
Waitrose Vintage Character (WAI)
Warre's Ruby (AUG, BYR)
Warre's Tawny (BYR)

£6.00 to £6.99

Non-vintage
Churchill's Finest Vintage Character (HUN)
Cockburn's Special Reserve (BO, WAI, WHI, CH, TES, HA, SAF)
Delaforce Special White Port (BOT)
Dow's Fine Ruby (AN)
Dow's Fine Tawny (AN)
Dow's Vintage Character (HOG)
Fonseca Bin 27 (HOG)
Quinta do Noval White (BYR)
Sandeman Founder's Reserve (OD)
Taylor Chip Dry White Port (BYR)
Taylor Special Ruby (HAH)
Taylor Special Tawny (HAH)
★Warre's Nimrod Old Tawny (NI)
Warre's Warrior (BYR)
1982
Dow's Late Bottled (MAJ)
Graham Late Bottled (NI)

1979
★Graham Late Bottled (HOG)

£7.00 to £8.99

Non-vintage
Churchill Dry White (IR, TAN, WW)
Churchill's Finest Vintage Character (IR, ASK, LOR, HAY, BAR, WW)
Cockburn's 10-year-old Tawny (WAI)
Cockburn's Fine Ruby (EL)
Cockburn's Special Reserve (BOT, BL, THR, AUG, WIL, OD, PD, UN, EL)
Delaforce His Eminence's Choice (IR, WIL, PD)
Dow's No. 1 White (AN)
Dow's Vintage Character (HAG, OD, WIL, AN)
★Fonseca 10-year-old Tawny (HOG)
Fonseca Bin 27 (WHI, CH, WAI, WIL, HAG, BE, HAH, GRE, BYR, BL, WRI, VIC, AI, PIP)
Fonseca Dry White (AS, PIP)
Graham 10-year-old Tawny (NI)
Offley Boa Vista (WIL)
Quinta do Noval Extra Dry White (GRE, AI)
Sandeman Founder's Reserve (WIL, AUG, BL)
Taylor Chip Dry White Port (WIL, HAG, DAV)
Warre's 10-year-old Tawny (AUG)
Warre's Warrior (AUG)
1984
Cockburn's Late Bottled (SAF)
Taylor Late Bottled (HOG, BL, TES, BO, THR)
1983
Fonseca Late Bottled (WIZ, HIG)
Ramos-Pinto Late Bottled (BEK)
Sandeman Late Bottled (THR)
Van Zellers Late Bottled Vintage (CH)
1982
Cockburn's Late Bottled (WHI)
Dow's Late Bottled (LOR)
Graham Late Bottled (BO, WHI, GRE, THR, AI)
Taylor Late Bottled (OD)
1981
Graham Late Bottled (BL, OD)
Sandeman Late Bottled (BL)
1980
Royal Oporto (TES)

£9.00 to £11.99

Non-vintage
Churchill's Finest Vintage Character (MV, VIN)
Cockburn's 10-year-old Tawny (WHI, TES, SAF, VIC, HA, THR)

Dow's 10-year-old Tawny (HAG, MV, AN)
Dow's Boardroom Tawny (HOG)
★Fonseca 10-year-old Tawny (WIZ, BYR, CH,
   AS, REI, BYR, HIG, PIP, VIN)
Fonseca Bin 27 (VIN)
Graham 10-year-old Tawny (GRE, BIB)
Martinez 10-year-old Tawny (STA, BAR)
Quinta da Ervamoira 10-year-old Tawny
   (BEK)
Quinta do Noval 10-year-old Tawny (BYR,
   WHI, AI, UN)
Sandeman 10-year-old Royal Tawny (OD)
Tanners Crusted (TAN)
★Taylor 10-year-old Tawny (GRE, WHI, BYR,
   WIL, BL, LAY, OD, PD, WRI, TAN, BOT)
Van Zellers 10-year-old Tawny (CH)
Warre's Nimrod Old Tawny (AUG)

Wellington Wood Port (BER)
1986
Churchill's Crusted Port Bottled 1986 (BY,
   LOR, IR)
Martinez Crusted (AV)
1985
Churchill's Crusted Port Bottled 1985 (CB,
   IR, HAY, BYR, BAR)
Fonseca 10-year-old Tawny (BAR)
1983
Offley Boa Vista (WHI)
Royal Oporto (HUN, WRI, DI)
1982
Quinta da Eira Velha (HA)
Sandeman (LO)
1980
Croft Quinta da Roeda (OD)
Warre Late Bottled (HAY)
1978
★Graham Quinta do Malvedos (NI)
1977
Offley Boa Vista (BL)
1976
Warre Late Bottled (WCL, MV, HAH)

────── **£12.00 to £14.99** ──────
Non-vintage
★Dow's 20-year-old Tawny (BO)
Graham 20-year-old Tawny (NI)
Martinez 20-year-old Tawny (STA)
Sandeman 20-year-old Tawny (BL, TES, OD)
1985
Gould Campbell (DI)
1983
Churchill's Quinta do Agua Alta (ASK, HAY)
Dow (BO)
Gould Campbell (GI, PIP)
Graham (BO)
Quarles Harris (GI)
Royal Oporto (TW, VIN)
Smith Woodhouse (GI)
★Taylor (BO)
Warre (BO, LO)
1982
Churchill (HUN, HAH, LAY, BER)
Croft (GI, LAY)
Martinez (AD)
Quinta do Noval (LAY, AD, DI)
Ramos-Pinto Tawny (BEK)
Sandeman (GI, AD)
1980
Delaforce Quinta da Corte (OD, CB)
Gould Campbell (BER)
Royal Oporto (AS)
1979
Dow Quinta do Bomfim (OD)
Warre's Late Bottled (VIC, TAN)
Warre's Quinta da Cavadinha (THR, LAY,
   PIP)
1978
Fonseca Guimaraens (LAY, GRE)
Graham Quinta do Malvedos (OD, WHI, GRE)
Taylor Quinta de Vargellas (AUG)
Warre's Quinta da Cavadinha (REI, BO, WAI)
1974
Fonseca Guimaraens (THR)
Taylor Quinta de Vargellas (HOG)

────── **£15.00 to £19.99** ──────
Non-vintage
Cockburn's 20-year-old Tawny (WHI, HA,
   VIC)
Dow's 20-year-old Tawny (HAG, AN)
Fonseca 20-year-old (BAR, PIP)
Graham 20-year-old Tawny (GRE)
Quinta da Bom Retiro 20-year-old Tawny
   (BEK, BO)
Quinta do Noval 20-year-old Tawny (WHI)
Taylor 20-year-old Tawny (BYR, WHI, EL,
   GRE, WIL, BOT, LAY, HAG)

Van Zellers 20-year-old Tawny (CH)
William Pickering 20-year-old Tawny (BER)
1985
Churchill (HAY, GI, HA, CH)
Cockburn (BIB, GI)
Croft (GI, TAN)
Dow (BIB, GI, BO, WHI)
Fonseca (BO)
Graham (GI, GRE, BO)
Sandeman (GI, BIB)
Smith Woodhouse (DI)
Taylor (GRE)
Warre (BIB, GI, CH, MV)
1983
Churchill's Quinta do Agua Alta (AD, LAY)
Cockburn (DAV)
Dow (GRE, OD, BYR, ! AY, DAV, AD)
Fonseca (BIB, MV)
Graham (BIB, DAV)
Offley Boa Vista (HA)
Quarles Harris (HA)
Smith Woodhouse (HAG, DI)
Warre (BIB, AUG, BYR, LAY, DAV, AD)
1982
Churchill (TW, WW)
Croft (VIC, DAV)
Quinta do Noval (HA, GI, VIC)
Royal Oporto (UN)
1980
Dow (BYR, DAV, LAY, BER, WIZ, OD)
Fonseca (GI, BYR, HA, BER, OL)
Graham (GI, BO, BYR, DAV, BER, HA)
Quarles Harris (HAH)
Sandeman (BYR)
Taylor (DAV, GRE, WHI, GI, LAY, OL, BER, THR)
Warre (GI, WCL, BYR, DAV, HA, OL, LAY, BER)
1978
Croft Quinta da Roeda (CB)
Taylor Quinta de Vargellas (HAH, LAY, TAN, OD, GRE, MAJ)
1977
Delaforce (BOT)
Gould Campbell (GI, BER)
Quarles Harris (BYR, BER)
Smith Woodhouse (WCL, GI, HA)
1975
Cockburn (AUG, BER)
Croft (BER, BL)
Dow (BER, BYR, LAY)
Fonseca (AUG, BER)
Quinta do Noval (WAI)
Sandeman (BER)
Warre (NI, BER, DAV, BYR, GI)
1970
Rebello Valente (WHI, GI)

─────── **£20.00 to £24.99** ───────
Non-vintage
Dow's 30-year-old Tawny (BO)
1988
Graham (BAR)
1985
Cockburn (VIC, DAV)
Dow (TAN, VIC, DAV)
Fonseca (CH, VIC)
Graham (VIC, DAV, TAN)
Taylor (BO, VIC)
Warre (TAN, VIC, WHI, DAV)
1983
Cockburn (BYR, VIC)
Fonseca (AD, VIC, BYR)
Graham (BYR, UN, VIC)
Taylor (TAN, OL, DAV, VIC)
Warre (UN, VIC)
1977
Graham (HAG, BIB)
Offley Boa Vista (VIC)
Royal Oporto (VIN)
Sandeman (GI, BYR)
Warre (BYR)
1975
Cockburn (BYR, AD)
Dow (AUG, PIP, WHI, OD)
Graham (BYR, BO, UN)
Quinta do Noval (AUG, BY)
Sandeman (AD, AUG, THR)
Taylor (BER, BYR, DAV)
Warre (AD, BO, AUG)
1970
Croft (BIB)
Delaforce (BER)
Dow (BIB)
Fonseca (BL)
Martinez (HA)
Warre (BL, BIB)
1967
Cockburn (NI, HA)
Fonseca Guimaraens (HAY)
1966
Gould Campbell (BER)
Offley Boa Vista (BER)

─────── **£25.00 to £29.99** ───────
1977
Croft (BYR, GI, BOT, PD, BER, TAN)
Dow (BOT, BO, GI, BER, ELL, BY, LAY, PD)
Fonseca (HAH, GI, AUG)
Graham (BYR, BOT, BO, GRE, ELL, LAY, PD, GI)
Quarles Harris (DI)
Smith Woodhouse (DI)
Warre (BIB, GI, DI, HAG, LAY, BO, ELL, BY)

1970
Cockburn (GI, CB, DAV, TAN, BAR)
Croft (GI, BY, BYR, DAV)
Dow (GI, BER, BYR)
Fonseca (LO, LO, BIB, GI, BYR, BER)
Graham (GI, WHI, AUG)
Offley Boa Vista (OL)
Quinta do Noval (GI, WHI, BER)
Sandeman (GI, BER)
Taylor (BIB, HAG, BL)
Warre (CB, GI, WHI, BER, LAY)
1966
Delaforce (BER)
1963
Rebello Valente (BER)
1960
Delaforce (HA)
Dow (LO)
1954
Graham Quinta do Malvedos (GI)

——————— £30.00 to £39.99 ———————
Non-vintage
Fonseca 30-year-old (BAR)
Taylor 40-year-old Tawny (GRE, BOT)
1983
Smith Woodhouse (UN)
1977
Croft (BY, CB, DAV)
Dow (CB, OD, DAV)
Fonseca (BER, BY, HA, ELL, AD)
Taylor (BO, DAV, UN)
1970
Cockburn (HA, OL)
Graham (LAY, BY, BYR, HA, DAV, BO)
Quinta do Noval (OL, VIN)
Taylor (LO, DAV, BY, BAR, BO)
1966
Croft (BL, BYR, WHI, OL)
Dow (WS, DAV)
Fonseca (WS)
Gould Campbell (OL)
Graham (GI, DAV)
Offley Boa Vista (TAN)
Quinta do Noval (GI, OL, TAN)
Smith Woodhouse (OL)
Taylor (GI, BYR, DAV)
Warre (BAR)
1963
Martinez (HA)
1960
Fonseca (OL)
Graham (GI, HAH, OL)
Taylor (DAV)
Warre (GI, HAH)

——————— £40.00 to £49.99 ———————
Non-vintage
Fonseca 40-year-old (BAR)
Quinta do Noval 40-year-old Tawny (AI)
Taylor 40-year-old Tawny (WIL, PD, UN, VIN)
1963
Croft (WS, GI, HAG)
Dow (TAN, GI)
Graham (GI)
Offley Forrester (WHI)
Quinta do Noval (GI)
Taylor (BIB)
Warre (BIB)
1960
Cockburn (TAN)
Warre (VIG)
1944
Royal Oporto (TW)

——————— £50.00 to £74.99 ———————
1963
Cockburn (TAN)
Sandeman (TW, OL)
Taylor (GI, BAR, REI, DAV, WHI)
Warre (GI, WHI, DAV)
1955
Cockburn (WHI)
Croft (BAR)
Fonseca (REI)
Offley Forrester (WHI)
Taylor (BIB)
Taylor 20-year-old Tawny (NI)

——————— £75.00 to £85.00 ———————
1955
Dow (GI)
Graham (GI, VIG)
1934
Dow (GI)
1917
Delaforce (GI)

——————— £155.00 to £175.00 ———————
1945
Croft (WY)
1935
Cockburn (REI)
1927
Cockburn (WY)
1924
Taylor (WY)

——————— c. £460.00 ———————
1931
Quinta do Noval (TW)

MADEIRA

――――― **Under £6.00** ―――――

Non-vintage

Bual Duke of Cumberland Blandy (GI, HOG)

Bual Justino Henriques (WIL, CH)

Malmsey Duke of Clarence Blandy (GI, HOG)

Malmsey Justino Henriques (WIL, CH)

Sercial Duke of Sussex Blandy (HOG)

Sercial Justino Henriques (WIL)

――――― **£6.00 to £7.99** ―――――

Non-vintage

5-year-old Bual Cossart Gordon (GRE, HOG, THR)

5-year-old Malmsey Cossart Gordon (GRE, HOG)

5-year-old Sercial Cossart Gordon (GRE, HOG, THR)

Bual Old Trinity House Rutherford & Miles (TAN, HAH, BE)

Finest Old Malmsey Cossart Gordon (IR)

Finest Old Sercial Cossart Gordon (IR)

Malmsey Blandy (NI, GRE, BL, OD, HAG, DAV, PD, BOT, VIN)

Malmsey Henriques & Henriques (ASK, VIG)

Rainwater Good Company Cossart Gordon (CH, ELL, IR, AD, AV)

Sercial Blandy (NI, GRE, OD, HAG, BOT, VIN)

Sercial Henriques & Henriques (ASK, VIG)

Verdelho Blandy (GRE, OD, BOT, VIN)

Verdelho Henriques & Henriques (ASK, VIG)

――――― **£8.00 to £9.99** ―――――

Non-vintage

Bual Cossart Gordon (BAR, HIC)

Finest Old Bual Cossart Gordon (HAY, LAY, PIP)

Finest Old Sercial Cossart Gordon (HAY, ELL, LAY, PIP)

Malmsey Cossart Gordon (BAR)

Sercial Cossart Gordon (BAR)

――――― **£10.00 to £14.99** ―――――

Non-vintage

★10-year-old Malmsey Blandy (HOG, THR, BOT, HAG, PD, GRE)

Bual Reserve Rutherford & Miles (BE)

Malmsey Henriques & Henriques (WW)

――――― **£15.00 to £19.99** ―――――

Non-vintage

10-year-old Malmsey Cossart Gordon (HIC)

Lamelino Special Reserve Sercial (WS)

Very Old Bual Duo Centenary Celebration Cossart Gordon (IR, HAH, WCL, CH, BAR, LAY, AD, ELL)

Very Old Sercial Duo Centenary Celebration Cossart Gordon (HAH, BAR, AD, ELL)

――――― **£20.00 to £29.99** ―――――

1954

Bual Henriques & Henriques (GRE)

1950

Sercial Rutherford & Miles (GRE)

――――― **£30.00 to £39.99** ―――――

1934

Malmsey Rutherford & Miles (GRE)

Verdelho Henriques & Henriques (GRE)

――――― **£50.00 to £71.99** ―――――

1952

Verdelho Cossart Gordon (VIG)

1950

Sercial Cossart Gordon (HA)

Sercial Leacock (VIG)

1934

Bual Cossart Gordon (REI)

1933

Malmsey Cossart Gordon (HA)

1905

Sercial Leacock (GI)

――――― **£110.00 to £125.00** ―――――

1930

Malmsey Quinta do Serrado 1830 (AD)

1927

Bual Quinta do Serrado 1827 (AD)

1898

Terrantez Cossart Gordon (REI)

UNITED STATES

CALIFORNIA RED

─────────── **Under £4.00** ───────────
Non-vintage
Lost Hills Red (BIB)
Sainsbury's Zinfandel (SAI)
1988
Asda Petite Sirah (ASD)
1986
★Glen Ellen Cabernet Sauvignon (BO)

─────────── **£4.00 to £5.99** ───────────
Non-vintage
Alexander Valley Red (AV)
Inglenook Cabernet Sauvignon (BOT, PD)
Trefethen Eshcol Red (BYR, HAG)
1988
E&J Gallo Zinfandel (PE)
Mountain View Pinot Noir (WAI)
1987
Firestone Merlot (CH, PD)
Glen Ellen Cabernet Sauvignon (AUG)
Hawk Crest Cabernet Sauvignon (WW)
★Robert Mondavi Cabernet Sauvignon
   (HUN, HAH)
Robert Mondavi Woodbridge Cabernet
   Sauvignon (PIP, THR)
Round Hill Zinfandel (WW)
1986
Inglenook Pinot Noir (PD)
Julius Wile Cabernet Sauvignon (AI, UP,
   THR)
Robert Mondavi Cabernet Sauvignon (VIC)
Stratford Cabernet Sauvignon (MAJ)
1985
Fetzer Zinfandel (TES)
Firestone Merlot (HOG)
Hawk Crest Cabernet Sauvignon (IR)
Paul Masson Cabernet Sauvignon (OD, WIL)
★Ridge Paso Robles Zinfandel (HOG)
1984
Round Hill Zinfandel (IR, ASK)
1983
Inglenook Petite Sirah (BOT)
Inglenook Zinfandel (BOT, PD)
1981
★Phelps Syrah (GRE, WHI, RAE)

─────────── **£6.00 to £7.99** ───────────
1988
Firestone Merlot (AMI, WHI)
Saintsbury Garnet Pinot Noir (BIB)

1987
Beaulieu Vineyards Pinot Noir (SAI)
Clos du Bois Merlot (AMI)
Fetzer Zinfandel (ALL)
Julius Wile Cabernet Sauvignon (STA)
La Crema Pinot Noir (SAI)
1986
Beaulieu Beautour Cabernet Sauvignon
   (BOT)
Beaulieu Vineyards Pinot Noir (BOT)
Buena Vista Cabernet Sauvignon (AMI, WHI)
Clos du Bois Merlot (PE, BYR, WHI, WS, NI,
   WCL, HAY)
Dry Creek Cabernet Sauvignon (BYR)
Firestone Ambassador's Vineyard Merlot
   (HAG)
Firestone Cabernet Sauvignon (WHI, WIL,
   VIG, HAY, THR, HAG, HAH)
Firestone Merlot (THR)
Firestone Pinot Noir (AMI, WHI)
Hawk Crest Cabernet Sauvignon (ASK, BO)
Heitz Zinfandel (WHI)
Lohr Cabernet Sauvignon (UP)
Sterling Cabernet Sauvignon (OD)
1985
Beringer Cabernet Sauvignon (VIC)
Buena Vista Zinfandel (WHI)
Clos du Val Zinfandel (BYR)
★Edna Valley Pinot Noir (GRE, THR)
Firestone Pinot Noir (VIN)
Mirassou Cabernet Sauvignon (UP)
Preston Zinfandel (GI)
Robert Mondavi Pinot Noir (HOG, HAH)
Trefethen Pinot Noir (VIC)
Wente Bros Cabernet Sauvignon (AUG)
1984
★Clos du Val Cabernet Sauvignon (BYR)
Firestone Pinot Noir (VIN)
Robert Mondavi Cabernet
   Sauvignon (HOG)
Shafer Merlot (GI)
1983
★Simi Cabernet Sauvignon (LAY)

─────────── **£8.00 to £9.99** ───────────
1988
Nebbiolo Podere il San Olivos (WCL)
★Saintsbury Pinot Noir (WS, BIB)
1987
Ridge Geyserville Zinfandel (OD, AMI)
Ridge Paso Robles Zinfandel (TAN, VIG)
Saintsbury Pinot Noir (HAH)

1986
Clos du Bois Merlot (HA, BIB, BAR)
Clos du Val Pinot Noir (REI)
Cuvaison Merlot/Zinfandel (BAR)
Newton Merlot (OD)
Ridge Geyserville Zinfandel (GRE, BYR)
Robert Mondavi Pinot Noir (PIP, AMI, UP)
Sanford Pinot Noir (HOG)
1985
Alexander Valley Cabernet Sauvignon (AV)
Buena Vista Cabernet Sauvignon (WIL)
Edna Valley Pinot Noir (HUN, HAG, VIG)
Newton Cabernet Sauvignon (OD)
Round Hill Cabernet Sauvignon (WW)
Rutherford Hill Merlot (AV)
1984
Clos du Bois Cabernet Sauvignon (HA)
Clos du Val Pinot Noir (CHA)
★Freemark Abbey Cabernet Sauvignon (AV)
Ridge York Creek Cabernet Sauvignon (RAE, GRE)
Robert Mondavi Pinot Noir Reserve (GRE)
Rutherford Hill Cabernet Sauvignon (AV, VIG)
Simi Cabernet Sauvignon (CB, LAY)
Trefethen Cabernet Sauvignon (BYR, RES, WS)
1981
Clos du Val Cabernet Sauvignon (BER)

──────── £10.00 to £11.99 ────────
1988
Au Bon Climat Pinot Noir (MV, WCL)
1987
Stag's Leap Cabernet Sauvignon (WW)
1986
Clos du Val Merlot (CHA, REI)
Cuvaison Cabernet Sauvignon (BY)
Iron Horse Cabernet Sauvignon (AMI)
Sanford Pinot Noir (WHI, UP, NI)
Trefethen Cabernet Sauvignon (AMI)
1985
Franciscan Cabernet Sauvignon (AN)
Grgich Zinfandel (RES)
Iron Horse Cabernet Sauvignon (VIG)
Ridge Geyserville Zinfandel (HAH)
Robert Mondavi Oakville Cabernet Sauvignon (NI, WHI)
1984
Acacia St Clair Pinot Noir (BYR, RES)
Cuvaison Cabernet Sauvignon (BY)
Robert Mondavi Oakville Cabernet Sauvignon (NI, WHI)
1982
Trefethen Cabernet Sauvignon (BER)

──────── £12.00 to £14.99 ────────
1987
Au Bon Climat Pinot Noir (MV, BAR)
1986
Acacia St Clair Pinot Noir (ALL)
Carmenet Cabernet Sauvignon (UP)
Freemark Abbey Cabernet Sycamore (AV)
Robert Mondavi Pinot Noir Reserve (WHI)
Stag's Leap Cabernet Sauvignon (BYR, BIB, ASK, BO)
1985
Calera Jensen Pinot Noir (BYR)
Joseph Phelps Cabernet Sauvignon (VIG)
Ridge Montebello Cabernet Sauvignon (VIG)
Robert Mondavi Pinot Noir Reserve (WHI)
Stag's Leap Cabernet Sauvignon (IR, IR)
1984
Grgich Hills Cabernet Sauvignon (RES)
Jordan Cabernet Sauvignon (LAY)
1983
Beaulieu Vineyards Georges de Latour Private Reserve Cabernet Sauvignon (BOT)
Carmenet Cabernet Sauvignon (VIG)
1982
Joseph Phelps Cabernet Sauvignon (VIG)
1981
Simi Reserve Cabernet Sauvignon (LAY, CB)
1975
★Cuvaison Cabernet Sauvignon (VIG)

──────── £15.00 to £19.99 ────────
1986
Calera Jensen Pinot Noir (WCL)
Philip Togue Cabernet Sauvignon (WW)
1985
Mount Eden Cabernet Sauvignon (WW)
1984
Stag's Leap Cabernet Sauvignon (VIG)
1983
Stag's Leap Cabernet Sauvignon (BER)
1982
Mayacamas Cabernet Sauvignon (BYR)
Ridge Geyserville Zinfandel (VIG)
1980
Ridge York Creek Cabernet Sauvignon (AD, VIG)

──────── £20.00 to £29.99 ────────
1985
Robert Mondavi Cabernet Sauvignon Reserve (VIG)
Stag's Leap Cask 23 Cabernet Sauvignon (IR)

1983
Robert Mondavi Cabernet Sauvignon
   Reserve (AMI)
Stag's Leap Cask 23 Cabernet Sauvignon
   (CB)
1980
Ridge Montebello Cabernet Sauvignon
   (AMI)
1979
Robert Mondavi Cabernet Sauvignon
   Reserve (BYR, RES)
1976
Mount Veeder Cabernet Sauvignon (VIG)

───────── £30.00 to £39.99 ─────────
1983
Mondavi/Rothschild Opus One (RAE)
1982
Heitz Martha's Vineyard Cabernet
   Sauvignon (AMI)
Mondavi/Rothschild Opus One (RES)
1978
Ridge Montebello Cabernet Sauvignon (AD)
1975
Robert Mondavi Cabernet Sauvignon (VIG)
1973
Sterling Cabernet Sauvignon Reserve (VIG)

───────── £40.00 to £50.00 ─────────
1983
Mondavi/Rothschild Opus One (WIL)
1981
Mondavi/Rothschild Opus One (BO, RES)
1976
Heitz Martha's Vineyard Cabernet
   Sauvignon (AD)

CALIFORNIA WHITE

───────── Under £4.00 ─────────
Non-vintage
E&J Gallo Sauvignon Blanc (BL, PD)
Lost Hills White (BIB)
Sainsbury's Chardonnay (SAI)
1987
E&J Gallo French Colombard (PE, UN)

───────── £4.00 to £5.99 ─────────
Non-vintage
Lost Hills Chardonnay (BIB)
Robert Mondavi Sauvignon Blanc (VIC)
Round Hill House White (ASK)
1989
Dry Creek Chenin Blanc (AMI)
Hawk Crest Chardonnay (WW)

★Robert Mondavi Woodbridge Sauvignon
   Blanc (WHI, PIP)
1988
Andrew Quady Essensia Orange Muscat
   ½ bottle (WHI)
Beringer Fumé Blanc (VIC)
Dry Creek Chenin Blanc (GRE, RAE)
Firestone Riesling (AMI)
Glen Ellen Chardonnay (AUG)
Jekel Johannisberg Riesling (SAI)
Robert Mondavi Woodbridge Sauvignon
   Blanc (WHI, AMI, NI)
Robert Mondavi Woodbridge Zinfandel (UP)

Round Hill Chardonnay (WW)
Sterling Sauvignon Blanc (OD)
1987
Clos du Bois Sauvignon Blanc (GRE)
Paul Masson Chardonnay (OD, WIL)
Robert Mondavi Woodbridge Sauvignon
   Blanc (NI, NI)
Sanford Sauvignon Blanc (THR)
Stratford Sauvignon Blanc (MAJ)
Wente Bros Chardonnay (GRE)
1986
Firestone Chardonnay (ASD)
1985
Preston Cuvée de Fumé (GI)
★Simi Sauvignon Blanc (LAY)

───────── £6.00 to £7.99 ─────────
Non-vintage
Sanford Sauvignon Blanc (HOG)
Trefethen Eshcol (AMI)
1988
Dry Creek Fumé Blanc (WHI)
Firestone Selected Harvest Johannisberg
   Riesling ½ bottle (UP, GRE, VIG)
Grgich Hills Fumé Blanc (EL)
Hawk Crest Chardonnay (IR, ASK, BAR)
Inglenook Chardonnay (BOT)
Stag's Leap Riesling (WW)
William Wheeler Sauvignon Blanc (BAR)

1987
Beaulieu Vineyards Sauvignon Blanc (BOT)
Buena Vista Chardonnay (RES)
Clos du Bois Chardonnay (THR)
Dry Creek Fumé Blanc (BAR)
Firestone Chardonnay (SAI, UP)
Mark West Gewurztraminer (ALL)
Pedroncelli Chardonnay (LAY)
Robert Mondavi Moscato d'Oro (WHI, AD)
Simi Sauvignon Blanc (REI)
Stag's Leap Sauvignon Blanc (BYR)
1986
Buena Vista Chardonnay (WHI)
Clos du Bois Chardonnay (RAE, BYR)
Clos du Val Sauvignon Blanc (REI)
Inglenook Chardonnay (PD)
Julius Wile Chardonnay (STA)
Mark West Gewurztraminer (WHI, BYR)
Monticello Chardonnay (AMI)
★Robert Mondavi Fumé Blanc (GRE, BYR,
  PIP, AD)
Robert Mondavi Moscato d'Oro (WHI)
★Wente Bros Chardonnay (UN)
William Wheeler Sonoma Chardonnay
  (BYR)
1985
Monticello Chardonnay (RES)
Newton Sauvignon Blanc (OD)
★Shafer Chardonnay (GI)
William Wheeler Sauvignon Blanc (HUN)
1984
Firestone Chardonnay (WIL)
Preston Sauvignon Reserve (GI)
1981
★Mark West Chardonnay (WHI)

──────── £8.00 to £9.99 ────────
Non-vintage
Sanford Chardonnay (HOG)
1989
Dry Creek Chardonnay (AMI)
1988
Matanzas Creek Sauvignon Blanc (HAH)
Rutherford Hill Jaeger Chardonnay (AV)
★Saintsbury Chardonnay (HAH, BIB)
Stag's Leap Chardonnay (VIG)
1987
Alexander Valley Chardonnay (AV)
Beringer Chardonnay (VIC)
Clos du Bois Chardonnay (HA)
★Edna Valley Chardonnay (HOG, RES, REI)
Frogs Leap Chardonnay (LAY)
Mark West Chardonnay (AMI)
Newton Chardonnay (OD)
Philip Togue Sauvignon Blanc (WW)

Robert Mondavi Chardonnay (BYR)
Simi Sonoma Chardonnay (REI)
1986
Chateau St-Jean Chardonnay (BYR)
Mark West Chardonnay (VIG, BAR)
Simi Mendocino Chardonnay (CB)
1985
Freemark Abbey Chardonnay (AV)
Robert Mondavi Chardonnay (GRE)
Robert Mondavi Oakville Fumé Blanc
  Reserve (NI)
Rutherford Hill Cellar Reserve
  Chardonnay (AV)
Simi Chardonnay (LAY)
1984
William Wheeler Sonoma Chardonnay
  (HUN)

──────── £10.00 to £11.99 ────────
1988
Acacia Chardonnay (AMI)
Au Bon Climat Chardonnay (MV, WCL)
Edna Valley Chardonnay (WCL, HAG, BAR)
Sonoma-Cutrer Chardonnay (AV)
1987
Clos du Val Chardonnay (REI)
Joseph Phelps Chardonnay (BYR, UP)
Saintsbury Reserve Chardonnay (HAH)
1986
Chalone Chardonnay (BYR)
Cuvaison Chardonnay (BAR)
Robert Mondavi Reserve Chardonnay (GRE)
Trefethen Chardonnay (AD)
1985
Monticello Chardonnay (BER)
Robert Mondavi Oakville Chardonnay (NI,
  WHI)
1984
Robert Mondavi Chardonnay (HUN)
1982
★Shafer Chardonnay (BO)

──────── £12.00 to £14.99 ────────
1988
Acacia Chardonnay (UP, HAH)
Au Bon Climat Chardonnay (BAR)
Matanzas Creek Chardonnay (HAH)
1987
Sanford Chardonnay (NI)
Stag's Leap Chardonnay (IR)
1986
Grgich Hills Chardonnay (EL)
Iron Horse Chardonnay (BER)
1985
Jordan Chardonnay (LAY)

1983
Simi Reserve Chardonnay (LAY)

─────── £15.00 to £19.99 ───────
1988
Far Niente Chardonnay (AV)
1987
Robert Mondavi Reserve Chardonnay (PIP)
ZD Chardonnay (BAR)

CALIFORNIA ROSÉ

─────── Under £5.00 ───────
Non-vintage
E&J Gallo Blush (BL)
1988
Robert Mondavi White Zinfandel (CH)

─────── £5.00 to £6.99 ───────
1989
Robert Mondavi White Zinfandel (PIP, AMI, NI)
1987
Robert Mondavi White Zinfandel (BOT, PD)

CALIFORNIA SPARKLING

─────── Under £12.99 ───────
1985
Schramsberg Blanc de Blancs (AD)

─────── £13.00 to £16.99 ───────
1984
Schramsberg Blanc de Blancs (WS, VIG)
1981
Schramsberg Blanc de Noirs (BO)

OTHER USA RED

─────── Under £6.00 ───────
1988
Covey Run Lemberger (HE)
1986
Texas Vineyards Ivanhoe Red (HE)

─────── £6.00 to £8.99 ───────
1987
Elk Cove Estate Pinot Noir (HE)
1986
Covey Run Cabernet Sauvignon (HE)

─────── £9.00 to £11.99 ───────
1987
Llano Estacado Cabernet Sauvignon (HE)
★Ponzi Pinot Noir (WW)

1986
Cameron Pinot Noir (BIB)
Pheasant Ridge Proprietors Reserve (HE)
1985
Rose Creek Mercer Ranch Cabernet Sauvignon (ASK)

─────── £12.00 to £15.99 ───────
1987
Eyrie Vineyard Pinot Meunier (WW)
Ponzi Pinot Noir Reserve (WW)
1986
Cameron Pinot Noir Reserve (BIB)

OTHER USA WHITE

─────── Under £6.00 ───────
1988
Columbia Crest Sauvignon Blanc (UP)
Covey Run Aligoté (HE)
Domaine Cordier Chenin Blanc (AUG)
Fall Creek Emerald Riesling (HE)
Snoqualmie Muscat Canelli (WW)
1987
Columbia Chardonnay (AUG)
Elk Cove Gewurztraminer (HE)
Fall Creek Emerald Riesling (HE)
1986
Covey Run Morio-Muskat (HE)
Texas Vineyards French Colombard (HE)
Texas Vineyards White Zinfandel (HE)
1985
Llano Estacado Dry Chenin Blanc (HE)
Texas Vineyards Ivanhoe Blanc (HE)

─────── £6.00 to £7.99 ───────
1988
Eyrie Pinot Gris (WW)
Fall Creek Sauvignon Blanc (HE)
1987
Eyrie Muscat Ottonel (WW)
1986
Covey Rise Chardonnay (IR)

─────── £8.00 to £9.99 ───────
1988
Llano Estacado Chardonnay (HE)
1987
Rose Creek Chardonnay (ASK)

─────── £10.00 to £13.99 ───────
1987
Covey Run Riesling Ice Wine ½ bottle (HE)
1986
Blackwood Canyon Chardonnay (WW)

AUSTRALIA

RED

──────── Under £4.00 ────────
Non-vintage
Asda Cabernet Sauvignon/Shiraz (ASD)
Sainsbury's Shiraz/Cabernet Sauvignon (SAI)
1988
★Penfolds Dalwood Shiraz/Cabernet Sauvignon (MAJ)
1987
Orlando Cabernet Sauvignon (HOG)
Orlando Jacob's Creek Red (AUS, SAF, AUG, DAV, HOG, BL)
1986
Orlando RF Cabernet Sauvignon (WIZ)
1985
Berri Cabernet Sauvignon/Shiraz (WAI)
★Wyndham's Cabernet Sauvignon Bin 937 (SAI)

──────── £4.00 to £4.99 ────────
Non-vintage
Penfolds Kalimna Shiraz Bin 28 (HOG)
1989
Rosemount Diamond Reserve Cabernet Sauvignon/Shiraz (NI)
Rosemount Diamond Reserve Dry Red (WHI)
1988
Hill-Smith Cabernet Sauvignon/Malbec (UP)
★Penfolds Koonunga Hill Cabernet Sauvignon/Shiraz (MAJ)
Rosemount Diamond Reserve Cabernet Sauvignon/Shiraz (CHA, NI)
Wyndham's Shiraz Bin 555 (MAJ)
1987
Berri Cabernet Sauvignon/Shiraz (ASD)
Brown Bros Shiraz (DI)
Lindeman Shiraz Bin 50 (WAI, WHI)
Orlando RF Cabernet Sauvignon (SAF, TAN, AUG, DI)
Rosemount Cabernet Sauvignon (ASD)
Tyrrells Long Flat Red (AV, PIP, LAY)
Wyndham's Shiraz Bin 555 (WHI)
Yalumba Cabernet Sauvignon/Shiraz (AUS)
1986
Brokenwood Cabernet Sauvignon/Shiraz (DI)
Brown Bros Meadow Creek Cabernet Sauvignon/Shiraz (WHI)

Brown Bros Shiraz (DI)
Lindeman Shiraz Bin 50 (WHI)
Mildara Shiraz (AUS)
Montrose Shiraz (BYR)
Penfolds Kalimna Shiraz Bin 28 (OD)
★Peter Lehmann Shiraz (BYR)
Rosemount Pinot Noir (WIZ)
Seaview Cabernet Sauvignon Reserve (OD)
Tyrrells Long Flat Red (AV, TAN)
Wyndham's Shiraz Bin 555 (GI)
Yalumba Cabernet Sauvignon (BYR)
1985
Brokenwood Cabernet Sauvignon/Shiraz (DI)
Hill-Smith Cabernet Sauvignon/Malbec (PD, BOT)
McWilliams Hanwood Cabernet Sauvignon (BYR)
Peter Lehmann Shiraz (HUN)
Peter Lehmann Shiraz/Cabernet Sauvignon (UP)
★Wynns Ovens Valley Shiraz (VIC)
1984
McWilliams Hanwood Cabernet Sauvignon (BYR)
Rouge Homme Shiraz/Cabernet Sauvignon (ASK)
Seaview Cabernet Sauvignon (CH)

──────── £5.00 to £5.99 ────────
1989
Rosemount Cabernet Sauvignon (NI)
Rosemount Shiraz (NI)
1988
Mildara Cabernet Sauvignon/Merlot (BOT)
Rosemount Cabernet Sauvignon (WHI, SAF, THR, CHA, NI, WRI, GRE)
Rosemount Shiraz (AUS, CHA, NI, DAV, WHI)
Yalumba Cabernet Sauvignon/Shiraz (AMI)
1987
Brown Bros Cabernet Sauvignon (DI, BY, PIP, WHI, AUS)
De Bortoli Shiraz (GRE)
Houghton Cabernet Sauvignon (GRE)
Lindeman Cabernet Sauvignon Bin 45 (BOT)
Mildara Cabernet Sauvignon/Merlot (BOT)
Penfolds Coonawarra Shiraz Bin 128 (AD)
Penfolds Koonunga Hill Cabernet Sauvignon/Shiraz (IR, VIG)
Rosemount Hunter Valley Shiraz (WHI)
Rosemount Pinot Noir (GRE, CHA)

Wynns Shiraz (THR)
Yalumba Cabernet Sauvignon/Shiraz (RES, LOR)
1986
Basedow Shiraz (BIB)
Brown Bros Cabernet Sauvignon (DI, BY, ASK, WHI, BL, PE, CH)
Brown Bros Shiraz (ASK, WHI, BYR, BO, WIL)
Hardy Nottage Hill Shiraz (WHI)
Lindeman Cabernet Sauvignon Bin 45 (AUG)
Mitchell Peppertree Shiraz (BAR)
Penfolds Kalimna Shiraz Bin 28 (THR, BYR, IR, AUS)
Peter Lehmann Shiraz (AUS)
Rosemount Cabernet Sauvignon (UP)
Rosemount Hunter Valley Shiraz (AI)
Rosemount Pinot Noir (AI)
Rosemount Shiraz (UP)
Rothbury Shiraz (BYR)
Wolf Blass Cabernet Sauvignon (WHI, GRE)
Yalumba Cabernet Sauvignon/Shiraz (HAG)
1985
Basedow Shiraz (BIB)
Chateau Tahbilk Cabernet Sauvignon (BYR, WCL, HAG)
Hardy Nottage Hill Shiraz (WHI)
Hill-Smith Cabernet Sauvignon (UP, AI)
Hill-Smith Shiraz (UP, AI)
Rosemount Cabernet Sauvignon (VIC, PD)
Rouge Homme Shiraz/Cabernet Sauvignon (UP, AUS, BAR)
★Taltarni Merlot (UP)
Wolf Blass Cabernet Sauvignon (WHI, AUG)
Wynns Ovens Valley Shiraz (AUS)
★Yalumba Pewsey Vale Cabernet Sauvignon (BYR)
1984
Brown Bros Shiraz (BOT, PD)
Idyll Cabernet Sauvignon/Shiraz (HOG)
Rouge Homme Shiraz/Cabernet Sauvignon (BR, AV)
Taltarni Shiraz (BYR)
1982
★Taltarni Cabernet Sauvignon (UP, HAG)

——————— **£6.00 to £7.99** ———————
1988
Balgownie Shiraz (RAE)
Rosemount Diamond Reserve Cabernet Sauvignon/Shiraz (HA)
★Schinus Molle Cabernet Sauvignon (AD)
1987
Brown Bros Koombahla Cabernet Sauvignon (BE)

Brown Bros Shiraz (TAN, AI, WRI, HIC)
Cape Mentelle Shiraz (RAE)
Cape Mentelle Zinfandel (RAE)

Hunter Estate Cabernet Sauvignon (WIC)
Jamiesons Run Coonawarra Red (AUS)
Mildara Cabernet Sauvignon (AUS)
Orlando St Hugo Red (AUS)
Redgate Cabernet Sauvignon (BYR)
Wyndham's Pinot Noir Bin 333 (WHI)
1986
Bowen Shiraz (BAR)
Brown Bros Koombahla Cabernet Sauvignon (HUN, BY, PIP, WHI, AUS, GRE)
Cassegrain Cabernet Sauvignon (BYR)
Coriole Shiraz (TAN)
★Hungerford Hill Coonawarra Cabernet Sauvignon (WRI)
Jim Barry Cabernet Sauvignon (TAN)
Orlando St Hugo Cabernet Sauvignon (SAI, OD)
Penfolds Cabernet Sauvignon Bin 222 (AUS)
Penfolds Cabernet Sauvignon/Shiraz Bin 389 (OD, THR, AUS)
Petersons Cabernet Sauvignon (BEK)
Pike Cabernet Sauvignon (BAR)
Rosemount Show Reserve Cabernet Sauvignon (BYR, BO, GRE, CHA, LOR, AUS)
Rothbury Estate Syrah (HA)
Seppelt Cabernet Sauvignon Black Label (WIZ, WHI, BAR)
Seppelt Shiraz Black Label (THR)
Wynns Coonawarra Cabernet Sauvignon (OD)
Yalumba Cabernet Sauvignon (AMI)
1985
Basedow Cabernet Sauvignon (TAN, HAY, BIB)
Botobolar St-Gilbert (HAG)
Campbells Shiraz (PIP)
Capel Vale Cabernet Sauvignon (PE)

Hardy Keppoch Cabernet Sauvignon/Shiraz (BYR)
Orlando St Hugo Cabernet Sauvignon (WIZ, WCL, WHI, BYR)
Penfolds Cabernet Sauvignon Bin 222 (HOG, THR)
Petersons Shiraz (BEK)
Rosemount Show Reserve Cabernet Sauvignon (UP, THR)
Rouge Homme Cabernet Sauvignon (ASK, BYR)
St Huberts Lilydale Pinot Noir (WAI)
Seppelt Cabernet Sauvignon Black Label (WHI, UP, VIC)
Seppelt Shiraz Black Label (THR, VIG)
Taltarni Merlot (REI)
Wynns Cabernet Sauvignon (TAN)
1984
Brown Bros Koombahla Cabernet Sauvignon (BYR, AI)
Cape Mentelle Shiraz (RAE)
Coriole Shiraz (BIB)
Huntington Cabernet Sauvignon/Merlot (UP, BIB)
Penfolds Cabernet Sauvignon/Shiraz Bin 389 (HOG, BO)
Saltram Mamre Brook Cabernet Sauvignon (AUS)
Yalumba Cabernet Sauvignon/Shiraz (BER)
1983
Krondorf Cabernet Sauvignon (AUS)
Rosemount Show Reserve Cabernet Sauvignon (BE)
Wynns Cabernet Sauvignon (BYR)

——————— **£8.00 to £9.99** ———————
1988
Balgownie Cabernet Sauvignon (RAE)
Jamiesons Run Coonawarra Red (AUS)
Moss Wood Cabernet Sauvignon (RAE)
1987
Balgownie Pinot Noir (RAE)
Cape Mentelle Cabernet Sauvignon (RAE)
Eileen Hardy Shiraz (OD)
Knappstein Cabernet Sauvignon/Merlot (AV)
★Lake's Folly Cabernet Sauvignon (LAY)
Moss Wood Cabernet Sauvignon (RAE)
Pikes Polish Hill River Shiraz (HAU)
Rosemount Pinot Noir (WHI)
1986
Adams & Wray Shiraz (BIB)
Balgownie Pinot Noir (RAE)
Chateau Reynella Cabernet Sauvignon (HA)

Hollicks Coonawarra Cabernet Sauvignon/Merlot (HAU)
Jeffrey Grosset Cabernet Sauvignon (UP)
Knappstein Cabernet Sauvignon (AV)
Moss Wood Pinot Noir (BYR, BYR)
Mount Edelstone Shiraz (AUS)
Yarra Burn Cabernet Sauvignon (BAR)
1985
Balgownie Cabernet Sauvignon (RAE)
Cullens Cabernet Sauvignon/Merlot (UP)
Penfolds Cabernet Sauvignon/Shiraz Bin 389 (BYR)
Wolf Blass President's Selection Cabernet Sauvignon (VIC, WHI, BOT, AUS)
1984
Balgownie Cabernet Sauvignon (RAE)
★Blue Pyrenees Estate Cabernet Sauvignon/Merlot/Shiraz (TAN)
Cullens Cabernet Sauvignon/Merlot (BYR)
Redgate Cabernet Sauvignon (RAE, VIG)
1983
Balgownie Cabernet Sauvignon (RAE, VIG)
Houghton Cabernet Sauvignon (HUN)
1980
★Idyll Cabernet Sauvignon/Shiraz (HOG)

——————— **£10.00 to £11.99** ———————
1988
Balgownie Pinot Noir (RAE)
Moss Wood Cabernet Sauvignon (MV, VIG)
Moss Wood Pinot Noir (RAE, BAR)
1987
Cape Mentelle Cabernet Sauvignon (TAN, VIG)
Lake's Folly Cabernet Sauvignon (AV)
Moss Wood Pinot Noir (MV)
Mountadam Pinot Noir (PIP)
Murray Robson Cabernet Sauvignon (RES)
Rosemount Giants Creek Pinot Noir (CHA)
Tyrrells Pinot Noir (AV, GRE)
1986
Cullens Cabernet Sauvignon/Merlot (BE)
Cyril Henschke Cabernet Sauvignon (AUS)
Lake's Folly Cabernet Sauvignon (VIG, AV, AUS)
Mountadam Cabernet Sauvignon (HIC)
Rosemount Kirri Billi Merlot (CHA, THR)
Yarra Yering Cabernet Sauvignon (UP)
1985
Cape Clairault Cabernet Sauvignon (BAR)
Penfolds St-Henri Cabernet Sauvignon/Shiraz (IR, AUS)
1984
Katnook Cabernet Sauvignon (GI)
Yarra Yering Cabernet Sauvignon (BAR)

1983
Geoff Merrill Cabernet Sauvignon (HUN)
Penfolds St-Henri Cabernet
  Sauvignon/Shiraz (CH)
Petaluma Cabernet Sauvignon (BYR)
1982
Penfolds St-Henri Cabernet
  Sauvignon/Shiraz (BO)

--------- £12.00 to £13.99 ---------
1986
Dalwhinnie Cabernet Sauvignon (BAR)
Penfolds Cabernet Sauvignon/Shiraz Bin
  389 (AV)
1985
Geoff Merrill Cabernet Sauvignon (UP)
Lindeman Limestone Ridge
  Shiraz/Cabernet Sauvignon (RAE, WHI)
Vasse Felix Cabernet Sauvignon (GRE)
1984
Chateau Xanadu Cabernet Sauvignon (BR)

--------- £14.00 to £15.99 ---------
1987
Yarra Yering Cabernet Sauvignon (WCL,
  VIG)
1986
Lindeman Pyrus (AUS)
1985
Lindeman St George Cabernet Sauvignon
  (UP, AV)
1984
Wolf Blass Black Label Cabernet
  Sauvignon (AI)
1983
Tyrrells Pinot Noir (VIG)

--------- £16.00 to £19.99 ---------
Non-vintage
Penfolds Cabernet Sauvignon Bin 707
  (HOG)
1986
Penfolds Cabernet Sauvignon Bin 707 (OD,
  WHI)
Penfolds Magill Shiraz (WHI)
1985
Penfolds Cabernet Sauvignon Bin 707 (VIG)
1984
Penfolds Cabernet Sauvignon Bin 707 (CH)
Penfolds Magill Shiraz (VIG)
1983
Penfolds Cabernet Sauvignon Bin 707 (BO)
1982
Moss Wood Cabernet Sauvignon (VIG)
Vasse Felix Cabernet Sauvignon (VIG)

--------- £25.00 to £30.00 ---------
1987
Yarra Yering Pinot Noir (AUS)
1983
Penfolds Grange Hermitage Bin 95 (AUS)
1982
Penfolds Grange Hermitage Bin 95 (IR, AUS,
  OD, THR, AD, WHI)

WHITE

--------- Under £4.00 ---------
Non-vintage
Berri Rhine Riesling (PD)
1989
Orlando Jacob's Creek
  Semillon/Chardonnay (SAF, HOG, AUG,
  DAV)
Orlando Jacob's Creek White (TES)
Penfolds Semillon/Chardonnay (WHI)
1988
★Hill-Smith Old Triangle Riesling (WAI,
  THR)
Orlando Jacob's Creek White (BL, WHI, DAV,
  WCL)
Penfolds Gewurztraminer/Riesling Bin 202
  (CH)
Penfolds Semillon/Chardonnay (WHI)
Stanley Spring Gully Rhine Riesling (BYR)
1987
Hill-Smith Old Triangle Riesling (ASD)
Orlando RF Chardonnay (HOG, WIZ)
1986
Stanley Spring Gully Rhine Riesling (GI)

--------- £4.00 to £4.99 ---------
1989
Brown Bros Dry Muscat (PIP, DI)
Brown Bros Orange Muscat & Flora ½
  bottle (HUN, PIP, WHI, DI)
Lindeman Chardonnay Bin 65 (OD)
Nottage Hill Chardonnay (OD)
Orlando RF Chardonnay (SAF, OD, AUS, TAN,
  DI)
Rosemount Diamond Reserve Dry White
  (BO, UP)
Rosemount Diamond Reserve
  Semillon/Sauvignon Blanc (NI)
★Rosemount Fumé Blanc (OD)
Tyrrells Long Flat White (AV, PIP)
Yalumba Rhine Riesling (BOT)
1988
Brown Bros Dry Muscat (BY, WHI, DI, MAJ)
Brown Bros Muscat Late Picked (BY, DI,
  BYR, PIP, HUN, WHI)

Brown Bros Orange Muscat & Flora ½ bottle (CH, BYR, WHI, BO, DI, WIL, PE, RAE, VIC)
Hardy Old Castle Rhine Riesling (BYR)
Hill-Smith Old Triangle Riesling (TAN)
Lindeman Chardonnay Bin 65 (WHI)
Lindeman Semillon/Chardonnay Bin 77 (OD)
McWilliams Chardonnay (BYR)
Mildara Chardonnay (VIC)
Orlando RF Chardonnay (SAF, WHI, WCL, AUG, DI)
Penfolds Gewurztraminer/Riesling Bin 202 (IR)

Penfolds Koonunga Hill Semillon/Chardonnay (AUS)
Peter Lehmann Semillon (UP)
Rosemount Chardonnay (WIZ, OD, ASD)
Rosemount Fumé Blanc (WIZ)
Rosemount Semillon/Chardonnay (WHI)
Seaview Chardonnay (CH)
Seppelt Moystin White (UP)
Tyrrells Long Flat White (AUS, AV, LAY, TAN)
Wyndham Estate Oak-aged Chardonnay (MAJ)
Wyndham's Chardonnay Bin 222 (STA, WHI)
Wynns Rhine Riesling (VIC)
1987
Brown Bros Muscat Late Picked (HAG, DI, ASK, WHI)
Hardy Chardonnay (BO)
Hill-Smith Old Triangle Riesling (BER)
Houghton Supreme Chenin Blanc/Muscadelle (WAI)
Leasingham Fumé Blanc (GI)
Lindeman Sauvignon Blanc Bin 95 (WHI)
Lindeman Semillon/Chardonnay Bin 77 (WHI)
Orlando RF Chardonnay (RAE)
Penfolds Semillon/Chardonnay (THR)
Peter Lehmann Semillon (BYR)

Rosemount Diamond Reserve Dry White (TES, WHI)
Rosemount Semillon/Chardonnay (WIZ, GI, WHI)
Rosemount Wood-Matured Semillon (ASD)
Wyndham's Chardonnay Bin 222 (GI, MAJ, WHI)
1986
Orlando RF Riesling (WHI)
Penfolds Gewurztraminer/Riesling Bin 202 (VIG)
Rosemount Fumé Blanc (SAI)
1985
Brown Bros Orange Muscat & Flora ½ bottle (BOT)
Hill-Smith Semillon (PD, BOT)
Idyll Gewurztraminer (HOG)
★Mitchelton Wood-Matured Semillon (WAI)

——————— £5.00 to £5.99 ———————
1989
Brown Bros Orange Muscat & Flora (AUS)
Krondorf Semillon (AUS)
Penfolds Semillon/Chardonnay (IR)
★Rosemount Chardonnay (SAF, WHI, THR, CH, AUS, CHA, UP, NI, WRI)
Rosemount Fumé Blanc (WHI, SAF, THR, GRE, AUS, BO, CHA, UP, WCL)
Rosemount Semillon/Chardonnay (NI)
Rothbury Brokenback Semillon (WHI)
1988
★De Bortoli Chardonnay (HOG)
Brown Bros Dry Muscat (THR, HAG, WIL, AD, BE, BO, GRE, VIC, BOT, HUN, HAY, TAN, AUG, AI)
Brown Bros Sauvignon Blanc (DI, PIP, WHI, AUS)
Brown Bros Semillon (BYR)
Lehmann Semillon/Chardonnay (AUS)
★Rosemount Roxburgh Chardonnay (CHA)
Rothbury Brokenback Semillon (WHI)
Rothbury Homestead Semillon (AUS)
Seppelt Chardonnay Gold Label (UP)
Wolf Blass Chardonnay (WHI, GRE, AUG)
Wyndham Estate Oak-aged Chardonnay (WHI)
Yalumba Semillon/Chardonnay (WCL)
1987
Brown Bros Dry Muscat (THR, BER)
★Brown Bros Muscat Late Picked (WIL, BO, GRE, PE, WRI, AI)
Brown Bros Sauvignon Blanc (BY, DI, WHI, OD)
Drayton Chardonnay (BYR, BYR)
Hardy Siegersdorf Rhine Riesling (UP)

Lindeman Chardonnay Bin 65 (PD)
Mitchelton Wood-Matured Marsanne (WAI)
Pewsey Vale Riesling (WCL, AUS)
Rosemount Semillon/Chardonnay (BO, NI)
Smith Chardonnay Riddoch (VIC)
Wolf Blass Chardonnay (WHI)
1986
Brown Bros Dry Muscat (PD, BL)
Hill-Smith Semillon (HAG)
Idyll Gewurztraminer (HAU)
Lindeman Sauvignon Blanc Bin 95 (PD)
1985
Brown Bros Semillon (ASK)
★Chateau Reynella Rhine Riesling (UP)
Penfolds Kaiser Stuhl Green Ribbon Rhine
  Riesling (VIG)
1984
★De Bortoli Late Harvest Selection Bin 3
  Reisling/Sauvignon (BAR)

——————— £6.00 to £7.99 ———————
1989
Balgownie Chardonnay (VIG)
Basedow Chardonnay (BIB)
Brown Bros Chardonnay (DI)
★Cape Mentelle Semillon/Sauvignon Blanc
  (RES, WW, BR, RAE, TAN, BAR)
Hardy Fumé Blanc (AUS)
Hunter Estate Chardonnay (BOD, WIC)
Krondorf Chardonnay (AUS)
Montrose Show Reserve Chardonnay (BAR)
★Moss Wood Semillon (RAE)
Peter Lehmann Semillon (BOD, WIC)
★Rothbury Brokenback Chardonnay (BIB)
Schinus Molle Sauvignon (AD)
Wynns Chardonnay (VIC)
1988
Allandale Sutherland Chardonnay (MAJ)
Basedow Chardonnay (HAY)
Basedow Semillon (HAY)
De Bortoli Chardonnay (GRE)
Brown Bros Chardonnay (BYR, DI, PE, BL,
  PIP, WHI, AI, TAN, WRI)
Cape Mentelle Semillon/Sauvignon Blanc
  (RAE, LAY)
Hungerford Hill Pokolbin Chardonnay (CB)
Jamiesons Run Coonawarra White (AUS)
Krondorf Chardonnay (BYR)
Moss Wood Wooded Semillon (RAE)
Peter Lehmann Fumé Blanc (AN)
★Plantagenet Chardonnay (WCL)
Richard Hamilton Chardonnay (BAR)
Rosemount Show Reserve Chardonnay (OD,
  BYR, WAI, CH, WHI, VIC, GRE, CHA, LOR, BE,
  UP, WCL, MAJ, BOT)

Rosemount Wood-Matured Semillon (UP)
Rothbury Chardonnay (HA)
Rouge Homme Chardonnay (BYR)
Schinus Molle Chardonnay (AD)
Seppelt Chardonnay Black Label (WHI, BER)
Henschke Tilleys Vineyard Semillon/Ugni
  Blanc (AUS)
Tisdall Chardonnay (RES)
Tisdall Semillon/Sauvignon (RES)
Tolleys Pedare Barossa Chardonnay Select
  Harvest (ASK)
Wolf Blass Chardonnay (PIP, WRI, AUS)
Wynns Chardonnay (BYR)
Yalumba Chardonnay (AUS)
1987
Basedow Chardonnay (UP)
Brown Bros Chardonnay (WIL, HUN)
Hill-Smith Chardonnay (AI)
Hollicks Coonawarra Riesling (HAU)
Houghton Gold Reserve Verdelho (VIC)
Hunter Estate Cabernet Sauvignon (BOD)
Leasingham Chardonnay (GI)
Moss Wood Wooded Semillon (RAE)
Penfolds Chardonnay (AUS)
★Petaluma Rhine Riesling (AUS)
Rosemount Show Reserve Semillon (WHI,
  CHA, GI, VIC)
Seppelt Chardonnay Black Label (WHI)
Terrace Vale Semillon (REI)
Wynns Chardonnay (WIZ)
1986
Drayton Chardonnay (HA)
Petersons Semillon (BEK, AUS)
Rosemount Show Reserve Chardonnay
  (SAI)
1985
Quelltaler Estate Wood-Aged Semillon
  (BER)
Rosemount Show Reserve Chardonnay
  (WIZ)
1984
Brown Bros Noble Late Harvest Riesling
  (AI)
Redgate Riesling (RAE)

——————— £8.00 to £9.99 ———————
1989
Moss Wood Wooded Semillon (RAE)
Pikes Polish Hill River Sauvignon Blanc
  (HAU)
1988
Cape Mentelle Chardonnay (BYR)
★Coldstream Hills Chardonnay (OD)
Knappstein Chardonnay (AV)
Lindeman Padthaway Chardonnay (BOT)

Mitchelton Chardonnay (WRI)
Moss Wood Chardonnay (BYR)
Pikes Polish Hill River Chardonnay (HAU)
★Tim Knappstein Fumé Blanc (GRE)
Wirra Wirra Sauvignon Blanc (AUS)
Wynns Chardonnay (THR)
1987
Capel Vale Chardonnay (PE, BAR)
Hardy Collection Chardonnay (HA)
Len Evans Chardonnay (AN)
Lindeman Padthaway Chardonnay (DAV)
Mitchelton Chardonnay (WRI)
Petersons Chardonnay (TAN, AUS)
Rothbury Reserve Chadonnay (AUS, VIG, RES)
Rouge Homme Chardonnay (WHI, LAY, DAV)
1986
Jeffrey Grosset Chardonnay (UP)
Lindeman Padthaway Chardonnay (TES)
Petaluma Rhine Riesling (VIG)
Rouge Homme Chardonnay (BR)
Wirra Wirra Chardonnay (AUS)
1985
Rouge Homme Chardonnay (AUS)

――――――― £10.00 to £12.99 ―――――――
1989
Moss Wood Chardonnay (RAE, AD, BAR)
Mountadam Chardonnay (HIC)
1988
Balgownie Chardonnay (RAE)
Cullens Sauvignon Blanc (UP)
Geoff Merrill Chardonnay (UP)
Lindeman Padthaway Sauvignon Blanc (UP)
Petaluma Botrytis Affected Riesling (AMI)
Rosemount Roxburgh Chardonnay (BYR)
Tyrrells Vat 47 Chardonnay (AUS)
Yarra Burn Chardonnay (TAN)
1987
Katnook Chardonnay (GI)
Montrose Show Reserve Chardonnay (BYR)
Moss Wood Chardonnay (HAG)
Mountadam Chardonnay (AUS)
Petaluma Chardonnay (AMI)
Rosemount Giants Creek Chardonnay (CHA, HA, THR)
1986
Dalwhinnie Chardonnay (UP)
Geoff Merrill Chardonnay (BYR)
Lakes Folly Chardonnay (LAY)
Petaluma Chardonnay (GRE, WCL, BYR, AUS, RES)
Rosemount Whites Creek Semillon (CHA)
Tyrrells Vat 47 Chardonnay (AV)

――――――― £13.00 to £15.99 ―――――――
1988
Cullens Chardonnay (UP)
1987
Dalwhinnie Chardonnay (BAR)
Petaluma Chardonnay (VIG)
Rosemount Roxburgh Chardonnay (WHI, GRE, UP, THR)
1986
Chateau Xanadu Chardonnay (BR)
Tarra Warra Chardonnay (BAR)

SPARKLING

――――――― Under £6.00 ―――――――
Non-vintage
★Angas Brut Rosé (WAI)
Seaview (AUS)
Yalumba Angas (AUS)
Yalumba Angas Rosé (AUS)

――――――― £12.50 to £13.50 ―――――――
Non-vintage
Croser (AUS)
Yalumba D (AUS)

FORTIFIED

――――――― Under £7.99 ―――――――
Non-vintage
★Baileys Liqueur Muscat (RAE)
Chambers Rosewood Liqueur Muscat (RAE)
Chateau Reynella 10-year-old Tawny (WAI)

――――――― £8.00 to £9.99 ―――――――
Non-vintage
All Saints Rutherglen Liqueur Muscat (UP)
Baileys Show Tokay (UP)
Brown Bros Liqueur Muscat (RAE)
Campbells Rutherglen Liqueur Muscat (ASD, BO)
Stanton & Killeen Liqueur Muscat (RAE, WHI, TAN, VIG, AUS)

――――――― £10.00 to £11.99 ―――――――
Non-vintage
Baileys Liqueur Muscat (BY)
Baileys Founders Liqueur Muscat (AUS)

――――――― £12.00 to £15.99 ―――――――
Non-vintage
Baileys Gold Label Liqueur Muscat (RAE)
Campbells Rutherglen Liqueur Muscat (AUS)
Chambers Special Liqueur Muscat (RAE)

NEW ZEALAND

RED

Under £5.00
1988
Cooks Pinot Noir (SAF)
★St-Helena Pinot Noir (THR)
1987
Cooks Cabernet Sauvignon (WHI)
★Montana Marlborough Cabernet
  Sauvignon (WHI, AUG, ASD, PIP, VIC)
1986
Cooks Cabernet Sauvignon (WHI, BYR, KA,
  WAI, VIC)
Montana Marlborough Cabernet
  Sauvignon (WHI, KA, BYR, WIL, GRE, BOT)

£5.00 to £6.99
1989
Montana Marlborough Cabernet
  Sauvignon (THR)
1988
Mission Cabernet Sauvignon/Merlot (KA)
1987
Babich Pinot Noir (WHI)
Montana Marlborough Cabernet
  Sauvignon (TAN, PD, GRE)
Ngatarawa Cabernet Sauvignon (KA)
Stoneleigh Cabernet Sauvignon (WHI, PIP,
  AI, HAH, BAR)
Villa Maria Cabernet Sauvignon (BYR, VIC,
  KA)
1986
Babich Pinot Noir (KA)
Cooks Cabernet Sauvignon (PD, MAJ, VIN)
Mission Cabernet Sauvignon/Merlot (KA)
Nobilo Pinotage (GRE, AV)
Stoneleigh Cabernet Sauvignon (UP, WHI, KA)

£7.00 to £8.99
1988
Brookfield's Cabernet Sauvignon (FIZ)
Redwood Valley Estate Cabernet
  Sauvignon (FIZ, PIP)
St-Helena Pinot Noir (LAY)
Stoneleigh Cabernet Sauvignon (ALL)
1987
★Cloudy Bay Cabernet Sauvignon/Merlot
  (BYR)
Hunter Pinot Noir (TAN, STA, KA)
Matua Valley Cabernet Sauvignon (MAJ,
  GRE, FIZ, WIZ)
St-Nesbit Cabernet Sauvignon (LAY, FIZ)

£9.00 to £10.99
1988
Brookfield's Estate Cabernet Sauvignon
  (RAE)
Cloudy Bay Cabernet Sauvignon (MV)
Dry Ridge Pinot Noir (REI)
1987
Matua Valley Cabernet Sauvignon (WCL,
  BO, YF)

£11.00 to £14.99
1988
Stonyridge Larose Cabernet (FIZ)
1987
Te Mata Coleraine Cabernet Sauvignon/
  Merlot (BYR)

WHITE

Under £5.00
Non-vintage
Nobilo Müller-Thurgau (DI)
1989
Matua Valley Brownlie Sauvignon (OD)
Montana Marlborough Chardonnay (WHI,
  OD, AUG, BO, PIP, SAF, VIC, UN, GRE)
★Montana Marlborough Sauvignon Blanc
  (WHI, OD, AUG, SAF, BOT, VIC, UN)
1988
Cooks Chenin Blanc (WHI, IR, DAV, TAN, KA)
1987
Cooks Chenin Blanc (GI, CH, IR)
Marlborough Gewürztraminer (WHI)
★Morton Estate Sauvignon Blanc (WIZ)

£5.00 to £5.99
1989
Babich Semillon/Chardonnay (WHI)
★Delegat's Sauvignon Blanc (WIZ, PIP)
Matua Valley Gewürztraminer (FIZ)
Montana Marlborough Chardonnay (THR,
  TAN, DAV, BAR)
Montana Marlborough Sauvignon Blanc
  (THR, TAN, DAV, BAR)
1988
Babich Sauvignon Blanc (BYR, HAY)
Cooks Chardonnay (BL, MAJ, DAV, VIN)
Delegat's Hawke's Bay Sauvignon Blanc
  (WHI)
Matua Valley Sauvignon Blanc (NI, GRE,
  FIZ)
Montana Marlborough Chardonnay (BL)

★Redwood Valley Late Harvest Rhine
  Riesling ½ bottle (VIC, FIZ)
Selaks Sauvignon Blanc/Semillon (WIZ)

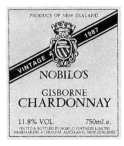

Stoneleigh Chardonnay (GRE)
Villa Maria Sauvignon Blanc (BYR)

——————— £6.00 to £7.99 ———————
1989
Brookfield's Gewürztraminer (FIZ)
Brookfield's Pinot Gris (FIZ)
★Cloudy Bay Sauvignon Blanc (KA, HAH,
  RAE)
Collards Sauvignon Blanc (BIB)
Morton Estate Sauvignon Blanc (PIP)
Nobilo Sauvignon Blanc (LOR, BO, BOT)
Redwood Valley Wood-Aged Sauvignon
  Blanc (FIZ)
Selaks Kumeu Estate Sauvignon Blanc
  (AD)
Stoneleigh Sauvignon Blanc (WHI)
Vidal Hawke's Bay Chardonnay (WHI)
Vidal Sauvignon Blanc (FIZ, RES)
1988
Babich Sauvignon Blanc (UP, GRE)
Babich Semillon/Chardonnay (VIC)
Brookfield's Chardonnay (KA)
Cloudy Bay Sauvignon Blanc (GI)
Coopers Creek Fumé Blanc (ALL)
Delegat's Sauvignon Blanc (ASK, KA, GI, REI,
  HA)
Hunter Gewürztraminer (STA, UP)
★Hunter Sauvignon Blanc (STA, UP, KA)
Hunter's Rhine Riesling (UP)
Morton Estate Sauvignon Blanc (BEK, BYR)
Nobilo Gewürztraminer (AV)
Nobilo Sauvignon Blanc (UP, DI)
Redwood Valley Chardonnay (FIZ)
Redwood Valley Sauvignon Blanc (MV, REI)
Selaks Sauvignon Blanc (BYR)
Stoneleigh Sauvignon Blanc (WHI, UP, KA,
  HAH, TAN, BAR, LAY, ALL, THR)
Vidal Sauvignon Blanc (KA)

1987
Coopers Creek Chardonnay (ALL)
Delegat's Chardonnay (ASK)
Morton Estate Chardonnay (WIZ, BEK)
Ngatarawa Chardonnay (BYR)
★Nobilo Gisborne Chardonnay (BYR, MAJ)
Selaks Chardonnay (WIL, RAE, KA)
Selaks Sauvignon Blanc/Semillon (WIL,
  RAE, BO, IR, KA)
Selaks Semillon (AD)
Stoneleigh Sauvignon Blanc (AI)
Villa Maria Sauvignon Blanc (KA)
1986
Delegat's Chardonnay (GRE, KA)
Delegat's Gisborne Chardonnay (WHI)
Redwood Valley Late Harvest Rhine
  Riesling ½ bottle (REI)
Selaks Semillon (WIL, IR)

——————— £8.00 to £9.99 ———————
1989
Cloudy Bay Sauvignon Blanc (LAY, HA, VIG)
Selaks Sauvignon Blanc (BAR, WS)
1988
Cloudy Bay Chardonnay (BO, MV, LAY, WCL,
  GI, RAE)
Giesen Chardonnay (CB, FIZ, KA, REI)
Hunter Sauvignon Blanc (HA)
Morton Estate Chardonnay (PIP)
Nobilo Dixon Chardonnay (UP, GRE)
Seifried Chardonnay (LAY)
Selaks Sauvignon Blanc (WIL, IR, PE)
1987
Hawke's Bay Sauvignon Blanc, Nautilus
  (TAN)
Ngatarawa Chardonnay (KA)
1986
Selaks Sauvignon Blanc/Semillon (PE)

——————— £10.00 to £11.99 ———————
1989
Cloudy Bay Chardonnay (RES)
1988
Babich Irongate Chardonnay (TAN, DAV)
Te Mata Elston Chardonnay (BYR, LAY)
1987
Te Mata Elston Chardonnay (CH)
1986
Selaks Founders Reserve Chardonnay
  (WIL)

——————— £12.00 to £13.99 ———————
1988
Kumeu River Noble Dry Sauvignon (AD)
Te Mata Elston Chardonnay (UP, VIG)

UNITED KINGDOM

WHITE

──────── Under £4.00 ────────

1989
★Biddenden Huxelrebe (HAC)
1988
★Hambledon (HAC)
1987
Meon Valley Madeleine Angevine (HAC)
1986
Penshurst Dry (STA)
Penshurst Reichensteiner (STA)
Westbury Madeleine Angevine/Sieger (HAC)

──────── £4.00 to £4.99 ────────

1989
Biddenden Ortega (HAC)
★Carr Taylor Reichensteiner (WAI)
Elmham Park Dry (HIC)
★Elmham Park Medium Dry (HIC)
Lamberhurst Priory Seyval Blanc (UP)
★Thames Valley Late Harvest Scheurebe
½ bottle (HAC)
Thames Valley Schönburger (HAC)
1988
Boze Down (HAC)
Bruisyard St Peter Müller-Thurgau (WIL, BO)
Elmham Park Medium Dry (HAC)
Headcorn Schönburger (HAC)
Headcorn Seyval Blanc (HAC)
Meon Valley Seyval Blanc (HAC)
★Pilton Manor Vintage Selection (WRI)
★Three Choirs Müller-Thurgau/
Reichensteiner (MAJ)
Wraxall (EL)
1987
Headcorn Wealdon White (HAC)
Lamberhurst Priory Reichensteiner (UP, WHI)
Nutbourne Manor Müller-Thurgau (HAC)
Penshurst Müller-Thurgau (HAC)
Pilton Manor Müller-Thurgau (MAJ)
Saxon Valley (DAV)
Tenterden (DAV)
Thames Valley Seyval (HAC)
1986
Chiddingstone Kerner (STA)
Chiltern Valley (HAG, CB)
Lamberhurst Priory Müller-Thurgau (WRI, HAC)
Lamberhurst Priory Seyval Blanc (VIC)

──────── £5.00 to £5.99 ────────

1989
★Breaky Bottom Müller-Thurgau (HAC)
★Nutbourne Manor Bacchus (HAC)
★Rock Lodge Müller-Thurgau Dry (HAC)
1988
Cane End (HAC)
Carr Taylor Reichensteiner (AUG)
Conghurst (HAC)
Nutbourne Manor Huxelrebe (HAC)
Nutbourne Manor Schönburger (HAC)
St George's Müller-Thurgau (ELL)
1987
Adgestone (HAG, WHI, WIL, VIC)
Barton Manor Müller-Thurgau (HA)
Chiltern Valley (BEK)
Chiltern Valley, Old Luxter's Reserve (HAG)
Pilton Manor Huxelrebe (WRI)
1986
Berwick Glebe (CB)
Heywood Special Reserve (HAC)
Staple St-James Müller Thurgau (VIC)

Wootton Seyval (HAG)

──────── £6.00 to £7.99 ────────

1989
Carr Taylor Schönburger (ELL)
Chiltern Valley, Old Luxter's Reserve (IR)
1987
Lamberhurst Schönburger (HAC)

SPARKLING

──────── £8.00 to £10.50 ────────

Non-vintage
Carr Taylor (HAC)
Meon Valley Sparkling (HAC)
1988
Rock Lodge Imperial Brut (HAC)

OTHER WINE REGIONS

ARGENTINA

──────── **Under £4.00** ────────
1989
Chenin Blanc Riesling, Flichman Clair (VIC)
1988
★Andean Chardonnay (GI)
Torrontes, Etchart (VIC)
1987
Andean Chenin Blanc (GI)
1986
Andean Malbec (GI)
1985
★Andean Cabernet Sauvignon (GI)
Andean Pinot Noir (GI)

AUSTRIA

──────── **Under £4.50** ────────
1987
★Grüner Veltliner Lenz Moser Selection (VIC)
Pinot Blanc Lenz Moser Selection (VIC)

BULGARIA RED

──────── **Under £3.00** ────────
Non-vintage
Bulgarian Cabernet Sauvignon (SAI, TES, BL, PE, VIC, LAY, BOT)
Bulgarian Cabernet Sauvignon/Merlot (ASD, RAE, AUG, UN, PD, BOT)
Mehana Red (WIW, PE)
Pavlikeni Cabernet Sauvignon/Merlot (WIW, MAJ, PE)
Petrich Cabernet Sauvignon/Melnik (WIW)
Suhindol Merlot/Gamza (WIW, MAJ)
1986
Bulgarian Cabernet Sauvignon (WHI, UN, DAV)
Haskovo Merlot (WIW, THR)
Plovdiv Cabernet Sauvignon (WIW, THR, WCL)
Suhindol Cabernet Sauvignon (WIW, THR)
★Svichtov Cabernet Sauvignon (WIW)
1985
★Bulgarian Cabernet Sauvignon (WAI, MAJ, OD, WHI, CH, BYR, BO, AI)
Haskovo Merlot (SAF, WIW, AUG)
Plovdiv Cabernet Sauvignon (WIW, SAF)
Sakar Mountain Cabernet Sauvignon (WIW)
Suhindol Cabernet Sauvignon (WIW, GRE, WIZ)
Svichtov Cabernet Sauvignon (WIW)
1984
Bulgarian Merlot (GRE, UN)
Haskovo Merlot (WIZ)
Oriahovitza Reserve Cabernet Sauvignon (WIW, THR)
Plovdiv Cabernet Sauvignon (WIW, BL, PD, BOT)
Suhindol Cabernet Sauvignon (IR)

──────── **£3.00 to £3.99** ────────
Non-vintage
Bulgarian Cabernet Sauvignon (AV)
Mavrud Asenovgrad (PD, BOT)
Oriahovitza Cabernet Sauvignon (BOT, PD)
Sakar Mountain Cabernet Sauvignon (MAJ, VIC, PD, BOT)
1986
Svichtov Cabernet Sauvignon (WIW, WHI)
1985
Lozitza Cabernet Sauvignon (WIW)
Oriahovitza Cabernet Sauvignon/Merlot (WIW)
Sakar Mountain Cabernet Sauvignon (WHI, WCL)
Svichtov Cabernet Sauvignon (WIW, WHI, MAJ, OD, WIZ, GRE)
1984
Oriahovitza Cabernet Sauvignon/Merlot (WIW, WIZ)
Oriahovitza Cabernet Sauvignon (BL, WCL)
Sakar Merlot (WIW)
Suhindol Gamza (WIW)
1983
Mavrud Asenovgrad (BYR, MAJ)
Oriahovitza Cabernet Sauvignon/Merlot (BYR, OD)
Oriahovitza Cabernet Sauvignon (AI, TAN, DAV, PE, UN, AV)
Sakar Mountain Cabernet Sauvignon (WHI, BYR, GRE, PE, TAN)
1981
Mavrud Asenovgrad (WAI, GRE, PE)
Oriahovitza Cabernet Sauvignon/Merlot (GRE)
Sakar Mountain Cabernet Sauvignon (BO, WIZ, OD)
1980
Mavrud Asenovgrad (WIL)
Sakar Mountain Cabernet Sauvignon (TES)

BULGARIA WHITE

──────── **Under £3.00** ────────

Non-vintage
Bulgarian Chardonnay (CH, WHI, WIL, WCL, BYR, VIC, LAY, AI)
Bulgarian Muscat/Ugni Blanc (ASD, RAE, DAV)
Bulgarian Riesling (ASD, WIL, MAJ, OD, BYR, WHI, PE, PD, UN, BOT)
Bulgarian Sauvignon Blanc (WIW, MAJ, GRE, OD, WHI, AUG, PD, WCL, BOT)
Choumen Riesling (AUG)
Mehana White (MAJ, WIL, WIW, PE, PE)
Preslav Chardonnay (WIZ)
Russe Riesling/Misket (WIW)
1988
Bulgarian Muscat/Ugni Blanc (BYR)
1987
★Khan Krum Chardonnay (OD, GRE, WIW, WIZ)

──────── **£3.00 to £3.99** ────────

Non-vintage
Bulgarian Chardonnay (AV)
Khan Krum Chardonnay (WHI, BOT, PD)
1987
Novi Pazar Chardonnay (WIW, WHI, MAJ)
1986
Khan Krum Chardonnay (BL, AI)
Novi Pazar Chardonnay (WHI)
1985
Novi Pazar Chardonnay (WIZ)

──────── **£4.00 to £4.99** ────────

Non-vintage
Mehana White (BAR)

CANADA

──────── **Under £6.00** ────────

1987
Inniskillin Maréchal Foch Red (GRE, AV)

──────── **£6.00 to £7.99** ────────

1988
Inniskillin Chardonnay (GRE, AV)
Inniskillin Riesling (AV)

CHILE RED

──────── **Under £4.00** ────────

1988
Santa Digna Cabernet Sauvignon, Torres (DI)

1987
★Caliterra Cabernet Sauvignon (LO)
Concha y Toro Cabernet Sauvignon/Merlot (NI)
★Errázuriz Panquehue Cabernet Sauvignon (SAF)
Santa Rita Maipo Cabernet Sauvignon (DI)
Undurraga Cabernet Sauvignon (AV)
1986
Caliterra Cabernet Sauvignon (HAU, BYR, LO)
Concha y Toro Cabernet Sauvignon (VIC, NI)
Concha y Toro Merlot (BOT, UN)
1985
★Concha y Toro Cabernet Sauvignon (GRE, WAI, BYR, UP, NI, UN)

──────── **£4.00 to £4.99** ────────

1989
Domaine Caperana Cabernet Sauvignon (BOD, WIC)
1988
★Villa Montes Cabernet Sauvignon (ELL)
1987
Canepa Estate Oak-Aged Cabernet Sauvignon (BOD)
1986
Cabernet Sauvignon Torres (WHI)
Concha y Toro Merlot (HIC)
★Cousiño Macul Don Luis Red (NI)
1985
★Undurraga Cabernet Sauvignon Reserve Selection (GRE)
1983
★Concha y Toro Casillero del Diablo (VIC, BYR)
★Cousiño Macul Antiguas Reservas Cabernet Sauvignon (VIC)
1982
Cousiño Macul Cabernet Sauvignon (UP)
1981
Cousiño Macul Antiguas Reservas Cabernet Sauvignon (BO, MV)

──────── **£5.00 to £5.99** ────────

1987
Cabernet Sauvignon Torres (PE, BAR)
★Los Vascos Cabernet Sauvignon (WIC)
Villa Montes Cabernet Sauvignon (STA)
1985
Cousiño Macul Antiguas Reservas Cabernet Sauvignon (NI)
1984
Cousiño Macul Antiguas Reservas Cabernet Sauvignon (ELL)

1983
Cousiño Macul Antiguas Reservas
Cabernet Sauvignon (AUG, NI, BOT, YF,
TAN)
Marqués de Casa Concha Cabernet
Sauvignon (TAN)

CHILE WHITE

──────── Under £4.00 ────────
1989
Caliterra Sauvignon Blanc (HAU)
★Undurraga Sauvignon Blanc (AV)
★Villa Montes Sauvignon Blanc (GRE)
1988
Concha y Toro Chardonnay (GRE, UP, NI)
Concha y Toro Sauvignon Blanc/Semillon
(GRE, UP, NI)
★Santa Digna Sauvignon Blanc, Torres (DI,
BYR, TAN)
1987
★Bellaterra Sauvignon Blanc, Torres (DI)
Concha y Toro Sauvignon Blanc (BYR)
Cousiño Macul Chardonnay (BO)
Santa Digna Sauvignon Blanc, Torres (BYR)

──────── £4.00 to £4.99 ────────
1989
Caperana Chardonnay (BOD)
Caperana Sauvignon Blanc (BOD, WIC)
Cousiño Macul Chardonnay (NI)
Errázuriz Panquehue Chardonnay (VIC)
Sauvignon Blanc Torres (UP)
Villa Montes Sauvignon Blanc (ELL)
1988
Concha y Toro Chardonnay (UN)
Cousiño Macul Chardonnay (BYR, GRE, YF)
Santa Digna Sauvignon, Torres (VIC)
Sauvignon Blanc Torres (AUG, UP)
1987
Gewürztraminer Torres (GRE)
Santa Digna Riesling, Torres (GRE)

──────── £5.00 to £5.99 ────────
1990
Villa Montes Chardonnay (ELL)
1989
Bellaterra Sauvignon Blanc, Torres (UP)
Cousiño Macul Chardonnay (TAN, HIC)
1988
Bellaterra Sauvignon Blanc, Torres (UP, PE)
1987
Bellaterra Sauvignon Blanc, Torres (HUN)
1986
Bellaterra Sauvignon Blanc, Torres (GRE)

CYPRUS

──────── Under £4.00 ────────
Non-vintage
Aphrodite Keo White (BYR, WHI, UN)
Othello Keo Red (WHI, BYR, UN)
St-Panteleimon Keo White (CH, WHI, BL, UN)

GREECE RED

──────── Under £3.00 ────────
Non-vintage
Demestica Achaia Clauss (CH, PD)
Mavrodaphne Patras, Kourtaki (WAI, VIC)
Nousa Tsantali (WHI)
1989
Kouros Nemea (WIZ)

──────── £3.00 to £4.99 ────────
1986
Kouros Nemea (AUG, UN)
1985
Naoussa, Naoussa Co-op. (AI)
1981
★Château Carras Côtes de Meliton (LO)

──────── £5.00 to £6.99 ────────
1986
Château Pegasus (AI)
1981
Château Carras Côtes de Meliton (VIC, WS,
GRE, TAN, HIC)
Château Carras Tête de Cuvée (WRI)
Meliton (VIC, WS, GRE, TAN, HIC)

GREECE WHITE

──────── Under £4.00 ────────
Non-vintage
Demestica Achaia Clauss (CH, BOT, WIL)
Imiglikos Tsantali (WHI)
Retsina Achaia Clauss (CH, PD, BOT)
Samos Muscat (WCL, MAJ, OD)
1988
★Kouros Patras (WIZ)

──────── £4.00 to £5.99 ────────
Non-vintage
Samos Muscat (VIC)
1987
Cephalonia Gentilini (BIB)

──────── c. £6.00 ────────
Non-vintage
Samos Nectar 10-year-old (TAN)

HUNGARY WHITE

──────── Under £3.00 ────────
Non-vintage
Hungarian Chardonnay (OD)
1989
Hungarian Chardonnay (WIW)
Hungarian Gewürztraminer (WIW)
Hungarian Sauvignon Blanc (WIW)
Móri Ezerjó (WIW)
1988
Hungarian Chardonnay (WIW)
Hungarian Gewürztraminer (WIW)
Hungarian Sauvignon Blanc (WIW)
Móri Ezerjó (WIW)
1987
Badacsonyi Pinot Gris (GRE)
Móri Ezerjó (WIW)
1985
Debroï Hárslevelü (GRE)

──────── £3.00 to £3.99 ────────
1986
★Tokay Szamorodni Sweet ½ litre (WIW)
1984
Tokay Szamorodni Dry ½ litre (WIW)

──────── £4.00 to £4.99 ────────
Non-vintage
Tokay Szamorodni Dry ½ litre (DI)
Tokay Szamorodni Sweet ½ litre (UN)
1986
★Tokay Aszú 3 Putts ½ litre (WIW)
1981
Tokay Aszú 5 Putts ½ litre (AI)

──────── £5.00 to £6.99 ────────
Non-vintage
Tokay Aszú 3 Putts ½ litre (LAY, UN, PE, DI,
   BOT, PD)
Tokay Aszú 4 Putts ½ litre (UN, DI)

┌─────────────────────────┐
│ *Please don't blame*   │
│ **Webster's** *or the*   │
│ *merchants listed if a* │
│ *wine is sold out or if the* │
│ *vintage you want is no* │
│ *longer available. Wine is* │
│ *a living entity and a* │
│ *limited commodity –*   │
│ *continuity of supply*   │
│ *cannot, alas, be*   │
│ *guaranteed.*   │
└─────────────────────────┘

Tokay Aszú 5 Putts ½ litre (LAY)
1984
Tokay Aszú 4 Putts ½ litre (WIW)
1983
Tokay Aszú 5 Putts ½ litre (WIW)
1982
Tokay Aszú 5 Putts ½ litre (OD)
1981
Tokay Aszú 3 Putts ½ litre (WIL, AD)
Tokay Aszú 5 Putts ½ litre (GRE)
1979
Tokay Aszú 3 Putts ½ litre (WHI, BO)
Tokay Aszú 4 Putts ½ litre (HAG, WIL, VIG)
★Tokay Aszú 5 Putts ½ litre (CH, WHI, BO)
1975
Tokay Aszú 3 Putts ½ litre (WRI)

──────── £7.00 to £9.99 ────────
Non-vintage
Tokay Aszú 5 Putts ½ litre (UN, DI, VIC)
1981
Tokay Aszú 3 Putts ½ litre (HA)
Tokay Aszú 5 Putts ½ litre (AD, WRI)
1979
Tokay Aszú 5 Putts ½ litre (TAN, WIL, VIG)

──────── c. £22.00 ────────
1976
Tokay Aszú Essencia ½ litre (WIW)

──────── £40.00 to £49.99 ────────
1968
Tokay Aszú Essencia ½ litre (AD)
1957
Tokay Aszú Essencia ½ litre (WIW, GRE)
1956
Tokay Aszú 5 Putts ½ litre (AD)

──────── £50.00 to £75.00 ────────
1957
Tokay Aszú Essencia ½ litre (VIG, HA, BER)
1945
Tokay Aszú 5 Putts ½ litre (VIG)
1924
Tokay Szamorodni Dry ½ litre (VIG)

HUNGARY RED

──────── Under £3.00 ────────
Non-vintage
Hungarian Pinot Noir (WIW)
1985
Soproni Kek-Frankos (GRE)
1984
Eger Bull's Blood (BO)

──────── **£3.00 to £3.99** ────────

1985
Eger Bull's Blood (AUG, PE, BOT)
1983
Eger Bull's Blood (AUG)
Hungarian Merlot (WIW)
1982
Hungarian Cabernet Sauvignon (WIW)
1979
Hungarian Pinot Noir (WIW)

ISRAEL

──────── **Under £6.00** ────────

Non-vintage
Segev No. 10 Medium Sweet Red (WIL)
1988
Golan Mount Hermon Dry White (AUG, WRI)

──────── **£6.00 to £7.99** ────────

1986
Gamla Galilee Cabernet Sauvignon (WRI)

LEBANON RED

──────── **Under £6.00** ────────

1982
★Château Musar (UP, HUN, WAI, GRE, WIZ,
    MAJ, LAY, HAG, WHI, CHA, TAN, HAU, IR, NI,
    AD, VIC, VIG, UN, AUG)
1981
Château Musar (BYR, GI, CH, WIL, BO, UP, AI)
1980
Château Musar (BYR, WIZ)
1979
Château Musar (UP, BYR)
1978
Château Musar (WIZ)

──────── **£6.00 to £9.99** ────────

1982
Château Musar (STA, ALL, ELL, PD, THR, BOT,
    AV)
1980
Château Musar (CHA, BAR, GI)
1979
Château Musar (CHA, GI, BAR)
1978
Château Musar (UP, GI, BAR)
1977
Château Musar (UP, GI)

──────── **£12.50 to £14.99** ────────

1975
Château Musar (GI, HAG, HAU, VIG)

──────── **£19.00 to £27.50** ────────

1967
Château Musar (GRE)
1966
Château Musar (VIG)

ROMANIA

──────── **Under £5.00** ────────

Non-vintage
Pinot Noir Dealul Mare (PE)
Romanian Merlot (GRE)
Sainsbury's Romanian Pinot Noir (SAI)
1988
Romanian Sauvignon Blanc (GRE)
1985
★Romanian Pinot Noir (CH)
1984
Classic Pinot Noir (GRE)
1979
Carpatenbogen Steiniger Pietraasele
    Edelbeerenlese (PE)
Muscat Ottonel White (HUN)

SOUTH AFRICA RED

──────── **Under £3.00** ────────

Non-vintage
★KWV Cabernet Sauvignon (HOG)
★KWV Shiraz (HOG)
1987
Pinotage Culemborg Paarl (WAI)
1986
KWV Roodeberg (WAI)

──────── **£3.00 to £3.99** ────────

Non-vintage
KWV Cabernet Sauvignon (UN, PD, PE, BOT)
KWV Roodeberg (BL, VIC, UN, PE, PD, BOT)
1987
KWV Pinotage (DAV, UP)
1986
KWV Cabernet Sauvignon (CH, UP)
KWV Paarl Cinsaut (CAP)
1985
KWV Pinotage (CAP, BYR, GRE)
KWV Roodeberg (CAP, CH, UP, AI)
Nederburg Pinotage (CAP)
1984
KWV Shiraz (BO, VIG)
1983
Diemersdal (BO)
KWV Roodeberg (GI, WHI)
1982
Diemersdal (CAP)

KWV Cabernet Sauvignon (GRE)
KWV Pinotage (LOR)
KWV Roodeberg (GRE)

——————— £4.00 to £4.99 ———————
Non-vintage
Drostdy Hof Rouge Select (GRE)
★Meerendal Shiraz (HOG)
1986
Backsberg Pinotage (BO)
Fleur du Cap Roodebloem (CAP)
1985
Nederburg Baronne (BAR)
Nederburg Paarl Cabernet Sauvignon (TAN)
Nederburg Pinotage (VIG)
Zonnebloem Shiraz (CAP)
1984
Nederburg Paarl Cabernet Sauvignon (CAP, WHI)
1982
Meerendal Pinotage (WIL)
★Nederburg Paarl Cabernet Sauvignon (UN)
1980
Nederburg Pinotage (WHI)

——————— £5.00 to £5.99 ———————
1986
Fairview Pinotage (WRI)
Zonnebloem Cabernet Sauvignon (WRI)
1985
Groot Constantia Pinotage (CAP)
1984
Nederburg Paarl Cabernet Sauvignon (WRI)
1983
Meerlust Cabernet Sauvignon (GI)
★Meerlust Rubicon (GI)
Nederburg Edelrood (WRI)

——————— £6.00 to £7.99 ———————
1986
Delheim Pinotage (BAR)
Pinotage Delheim Kaelenhof (PE)
1985
Groot Constantia Pinotage (WRI)
Meerlust Rubicon (CAP)
1984
Groot Constantia Cabernet Sauvignon (BYR, CAP)
Zandvliet Shiraz (WRI, GRE)
1983
Meerlust Cabernet Sauvignon (WHI, CAP, IR)
1982
Meerlust Rubicon (HOG)
Groot Constantia Heerenrood (CAP)

——————— £8.00 to £9.99 ———————
1987
Rustenberg Cabernet Sauvignon (AV)
1984
★Hamilton Russell Grand Vin Rouge (VIG)
Meerlust Cabernet Sauvignon (WRI)
Meerlust Rubicon (GRE)
Rustenberg Cabernet Sauvignon (VIG)
1983
Meerlust Cabernet Sauvignon (WRI, VIG, GRE)
Meerlust Rubicon (WRI)
Stellenryk Cabernet Sauvignon (CAP, WRI)
1982
★Uitkyk Carlonet (CAP)
1975
Meerlust Rubicon (VIG)

SOUTH AFRICA WHITE

——————— Under £3.00 ———————
Non-vintage
KWV Chenin Blanc (HOG)
KWV Riesling (HOG)
★KWV Steen (HOG)
1988
KWV Chenin Blanc (WAI)

——————— £3.00 to £3.99 ———————
Non-vintage
Grunberger Stein (WIL)
KWV Chenin Blanc (BL, VIC, UN, PE, PD, BOT)
KWV Riesling (UN, PD, BOT)
KWV Sauvignon Blanc (VIC, BOT)
1989
KWV Chenin Blanc (BO, DAV, WRI, HIC)
KWV Steen Special Late Harvest (HIC)
1988
KWV Chenin Blanc (CAP, BYR, CH, GRE, WRI, AI)
KWV Pinotage (BO)
KWV Riesling (CAP)
KWV Steen (CAP, BYR, CH, DAV, TAN)
KWV Steen Special Late Harvest (CAP, BO)
Nederburg Stein (CAP)
1987
KWV Cape Bouquet Blanc (WHI)
KWV Chenin Blanc (LOR, GI, WHI)
KWV Laborie (CAP)
KWV Riesling (GRE, UP)
1986
KWV Laborie (CAP)
KWV Riesling (WHI)
KWV Roodeberg (BO)
KWV Steen (WHI)

───── £4.00 to £5.99 ─────

1988
Koopmanskloof Blanc de Marbonne (WHI, CAP)
le Bonheur Blanc Fumé (CAP)
l'Ormarins Rhine Riesling (CAP)
Uitkyk Carlsheim (CAP)
de Wetshof Rhine Riesling (CAP, HOG)
de Wetshof Sauvignon Blanc (CAP, HOG)
1987
Koopmanskloof Blanc de Marbonne (CAP)
Nederburg Fonternel (GRE)
★l'Ormarins Sauvignon Blanc (WHI)
Theuniskraal Riesling (HOG)
de Wetshof Rhine Riesling (WHI, CAP, GRE)
1986
Nederburg Paarl Riesling (GRE, WHI)
de Wetshof Rhine Riesling (WIL)
1985
Kanonkop Sauvignon Blanc (CAP)

───── £6.00 to £8.99 ─────

1988
Backsberg Sauvignon Blanc (WRI)
1987
KWV Noble Late Harvest (WHI, VIG)
Simousig Late Harvest Gewürztraminer (BAR)

SOUTH AFRICA ROSÉ

───── Under £4.00 ─────

1988
KWV Cabernet Sauvignon Blanc de Noir (CAP)
Nederburg Rosé (CAP)

SOUTH AFRICA SPARKLING

───── Under £6.50 ─────

Non-vintage
KWV Mousseux Blanc Cuvée Brut (CAP)
Nederburg Première Cuvée Brut (CAP)
1988
JC Le Roux Sauvignon Blanc (CAP)
Laborie Blanc de Noir (CAP)

SOUTH AFRICA FORTIFIED

───── Under £3.00 ─────

Non-vintage
Cavendish Cape Medium Dry (HOG, WAI)
Mymering Pale Extra Dry (HOG, CAP)
Onzerust Medium (HOG, CAP)
Renasans Dry Amontillado (HOG)

───── £3.00 to £4.49 ─────

Non-vintage
Cavendish Cape Extra Dry (CAP)
Cavendish Fine Old Ruby (HOG, CAP)
Onzerust Medium (HAG, DI)
Renasans Pale Dry (HAG, DI)

SWITZERLAND

───── Under £7.00 ─────

1986
Dôle Romane Orsat Gamay (GRE)
Johannisberg Vent d'Est Orsat Sylvaner (GRE)

───── c. £9.50 ─────

1986
Domaine de la Bolliattaz, Villette (TAN)

YUGOSLAVIA WHITE

───── Under £4.00 ─────

Non-vintage
Lutomer Laski Riesling (ASD, TES, UN)
Tesco Laski Riesling (TES)
1989
Traminer, PPK Kutjevo Winery (BOD)
1983
Beli Burgundec Pinot Blanc (BYR)

YUGOSLAVIA RED

───── Under £4.00 ─────

1988
★Alpi Juliana Merlot (BOD)
1987
★Alpi Juliana Cabernet Sauvignon (BOD)
Slovin Cabernet Sauvignon (WHI)
1986
★Milion Merlot (WAI)
1985
Mordi Cabernet Sauvignon (BYR)
Mordi Pinot Noir (BYR)
Slovin Cabernet Sauvignon (BYR, WIL)
1984
Milion Merlot (OD)
1983
Slovin Black Label Cabernet Sauvignon (WHI)

ZIMBABWE

───── Under £3.50 ─────

1986
Flame Lily Premium Dry White (GRE)
Flame Lily Red (GRE)

CELLARING, SERVING AND TASTING WINE

Closely-packed builders' rubble or someone else's living room, rather than a cellar, is all you're likely to find these days under most people's floorboards. So if you want to store your wine, finding the right place can be a problem.

Cellars, though, are the *ideal* place to store wine – dark, cool (around 12°C/54°F is best), with no great temperature changes between winter and summer, and well out of the path of wagging tails and scampering feet. But don't despair if all you have is a broom cupboard or a few square feet under the bed. Almost any cupboard can be adapted for storing wine – and a little insulation can be improvised to protect the bottles even in the most severely overheated flat. Wine is remarkably resilient stuff. Break all the rules – leave it upright for weeks on the kitchen window sill – and you'll be surprised how few wines will actually suffer.

Wines you intend to keep for months or years need a little more care. Heat really is the greatest enemy. Like any other chemical reaction, the natural development of wine speeds up as the temperature rises, and warm wine will age and spoil more quickly, while badly bottled wines might re-ferment. So avoid storing your long term bottles near the stove, by the central heating pipes or even in the garage if it is subject to a blast of heat whenever the sun shines. Light has been shown to damage wines. And long keepers should lie on the sides – corks may dry out if the bottles are left for many months upright, allowing in damaging air. It takes some time, though, for a properly capsuled bottle to come to any harm.

If you really are worried about your wine storage, get someone else to keep it for you. Fine wines needing long ageing are best looked after by a wine merchant, and many will cellar your wine for between £2 and £3.50 per case per year.

SERVING

TEMPERATURE We've been conditioned to expect our red wines at 'room' temperature and our white wines chilled. But if the temperature of your room is 70°F or if Britain is suffering an unusual heatwave, red wines will taste nothing but soupy and flat served at 'room temperature'. Decide what you want from your wine, and treat it accordingly. Light reds often taste far fresher chilled, and full-bodied whites show at their best when cooled only lightly. On a hot day even full-bodied reds will need to be served cooler. Cooling can give a wine a freshness it will not display at room temperature. An hour in the fridge is enough for light whites and rosés, half an hour for fuller whites and rosés and light reds.

If you're caught short of cold wine, a quarter of an hour in the freezer will certainly do the wine no harm. Ice buckets filled with ice *and* water will chill a bottle quicker than ice alone, and, in desperation, a cube in the glass is a perfectly reasonable solution for an everyday wine. Once your bottle is cold, plastic insulating sleeves are a good alternative to ice buckets. Warming up wine is more difficult. You could pour it into a warm, not hot, decanter, or just be patient, and cup the glass in your hands.

DECANTING Many fine, old wines are never tasted at their best because they are decanted too soon. The fruit and aromas of old wines are delicate and fleeting, and if you follow the traditionalists' advice and decant an hour or two before drinking, they may be off and away on the dining room air long before you get your nose into a glass. Old wines oxidize and develop vinegary flavours very quickly on exposure to air. The safest bet is to open and decant immediately before serving, and the older the wine, the more vital this is.

There is a *good* reason for decanting old wines. Many old red wines have thrown a sludgy, gritty deposit in the bottle, and the clear wine must be poured off the solids very carefully in one single action if everyone is not to drink a glassful of sludge. Simply stand the bottle upright for a day or two to allow the deposit to settle, then very gently remove the cork (a Screwpull or Spinhandle corkscrew is gentlest) and, with a light (torch, lightbulb or the traditional candle) under the bottle, pour the wine gently off the sludge, stopping when you see the deposit or the cloudy wine above it heading into the neck of the bottle.

OPENING 'Warning: direct this bottle away from people before opening!' Champagne bottles are unlikely ever to bear the French translation, but that was the message on a piece of plastic wrapped around the capsule of a bottle of American fizz I opened the other day. Over-reaction, perhaps to a lawsuit brought by an angry recipient of a flying cork, but nevertheless wise advice. Hold Champagne corks firmly as you remove the wire, then twist the bottle gently, disturbing the bottle as little as possible and keeping a glass at hand to catch accidental fountains.

Still wines are less problematic. Remove the foil or plastic capsule completely, or cut it beneath the bottle lip (especially important with old-fashioned – poisonous – lead capsules). If the cork won't budge, try holding the bottle neck for a few moments under hot running water. For corks that drop into the bottle, there's a spindly-legged plastic gadget called a 'decorker'. The easiest corkscrews are Screwpulls, especially the Spinhandle version, and Screwpull also do a labour-saving foil-cutter.

Taste a little of each bottle after opening, even if you've just finished a bottle of the same thing – bottles from the same batch do vary.

KEEPING LEFT-OVERS There are three gadgets on the market to help you keep wine fresh once it's been opened. The cheapest in the long term (at around £7 for the gadget and two stoppers) is the Vacu-Vin, which sucks air out through a special rubber stopper, leaving a vacuum over the remaining wine inside the bottle. This works well if you are able to finish up the bottle within a few days, though it sucks out some aroma, too. The other two devices protect the wine under a blanket of inert gas – nitrogen and carbon dioxide combined. The Wine Preserver (about £4) is a simple aerosol with a long plastic tube. It takes practice to squirt the right amount, but this, too, works well so long as you drink up the bottle in a couple of goes. Best, but by far the most expensive, is the Mini Wine Machine. A plastic tube and stopper remain in place until the bottle is finished, and as wine is drawn out through the tube and stopper, the bottle fills with inert gas from a detachable pressurized canister. We've tested them, and with this one, wines taste as fresh after ten days of opening as when first opened. The snag is, it costs £30, but one canister should last for 50 bottles.

GLASSES The reason that professional wine tasters use stemmed, tulip-shaped glasses rather than plastic beakers is all to do with learning the maximum amount about a given wine in the shortest possible time. Tulip-shaped glasses are generally reckoned to be the best since they concentrate the wine's aromas, and the stem prevents the hand from warming the wine as well as keeping any skin scent away from the taster's nose. But unless you're tasting professionally, it really is immaterial what you use. Of course fine, thin glass is likely to enhance the experience of drinking fine wine. But even glass slippers will do, providing, that is, they're clean and free from smells.

TASTING

LOOKS You can tell a lot about a wine just from looking. Sound wines are bright and clear (crystals are natural and no problem at all). Cool regions make pale wines, warm areas darker wines. Young reds will be purple to purple-black, gradually turning red, then orange then brown with age. Good dry white wines from cool climates will be pale whitish-yellow; warm-climate whites a deeper yellow, both yellowing more with age. Orange or brown shades are a sign of oxidation. Sweet wines are a deeper yellow from the outset, turning orange then brown with age. Tiny bubbles generally mean a young, fresh wine.

SMELL Good wines should smell clean and fruity. Swilling it round the glass will release more aroma. Professionals who are tasting on a daily basis and may taste up to a hundred wines on a busy day, have the chance to regularly refresh their palate memory and should be able to identify details such as the grape variety, country of origin, and so on. But the days of the 'fifth vine on the left, bottom south-east corner of the vineyard' party game are really no longer with us. Life for the blind-taster certainly used to be simpler when all the Cabernet in the world came from Bordeaux and all the Pinot Noir from Burgundy – but today even the best, most experienced of tasters may confuse a California wine with an Australian, an Italian with a French. But even the most inexperienced of wine drinkers is likely to be able to identify more than they realize. Red Rioja, for instance, tends to be an easily recognizable style, and usually everyone can pick out the grapiness of a Gewürztraminer or a Muscat.

Most wine faults can also be picked out in a single sniff: the cardboardy, sherry-like smell of oxidation, vinegary smells caused by bacteria at some stage during the wine's maturation, musty smells from the cork (corked wine) or from dirty barrels or mouldy cellars, the catch-in-your-throat dirty smell of sulphur dioxide, used as a preservative.

TASTE Try to dissect the different elements of the wine: sweetness, fruitiness, sharp acidity, tough tannin and alcohol, as well as specific flavours, of grape variety, oak, or other things. Then there's alcohol, anything from five per cent by volume in some Italian *spumante* wines to a whacking great 13 per cent in wines like Châteauneuf-du-Pape. The more alcohol there is, the bigger the wine will feel in the mouth, and a lot of alcohol will give your mouth a burning, spirity sensation. The hotter the climate, the more alcoholic the wine is likely to be. And with young, fortified wines, the spirit will be very noticeable before it has had a chance to blend in with the other elements in the wine – just try a young port.

Tarter, more acid wines will tend to come from cooler countries and vintages, though many hot countries add acidity to their wines. Tough, dark reds are more likely to come from hot places. The youngest and best-made wines will tend to have most fruit, and certain grape varieties make fruitier wines than others. Once you have spat or swallowed, wait a moment before the next gulp. The taste of a good wine lingers.

RESTAURANTS

Most wine is drunk with meals, and whatever marvels you may have down in the cellar or up in the loft, there comes a time when you want to brave the restaurant mark-ups. Many of the finest restaurants have lousy wine lists, but you will rarely eat an entirely bad meal in a restaurant with superlative wines. This is a selection of restaurant wine lists for the wine lover ... the cream of the country's good lists. Not all of them are long, but on each there is hardly a wine that will prove disappointing, and plenty that will have you positively purring with pleasure.

EAST ANGLIA

The Crown *90 High Street, Southwold, Suffolk IP18 6DP (0502) 722275* Stunning selection from Adnams, who own the hotel. The Italian selection is unusually good, but there are exceptional French wines, too, especially from the Loire, Rhône, Burgundy and Bordeaux, including some mature wines. California wines include Cabernets back to 1974. Fine wines also come by the glass from the Cruover machine (it keeps opened wines fresh).

The Fountain House *The Street, East Bergholt, Colchester, Essex CO7 6TB (0206) 298232* An interesting, often unusual selection of top names from Australia, Italy, Germany, the major areas of France.

Hintlesham Hall *Hintlesham, Suffolk IP8 3NS (047 387) 268* Well-balanced list of tempting wines from Bordeaux, Burgundy, Rhône, Germany and Australia, with a fine selection of half bottles.

The Starr *Market Place, Great Dunmow, Essex CM6 1AX (037187) 4321* Limited but good selection mostly from France, with good Burgundies, clarets including a list of second wines, Beaujolais, and a few serious wines from elsewhere.

LONDON & HOME COUNTIES

Bibendum *Michelin House, 81 Fulham Road, London SW3 6RE 071-581 5817* Long list of clarets and good Burgundies and short but excellent selection from the Loire, Alsace, Rhône, Germany, Italy, California and Australia.

Boulestin *1a Henrietta Street, London WC2E 8PS 071-836 7061* An expensive list, over 250 entries, but very strong on claret and some good Sauternes.

Cavaliers *129 Queenstown Road, London SW8 3RH 071-720 6960* Relatively short but excellent list, notable expecially for Loires (including old vintages) and Burgundies.

Corney & Barrow *118 Moorgate, London EC2M 6UR 071-628 2898; 109 Broad Street, London EC2N 1AP 071-638 9308; 44 Cannon Street, London EC4N 6JJ 071-248 1700* When a restaurant is run by a wine merchant you expect the list to be good. France dominates, but there are fine wines from around the world, albeit at decidedly London prices.

La Giralda *66 Pinner Green, Pinner, Middlesex HA5 2AB 081-868 3429* Exclusively Spanish list, concentrating on Rioja, but there are several vintages of Torres Gran Coronas Black Label (back to 1971) and of Valbuena and Vega Sicilia.

L'Incontro *87 Pimlico Road, London SW1W 8PH 071-730 6327* Wine in Italian restaurants has been a joke for too long. By the simple expedient of taking the new generation of Italian wines (notably from Tuscany and Piedmont) seriously, L'Incontro has produced easily the best Italian list in the country.

RSJ *13A Coin Street, London SE1 8YQ 071-928 4554* Good French list with a particularly fine and extensive Loire section.

Tate Gallery Restaurant *Millbank, London SW1P 4RG 071-834 6754* Fine, mature wines – especially clarets, but also Germans, ports, Sauternes and even mid-'70s California Cabernet at ungreedy mark-ups.

Waltons *121 Walton Street, London SW3 071-584-0204* Excellent list of domaine-bottled Burgundies and fine clarets.

MIDLANDS

Bell Inn *Aston Clinton, Bucks HP22 5HP (0296) 630252* A fine globe-trotting list that benefits from the associated Gerard Harris wine shop over the road. Virtually the entire retail list is available in the restaurant, although with higher mark-ups. Some bottles (notably mature clarets) need to be ordered up from the cellar in advance. Loire, Rhône, Provence and Alsace are well served.

The Evesham Hotel *Cooper's Lane, off Waterside, Evesham, Worcs WR11 6DA (0386) 765566* Wines from *everywhere* (Algeria, Brazil, Turkey, Canada, Israel, India, Mexico, Romania, Oregon, Washington, Virginia, Texas, Idaho) plus good Italians, Portuguese, Spanish, Australian and New Zealand wines – only France doesn't get a look-in. Prices are low.

French Partridge *Horton, Northampton NN7 2AP (0604) 870033* Long and excellent list of German and French wines.

Lake Isle *16 High St East, Uppingham LE15 9PL (0572) 822951* The basic list, with world coverage, a generous supply of half bottles, and that rarity, sound Burgundy, is supported by a selection of very fine wines.

Old Bridge Hotel *1 High Street, Huntingdon, Cambs PE18 5QT (0480) 52681* Excellent all-round list with a particularly fine selection of Burgundies.

Croque-en-Bouche *221 Wells Road, Malvern Wells, Worcs WR14 4HF (068 45) 65612* Spectacular wine list from around the world, good value for budget and top class wines, often well below auction prices. Exceptional Loires and Rhônes.

Sir Charles Napier Restaurant *Sprigg's Alley, Chinnor, Oxon OX9 4BX (0494 48) 3011* Small but well chosen selection from Burgundy and the Loire, some good Italians and a few from Australia and California.

Stapleford Park, *near Melton Mowbray, Leics LE14 2EF (057 284) 522* Bob Payton's philosophy is that 'drinking wine should be an enjoyable experience, not an intellectual one,' and the list helps by being organized into styles: dry and flinty, rich and buttery, light and fruity. His American roots have ensured a good selection from California.

NORTH-EAST

Epworth Tap *9-11 Market Place, Epworth, South Yorks DN9 1EU (0427) 873333* Long and mouthwatering list from France, Italy, California and a scattering from elsewhere, all at extremely low prices.

The George *71 St Martin's, Stamford, Lincs PE9 2LB (0780) 55171* Top Burgundies, fine clarets and a good, brief range from elsewhere in France and the rest of the world.

NORTH-WEST

The Old Vicarage Country House Hotel *Witherslack, Grange-over-Sands, Cumbria LA11 6RS (044852) 381* Excellent, French list, strong on clarets and domaine-bottled Burgundies.

Porthole Eating House *3 Ash St, Bowness-on-Windermere, Cumbria LA23 3EB (096 62) 2793* Burgundy and Bordeaux are the longest suits, but the aces come from Italy, Spain, Australia and New Zealand, with a full house of Germans.

Village Restaurant *16 Market Place, Ramsbottom, Greater Manchester BL0 9HT (070 682) 5070* The best cellars are put together by enthusiasts. Chris Johnson organizes his 160-bottle, round-the-world list by grape variety, and offers a selection by the glass to accompany the day's menu. A full stock-list is also available, and there are wine-tasting dinners.

SCOTLAND

Champany Inn *Champany, West Lothian EH49 7LU (050683) 4532* Great tome of a list with a remarkable collection of Burgundies from both *négociants* and top producers. But also fine clarets up to top growths and back to 1945, good wines from the rest of France, Italy, Spain, Germany, Australia and California.

Cross *25-27 High St, Kingussie, Highland PH21 1HX (054 66) 1762* Wine is a hobby for Tony Hadley, and the passion shows. Classic French wines, including the Loire and Alsace, form the backbone, fleshed out with sweet wines, a generous supply of half bottles, and contributions from Germany, Spain, Portugal, California, Australia and New Zealand.

Harding's *2 Station Road, North Berwick, East Lothian, EH39 4AU (0620) 4737* Chris Harding is from Australia, like most of his wines. Moss Wood and Cape Mentelle from Western Australia; Coldstream Hills and Yarra Yering from Victoria; Lindemans and Penfolds (including four vintages of Grange) from South Australia; Rosemount and Tyrrell from New South Wales.

Peat Inn *Peat Inn, Fife KY15 5LH (033 484) 206* Although the strengths are principally among traditional and classic wines, the New World gets a look in, and prices and half bottles are reasonable.

La Potinière *Main Street, Gullane, Edinburgh EH31 2AA (0620) 843214* Unbelievably cheap, exclusively French. Impeccable and wide choice of wines from all the main areas.

The Ubiquitous Chip *12 Ashton Lane, Glasgow G12 8SJ 041-334 5007* Claret and Burgundy are the strength of this long list, but the selection from elsewhere in the world is unusual and imaginative, too. Mark-ups are very modest, even on fine, old vintages.

SOUTH-EAST

Moonrakers Restaurants *High Street, Alfriston, East Sussex BN26 5TD (0323) 870472* Short but excellent list of German, Italian, Spanish and French wines.

WALES

Meadowsweet Hotel *Station Rd, Llanrwst, Gwynedd LL26 0DS (0492) 640732* An extensive, all-round list with something for everybody.

Walnut Tree Inn *Abergavenny, Gwent NP7 8AW (0873) 2797* Especially strong on French wines, particularly mature clarets,

but good shorter selections of Loire, Provence, Rhône, Alsace and Burgundy, and some unusual Italian wines imported by the restaurant on an above average Italian list.

WEST AND SOUTH-WEST

Bowlish House *Wells Road, Shepton Mallet, Somerset BA4 5JD (074934) 2022* Unusually laid out by wine style, this list is strong on New World as well as having some very fine clarets and an excellent selection of dessert wines.

Brookdale House *North Huish, South Brent, Devon TQ10 9NR (054 882) 402* Eighty-strong list of mouthwateringly interesting wines from France, Spain and the New World: really top New Zealand, Australian, Californian and Oregon wines, top growers' Burgundies.

Castle Hotel *Castle Green, Taunton, Somerset TA1 1NF (0823) 272671* This is one of those lists where, instead of looking through it to choose a bottle, you just think of a wine and ask for it; the chances are it will be in there somewhere, especially if it comes from France or Germany.

Gidleigh Park *Chagford, Devon TQ13 8HH (064 73) 2367* Extraordinary list of American wines, including many elderly vintages, backed up by excellent Burgundies and clarets, wonderful Rhônes and Alsace.

Harvey's *12a Denmark St, Bristol BS1 5DQ (0272) 277665* Absolutely magnificent for claret, especially mature and venerable vintages. It has what must be the best selection of Château Latour vintages outside the château's own cellars.

Hope End Country House Hotel *Ledbury, Hereford HR8 1JQ (0531) 3613* Excellent, largely French list, especially good for Burgundies but also fine Loires, Rhônes and clarets. Outstanding selection of half bottles.

Queen Anne Restaurant *Buckland-Tout-Saints Hotel, Goveton, Kingsbridge, Devon TQ7 2DS (054885) 3055* Good all-round list with especially fine Burgundies.

MERCHANT DIRECTORY

Abbreviations used in the Merchant Directory are as follows. **Credit cards** Access (ᴀᴄ), American Express (ᴀᴇ), Diners Club (ᴅᴄ), Visa/Barclaycard (ᴠ). The following services are available where indicated: **C** cellarage, **EP** *en primeur* offers, **G** glass hire/loan, **M** mail order, **T** tastings and talks.

Adnams   AD
The Crown, High Street, Southwold, Suffolk IP18 6JW (0502) 724222 **Hours** Mail order dept Mon–Fri 9–5, The Cellar and Kitchen Store (Southwold collection) Mon–Sat 10–6.30 (Jan only, Tue–Fri 10–5, Sat 10–6.30); The Wine Shop, South Green, Southwold, Suffolk IP18 6EW (0502) 722138 **Hours** Mon–Sat 10–7.15; The Grapevine, 109 Unthank Road, Norwich NR2 2PE (0603) 613998 **Hours** Mon–Sat 9–9. **Credit cards** AC V. **Discounts** £3 per case if collected (off mail-order price). **Delivery** £3.50 1 case, free 2 or more cases mainland UK. **Minimum order** 1 mixed case. **C EP G M T**
Very go-ahead and comprehensive list, giving one of the widest selections in the country, as well as particularly reliable basic wines, all backed up by the highly readable and often controversial comments of wine director Simon Loftus.

James Aitken & Son   AI
53 Perth Road, Dundee DD1 4HY (0382) 21197 **Hours** Mon–Sat 8.30–5.45. **Discounts** 5% unsplit case, 5% 2 or more mixed cases. **Delivery** Free within Dundee. **Minimum order** 1 mixed case. **C G M T**
French specialist, excellent range of malt whiskies and a very tasty delicatessen.

H. Allen Smith   ALL
24-25 Scala Street, London W1P 1LU, 071-637 4767 **Hours** Mon–Fri 9.30–6.30, Sat 10–1; 56 Lamb's Conduit Street, London WC1N 3LW, 071-405 3106 **Hours** Mon–Fri 9.30–6.30, Sat 10–1. **Credit cards** AC AE DC V. **Delivery** Free central London 1 case or more, outer London 3 cases or more. **C G M T**
Shops with a strong Iberian emphasis and a good range of French and Australian wines.

Les Amis du Vin   AMI
19 Charlotte Street, London W1P 1HB, 071-636 4020; 51 Chiltern Street, London W1M 1HQ, 071-487 3419 **Hours** Mon–Fri 10.30–7, Sat 10.30–5; The Winery, 4 Clifton Road, London W9 1SS, 071-286 6475 **Hours** Mon–Fri 10.30–8.30, Sat 10–6.30. **Credit cards** AC AE DC V. **Discounts** 5% unsplit cases for non-members, 10% for members (5% per bottle). **Delivery** Free 2 or more cases worth over £75, otherwise £5 per order. **Minimum order** 1 mixed case. **C EP G M T**
Traditional wine shops and club. Californian, Australian and French country wines strong. Regular list supplemented by additional offers.

André Simon   AN
14 Davies Street, London W1Y 1LJ, 071-499 9144; 50-52 Elizabeth Street, London SW1W 9PB, 071-730 8108; 21 Motcomb Street, London SW1X 8LB, 071-235 3723 **Hours** Mon–Sat 9.30–8.30. **Credit cards** AC AE V. **Delivery** Free in central London. **C EP G T**
Revitalized central London chain, with first-class selections of fine and rare wines from both the Old World and New, very fair prices.

ASDA   ASD
Asda House, Southbank, Great Wilson Street, Leeds LS11 5AD (0532) 435435 **Hours** Mon–Fri 9–8, Sat 8.30–8, open most bank hols. **Credit cards** AC V. **T**
Over 193 shops throughout the UK. Quality / price ratio is excellent.

Ashley Scott   AS
PO Box 28, The Highway, Hawarden, Deeside, Clwyd CH5 3RY (0244) 520655 **Hours** 24-hr
answerphone. **Discounts** 5% unsplit case. **Delivery** Free in north Wales, Cheshire, Lancs,
Merseyside. **Minimum order** 1 mixed case. **G M T**
Small but balanced range, with one or two well-priced specials in every section.

Askham Wines   ASK
Newark, Notts NG22 0RP (077 783) 659, fax (077 783) 659 **Hours** Mon–Fri 9–5.30, Sat
9–12. **Discounts** By arrangement. **Delivery** Free for orders over £50 UK mainland.
Minimum order 1 mixed case. **G M T**
Strong on France, Portugal, New World, especially California and Pacific North-West.

Augustus Barnett   AUG
3 The Maltings, Wetmore Road, Burton-on-Trent, Staffs DE14 1SE (0283) 512550 **Hours**
Variable, most open till 10pm. **Credit cards** AC AE V. **Discounts** For large orders. **G T**
*A chain undergoing a revival, wines from all corners of the world, including Chile, Portugal,
Australia, New Zealand, USA, Spain, Italy and regional France.*

Australian Wine Centre   AUS
'Down Under', South Australia House, 50 Strand, London WC2N 5LW, 071-925 0751, fax
071-839 9021 **Hours** Mon–Fri 10–7, Sat 10–4. **Credit cards** AC V. **Discounts** 5% 1 mixed
case cash order collected. **Delivery** Free anywhere in UK for orders over £75, otherwise £5
delivery charge. **G M T**
*Over 200 wines from all over Australia. Good, informative list; some specials unavailable
elsewhere. Also mail order: The Australian Wine Club (free membership).*

Avery's   AV
7 Park Street, Bristol BS1 5NG (0272) 214141 **Hours** Mon–Sat 9–6. **Credit cards** AC V.
Discounts By negotiation. **Delivery** Free 2 cases or more, otherwise £5.50 per
consignment. **C EP G M T**
*Traditional Bristol wine merchants, with a special interest in fine Burgundy. John Avery
was one of the pioneer importers of New World wines, so California, Australia, New Zealand
and Chile feature in the list. Daily tastings in shop; major tasting annually.*

Barnes Wine Shop   BAR
51 High Street, Barnes, London SW13 9LN, 081-878 8643 **Hours** Mon–Sat 9.30–8.30, Sun
12–2. **Credit cards** AC V. **Discounts** 5% mixed case, larger discounts negotiable. **Delivery**
Free in London. **Minimum order** 1 mixed case. **C G M T**
*Very reliable operation with wines chosen by ex-Cullen's wine wizard James Rogers. It is
strong in Australia, New Zealand and the US. Bin end lists often very good.*

Bedford Fine Wines   BE
Faulkner's Farm, The Marsh, Carlton, Bedford MK43 7JU (0234) 721153, fax (0234)
721145 **Hours** Open office **hours** or by arrangement. **Discounts** On preferred wines.
Delivery Free in Bedford, Luton and St Albans areas for minimum order of £80.
Minimum order 1 mixed case.
Particularly strong on mature claret, also frequent bin end specials and other offers.

Berkmann Wine Cellars   BEK
12 Brewery Road, London N7 9NH, 071-609 4711 **Hours** Mon–Fri 9–5.30, Sat 10–2.
Closed: Bank holiday weekends. **Credit cards** AC V. **Discounts** £2 per case collected.
Delivery Free in London; elsewhere £4.50 1 case, £2.50 2 cases, £1.50 3–4 cases, free 5 or
more cases. **Minimum order** 1 mixed case. **C EP G M T**
The people for Georges Duboeuf's Beaujolais and his white wines of the Mâconnais.

Berry Bros & Rudd   BER
3 St James's Street, London SW1A 1EG, 071-839 9033 **Hours** Mon–Fri 9.30–5; The Wine
Shop, Hamilton Close, Houndmills, Basingstoke, Hants RG21 2YH (0256) 23566 **Hours**
Mon–Fri 9–5, Sat 9–1. **Credit cards** AC DC V. **Discounts** 3–7.5% according to quantity.
Delivery Free 1 case or more. **C EP G M T**
*At the same address in St James's for two and half centuries. Claret, Burgundy and Vintage
port are the strong points, with a good selection of Rhine and Mosel too.*

Bibendum   BIB
113 Regents Park Road, London NW1 8UR, 071-722 5577 **Hours** Mon–Sat 10–8. **Credit
cards** AC AE V. **Delivery** Free in London (same day service); elsewhere £4.95 per
consignment. **Minimum order** 1 mixed case. **C EP G M T**
*Good on claret – petits châteaux and Classed Growths alike. French country wines feature
prominently, also California. Specialist offers accompanied by tastings.*

Blayneys   BL
Riverside Road, Sunderland SR5 3JW, 091-548 4488 **Hours** Mon–Sat 10–10, Sun 12–2,
7–9.30. Closed: Christmas day. **Credit cards** AC V. **Discounts** 5% mixed case. **G T**
The leading chain in the north-east. Now with 23 branches in Birmingham.

Booths Fine Wines   BO
4–6 Fishergate, Preston, Lancs PR1 3LJ (0772) 51701 **Hours** Mon–Fri 9–5. **Credit cards**
AC V. **Delivery** £2 per case 1–5 cases, free 5 cases or more, UK mainland. **Minimum order**
Warehouse only 1 mixed case. **G M T**
*20 shops spread through the north-west. Varied selection of excellent wines at excellent
prices; strong on France but a good showing in the New World.*

Bordeaux Direct   BOD
New Aquitaine House, Paddock Road, Reading, Berks RG4 0JY (0734) 481718, fax (0734)
471928 **Hours** Mon–Fri 10.30–7 (Thu till 8), Sat 9–6; 24-hr answerphone. **Credit cards** AC
AE DC V. **Discounts** On special offers. **Delivery** Free for orders over £50. **G EP M T**
*The original 'direct from the vineyard' company. Has office near St-Émilion and own
vineyard, but expanding to include wines from elsewhere. There are also six specialist shops
in the London / Thames valley area.*

Borg Castel   BOR
Samlesbury Mill, Goosefoot Lane, Samlesbury Bottoms, Preston, Lancs PR5 0RN (0254 85)
2128 **Hours** Mon–Fri 10–5, Thu 7–9.30pm, first Sun of month 12–4. **Discounts** 6 or more
cases. **Delivery** Free 1 case or more within 30 mile radius. **C G M T**
Good quality; attractive prices. Mainly European selection.

Bottoms Up   BOT
Astra House, Edinburgh Way, Harlow, Essex CM20 2BE (0279) 451145 **Hours** Daily 10–10
(most stores). **Credit cards** AC AE DC V. **Discounts** 5% mixed case. **Delivery** Free orders
over £20. **G T**
*Loads of exciting wines, particularly strong on New World. They plan massive expansion. If
they keep to the path – thumbs up.*

Broad Street Wine Company   BR
The Holloway, Market Place, Warwick CV34 4SJ (0926) 493951 **Hours** Mon–Fri 9–6, Sat
9–1. **Credit cards** AC V. **Delivery** Price according to quantity; free 6 or more cases.
Minimum order 1 mixed case. **G M T**
Specialize in Alsace and Burgundy. Largest collection in the UK of vintage cognacs.

Anthony Byrne Fine Wines   BY
88 High Street, Ramsey, Huntingdon, Cambs PE17 1BS (0487) 814555; 88 High Street, Ramsey, Cambs PE17 1BS (0487) 814555 **Hours** Mon–Sat 9–5.30. **Credit cards** AC V. **Discounts** 5% mixed case, 10% unsplit case. **Delivery** £2.50 less than 2 cases, free 2 or more cases. **C EP G M T**
One of the best Burgundy lists. Quality wines from Germany, Australia and California.

D. Byrne   BYR
12 King Street, Clitheroe, Lancs BB7 2EP (0200) 23152 **Hours** Mon–Wed, Sat 8.30–6; Thu–Fri 8.30–8. **Discounts** 5% unsplit case. **Delivery** £4 1 case, £3.50 2 cases, free 2 cases or more. **Minimum order** 1 case. **C EP G M T**
Variety and bargains – strong on claret, Germany, Australia, California and Chile.

Cape Province Wines   CAP
1 The Broadway, Kingston Road, Staines, Middx TW18 1AT (0784) 451860/455244, fax (0784) 469267 **Hours** Mon–Sat 9–9, Sun 12–1. **Credit cards** AC V. **Delivery** Locally and London £4; UK mainland varies with quantity. **Minimum order** 6 bottles. **G M T**
Specialists in South African wines.

Chaplin & Son   CH
35 Rowlands Road, Worthing, Sussex BN11 3JJ (0903) 35888 **Hours** Mon–Sat 8.45–5.30 (Fri till 6). **Credit cards** AC V. **Discounts** 5% mixed case. **Delivery** Free within 7 mile radius, 1 mixed case or more. **G M T**
A bit of everything in this list – claret, Burgundy, Australia, Italy and so on.

Châteaux Wines   CHA
11 Church Street, Bishop's Lydeard, Taunton, Somerset TA4 3AT (0454) 613959. Mail/phone orders only. **Hours** Mon–Fri 9–5.30, Sat 9–12.30. **Credit cards** AC V. **Discounts** Negotiable. **Delivery** Free 1 case or more UK mainland. **Minimum order** 1 case (usually unsplit). **C EP M T**
Concentrates on Lebanese Château Musar, Australian, Californian and Laurent Perrier fizz.

Corney & Barrow   CB
12 Helmet Row, London EC1V 3QJ, 071-251 4051; 44 Cannon Street, London EC4, 071-248 1700; 190 Kensington Park Road, London W11, 071-221 5122; 118 Moorgate, London EC2, 071-638 3125; 31 Rutherland Square, Edinburgh EH1 2BW, 031-556 7142 **Hours** Mon–Fri 9–5.30; 24-hr answerphone. **Credit cards** AC V. **Delivery** Free London 2 cases or more, elsewhere 3 cases or more. **C EP G T**
Excellent claret list. Some great names in Burgundy and New World too.

Davisons Wine Merchants   DAV
7 Aberdeen Road, Croydon, Surrey CR0 1EQ, 081-681 3222 **Hours** Usually 10–2, 5–10 daily. **Credit cards** AC V. **Discounts** 8.5% mixed case. **Delivery** Free locally. **EP G T**
Strong on claret, petits châteaux, Burgundy and vintage ports bought en primeur.

Direct Wine Shipments   DI
5/7 Corporation Square, Belfast BT1 3AJ (0232) 238700/243906 **Hours** Mon–Fri 9–6 (Thu till 8); Sat 10–5. **Credit cards** AC V. **Discounts** 5% unsplit case. **C EP M T**
A lot of very good wines at good prices on this list.

Domaine Direct   DOM
29 Wilmington Square, London WC1X 0EG, 071-837 3521 **Hours** Mon–Fri 9–6. **Delivery** Free within London. **Minimum order** 1 mixed case. **EP G M T**
Burgundy specialists with a selection of the best domaines in recent vintages.

Eldridge, Pope & Co EL
Weymouth Avenue, Dorchester, Dorset DT1 1QT (0305) 251251; mail order (0345) 078521
Hours Mon–Sat 9–5.30. **Credit cards** AC V. **Discounts** On application. **Delivery** £3.60 1
case, £6.50 2–3 cases, free 4 or more cases. **C M T**
*Informative, all-embracing, high quality list with many rarities – port, for instance, back to
1917 – but also spreading outside the classic European areas to good effect.*

Ellis, Son & Vidler ELL
Cliffe Cellars, 12-13 Cliffe Estate, Lewes, East Sussex BN8 6JL (0273) 480235 **Hours**
Mon–Fri 8–5. **Credit cards** AC V. **Delivery** Free 5 cases or more. **C EP G M T**
*Go to them for bourgeois and cru classé claret, and French country wines; also Loire and
German specialists.*

Fine Wines of New Zealand FIZ
PO Box 476, London NW5 2NZ, 071-482 0093 **Hours** Mon–Sat 9–5. **Delivery** £7 mixed
case except for special offers. **Minimum order** 1 mixed case. **M T**
*Small outfit with wines from every wine producing area in New Zealand – at keen prices
given the quality.*

M. & W. Gilbey GIL
The Eton Wine Bar, 82-83 High Street, Eton, Windsor, Berks SL4 4AF (0753) 854921/
855182, fax (0753) 868384; The Eton Wine Bar, 1 Market Square, Old Amersham, Bucks
HP7 0DF (0494) 727242, fax (0494) 431243 **Hours** Daily, hours variable. **Delivery** £6.90
per single case, free 2 cases or more. **Minimum order** 1 unsplit case. **G M**
Short list of well-chosen French wines with Burgundy and the Loire looking good.

Grape Ideas GI
3–5 Hythe Bridge Street, Oxford OX1 2EW (0865) 722137/724866 **Hours** Mon–Sat 10–7,
Sun 11–2; 2 Canfield Gardens, London NW6 3BS, 071-328 7317/624 0254 **Hours** Mon–Sat
11–8, Sun 12–2. **Credit cards** AC V. **Discounts** £1.20 mixed case. **Delivery** Free locally,
elsewhere £6. **Minimum order** 1 case for mail order, no minimum in shop. **C EP G M T**
*Warehouse operation with good European wines and better than average New World spread.
Magnificent fine wine department franchised to Fine Vintage Wines.*

Peter Green GRE
37A-B Warrender Park Road, Edinburgh EH9 1HJ, 031-229 5925 **Hours** Mon–Fri
9.30–6.30, Sat 9.30–7. **Discounts** 5% most unsplit cases. **Delivery** £5.50 1 case; £3.50 each
additional case. **G M T**
*Imaginative list of wines from all round the world, with some particularly good buys in
France. Good selection of half bottles. Hold an annual tasting, usually in October.*

Harcourt Fine Wine HAC
3 Harcourt Street, Marylebone, London W1H 1DS, 071-723 7202, answerphone 071-724 5009, fax 071-723 8085 **Hours** Mon–Fri 9.30–6.30, Sat 10–5. **Credit cards** AC AE V. **Discounts** 5% mixed case, additional for larger quantities. **Delivery** Per bottle or per case, free 3 or more cases in London. **G M T**
Useful outlet for quality wines from English vineyards. Large range of German wines.

Gerard Harris Fine Wines HAG
2 Green End Street, Aston Clinton, Aylesbury, Bucks HP22 5HP (0296) 631041 **Hours** Tue–Sat 9.30–8. **Credit cards** AC V. **Discounts** 10% mixed case (except claret, Burgundy, port). **Delivery** Free locally 1 case or more. **Minimum order** 1 mixed case for delivery, no minimum in shop. **C EP G M T**
Strong points are Bordeaux and Germany; other countries and regions are well covered.

Roger Harris Wines HAW
Loke Farm, Weston Longville, Norfolk NR9 5LG (0603) 880171/2 **Hours** Mon–Fri 9–5. **Credit cards** AC AE DC V. **Discounts** 2 cases £1 per case, 5 cases or more £1.50 per case. **Delivery** Free UK mainland. **Minimum order** 1 mixed case. **C EP M T**
Beaujolais specialist par excellence *with over 60 different wines, plus white Mâconnais.*

John Harvey & Sons HA
31 Denmark Street, Bristol BS1 5DQ, 0272-268882 **Hours** Mon–Fri 9.30–6, Sat; The Hard, Portsmouth PO1 3DT (0705) 825567 **Hours** Mon–Fri 9.30–6. **Credit cards** AC AE DC V. **Discounts** Quantity discounts. **Delivery** Free 2 cases or more UK mainland. **C EP M T**
Sherry (Harvey's), port (Cockburn's), and claret (close association with Château Latour) are the strengths. Regular en primeur *offers for claret and Burgundy.*

Richard Harvey Wines HAY
Home Farm, Morden, Wareham, Dorset BH20 7DW (092 945) 224. **Discounts** 2.5% 1 case, 5% 6 cases or more. **Delivery** Free within 30 miles for 3 or more cases. **Minimum order** 1 mixed case. **C EP G M T**
A small firm with a bit of everything, all from reputable producers.

Haughton Fine Wines HAU
Chorley Green Lane, Chorley, Nantwich, Cheshire, CW5 8JR (0270 74) 537/(0836 597) 961, fax (0270 74) 233 **Hours** Mon–Fri 9–5.30, Sat 9.30–12.30; 24-hr answerphone. **Credit cards** AC V. **Discounts** For quantity orders. **Delivery** Free within 30 miles, elsewhere 6 cases or more. **Minimum order** 1 mixed case. **G M T**
Barely four years old and already with a growing reputation for their varied list. Strong on Australian wines, French wines, with a selection of 'tasting cases' for newcomers.

All the companies listed in the Merchant Directory have wines featured in the Price Guides (pages 243–393). Abbreviations used in the Directory are as follows: **Credit cards** *Access (AC), American Express (AE), Diners Club (DC), Visa/Barclaycard (V). The following services are available where indicated:* **C** *cellarage,* **EP** *en primeur offers,* **G** *glass hire/loan,* **M** *mail order,* **T** *tastings and talks.*

Haynes Hanson & Clark   HAH
17 Lettice Street, London SW6 4EH, 071-736 7878 **Hours** Mon–Thu 9–7, Fri 9-6; 36
Kensington Church Street, London W8 4BX, 071-937 4650 **Hours** 9.30–7. **Discounts** 10%
unsplit case. **Delivery** Free central London, elsewhere 5 cases or more. **Minimum order**
Warehouse only 1 case. **EP G M T**
The list is dominated by France, but includes a new range of Antipodean wines and new
Californian shipments – both areas expanding in their list. Burgundy is a speciality.

Douglas Henn-Macrae   HE
81 Mackenders Lane, Eccles, Maidstone, Kent ME20 7JA (0622) 710952 **Hours** Phone
enquiries only Mon–Sat to 10pm. **Credit cards** AC V. **Discounts** Subject to quantity.
Delivery Free 5 or more cases UK mainland; otherwise £5.75 per order. **Minimum order**
1 case. **M T**
Fascinating list concentrating on just two areas – a selection of German wines from the
Nahe, Hessische Bergstrasse, Württemberg and Rheinpfalz, and a remarkable array of US
Oregon and Washington wines, and the only Texan wine importer in Europe. Probably the
longest German red wine list in this country, and a wide range of older rarities.

Hicks & Don   HIC
4 The Market Place, Westbury, Wilts BA13 3EA (0373) 864723, fax (0373) 858250. Head
office: Park House, Elmham, Dereham, Norfolk NR20 5AB (036 281) 571 **Hours** Mail order,
also by phone and fax. **Credit cards** AC V. **Discounts** For quantity, on certain wines.
Delivery Under 3 cases £3 per case, over 3 cases free UK mainland. **Minimum order** 1
mixed case. **C EP G M T**
Strong on opening offers of claret, Burgundy, cru Beaujolais, port and the Rhône. Fine
sherries from Barbadillo. A selection of lesser known French wines, as well as the classics.

High Breck Vintners   HIG
Spats Lane, Headley, Bordon, Hants GU35 8SY (0428) 713689 **Hours** Mon–Fri 9.30–6, Sat
9.30–1, later by arrangement. **Delivery** £6 for 1–3 cases, free large quantities. **Minimum**
order 1 mixed case. **EP G M T**
Pretty catholic selection from interesting French producers, particularly Alsace, Bordeaux
and the Loire – nice Germans from Deinhard, but not a lot from the rest of the world.

J.E. Hogg   HOG
61 Cumberland Street, Edinburgh EH3 6RA, 031-556 4025 **Hours** Mon–Tue, Thu–Fri 9–1,
2.30–6; Wed, Sat 9–1. **Delivery** Free 12 or more bottles within Edinburgh. **G M T**
Claret buyer's delight. This little shop frequently has a queue of Edinburgh's most canny
wine enthusiasts outside. Mature claret and Burgundy are excellent, as are malt whiskies.

Hungerford Wine Company   HUN
Unit 3, Station Yard, Hungerford, Berks RG17 0DY (0488) 683238, fax (0488) 684919
Hours Mon–Fri 9–5.30, Sat 9.30–5. **Credit cards** AC AE DC V. **Discounts** 5% case.
Delivery Free within 15 mile radius 1 case, elsewhere 5 cases or more. **C EP G M T**
The ebullient Nick Davies has a list of over 1000 wines. Very good value en primeur offers for
Bordeaux, Rhône and port.

Irvine Robertson Wines   IR
10/11 North Leith Sands, Edinburgh EH6 4ER (031) 553-3521; in association with Graham
MacHarg Fine Wines, Fowberry Tower, Woder, Northumberland NE71 6ER (06685) 274
Hours Mon–Fri 9–5.30. **Discounts** On 5 cases or more. **Delivery** Free locally, elsewhere 3
cases or more. **Minimum order** 1 mixed case. **E G M T**
Remarkably good range of first class stuff worldwide. You'd expect good claret and
Burgundy from an ex-Justerini & Brooks man, but they're also excellent on New World.

J.C. Karn & Son Ltd.   KA
7 Lansdown Place, Cheltenham, Glos GL50 2HU (0242) 513265 **Hours** Mon–Fri 9.30–6,
Sat 9.30–1.30. **Discounts** 5% mixed case. **Delivery** Free in Glos. **G M T**
Personally selected list, particularly good on New Zealand; also strong in the Loire,
especially domaine wines from Touraine.

Lay & Wheeler   LAY
Head office and shop: 6 Culver Street West, Colchester, Essex CO1 1JA (0206) 764446
Hours Mon–Sat 8.30–5.30; Wine Market, Gosbeck's Road, Shrub End, Colchester, Essex
CO2 9JT (0206) 764446 **Hours** Mon–Sat 8–8. **Credit cards** AC V. **Discounts** 1½% 4–11
cases, 3% 12 cases or more. **Delivery** Free locally 1 case, elsewhere 2 cases or more. **C EP
G M T**
Colchester wine merchants with one of the most comprehensive lists in the country, with
some of the best producers in each region. The claret is particularly good, but the others take
a lot of beating.

Laymont & Shaw   LA
The Old Chapel, Mill Pool, Truro, Cornwall TR1 1EX (0872) 70545 **Hours** Mon–Fri 9–5.
Discounts On more than 2 cases. **Delivery** Free. **Minimum order** 1 case. **G M T**
Spanish specialists and pioneers – not just Rioja, but Penedés, La Mancha, Navarra,
Malaga and several others.

London Wine   LO
Chelsea Wharf, 15 Lots Road, London SW10 0QF, 071-351 6856 **Hours** Mon–Fri 9–9, Sat
10–7, Sun 10.30–5.30. **Credit cards** AC AE DC V. **Discounts** On very large orders. **Delivery**
Free locally. **Minimum order** 1 mixed case. **EP G M T**
Revitalized warehouse operation with an increasingly good selection of whatever wines are
in vogue at the present time. Fine wine investment advice, wine exchange, sale or return
service.

Lorne House Vintners   LOR
Unit 5, Hewitts Industrial Estate, Elmbridge Road, Cranleigh, Surrey GU6 8LW (0483)
271445 **Hours** Mon–Fri 9–5.30, Sat 9–1. **Discounts** Negotiable. **Delivery** Free 2 cases or
more within 25 miles central London, or £5 per consignment. **Minimum order** 1 mixed
case. **G M T**
These are the Muscadet specialists, but they have other wines as well and are at present
expanding into other areas of France.

Majestic Wine Warehouses   MAJ
421 New Kings Road, London SW6 4RN, 071-731 3131, fax 071-736 1113; 14 branches in
London; also in Acocks Green, Amersham, Birmingham, Bristol, Cambridge, Croydon,
Gloucester, Guildford, Ipswich, Leeds, Maidenhead, Norwich, Oxford, Poole, Reading, St
Albans, Salisbury, Stockport, Swindon, Taunton, Walsall **Hours** Mon–Sat 10–8, Sun 10–6.
Closed: 25–27 Dec, 1 Jan. **Credit cards** AC AE DC V. **Delivery** Free locally. **Minimum
order** 1 mixed case. **EP G M T**
Very much the market leader in wine warehouses. An enormous range going from some of
England's most unashamedly plonky plonk to top line Bordeaux, Burgundy, port, etc. Keen
prices, good tastings, and a nice line in music on the stereo. 700 wines, friendly and
knowledgeable staff.

Marks & Spencer   MAR
Michael House, Baker Street, London W1A 1DN, 071-935 4422; 264 licensed stores all over
the country **Hours** Variable. **Discounts** 12 bottles for the price of 11.
Expanding list of 200 wines, 40 of which are vintage selection.

Moreno Wines MOR
2 Norfolk Place, London W2 1QN, 071-706 3055 **Hours** Mon–Fri 9–8, Sat 10–8; 11
Marylands Road, London W9 2DU, 071-286 0678 **Hours** Mon–Fri 9–9, Sat 10–9, Sun 12–2.
Credit cards AC V. **Discounts** 5% mixed case. **Delivery** Free locally, elsewhere 4 cases or
more. **G M T**
*Largest range of Spanish wines in the country. Over 500 Riojas, Penedés, Navarra, Jumilla,
Cariñena, Priorato, Somontano, Rueda, Galicia, León, Alella, Ribera del Duero,
Valdepeñas, Valencia, Toro and a fine selection of sherries, brandies and liqueurs.*

Morris & Verdin MV
28 Churton Street, London SW1V 2LP, 071-630 8888 **Hours** Mon–Fri 9.30–5.30, Sat 10–3.
Discounts On 5 cases or more. **Delivery** Free central London and Oxford, elsewhere 5
cases or more. **Minimum order** 1 mixed case. **C EP G M T**
Tip-top for Burgundy, but very good for Alsace, Loire and Australian single estates.

James Nicholson NI
27A Killyleagh Street, Crossgar, Co. Down, Northern Ireland BT30 9DG (0396) 830091, fax
(0396) 830028 **Hours** Mon–Sat 10–7. **Credit cards** AC V. **Discounts** Variable on mixed
case. **Delivery** Free Northern Ireland for 1 case or more, mainland nominal postage. **C EP
G M T**
Extensive French list, plus other countries including the New World.

Oddbins OD
31-33 Weir Road, London SW19 8UG, 081-879 1199 **Hours** Mon–Sat 9–9, Sun 12–2 and
7–9 except Scotland. Closed: Christmas. **Credit cards** AC AE V. **Discounts** 5% unsplit case
wine, 7 bottles Champagne for the price of 6. **Delivery** Available locally for most shops.
Free with reasonable order. **G T**
Their range is among the best of the high street wine merchants, with over 500 wines.

Old Street Wine Company OL
309 Old Street, London EC1V 9LE, 071-729 1768 **Hours** Mon–Fri 10–7, Sat 11–3. **Credit
cards** AC V. **Discounts** 5% mixed case, pay and carry or local delivery. **Delivery** Free EC1
and EC2 1 mixed case or more, other London areas 3 cases or more. **EP G M T**
Very strong on Loire and French country wines; also good list (and stocks) of vintage ports.

Thos. Peatling PE
Westgate House, Bury St Edmunds, Suffolk IP33 1QS (0284) 755948 **Hours** Variable.
Credit cards AC AE V. **Discounts** 5% mixed case. **Delivery** Free within East Anglia,
elsewhere 5 or more cases. **C G M T**
Over 800 wines, strong in France – good value petits châteaux. Fine German and Spanish.

Peter Dominic   PD
Astra House, Edinburgh Way, Harlow, Essex CM20 2BE (0279) 451145 **Hours** Variable,
many stores open late and Sun. **Credit cards** AC AE DC V. **Discounts** 5% mixed case.
Delivery Available from most stores, free orders over £20. **G M T**
*About 700 branches nationwide, from Elgin to Penzance. They stock a range of over 800
wines from around the world.*

Christopher Piper Wines   PIP
1 Silver Street, Ottery St Mary, Devon EX11 1DB (0404) 814139/812197 **Hours** Mon–Sat
9–6. **Credit cards** AC V. **Discounts** 5% mixed case, 10% 3 cases or more. **Delivery** Free in
south-west 4 or more cases, elsewhere 6 or more cases. **Minimum order** 1 mixed case.
C EP G M T
*Chris Piper is one of the very few English merchants who is also a wine producer in France
at Brouilly (Château des Tours). Specializes in domaine-bottled wines and works very
closely with producers, especially in Burgundy and the Rhône.*

Raeburn Fine Wines and Foods   RAE
23 Comely Bank Road, Edinburgh EH4 1DS, 031-332 5166 **Hours** Mon–Sat 9–7.
Discounts 5% unsplit case, 2.5% mixed case. **Delivery** Price negotiable, all areas covered.
C EP G M T
Prices are excellent, and many of the world's greatest wines are hiding on the shelves.

Reid Wines   REI
The Mill, Marsh Lane, Hallatrow, Bristol BS18 5EB (0761) 52645, fax (0761) 53642 **Hours**
Mon–Fri 9–5.30, weekends by arrangement; Wine Warehouse, Unit 2, Block 3, Vestry
Trading Estate, Oxford Road, Sevenoaks, Kent TN14 5NL (0732) 458533 **Hours** Mon–Fri
9–6, Sat 9–1. **Credit cards** Sevenoaks only: AC V. **Discounts** Sevenoaks only: 5% on orders
over £250. **Delivery** Free within 25 miles of Sevenoaks and Hallatrow (Bristol). **C EP G M T**
*Good selection of top quality wines from all the classic areas of Europe and from some of the
new wine areas of the world; also many fine and rare wines and a witty wine list.*

La Reserve   RES
56 Walton Street, London SW3 1RB, 071-589 2020; Le Picoleur, 47 Kendal Street, London
W2, 071-402 6920 **Hours** Mon–Fri 10–8, Sat 10–6; Le Sac à Vin, 203 Munster Road,
London SW6 6BX, 071-381 6930 **Hours** Mon–Sat 12–9.30, Sun 12–2, 7–9. **Credit cards** AC
V. **Discounts** For case quantities. **Delivery** Free in central London, will deliver
throughout the country. **C EP G M T**
*Fine old and rare wines are the speciality, especially from Burgundy and Bordeaux. Lots of
good quality wines, particularly from single domaines, and older vintages.*

Safeway   SAF
6 Millington Road, Hayes, Middx UB3 4AY, 081-848 8744 **Hours** Mon–Sat 8–8 (Fri till 9).
Credit cards AC V (ex Penzance).
*The surprise supermarket success story of the 1980s. After years of underachieving Safeway
is dramatically back in the leading pack of high street wine cellars.*

Sainsbury   SAI
Stamford House, Stamford Street, London SE1 9LL, 071-921 6000. Main branches: Bath,
Cambridge, Chester, Crayford (Kent), Guildford, Leeds, London (Camden, Chiswick,
Cromwell Road, Fulham, Hampton, Harringay, Ladbroke Grove, Nine Elms, Pinner,
Wandsworth), Oxford, Sheffield, York. Savacentres: Edinburgh, London Colney, Merton
(south-west London), Reading **Hours** Variable, many stores open late.
*The country's largest wine retailer. Increasingly imaginative list enlivened by a vintage
selection of fine wines available from 238 main stores with the widest selection of 300 wines
available in 30 branches and 4 Savacentres.*

Stapylton Fletcher   STA
3 Haslemere, Sutton Road, Maidstone ME15 9NE (0622) 691188 **Hours** Mon–Fri 8–6, Sat
8.30–12.30. **Credit cards** AC V. **Discounts** £1.15 per case for 6–11 cases, £2.30 for 11 cases
or more. **Delivery** £1.15 for any quantity UK mainland. **Minimum order** 1 mixed case.
C EP G M T
Increasingly good wide ranging list; France, Italy, New World and decent English too!

Tanners   TAN
26 Wyle Cop, Shrewsbury, Shropshire SY1 1XD (0743) 232400 **Hours** Mon–Sat 9–5.30.
Credit cards AC AE V. **Discounts** On 6 unsplit cases or more. **Delivery** £4.50 per case; free
over £75. **EP G M T**
Good clarets, Burgundies and California among others. Regular newsletter.

Tesco   TES
Delamare Road, Cheshunt, Herts EN8 9SL (0992) 32222. 362 licensed branches **Hours**
Variable. Open Sunday in Scotland. **Credit cards** AC V.
An ever-improving list; wines from all over the world.

Thresher   THR
Sefton House, 42 Church Street, Welwyn Garden City, Herts AL8 6PJ (0707) 328244
Hours Mon–Sat 9–9 or 10–10, Sun 12–2, 7–9.30. Closed Sun in Scotland. **Credit cards** AC
V. **Discounts** 10% on unsplit cases. **Delivery** Free, selected branches only.
Over 940 branches nationwide, with a wine selection of over 300 different lines.

T. & W. Wines   TW
51 King Street, Thetford, Norfolk IP24 2AU (0842) 765646 **Hours** Mon–Fri 9.30–5.30,
Sat 9.30–2.30. **Credit cards** AC AE DC V. **Delivery** Free 4 cases or more UK mainland.
C EP G M
Good people to hunt out old and rare wines. Specialists in half bottles.

Unwins   UN
Birchwood House, Victoria Road, Dartford, Kent DA1 5AJ (0322) 72711/7; 300 specialist
off-licences throughout the south-east of England **Hours** 10–10. **Credit cards** AC AE DC V.
Discounts 10% mixed case. **G M T**
All the world's major wine-producing areas are covered by this family run company.

Upper Crust   UP
3–4 Bishopsmead Parade, East Horsley, Surrey KT24 6RT (04865) 3280 **Hours** Mon–Sat
9–9, Sun 12–2, 7–9. Closed 25 Dec only. **Credit cards** AC V. **Discounts** For cash or cheque
payments only, 5% on 1 case, 2.5% on Champagne case. **Delivery** Free within 25 miles,
otherwise cost according to quantity. **C EP G M T**
Award-winning retailers. Very good on France; other countries covered in less detail.

Valvona & Crolla   VA
19 Elm Row, Edinburgh EH7 4AA, 031-556 6066 **Hours** Mon–Sat 8.30–6. Closed: 1–7 Jan.
Credit cards AC V. **Discounts** 5% mixed case. **Delivery** £5.80 mixed case, free for orders
over £100. **G M T**
One of the best selections of Italian wine in the UK – regular special offers.

Victoria Wine   VIC
Brook House, Chertsey Road, Woking, Surrey GU21 5BE (048371) 5066. Nearly 900
branches throughout Great Britain **Hours** Variable, usually Mon–Sat 9–6 (high street),
10–10 or 10–2, 5–10 (local shops); Sun 12–2, 7–9. **Credit cards** AC AE DC V. **Discounts** 5%
mixed case. **G M T**
France is well represented and Italy too. A good New World spread.

La Vigneronne
VIG

105 Old Brompton Road, London SW7 3LE, 071-589 6113 **Hours** Mon–Fri 10–9, Sat 10–8, Sun 12–2.30. **Credit cards** AC AE DC V. **Discounts** 5% mixed case collected. **Delivery** Free locally, elsewhere £5.00 per delivery under £100 in value, £3.50 for £100–£250, over £250 free. **C EP G M T**

Fascinating list, strong on classic French – also the place for exceptional Alsace wines, Provençal rarities, outstanding Californians and Aussies.

Vintage Wines
VIN

116 Derby Road, Nottingham NG1 5FB (0602) 476565/419614 **Hours** Mon–Fri 9–5.30, Sat 9–1. **Credit cards** AC V. **Discounts** 10% mixed case. **Delivery** Free within 20 miles. **G M T**

Useful merchant with a traditional taste who takes particular care with his house wines.

Waitrose
WAI

Doncastle Road, Southern Industrial Area, Bracknell, Berks RG12 4YA (0344) 424680. 89 licensed supermarkets **Hours** Mon–Tue 9–6, Wed 9–8, Thu 8.30–8, Fri 8.30–9, Sat 8.30–5.30. **Discounts** 5% for over £100 of wine or any whole case of wine. **Delivery** Carriage to car service. **G**

An incredibly good range of wines from all round the world, always at competitive prices.

Whitesides of Clitheroe
WHI

Shawbridge Street, Clitheroe, Lancs BB7 1NA (0200) 22281 **Hours** Mon–Sat 9–5.30. **Credit cards** AC V. **Discounts** Dependent on amount. **G T**

A good all-round selection. New wine club, including tours, talks and tastings.

Willoughby's
WIL

53 Cross Street, Manchester M2 4JP 061-834 6850; 1 Springfield House, Water Lane, Wilmslow, Cheshire (0625) 533068; 100 Broadway, Chadderton, Oldham, Lancs OL9 0AA 061-620 1374; in association with: George Dutton and Son, Godstall Lane, St Werburgh Street, Chester CH1 1LJ (0244) 321488; and Thomas Baty and Sons, 37-41 North John Street, Liverpool L2 6SN 051-236 1601 **Hours** Mon–Sat 9–5. **Credit cards** AC V. **Discounts** By arrangement. **Delivery** Free locally. **C EP G M T**

Specializes in Champagne, Bordeaux, Burgundy, but good varied worldwide selection with over 800 wines from 19 countries, supported by a large range of spirits and fortified wines.

Windrush Wines
WW

The Barracks, Cecily Hill, Cirencester, Glos GL7 2EF (0285) 650466 **Hours** Mon–Fri 9–6; 3 Market Place, Cirencester, Glos GL7 2PE (0285) 657807 **Hours** Mon–Sat 9–6. **Discounts** In bond and ex-cellar terms available. **Delivery** Free. **Minimum order** 1 mixed case. **C EP G M T**

Specialists in fine single-estate wines. While the emphasis lies on France, they have also established a reputation for the best wines from California and the Pacific North-West.

Wine Club
WIC

New Aquitaine House, Paddock Road, Reading, Berks RG4 0JY (0734) 481713, fax (0734) 471928 **Hours** Mail order, 24-hr answerphone. **Credit cards** AC AE DC V. **Discounts** On special offers. **Delivery** Free orders over £50. **EP M T**

Associate company is Bordeaux Direct. Membership fee is £5 per annum.

Wine Society
WS

Gunnels Wood Road, Stevenage, Herts SG1 2BG (0438) 741177 **Hours** Mon–Fri 9–5; showroom Mon–Fri 9–6 Sat 9–1. **Credit cards** AC V. **Delivery** Free 1 case or more. **C EP G M T**

You have to be a member to buy wines from this non-profit-making co-operative. One of their aims is to seek out new wines. They also offer an outstanding range of classic wines.

Winecellars   WCL
153-155 Wandsworth High Street, London SW18 4JB, 081-871 2668 **Hours** Mon–Sat
10.30–8.30; The Market 213-215 Upper Street, London N1 1RL, 071-359 5386 **Hours** daily
9–9. **Credit cards** AC V. **Discounts** 10% mixed case. **Delivery** Free within M25 boundary,
2 cases or more UK mainland. **Minimum order** 1 mixed case. **C G M T**
One of the most exciting ranges of wine in London. England's leading Italian specialist .

Wines of Westhorpe   WIW
Field House Cottage, Birch Cross, Marchington, Staffs ST14 8NX (0283) 820285, fax (0283)
820631 **Hours** Mon–Fri 9–5.30. **Credit cards** AC V. **Discounts** According to quantity.
Delivery Free on UK mainland. **Minimum order** 1 mixed case. **M T**
The Eastern European experts with a good range of Bulgarian and Hungarian wines.

Wizard Wines   WIZ
6 Theobald Court, Theobald Street, Borehamwood WD6 4RN, 081-207 4455 **Hours** Phone
for details of local branch opening **hours. Credit cards** AC AE V. **Discounts** 5% 10 or more
unsplit cases. **Delivery** Within 20 mile radius; £4 per case, free orders over £100. **G T**
Huge range, low price. They offer more really cheap wine than anyone else.

Wright Wine Company   WRI
The Old Smithy, Raikes Road, Skipton, N. Yorks BD23 1NP (0756) 700886 **Hours** Mon–Sat
9–6, including bank holidays. **Discounts** Wholesale price unsplit case, 5% mixed case.
Delivery Free within 30 miles. **G T**
Large selection of brandies, malt whiskies, liqueurs. Interesting wines from the New World.

Peter Wylie Fine Wines   WY
Plymtree Manor, Plymtree, Cullompton, Devon EX15 2LE (088 47) 555, fax (088 47) 557
Hours Mon–Fri 9–6.30. **Discounts** Unsplit case. **Delivery** London 3 or more cases free;
1–2 cases and UK mainland £8 for 1 case then £6 per case. **C M**
Over 1000 wines concentrating on Bordeaux. Classic selections. Varied large bottle sizes.

Yapp Brothers   YAP
The Old Brewery, Mere, Wilts BA12 6DY (0747) 860423, fax (0747) 860929 **Hours** Mon–
Fri 9–5, Sat 9–1. **Credit cards** AC V. **Discounts** On 5 or more cases. **Delivery** £2.50 1 case,
free more than 1 case. **C EP G M T**
Loire and Rhône specialists. Also an extensive range of Provence wines.

Yorkshire Fine Wines   YF
Nun Monkton, York YO5 8ET (0423) 330131 **Hours** Mon–Fri 9–5. **Credit cards** AC V.
Discounts 4% cash on delivery. **Delivery** Free in northern England, elsewhere 5 or more
cases. **Minimum order** 1 mixed case. **C G M T**
Champagnes in different sizes and a fine French range. Well balanced all round coverage .

REGIONAL DIRECTORY

LONDON

H. Allen Smith	ALL
Les Amis du Vin	AMI
André Simon	AN
Australian Wine Centre	AUS
Barnes Wine Shop	BAR
Berkmann Wine Cellars	BEK
Berry Bros & Rudd	BER
Bibendum	BIB
Bottoms Up	BOT
Corney & Barrow	CB
Davisons	DAV
Domaine Direct	DOM
Ellis Son & Vidler	ELL
Fine Wines of NZ	FIZ
Grape Ideas	GI
Harcourt Fine Wines	HAC
Haynes Hanson & Clark	HAH
London Wine	LO
Moreno Wines	MOR
Morris & Verdin	MV
Old Street Wine Co	OL
La Reserve	RES
Unwins	UN
La Vigneronne	VIG
Winecellars	WCL

SOUTH-EAST AND HOME COUNTIES

Bedford Fine Wines	BE
Berry Bros & Rudd	BER
Bordeaux Direct	BOD
Bottoms Up	BOT
Cape Province Wines	CAP
Chaplin & Son	CH
Ellis Son & Vidler	ELL
M. & W. Gilbey	GIL
Gerard Harris	HAG
Douglas Henn-Macrae	HE
High Breck Vintners	HIG
Hungerford Wine Co	HUN
Lorne House Vintners	LOR

Reid Wines	REI
Stapylton Fletcher	STA
Unwins	UN
Upper Crust	UP
Wine Club	WIC
Wine Society	WS
Wizard Wine	WIZ

WEST AND SOUTH-WEST

Averys	AV
Bottoms Up	BOT
Châteaux Wines	CHA
Eldridge, Pope & Co	EL
John Harvey & Sons	HA
Richard Harvey Wines	HAY
Hicks & Don	HIC
J.C. Karn	KA
Laymont & Shaw	LA
Christopher Piper	PIP
Reid Wines	REI
Windrush Wines	WW
Peter Wylie	WYL
Yapp Brothers	YAP

EAST ANGLIA

Adnams	AD
Anthony Byrne	BY
Roger Harris Wines	HAW
Hicks & Don	HIC
Lay & Wheeler	LAY
Thos. Peatling	PE
T. & W. Wines	TW

MIDLANDS

Askham Wines	ASK
Blayneys	BL
Broad Street Wine Co.	BR
Grape Ideas	GI
Tanners	TAN
Vintage Wines	VIN
Wines of Westhorpe	WIW

NORTH

Blayneys	BL
Booths	BO
Borg Castel	BOR
D. Byrne	BYR
George Dutton & Son	WIL
Haughton Fine Wines	HAU
Whitesides of Clitheroe	WHI
Willoughbys	WIL
Wright Wine Company	WRI
Yorkshire Fine Wines	YF

WALES

Ashley Scott	AS

SCOTLAND

James Aitken	AI
Corney & Barrow	CB
Peter Green	GRE
J.E. Hogg	HOG
Irvine Robertson Wines	IR
Raeburn Fine Wines	RAE
Valvona & Crolla	VA

NORTHERN IRELAND

Direct Wine Shipments	DI
James Nicholson	NI

COUNTRYWIDE

ASDA	ASD
Augustus Barnett	AUG
Majestic	MAJ
Marks & Spencer	MAR
Oddbins	OD
Peter Dominic	PD
Safeway	SAF
Sainsbury	SAI
Tesco	TES
Thresher	THR
Victoria Wine	VIC
Waitrose	WAI

WINE TERMS

Acidity Naturally present in grapes, it gives wine a refreshing tang. The main wine acids are: acetic, carbonic, citric, malic, tannic and tartaric.

Ageing For fine wines, and for many ordinary reds, ageing is essential. The process, lasting months or years, takes place in wooden barrels, then often continues in bottle.

Alcoholic content The alcoholic strength of wine, usually shown as a percentage of the total volume.

Appellation d'origine contrôlée Official designation in France guaranteeing a wine by geographical origin, grape variety and production method; abbreviated as AC or AOC.

Approved viticultural area Californian appellation system, introduced in 1980s and still in infancy; abbreviated as AVA.

Assemblage In Bordeaux and Champagne, final cask-to-cask blending of fine wines.

Auslese German term for 'selected'; applied to sweet QmP wine made from late-picked bunches of grapes.

Back-blending New Zealand term for adding unfermented grape juice to wine to sweeten it.

Barrique Small French oak barrel, holding 225 litres.

Beerenauslese German term for 'berry selection', referring to very sweet QmP wine made from single berries, left on the vine for late harvest.

Bereich German term for a wine-producing district.

Bin number Australian system of numbering wine by batches for identification purposes; sometimes also used in brand names.

Blanc de blancs White wine, especially Champagne, made only from white grapes; the rarer *blanc de noirs* is white wine from black grapes.

Blush wine Pink wine, usually sweetish, originally made from black Zinfandel grapes in California; now also made in Europe from other varieties.

British wine Wine made in the UK from imported, dehydrated must which is reconstituted, then fermented.

Brut French term for unsweetened; usually applied to sparkling wine.

Carbonic maceration Red wine-making method traditional to Beaujolais but now used in other warm-climate areas. The grapes, whole and uncrushed, are fermented in a closed vat to give a light, fruity wine for young drinking.

Cava In Spain and Portugal, Champagne-method sparkling wine.

Cepa/cépage Spanish/French for grape variety.

Chaptalization Permitted addition of sugar during fermentation to increase alcoholic strength.

Classico Italian term for the original, central zone of a DOC area; usually produces superior wine.

Cold/cool fermentation Long, slow fermentation at low temperature to give maximum freshness and fruit. Crucial for white in hotter climates.

Côtes, coteaux French for slopes.

Crémant French Champagne-method sparkling wine from Alsace, the Loire and Burgundy. In Champagne applies to wines with fewer bubbles.

Cru French word, literally 'growth', used to describe a single vineyard.

Cru classé French term, literally 'classed growth', indicating that a vineyard is included in the rating system.

Cuve close Method of making sparkling wine in which the second, fizz-forming fermentation takes place in closed tanks.

Denominación de origen Spanish equivalent of the French *appellation d'origine contrôlée*; abbreviated as DO.

Denominazione di origine controllata Italian equivalent of the French *appellation d'origine contrôlée*; abbreviated as DOC. If *e garantita* is added (DOCG), it indicates a top-quality wine.

Élevage French term covering all wine-making processes between fermentation and bottling.

Embotellado de origen Spanish for estate-bottled.

Engarrafado na origem Portuguese for estate-bottled.

En primeur Wine offered for sale immediately after the vintage, while still in cask; often the best way of buying top-class reds.

Estate-bottled Wine bottled on the premises where it has been made.

Fermentation Wine is subject to two fermentations. First, the essential alcoholic fermentation when yeasts convert grape sugars into alcohols. Second, the malolactic fermentation when sharp malic acid turns into milder lactic acid. The malolactic softens reds and full whites, but with young whites it is often prevented to preserve freshness.

Fining Clarifying wine by adding coagulant, traditionally egg white, to the surface; as this descends through the wine it collects all impurities.

Flor A special yeast which grows on the surface of certain wines, especially sherry, in barrel; it inhibits oxidation and creates a special taste.

Fortified wine High-strength wine made by adding in extra alcohol.

Garrafeira Portuguese term for a selected wine which has been aged and is usually superior quality.

Governo In Chianti, traditional practice of adding raisined grapes to the fermented wine to induce slight re-fermentation; this softens the wine and gives it a prickle.

Hock English name for any German wine made along the Rhine.

Hybrid Grape variety bred from a European *Vitis vinifera* and an American vine species; as opposed to a crossing which is bred from two *vinifera* varieties.

Kabinett Lightest and driest category of German QmP wines.

Maderization Browning of white wines caused by age or poor storage.

Marc Mush of skins, stalks and pips left behind after grapes have been pressed.

Mildew Common fungus disease affecting vines. Oidium (powdery mildew) attacks leaves and shoots; downy mildew destroys leaves and shrivels fruit.

Millésime French for vintage date.

Must Grape juice or crushed grapes before fermentation.

Négociant In France, merchant or shipper who buys in wine from growers, then matures, maybe blends, and sells it.

Noble rot Fungus (*Botrytis cinerea*) which, in warm autumn weather, can attack white grapes, shrivel them and thus concentrate the sugars to produce quality sweet wines.

Oak Traditional wood for wine barrels; during ageing it imparts important flavours such as vanillin and tannin.

Organic wine Made with the least possible use of artificial substances both in the vineyard and winery.

Oxidation Over-exposure of wine to air causing bacterial decay and loss of fruit.

Pasteurization Cheaper wines are often pasteurized – sterilized by heating – to prevent bacterial decay. Unsuitable for fine wines as it inhibits bottle ageing.

Phylloxera Vine aphid which devastated viticulture worldwide in the nineteenth century. Now prevented by grafting European vines on to phylloxera-resistant American rootstocks.

Qualitätswein bestimmter Anbaugebiete German wine quality designation; abbreviated as QbA.

Qualitätswein mit Prädikat German wine top-quality designation; abbreviated as QmP.

Quinta Portuguese for estate or farm.

Racking Gradual clarification of wine by transferring it from one barrel to another, leaving the lees or sediment behind.

Rancio Deliberately oxidized white wine, popular in Catalonia and Languedoc-Roussillon. *Rancio* is deep amber with high alcohol and a caramel flavour.

Récoltant French term for grower.

Récolte French for crop or vintage.

Região demarcado Portuguese for demarcated wine region; abbreviated as RD.

Reserva Spanish term applied to wine, usually better quality, which has been aged for a minimum period before release. A *gran reserva* wine has longer ageing.

Riserva Italian DOC or DOCG wine aged for a specified period.

Second wine Wine from a designated vineyard which is sold separately from the main production, under a different name.

Sediment Residue thrown by wine, especially red, as it ages in bottle.

Sekt German term for sparkling wine.

Sparkling wine Wine which undergoes a second fermentation either in bottle (Champagne-method) or in a closed tank (*cuve close*); the carbon dioxide given off is trapped in the wine as bubbles.

Spätlese German QmP wine, slightly sweeter than Kabinett.

Sulphur Commonly used in vinification as a disinfectant for equipment; as an anti-oxidant on fresh-picked grapes; to delay or halt fermentation and as a preservative.

Sur lie French for 'on the lees', applied to a wine bottled direct from fermentation vat or cask, thus gaining extra flavour from the sediment or lees.

Süssreserve German term for unfermented grape juice added to wine just before bottling to increase its sweetness.

Tannin Bitter element in red wine; from grape skins, stems and oak barrels.

Trockenbeerenauslese Sweetest category of German QmP wine, made from individually selected 'noble rot' grapes.

Ullage Small air space left at the top of a bottle or cask; too much causes oxidation.

Varietal Wine made from and named after a single grape variety.

Vin délimité de qualité supérieure Second category of French quality control for wines, between *appellation contrôlée* and *vin de pays*; likely to be phased out. Abbreviated as VDQS.

Vin doux naturel French term for fortified sweet wine, mostly from the Midi. Abbreviated as VDN.

Vinho verde Portuguese term for young wine; also refers to demarcated region in the north-west.

Vitis vinifera Vine species, native to Europe and Central Asia, from which almost all the world's wine is made.

USEFUL ADDRESSES

WINE AUCTIONEERS

Bigwood Auctioneers The Old School, Tiddington, Stratford-Upon-Avon CV37 7AW (0789) 69415

Christie's 8 King Street, St James's, London SW1Y 6QT 071-839 9060

Christie's Scotland 164-166 Bath Street, Glasgow G2 4TG 041-332 8134

Christie's South Kensington 85 Old Brompton Road, London SW7 3LD 071-581 7611

International Wine Auctions 40 Victoria Way, London SE7 7QS 081-293 4992

Lacy Scott 10 Risbygate Street, Bury St Edmunds, Suffolk IP33 3AA (0284) 763531

Lithgow & Sons Auction Houses, Station Road, Stokesely, Middlesbrough, Cleveland TS9 7AB (0642) 710158

Phillips, Son & Neil 39 Park End Street, Oxford OX1 1JD (0865) 723524

Sotheby's 34 New Bond Street, London W1A 2AA 071-493 8080; Summers Place, Billingshurst, West Sussex RH14 9AD (040381) 3933; 28 Watergate Street, Chester CH1 2NA (0244) 315531; 146 West Regent Street, Glasgow G2 2RQ 041-221 4817

Straker, Chadwick & Sons Market Street Chambers, Abergavenny, Gwent NP7 5SD (0873) 2624

WINE CLUBS

Les Amis du Vin 19 Charlotte Street, London W1P 1HB 071-636 4020

Laytons Wine Vaults 20 Midland Road, London NW1 2AD 071-387 8235

Le Nez Rouge 12 Brewery Road, London N7 9NH 071-609 4711

The Wine Club New Acquitaine House, Paddock Road, Reading, Berkshire RG4 0JY (0734) 481711

Wine Mine Club Vintner House, River Way, Harlow, Essex CM20 2EA (0279) 416291

The Wine Society Gunnels Wood Road, Stevenage, Herts SG1 2BG (0438) 741177

ORGANIC WINE SPECIALISTS

Cooper's Natural Foods 17 Lower Marsh, London SE1 7RJ 071-261 9314

HDRA Sales Ltd National Centre for Organic Gardening, Ryton Gardens, Ryton-on-Dunsmore, Coventry CV8 3LG (0203) 303517

Vinceremos Ltd Unit 10, Ashley Industrial Estate, Wakefield Road, Ossett, West Yorkshire WF5 9JD (0924) 276393

Vintage Roots 25 Manchester Road, Reading, Berks RG1 3QE (0734) 662569

West Heath Wine West Heath, Pirbright, Surrey GU24 0QE (048 67) 6464

WINE TOUR OPERATORS
Abreu Travel 109 Westbourne Grove, London W2 4UL 071-229 9905

Arblaster & Clarke 104 Church Road, Steep, Petersfield GU32 2DD (0730) 66883

Blackheath Wine Trails 13 Blackheath Village, London SE3 9LD 081-463 0012

Excalibur Holidays of Distinction 221 Old Christchurch Road, Bournemouth BH1 1PG (0202) 298963

Moswin Tours Ltd PO Box 8, 52b London Road, Oadby, Leicester LE2 5WX (0533) 714982/719922

Vintage Wine Tours 8 Belmont, Lansdown Road, Bath BA1 5DZ (0225) 315834/315659

The Wine Club New Aquitaine House, Paddock Road, Reading RG4 0JY

World Wine Tours 4 Dorchester Road, Drayton St Leonard, Oxfordshire OX10 7BH (0865) 891919

VISITING VINEYARDS

This is a list of the main English (and Welsh) vineyards which welcome visitors *without an appointment*. Most other vineyards will allow visitors by appointment, and you should contact the English Vineyards Association Ltd, 38 West Park, London SE9 4RH Tel. 081-857 0452 and ask for their complete list of *English Vineyards Open to the Public*. The size of each vineyard is indicated, and **W** means that it has its own winery. Many vineyards have a shop and almost all will sell their wine direct to visitors.

Adgestone Vineyard Ltd (3 hectares) **W** K.C. Barlow, Upper Road, Adgestone, Sandown, Isle of Wight (0983) 402503

Arundel (0.5 hectares) **W** J. & V. Rankin, Church Lane, Lyminster, Arundel, West Sussex (0903) 883393

Bardingley (0.8 hectares) **W** H.B. Smith & I. Winter, Babylon Lane, Hawkenbury, Staplehurst, Kent (0580) 892264

Barton Manor (4.1 hectares + 4) **W** Mr & Mrs A.H. Goddard, Whippingham, East Cowes, Isle of Wight (0983) 292835

Biddenden (8.3 hectares) **W** R.A. Barnes, Little Whatmans, Biddenden, Ashford, Kent (0580) 291726

Breaky Bottom (2.3 hectares) **W** Peter Hall, Rodmell, Lewes, East Sussex (0273) 476427

Broadfield (6 hectares) Mr & Mrs Keith James, Broadfield Court Estate, Bodenham, Hereford (056884) 483

Bruisyard (4 hectares) **W** Mr & Mrs I.H. Berwick, Church Road, Bruisyard, Saxmundham, Suffolk (072 875) 281

Brympton d'Evercy (0.4 hectares) Charles E.B. Clive-Ponsonby-Fane, Yeovil, Somerset (093 586) 2528

Capton (0.2 hectares) **W** Mr & Mrs E.B. Kain, Capton, Dartmouth, Devon (080 421) 452

Carr Taylor (8.75 hectares) **W** David & Linda Carr Taylor, Westfield, Hastings, East Sussex (0424) 752501

Cavendish Manor (4 hectares) B.T. Ambrose, Nether Hall Manor, Cavendish, Sudbury, Suffolk (0787) 280221

Chilford Hundred (7.4 hectares) **W** Simon Alper, Chilford Hall, Balsham Rd, Linton, Cambridge (0223) 892641

Chilsdown (5 hectares) **W** Ian & Candy Paget, The Old Station House, Singleton, Chichester, West Sussex (0243 63) 398

Coxley (3.5 hectares) W. Austin, Coxley, Wells, Somerset (0749) 73854

Croffta (1.2 hectares) J.L.M. Bevan, Groes-Faen, Pontyclun, Mid-Glamorgan (0443) 223876

Elham Valley (1 hectare) **W** Vera Allen and Peter Warden, Breach, Barham, Kent (0227) 831 266

Elms Cross (1.5 hectares) **W** A.R. Shaw, Elms Cross, Bradford-on-Avon, Wilts (022 16) 6917

English Wine Centre (0.4 hectares) Christopher Ann, Drusillas Roundabout, Alfriston, East Sussex (0323) 870532 or 870164

Felsted (5.2 hectares) **W** M. Lilley & Ms B.E. Cole, Crix Green, Felsted, Essex (0245) 361504

Highwaymans (11 hectares) P. Fisher, Heath Barn Farm, Risby, Bury St Edmunds, Suffolk (0284) 810001

La Mare (2 hectares) **W** R.H. and A.M. Blayney, St Mary, Jersey, Channel Islands (0534) 81178

Lamberhurst (20 hectares) **W** K. McAlpine, Ridge Farm, Lamberhurst, Tunbridge Wells, Kent (0892) 890844 or 890286

Leeds Castle (1 hectare) Maurice Bristow, Leeds Castle, Kent (0622) 765400

Loddiswell (2.4 hectares) R.H. & B.E. Sampson, Lilwell, Loddiswell, Kingsbridge, Devon (0548) 550221

Lymington (2.5 hectares) **W** C.W & M.M. R. Sentance, Wainsford Road, Pennington, Lymington, Hants (0590) 672112

Meon Valley (3.4 hectares) C.J. & K. Hartley, Hill Grove, Swanmore, Southampton, Hants (0489) 877435

Moorlynch (6 hectares) **W** Mr and Mrs T Rees, Moorlynch, Bridgwater, Somerset (0458) 210393

Nutbourne Manor (7.5 hectares) J.J. Sanger, Nutbourne, Pulborough, West Sussex (07983) 3554

Penshurst (5 hectares) **W** D.E. Westphal, Grove Road, Penshurst, Kent (0892) 870255

Pilton Manor (9 hectares) **W** J. Dowling, Pilton, Shepton Mallet, Somerset (074 989) 325

Polmassick (0.75 hectares) Barbara Musgrave, Polmassick, St Ewe, St Austell, Cornwall (0726) 842239

St George's (8 hectares) **W** Gay Biddlecombe, Waldron, Heathfield, East Sussex (043 53) 2156

St Nicholas of Ash (1 hectare) **W** Wilkinson family, Moat Lane, Ash, Canterbury, Kent (0304) 812670

Sedlescombe (organic) (2.8 hectares) **W** W.R. Cook, Staplecross, Robertsbridge, East Sussex (058 083) 715

Staple (3 hectares) **W** W.T. Ash, Church Farm, Staple, Canterbury, Kent (0304) 812571

Steyning (2.5 hectares) Joyce Elsden, Nash Country Hotel, Horsham Road, Steyning, West Sussex (0903) 814988

Tenterden (5.1 hectares) **W** K. Dawson, Spots Farm, Small Hythe, Tenterden, Kent (05806) 3033

Thames Valley (10.3 hectares) Jon Leighton, Stanlake Park, Twyford, Reading, Berks (0734) 340176 or 320025

Three Choirs (14.5 hectares) **W** T.W. Day, Rhyle House, Welsh House Lane, Newent, Gloucester (053 185) 223 or 555

Westbury (6.5 hectares) **W** B.H. Theobald, Westbury Farm, Purley, Reading, Berks (073 57) 3123

Wootton (2.4 hectares) **W** Major C.L.B. Gillespie, North Wootton, Shepton Mallet, Somerset (074 989) 359

Wraxall (2.2 hectares) **W** A.S. Holmes and Ptns, Shepton Mallet, Somerset (074 986) 486 or 331

INDEX

Webster's is an annual publication. We welcome your suggestions for next year's edition.

ACKNOWLEDGEMENTS

Our thanks especially go to the following (members of the trade and others) who have generously put information and expertise at the disposal of the guide: Avril Abbott, Jim Ainsworth, Burton Anderson, Tim Atkin, William Bolter, Stephen Brook, Gordon Brown, Allan Cheesman, Philip Contini, the staff at Davy's, Newcomen St branch, Nicholas Faith, Food and Wine From France, German Wine Information Service, David Gleave MW, James Halliday, João Henriques, Portuguese Government Trade Office, Jane Hunt MW, Italian Trade Centre, Ian Jamieson MW, Jacquie Kay, Bruce Kendrick, Tony Keys, Willie Lebus, Giles MacDonogh, the staff at Mayor Sworder, Richard Mayson, Kathryn McWhirter, Charles Metcalfe, Christopher Milner, Jasper Morris MW, James Rogers, Anthony Rose, Richard Tanner, Larry Walker, Marcel Williams, Wines from Spain.